International Energy Governance

International Energy Governance

Selected Legal Issues

Rafael Leal-Arcas

Reader in Law, Queen Mary University of London, UK

Andrew Filis

Research Associate, Queen Mary University of London, UK

Ehab S. Abu Gosh

Research Associate, Queen Mary University of London, UK

Edward Elgar

Cheltenham, UK • Northampton, MA, USA

Published by
Edward Elgar Publishing Limited
The Lypiatts
15 Lansdown Road
Cheltenham
Glos GL50 2JA
UK

Edward Elgar Publishing, Inc.
William Pratt House
9 Dewey Court
Northampton
Massachusetts 01060
USA

A catalogue record for this book
is available from the British Library

Library of Congress Control Number: 2014950733

This book is available electronically in the ElgarOnline.com Law Subject Collection, E-ISBN 978 1 78471 150 4

FSC
www.fsc.org
MIX
Paper from responsible sources
FSC® C013056

ISBN 978 1 78471 149 8

Typeset by Columns Design XML Ltd, Reading
Printed and bound in Great Britain by T.J. International Ltd, Padstow

Summary of contents

Contents

PART IV LOOKING FORWARD: BRIDGING THE POLICY OBJECTIVES OF ENERGY, TRADE, AND ENVIRONMENT

Figures

Tables

Acknowledgements

This book was conceived while I was a Marie Curie COFIT senior research fellow thanks to the generosity of the FP7 program of the European Commission, which resulted in the publication of my book entitled *Climate Change and International Trade* (Edward Elgar Publishing, 2013). While writing that book, I started thinking about the close links between climate change mitigation and energy-related issues. The broad thematic scope of this current book brings together various legal aspects of international energy governance, such as international trade liberalization, investment protection, environmental protection, energy security, and energy transit, which I have studied in my previous books: *Theory and Practice of EC External Trade Law and Policy* (Cameron May, 2008), *International Trade and Investment Law: Multilateral, Regional and Bilateral Governance* (Edward Elgar Publishing, 2010), and *Climate Change and International Trade* (Edward Elgar Publishing, 2013). This time around, the book looks at all these legal aspects and others from an international energy governance perspective.

I was fortunate enough to serve as a fellow at the Energy Charter Secretariat during the final stages of this book. That experience enabled me to see first-hand the intricacies of international energy policymaking. I thank my colleagues at the Energy Charter Secretariat for inviting me to be part of their home.

I am very grateful to my co-authors Andrew Filis and Ehab Abu-Gosh for uniting efforts to make this project a reality. I am also very grateful to Tarun Krishnakumar, Tathagata Choudhury, Ishita Sharma, and Catherine Wilmarth for their research input at various stages of the writing of this book. Lastly, I am most indebted to my wife for her tireless efforts to help.

Note for the reader: As is the case with legal research, at one point, one needs to draw the line, since there are constant developments in law and policy-making. Therefore, the cut-off date for this book was April 2014. Any new developments in legislation, case law, or policy related to the theme of this book after that date have not been included.

Rafael Leal-Arcas
April 2014

Introduction

This book deals with selected legal issues relating to interstate systems of energy governance. In this respect, the *systems* within scope are both institutional and normative frameworks, and, as is often the case, it is their interplay that provides levels of governance. International law as it stands today is not well equipped to handle interstate energy governance issues fully. This legal deficiency affects energy security negatively. If the currently fragmented and multi-layered interstate energy governance regime were streamlined for greater legal cohesiveness and international political and economic cooperation, it would promote energy security.

Before referring to the structure of our book, we would like to refer to the general premise that underpins our thinking about interstate energy governance. Energy 'governance' at the 'interstate' level takes place in a manner that is 'fragmented'. In this context, 'governance' could refer to any instance of interstate cooperation ranging from *ad hoc* to institutionalized, one-off to on-going, binding to voluntary, etc. When we bring in the notion of 'energy', governance could be taking place along different areas of interstate cooperation that are ostensibly (e.g., energy transit, energy market liberalization, energy exploration, *et cetera*) or incidentally (e.g., including trade, investment, environmental protection) linked to energy. Moreover, this governance could be taking place in a manner that is not universal, co-extensive, or coherent. For instance, while there is some interstate cooperation pertaining to energy investments, this is merely 'cooperation' or governance arising from the various interstate agreements that include norms relevant to energy investments, and which again is governance that is not necessarily relevant to all states concerned. For instance, while the Energy Charter Treaty[1] contains energy investment protection norms and is a significant element of the interstate energy governance system, its normative scope is far from universal.

In this respect, as we discuss in Chapter 1, while there may be instances of interstate energy governance, these are not coherently

[1] Incidentally, the Energy Charter Treaty is not solely concerned with energy investment protection.

inter-related, for they involve disparate levels of participation, normativity, and/or thematic scope. This is unsurprising given that the residual state of affairs regarding interstate energy governance is an artifact of how interstate relations and cooperation have been conducted throughout history – namely in successive rounds, with disparate purposes involving variable groups of participants. However, while there is no truly universal energy governance system, this is not to say that there is very little to say about interstate energy governance, or about the legal issues that arise in relation to it. On the contrary, this book addresses numerous legal issues and disputes that have arisen in the area of energy and natural resources, and the ability or lack thereof for current interstate energy governance systems to handle them.

A supplementary premise that underpins how we understand the legal aspects of interstate energy governance pertains to how international law may be perceived by some – i.e., a tendency to deal with international law in terms of thematic bundles along the lines of neologisms such as 'international energy law', 'international economic law', *et cetera.* While the running theme of our compilation of chapters is interstate energy governance, we certainly do not espouse the view that the various legal issues in scope are somehow aspects of some creature termed 'international energy law'. What we do is highlight the likely *legal issues* that arise at the juncture of interstate energy governance or that relate to it. We do not take these as amounting to some discrete area of international law in its proper sense.

While the various parts and chapters of this book are compiled based on their general subject matter (i.e., interstate energy governance), they do not necessarily share identical levels of depth of inquiry and analysis regarding the matters within their respective scopes. For instance, while Chapters 7 and 8 both discuss the renewable energy cause within the context of the World Trade Organization (WTO), Chapter 7 does this in greater depth, whereas Chapter 8 does this to the extent that we consider necessary to illustrate how, and to what degree, European Union (EU) renewable energy policy development is *also* restrained by WTO law. Again, while Chapter 1 explores, amongst other things, the overall institutional architecture that pertains to energy governance at the multilateral level, many of the various institutions referred to in Chapter 1 surface again in various chapters of this book, given that they are discussed within the context of specific perspectives of energy governance. In that respect, while there is some inevitable overlap between the various chapters, we want to point out that this overlap is neither repetitive *per se* nor gratuitous.

Finally, we make some theoretical points in order to situate the legal issues in scope against the backdrop of general international law. This is most noticeable in Chapter 4 (where we discuss the normative context for resolving territorial delimitation disputes in light of recent energy exploration attempts in the easternmost part of the Mediterranean), Chapter 5 (where we comment on the normative context for sovereign states to relinquish aspects of their sovereignty to supranational institutions), Chapter 6 (where we comment on normative conflicts between legal regimes, and the juridical tools to overcome them), and Chapter 7 (where we comment on how multiple policy objectives and their related norms can be integrated within an international legal system). In that respect, these references to the broader international law system seek to bring a more macro-normative approach to the issue of interstate energy governance.

STRUCTURE OF THE BOOK

This book is divided into four parts. Part I (Chapters 1–4) explores selected high-level legal issues that arise in relation to interstate energy governance. After a high-level overview in Chapter 1 of the institutional architecture and fields of cooperation involved in interstate energy governance, Chapter 2 discusses the high-level multilateral energy trade system. Chapter 3 explores the relationship between energy, trade and environmental protection in order to contextualize the conservation of exhaustible natural resources and its implications for oil trade. It also highlights ways in which the fragmented energy governance system impacts the conservation of oil resources and restricts its protection. Chapter 4 explores certain legal considerations relating to the law of the sea in order to tease out their implications for energy exploration in the Eastern Mediterranean Basin.

Chapter 1 provides an overview of the various institutions and normative systems that come to combine into a 'global energy governance system' of sorts. It aims to equip the reader with an account of what we deem to be the most notable aspects of a putative global energy governance system. For an 'at-a-glance' understanding of this system, one could refer to the various tables in Chapter 1, which list the different institutions vis-à-vis their scope and what we deem to be their normativity. While it discusses the overlaps that exist within this putative system, Chapter 1 also comments on the gaps that seem to exist, particularly within the context of global energy security objectives.

Chapter 2 discusses energy trade within the World Trade Organization (WTO). Energy trade flows within the scope of the WTO make energy trade one of the most significant trade sectors. Although there are several factors examined in this chapter which explain why international trade in energy has been treated differently from other trade sectors and products in the world trading system, it cannot be said that energy trade is treated any differently from other trade sectors within the context of the WTO. Chapter 2 presents various arguments in favor of treating energy trade as a special trade sector within the WTO.

Chapter 3 analyzes the conservation of exhaustible natural resources in the context of the General Agreement on Tariffs and Trade (GATT) and the WTO. The WTO notion of conservation of exhaustible natural resources constitutes an important WTO vehicle for bridging trade liberalization objectives and environmental protection objectives in order to achieve sustainability. Chapter 3 discusses the normative dispensations that exist within the WTO system in relation to the conservation of natural resources. It also discusses their application in WTO cases and the likely implications for the conservation of oil resources vis-à-vis the WTO system.

Chapter 4 relates to energy exploration attempts in the easternmost part of the Mediterranean, a region compounded by the discovery of underwater energy resources in maritime territories which are subject to competing claims from regional actors. The law of the sea becomes an important element of interstate energy governance, given that it regulates such significant legal questions as the delimitation of maritime areas between states.

Part II of this book (Chapters 5 and 6) deals with selected legal aspects of EU energy governance.

Chapter 5 seeks to equip the reader with an overview of the key legal considerations behind EU energy policy in order to provide insights into the complexities of EU energy security, including the plurality of actors in EU energy policy, the lack of an overall exclusive energy policy remit on the part of the EU authorities, and the disparity of energy interests among EU Member States. It analyzes the legal aspects of EU energy policy, focusing on the changes brought by the Treaty of Lisbon and the challenges the EU faces when aiming for a common energy security policy. It also analyzes how the EU's 'shared' competence in the energy field affects the energy security of its member states.

Unlike Chapter 5, which is more concerned with what happens behind the EU parapet, Chapter 6 is concerned with the outer aspects of EU energy policy and the EU's relationship with neighboring and not-so-neighboring states and regions. Chapter 6 does this by, among other things, discussing the systemic relationship of the EU with institutional and normative systems such as the Energy Charter Treaty and the Energy Community, which, as we demonstrate, owe their existence to efforts on the part of the EU to promote its energy interests and enhance its energy security.

Part III of this book (Chapters 7 and 8) examines selected legal aspects that arise from the promotion of renewable energy in the WTO and EU contexts, and identifies certain shortcomings, pointing to the need for clearer rules and stronger governance in order to promote the use of renewable energy worldwide. Arguably, the use of renewable energy will help towards energy security regionally and climate change mitigation globally.

Chapter 7 examines selected legal issues relating to the multilateral trade system and renewable energy promotion. It argues that the WTO rules are capable of promoting environmental protection objectives. It provides an overview of the sort of legal considerations most likely to arise at the juncture of the WTO and renewable energy promotion. The chapter discusses the evolution of the GATT/WTO system into one that, ultimately, is better equipped to balance trade-related objectives with those relating to environmental protection.

Chapter 8 examines selected legal issues regarding the promotion of renewable energy within the EU and in relation to the EU's obligations under the WTO system. Both energy and the EU, albeit for different reasons inherent to them, are complex affairs. At the juncture between EU renewable energy policy and WTO rules, a number of issues have trade-restrictive effects, which may be justified under environmental protection objectives, including the propagation of renewable energy. Striking the balance between multiple objectives is key for a functional multilateral system. In recent years, the WTO system has evolved to better accommodate environmental protection objectives. However, questions remain around unilateral measures that do not necessarily flow from international practice or from international standards, as well as the differential treatment between tradables, depending on their process and production methods.

Finally, Part IV of this book (Chapter 9) presents the future of interstate energy governance from a sustainability point of view by linking multiple policy objectives: energy, trade, and the environment. Chapter 9 presents an analysis of sustainable development goals in the context of two mega-regional trade agreements: the Transatlantic Trade and Investment Partnership (TTIP) and the Trans-Pacific Partnership (TPP). It examines the implications for energy within the TTIP and TPP, concluding that, there too, there is room for greater coherence when it comes to promoting sustainable energy. Chapter 9 comments on those aspects of the agreements in scope that are likely to have important implications for how efficiently the energy, trade, and environmental protection objectives of their respective participants are balanced against each other. These preferential trade agreements are likely to present a more efficient vehicle than the multilateral trading platform, as it currently stands, when it comes to reconciling the above trinity of objectives in a way that may promote sustainable development.

PART I

Interstate energy governance: selected legal issues from trade, environment and law of the sea

CONCEPTUALIZATION OF PART I

Some definitional issues first: a valid definition of global energy governance is the fact of 'making and enforcing rules to avoid the collective action problems related to energy at a scale beyond the nation-state'.[1] By *global energy economy*, the authors mean a closed system or totality that one could consider to exist that contains the total global energy supply as well as the institutions and infrastructure that facilitate, or are engaged by, energy supply flows. This necessarily contains the global markets and any other pertinent systems and processes.

What we mean by *global energy security* is the satisfaction of humankind's energy needs to maintain lifestyle levels in the developed world and to promote development and improve the quality of life across the world, including least-developed and developing countries. However, this notion still remains unclear. Depending on subjective factors, such as the distinct policy priorities of each State, this definition may be extended to mean 'affordable' and/or 'sustainable' energy. What is more, when discussed within the context of energy producing/net-exporting

---

[1] Sovacool, B. & Florini, A. 'Examining the Complications of Global Energy Governance' (2012) *Journal of Energy and Natural Resources Law*, Vol. 30, No. 3, p. 238.

States, this could be stretched to mean security of *demand*.[2] However, when energy security is discussed in *global* terms, its content is less precise, and the deployment of the term *global energy security* can be deceptive.[3] So whilst domestic *energy security* is a straightforward concept, it is less so at the international level, as it leaves several questions unaddressed, including: What does 'global' mean in this context? Is it achievable in the current normative and broader systemic setting? Who/which body is charged with the responsibility of addressing global energy security needs? What changes would be necessary to achieve this? What are the implications for State sovereignty? Whilst this book does not attempt to address all of these questions, it proceeds on the following bases: that a global energy security that is truly global should seek to address the universal collective needs of humanity, and that a global energy security strategy ought to be bifurcated in that it should aim to negate all zero-sum approaches to energy security, and to fully explore all non-polluting non-exhaustible/renewable energy sources through projects based on the broadest possible international cooperation.[4]

---

[2] See Victor, D. & Yueh, L. 'The New Energy Order: Managing Insecurities in the Twenty-First Century' (2010) *Foreign Affairs*, Vol. 89, No. 1, pp. 61–73, where this notion is cited as the position of the Organization of the Petroleum Exporting Countries.

[3] Taylor, J. & Van Doren, P. 'The Energy Security Obsession' (2008) 6 *Geo. J.L. & Pub. Pol'y* 475; Smith, M. & Htoo, N. 'Energy Security: Security for Whom?' (2008) 11 *Yale Hum. Rts. & Dev. L.J.* 217.

[4] By promoting reliance on less polluting energy resources, one must be cautious not to give rise to problems elsewhere. For instance, the diversion of land and water resources to produce plant-derived ethanol may pose threats to food security, with severe repercussions for global food security needs. See e.g., concerns expressed on the Food and Agriculture Organization website (available at http://www.fao.org/energy/befs/en/). Furthermore, see Zarrilli, S. 'The Development of the Emerging Biofuels Market', in Goldthau, A. & Witte, J.M. (eds) *Global Energy Governance: the New Rules of the Game* (Washington, DC: Brookings Institution Press, 2010) at p. 73 onwards for an exposition of the main contours of the emerging biofuels market, including key figures, trends, and the features of the structure of this market. Moreover, see the 2009 World Bank report *Global Economic Prospects 2009: Commodities at the Cross-Roads*, where it is stated (at p. 7) that: 'because farmers have responded to high maize prices by increasingly growing maize in fields where they once grew wheat and soybeans, prices of these (and other) commodities have also become increasingly sensitive to oil prices. Given that the energy market is much larger than the market for maize (if all the world's maize were used to produce biofuels, it would only meet 8 percent of energy demand), biofuel demand has the potential

Although energy security is a concern common to all sovereign actors, it is currently not a collective objective as is, for instance, human security (i.e., the prohibition of aggression) under the UN Charter. What we witness when we examine instances of interstate cooperation in relation to energy security is that most of these are concerned with partial – not universal – energy security needs, namely the needs of the States involved. As discussed above, the furthest States go in terms of *global* energy governance is to deal with matters that engage energy in a thematically fragmented manner and to the extent that it is politically acceptable to them. The furthest they go in addressing their energy security needs is to the extent that each State deems a collective approach to yield more favorable results than going it alone. In terms of interstate cooperation on energy security, the furthest States go appears to be limited to engaging in bilateral arrangements, to setting up regional arrangements – for example, the NAFTA and the European Union/European Economic Area (and their bilaterals with significant producer and transit States such as Russia[5] and Ukraine,[6] respectively) – or to set up other types of multilateral sector-specific arrangements, the example *par excellence* being the Energy Charter Treaty regime. In that respect, current interstate energy security arrangements are far from *global*. That said, it would be interesting to see whether the combined effect of these different regimes actually enhances global energy security in the sense that, arguably, the proliferation of preferential trade arrangements (PTAs) – for example, customs unions and free trade areas – has contributed to trade liberalization.

We have listed energy security as a theme relevant to instances of institutionalized energy-related international cooperation. For its part, energy security is an imprecise term in both the domestic and global

---

to change permanently the nature (and price) of agricultural commodities. *The International Energy Agency (IEA), for example, suggests that biofuel demand for grains could increase by 7.8 percent a year over the next 20 years (compared with 1.2 percent annual increases for food demand). If this prognosis is borne out, 40 percent of global grain production could be going to biofuels by 2030*' (emphasis added).

[5] See http://ec.europa.eu/trade/creating-opportunities/bilateral-relations/countries/russia/ for a run-down on EU-Russia trade relations. The main EU imports from Russia are oil and gas. The EU is the largest foreign investor in Russia.

[6] For instance, the EU concluded a deep and comprehensive free trade agreement with Ukraine. See http://ec.europa.eu/trade/creating-opportunities/bilateral-relations/countries/ukraine/

context.[7] What is more, the various themes we have listed above interact. For instance, arguably, an effective trade system and energy transit system enhances energy security for those economies concerned in the relevant instances of international cooperation. At the domestic level, a single agent – for example, the State – is the authority that adopts measures towards the energy security of the territory/economy that it controls.[8] Such an agent is not omnipotent in its attempts towards energy security, given that the latter often relies on factors – for example, availability and price of energy commodities – over which such a sovereign actor might have little or no control. At the global level, there is a plurality of actors[9] who have influence over the global energy economy. Whilst energy security is a concern of all sovereign actors, this reality unites all such actors to the extent that global energy security becomes a common concern. The plurality of actors and the variety of interests at play – for example, interests across the national-regional-universal spectrum and the public-private spectrum – mean that, at the global level, the achievement of global energy security becomes less feasible, and that no truly universal regime exists charged with the task of providing governance for the global energy economy or for addressing energy security interests.[10]

---

[7] Bhattacharyya, S. *Energy Economics: Concepts, Issues, Markets, and Governance* (London: Springer, 2011); Korkmaz, D. 'Internal and External Dynamics of European Energy Security' (2010), accessible at http://www.jhubc.it/ecpr-porto/virtualpaperroom/034.pdf; Smith, M. & Htoo, N. 'Energy Security: Security for Whom?' (2008) 11 *Yale Hum. Rts. & Dev. L.J.* 217; Taylor, J. & Van Doren, P. 'The Energy Security Obsession' (2008) 6 *Geo. J. L. & Pub. Pol'y* 475; Victor, D. & Yueh, L. 'The New Energy Order: Managing Insecurities in the Twenty-first Century' (2010) *Foreign Affairs*, Vol. 89, No. 1, pp. 61–73.

[8] Graetz, M.J. *The End of Energy: The Unmaking of America's Environment, Security, and Independence* (Cambridge, Mass.: MIT Press, 2011).

[9] Korkmaz, D. 'Internal and External Dynamics of European Energy Security' (2010), accessible at http://www.jhubc.it/ecpr-porto/virtualpaperroom/034.pdf; Sovacool, B. & Florini, A. 'Examining the Complications of Global Energy Governance' (2012) *Journal of Energy and Natural Resources Law*, Vol. 30, No. 3; Sovacool, B.K. (ed.) *The Routledge Handbook of Energy Security* (Abingdon: Routledge, 2011).

[10] Goldthau, A. & Witte, J.M. (eds) *Global Energy Governance: The New Rules of the Game* (Washington, DC: Brookings Institution Press, 2010); Korkmaz, D. 'Internal and External Dynamics of European Energy Security', (2010), accessible at http://www.jhubc.it/ecpr-porto/virtualpaperroom/034.pdf; Sovacool, B. & Florini, A. 'Examining the Complications of Global Energy Governance' (2012) *Journal of Energy and Natural Resources Law*, Vol. 30, No.

There is a patchwork of institutions that seek to facilitate and regulate matters that engage energy at the interstate level. One such institution is the WTO, which provides degrees of governance over the trade flows between its members to the extent that they fall within WTO norms. The WTO does not currently handle energy commodities any differently than other tradable commodities. In that sense, it provides governance over the trade aspects of energy flows between its membership. Another example is the IEA, which provides a degree of energy security governance for its limited membership. A further example is the implications of the Energy Charter Treaty (ECT), which provides some rules-based energy governance – namely over the investment protection aspects of energy between contracting States.[11] A multitude of institutions exist which provide degrees of governance over aspects of energy at the interstate level.[12]

The effect of this patchwork of institutions and regimes amounts to a global energy governance system of sorts. However, such a putative system is neither cohesive nor unitary; nor does it provide cohesive global governance over energy.[13] This putative system presents some overlaps in that, for example, the WTO system may extend over the trade aspects of energy, but also contains provisions that extend over the environmental impacts of trade in energy, whilst the regimes under the United Nations Convention on Climate Change (UNFCCC) and its Kyoto Protocol may also address the environmental impacts of energy. Similarly, there is overlap between the WTO system and the ECT-related

---

3; Kuzemko, C. (ed.) *Dynamics of Energy Governance in Europe and Russia* (Basingstoke: Palgrave Macmillan, 2012); Anceschi, L. et al. (eds) *Energy Security in the Era of Climate Change: The Asia-Pacific Experience* (Houndmills: Palgrave Macmillan, 2011).

[11] Lowenfeld, A.F. *International Economic Law* (Oxford: Oxford University Press, 2008); Selivanova, Y. (ed.) *Regulation of Energy in International Trade Law: WTO, NAFTA, and Energy Charter* (Alphen aan den Rijn: Wolters Kluwer, 2011); Wälde, T. *The Energy Charter Treaty: An East-West Gateway for Investment and Trade* (London, The Hague, Boston: Kluwer Law International, 1996).

[12] Goldthau, A. & Witte, J.M. (eds) *Global Energy Governance: The New Rules of the Game* (Washington, DC: Brookings Institution Press, 2010); Sovacool, B. & Florini, A. 'Examining the Complications of Global Energy Governance' (2012) *Journal of Energy and Natural Resources Law*, Vol. 30, No. 3; Victor, D. & Yueh, L. 'The New Energy Order: Managing Insecurities in the Twenty-first Century' (2010) *Foreign Affairs*, Vol. 89, No. 1, pp. 61–73.

[13] Bhattacharyya, S. *Energy Economics: Concepts, Issues, Markets, and Governance* (London: Springer, 2011); Baumann, F. 'Europe's Way to Energy Security. The Outer Dimensions of Energy Security: From Power Politics to Energy Governance' (2010) *European Foreign Affairs Review*, Vol. 15, No. 1.

system regarding the trade, investment, and environmental protection aspects of energy between the memberships they share.

Finally, whilst energy supply and the normative framework around the global energy economy are important features of the latter, one should also not lose sight of the fact that other factors/phenomena with significant implications for the global energy economy exist. For instance, global markets and market dynamics, whilst facilitated by the normative framework under review, are formidable forces that transcend it. On that point, given that these ultimately dictate the allocation of a great part of the energy supply, perhaps it is global markets – that after all are transnational – that by default fill in the gaps in the global energy governance edifice. What is more, the rise of national oil and or gas companies (let us use the shorthand 'NOCs') and the activity of some of these abroad have important implications for the global energy economy.

In sum, there is neither some overarching top-down[14] universal arrangement to provide interstate energy governance nor is there one to deal with global energy security *per se*. Numerous instances of interstate cooperation, which converge on their association to energy, intersect to weave together a normative patchwork with implications for the global energy economy, and, consequently, for global energy security. As one might imagine the case with such default arrangements to be, despite the overlaps,[15] gaps emerge when one assesses the emerging system through a particular prism, in our case, through that of its implications for global energy security. Where there is almost universal governance over an energy-related matter (e.g., the WTO system in relation to governance of a large proportion of global energy trade), there is usually insufficient

---

[14] A top-down approach refers to the way in which an agreement is managed, which is essentially based upon a multilateral/universal membership. A top-down approach to a problem is a situation that begins at the highest conceptual level and works down to the details, i.e., an approach in which an agenda for negotiations that defines the overall shape of the agenda is prepared first, before considering how to deal with individual components. Within formal international organizations, top-down architecture and centralization are to be found, for instance, in the International Monetary Fund and the World Bank Group. The decision-making process of these two institutions differs from that of the UNFCCC, where consensus is required. Based upon international agreements, operations are managed by bodies representing Member States within the charter of the organizations concerned. Top-down architectures have been seen to have difficulties in adjusting to new challenges. See Lowenfeld, A. *International Economic Law*, 2nd ed. (Oxford: Oxford University Press, 2008), at pp. 610–622, 644 et seq.

[15] See Table 1.3 in Chapter 1.

cohesion with other areas of interstate cooperation over distinct yet interlinked energy-related issues (e.g., environmental protection, investment protection, and anti-corruption, to name but a few).[16]

[16] In relation to this point, should there be sufficient political will, the WTO could amend rules to encourage subsidies in the development of renewable energy and the diffusion of environmental goods and services, along with changing rules, to encourage environmental methods of production, which would consequently make it WTO-compliant to discriminate between 'like' products, e.g., CO_2-free or CO_2-low laptops or tires. In other words, if WTO rules were amended, then some discrimination between 'like' products – e.g., no tariffs for popular electronic goods such as laptops that have low or no CO_2 emissions and higher tariffs for CO_2-heavy laptops – could be accommodated within the WTO system. This would then allow for environmental objectives to be given more weight in cases that pitch trade versus environmental concerns.

1. A fragmented global energy governance

I. INTRODUCTION TO GLOBAL ENERGY GOVERNANCE: AN INESCAPABLE EVENTUALITY OR AN ELUSIVE DREAM?

Energy engages almost every aspect of human endeavor in modern times. In the words of the Secretary-General of the United Nations (UN) Ban Ki-moon: 'it is unimaginable that today's economies could function without electricity and other modern energy services. From job creation to economic development, from security concerns to the status of women, energy lies at the heart of all countries' core interests'.[1] Moreover, according to the International Energy Agency (IEA), 'energy alone is not sufficient for creating the conditions for economic growth, but it is certainly necessary. It is impossible to operate a factory, run a shop, grow crops or deliver goods to consumers without using some form of energy'.[2] Furthermore, energy is the mainstay of today's economy in the developed world, in the rapidly industrializing developing world, and in other parts of the world. Such is its importance to the modern economy that energy security has been linked to national security. Yet one in five people in the world today has no access to electricity,[3] and there are large inequalities in per capita electricity consumption across countries (see Figure 1.1). Such inequalities often have their roots in history, but some crucial questions arise: Is the global energy economy being collectively managed in an effective way that is steering us towards greater energy

---

1 'Sustainable Energy for All' 2011, p. 2, available at http://www.un.org/wcm/webdav/site/sustainableenergyforall/shared/Documents/SG_Sustainable_Energy_for_All_vision_final_clean.pdf

2 http://www.worldenergyoutlook.org/resources/energydevelopment/accesstoelectricity/

3 Hongbo, W., Keynote address at the Sustainable Energy for All Ministerial Panel, Abu Dhabi International Renewable Energy Conference, 15 January 2013. Available at http://www.un.org/en/development/desa/usg/statements/mr-wu/2013/01/sustainable-energy-for-all-2.html

security for all? Is the global governance framework for energy security comprehensive and inclusive?

Understandably, therefore, any inordinate disruption to energy supplies – the 'oxygen' of the economy[4] – would make any State's government particularly twitchy. Power cuts and fuel shortages are the sort of events that have repercussions for all fields of economic activity and that powerfully impress images of State failure on the public imagination. This – coupled with the fact that the current mainstay of energy supply disproportionately relies on fossil fuels (i.e., petroleum, gas, and coal)[5] that are finite, unevenly distributed, and highly polluting – necessarily makes energy an ostensibly global issue given, amongst other things, energy's climatic, transport, and economic development implications. In other words, it is a common concern for all of humanity.

Initial investigation has revealed that 'global energy governance' today is a theoretical concept that does not exist in actuality; there is a marked absence of a global mechanism – or cohesive set of mechanisms – purposely set up by the international community to address its collective energy security needs. What we have instead is a mixed bag of incidental outcomes arising from an array of disjointed institutions and processes operating at various scales (bilateral, regional, etc.), often each with its own selective membership. The various initiatives span a wide range of energy-related topics pertinent to various countries, such as trade,[6] investment protection,[7] and climate change,[8] that are not necessarily

---

[4] See Peter Voser's foreword to the World Economic Forum 2012 'energy vision update' report titled *Energy for Economic Growth* (at p. 2), available at http://www3.weforum.org/docs/WEF_EN_EnergyEconomicGrowth_IndustryAgenda_2012.pdf

[5] In 2009, 80.9% of the 12,150 million tons of oil equivalent (Mtoe) global primary energy supply came from fossil fuels. In 1973, 86.6% of the total global primary energy supply of 6,111 Mtoe came from fossil fuels. Although the share of coal and gas has increased with the rising cost of oil within the fossil-fuel mix of primary energy supply over that period, oil continues to be the dominant primary energy source, e.g., 46% during 1973 and 32.8% during 2009. See International Energy Agency, Key World Energy Statistics (2011) at p. 6.

[6] Leal-Arcas, R. 'Proliferation of Regional Trade Agreements: Complementing or Supplanting Multilateralism?' (2011) *Chicago Journal of International Law*, Vol. 11, No. 2, pp. 597–629.

[7] Leal-Arcas, R. 'The Multilateralization of International Investment Law' (2009) *North Carolina Journal of International Law and Commercial Regulation*, Vol. 35, Issue 1, pp. 33–135.

[8] Leal-Arcas, R. 'Unilateral Trade-related Climate Change Measures' (2012) *The Journal of World Investment and Trade*, Vol. 13, No. 6, pp. 875–927.

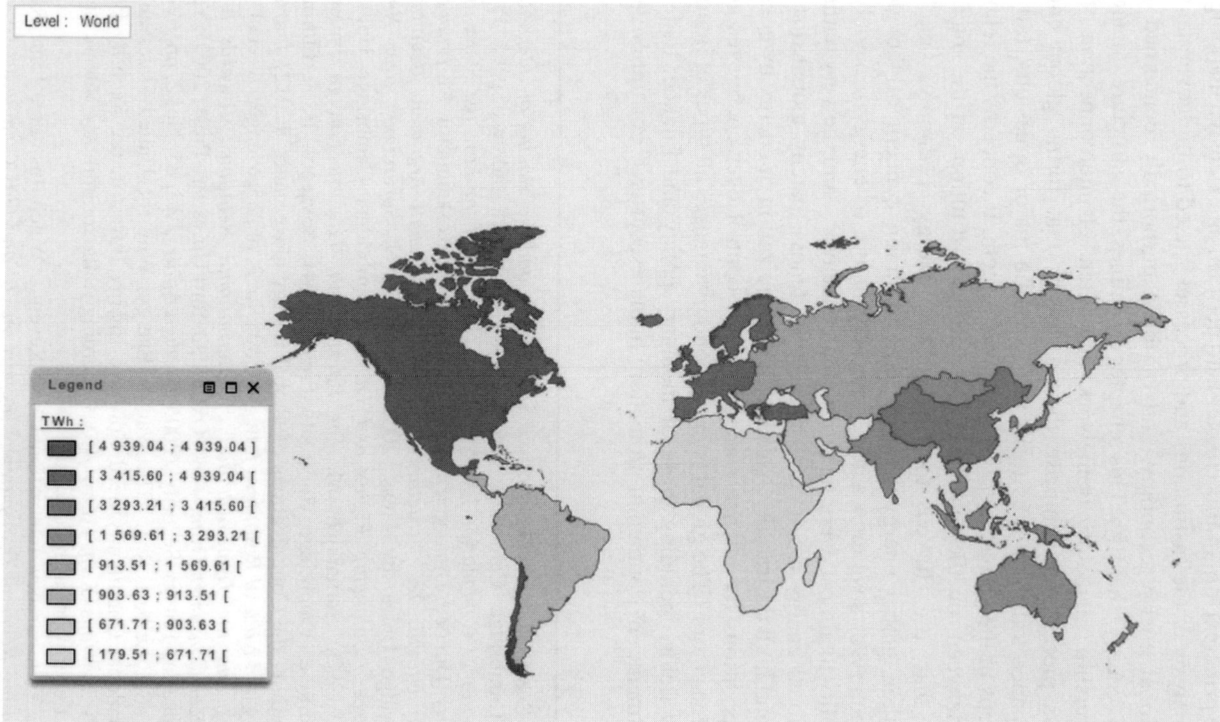

Source: © 2010 OECD/IEA – Software: © Articque, All rights reserved.

Figure 1.1 Per capita electricity consumption (2010)

functioning in coordination with each other. Overall, the global energy governance regime appears to be highly fragmented.

The principal aim of this chapter is to perform an extensive mapping-out and analysis of the institutions and processes linked to the governance of the global energy economy, and of those purportedly concerned with global energy security. This chapter examines the structure, mandate, membership, regulatory framework, and extent of interconnection of the various pieces that comprise the patchwork that forms global energy governance today. It aims to identify specific major omissions, failings, and gaps in the global energy governance system. It concerns the relationship between, on the one hand, the various institutions at the interstate level that are linked to the global energy economy, and, on the other, global energy security as a common concern of the global community of sovereign actors. The very nature of energy – namely, its centrality to almost every field of human endeavor – and the very nature of traditional energy resources – namely finiteness, patchy global distribution, and high desirability – lead to the politicization of energy by creating the conditions for intense competition for control over energy resources between actors.[9] The global energy economy engages all types of interstate policy fields, including those of monetary policy and finance; trade and investment; environmental protection; human security;[10] corruption;[11] and

---

[9] See Anghie, A. *Imperialism, Sovereignty, and the Making of International Law* (Cambridge: Cambridge University Press, 2007); Andrews-Speed, P. (ed.) *International Competition for Resources: The Role of the Law, the State, and of Markets* (Dundee: Dundee University Press, 2008); Koskenniemi, M. *From Apology to Utopia: The Structure of International Legal Argument* (Cambridge: Cambridge University Press, 2005); Schrijver, N. *Sovereignty over Natural Resources: Balancing Rights and Duties* (Cambridge: Cambridge University Press, 1997); Sornarajah, M. *The International Law on Foreign Investment* (Cambridge: Cambridge University Press, 2004); Sovacool, B. & Florini, A. 'Examining the Complications of Global Energy Governance' (2012) *Journal of Energy and Natural Resources Law*, Vol. 30, No. 3, p. 235; Wenger, A. et al. (eds) *Energy and the Transformation of International Relations: Towards a New Producer-Consumer Framework* (Oxford: Oxford University Press, 2009); Yergin, D. 'Ensuring Energy Security' (2006) *Foreign Affairs*, Vol. 85, No. 2, pp. 69–82.

[10] See Leibert, R.A. 'The War on Energy: Why the United States and the International Community need Cohesive Energy Infrastructure Security Policy' (2007) 29 *Hous J Int'l Law* 453 (regarding calls for military intervention to protect energy infrastructures).

[11] Transparency International and Revenue Watch Institute, Joint Report, *Promoting Revenue Transparency*: *Report on Oil and Gas Companies*, 2011.

energy security.[12] Whilst energy supply and consumption are important aspects of the global energy economy,[13] they do not exist in an equilibrious relationship. Rather, they are heavily mediated by political considerations and by the very operation of global markets, which dictate the extent to which energy needs are ultimately met.[14] Moreover, this chapter seeks to enumerate and discuss the principal normative aspects of the global energy economy, including the relevant institutional architecture and legal norms involved in its *governance*.[15]

Argument

We argue that the currently fragmented and multi-layered global energy governance is not conducive to energy security that is truly global for a number of reasons. Despite the seeming overlaps between institutions and regimes dealing with the global energy governance system, gaps seem to emerge were one to examine it in relation to its capacity to address global energy governance issues.[16] It is not surprising that the current governance system over the global energy economy fails to address global energy security needs. A plausible way to improve global energy security for the near future is to promote more cohesive models and methods of interstate cooperation and to promote more cohesive collaboration among the various institutions and processes that are connected to the global energy economy. It is necessary to address the weaknesses of the current energy governance system due to its fragmented nature through cooperation and partnerships, whether bilaterally, regionally or multilaterally. A thorough assessment of the evolution and workings of the current global energy governance regime is necessary, for which we need to consider the following factors:

---

12 Luciani, G. *Security of Oil Supplies: Issues & Remedies* (Deventer, the Netherlands: Claeys & Casteels, 2013).

13 Yergin, D. *The Prize: The Epic Quest for Oil, Money and Power* (New York: Free Press, 2008); Yergin, D. *The Quest: Energy, Security, and the Remaking of the Modern World* (New York: Penguin Press, 2011).

14 Yergin, D. 'Ensuring Energy Security' (2006) *Foreign Affairs*, Vol. 85, No. 2, pp. 69–82.

15 Other commentators have tried a similar exercise. See Sovacool, B.K. & Florini, A. 'Examining the Complications of Global Energy Governance' (2012) *Journal of Energy & Natural Resources Law*, August.

16 Bhattacharyya, S. *Energy Economics: Concepts, Issues, Markets, and Governance* (London: Springer, 2011); Florini, A. & Sovacool, B.K. 'Who Governs Energy? The Challenges Facing Global Energy Governance' (2009) 37 *Energy Policy*, pp. 5239–5298.

Lack of cohesiveness of the energy governance system

That is to say, the energy governance system exists incidentally as an aggregation of various institutions and processes linked to the energy economy. In fact, very little suggests that the international community handles the global energy economy as a cohesive entity or concept. In this respect, it lacks the ontological basis – that is to say, both the mandate and the cohesive structure – to address global energy security.

Fragmentation of the global energy governance regime

Firstly, the fragmentation of the global energy governance regime reflects the progressive nature of its development. For instance, in 1947 a number of sovereign actors came together to lay down arrangements for the General Agreement on Tariffs and Trade to provide disciplines focusing on global trade. Some years later, several States ratified the Kyoto Protocol in order to deal with greenhouse gas (GHG) emissions in the context of climate change mitigation. Although neither of the two examples (namely the trading system and the climate change regime) is exclusively concerned with the global energy economy, they are significant elements of the global energy economy's trade and climate change aspects, respectively.

Secondly, the fragmentation of the governance system over the global energy economy may also be viewed as reflecting the fact that sovereign States engage with one another to the extent that it is in their national interest to do so. Efforts among States to promote their collective – let alone universal – energy security are considerably undercut by systemic constraints: namely by the very nature of international relations that are profoundly conditioned by market dynamics and by the fact that the international community is composed of States fiercely defensive of their respective national interests.[17]

Plethora of relevant entities

There is a plurality of international institutions, organizations and bodies that affect the global energy economy. Moreover, there is an obvious diversity of interests, including conflicts of interests, at the national, regional and international levels, pertaining to the energy economy and energy security. This plurality of international organizations relating to global energy as well as the diversity and variety of energy interests

---

[17] See generally Wenger, A. et al. (eds) *Energy and the Transformation of International Relations: Towards a New Producer-Consumer Framework* (Oxford: Oxford University Press, 2009).

illustrate the sophisticated and fragmented complexity of global energy governance.[18] At the same time, they render global energy economy governance not only highly fragmented, but also incoherent, controversial and unstable, encompassing several conflicts of interests.

Diversity of energy sources

Current over-reliance on traditional sources of energy (e.g., coal, petroleum, natural gas), which are finite and patchily distributed, leads to intense competition and renders energy security that is truly global less attainable.[19] There have even been calls to defend energy infrastructure militarily.[20] Were we to shift reliance on energy production to the exploitation of renewables (e.g., power derived from the sun, wind, oceans, and from the heat of the earth), which are abundant, more sustainable and distributed more widely, the zero-sum logic that underlines interstate energy relations could become obsolete.

Pursuit of national interests

For the most part, the genesis and evolution of international law suggests it to be a creature of consent between hegemonic States and, in the final analysis, to reflect the balance of their interests.[21] The international community is merely a totality of disparate actors in that sovereign States have distinct interests and disparate levels of economic strength. Interstate cooperation takes place to the extent that the interests of the most influential States sufficiently coincide. On certain aspects of the global energy economy – namely in relation to its trade aspects – there is sufficient agreement of interests that has resulted in degrees of global governance; on others, there is not. For instance, the exploration, extraction, production and allocation of energy resources currently take place on a very different footing to that of addressing global energy security. Namely, it takes place to the extent that it is profitable to the

---

[18] See generally, Van de Graaf, T. *The Politics and Institutions of Global Energy Governance* (Houndmills: Palgrave Macmillan, 2013).

[19] Andrews-Speed, P. (ed.) *International Competition for Resources: The Role of the Law, the State, and of Markets* (Dundee: Dundee University Press, 2008).

[20] See for instance Leibert, R.A. 'The War on Energy: Why the United States and the International Community need Cohesive Energy Infrastructure Security Policy' (2007) 29 *Hous J Int'l Law* 453.

[21] Koskenniemi, M. *From Apology to Utopia: The Structure of International Legal Argument* (Cambridge: Cambridge University Press, 2005); Anghie, A. *Imperialism, Sovereignty, and the Making of International Law* (Cambridge: Cambridge University Press, 2007).

actors at the various stages of energy exploration and exploitation.[22] In an increasingly more globalized economy in which, to paraphrase Henry Kissinger, sovereign States consider their national interests over their *ad-hoc* alliances, it is perhaps naïve to currently expect there to be sufficient political will to set up a global energy security governance regime. Or rather, it is perhaps naïve to consider that the international community is composed of States that are economically equal or whose interests are sufficiently aligned to make such a global governance regime likely.

Starting from a universal perspective, it becomes clear that there is no unitary, cohesive and comprehensive universal regime exclusively set up to address global energy security. One may view the UN Charter, and the organization it has set up, as providing some loose top-level global governance that has incidental implications for the global economy, including for the global energy economy. For instance, it contains a normative framework with which interstate relations ought to comply. It effectively prohibits international acts of aggression and preserves sovereign prerogatives over domestic matters, including the management of natural resources and especially of energy-related resources.[23] Other than this, arguably, there is neither a universal regime nor norms that could be said to be truly universal or that may be universally espoused. This is particularly the case in relation to the position under general international law relating to the protection of investor interests.[24]

Whilst one witnesses instances of interstate cooperation on energy security, these are evidently not global. For instance, although the regime under the Energy Charter Treaty – principally concerned with promoting trade and investment interests in the energy/extractive industries of its members – may, at best, promote the energy security of its membership, it is not of universal scope. Indeed, by addressing the energy security of its limited membership, such a regime may incidentally undermine global energy security in ways that will be analyzed later. Consequently, interstate efforts relating to energy security have not gone as far as to address global energy security needs. In that respect, the current plethora of institutions and processes linked to the global energy economy cannot be held to go far enough, in their combined effect, to address global

[22] Victor, D. & Yueh, L. 'The New Energy Order: Managing Insecurities in the Twenty-first Century' (2010) *Foreign Affairs*, Vol. 89, No. 1, pp. 61–73.

[23] Schrijver, N. *Sovereignty over Natural Resources: Balancing Rights and Duties* (Cambridge: Cambridge University Press, 1997).

[24] Sornarajah, M. *The International Law on Foreign Investment* (Cambridge: Cambridge University Press, 2004).

energy security. There is a misalignment between their various purposes, which results in gaps and in an overall systemic failure when addressing global energy security.

Given the enormity of the subject's scope, it would be reasonable to assume that there is a high degree of international cooperation around the governance of energy.[25] In reality, as shall become clearer later, global energy governance – if indeed such a thing exists – is fragmented along thematic lines, and is normatively patchy at that (see Table 1.1). This is unsurprising given the realities of international cooperation. International cooperation does not occur on a disinterested basis; it occurs to the extent that it draws in the most influential States relevant to the matter in hand, and, conceivably, when their respective interests are sufficiently accommodated.[26]

Following this introductory Section I, Section II provides a discussion on international cooperation in energy. Section III includes some key figures around global energy supply and consumption to gauge the extent of the global energy economy. Section IV then examines what might be the impact of the key aspects of the global energy economy on global energy security. Section V concludes the chapter and offers recommendations and proposals on how to improve the currently fragmented global energy governance system and how to promote greater global energy security.

II. INTERNATIONAL COOPERATION IN ENERGY

The interests that underpin a State's response to a call for international cooperation are much broader than its specific interests in relation to the particular global policy issue at hand. States may be motivated to adopt a particular position on account of their subjective interests, which many a learned analyst would labor to understand, just as a psychoanalyst delves beyond the phenomenological to deduce some rational basis in his/her subject's behavior. All kinds of horse-trading between States habitually takes place through diplomatic means that, incidentally, are outside the scope of the present chapter. However, it is helpful to bear this in mind

[25] For more details, see Dubash, N. & Florini, A. 'Mapping Global Energy Governance' (2011) *Global Policy*, Vol. 2, Special issue, pp. 6–18; Hirst, N. & Froggatt, A. 'The Reform of Global Energy Governance' *Grantham Institute for Climate Change, Discussion Paper No. 3*, 2012.

[26] See Goldsmith, J. & Posner, E. *The Limits of International Law* (Oxford: Oxford University Press 2005).

Table 1.1 Gauging normativity

	Number of members	Normativity	Potential for global energy security
UN	193	Treaty-based legal relations. UN Charter and other UN agreements create legal relations	Potentially enormously positive; however, its potential is fraught by political realities. Top-down regime *par excellence*, with no express mandate for global energy policy
EU/EEA	28/30[a]	Treaty-based economic relations. Successive EU treaties have deepened and widened legal relations among its Member States	Sophisticated energy policy that advances the energy security of its membership. Its potential for the global setting is unclear
NAFTA	3	Treaty-based economic relations	Unclear
ASEAN /AFTA	10	Treaty-based economic relations	Unclear
ECC	54	Treaty-based economic relations.	Potentially positive through the facilitation of energy investments and flows
GECF	13	Low – discussion forum	Uncertain. The GECF purports to be set up to promote its members' sovereign rights over their gas endowments and to promote security of energy demand. In that sense, it is a producer association. That said, the exchange of energy data between its membership could help better plan the exploration of gas reserves and thus contribute to global energy security.
G8/G8+5	8/13	Low – discussion forum	Potentially positive
G20	20	Low – discussion forum	Potentially positive
IEA	29	Set up within the framework of the OECD creating legal obligations	Potentially positive if all energy-significant States are engaged
IEF	75	Low – discussion forum	Positive through the wide level of participation and the sharing of energy-related data.
MEF	17	Low – discussion forum	Potentially positive, particularly in relation to sustainable/green energy security.

	Number of members	Normativity	Potential for global energy security
OPEC	12	Medium – although OPEC status and effect are unlike a legal treaty-based organization, it is more than a discussion forum for its membership	Uncertain. OPEC arose as a backlash to historic dominance by Western oil companies. OPEC could be seen as progressive when compared with the previous state of play. On the other hand, manipulating supply could harm global energy security.
UNFCCC	195	Medium – parties are grouped into categories with distinct legal obligations under the UNFCCC/Kyoto Protocol to take environmental protection measures	Unclear
WPC	65	Low – discussion forum	Positive
WTO	160	Treaty-based economic relations. Several legal agreements	Uncertain. Potentially positive by facilitating trade in energy commodities (including fuel and technology)

Note: [a] At the time of writing this chapter, Croatia, the 28th and newest EU Member State, was provisionally applying the agreement creating the EEA.

in understanding why it might be politically unrealistic to achieve concerted cohesive action over certain global policy issues.

Effective international cooperation often involves the setting up of institutions and the laying down of normative frameworks – that is to say, the rules of the game by which all parties ought to abide. Regarding international cooperation, at one end of the spectrum we witness sophisticated institutions with rules and effective enforcement mechanisms, and at the other end of the spectrum there are talking shops, for example transnational policy networks/global public policy networks, where States engage in discussions over global issues and where concrete decisions on action are made only when this is politically acceptable to them.[27]

In relation to energy, international cooperation is necessary because of the high level of uncertainty in the markets. International cooperation occurs along thematic lines and in successive waves, rather than in a universal joined-up manner. Consequently, the global energy governance

---

[27] See for instance the work by Paul Thurner and Alexander Hatzold, 'Inter-Organizational Networks in the Global Energy Sector. Part I: The IGO-Network in Fossil Fuels', June 2010, not published, available at http://www.asna.ch/fileadmin/user_upload/2010/Papers/Thurner-Hatzold_Paper.pdf

structure is not unitary and cohesive. Rather, one finds it to be fragmented and patchy. Surveying the global energy-related landscape from a 2012 standpoint, it is evident that no purposively set-up universal expansive top-down arrangement exists that draws in the entire international 'community' over all energy-related matters. Rather, what appears to emerge is a patchwork of instances of international cooperation broadly or more directly linked to energy. In that sense, 'global energy governance' is an artificial abstraction that unjustifiably suggests universality and a degree of cohesion and comprehensiveness which is not reflected in reality. In our view, it would be more in keeping with reality to approach the global energy economy as one where, whilst there is no global energy governance *per se*, there exist instances of interstate activity/international cooperation in matters that are linked to energy. During the course of this chapter, we shall examine several fields of international cooperation, and instances therein, with implications for the global energy economy.

As one might expect, assessing whether the current state of play is satisfactory is contingent on subjective factors such as the objectives and values of the agent that carries out such an assessment. Returning to the concept of an international 'community' – this abstraction can also be misleading in that it may unjustifiably suggest a grouping of States of equivalent or similar qualities. In reality, the international community of sovereign States involves a heterogeneous 'community' of States with divergent interests and disparate levels of economic might and, therefore, influence in the increasingly globalized world. In that respect, whilst one State might view existing 'global energy governance' arrangements as frightfully inadequate, another might view them as perfectly adequate, with all the shades of opinion between these two poles.

Other agents that might aspire to approach this issue in a professedly disinterested manner – for example, social scientists from across the disciplinary spectrum – may, for instance, take a realist view of the existing arrangement as amounting to a global energy governance system *of sorts* that has risen both organically and in response to the political expediencies that ultimately underscore all interstate activity. Such an approach is less concerned with pronouncing on suitability; rather, it is more concerned with understanding the phenomenon and its causes. In that regard, the existing fragmentation in the field of energy is an artifact of the realities of international cooperation. For instance, international cooperation may take place in a non-linear and patchy manner. It may develop against too many variables such as the composition of the parties involved, their respective interests and historical grievances, the power relations at play, and the purported policy objectives of cooperation, *inter alia*. In figurative speech, it is as if one were carrying a tower of wobbly jelly whilst balancing on a unicycle with the earth beneath trembling. There are too many considerations at play, too wide a disparity between the actors and too much dissonance in their respective sets of interests.

Another view by a professedly disinterested agent might be more concerned with carrying out an assessment of the current arrangement through the prism of some external factor such as, in our case, the implications of the existing state of play regarding global energy governance for global energy security. Such an investigation, therefore, may potentially conclude that the current situation is not satisfactory. Again, with a potential plethora of opinions between these two approaches.

One might also – correctly in our view – start from the position that there is no global energy governance *per se* and that, rather, what could be held to exist are instances of degrees of international governance over discrete matters that are linked to energy. Let us call this international governance 'interstate', which, incidentally, is hardly ever global. At most, some examples of interstate governance are not 'energy governance' *per se*, although they engage various aspects of energy. For instance, the WTO system – which plays a significant part in the 'global' governance of energy trade – neither exclusively, nor specifically, nor formally focuses on energy trade. It extends to all intra-WTO trade, irrespective of the trade sector (to the extent that its members have previously agreed in their specific schedules of trade concessions upon forming, or acceding to, the WTO). In that respect, the WTO's significance to global energy trade is incidental, though not inconsiderable, given its importance to the global trade system *per se*.

Moreover, the WTO also may sensibly be held to relate to the global environmental protection system, given that it contains provisions that could sensibly be considered to be part of the overall composite normative framework on environmental protection. In addition, the WTO also contains provisions relevant to intellectual property rights (IPRs) protection and to the freedom of transit (of commodities), which are matters that enhance the trade aspects of energy. In that regard, the WTO regime extends to more than one matter linked to energy, namely to trade in energy, environmental protection, and transit aspects.

Further examples are the European Union (EU) and the European Economic Area (EEA), which are sophisticated regional trade agreements, and customs union arrangements that provide for detailed policies on, amongst other things, energy markets, environmental protection, investment protection, and transit issues; all of which are matters linked to energy. In that respect, both examples cited – namely, the WTO and the EU/EEA – are neither exclusively concerned nor purposely set up to deal with the energy economy of their respective membership. This is diagonally different from, for instance, the regime set up under the Energy Charter Treaty (ECT), which contains provisions on trade and on environmental and investment protection, and which is expressly concerned with the energy sectors of, or the *energy economy* between, its members. Rather, what the WTO and EU/EEA do is apply to the energy economies of their respective membership and, therefore having implications for their energy security through their operations. All three examples (i.e., the WTO, the EU/EEA, and the ECT) shall be explored subsequently.

The advent of the UN order, industrialization, and progressive economic integration between States have arguably led to international relations becoming more standardized and disciplined than they had been before and during the colonial era. Those times had involved contests for resources and trade posts between, amongst others, American, British, French, Prussian, Spanish, and Russian imperialisms that were ostensibly driven by mercantilist considerations. One might consider this transformation in reality to be more formal than substantive in that the persistent trend in recent history – namely in the post-World-War-II era – regarding globalization is essentially about the unbridled speculation of capital through, amongst other things, market penetration in the quest for returns higher than those possible domestically. This almost universal commitment of the industrialized world to trade liberalization – in other words, by those economies whose industries are better placed to commercially exploit the commercial opportunities that further liberalization makes possible – on terms favorable to it points towards a neo-mercantilist dimension in their economic relations. This return to neo-mercantilist ways becomes more evident at times of economic downturn, when protectionism becomes increasingly more appealing as a policy option for trade.[28]

[28] See EU Commission, *Ninth Report on Potentially Trade Restrictive Measures Identified in the Context of the Financial and Economic Crisis*, 2012 (available at http://trade.ec.europa.eu/doclib/docs/2012/june/tradoc_149526.pdf). Do note, however, that in April 2010 the World Bank had looked at protectionism and, although it concluded that 'there is no widespread increase in protectionism via tariff policies since the global financial crisis has unfolded', it had looked at the causality between economic downturn, the collapse in trade, and protectionism in the reverse manner – namely to assess to what extent any instances of protectionism had caused the collapse in trade. See the abstract to World Bank Policy Research Work Paper 5274 'Is Protectionism on the Rise? Assessing National Trade Policies during the Crisis of 2008', Hiau Looi Kee et al., April

Returning to the fact that historically in modern times the mainstay of energy derives from resources that are finite and unevenly distributed across the globe, the pursuit of energy security on the part of each State necessarily involves a zero-sum mentality that encourages neo-mercantilist approaches to energy trade. For instance, despite the increased consolidation and fluidity of the global oil markets, large amounts of oil are bound in contracts and bilateral investment treaties between net producer States and downstream actors (e.g., domestic and foreign oil distribution companies). Furthermore, extensive reserves are held by States, thus impacting global oil supply.[29] In terms of further examples, net consumer States – the People's Republic of China being a case in point – engage in interstate relations with the clear aim of securing a steady energy supply for their ever-increasing domestic needs.[30] For oil producing net exporter States, there are efforts to collude in relation to supply in order to secure demand (and therefore steady revenues from their supplies)[31] and to promote market dominance for their energy sector actors, with the Russian Federation's Gazprom being a case in point.[32]

That said, States continue to engage multilaterally to secure their energy needs, and there are instances of interstate cooperation that shall be explored below. Briefly citing the EU as an example of this, it has developed a sophisticated long-term common energy policy that promotes the energy security of its 28 Members. Therefore, there is a need to improve international cooperation.

2010 (available at https://openknowledge.worldbank.org/bitstream/handle/10986/3761/WPS5274.pdf?sequence=1).

[29] Roughly 50% of global oil supplies are made available on global markets with no restrictions on who ends up being the purchaser. See Goldthau, A. & Witte, J.M. 'The Role of Rules and Institutions in Global Energy: An Introduction', in Goldthau A. & Witte, J.M. (eds) *Global Energy Governance: the New Rules of the Game* (Washington, DC: Brookings Institution Press, 2010) at pp. 4–5.

[30] In relation to instances of energy diplomacy, see Goldthau, A. 'Energy Diplomacy in Trade and Investment in Oil and Gas', in Goldthau A. & Witte, J.M. (eds) *Global Energy Governance: the New Rules of the Game*, (Washington, DC: Brookings Institution Press, 2010) at pp. 25–47.

[31] OPEC being a case in point. See Goldthau A. & Witte, J.M. (eds) *Global Energy Governance: the New Rules of the Game* (Washington, DC: Brookings Institution Press, 2010) at p. 4, footnote 2.

[32] Goldthau, A. 'Energy Diplomacy in Trade and Investment of Oil and Gas', in Goldthau A. & Witte, J.M. (eds) *Global Energy Governance: the New Rules of the Game* (Washington, DC: Brookings Institution Press, 2010) at p. 28.

III. FACTS AND FIGURES AROUND ENERGY SUPPLY AND CONSUMPTION

The latest figures available indicate that during 2010 global primary energy supply stood at 12,717 million tons of oil equivalent (Mtoe) – or 12.71 trillion tons of oil equivalent.[33] In terms of global final energy consumption, this was around the 8,677 Mtoe (8.6 trillion toe) mark.[34] During 2010, global supply of energy exceeded global consumption by 4,040 Mtoe (c. 4 trillion toe). For 2009, global energy supply exceeded consumption by 3,797 Mtoe (3.7 trillion toe).[35] In relation to 2008 figures,[36] global supply exceeded consumption by 3,839 Mtoe (3.8 trillion toe). For good measure, let us examine the 2005, 2006 and 2007 figures for an insight into global energy trends before the outbreak of the 2008 global financial crisis. In 2005, global supply exceeded consumption by 3,523 Mtoe (3.5 trillion toe). In 2006, supply exceeded consumption by 3,657 Mtoe (3.6 trillion toe).[37] In 2007, the supply surplus stood

---

[33] See International Energy Agency, *2012 Key World Energy Statistics* (OECD/IEA, 2012), at p. 8.

[34] Ibid., at p. 28.

[35] See International Energy Agency, *2011 Key World Energy Statistics* (OECD/IEA, 2011), at pp. 6 & 28. Final consumption globally during 2009 was 8,353 Mtoe. The breakdown is: 41.3% from oil; 17.3% from electricity; 15.2% from natural gas; 12.9% biofuels and waste; 10% from coal and peat; and 3.2% from other sources, including renewable non-emitting sources. Note that electricity requires the input of one of the primary resources, or the harnessing of renewable sources, for it to be produced, rather than being a primary energy resource itself. See also Bhattacharyya, S. *Energy Economics: Concepts, Issues, Markets, and Governance* (London: Springer, 2011), for economic analyses surrounding energy.

[36] See International Energy Agency, *2010 Key World Energy Statistics* (OECD/IEA, 2010).

[37] All figures have been taken from International Energy Agency reports for 2007, 2008, and 2010. Note that annual figures are published in the reports after two years, e.g., 2005 figures were published in the 2007 report, and so on. Reports used are available at http://www.iea.org/textbase/nppdf/free/2007/key_stats_2007.pdf (last accessed 2013); http://www.iea.org/textbase/nppdf/free/2008/key_stats_2008.pdf (last accessed 2013); and http://www.iea.org/textbase/nppdf/free/2010/key_stats_2010.pdf (last accessed 2013).

at 3,743 Mtoe.[38] Firstly, in a world that is patchily industrialized, no energy supply surplus is excessive or redundant when it could be put to good use, particularly when so many people go without electricity in the 21st century.[39] However, this persistent energy supply surplus (see Table 1.2) might have serious implications for investment in the upstream side of this sector given that it may signal to investors a less profitable field of speculation, since demand appears uncertain.[40] This is not to be dismissed lightly, given that IEA projections call for investments of at least USD 6.3 trillion by 2030 for the oil sector alone[41] to meet growing global energy demand.[42]

Whilst the quantification of the global energy supply and consumption is relatively straightforward, this is not so for the total energy needs of humankind. Historical supply and consumption figures, whilst helpful, present an incomplete picture of *global* energy needs given that they do not gauge what may be the necessary energy needs of the developing countries in order to harmonize global development levels. For instance, how might these figures be used to deduce the total energy requirements for upwardly harmonizing global industrialization levels to achieve parity in the standards of life for the whole of humanity? Whilst energy security alone is clearly not sufficient to achieve this, it remains a key factor given that industrialization is a complex matter relying on a multitude of other economic and social factors.

---

[38] In 2007, 12,029 Mtoe (c.12 trillion toe) of energy were produced globally, and 8,286 Mtoe (8.2 trillion toe) of energy were consumed globally. See International Energy Agency, *2009 Key World Energy Statistics* (OECD/IEA, 2009), at pp. 6 & 28.

[39] There are currently nearly two billion people that go without modern forms of energy such as electricity. See the World Bank Report 'Meeting the Challenge for Rural Energy and Development', foreword, available at http://siteresources.worldbank.org/INTENERGY/Resources/Rural_Energy_Development_Paper_Improving_Energy_Supplies.pdf

[40] See Victor, D. & Yueh, L. 'The New Energy Order: Managing Insecurities in the Twenty-first Century' (2010) *Foreign Affairs*, Vol. 89, No. 1, pp. 61–73, at p. 61.

[41] See International Energy Agency, *World Energy Outlook 2008* (OECD/IEA, 2008), p. 89.

[42] Incidentally, for the entire energy sector, the IEA calls for investments of USD 33 trillion by 2035. See the International Energy Agency's 2010 World Energy Outlook report, p. 93.

Table 1.2 Global energy figures (all figures in million tons of oil equivalent)*

Year	Global production	Global consumption	Surplus
2012[a]	n/a[b]	12,476	n/a
2011[c]	n/a[d]	12,274	n/a
2010[e]	12,717	8,677	4,040
2009[f]	12,150	8,353	3,797
2008[g]	12,267	8,428	3,839
2007[h]	12,029	8,286	3,743
2006[i]	11,741	8,084	3,657
2005[j]	11,435	7,912	3,523

Notes: * We have drawn from two different sets of data for this compilation. The 2007–2010 figures are compiled from the IEA's publications, whilst figures for 2011 and 2012 are from British Petroleum's publications. This is due to the fact that, as of June 2013, the IEA's latest figures did not extend to the years 2011 and 2012. Do also note that the IEA set of data covers oil, gas, coal, nuclear, hydroelectricity, combustible renewables and waste, and *others*, by which the IEA means solar, wind, heat, and geothermal energy. The IEA provides figures for these sources for global energy production and consumption, whereas British Petroleum (BP) only provides figures for these sources for global energy consumption. Moreover, in relation to global energy production, BP's 2012 and 2013 reports only provide figures for oil, gas, and coal. [a] The figures listed for 2012 are calculated on the basis of the sums on oil, gas, and coal production and consumption during 2012 as these appear in the *BP Statistical Review of World Energy June 2013* (http://www.bp.com/content/dam/bp/pdf/statistical-review/statistical_review_of_world_energy_2013.pdf) (at pp. 10, 11, 24, 25, 32, and 33). [b] The BP figures omit global production figures for primary energy generated via nuclear, hydroelectricity, renewables (solar, geothermal, heat, and wind), and combustible renewables (biofuel) and waste, all of which are included in the IEA's estimates for the years for which IEA reports have been published. In 2012, global energy production of oil, gas, and coal amounted to 10,997 Mtoe. [c] The figures listed for 2011 are calculated on the basis of the sums on oil, gas, and coal production and consumption during 2011 as these appear in the *BP Statistical Review of World Energy June 2012* (http://www.bp.com/content/dam/bp/pdf/Statistical-Review-2012/statistical_review_of_world_energy_2012.pdf) (at pp. 10, 11, 24, 25, 32, and 33). [d] The BP figures omit global production figures for primary energy generated via nuclear, hydroelectricity, renewables (solar, geothermal, heat, and wind), and combustible renewables (biofuel) and waste, all of which are included in the IEA's estimates for the years for which IEA reports have been published. In 2011, global energy production of oil, gas, and coal amounted to 10,906 Mtoe. [e] See International Energy Agency, *2012 Key World Energy Statistics*, OECD/IEA, 2012 (at pp. 8 & 28). [f] See International Energy Agency, *2011 Key World Energy Statistics*, OECD/IEA, 2011 (at pp. 6 & 28). [g] See International Energy Agency, *2010 Key World Energy Statistics*, OECD/IEA, 2010 (at pp. 6 & 28). [h] See International Energy Agency, *2009 Key World Energy Statistics*, OECD/IEA, 2009 (at pp. 6 & 28). [i] See International Energy Agency, *2008 Key World Energy Statistics*, OECD/IEA, 2008 (at pp. 6 & 28). [j] See International Energy Agency, *2007 Key World Energy Statistics*, OECD/IEA, 2007 (at pp. 8 & 28).

IV. FIELDS OF INTERSTATE COOPERATION RELATING TO ENERGY

Below is an analysis of some key aspects of energy governance: trade, investment, environmental protection, energy transit, energy security and other phenomena with implications for the global energy economy (see Figure 1.2 for a graphic view of the various aspects of energy governance). To that end, this section provides an analysis of the relevant institutions in each one of the aspects mentioned above. Another key legal aspect of international energy governance not covered in this chapter (but in Chapter 4 below) is the law of the sea. The purpose of examining the various institutions and processes is to establish how open they are to a more cohesive governance of the global energy economy and whether they lead to greater global energy security. Overall, the institutions and processes linked to the global energy economy appear to impact global energy security in the following ways:

- Negatively, by creating obstacles, as in the case of the Organization of the Petroleum Exporting Countries (OPEC) with its prescribed production restrictions, or, potentially, with institutions that promote energy security interests specific to their memberships (for instance, the EU, the Energy Charter Treaty, and the NAFTA) in a way that may undermine the energy security of outsiders;
- Positively, through the work of the UN inter-agency mechanism on energy security, or through the work of the International Energy Agency (IEA), whose members have taken precautionary steps by setting up and contributing to an emergency oil reserve to draw from when events threaten their energy security, without undermining the energy security of outsiders. Moreover, positive impacts can take place thanks to cooperation between producing and consuming countries through the creation of the International Energy Forum (IEF), where 75 countries gather to promote global energy security through data sharing, data analysis and dialogue. Another example of positive global cooperation is the joint report by the IEA, OPEC, the Organisation for Economic Co-operation and Development (OECD) and the World Bank on fossil-fuel and other energy subsidies, which highlights the extent of subsidies and other support for fossil-fuel production and consumption as

well as the economic and environmental benefits from reform in energy subsidies;[43] or

- Ambivalently/inconclusively, by containing aspects that could be considered to both support and undermine global energy security, as in the case of the WTO, which, on the one hand, by streamlining trade in energy commodities, may be contributing to global energy security, whilst, on the other, by facilitating the allocation of energy resources to the highest bidders, may be undermining global energy security by leading to the exclusion of others.

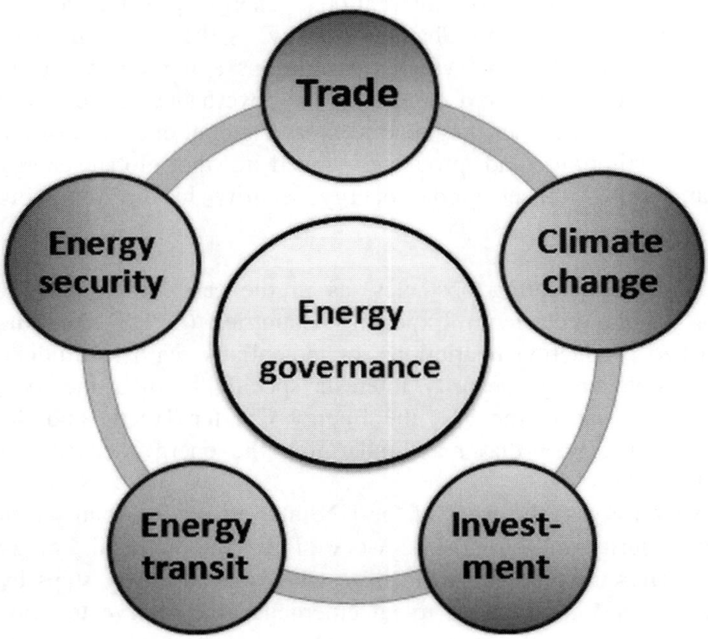

Figure 1.2 The various aspects of energy governance

[43] IEA, OPEC, OECD & World Bank 'Joint report by IEA, OPEC, OECD and World Bank on fossil-fuel and other energy subsidies: An Update on the G20 Pittsburgh and Toronto Commitments' (2011).

A. Trade

International trade allows energy supply to expand and travel transnationally.[44] Despite this link between trade and energy, it is surprising that the trade regime has not dealt with energy issues more directly. At the international level, there is no truly universal framework exclusively governing global trade, let alone governing global trade in energy. In its absence, a multi-layered patchwork of regimes has emerged, the largest cog of which is the WTO. If one were to take this patchwork to amount to an overarching global *energy trade* governance system, it would surely contain various elements, including: the WTO, the trade aspects of various preferential trade arrangements (PTAs) – for example, the EU, the North American Free Trade Agreement (NAFTA), and the Association of Southeast Asian Nations (ASEAN), amongst others – along with the trade aspects of organizations with a specific focus on energy, an example *par excellence* being the Energy Charter Conference. In that respect, none of these institutions possesses vertical exclusive competence over global energy trade, or over one another. Rather, it is more their interplay that one might consider as providing a degree of global governance over energy trade, with each component's scope limited to its specific membership.[45]

---

44 For an overview of trade in energy, see Waelde, T. & Gunst, A. 'International Energy Trade and Access to Energy Networks', in UNCTAD, *Energy and Environmental Services: Negotiating Objectives and Development Priorities* (UNCTAD/DITC/TNCD/2003/3), pp. 118–163, available at www.unctad.org/en/docs/ditctncd20033p1_en.pdf; F. Botchway, 'International Trade Regime and Energy Law' (2001) 28 *Syracuse J of Int'l Law*, pp. 1–17; Zarrilli, S. 'The Doha Work Programme: possible impact on energy trade and on domestic policies in energy-producing developing countries' (2003) *Journal of Energy and Natural Resources Law*, Vol. 21, No. 4, p. 399.

45 There are exceptions to this; for instance, the ECT and NAFTA regimes systemically show deference towards the WTO regime, were there to be any conflict. See Leal-Arcas, R. *International Trade and Investment Law: Multilateral, Regional and Bilateral Governance* (Cheltenham: Edward Elgar, 2010), Part 3; Leal-Arcas, R. 'Choice of Jurisdiction in International Trade Disputes: Going Regional or Global?' (Winter 2007) *Minnesota Journal of International Law*, Vol. 16, No. 1, pp. 1–59.

1. The World Trade Organization

The WTO is the most widely acceded organization to multilateral trade in existence.[46] Most energy-significant States – be it in terms of consumption or production – are within its fold. Notably, Russia became a fully-fledged WTO Member in August 2012, and the greater part of the remaining energy-significant States that are currently not WTO Members – including Azerbaijan, Belarus, Iran, Iraq, Kazakhstan, Libya, and Sudan – are in the process of negotiations to accede to the WTO.[47] The WTO governs trade relations among its members. Trade in energy-related commodities among WTO Members also falls within its remit. In that sense, the WTO system is an important element of the global energy economy in relation to the trade aspects of the global energy economy.

WTO figures suggest that at least 18% of total intra-WTO trade involves energy goods[48] – in other words, almost one in five US dollars spent on intra-WTO trade in goods is spent on energy. Despite this fact, the WTO does not handle the energy trade sector any differently from any other trade sector. Where the WTO system discriminates is in providing separate regimes for commodities that are deemed to be either 'goods' or 'services'. However, this distinction cuts across the trade sectors and treats energy trade – be it in goods or services – indiscriminately. Namely, those regimes are, in relation to 'goods', the General Agreement on Tariffs and Trade (GATT) and, in relation to 'services', the

---

[46] The WTO membership currently stands at 160 Members (see http://www.wto.org/english/thewto_e/whatis_e/tif_e/org6_e.htm). Compare this to the membership of the United Nations, which currently stands at 193 (see http://www.un.org/en/aboutun/index.shtml).

[47] Turkmenistan seems to be in no rush to join the WTO. Presumably, this might be to keep its significant export flows of energy outside the ambit of WTO disciplines, given that the latter extend beyond direct trade considerations to include norms on export restrictions and preferential trade practices, subsidies, and intellectual property rights (IPRs). This may be particularly significant to Turkmenistan, given its close energy export relationship with China and Iran, including subsidies and intellectual property rights protection. Turkmenistan is a net exporter of electricity (circa 1.5 billion kWh per annum in 2009), oil exporter (circa 40,160 barrels per day in 2009) and natural gas exporter (24.9 billion m^3 per annum in 2010). It has 600 million barrels of proved oil reserves and 7.5 trillion m^3 of natural gas reserves (in 2012), whilst it produces circa 15 billion kWh of electricity annually (in 2009). See CIA Factbook resource available at https://www.cia.gov/library/publications/the-world-factbook/geos/tx.html (all figures cited as appeared in late November 2012).

[48] See WTO, 'World Trade Report 2010: Trade in Natural Resources' (2010), p. 54, where it is stated that during 2008 fuels alone made up 18% of total intra-WTO trade in goods.

General Agreement on Trade in Services (GATS).[49] Incidentally, trade in services is considerably less liberalized than trade in goods, given the idiosyncrasies of cross-border services transactions. Returning to the energy sector, it is worth noting that there is disagreement as to whether electricity as a tradable commodity ought to be classified as a good or a service.[50] Further, as the world shifts towards renewable energy (however expensive the process of moving away from fossil fuels to renewables may be),[51] longer distances of electricity transportation are envisaged. Such a development could be a reason for creating an energy-specific multilateral trade agreement.[52] In such a case, would the WTO be the right forum to design a framework agreement on trade in energy?[53] Is such an agreement necessary and realistic? Or is it more realistic to add energy-related provisions to the current WTO rules, which would imply avoiding the complex process of ratification of a new international agreement?

Whilst it is true that the WTO system does not discriminate in any way when it comes to trade in energy, it is also true that the WTO system allows for concerns potentially linked to energy – chiefly in relation to the conservation of natural resources,[54] the protection of the

---

49 Other multilateral and plurilateral agreements adopted within the WTO may also apply to trade in goods or services. See http://www.wto.org/english/docs_e/legal_e/final_e.htm for a list of potentially relevant agreements.

50 See Pierros, P. 'Exploring Certain Trade-related Aspects of Energy under GATT/WTO: Demarcation Questions Regarding Electricity' (1999) *Int. Trade L. and Regulation* Vol. 5, No. 1, pp. 26–27, where he explores how electricity is dealt with under the EU, NAFTA, and WTO regimes.

51 However, there is currently a shale gas revolution in the USA. Further, coal and other highly polluting hydrocarbons are on the increase. See for instance Yang, A. & Cui, Y. 'Global Coal Risk Assessment: Data Analysis and Market Research' WRI Working Paper, World Resources Institute, 2012, where it is reported that more than 1,000 coal-fired plants were being proposed across 59 States as of 2012.

52 See notably the work by Cottier, Thomas et al. 'Energy in WTO Law and Policy', in Cottier, T. & Delimatsis, P. (eds) *The Prospects of International Trade Regulation: From Fragmentation to Coherence* (Cambridge University Press, 2011).

53 Ibid.

54 Article XX(g) GATT. For further details, see Abu-Gosh, E. & Leal-Arcas, R. 'The Conservation of Exhaustible Natural Resources in the GATT and WTO: Implications for the Conservation of Oil Resources' (2013) *The Journal of World Investment and Trade*, Vol. 14, No. 3.

environment,[55] or the protection of human, animal or plant health or life from pathogens in imports[56] – to modify the effect of core WTO rules. That is not to say, however, that it treats this sector differently; it is simply to say that concerns *potentially* linked, rather than *inherent*, to energy may modify the application of core WTO rules. This, however, is not unique to energy tradables/the energy sector, as these concerns may well be cited in relation to other trade sectors, including foodstuffs and chemicals.

For the purposes of the present chapter, however, it will suffice to sum up the overall WTO system as one that fails to provide universal/global governance over all energy-related trade. Moreover, the WTO does not provide separate rules for energy trade, nor does it exclude it. Consequently, WTO rules are fully applicable to trade in energy as well as to energy goods and services by default.

2. Preferential trade arrangements

As discussed above, international cooperation comes in a range of forms. States engage bilaterally and multilaterally to set up regimes of varying degrees of normativity. Preferential trade arrangements (PTAs) – for example, free-trade agreements (FTAs)/regional trade agreements (RTAs), and customs unions (CUs) – are invariably treaty-based regimes under public international law that create legal relations between States.

In most cases, these PTAs complement rather than undermine the wider multilateral trade system – namely the WTO – so that the trade aspects of the PTAs along with the WTO system may sensibly be considered elements of an overarching normative framework/governance system for global trade.[57] The WTO system contains provisions that accommodate the PTA phenomenon.[58] What is more, on balance, the proliferation of PTAs has not undermined the multilateral trade system; rather, their interplay may have made for a more – not less – liberalized

---

55 Article XX(b) GATT. See also the analysis by Schrijver, N. *Development without Destruction: The UN and Global Resource Management* (Bloomington, IN: Indiana University Press, 2010).

56 Article 2 of the Sanitary and Phytosanitary Agreement.

57 Leal-Arcas, R. 'Proliferation of Regional Trade Agreements: Complementing or Supplanting Multilateralism?' (2011) *Chicago Journal of International Law*, Vol. 11, No. 2, pp. 597–629.

58 See Article XXIV GATT in relation to goods and Article V GATS in relation to services. For an exposition on the FTA phenomenon vis-à-vis the WTO multilateral system, see Mavroidis, P. 'WTO and PTAs: A Preference for Multilateralism? (or the Dog That Tried to Stop the Bus)' (2010) *Journal of World Trade*, Vol. 44, No. 5, pp. 1145–1154.

market and globalized world.[59] For instance, PTAs such as the European Economic Area (EEA),[60] the NAFTA, and the ASEAN Free Trade Area (AFTA)[61] have liberalized trade between their respective memberships whilst not making trade relations more onerous for their external trade partners.[62] What is more, the PTAs cited above go further than the multilateral trade system in that they provide for energy-sector-specific disciplines.

Let us examine perhaps the most comprehensive out of these three PTAs. The body of EU internal market rules that the EEA espouses is highly developed in that it contains several EU legislative acts that govern or otherwise relate to energy trade.[63] What is more, there is a distinct portfolio in the EU Commission for energy matters, including a long-term EU energy security strategy.[64] In that sense, the EEA/EU structure goes well beyond energy trade to also provide energy security governance in relation to its members.[65] The EU, in that sense, is an

---

[59] See Sapir, A., 'The Political Economy of EC Regionalism'(1998) *European Economic Review*, Vol. 42, pp. 717–732.

[60] The EEA is a free-trade area formed on the basis of an agreement between, on the one hand, all but one of the Members of the European Free Trade Association (EFTA) (namely Switzerland) and, on the other, the countries of the European Union (EU). The entire EU internal market *acquis* – save for that on fisheries and agriculture – applies to the EEA. See http://eeas.europa.eu/eea/ for more details on the EEA.

[61] AFTA is based on the 1992 Agreement on the Common Effective Preferential Tariff Scheme for the ASEAN Free Trade Area (AFTA-CEPT Agreement) signed in Singapore on 28 January 1992. See Article 2.A of the Framework Agreements on Enhancing ASEAN Economic Cooperation, Singapore, 28 January 1992 (within the context of the AFTA-CEPT Agreement) in relation to the duty for trade cooperation.

[62] See for instance, the Appellate Body report in *Turkey – Restrictions on Imports of Textile and Clothing Products*, of 22 October 1999 (WT/DS34/AB/R), in which the WTO Appellate Body found that, although FTAs and CUs are permitted to confer exclusive privileges to parties to them, they may not, consequently, introduce more restrictive trade terms for third parties. In that case, in forming a CU with the EU, Turkey introduced quantitative restrictions that engaged, amongst other things, Article XI GATT.

[63] See http://www.energy.eu/#directives. See also Deketelaere, K. (ed.) *Codex EU Energy Law* (Berlin: Lexxion, 2012).

[64] For more information, see http://ec.europa.eu/energy/index_en.htm. See also http://ec.europa.eu/energy/energy2020/roadmap/index_en.htm in relation to longitudinal strategies.

[65] For more detailed analysis, see Leal-Arcas, R. & Filis, A. 'Conceptualizing EU Energy Security through an EU Constitutional Law Perspective' (Spring 2013) *Fordham International Law Journal*, Vol. 36.

instance of interstate cooperation that is remarkably comprehensive in relation to energy. Whilst the EU has not been purposely set up to deal with the energy security of its membership,[66] its comprehensive and sophisticated nature has led it to pursue its, amongst other things, environment, trade,[67] investment, and energy-security policy objectives in the most cohesive of manners.

Whilst this might seem to run against our earlier assertion that the global energy governance system is fragmented, and that, for the most part, interstate cooperation occurs along thematic lines, we would suggest that the EU be viewed as an exception – albeit an admirable one – to the rule. It should be borne in mind that the EU is primarily concerned with the internal market of its Member States and its *en bloc* economic relations with the outside world. Whilst the EU might lack the political mandate to expand its remit at will, it possesses the clout and global legitimacy, which flow from its institutional capacity and overall positive external relations, to take cohesive action. What is more, the EU and the US account for about half of global GDP, a third of global trade flows, and possess 'the most integrated relationship in the world'.[68] In 2007, they set up the Transatlantic Economic Council (TEC) with a view to deepening their integration, including through cooperating on energy-related matters.[69]

When one views the EU through the prism of global energy governance, the EU is merely an element – albeit unparalleled in its comprehensiveness – of the global energy governance system that seems to emerge. It contains provisions on trade, energy security and investment protection, all of which are matters that engage the energy sector. In that

---

66 Having said that, one should bear in mind the fact that the EU has its origins in the European Coal and Steel Community, which was set up to lock key resources between the historically belligerent German and French nations under a common administration to make armed conflict less likely. For the constitutive treaty that established that institution, see http://europa.eu/legislation_summaries/institutional_affairs/treaties/treaties_ecsc_en.htm

67 See for instance Leal-Arcas, R. *Theory and Practice of EC External Trade Law and Policy* (London: Cameron May, 2008), for a comprehensive analysis of EU trade law. See also Leal-Arcas, R. 'Reflections on EU International Trade Law: An Introspective View' (2012) *Frontiers of Law in China*, Vol. 7, No. 1, pp. 1–20.

68 See http://ec.europa.eu/trade/creating-opportunities/bilateral-relations/countries/united-states/

69 See the December 2010 TEC joint statement that mentions cooperation in, amongst other things, energy matters. See http://www.whitehouse.gov/sites/default/files/TEC_Joint_Statement_12-17-10.pdf

sense, it provides *incidental* governance – albeit limited to its 28 Member States – over a range of energy-related matters. From that point of view, the EU's inception and dynamic evolution could certainly serve as an effective blueprint for other such systems, were the necessary political will to materialize.

Briefly referring to the other PTAs mentioned above, NAFTA devotes an entire chapter in its constituent agreement[70] to energy trade among its three (energy-significant) members – Canada, Mexico,[71] and the US. The ASEAN-dominated AFTA, for its part, obliges its Members to cooperate on energy matters, including the production and supply of energy.[72] For the purposes of this chapter, we have considered it sufficient to refer to the above three examples of PTAs to highlight their relationship to a global *energy trade* governance system.[73]

3. The Energy Charter Conference

The Energy Charter Conference is an intergovernmental organization set up under the ECT,[74] mentioned earlier, to administer its provisions and acts as the decision-making body for the Energy Charter process.[75] One can think of the ECT as Plan B to what had been Plan A of Western net energy importing States – namely the developed West – to conclude an energy-specific agreement within the context of the GATT/WTO system.[76] Part II of the ECT (Articles 3–9) is devoted to trade. What is more, it contains provisions that promote WTO obligations and that make clear

---

[70] Chapter VI (Articles 601–608) of NAFTA, 32 ILM (1993).

[71] Certain reservations on the part of Mexico have been subsumed into the NAFTA Agreement (see Annexes 602.3 and 603.6).

[72] See Article 2B of the Framework Agreements on Enhancing ASEAN Economic Cooperation. It is preceded by Article 2A, which places a duty on members for trade cooperation. Article 2B relates to the duty to cooperate in 'industry, minerals, and energy', and contains provisions relating to, amongst other things, research and development, the sharing of know-how and the exploration and production of energy resources. In that sense, it may also be considered an aspect of a broader governance of energy framework between AFTA Members.

[73] One could think of other major PTAs under negotiation as of 2013, where energy security may play an important role. These are the Trans-Pacific Partnership, the Regional Comprehensive Economic Partnership, and the Transatlantic Trade and Investment Partnership.

[74] UNTS 2080/1999.

[75] For background information, see http://www.encharter.org/index.php?id=25

[76] See generally Wälde, T. (ed.) *The Energy Charter Treaty: An East-West Gateway for Investment and Trade* (London: Kluwer Law International, 1996).

that the ECT regime in no way weakens the obligations ECT parties owe under the WTO.[77]

Unlike the PTAs discussed above, not only is the ECT regime not location-restricted/regional, it is a single-sector multilateral agreement in that it exclusively deals with the energy sectors of parties to it. In this sense, it is worth noting that, for the purposes of the WTO, the ECT regime cannot be considered an RTA/FTA, given that WTO rules require that substantively all trade areas fall within the scope of such an interstate arrangement.[78] Nevertheless, the specificity of the ECT's trade aspects – that is, the exclusive focus on energy – makes this regime also an important feature of the putative overall *global* energy trade governance edifice.[79] What is more, the ECT regime also extends to other energy-related matters, including investment and environmental protection, with a focus on their interplay with energy exploration and trade.

Incidentally, it is worth noting that in November 2012 ECT parties agreed to begin the process of updating the ECT during successive rounds of negotiations – known as the *Warsaw Process* – to take place in Warsaw, Poland. This has been argued as necessary to meet current demands and to also draw in membership from other regions.[80]

4. The Organization of the Petroleum Exporting Countries

The Organization of the Petroleum Exporting Countries (OPEC) has been included as an element of the putative global energy trade governance edifice, given that OPEC members control roughly 81% of global oil reserves,[81] about 43% of global oil production, and 60% of global oil trade, thus affording it considerable influence over global oil supply.[82]

---

77 See Article 4 ECT, which prohibits derogation from the GATT, and Annex G to ECT, which conditions the exercise of WTO rules between ECT Members.

78 See Article XXIV:8(b) GATT, the Understanding on the Interpretation of Article XXIV GATT and Article V:1(a) & (b) GATS.

79 For further details on the link between trade regulation and the ECT, see Frasl, I. 'The Trade Rules of GATT and Related Instruments and the Energy Charter Treaty', in Waelde, T. (ed.), *The Energy Charter Treaty: An East-West Gateway for Investment and Trade* (Kluwer Law International, 1996), Chapter 21.

80 See http://www.encharter.org/index.php?id=21&id_article=334&L=0

81 For an overview of statistics, see OPEC, '2014 Annual Statistical Bulletin', OPEC, 2014, available at http://www.opec.org/opec_web/en/press_room/178.htm

82 See http://alturl.com/s8oib, where it is stated that during 2005, the annual share of production had been 41.7%. See also the answer to question 'Does

This has implications for trade volumes and flows of oil, given that, as we have seen earlier, oil remains a significant share of the primary energy supply. Compare this degree of influence with that of the next-in-size groups of producers, namely those involved in the Organisation for Economic Co-operation and Development (OECD) and in the Commonwealth of Independent States (CIS)[83] – that is, the transition economies that had formerly been part of the Soviet Union – which, during 2005, produced just 23.8% and 14.8% of global oil production respectively.[84]

OPEC is ostensibly concerned with defending the interests of the 12 oil producing/exporting States that are OPEC members.[85] In that sense, it can more appropriately be considered an institutionalized cartel with potentially trade-distortive implications for global oil trade and, therefore, for the global energy economy, particularly when its membership colludes to set production quotas. Furthermore, OPEC has a negative impact on global energy security by creating obstacles with its prescribed production restrictions. Given that the majority of its members – with the exception of Algeria, Iraq, and Iran – are WTO Members, the compliance of their OPEC-related activities with the WTO system comes under examination. However, imposing production quotas, whatever the trade implications, is not, in itself, WTO inconsistent. Whilst the WTO unequivocally prohibits quantitative restrictions – including those that are export and import related – on trade flows (namely through Article XI GATT), it is unlikely that this prohibition will extend to the pre-extractive stage of energy resources.

Once resources have been extracted and are in tradable form, they ought not be subject to quantitative restrictions that are otherwise not WTO-compliant. In other words, WTO disciplines – as they currently stand – do not extend to the pre-extraction/production stage of energy.

OPEC control the oil market?' in the FAQ section on the OPEC website at http://www.opec.org/opec_web/en/press_room/178.htm (last accessed 2013), where the figures of 43% annual share of global oil production and 60% annual share of global oil trade have been listed by OPEC.

[83] The CIS is a loose, quasi-economic association of independent States following the dissolution of the USSR. Its membership today comprises Azerbaijan, Armenia, Belarus, Kazakhstan, Kyrgyzstan, Moldova, Russia, Tajikistan, Turkmenistan (unofficial associate member), Uzbekistan, and Ukraine (officially not a member). International agreements have been signed within its auspices towards the progressive development of a free-trade area between parts of or its entire membership. See http://en.ria.ru/infographics/20100821/160274561.html.

[84] Compare these figures with OPEC's 41.7% annual share of global oil production in 2005. See http://alturl.com/yhq8u (last accessed 2013).

[85] http://www.opec.org/opec_web/en/about_us/25.htm

This could be understood to preserve the voluntarist basis upon which WTO members have acceded to the WTO, and to safeguard the sovereign prerogatives – in our case, in relation to sovereignty over natural resources from incursions not otherwise justified under the existing state of public international law.

5. The Gas Exporting Countries Forum

The Gas Exporting Countries Forum (GECF) could be understood as the OPEC-equivalent for net natural gas producers, albeit a more influential institution. It counts amongst its membership 13 producers over four continents, namely Algeria, Bolivia, Equatorial Guinea, Egypt, Iran, Libya, Nigeria, Oman, Qatar, Russia, Trinidad and Tobago, United Arab Emirates, and Venezuela.[86] It represents 70% of gas reserves, 38% of global pipeline trade, 85% of global production of liquefied natural gas (LNG),[87] 45% of global gas production and 90% of global gas trade in all its forms.[88] The realities inherent to gas – for example, cost-intensive processing to transport outside of pipeline infrastructure by liquefying and then regassing – have contributed to a less globalized gas market.[89] It remains to be seen what the GECF's implications shall be for the global gas supply and the global energy economy at large; whether it would seek to mimic OPEC or take an altogether different approach so as to unify the global gas market by encouraging the membership-wide development of infrastructure to process and transport gas and, thus, to contribute to global energy security.

---

86 See http://www.gecf.org/aboutus/faq. Iraq, Kazakhstan, the Netherlands, and Norway have 'observer' status.

87 'GECF members together control over 70% of the world's natural gas reserves, 38% of the pipeline trade and 85% of the liquefied natural gas (LNG) production. The three largest reserve-holders in the GECF – Russia, Iran and Qatar – alone hold about 57% of global gas reserves'. See GECF FAQ's, 'Who are GECF Member Countries? What is the total strength of GECF now?' available at http://www.gecf.org/aboutus/faq

88 These figures are based on an analysis of BP in 2008, Statistical Review of World Energy, as cited by Dick de Jong et al. in Goldthau A. & Witte, J.M. (eds) *Global Energy Governance: the New Rules of the Game* (Washington, DC: Brookings Institution Press, 2010) at p. 227.

89 See de Jong, D. et al. 'The Evolving Role of LNG in the Gas Market', in Goldthau A. & Witte, J.M. (eds) *Global Energy Governance: the New Rules of the Game* (Washington, DC: Brookings Institution Press, 2010) at pp. 221–245.

B. Investment

What has so far been said in relation to the global trade system could also be said regarding the global investment protection system. Namely, no truly universal framework exists,[90] let alone one concerned with global investment protection in energy. What one might imagine to exist is a putative composite framework constituted by various independent elements. As discussed above, the international community is neither monolithic nor homogenous; it is made up of numerous States that could broadly be lumped together in different groups in relation to their economic strength and levels of industrialization/development. In that respect, the interests of least or less developed countries on the question, say, of foreign investment interests protection had, in the past, not been identical to those of the developed world.[91] This is less the case now, following the end of the Cold War, where it appears that whatever misgivings existed on the part of the less industrialized world about capitalist-based paths to development seem to have subsided, given that States in the less industrialized world seek to outcompete one another in their quest to attract foreign direct investment and to further integrate into the global economy.

Although investment is a major issue for energy production, in relation to the global governance of energy investments, there is no overarching regime. In fact, without access to energy, our daily lives would collapse. One might imagine that the various existing investment regimes converge to the extent that their respective provisions apply to the energy sectors of their respective memberships to form a putative global energy-related investment governance regime that is multi-layered, the layers of which are non-uniform and non-coextensive.

---

90 See for instance Leal-Arcas, R. 'The Multilateralization of International Investment Law' (2009) *North Carolina Journal of International Law and Commercial Regulation*, Vol. 35, Issue 1, pp. 33–135.

91 The adoption of multilateral frameworks for investment protection within the context of the WTO and the OECD has been unsuccessful, given the difficulties of securing the buy-in from least and less developed countries. See Sornarajah, M. *The International Law on Foreign Investment* (Cambridge: Cambridge University Press, 2004), Chapter 6. See also Schrijver, N. *Sovereignty over Natural Resources: Balancing Rights and Duties* (Cambridge: Cambridge University Press, 1997), Chapter 6, at pp. 187–190.

1. Energy Charter Conference

Earlier we discussed the ECT regime's trade aspects. The ECT's purported aim according to Article 2 (Purpose of the Treaty) is to establish 'a legal framework in order to promote long-term co-operation in the energy field, based on complementarities and mutual benefits, in accordance with the objectives and principles of the Charter'. The ECT's facilitates the exploration of the energy sectors of the 49 States[92] that have ratified it so far.[93] It does this principally by legally obligating parties to it to respect foreign investment interests in their jurisdictions and to offer more robust investment protection[94] than that which appears to exist under general international law.[95] The ECT investment protection

---

[92] The last country to join the ECC was Afghanistan, in 2013. See http://www.encharter.org/index.php?id=21&id_article=349&L=0

[93] See http://www.encharter.org/index.php?id=61&L=0 for a list of members and observers. There are 54 members. Also note that parties that have ratified may withdraw; however, this cannot be until five years post-ratification. Parties who had ratified before withdrawing from the ECT remain bound by ECT investment protection obligations for 20 years post-withdrawal (see Article 47 ECT). For those parties who have signed but not ratified, it is possible to withdraw with effect from within a shorter timeframe – namely 60 calendar days (see Article 45(3)(a)), as has been the case with Russia, which had not ratified the ECT before its notification to the Energy Charter Secretariat to withdraw from the provisional application of the ECT. See Leal-Arcas, R. *International Trade and Investment Law: Multilateral, Regional and Bilateral Governance* (Cheltenham: Edward Elgar, 2010), Chapter 7; Leal-Arcas, R. 'The EU and Russia as Energy Trading Partners: Friends or Foes?' (2009) *European Foreign Affairs Review*, Vol. 14, Issue 3, pp. 337–366. See also Hober, K. 'Arbitrating Disputes under the Energy Charter Treaty' (2009) *Oil, Gas & Energy Law Journal (OGEL)*, 2.

[94] See Part III ECT (Articles 10 to 17), which exclusively deals with obligations to protect foreign investment, thus elevating investor interests to legally protected rights flowing from the ECT. These include the right to compensation (see Article 12(2) ECT, which embeds the Hull formula of compensation that is 'prompt, adequate, and efficient' named after Cordell Hull, the US Secretary of State in 1938, who articulated the US's position in relation to the expropriations of its interests carried out in Mexico during the Mexican Revolution of 1910). For further details, see Leal-Arcas, R. 'The Multilateralization of International Investment Law' (2009) *North Carolina Journal of International Law and Commercial Regulation*, Vol. 35, Issue 1, pp. 33–135. The ECT also heavily restricts sovereign rights of expropriation so that expropriations may be permissible to the extent they are ECT-compliant (see Article 13 ECT).

[95] For a fuller analysis of the protection that might exist under general international law, see Sornarajah, M. *The International Law on Foreign Investment* (Cambridge: Cambridge University Press, 2004), at pp. 135ff.

regime is essentially the only multilateral investment treaty that exclusively deals with the energy sector and as such – despite its limited membership – it is a principal element in the putative global governance system in relation to energy-related investments.[96]

As it currently stands, the ECT does not apply the Most-Favored-Nation (MFN) treatment[97] or National Treatment (NT)[98] at the pre-investment stage. This therefore leads us to conclude that the ECT neither obligates its parties to liberalize their energy markets and to open up their energy sectors to foreign investment, nor does it provide energy exploitation contracts to all ECT parties on a non-discriminatory basis.[99] The ECT only obligates parties to ensure that, once foreign investments have been accepted into their territories, they provide ECT protection, including MFN and NT, to such investments. Broadly, the ECT provides disciplines for energy sector foreign investment once this has been welcomed in the territory of an ECT party. In sum, once investments

---

[96] Do note, however, that the ECT's efficacy has significantly been undercut by the withdrawal of Russia from the ECT's provisional application, a State of considerable energy-relevance in terms of energy-related natural resource reserves. On the Russian proposal regarding an energy security convention, see also Belyi, A., Nappert, S. & Pogoretskyy, V. 'Modernizing the Energy Charter Process? The Energy Charter Conference Road Map and the Russian Draft Convention on Energy Security' (2011) *Journal of Energy and Natural Resource Law*, Vol. 29, No. 3.

[97] As defined in an UNCTAD report, MFN treatment in the context of international investment law means that 'a host country treats investors from one foreign country no less favourably than investors from any other foreign country'. See UNCTAD, *Most-Favoured-Nation Treatment*, UNCTAD Series on Issues in International Investment Agreements (New York and Geneva, United Nations, 1999), p. 1. For further detail, see Newcombe, A. & Paradell, L. *Law and Practice of Investment Treaties: Standards of Treatment* (Alphen aan den Rijn: Kluwer Law International, 2009), Chapter 5.

[98] As defined in an UNCTAD report, national treatment is the principle whereby a host country extends to foreign investors treatment that is at least as favorable as the treatment that it accords to national investors in like circumstances. In this way, the national treatment standard seeks to ensure a degree of competitive equality between national and foreign investors. See UNCTAD, *National Treatment*, UNCTAD Series on Issues in International Investment Agreements (New York and Geneva: United Nations, 1999), p. 1. For further detail, see Newcombe, A. & Paradell, L. *Law and Practice of Investment Treaties: Standards of Treatment* (Alphen aan den Rijn: Kluwer Law International, 2009), Chapter 4.

[99] See the section entitled 'An Introduction to the Energy Charter Treaty' of the *Energy Charter Treaty and Related Documents: A Legal Framework for International Energy Cooperation* (at p. 14).

have been accepted by ECT parties in their territories, they must provide indiscriminate treatment to all foreign investors, as well as between foreign investors and domestic investors (that is to say, on the MFN and NT bases). Russia's notification to withdraw from the provisional application of ECT has undercut the clout of the ECT, given Russia's significance in terms of its energy exports.

The ECT is therefore a regime that promotes, amongst other things, investment protection in the energy sectors of its parties. The provisions are more robust than those under general international law. Thus the ECT may be viewed as an element of the global energy economy in relation to the investment aspects of the global energy economy.

2. The World Trade Organization system

Within the context of the UN, there have been efforts to set up a comprehensive trade regime (the International Trade Organization, the ITO) that would have contained, amongst other things, investment protection provisions. These efforts were ultimately unsuccessful. Whilst the trade-specific aspects of that ill-fated regime, that is, the ITO, survived in the GATT and its eventual evolution into the WTO system,[100] this had not been the case with its investment protection aspects. However, the necessity for an overarching investment protection regime found some expression within the WTO at a later stage in that the WTO Agreement on Trade-related Investment Measures (TRIMs), and the GATS contain provisions related to investment protection. These do not single out energy trade, or any other trade sector, but their provisions may apply to measures taken by WTO Members that seem to be WTO-inconsistent.

For instance, the Annex to the TRIMs Agreement includes an illustrative list of the sort of trade-related investment measures in relation to goods that might violate core WTO obligations. Namely, discouraging the use of imported parts, or encouraging the use of domestically-produced parts, in the domestic production process may amount to a *prima facie* breach of Article III GATT in relation to the duty to provide national treatment to goods that are imported. Restricting the importation of parts to be used in the domestic production process, the exportation of goods, or restricting access to foreign exchange may all amount to a *prima facie* breach of Article XI GATT. Presumably, both such measures

---

[100] For more details on the ill-fated International Trade Organization under the 1948 Havana Charter and on investment matters within WTO, see http://www.wto.org/english/thewto_e/whatis_e/tif_e/bey3_e.htm and http://www.wto.org/english/tratop_e/invest_e/invest_e.htm

may harm foreign investment interests as they condition how those investments must be used in ways that may be against the interests of the investors.

Whilst the TRIMs Agreement does not single out the energy sector, it provides a layer of protection for foreign investment interests in the energy sector in that it discourages export restrictions, prohibits requirements that investors favor domestically produced goods in the production process, and prohibits importation restrictions on parts that are used in the production process.

Similarly, whilst the GATS does not single out the energy sector, its provisions apply to all sectors of trade in services in which market-access specific commitments on the part of each WTO Member have been made to the extent that they have stated in their respective schedules. Depending on how trade in services takes place – that is to say, depending on the modality of the provision of services – it may be necessary for the service provider to set up operations in a host territory in order to render services to consumers in that territory.[101] Those operations require investments, and those investments require sufficient degrees of protection.

The GATS promotes sufficient protection of foreign investor interests in trade in services. It prohibits discriminatory and other bad faith restrictions on such operations, including in relation to foreign investment interests.[102] It does not single out the energy sector nor does it apply to it on the strength of the energy sector alone. Rather, it may apply to it to the extent that the WTO member that has taken the offending measure has made specific commitments in their schedules that relate to the energy sector.

In conclusion, given the broad membership of the WTO and on account of the potential engagement of the TRIMs Agreement and the GATS, the WTO becomes an important element of the putative global governance regime over energy-related investments.

3. Proliferation of bilateral and multilateral investment treaties

As discussed previously, States contract legal relationships with one another in all manner of configurations, for example bilateral, multilateral, regional or on the basis of specific shared interests (e.g., ECT and the energy sector). The explosion in bilateral investment treaties

---

[101] As contemplated in Article I:2(c) GATS.

[102] See Article XVI on market access obligations and Article XI in relation to the prohibition of restrictions over transfers and payments.

(BITs)[103] makes this phenomenon a significant element of the putative global investment protection governance system in that it provides a further layer of investment protection to the extent that an interstate relationship may also be conditioned by the existence of a BIT. It is worth noting that the proliferation of BITs does not in itself lead to the crystallization of investment protection norms in international customary law.[104] In that respect, one should not deduce that the norms contained in such agreements – however widely these might be witnessed – amount to international custom binding on all States. Rather, one should understand the BIT practice to amount, along with the other elements under review, to a putative global energy investment governance system. Whilst this phenomenon does not single out the energy sector *per se*, its incidence is particularly relevant to energy diplomacy.[105]

4. The Convention on the Settlement of Investment Disputes

The 1965 Convention on the Settlement of Investment Disputes between States and Nationals of Other States (ICSID Convention)[106] sets up a

---

[103] BITs form the bulk of international investment agreements (IIAs), namely 2,833 out of 3,164 IIAs. Thirty-three out of the 47 IIAs signed in 2011 were BITs. Sixty-nine BITs were signed in 2010. The number of BITs may be decreasing annually; however, regionalism (through regional trade agreements/free trade agreements and customs unions) is on the increase. See UN Conference on Trade and Development, *World Investment Report 2012: Towards a New Generation of Investment Policies* (UNCTAD, 2012), at pp. xx, cvii & 84. See also Leal-Arcas, R. 'Proliferation of Regional Trade Agreements: Complementing or Supplanting Multilateralism?' (2011) *Chicago Journal of International Law*, Vol. 11, No. 2, pp. 597–629; Leal-Arcas, R. *International Trade and Investment Law: Multilateral, Regional and Bilateral Governance* (Cheltenham: Edward Elgar, 2010), Part 2; Leal-Arcas, R. 'The Multilateralization of International Investment Law' (2009) *North Carolina Journal of International Law and Commercial Regulation*, Vol. 35, Issue 1, pp. 33–135; Leal-Arcas, R. 'The Fragmentation of International Trade Law: Is Now the Time for Variable Geometry?' (2011) *The Journal of World Investment and Trade*, Vol. 12, No. 2, pp. 145–195.

[104] See Schrijver, N. *Sovereignty Over Natural Resources: Balancing Rights and Duties* (Cambridge: Cambridge University Press, 1997), Chapter 6, in relation to the view that this proliferation of BITs, though illustrative of State practice, 'may not in itself be able to reflect or generate customary international law including *opinio juris communis*' (at p. 193).

[105] See for instance EU efforts to engage Russia and the Ukraine in separate bilaterals discussed above. For further information on each EU trade negotiation partner, see http://ec.europa.eu/trade/creating-opportunities/bilateral-relations/

[106] 4 ILM 532 (1965).

dispute resolution regime for investment disputes between a host State and a national of another State. Out of 158 States that have signed the ICSID Convention, 147 have ratified it. Given such wide membership, it is an important element of the putative global investment protection governance regime. That said, it should be noted that whether it offers robust protection *per se* is highly dependent upon the norms that may come to apply to a particular dispute. As the ICSID Convention provides for arbitration on the basis of the domestic law of the host State, 'including its rules on the conflict of laws and such other rules of international law as may be applicable',[107] investment protection under ICSID can be patchy, given the disparity between the investment-protection regimes of States parties to ICSID.

C. Environmental Protection

As has been the case with the other aspects of energy mentioned above, environmental protection is also a field of interstate activity that lacks an overarching universal governance framework that is cohesive.[108] Legal obligations at the interstate level flow from a variety of legal agreements that, taken cumulatively, could be construed to amount to an overarching environmental protection regime, albeit to the extent that its constituent elements apply to their respective disparate sets of members.

There is a plethora of international legal agreements that promote environmental protection to the extent that these bind the parties that have ratified them.[109] As has been the case with the other aspects of energy, there is no universal governance regime in relation to the environmental aspects of energy. A patchwork of regimes and provisions could be understood to amount to a putative global governance regime

---

[107] See Article 42(1) ICSID Convention.

[108] See Helm, D. *The Carbon Crunch: How We're Getting Climate Change Wrong – and How to Fix It* (New Haven, CT: Yale University Press, 2012).

[109] See e.g., Part XII of the 1982 UN Convention on the Law of the Sea on the Protection and Preservation of the Marine Environment; the 1985 Vienna Convention on the Protection of the Ozone Layer and its 1987 Protocol (Montreal Protocol); the 1989 Basel Convention on the Control of Transboundary Movements of Hazardous Wastes and their Disposal; the 1992 UN Framework Convention on Climate Change and its 1997 Protocol (Kyoto Protocol); and the 1992 Convention on Biological Diversity. For an analysis of some of these agreements, see Leal-Arcas, R. *Climate Change and International Trade* (Cheltenham: Edward Elgar, 2013), Chapters 3–6.

over the environmental aspects of energy.[110] The level of interstate cooperation to meaningfully govern the interplay between energy and the environment is frightfully poor given that fossil-fuel combustion is responsible for 82% of anthropogenic greenhouse gas emissions.[111] The value of global energy consumption is annually somewhere around USD 3 trillion, which amounts to about 7% of global GDP.[112] Apparently, it could cost as much to meaningfully contain CO_2 emissions.[113] The 2006 Stern Review projects that to contain CO_2 emissions by 2050 to necessary levels could cost anything between 1% and 3.5% of annual global GDP,[114] which, alone, makes the case for colossal capital investments on the part of all States according to their polluting history and economic ability.[115]

---

[110] See Schrijver, N. *Sovereignty over Natural Resources: Balancing Rights and Duties* (Cambridge: Cambridge University Press, 1997), Chapter 8, for a fuller analysis on the interplay between natural resources – including those that are energy-related – and international environmental law.

[111] See the 2001 figures published by the US Energy Information Agency at http://www.eia.gov/oiaf/1605/ggccebro/chapter1.html

[112] See Blyth, W. 'How do Emerging Carbon Markets Influence Energy Sector Investments?', in Goldthau A. & Witte, J.M. (eds) *Global Energy Governance: the New Rules of the Game* (Washington, DC: Brookings Institution Press, 2010), Chapter 7, at p. 133. Note that during 2011, global gross world product (GWP) stood at USD 70 trillion, according to the World Bank (see figures at http://search.worldbank.org/data?qterm=global%20gdp&language=EN), and anything between USD 69.99 and 80.33 trillion, according to the CIA (see https://www.cia.gov/library/publications/the-world-factbook/geos/xx.html).

[113] See International Energy Agency, *World Energy Outlook 2008*, at p. 47, where different scenarios for climate change action are outlined, including the range of costs associated with these.

[114] See the Executive Summary to the *Stern Review: The Economics of Climate Change*, at p. 12 (available at http://goo.gl/7tFXJ).

[115] Were it politically feasible, some international organization within the context of the UN could be constituted, in which all States assume robust obligations in line with their polluting history and beyond the level of differentiation that the UNFCCC accommodates. This could assist in quantifying the level of contributions each State should make for the development of the vast infrastructure necessary to macro-manage and exploit all possible renewable resources. This infrastructure ought to remain a public good under the management of that international organization in the manner that the International Seabed Authority, pursuant to the UN Convention on the Law of the Sea, manages those resources which lie outside the jurisdictional reach of States, and that are considered the 'common heritage of mankind'. See UNCLOS Part XI, Articles 136 and 156–158. As has been the case elsewhere, solutions exist. It is

1. United Nations Framework Convention on Climate Change and its Kyoto Protocol

The 1992 United Nations Framework Convention on Climate Change (UNFCCC) encourages parties to it to reduce greenhouse gas (GHG) emissions, whilst its 1997 Kyoto Protocol mandates that those who have ratified the Protocol not exceed the permissible GHG emission levels under that instrument.[116] Within the context of the UNFCCC, States have also agreed a set of propositions contained in the 2007 Bali Action Plan[117] on next steps after the expiry of the first phase of the Kyoto Protocol, which took place at the end of 2012.

The strength of the Kyoto Protocol lies in that it has 192 parties of which 191 have ratified it, with the prominent exception of the United States; its weakness lies in that it is of little consequence in the greater scheme of things.[118] Note, for instance, that the most onerous aspect of the UNFCCC regime is that the EU plus the 36 Annex B States that are parties to the Kyoto Protocol ensure that they reduce their 1990-level of emissions by at least 5% within the five-year period between 2008 and 2012.[119] This is not surprising given that States – particularly at the international level – are loath to assume restrictions on their GHG emitting that may compromise the competitiveness of their industries.

---

the political expediencies at play between national capitalisms that make such meaningful cohesive action difficult.

[116] See http://unfccc.int/kyoto_protocol/items/2830.php/ for a run-down on the Kyoto Protocol. For a comprehensive analysis, see Leal-Arcas, R. *Climate Change and International Trade* (Cheltenham: Edward Elgar, 2013), Chapter 5; Leal-Arcas, R. 'Kyoto and the COPs: Lessons Learned and Looking Ahead' (2011) *Hague Yearbook of International Law*, Vol. 23, pp. 17–90.

[117] See http://unfccc.int/resource/docs/2007/cop13/eng/06a01.pdf.

[118] It is astonishing to note that the Clean Development Mechanism under the UNFCCC has only resulted in a 1% containment of global CO_2 levels. See Blyth, W. 'How Do Emerging Carbon Markets Influence Energy Sector Investments?' in Goldthau A. & Witte, J.M. (eds) *Global Energy Governance: the New Rules of the Game* (Washington, DC: Brookings Institution Press, 2010) at p. 146.

[119] See Article 3.1 of the Kyoto Protocol in relation to this duty, and Annexes A and B of the Kyoto Protocol in relation to the greenhouse gases and to the States, respectively, to which this duty extends. Do note that it does not extend to the US, which has not ratified the Kyoto Protocol, nor to Canada, which withdrew from the Kyoto Protocol. Kyoto Protocol Annex B States are required to restrict their aggregate emissions by at least 5% below 1990 levels, whilst parties to Annex I of the UNFCCC must restrict their emissions to levels based on a formula contained in Article 3 of the Kyoto Protocol.

Consequently, consensus on such an acute matter, as is the case for climate change mitigation, ends up being achieved on a lowest-common-denominator basis.[120]

Perhaps whatever has been agreed is as good as it gets under the present circumstances. Although this might be the case, it is neither sufficient nor satisfactory, given what is at stake.[121] As an example, it is relevant to mention one of the outcomes of the Conference of the Parties (COP)-18 in Doha, where New Zealand, Japan, Russia, and Canada refused to take on commitments for the second phase of the Kyoto Protocol. This translates mathematically into the Kyoto Protocol only covering 15% of global GHG emissions.[122]

An interesting feature of the UNFCCC regime and its Kyoto Protocol is the co-option of markets as part of the solution – or more worryingly, in our view, the penetration of the market/speculation into a field of common concern and endeavor. Namely, there is a global market for carbon emission credits subsequent to the advent of the UNFCCC-related regimes. A recent World Bank report has quantified the value of this market to be around USD 176 billion in 2011 alone, involving 10.3 billion tons of CO_2 equivalent (CO_2e).[123]

---

[120] Leal-Arcas, R. 'Is the Kyoto Protocol an Adequate Environmental Agreement to Solve the Climate Change Problem?' (Winter 2001) *European Environmental Law Review*, Vol. 10, Issue 10, pp. 282–294.

[121] Alternative approaches to climate change mitigation have been proposed. See for instance, Leal-Arcas, R. *Climate Change and International Trade* (Cheltenham: Edward Elgar, 2013), Chapters 6–8; Leal-Arcas, R. 'Alternative Architecture for Climate Change: Major Economies'(2011) *European Journal of Legal Studies*, Vol. 4, Issue 1, pp. 25–56; Leal-Arcas, R. 'Top-down versus Bottom-up Approaches for Climate Change Negotiations: An Analysis' (December 2011) *The IUP Journal of Governance and Public Policy*, Vol. 6, No. 4, pp. 7–52; Leal-Arcas, R. 'A Bottom-up Approach for Climate Change: The Trade Experience'(2011) *Asian Journal of Law and Economics*, Vol. 2, Issue 4, pp. 1–54; Leal-Arcas, R. & Filis-Yelaghotis, A. 'Geoengineering a Future for Humankind: Some Technical and Ethical Considerations' (2012) *Carbon and Climate Law Rev*, Vol. 6, No. 2, pp. 128–148.

[122] Earth Negotiations Bulletin, 'Summary of the Doha Climate Change Conference' (11 December 2012) IISD, Vol. 12, No. 567, p. 26.

[123] See Kossoy, A. & Guigon, P. *State and Trends of the Carbon Market 2012* (Washington, DC: World Bank, 2012), at p. 9.

2. World Trade Organization

The WTO[124] has been listed here given that the protection and preservation of the environment is included in the purported aims of the WTO's constituent instrument, that is, the Marrakesh Agreement Establishing the World Trade Organization.[125] However, there are no specific agreements contracted within the WTO context – with the exception of the Agreement on Sanitary and Phytosanitary Measures (SPS Agreement) – that are principally concerned with environmental matters. What exists is a number of provisions relating to concerns about human, animal, and plant health or life. These provisions might justify *bona fide* – that is to say, agreements that are neither intentionally protectionist nor discriminatory – trade-restrictive measures on the part of WTO members aimed at protecting the environment.[126] The ongoing Doha Development Agenda negotiations feature the relationship between the multilateral trade system and the environment.

There is also a purposely set-up body within the WTO – the Committee on Trade and Environment (CTE) – created under the 1994 Ministerial Decision on Trade and Environment with a broad mandate that effectively functions as a talking-shop on the interplay between trade and the environment for the WTO Members that have joined it.[127]

In sum, given that the WTO is principally concerned about disciplining trade within its membership, arguably, its environmental protection aspects are incidental to the entire WTO project. That said, the WTO is a dynamic organization in which suitable diplomatic mechanisms exist for its membership to consider adopting subsequent norms, or to modify the interpretation of the existing norms to allow for current broader policy

---

124 See http://www.wto.org/english/tratop_e/envir_e/envt_intro_e.htm in relation to the environment within the WTO context.

125 See the Marrakesh Agreement Establishing the World Trade Organization, first recital. On the world's resources, see also Schachter, O. *Sharing the World's Resources* (New York: Columbia University Press, 1977).

126 See for instance Articles XX and XI GATT; various provisions in the Agreement on the Application of Sanitary and Phytosanitary Measures, including Article 2.1; provisions of the Agreement on Technical Barriers to Trade; and Article XIV(b) GATS. There are a number of cases dealt with by the adjudicative agency of the WTO that engage the environment; for a list of disputes per subject, see http://www.wto.org/english/tratop_e/dispu_e/dispu_subjects_index_e.htm

127 See http://www.wto.org/english/tratop_e/envir_e/wrk_committee_e.htm for background information on the CTE.

concerns – including over the environment – to be sufficiently accommodated.[128] This is a matter that requires sufficient political will.

Finally, in relation to the global governance of energy implications for the environment, the WTO, on account of its very broad membership, should be considered an important cog of any such putative system.

3. Energy Charter Conference

The Energy Charter Conference (ECC) and the regime under the ECT are essentially about the energy security of the ECC membership and parties to the ECT. The principal concerns of this regime surround the investment protection and trade aspects of energy. That said, the ECT contains provisions that relate to the environment.[129] In fact, an entire Protocol – the Energy Charter Protocol on Energy Efficiency and Related Environmental Aspects (PEEREA) – to the ECT relates to the environmental aspects of energy. The majority of the ECT parties have ratified the PEEREA.[130]

4. European Union

The EU is a comprehensive PTA of its own kind with sophisticated provisions in relation to, amongst other things, the protection of the environment. Articles 191 to 193 of the Treaty on the Functioning of the European Union (TFEU) contain the high-level coordinates of EU environmental policy. This is supplemented by a vast array of EU legislation.[131] What is more, the EU has set up a sophisticated emissions trading scheme (EU ETS) under which it is progressively drawing all

---

[128] See Article IX:2 of the WTO Agreement. Under it, the WTO Ministerial Conference and the General Council have exclusive authority to decide on questions of interpretation on a three-fourths majority. Though greater use of this mechanism could be to promote environmental objectives, in reality, the same difficulties of majority vote would be encountered in those *fora* to secure the requisite consensus to do this. It is worth noting that the WTO Dispute Settlement Body (DSB), tasked with adopting reports issued by the WTO judicial agency (namely the Appellate Body, following a Panel determination), is the *alter ego* of the General Council, the highest level diplomatic decision-making body of the WTO. In that regard, processes are in place to expedite the promotion of environmental objectives over those concerned with trade. In other words, the apparent idleness here is political, not systemic.

[129] See Article 19 ECT.

[130] See http://www.encharter.org/fileadmin/user_upload/document/PEEREA_ratification_status.pdf for details on ratification.

[131] EU environmental legislation is available at http://europa.eu/legislation_summaries/environment/index_en.htm.

major polluting industries, including aviation and prospectively the shipping industry.[132] This has annoyed many a non-EU State, given that the EU ETS has been extended to all airline operators with flights that enter, or depart from, EU territory; moreover, it has also been opposed by the EU aviation industry.[133] Following this sustained opposition, the EU caved in and announced a year-long moratorium on 12 November 2012 that suspends the application of the EU ETS on flights that are not entirely limited to EU territory.[134]

Despite the protectionist stance of the aviation sector, and of a few non-EU States, the EU ETS should surely be supported and replicated, given that it goes far beyond any other instance of interstate cooperation on the protection of the environment taken within the context of the UNFCCC or the WTO.[135] The EU ETS has proven worthwhile in that, during 2011, of the 8,081 million tons of CO_2e that were globally traded through emission credits, 7,853 million tons of CO_2e were traded through the EU ETS – in other words, the value of EU ETS transactions was USD 147.8 billion, whereas global transactions were USD 148.8 billion.[136] Since the EU ETS relates to the climate change aspects of GHG emissions – including those caused by the consumption of fossil fuels – within EU territory, it could be viewed as an element of the global energy economy in relation to the climate change aspects of the global energy economy.

5. North American Free Trade Agreement

Similarly to the WTO, the NAFTA includes provisions that permit *bona fide* trade-restrictive measures concerned with the protection of the environment.[137] It goes further, to condition how GATT/WTO provisions in relation to the environment may be applied among NAFTA parties.

---

[132] Fuller background information on the EU ETS is available at http://ec.europa.eu/clima/policies/ets/index_en.htm. See also Leal-Arcas, R. 'Unilateral Trade-related Climate Change Measures' (2012) *The Journal of World Investment and Trade*, Vol. 13, No. 6, pp. 875–927.

[133] See http://ictsd.org/i/news/bridgesweekly/134007. Also, note that China, India, and Saudi Arabia, amongst others, have instructed their airlines to not comply with the EU carbon tax. See Leung, A. & Suhartono, H. 'China Airlines Won't Pay EU Carbon Tax' *Reuters*, January 6, 2012.

[134] See http://ictsd.org/i/news/bridgesweekly/134007/

[135] See Kossoy, A. & Guigon, P. *State and Trends of the Carbon Market 2012* (Washington, DC: World Bank, 2012), pp. 73–104, in relation to initiatives elsewhere, including Australia, South Korea, and the USA.

[136] Ibid, at p. 10.

[137] See Article 2101 NAFTA.

Although it has similar provisions to the WTO system in relation to permissible trade-restrictive measures taken on environmental grounds, it places greater emphasis on their potential trade implications in assessing their permissibility.[138] In that sense, it appears to prioritize the trade aspects over the environmental protection aspects of intra-NAFTA trade (including of intra-NAFTA energy trade).

D. Energy Transit

Global energy consumption continues to draw heavily on primary energy resources that, in addition to being highly polluting, are finite and patchily distributed across the globe. Very few States are truly energy sufficient and energy independent, hence the importance of transnational policy networks.[139] Against this backdrop, it is no surprise that the cross-border and cross-regional transportation of energy resources (hereinafter 'energy transit') is no new phenomenon. This energy transit relies on a variety of means, including vessels and other means of transportation, and conduits such as cross-border overland and underwater pipelines, for bringing energy goods to markets. For instance, States such as Turkey and Ukraine are important energy transit States for EU energy imports from the Caspian Sea region and from Russia.[140] Spats between, for instance, energy exporting States and transit States may cause shocks to energy flows that have negative implications for consumer States' energy security. One such incident was the Russia-Ukraine dispute, which brought the issue of energy transit sharply into focus by affecting EU energy markets and consumers, given that up to 20% of EU gas supplies transit via Ukraine.[141]

---

[138] See Article 715.2 NAFTA.

[139] Literature has been published on transnational policy networks. See for instance Slaughter, A.-M. *A New World Order* (Princeton, NJ: Princeton University Press, 2004) (arguing that global governance is done through a complex global web of government networks by, for instance, exchanging information transnationally to solve global issues).

[140] See for instance the report for the Committee on Foreign Relations; US Senate, 'Energy and Security from the Caspian to Europe,' 112th Congress, Second Session, 12 December 2012.

[141] See the 2011 EU Commission Communication to the European Parliament, the Council, the European Economic and Social Committee, and the Committee of the Regions, 'On security of energy supply and international cooperation – "The EU Energy Policy: Engaging with Partners beyond Our Borders"', 7 September 2011 (COM(2011) 539 final), at p. 5. The IEA estimates

Interstate cooperation in relation to energy transit issues is less institutionalized than other areas of interstate cooperation engaging energy (such as trade, investment protection or environmental protection) since there are no international agreements solely devoted to transit; rather, there are norms here and there that come together to produce some sort of interstate governance framework for transit. The *freedom of transit* provisions of a number of international agreements and the *freedom of transit* norms of general international law (that is to say, norms not flowing from particular international law) are important elements of whatever interstate governance exists in relation to energy transit.

1. UN and its legal order

On the occasion of the adoption of the 1958 Convention on the High Seas,[142] which enshrined the notion of a *freedom of transit* in a multilateral international agreement – an innovation up to that point – Lauterpacht carried out a comprehensive review of the notion of *freedom of transit* in international law, linking it to historical notions and to practices that had taken place between States, be these practices due to conventional or customary norms or due to other circumstances. In that respect, the legal notion of *freedom of transit* and its implications for such acute matters – such as sovereign prerogatives (e.g., to exclude others from their territory) and the voluntarist nature of international law – may properly be understood with reference to Lauterpacht's extensive study.[143] There is some debate as to the status of the notion of *freedom of transit* under customary international law.[144] This has implications for energy transit. In the absence of *freedom of transit* norms that flow from

---

that up to 84% of Russian gas supplies to the EU transit through Ukraine. See http://www.iea.org/countries/non-membercountries/ukraine/.

[142] 450 UNTS 11. Done in Geneva on 29 April 1958 and entered into force on 30 September 1962. This international legal agreement at the time involved 46 signatories and currently involves 63 parties. See its status at http://treaties.un.org/pages/ShowMTDSGDetails.aspx?src=UNTSONLINE&tabid=2&mtdsg_no=XXI-2&chapter=21&lang=en#Participants.

[143] Lauterpacht, E. 'Freedom of Transit in International Law' (1958) *Transactions of the Grotius Society*, Vol. 44, Problems of Public and Private International Law, Transactions for the Year 1958–59.

[144] For instance, Lothar Ehring and Yulia Selivanova refer to this as a controversial notion that cannot be assumed to be reflected in customary international law. Their argument is predicated on the view that given that States had historically included transit provisions frequently in their bilateral treaties, that this may suggest the absence of an equivalent binding norm in customary

international agreements relevant to the States concerned, it remains unclear to what extent general international law countenances *freedom of transit*.

Successive international agreements adopted within the context of the UN – namely, the 1958 Convention on the High Seas,[145] the 1958 Convention on the Territorial Sea and Contiguous Zone,[146] the 1958 Convention on the Continental Shelf,[147] and the 1982 Convention on the Law of the Sea (UNCLOS)[148] – have come to strengthen the notion of

---

international law. See Ehring, L. & Selivanova, Y. 'Energy Transit', in Selivanova, Y. (ed.) *Regulation of Energy in International Trade Law: WTO, NAFTA, and Energy Charter* (Alphen aan den Rijn: Wolters Kluwer 2012), at pp. 51–52.

145 See Article 3 of the Convention on the High Seas.

146 See Section III *Right of Innocent Passage* (Articles 14–20), which restricts sovereign acts in the territorial sea of coastal States to the extent that the right of innocent passage is protected.

147 See Articles 4 and 5.1 UNCLOS. Furthermore, whilst this international agreement allows coastal States to set up safety zones around their continental shelf installations from which to curtail the freedom of navigation and of laying cables or pipelines by third States, these safety zones should not exceed 500 meters beyond the installations in question (see Articles 15.2 and 15.3 UNCLOS).

148 UNCLOS has come to revolutionize international maritime law by codifying norms over a wide range of maritime issues, including the delimitation of the territorial sea, continental shelf, and exclusive economic zone of coastal States, and the rights and obligations of third party States, including landlocked States. What is more, it promotes the *freedom of transit* in that several UNCLOS provisions touch upon transit/navigation and communication matters. Whilst UNCLOS lays down extensive rules that enshrine coastal States' rights to their territorial sea and other adjacent maritime areas, it also places restrictions on their sovereign control of these maritime areas in order to promote the interests of other States to navigation and communication. For instance, Part II, Section 3 (Articles 17–32) relates to the right of innocent passage through the territorial sea of coastal States; Part III, Section 2 (Articles 34–44) relates to the rights of States concerning the use of straits for international navigation; Part III, Section 3 relates to innocent passage (Article 45); Article 58 relates to the rights and obligations of other States in the exclusive economic zone of coastal States; Part IV, Article 79 relates to the rights of other States to lay cables and pipelines on the continental shelf of coastal States; Part VII, Article 87 relates to the freedom of the high seas, and Article 90 on the rights of navigation on the high seas; Part X (Articles 124–132) relates to the rights of landlocked States to and from the sea and their freedom of transit. For analyses on the delimitation of exclusive economic zones specifically in the Eastern Mediterranean Basin, see Abu-Gosh, E. & Leal-Arcas, R. 'Gas and Oil Explorations in the Levant Basin: The Case of Lebanon and Israel' (2013) *Oil, Gas & Energy Law Journal*, Vol. 11, Issue 3, pp. 1–32; Filis, A. and Leal-Arcas, R. 'Legal Aspects of Inter-State Maritime

freedom of transit in modern international maritime law. In that respect, these international agreements may be important elements to the notion of maritime energy transit – and, consequently, to interstate governance of energy transit – to the extent that the States concerned are parties to these agreements. What is more, where these agreements are inapplicable, one would have to identify the strictures of customary international law that come to bear in such matters.

2. World Trade Organization

Within the WTO legal order, Article V GATT enshrines the *freedom of transit* of such commodities deemed to be *traffic in transit* (Article V:1). What is considered for the purposes of the WTO system to be *traffic in transit* are commodities from State X that are temporarily traversing the territory of State Y in order to be consumed in one (or more) third State. Under Article V, such *traffic in transit* ought to be exempt from customs duties and other encumbrances.[149] Moreover, Article V:2 expressly requires that the 'most convenient' route for international transit be made available to such traffic. This means whatever route is most convenient for the purposes of international trade, rather than for the purposes of the transit State. However, it is not entirely clear how the tension is resolved between what is convenient to the transit State and what is convenient to the exporting and/or importing States.[150] As in the entire WTO legal system, Article V (namely Article V:2 & V:5) prohibits the application of the *freedom of transit* in a manner that discriminates between WTO members. What is more, as also is the case with other WTO provisions, Article V does not single out energy commodities, or any other type of commodity for that matter. In that sense, Article V incidentally, rather than expressly, applies to the transit of energy commodities, given that it is a general provision with scope over all intra-WTO trade in goods. That said, it is less clear what the implications of Article V are for energy commodities that are being transported via fixed infrastructure through the territory of a transit State. Does Article V mandate that a transit State ought to make, say, gas or oil pipelines in its territory – in other words, infrastructure that is fixed to its territory – available to all its WTO peers in an even-handed manner?

Delimitation in the Eastern Mediterranean Basin' (2013) *Oil, Gas & Energy Law Journal*, Vol. 11, Issue 3, pp. 1–23.

149 Article V:3 GATT.

150 See Azaria, D. 'Energy Transit under the Energy Charter Treaty and the General Agreement on Tariffs and Trade' (2009) *Journal of Energy & Natural Resources Law*, Vol. 27, No 4, at pp. 570–574, who highlights this ambiguity.

There is some controversy around this point. Azaria argues that we cannot assume that Article V applies automatically to such infrastructure.[151] Cossy, on the other hand, argues that nothing in the wording of Article V suggests that transportation via fixed structures ought to be excluded under Article V. She refers to the express exclusion in Article V of aircraft in transit and therefore seeks to argue that transit through fixed infrastructure falls within Article V.[152] Faced with the strength of these arguments, and given what is at stake – namely the imposition of a potentially wider and more onerous obligation on WTO members that could amount to an unjustified incursion on their sovereign prerogatives – we consider Azaria's to be the better view.

It should be noted that *freedom of transit* within the WTO system has not much concerned the WTO's dispute resolution mechanism. There is a 2009 report by a WTO Panel[153] in which they interpreted the Article V *freedom of transit* as one that must be extended by a WTO member to all traffic in transit via the most convenient routes for the purposes of the trading WTO peer who wishes its goods to traverse the territory of the

---

151 Azaria argues that we cannot assume that Article V applies automatically to such infrastructure. Azaria argues this point by relating it to how the *freedom of transit* is envisaged elsewhere – namely in the ECT. ECT Article 7 expressly applies to fixed infrastructures. Incidentally, Azaria also makes a finer point about the possible interplay of Article V GATT and Article 7 ECT to state that, whilst GATT systemically influences the interpretation of ECT norms (for instance, Article 4 ECT expressly mandates non-derogation from GATT obligations, and, notably, the ECT mentions the term 'GATT' on 100 occasions), the reverse is not the case. See Azaria, D. 'Energy Transit under the Energy Charter Treaty and the General Agreement on Tariffs and Trade' (2009) *Journal of Energy & Natural Resources Law*, Vol. 27, No. 4, at p. 571. Furthermore, she argues that the interpretation of Article 7 ECT is not influenced by Article 5 GATT, in that Article 7 ECT, on its own strength, mandates ECT contracting parties – who incidentally are also GATT/WTO parties – to facilitate transit, including via fixed pipes. Article V GATT does not condition this effect. Nor does the Article 7 ECT norm, on its own strength, condition how Article V GATT ought to be applied between WTO parties *inter se*.

152 Cossy seems to rely on the interpretative principle that to expressly refer to one matter would imply the exclusion of whatever is not mentioned (namely *expressio unius est exclusio alterius*) by arguing that transit through fixed structures is within the scope of Article V. See Cossy, M. 'Energy Transport and Transit in the WTO', in Pauwelyn, J. (ed.) *Global Challenges at the Intersection of Trade, Energy, and the Environment* (Geneva: Centre for Trade and Economic Integration, 2010), pp. 113–121.

153 See WTO Panel Report, *Colombia – Indicative Prices and Restrictions on Ports of Entry*, WT/DS366/R (20 May 2009).

former. The case involved the restriction on the part of Colombia of the points of entry for imports and for traffic in transit relating to textiles, apparel, and footwear. This restriction was underpinned by Colombia's concerns on the smuggling of such goods via Panama. The Panel found the measure inconsistent with Article V in that it restricted access in ways that were not convenient to trade flows, and in ways that discriminated between goods and the between places of origin. This offended the requirement for unrestricted and non-discriminatory access for traffic in transit under Article V. The Panel's finding, however, has no special relevance to energy transit. What is more, it does not address whether *freedom of transit* under Article V within the WTO context extends to fixed infrastructure such as gas and oil pipelines. This is hardly surprising, given that the dispute in question did not relate to energy resources.[154]

3. Energy Charter Conference

Within the ECT regime, freedom of transit is considered 'a critical issue for the collective energy security [of ECT parties] ... since energy resources are increasingly being transported across multiple national boundaries on their way from producer to consumer'.[155] Article 7 ECT is a far more comprehensive provision than Article V GATT, not least due to Article 7 ECT being part of an energy sector specific regime. Similarly to Article V GATT, Article 7 prohibits discrimination in how the freedom of transit is extended between ECT parties.[156] Furthermore, Article 7

---

[154] See Ehring, L. & Selivanova, Y. 'Energy Transit', in Selivanova, Y. (ed.) *Regulation of Energy in International Trade Law* (Alphen aan den Rijn: Wolters Kluwer International, 2012), Chapter 2.

[155] See Energy Charter Secretariat, *The Energy Charter Treaty and Related Documents: A Legal Framework for International Energy Cooperation* (2004), at p. 15.

[156] See Article 7§1 & 7§3. However, under Article 7§3, discrimination due to 'an existing international agreement' would not necessarily amount to a breach. In that sense, while there is a general *erga omnes partes* obligation to extend the freedom of transit 'in a manner no less favorable', this is displaced when there is a particular legal agreement in place. In that respect, the 'most favored nation' principle – that is to say, that a party extend towards all parties the most favorable conditions that are enjoyed by another party – does not apply to the Article 7 ECT freedom of transit. Also, note that Article 7§8 states that: 'Nothing in this Article shall derogate from a Contracting Party's rights and obligations under international law including customary international law, existing bilateral or multilateral agreements, including rules concerning submarine cables and pipelines', thus elevating particular norms that may exist.

contains provisions on dispute resolution,[157] and expressly refers to the *freedom of transit* extending to such fixed infrastructure as oil and gas pipelines.[158] Unsurprisingly for an energy-focused regime, ECT provides the most elaborate governance for energy transit between its parties.

Shortly after the ECT came into force in 1998, the ECC decided in 2000 to launch negotiations for more specific rules on energy transit for the adoption of a separate *Transit Protocol* that have yet to result in any such agreement. These negotiations started in 2000 and were concerned with matters such as secure, efficient, uninterrupted, and unimpeded transit; the efficient use of transit infrastructure, and the facilitation of construction and/or updating of transit infrastructure. However, on 29 November 2011, the ECC repealed the negotiation mandate for a Transit Protocol. This has not fully closed the door to future negotiations. The ECC Trade and Transit Group intended to consult on the prospects of future negotiations and to make recommendations to the ECC.[159]

4. North American Free Trade Agreement

According to the website of the US Department of Transportation's Federal Motor Carrier Safety Administration, the principal means of commercial transportation between the parties to NAFTA – namely Canada, Mexico, and the US – is territorial and vehicular via trucks.[160] At that site, there is a rundown of the principal provisions with implications for transit issues. US trucks are not permitted to operate in Mexico, whilst Mexican truck operations are restricted to certain border zones within the US.[161] This is despite the initial plan for these restrictions to be entirely phased out between 1995 and 2000. This evidently places restrictions on transportation; however, it is not clear what the *freedom of transit* implications are concerning, say, traffic in transit originating in the territory of one NAFTA member, traversing the territory of either of the other NAFTA members and destined for

---

[157] Namely Article 7§6 & 7§7.

[158] See Article 7§10 (b). However, ECT parties are bound by a list of *understandings*, including one on Article 7 ECT. See Declaration with respect to Article 7, Energy Charter Secretariat, *The Energy Charter Treaty and Related Documents: A Legal Framework for International Energy Cooperation* (at p. 31).

[159] As of April 2013, no announcements had been publicized on the resumption of Transit Protocol negotiations. See the historical rundown in relation to the Transit Protocol negotiations and related activity at http://www.encharter.org/index.php?id=37

[160] http://www.fmcsa.dot.gov/intl-programs/naftatrans.htm (last accessed 2013).

[161] Ibid.

consumption in the remaining NAFTA member and/or any other State. What appears to have been happening is that traffic in transit, say, from Mexico to Canada or any other point in the US was required to be unloaded and then reloaded on other trucks in a buffer zone within the US for onward transportation.[162]

Mexico appended Annex 602.3 to NAFTA to reserve the exclusive right to strategic activities, including the transportation of energy.[163] Whilst it is not clear what the implications for the *freedom of transit* may be in terms of Canada or US energy transit traversing Mexico for consumption to a third State, this appears to be a significant restriction to unbridled access to each other party's road infrastructure.

In relation to energy transit, the reservation on the part of Mexico illustrates that it is less free than general traffic in transit. All three NAFTA parties are WTO members. In that respect, the relationship between their obligations to ensure that there be *freedom of transit* according to Article V GATT and their NAFTA commitments and reservations would be of particular interest in instances where another WTO member such as Nicaragua commissions Mexican transportation services to transfer coal from Nicaragua to Canada, via Mexico and the US. In this arrangement, a third party – namely Nicaragua – would want to argue that the loading and reloading requirement breaches its *freedom of transit* rights under Article V.

5. Association of Southeast Asian Nations

ASEAN provides for some governance of transit between its members. However, this is not energy sector specific, although it does extend over energy goods in transit, given that these have not been excluded. Similar to the WTO's Article V GATT regime, Article 5 of the 1998 ASEAN Agreement on the Facilitation of Goods in Transit relates to the freedom of transit, to which it refers in Article 3 and throughout the Agreement as 'transit transport'. Furthermore, the 2009 ASEAN Agreement on the Facilitation of Inter-State Transport further supports the freedom of transit of ASEAN members by obligating parties to that Agreement to grant each other the right to 'inter-state transport' by allowing transport operators of each party to undertake transport of goods into and/or from the territories of the other parties, and to grant the right to load and

162 See http://www.fmcsa.dot.gov/intl-programs/naftatrans.htm (last accessed 2013) for a more expansive version. See also the following article on this matter referring to a brief piloting of lifting these restrictions: http://transportationnation.org/2011/10/25/first-ever-mexican-truck-crosses-border-under-nafta/

163 See Annex 602.3: Reservations and Special Provisions.

discharge goods destined for or coming from other parties.[164] The 2009 Agreement defines 'inter-state transport' as transport of goods and the movement of means of transport into and/or from parties to that Agreement.[165]

Neither the 1998 nor the 2009 Agreement makes any reference to traffic in transit/transit transport/interstate transport in relation to fixed infrastructure such as pipelines, or even to energy, for that matter.[166] That said, energy-specific agreements exist within the context of ASEAN. The 1986 ASEAN Agreement on Energy Cooperation sets out the fields of cooperation. This Agreement was amended by the 1995 Protocol to add further fields of interstate cooperation, including over the transportation and distribution of energy.[167] This is an element of the governance of energy transit within the context of ASEAN.

Furthermore, a 2002 Memorandum of Understanding between ASEAN members on the trans-ASEAN Gas Pipeline requires parties to conduct relevant studies on several cross-border matters, including transit issues.[168] There is also a 2007 Memorandum of Understanding on the ASEAN Power Grid that lays the foundations for cooperation over the progressive development of an ASEAN-wide electricity power grid, which would also be viewed as an important element of ASEAN governance over energy transit.

---

[164] See Article 5.1 (a) & (b).

[165] See Article 3(e).

[166] The 1998 Agreement (at Article 3(c)) refers to *means of transport* to mean: 'road vehicles, railway rolling stock, sea and inland waterways craft and aircraft' and the 2009 Agreement (at Article 3(f)) refers to *means of transport* to mean: 'road vehicle, including those on-board roll-on/roll-off vessels'.

[167] See Article 1 of the 1995 Protocol, which amends Article 1.2 of the 1986 Agreement so as to include the 'processing, handling, transport and distribution of various energy forms' as a field of cooperation between the parties to that Agreement. See http://www.asean.org/news/item/protocol-amending-the-agreement-on-asean-energy-cooperation-bangkok-15-december-1995.

[168] See Article III(f), which refers to: 'acceptable measures which would facilitate the issuance of permits, licenses, consents, or other authorizations for transit Pipelines and natural gas being transported through the territory of such Member Country' as the transit issues within scope of this duty to carry out studies. For more information on the gas pipeline project, see http://www.petronas.com.my/our-business/gas-power/gas-processing-transmission/Pages/gas-processing-transmission/trans-asean-gas-pipeline.aspx.

6. European Union

The freedom of movement of goods across the EU is constitutionally entrenched.[169] This applies to energy flows across EU territory. However, the EU also has energy-specific legislation in place to facilitate the integration of the energy markets across the EU.[170] Currently, the EU energy market and its infrastructure are not fully integrated. This is not down to the lack of a normative framework, but to the economic and geographic relations of energy. According to the TFEU, EU energy policy ought to aim at the promotion of the interconnection of energy networks.[171] The EU seeks to fully integrate its 28 members' electricity and gas markets by 2014 into the Internal Energy Market (IEM).[172]

The EU has drawn several neighboring States into energy relations on the basis of the Energy Community Treaty[173] with the aim of enhancing EU energy security by promoting regulatory convergence amongst the parties with a view to future integration of their respective gas and electricity markets.[174] In that respect, intra-EU energy transit and energy transit with neighboring partners are certainly no afterthought within the EU order. The TFEU (Article 26 and Title XXI TFEU) along with EU policies pursuant to it (e.g., the IEM and the Energy Community) are

---

169 Article 26 TFEU.

170 Under Article 4§1(i) TFEU, *energy*, in its wide sense, is expressly referred to as a matter of shared competence. This allows the EU to act (including to legislate) in relation to energy in a manner that is proportionate and effective without unduly encroaching on the sovereign rights of EU member states. That said, certain energy-related matters are the exclusive competence of the EU under Article 3 TFEU, given that they may engage the competitive conditions of energy trade within the internal market, the question of tariffs when third-country energy commodities cross an EU border.

171 Article 194§1(d) TFEU.

172 Communication from the Commission to the European Parliament, the Council, the European Economic and Social Committee, and the Committee of the Regions, 'Energy Roadmap 2050', Brussels, 15 December 2011 (COM(2011) 885 final), (p. 19).

173 http://www.energy-community.org/portal/page/portal/ENC_HOME/ENERGY_COMMUNITY/Legal/Treaty

174 The European Commission states that the Energy Community ought to be promoted with third party States who are negotiating or concluding an FTA with the EU. See Communication from the Commission to the European Parliament, the Council, the European Economic and Social Committee, and the Committee of the Regions, On Security of energy supply and International Cooperation, 'The EU Energy Policy: Engaging with Partners beyond Our Borders', Brussels, 7 August 2011, COM (2011) 539 final (at p. 7).

important elements of EU governance over energy transit within the EU and several neighboring third party States.

So far, the above provisions relate to energy transit within the EU, but not with the outside world. However, the relationship of the EU with the outside world also contains *freedom of transit* obligations. For instance, the EU alongside its 28 members (and the broader membership of the EEA) are parties to the WTO and thus subject to GATT Article V *freedom of transit* obligations owed to WTO members. What is more, the EU is also a member of the ECT – in that respect, ECT Article 7 *freedom of transit* obligations (which, as we have seen, are energy specific and extend to transit through fixed infrastructure) that are owed to its ECT peers must also be respected.

E. Energy Security

As mentioned above, what we ultimately mean by *global energy security* is the satisfaction of humankind's energy needs to maintain lifestyle levels in the developed world and to promote development and improve the quality of life across the world, including least-developed and developing countries. Although *energy security* at the nation-state level is a more straight-forward concept, this is not the case at the global level, where the deployment of this term can be deceptive.[175] Whilst energy security is a concern common to all sovereign actors, it is currently not a collective objective, as is, for instance, human security (i.e., the prohibition of aggression) under the United Nations (UN) Charter. Moreover, the aim of energy is to be affordable, secure, and sustainable. Yet the world is still far from achieving these goals.

The global energy economy is a reality that exists not because it has been set up or otherwise prescribed. When we discuss, say, the *global* governance systems for trade (discussed above) or monetary matters (e.g., the interplay between, say, the International Monetary Fund, the Bank for International Settlements and any other relevant bodies), we examine their constituent elements and analyze their mandates and effects. However, when we look at the global energy economy, we are not examining a system *per se*; rather, we are examining an expansive reality – a totality that encompasses *inter alia* energy needs, supplies, infrastructure, processes, and institutions – to which we retrospectively link a plethora of institutions and other related elements.

---

[175] Taylor, J. & Van Doren, P. 'The Energy Security Obsession' (2008) 6 *Geo. J.L. & Pub. Pol'y* 475; Smith, M. & Htoo, N. 'Energy Security: Security for Whom?' (2008) 11 *Yale Hum. Rts. & Dev. L. J.* 217.

From the dawn of human society there have been energy needs, on the one hand, and energy resources, on the other. One could argue that the global energy economy conceptually takes shape only once we start asking questions about energy needs, energy flows, energy costs, environmental impacts of energy use, and so on. In such cases, we actively attempt to put together the puzzle that is the global energy economy. Arguably, is it not the case that interstate cooperation in relation to all energy matters is essentially entirely conditioned, if not driven, by States' energy security needs? In other words, is there not a special relationship between energy security and the global energy economy? One perhaps that is not seen when we relate the other fields of interstate cooperation under review – namely environmental protection, investment protection, and trade – to the notion of the *global energy economy*.

As is the case for the other fields under review, energy security is also a field of interstate cooperation that has not amounted to effective global energy governance. There are various instances of interstate cooperation at play that may be taken to amount to some sort of overall energy security governance structure that neglects to address in any effective manner the *global* aspects of energy security. Below we list the most ostensible instances of interstate cooperation that are concerned with, or contain provisions on, collective energy security.

1. International Energy Agency

Due to its name, arguably, the most supposedly relevant body in connection to energy security appears to be the International Energy Agency (IEA), an offshoot of the Organisation for Economic Co-operation and Development (OECD). The IEA is ostensibly concerned with the energy security of its membership to the extent that it legally obligates them to hold oil reserves equivalent to 90 days of their oil consumption.[176] Moreover, the IEA membership conditions include that a candidate meet the criteria of the OECD.[177] Currently IEA membership stands at 29 States. The IEA was set up to defend its membership's interests with respect to their collective energy security. In that sense it is not concerned with global energy security *per se*. That said, were there to be similar

---

[176] Namely through the IEA's Coordinated Emergency Response Mechanism. See http://www.iea.org/topics/energysecurity/ for further information.

[177] Not all OECD Members have chosen to become members of the IEA. The IEA applies a second set of criteria, including the ability of prospective members to assist with energy shocks by contributing collective energy security efforts to IEA membership. For more details, see http://www.iea.org/aboutus/faqs/membership/

examples to those of the IEA springing up regionally, one might consider their implications for global energy security to be potentially positive, as has arguably been the case concerning the relationship between the proliferation of PTAs and global trade liberalization.[178] This successful bottom-up approach[179] in trade governance could be emulated for the case of energy security governance.

The IEA membership criteria seriously undercut the potential of the IEA to expand its reach. Traditionally, the IEA has been a club of consumers. In that respect, the fact that acutely significant States in terms of energy-resource deposits – including Russia, Iran, and Kazakhstan, as well as other countries in the Middle East, Central Asia, Latin America, and Africa – are not represented in this body is not surprising. Broadening its membership to include States with proven energy resources would significantly augment the capacity of the IEA to respond to energy shocks. Also, broadening its membership by drawing in the emerging net consumers, that is China and India,[180] would help give this body more clout, as it currently fails to represent the entire community of net consumers by a significant margin. Notably the OECD share of global energy consumption has steadily decreased since 1990, which, the IEA projects, is likely to account for roughly 25% by 2035.[181] Expanding its membership presumably poses political difficulties as this may require its

---

[178] See Mavroidis, P. 'WTO and PTAs: A Preference for Multilateralism? (or the Dog That Tried to Stop the Bus)' (2010) *Journal of World Trade*, Vol. 44, No. 5, pp. 1145–1154.

[179] A bottom-up approach to a problem is one that begins with details and works up to the highest conceptual level, such as 'a bottom-up model of the reading process'. Bottom-up architecture and decentralization are to be found, for instance, in the field of investment protection, which continues to rely upon bilateral agreements and has not formally embraced multilateralism. There are more than 2,800 bilateral investment protection agreements of diverging content. For an overview of the latest figures characterizing the decentralized landscape of international investment rules, see UNCTAD, *UNCTAD World Investment Report 2010: Investing in a Low-Carbon Economy* (New York and Geneva: UNCTAD, 2010), 81ff, http://www.unctad.org/en/docs/wir2010_en.pdf

[180] Note that the IEA projects that India and China would account for roughly 45% of the anticipated increase in global energy consumption between 2005 and 2035, which means more GHG emissions in the case of India since it does not have a policy on renewables. See IEA, *World Energy Outlook 2007: China and India Insights*, Executive Summary (at p. 3), available at http://www.iea.org/Textbase/npsum/WEO2007SUM.pdf

[181] In 1990 the OECD's share of global energy consumption stood at around 50%; by 2010 it had dropped to about 40%, and by 2035 the IEA projects it will stand at around 25%. See the presentation prepared by Maria Argiri on the 2010

core membership – for example, the founding members of the IEA/OECD – to redraft their membership criteria to make these more inclusive.

For instance, those requirements that relate to free-market conditions may be anachronistic, given that, in a post-Cold War increasingly globalized world, most States – including China[182] – opened up their economies to unprecedented degrees. In that sense, criteria in relation to the opening up of markets could be more easily amended. However, the abandonment of the criteria relating to liberal democratic processes is a separate matter. The current globalized arena is significantly different than it was during the post-World-War-II years. The purported values of those world powers that at the time set up the principal international institutions of the global economy might have to be recast to meet their current political expediencies. Perhaps we see the sacrifice of such principles on the part of the OECD/IEA club in order to draw in China and other net consumers for the purposes of becoming more relevant.[183] Indeed, as of April 2013, the IEA was planning to welcome China and another six emerging economies[184] to the IEA as associated members of the IEA for purposes of data sharing.[185]

It should be noted that the IEA seeks to engage with non-members primarily in the field of transparency and data sharing. If there are two great challenges that the international community seems to face in relation to global energy security, these surely relate to insufficient data sharing and upstream investments for future demand. For instance, supply and demand data may be difficult to obtain from States such as Saudi Arabia because such States might be unwilling or unable to submit

---

IEA World Energy Outlook report on renewables in MENA, available at http://www.oecd.org/mena/investment/46769903.pdf, p. 5.

182 In relation to China, see Staiger, R. & Sykes, A. (2010) '"Currency Manipulation" and World Trade' *World Trade Review*, 9, pp. 583–627, regarding the degree to which China has opened up its economy to world trade. This article seeks to put into context the accusations that China manipulates its currency for export purposes by citing relevant International Monetary Fund and WTO norms, and concludes that the accusations are legally baseless. It has been cited here due to the impressive analysis regarding the degree of liberalization of the Chinese economy following its accession to the WTO in 2001.

183 This situation reminds us of one of Groucho Marx's quips: 'Those are my principles, and if you don't like them … well, I have others'.

184 These are India, Russia, Brazil, South Africa, Mexico, and Indonesia.

185 Makan, A. & Blas, J. 'IEA plans to welcome China into the fold' *Financial Times*, London, 4 April 2013, available at http://www.ft.com/cms/s/0/9d6e0c00-9d3e-11e2-88e9-00144feabdc0.html#axzz2PWEPXmAF

accurate data.[186] The IEA seeks to encourage non-states to share data in order to build a more accurate picture around global energy volumes and trends.[187]

2. International Energy Forum

It is encouraging to note the recent efforts by the IEA and OPEC, which arguably represent opposing interests, to find sufficient common ground to work together. This has resulted in the International Energy Forum (IEF), which is an *ad hoc* forum of informal dialogues. The IEF boasts a membership of 75 countries, six continents, and covers 90% of the world's oil and gas supply and demand with a vision of making possible 'global energy security through dialogue'.[188] It has a Charter, which is not a legal document, but a political commitment of 'key governments to a dialogue process which builds trust among member countries'[189] which has been signed by all 75 members.

The advantage of this body is that it includes transition economies[190] and those of Brazil, China, and India. This is important, given that it is the emerging economies – the powerhouses, or rather, the workshops, of the globalized world – whose energy consumption is increasingly eclipsing that of the industrialized world.[191] Moreover, along with net producers and net consumers, it draws in transit States. In that respect, it is as representative as these instances of interstate cooperation come. Whilst it does not create legal obligations, the IEF seeks to foster cooperation in

---

186 That said, a promising dialogue is underway between the IEA and OPEC in connection to 'bringing more transparency to oil markets by providing data on oil production and trade' through the *ad hoc* International Energy Forum. See Victor, D. & Yueh, L. 'The New Energy Order: Managing Insecurities in the Twenty-first Century' (2010) *Foreign Affairs*, Vol. 89, No 1, pp. 61–73 (at p. 67).

187 There is informal cooperation between the IEA and China, India, Russia, Brazil, and other non-member states. View a list of non-member countries and see how the IEA interacts with them by clicking on each state at http://www.iea.org/countries/non-membercountries/

188 http://www.ief.org/about-ief/what-is-the-ief/member-countries.aspx

189 http://www.ief.org/about-ief/what-is-the-ief/mission/charter.aspx

190 The locution 'transition economies' refers to those countries moving from command economies (e.g., former Soviet Union republics and those in Eastern Europe) to market economies.

191 To see the impact of emerging economies vis-à-vis the EU in the trade field, see Leal-Arcas, R. 'The European Union and New Leading Powers: Towards Partnership in Strategic Trade Policy Areas' (2009) *Fordham International Law Journal*, Vol. 32, Issue 2, pp. 345–416.

relation to the energy needs of its membership, chiefly through facilitating dialogue and data-sharing within its membership.[192]

The IEF has been successful in that it has led to the formation of the Joint Organizations Data Initiative (JODI)[193] that brings together several institutions, including the IEF, IEA, OPEC, Eurostat (i.e., the EU official statistics body), Asia-Pacific Economic Cooperation (APEC), Latin American Energy Organization (OLADE) and the United Nations Statistics Division (UNSD). JODI is a remarkable development when one considers the state of play twenty years ago. The IEF was formed in 1991 and JODI in 2001. Prior to that, cooperation seemed to divide along consumer/producer lines in the IEA and OPEC fora.

3. World Petroleum Council

A further institution that might also be relevant to energy security is the World Petroleum Council (WPC),[194] which entered its 75th year of operation in 2008. The WPC includes more than 60 Members and purports to represent every continent and every interest/aspect of the petroleum and gas sectors.[195] It does not, however, provide any governance of these sectors and its efforts focus on facilitating dialogue. In that respect, perhaps the advent of the IEF has rendered this initiative less relevant to the overall global governance system. However, where it does differ is that it purports not only to include States, but to also include international oil companies (IOCs) and national oil companies (NOCs) amongst its Members.

---

[192] See Sections I (2–4) and II of the IEF Charter, available at http://www.ief.org/_resources/files/pages/ief-charter/ief-charter.pdf

[193] In 2000, during the course of their 7th Ministerial meeting in Riyadh, IEF energy ministers called for improved energy data collection processes that resulted in the formation of JODI Oil in 2001. Six international organizations (Asia-Pacific Economic Cooperation (APEC), Eurostat, IEA, Latin American Energy Organization (OLADE), OPEC and the United Nations Statistics Division (UNSD)) launched in 2001 the Joint Oil Data Exercise, whose primary goal was 'to raise the awareness of all oil market players to the need for more transparency in oil market data'. See http://www.jodidata.org/about-jodi/history.aspx. See also information available at http://www.jodidata.org/about-jodi.aspx.

[194] See http://www.world-petroleum.org/index.php?/Introduction/introduction.html

[195] http://www.world-petroleum.org/index.php?/Members/list-of-members.html.

4. The Group of Eight (G8)

The leaders of the world's most industrialized States – namely Canada, France, Germany, Italy, Japan, Russia, the United Kingdom, and the USA – converge annually for discussions on a range of macro-economic matters.[196] While this *ad hoc* forum has a broad remit rather than one limited to energy matters, it is interesting to note that energy played a part in its establishment, which was triggered by France calling for meetings to discuss concerted responses to the 1973 oil crisis. Energy, however, has come to be discussed within the context of the G8, with the leaders of the States involved during the Camp David Summit, calling for market-based solutions to energy security and to climate change.[197] It is worth noting that at the 2006 St Petersburg Summit hosted by Russia, Russia called for a rethinking of energy security to emphasize the mutual dependencies between consumer and producer States.[198]

The G8's recent steps to occasionally include the next five economies – Brazil, China, India, Mexico, and South Africa – make this a forum that includes two significant producer/net exporter States (Brazil and Mexico) and two significant net consumers (China and India), who, as pointed out earlier, are projected to account for as much as 45% of the increase of global energy consumption by 2035.[199] In that sense, the G8+5 arrangement lends itself perfectly to interstate cooperation on energy security.

---

[196] See background information at http://www.canadainternational.gc.ca/g8/index.aspx?view=d (last accessed 2013).

[197] See May 2012 Factsheet on G8 Action on Energy and Climate Change, at http://www.canadainternational.gc.ca/g8/summit-sommet/EC-2012-05-19.aspx?view=d (last accessed 2013). See also Kohl, W. 'Consumer Country Energy Cooperation: The International Energy Agency and the Global Energy Order', in Goldthau A. & Witte, J.M. (eds) *Global Energy Governance: the New Rules of the Game* (Washington, DC: Brookings Institution Press, 2010) at pp. 202–203.

[198] See the official G8 Russia 2006 summit web page, where a Russian Presidential aide called for the G8's approach to energy security to be: 'based on the assumption that we need to find new ways of ensuring energy security, differing from those used by OPEC countries. The notion of energy security should be based on more finely balanced principles. We need mutual dependence'. Available at http://en.g8russia.ru/news/20060427/1148579.html (last accessed 2013)

[199] See for instance the Gleneagles 2005 Summit hosted by the UK Government, where the leaders of the plus five States had also made pledges in relation to antiterrorist action.

5. The Group of Twenty (G20)

Similarly, the G20[200] has been included here due to its general clout. It is a forum that includes the 20 most influential and economically significant States concerned with macroeconomic matters.[201]

> [The G20] brings together important industrial and emerging-market countries from all regions of the world. Together, member countries represent around 90 per cent of global gross national product, 80 per cent of world trade [including intra-EU trade] as well as two-thirds of the world's population. The G-20's economic weight and broad membership gives it a high degree of legitimacy and influence over the management of the global economy and financial system.[202]

The G20 is not a body charged with energy security *per se*. It has, however, been listed here as it includes most energy-consuming (including the EU, China, India, and the US) and energy-producing (including Brazil, Mexico, Russia, and Saudi Arabia) behemoths. Given that energy is so crucial to almost every field of human endeavor, this *ad hoc* body and its edicts could be considered an element of the putative global governance system over energy security. One can see, for instance, the

---

200 The Group of Twenty (G20) finance ministers and Central Bank governors was established in 1999. The inaugural meeting of the G20 took place in Berlin, hosted by German and Canadian finance ministers. 'By contributing to the strengthening of the international financial architecture and providing opportunities for dialogue on national policies, international cooperation, and international financial institutions, the G20 helps to support growth and development across the globe'. See http://www.g20.org/about_what_is_g20.aspx

201 The members of the G20 are the finance ministers and central bank governors of 19 countries: Argentina, Australia, Brazil, Canada, China, France, Germany, India, Indonesia, Italy, Japan, Mexico, Russia, Saudi Arabia, South Africa, South Korea, Turkey, the United Kingdom, and the United States. The European Union is also a member, represented by the rotating Council presidency (since the entry into force of the Lisbon Treaty, it is the European Council president) and the European Central Bank. To ensure that global economic fora and institutions work together, the Managing Director of the International Monetary Fund (IMF) and the President of the World Bank, plus the chairs of the International Monetary and Financial Committee and Development Committee of the IMF and World Bank, also participate in G20 meetings on an ex-officio basis. See Leal-Arcas, R. *International Trade and Investment Law: Multilateral, Regional and Bilateral Governance* (Cheltenham: Edward Elgar, 2010) at p. 18, fn 15. The G20 'promotes open and constructive discussion between industrial and emerging-market countries on key issues related to global economic stability'. See http://www.g20.org/about_what_is_g20.aspx (last accessed 2013)

202 See http://www.g20.org/about_what_is_g20.aspx (last accessed 2013).

specific commitments that G20 Members made at the Los Cabos 2012 summit in Mexico over a range of matters, including in some cases energy.[203] Given that 84% of global fossil-fuel emissions[204] are generated by G20 Members, the G20 could be an important forum for cohesive action over energy security and climate change.

6. Major Economies Forum on Energy and Climate

The Major Economies Forum on Energy and Climate (MEF) was initiated in 2007 by the Bush administration under the name 'Major Emitters Forum'[205] and launched by the Obama administration on March 28, 2009. The MEF 'is intended to facilitate a candid dialogue among major developed and developing economies',[206] help generate the political leadership necessary to achieve a successful outcome at future UN climate change conferences, and 'advance the exploration of concrete initiatives and joint ventures that increase the supply of clean energy while cutting GHG emissions'.[207] The MEF would provide for significant GHG limitations with credible assurances for compliance.[208] The MEF partners comprise: Australia, Brazil, Canada, China, the EU, France, Germany, India, Indonesia, Italy, Japan, Korea, Mexico, Russia, South Africa, the UK, and the US.[209] Bringing together these major emitters, which were responsible for around 75% of GHG emissions in the world

---

[203] See http://www.g20.org/images/stories/docs/g20/conclu/Policy_Commitments_By_G20_Members.pdf (last accessed 2013) for a list of commitments where, amongst others, Argentina pledges to reduce household energy subsidies (presumably to make more oil available on global markets) and Brazil pledges to devote USD 45 billion in energy investments between 2011 and 2014.

[204] Source: http://www.g20.org/index.php/en/numeralia (last accessed 2013).

[205] The name was changed because, according to the members, the initial name sounded like an oligopoly of polluters. The MEF has gone through a number of name changes. Other proposed names were the Major Economies Process on Energy Security and Climate Change (http://2001-2009.state.gov/g/oes/climate/mem/index.htm) and Major Economies Meeting on Energy Security and Climate Change (http://georgewbush-whitehouse.archives.gov/news/releases/2007/09/20070927.html).

[206] http://www.majoreconomiesforum.org/about.html

[207] Ibid.

[208] Stewart, R. et al. 'Strategic Analytics for Building a Global Climate Regime Bottom-Up', pp. 4–5, paper presented at the conference 'Reaching International Cooperation on Climate Change Mitigation', December 21–23, 2011 (unpublished paper; on file with author).

[209] See Major Economies Forum on Energy and Climate, available at http://www.majoreconomiesforum.org/about/descriptionpurpose.html

as of 2009 (these numbers include land-use change),[210] will increase the likelihood of reaching a climate change agreement, as the MEF is a more efficient negotiating forum than the UNFCCC.[211] Furthermore, an agreement amongst them would be almost as valuable as an agreement amongst all UNFCCC parties in terms of absolute GHG emissions reductions, since most GHGs come from the MEF partners.[212]

Bringing together 17 major economies, including energy net consumer economies such as the EU, India, China, and the US, alongside energy net producers such as Brazil, Russia, and Mexico, the MEF was set up at the instance of the US to act as a negotiations' anteroom for the most emissions-significant economies to decide on action within the context of the wider UN negotiations on climate change. Purportedly, the MEF is also concerned with: '… advanc[ing] the exploration of concrete initiatives and joint ventures that increase the supply of clean energy while cutting greenhouse gas emissions'.[213] Whilst this is an important forum – and a commendable one, given that it is essentially about the interplay between energy and climate change – its capacity to address global energy security concerns is restricted. This is because most major net energy producers (including all OPEC members), except for Indonesia, do not participate; a fact that substantially undercuts its capacity to address global security concerns.

From the instances of interstate cooperation engaging energy security concerns, the G8, G8+5, and G20 could be distinguished from the other examples on the basis that discussions are high level and on a broad range of topics. Although they are not topic-specific – unlike, say, the IEF and the MEF, which focus on energy and energy and climate change, respectively – these are more akin to, albeit much less inclusive than, the UN's deliberative chamber, namely the General Assembly (UNGA), an institution that allows its members to discuss and to pass resolutions that may, potentially, be put to the UN Security Council or to specific UN members to take action,[214] or put through the UN legislative process with

---

[210] Broder, J. 'Clinton Says US is Ready to Lead on Climate', *The New York Times*, 27 April 2009, available at http://nyti.ms/huEbYb

[211] Oye, K. 'Explaining Cooperation under Anarchy' (1985) *World Politics*, Vol. 38, No. 1, p. 21.

[212] Leal-Arcas, R. 'Top-down Versus Bottom-up Approaches for Climate Change Negotiations: An Analysis' (December 2011) *The IUP Journal of Governance and Public Policy*, Vol. 6, No. 4, pp. 7–52, at 44–45.

[213] See http://www.majoreconomiesforum.org/about.html

[214] See Article 10 UN Charter.

a view to the adoption of a legally binding interstate agreement.[215] Examining the international order, there is no shortage of legislative means to make cohesive concerted action a reality. Rather, it is the political challenges that top-down approaches seem to face that explain the proliferation of exclusive forums such as the G8, G20, MEF, and so on. In that sense, one could analyze the resolutions of such high-level fora to deduce how international policy might develop over the following years. It is encouraging to note that energy and climate change have made it to the agenda of such fora relatively recently.[216] Let us hope that this will translate into more cohesive action on the implications of energy consumption for the environment and for global energy security.

F. Other Phenomena with Implications for the Global Energy Economy

As discussed above, the global energy economy is a reality. The global energy order involves various fields of interstate cooperation on aspects of energy. In that sense, there are various fields of governance to varying degrees of normativity. There are, however, phenomena outside the context of interstate cooperation, as described above, that have significant implications for the global energy economy. So although this chapter is mainly focused on institutions and processes, we recognize that the global energy economy is not simply the sum of structures relevant to it and that there is more to it. For instance, national oil companies and global markets – although facilitated by numerous institutions and processes within their scope – are actually formidable forces that transcend these structures.

Let us now analyze how the rise of national oil companies (NOCs) has impacted global markets.

1. National oil companies

One such phenomenon outside the interstate cooperation context is the advent of NOCs, to the cost of international oil companies (IOCs). The advent of NOCs for its most part has happened following the decolonization process. NOCs currently control more than 80% of global oil and gas reserves.[217] The top 13 out of 20 oil companies are now NOCs.[218] In that respect, their implications for global energy security could be

[215] See Article 13 UN Charter.

[216] Particularly the G8, from the 2005 Gleneagles summit onwards.

[217] See Goldthau, A. & Witte, J.M. 'The Role of Rules and Institutions in Global Energy: An Introduction', in Goldthau, A. & Witte, J.M. (eds) *Global*

considerable. Moreover, one should bear in mind the extra-territorial obligation of States to hold their companies responsible for their actions abroad.

The advent of NOCs has led to the transformation of energy exploration and the decoupling of the upstream and downstream aspects of the sector. Previously, a few private – mainly UK and US[219] – IOCs had come to dominate oil exploration through the – at times, aggressive – patronage of their home States, and by committing host States to long-term contracts.[220] The wave of disputes, and their sticky resolution, that arose during the decolonization process through the assertion of sovereignty over natural resources by newly founded States has been the main impetus behind the adjustment of the international legal system to promote investment-protection norms.[221] One might have imagined that this rise in *resource nationalism* would have harmed markets. However, this is far from clear. In fact, it may have had an opposite effect on global markets. Previously IOCs dominated the production, along with the refinement and distribution aspects, of oil. Consequently, the rise of NOCs took production largely out of IOC hands, thus making more oil available on the global markets outside traditional vertically integrated

---

Energy Governance: the New Rules of the Game (Washington, DC: Brookings Institution Press, 2010) at p. 15.

218 Jaffe, A. & Soligo, R. 'State-Backed Financing in Oil and Gas Projects', in Goldthau, A. & Witte, J.M. (eds) *Global Energy Governance: the New Rules of the Game* (Washington, DC: Brookings Institution Press, 2010) at p. 107.

219 See the US Federal Office of the Historian's note on the 'Seven Sisters' at http://history.state.gov/milestones/1921-1936/RedLine

220 These matters have been well documented by, amongst others, Anglie, A. *Imperialism, Sovereignty and the Making of International Law* (Cambridge: CUP, 2004); Stevens, P. in 'Oil Wars: Resource Nationalism and the Middle East,' in Andrews-Speed, P. (ed.) *International Competition for Resources: The Role of Law, the State, and of Markets* (Dundee: Dundee University Press, 2008), Chapter 2; and Schrijver, N. *Sovereignty Over Natural Resources: Balancing Rights and Duties* (Cambridge: CUP 1997).

221 This has been done through, amongst other things, contracts between States and private investors, in which the former waive sovereign immunity-to-suit in foreign adjudicative fora so that the latter are able to enforce arbitration outcomes, and through the adoption of State-to-State legal agreements that obligate States to offer degrees of protection for property interests, including over investment interests (e.g., through the European Convention for the Protection of Human Rights and Fundamental Freedoms (ECHR), the ECT regime, and other aspects of investment protection discussed in this chapter). See also Bishop, R.D. 'International Arbitration of Petroleum Disputes: The Development of a "Lex Petrolea"', YCA 1998.

operations run by IOCs. Moreover, the decoupling of the upstream (i.e., the operations concerned with exploration and extraction of energy commodities) and downstream (i.e., the operations concerned with getting energy commodities to consumers) aspects of the oil supply has increased the number of actors and potentially has contributed to more healthy competition in this sector.[222]

That said, the rise of NOCs could potentially harm investments in that some NOCs divert a sizeable share of oil revenue into social projects aimed at raising the living standards of their populations.[223] However, it should also be noted that IOCs have similar obligations in that they use revenues for shareholder payouts. Moreover, within the parameters of global markets, IOCs develop production capacity to the extent that it is profitable to do so. Any matter that might potentially undermine energy supply investments is a cause for concern, given that the IEA projects that monumental sums need to be committed in order to meet the increase in global energy consumption by 2035. There are also concerns around NOCs lending themselves to corrupt regimes that are incapable of exploiting State resources for the collective good, and who run these NOCs as personal fiefdoms.[224]

2. Global markets

Global markets, including financial markets, are formidable forces in the globalized world. Trade amongst people has been happening for more

---

222 See Goldthau, A. & Witte, J.M. 'The Role of Rules and Institutions in Global Energy: An Introduction,' in Goldthau, A. & Witte, J.M. (eds) *Global Energy Governance: the New Rules of the Game* (Washington, DC: Brookings Institution Press, 2010) at p. 4.

223 Venezuela's NOC – Petroleos de Venezuela, S.A. (PDVSA) – is a case in point. It diverts around USD 60 billion annually towards social projects. Between 1998 and 2009, there has been a 50% loss of productive capacity, namely from 3.8 million barrels per day to 2 million barrels per day, respectively. See Jaffe, A. & Soligo, R. 'State-Backed Financing in Oil and Gas Projects', in Goldthau, A. & Witte, J.M. (eds) *Global Energy Governance: the New Rules of the Game* (Washington, DC: Brookings Institution Press, 2010) at p. 110.

224 See the example whereby the World Bank had sought to place conditions on how shares of Chad's oil revenues were to be ring-fenced for developmental purposes and thus placed outside the immediate budgetary scope of the Chad government by binding the latter into agreements it later reneged on. This arrangement was aimed at securing intergenerational rights to the benefits that Chad's oil revenues could fund. See Leibold, A. 'Aligning Incentives for Development: the World Bank and the Chad-Cameroon Oil Pipeline' (2011) *Yale J., Int'l Law*, Vol. 36, pp. 167–204.

than 5,000 years, and was a key factor in the development of human civilization.[225] In that sense, markets precede international institutions and rules. Institutions and rules were subsequently developed to streamline interstate economic transactions and to entrench, in modern times, market-based systems with the higher aim of capitalist expansion.[226] In that sense, global markets, including financial markets, should not simply be viewed as stemming from the operation of international institutions and rules; rather, they should be understood as realities whose implications are broader than those of the institutions and rules in place.

The fundamental dynamic that drives markets is the search on the part of capital-possessing entities to find fields of speculation where there are reasonable prospects for profit. When capital-possessing entities exhaust domestic fields of speculation, or where they consider higher rates of profit to exist outside the domestic realm, they push their governments to pursue market-friendly foreign policy. This is reflected in developments in the multilateral trade system (which has become increasingly more liberalized with the successive reduction in the level of trade tariffs), in the successive integration of economies (e.g., EU, NAFTA, and FTAs in Latin America and in Asia), in the liberalization of financial markets with money being a tradable commodity in its own right and the removal of many capital exchange controls, and in the deregulation of credit over the last 30 years. In the field of energy production and pricing, the operation of non-traditional actors – for example, financiers and speculators, rather

---

225 See Overy, R. (ed.) *Complete History of the World* (London: Times Books/Harper Collins Publishing, 2008) at p. 55, where it is stated: 'Trade and exchange were important in the expansion of the first civilizations. The possession of prestige goods and the desire to acquire more resources were instrumental in the emergence of the first empires in Mesopotamia'.

226 The setting up of institutions and rules reflects the concerted efforts of the Western group of World War II victors to set up a world order that preserved their interests. Philippe Sands considers the advent of international institutions and rules, and the strengthening of international law, as a reflection of Anglo-American efforts towards the creation of a global rules-based system to entrench their own economic and social interests. This system arose against the backdrop of the Cold War to contain the threat of communist expansion. See Sands, P. *Lawless World: The Whistle-blowing Account of how Bush and Blair are Taking the Law into Their Own Hands* (London: Penguin, 2006) at p. 13. See also Kagan, R. *Paradise and Power: America and Europe in the New World Order* (London: Atlantic Books, 2003) at p. 71.

than oil companies alone – has implications for energy pricing[227] and, consequently, for energy security.

V. CONCLUSION AND RECOMMENDATIONS

There is not a single international organization that deals with global energy governance, nor is there a single agreement that deals with energy in a comprehensive manner. Instead, there are a multitude of instances of interstate cooperation that touches upon energy and thus the global energy economy. The realities of interstate cooperation – namely the nonlinear and *ad hoc* occurrence of cooperation – have led to matters relating to energy being dealt with in a manner that lacks absolute cohesion. There is a wide range of institutions that pertain to the global energy economy; yet there is a misalignment between their respective purposes and mandates. As can be seen in Table 1.3, although there is a degree of overlap between the remits of a number of relevant institutions, there is insufficient cohesiveness between them.[228] In that respect, the fragmentation of international law is simply a reflection of the realities of interstate cooperation. Though jurisprudential tools exist to cohesively integrate the international obligations of States in a manner that such obligations be discharged sympathetically *inter se*,[229] the issue is essentially political and can be more effectively addressed through those

---

[227] See Lenzner, R. 'Speculation in Crude Oil Adds $23.39 to the Price per Barrel', *Forbes*, 27 February 2012 (on how speculation in futures markets might add USD 23 per barrel to oil prices). Available at http://www.forbes.com/sites/robertlenzner/2012/02/27/speculation-in-crude-oil-adds-23-39-to-the-price-per-barrel/

[228] For instance, in terms of monetary policy, we see that the WTO systemically defers such policy questions to be resolved first within the context of the IMF. There are occasionally accusations between some WTO members of currency manipulation. The IMF provides degrees of governance over monetary policies to ensure that these are in line with its Articles of Agreement. Invariably, disputes about appropriate levels of currency valuation involve trade interests. This explains why WTO Members might see this as the appropriate regime within which to resolve such disputes. Article XV:9 GATT, however, indicates that exchange measures in line with IMF obligations should not be opposed under the GATT. See Staiger, R. & Sykes, A. (2010) '"Currency Manipulation" and World Trade' *World Trade Review* 9, where the relationship between IMF and WTO is discussed.

[229] See McLachlan, C. 'The Principle of Systemic Integration and Article 31(3)(C) of the Vienna Convention' (April 2005) *International & Comparative Law Quarterly (ICLQ)*, Vol. 54, pp. 279–320, for an exposition of the means to

means. In reality, obligations are discharged outside the remit of judicial processes, and, when disputes arise, not all of these end up before an adjudicative agency. So it is one thing to ask how these obligations ought to be discharged, but what ends up happening on the ground is quite another.

In relation to instances of interstate cooperation relating to energy security, the furthest the broader community of States goes is to set up talking-shops and to share data through the IEF and JODI. More robust regimes extending to energy security do exist, although these are restricted in their scope, for example the EU, IEA, and ECT. In that sense, it would not be inaccurate to claim that the seeds have been sown for a global energy security governance system to potentially take root in future (namely the IEF and its wide participation). However, the existing global energy security governance system is ineffective.

We might want to take the normative patchwork that emerges to amount to a global energy governance system of sorts. However, in our view, it is more accurate to describe it as an aggregation of stand-alone instances of interstate cooperation that relate to energy, but that insufficiently link up on other levels, including scope and governance. In that sense, there is currently insufficient cohesive governance amongst the various fields of energy-related interstate cooperation to justify the presumption of an emerging global governance system. Nor is it helpful that much of the literature refers to *global energy governance* without sufficiently highlighting the arbitrary nature of this abstraction. Though we might see much merit in such a system, it is more accurate to talk about governance in the specific themes that engage, or otherwise relate to, global energy governance, which incidentally is never truly *global*, though there are examples of near universal reach – for example, the WTO in relation to trade and the UNFCCC in relation to environmental protection.

The current state of play in terms of global energy governance has implications for global energy security in that, arguably, the absence of an overarching, truly universal regime has meant that states continue to engage in interstate cooperation along bilateral, regional, multilateral – yet never universal – lines to secure access to energy resources. Let us refer to these as 'bottom-up approaches'. The EU is keen to entangle Russia and Ukraine, amongst others, in PTAs, whilst China and Russia

---

achieve integration among norms flowing from different special regimes or other areas of international law, and how these have been deployed by the International Court of Justice, the WTO Panels and Appellate Body, and the Court of Justice of the European Union.

engage in energy diplomacy, which could have implications for energy supply and therefore global energy security.

IEA members are legally obligated to hold 90 days' worth of oil reserves in order to address potential energy supply disruptions. This allows them to assist one another in such an eventuality. The EU, in its sophistication, creates more rational market conditions within its internal market. It also engages in external relations to advance its members' energy security needs. Other interstate instances of cooperation take similar steps. The question is: do these somehow contribute to greater energy security for the international community, or do they, given that the bulk of energy supply continues to derive from finite resources, perpetuate zero-sum dynamics in energy-security related interstate relations? Research would be welcome to assess whether these 'bottom-up' instances of interstate cooperation in relation to energy security have an effect similar to how PTAs seem to enhance the overall multilateral system (discussed above regarding PTAs and the WTO), and to assess what the specific and accumulative implications of each institution and issue might be upon global energy security. For instance, do they enhance or undermine prospects for global energy security? Given that the aim of energy security should be global, would a bottom-up regime of regions working together be the most effective way forward? Just as the IEA acts in the context of the OECD countries, similar arrangements could be created in other regions/groupings of the world. This could be achieved thanks to the inclusion of strong energy chapters in regional trade agreements (such as the Trans-Pacific Partnership, the Southern African Development Community, and the East African Community, to name a few examples).

Top-down approaches, for their part, are undoubtedly more effective when supported by efficient dispute resolution and enforcement mechanisms. However, they are also less likely to be adopted in such a sensitive field of cooperation as energy security. Top-down instances such as the IEF, whilst laudable and to be encouraged and further strengthened, are less powerful, given that they are limited to facilitating dialogue and data-sharing.

The key question is: What is to be done to push the most influential States towards adopting policies that meaningfully address energy security in a manner that promotes environmental protection and economic development? Any such solution must surely include policies that promote the full exploration of renewables and the dramatic reduction of fossil-fuel emissions. This is likely to be opposed not only by energy net exporter States but also by other economies – including net importers – whose NOCs (e.g., in the case of China) and IOCs (e.g., British

Petroleum, ExxonMobil, Shell, and others) are likely to be harmed by such policies. In today's globalized world, the implications could be far-reaching. Within the parameters of the market-based global order, how could the private sector and the existing actors in energy exploration be sufficiently enticed to progressively replace the currently fossil-fuel dominated energy mix with one exclusively based on renewables? To that end, should states pool funds to subsidize the existing actors such as IOCs and NOCs? Should they set up large-scale infrastructure under common ownership? Or should they leave it to markets to make the transition to renewables at their own pace?[230] These are ultimately political questions that engage economic relations that are, ultimately, resolved in relation to the political values that the dominant State actors promote in relation to the global economy.

Table 1.3 is intended to offer an at-a-glance snapshot of what area of policy each regime extends to, without going into too much detail concerning the specifics of each regime/institution. The table explains for most, if not all, institutions what their relationship to each field of international cooperation included in the chapter is likely to be. For instance, the UN is chiefly about security. In that respect, it is not charged with energy security or trade or investment matters. Nor is it charged with environmental protection; however, the UNFCCC has been adopted within its auspices.

---

[230] Fossil fuels, although finite, remain abundant and reserves exist to fuel consumption for many years ahead. In that respect, it remains more profitable for market actors to exploit these until their exhaustion. However, such an approach does not acknowledge the environmental cost, which could be partially quantified in relation to the cost to adopt climate change mitigation and adaptation measures, nor does it factor in the broader implications – e.g., on intergenerational rights to the amenity that the environment offers. When the exploration of fossil fuels is considered in terms of its broader implications for the environment and for human security (where, e.g., conflict results because of competition to control finite resources, such as was the case in both Iraq wars, Sudan internecine conflict, and so on), the social and environmental costs outweigh the fiscal gain that accrues to a few actors, namely to NOCs and to IOC shareholders. This starkly illustrates how the well-being of the environment and the life it sustains, including seven billion human beings, is subjugated to the economic interests of actors in global energy markets.

Table 1.3 At a glance: institutions vis-à-vis fields of interstate cooperation relating to energy

	Trade	Investment	Development	Environment	Energy transit	Energy security
UN	Partially. See the UN Conference on Trade and Development, chiefly concerned with the interests of developing States.	Partially, through the promotion of ICSID in relation to investment disputes.	Partially. See the UN Conference on Trade and Development expressly focused on the interests of developing States.	Yes – e.g., UNFCCC and its Kyoto Protocol	Partially to the extent that the right of innocent passage and the freedom of transit in maritime areas have been protected in international agreements adopted within the context of the UN by a substantial number of coastal states.	No express mandate. The effect of the UN Charter (and of its normative framework) on energy security is unclear. The UN Charter preserves State sovereignty (including over natural resources) and expressly prohibits unlawful external intervention.
EU	Yes. There is a single market among the 28 EU Member States and other neighboring States through the EEA.	Yes – The EU is based on the four fundamental freedoms of movement of goods, services, capital, and labor. The free movement of capital relies on investment protection.	Yes. See Cotonu Agreement and the EU's Generalized System of Preferences.	Yes. See for instance the EU's emissions trading scheme.	Yes. Intra-EU energy transit protected and promoted. Also EU bound by transit provisions of WTO and ECT.	Yes. EU energy policy includes external and internal aspects. External in that it pursues external action that advances EU energy security, and internal in that it legislates to further integrate the internal energy market.

NAFTA	Yes, by integrating the markets among its three Members.	Yes	No express mandate.	No express mandate. However, various NAFTA provisions (e.g., Articles 103, 104, 715, 906, 907, and 1114) relate to the rights of parties in relation to their environmental objectives.	Unclear. Intra-NAFTA restrictions apply to transit and transport.	Unclear – potentially positive implications by making energy markets more fluid among its three Members.
MEF	Partially in all areas by *ad hoc* commitments arising from discussions between its members.					
ASEAN	Yes	Yes	Yes	Yes	Yes. Trans-ASEAN gas and electricity projects underway.	Yes
ECC	Yes	Yes – an example *par excellence* regarding protection	Purportedly so. Unclear how this takes place.	Purportedly so. Unclear how this takes place.	Yes. Freedom of transit consolidated in Article 7 ECT. Express reference to fixed infrastructure.	Yes, in relation to its membership
G8	Partially in all areas by *ad hoc* commitments from time to time by its members					
G20	Partially in all areas by *ad hoc* commitments from time to time by its members					

	Trade	Investment	Development	Environment	Energy transit	Energy security
GECF	Yes – gas producer interest group.	No	No express mandate.	GECF argues that the promotion of gas over other hydrocarbons is better for the environment. It is unclear, however, what other measures are taken within GECF to address environmental degradation.	GECF members exchange information and know-how in relation to, among other things, transportation technologies. It is unclear to what extent this enhances energy transit.[a]	No express mandate. GECF is more concerned with energy (gas) demand security in the interests of its members.
IEA	No express mandate.	No express mandate.	No express mandate.	Purportedly so by listing 'environmental awareness' as one of its four principal focuses.	Not expressly.	Yes, through the obligation for stockpiles.
IEF	No	No	No	No	Not expressly.	Potentially positive implications, by facilitating much needed data-sharing between energy consumers and producers.
OPEC	Yes – oil producer interest group	No	No	No	No	No, though it is concerned with OPEC members' security of energy *demand*.

WPC	Potentially positive implications for all these fields of interstate cooperation by facilitating dialogue.					
WTO	Yes – multilateral trade regime *par excellence*.	Partially – see the TRIMs Agreement and GATS.	Partially – see WTO's Special and Differential Treatment.	No express mandate. However, various relevant provisions and the SPS Agreement relate to environmental concerns (see relevant WTO entry in the chapter).	Yes. Freedom of transit consolidated in Article V GATT. Unclear what the implications are for energy transit through fixed infrastructure.	No express mandate. However, WTO provisions support energy flows through freedom of transit and by prohibiting quantitative restrictions on tradable commodities.

Note: [a] See http://www.gecf.org/aboutus/gecf-objectives

2. Energy as a special sector in the World Trade Organization

I. INTRODUCTION

For decades, trade in energy has been treated as a special case of international trade, different from other trade sectors and products. In fact, it is safe to consider the energy trade sector as one of the most significant trade sectors – actually *the* most – for a variety of reasons, including its unique characteristics and the unprecedented challenges confronting it. Moreover, the ongoing debate over the applicability/ inapplicability of the General Agreement on Tariffs and Trade (GATT)/ World Trade Organization (WTO) disciplines to trade in energy further sets this sector apart. One school of thought believes that international trade in energy is included in and is subject to GATT/WTO disciplines. It holds that international trade in energy is governed by WTO law, like any other trade in goods or services, and that it is not excluded from the coverage of the GATT/WTO law. The other school of thought holds that a combination of factors has led, *de facto*, to the exclusion of energy trade from the scope of GATT/WTO disciplines. To support their arguments and arrive at their conclusions, both schools of thought have examined the creation of the GATT, its founding members, the various multilateral trade negotiations, the purposes and objectives behind the GATT, the GATT rounds of multilateral trade negotiations, the Uruguay Round and the establishment of the WTO, and even aspects of the Doha Round of multilateral trade negotiations.

This chapter argues that, although trade in energy in general and trade in petroleum in particular were not clearly and directly included in any of the GATT provisions, according to GATT history, the contracting parties discussed energy-related matters during various rounds of GATT negotiations and, therefore, the presumption is that GATT/WTO disciplines apply to trade in energy. Had parties to the GATT not wanted energy in the trade agenda, they would have expressly mentioned so. It is therefore presumed that, since trade in energy was not expressly excluded from the GATT provisions, the GATT/WTO system applies to trade in energy.

After this short introduction, Section II presents an overview of the international trade system and the reasons why trade in energy has been treated differently from other trade sectors and products, while Section III analyzes the special characteristics of energy. Section IV presents the challenges in global energy trade, while Section V analyzes the link between WTO law and energy trade. It provides a chronological evolution of international trade in energy, starting with the International Trade Organization (ITO) (which eventually did not come into being) and the creation of GATT in 1947, the various rounds of GATT negotiations, the subsequent accession of energy exporting countries to the GATT, the WTO era and energy trade, and the accession of energy-rich countries to the world trading system since 1995, all of which with a view to determining whether GATT/WTO law applies to trade in energy. It further discusses certain unresolved energy trade issues. Section VI concludes the chapter with the view that trade in energy is governed by, and subject to, the GATT/WTO umbrella.

II. THE INTERNATIONAL TRADE SYSTEM

It is important to review the main characteristics of the multilateral trade system before addressing the main issue of this chapter.

A. The General Agreement on Tariffs and Trade (GATT)

In the aftermath of World War II, in 1947, 23 countries negotiated a multilateral agreement for tariff reductions.[1] The outcome of this negotiation was the genesis of the General Agreement on Tariffs and Trade (GATT).[2] The GATT entered into operation in January 1948 on a provisional basis.[3] The GATT was enacted during the aftermath of World

[1] See Hoekman, B. & Mavroidis, P. *The World Trade Organization: Law, Economics and Politics* (London: Routledge, 2007) at p. 8; Hoekman, B. & Mavroidis, P. *The Political Economy of the World Trading System* (Oxford: Oxford University Press, 2011) at p. 47.

[2] See the General Agreement on Tariffs and Trade, Oct. 30, 1947, 61 Stat. A-11, T.I.A.S. 1700, 55 U.N.T.S. 194.

[3] See Jackson, J, Davey, W.J. & Sykes, A.O. *Legal Problems of International Economic Relations: Cases, Materials and Text on the National and International Regulation of Transnational Economic Relations* (St Paul, MN: west Publishing Co, 5th ed. 2008) [hereinafter Jackson] at p. 219 (explaining that some countries required parliamentary ratifications in order to apply some articles of the GATT and therefore, in late 1947, signed the Protocol of

War II, in 1947.[4] It came into operation as an international treaty that contained a series of over two hundred agreements, protocols, and other documents. It dealt almost entirely with trade in products.[5] Although intended to be an agreement to organize international trade in goods, since its creation the GATT has been the central international multilateral trade treaty, and has operated as an organization.[6] The GATT's establishment sought to achieve several purposes, one of the most essential purposes of which was to improve worldwide economic growth and to free and liberalize global trade.[7] These goals were assumed to be achieved by disallowing governments from imposing or continuing a variety of measures which restrain or distort international trade, such as tariffs, quotas, internal taxes and regulations.[8]

The GATT contains significant basic provisions that regulate international trade with respect to government actions, namely: the 'Tariff Schedules' provision, where each country commits to limiting its tariffs to a negotiated level on particular items;[9] the 'non-discrimination obligation' principle, which includes the 'Most-Favored-Nation' clause and which imposes on a country the duty to provide equal treatment to all the countries it imports from,[10] and the 'National Treatment' clause, which rules that imported goods shall be treated no worse than domestically produced goods;[11] and the 'prohibition on quotas' principle, which

---

Provisional Application (PPA), which came into force on January 1, 1948. Under the PPA, the signatories applied the GATT as a provisional treaty to operate under the umbrella of the International Trade Organization, which was never established).

4 See Jackson at p. 219.

5 See Jackson at pp. 215, 222.

6 Ibid.; Jackson, J.H. 'The WTO "Constitution" and Proposed Reforms: Seven "Mantras" Revisited' (2001) 4 *J. Int'l Econ. L.* 67, 68 (explaining that a primary objective of the GATT founders in the aftermath of World War II was to avoid another war by reducing the economic conditions that were seen as conducive to conflict).

7 See Jackson at pp. 217–221 (noting there was no intention to make the GATT the principal international trade organization when the original idea was to create an International Trade Organization (ITO). However, the US could not get congressional approval for the ITO (Havana) Charter. This meant the death of the ITO, and the GATT became the default central organization for coordinating national policies on international trade).

8 Ibid. at p. 215.

9 Ibid. at p. 222; Article II of the GATT.

10 Article I of the GATT; Jackson at p. 222.

11 Article III of the GATT; Jackson at p. 222.

prohibits quantitative restrictions on the import and export of goods.[12] In addition to these substantive provisions, the GATT includes a number of general and particular exceptions.[13]

Although the establishment and operation of the GATT were meant to govern and promote international trade matters, the GATT faced a variety of problems that constituted substantial impediments to its operation and the fulfillment of its objectives.[14] One of these major problems related to the use of the GATT in resolving disputes between its contracting parties.[15] It is important to note that the GATT Panels' decisions were not binding and were adopted by a 'consensus' approach, which limited the efficiency of resolving disputes between contracting parties.[16]

B. The World Trade Organization (WTO)

The WTO was established in 1994 by the Marrakesh Agreement and replaced the GATT in January 1995.[17] The Uruguay Round results led to the creation of the WTO as a developed international organization and treaty structure, which includes almost 30 legal agreements and supplementary decisions. All its members become subject to all of the annexed agreements as a single package, except the plurilateral agreements.[18] Currently, the WTO has 160 Member States, which are subject to the WTO rules and agreements in their direct and indirect international trade conducts. The WTO was founded as an improved successor to the GATT, and it was intended to be a very developed system for facilitating and unifying international trade, with the aim of eliminating protectionism and promoting free and globalized trade.[19] Notably, the structure of the WTO distinguishes it as an international organization with a legal personality. The WTO agreements encompass several annexes,[20] including Annex 1A that

---

12 Article XI:1 of the GATT; Jackson at p. 222.

13 See Jackson at p. 216.

14 Ibid. at pp. 220–221.

15 Ibid. at pp. 220–222.

16 Ibid.

17 See Marrakesh Agreement Establishing the World Trade Organization, Apr. 15, 1994, 1867 U.N.T.S. 154, 33 I.L.M. 1144.

18 See Jackson at p. 217.

19 Ibid.

20 Ibid. at pp. 226–227 (describing the agreements that are included in the WTO agreements: Annex 1A, the General Agreement on Tariffs and Trade 1994; Annex 1B, the General Agreement on Services; Annex 1C, the agreement on Trade-Related Aspects of Intellectual Property (TRIPS); Annex 2, the Dispute Settlement Understanding (DSU); Annex 3, the Trade Policy Review Mechanism

consists of GATT 1994.[21] This Annex is substantively the same as GATT (1947) with a number of understandings on how the GATT should be interpreted.[22]

Moreover, multilateral agreements within the WTO stipulate that Member States manage their trade in accordance with the main operative provisions of the GATT with respect to the use of non-discriminatory measures such as the Most Favored Nation clause[23] and the National Treatment clause.[24] The WTO also discourages quantitative prohibitions or restrictions on imports or exports of products through the General Elimination of Quantitative Restrictions provision.[25] Further, it promotes competition by encouraging the reciprocal reduction and elimination of tariffs and trade barriers.[26] In addition to these intrinsic obligations, WTO

(TPRM); Annex 4 contains the four agreements which are 'optional', termed 'plurilateral agreements').

[21] See General Agreement on Tariffs and Trade 1994, Apr. 15, 1994, Marrakesh Agreement Establishing the World Trade Organization, Annex 1A, The Legal Texts: The Results of the Uruguay Round of Multilateral Trade Negotiations 17 (1999), 1867 U.N.T.S. 187, 33 I.L.M. 1153 (1994) [hereinafter GATT 1994].

[22] See Jackson at p. 216.

[23] Article I of the GATT; Jackson at p. 475.

[24] Article III of the GATT; Jackson at p. 540.

[25] Article XI of the GATT; Jackson at pp. 423–424.

[26] In spite of these rules and provisions, some domestic environmental policies could, either directly or indirectly, discriminate against imports from other WTO Members, or may somehow result in quantitative restrictions. The following are examples of measures that have (at least *prima facie*) been at odds with the above mentioned GATT provisions: applying a minimum-size requirement to imports of lobsters (*United States – Prohibition of Imports of Tuna and Tuna Products from Canada*, GATT Panel Report, adopted 22 February 1982, BISD 29S/91); embargoing imports of tuna not caught in a way that minimizes the risk to dolphins (*United States – Measures Concerning the Importation, Marketing and Sale of Tuna and Tuna Products*, WT/DS381/AB/R); taxing sales of vehicles not in compliance with mandated fuel economy standards (*United States – Imposition of Import Duties on Automobiles from Japan under Sections 301 and 304 of the Trade Act of 1974*, WT/DS6); composition standards for conventional and reformulated gasoline (*United States – Standards for Reformulated and Conventional Gasoline*, WT/DS2/AB/R); placing an embargo on imports of shrimp that were not captured using technology that minimizes harm to turtles (*United States – Anti-Dumping Measures on Shrimp and Diamond Sawblades from China*, WT/DS422); imposing export restraints on a number of raw materials (*China – Measures Related to the Exportation of Various Raw Materials*, WT/DS394/AB/R, WT/DS395/AB/R, WT/DS398/AB/R).

agreements contain many transparency and notifications requirements.[27] The result has been a successful lowering of tariffs and reduction of quotas, which has paved the way for focusing on other, less apparent blocks, including environmental health and safety (EHS) regulation, that hinders trade and may constitute a type of protectionism. Developing countries in particular have expressed concern that EHS regulations on the part of developed countries may be a cover for protectionist measures against their products, or a means by which to impose tougher environmental standards on them in a form of 'eco-imperialism'.[28]

In addition, it should be emphasized that the WTO has the most powerful intergovernmental dispute resolution mechanism of any international agreement.[29] In joining the WTO, Member States are held to the prescribed procedures and subject to mandatory jurisdiction, pursuant to the terms of the Dispute Settlement Understanding (the DSU).[30] The DSU is 'obligatory on all members' and comprises (for the first time) a

---

27 See e.g., Article X of the GATT; Article III of the GATS; Article 63 of the TRIPs; Articles 2 and 10 of the Agreement on Technical Barriers to Trade (TBT); Article 7 of the Agreement on the Application of Sanitary and Phytosanitary measures (SPS); Qin, J.Y. '"WTO-Plus" Obligations and Their Implications for the World Trade Organization Legal System: An Appraisal of the China Accession Protocol' (2003) *Journal of World Trade*, Vol. 37, No. 3, pp. 483–522 at p. 491.

28 See Cheyne, I. 'The Precautionary Principle in EC and WTO Law: Searching For a Common Understanding' (2006) *Env. L. Rev.* Vol. 8, No. 4, pp. 257–277; Gonzalez, C.G. 'Beyond Eco-Imperialism: An Environmental Justice Critique of Free Trade' (2001) *Denver University Law Review*, Vol. 78, No. 4, pp. 979–1016; Lal, D. 'Eco-Fundamentalism' (1995) *International Affairs*, Vol. 71, No. 3, pp. 515–528.

29 See Keohane, R.O., Moravcsik, A. & Slaughter A. 'Legalized Dispute Resolution: Interstate and Transnational' (2000) *International Organization*, Vol. 54, pp. 457–488; Sutherland Report, 'The Future of the WTO: Addressing Institutional Challenges in the New Millennium' (2004), pp. 49–59; Ali, A. 'Non-Compliance and Ultimate Remedies Under the WTO Dispute Settlement System' (2003) *Jour. Pub. Int'l Affairs*; Leal-Arcas, R. 'Comparative Analysis between NAFTA's Chapter 20 and the WTO's Dispute Settlement Understanding' (2011) *Transnational Dispute Management*, Vol. 8, No. 3, pp. 1–25.

30 See Understanding on Rules and Procedures Governing the Settlement of Disputes, Marrakesh Agreement Establishing the World Trade Organization, Annex 2, The Legal Texts: The Results of the Uruguay Round Of Multilateral Trade Negotiations 354 (1999), 1869 U.N.T.S. 401, 33 I.L.M. 1226 (1994) [hereinafter DSU].

'unitary dispute settlement mechanism covering all the agreements listed in Annex 1' of the Marrakesh Agreement establishing the WTO.[31]

The DSU is one of the most important new features of the WTO. It establishes a system of review and procedures for situations such as a WTO member complaining that the actions or policies of another member have harmed it through a violation of WTO rules. Typically, a complaint would be followed by consultations, possible arbitration, the formation of a panel of experts, and the Panel ruling. If the decision of the Panel is not appealed, it becomes binding after being adopted by the Dispute Settlement Body (DSB), which is a WTO body that rules on dispute settlement cases under the DSU.[32] If the decision of the Panel is appealed, then the Appellate Body hears the appeal and its final decision becomes a binding decision, after being adopted by the DSB.[33] The WTO's system of settling disputes provides for specific deadlines, and is therefore quicker than the old GATT system. Its functioning is more automatic, which entails fewer obstacles compared to the GATT system. The rules concerning the establishment of the findings process are more detailed than they were under the GATT system. Panel reports and Appellate Body rulings can be overturned only by a unanimous vote of the Dispute Settlement Body (DSB). The DSB consists of all members of

---

[31] Annex 1A (GATT 1994), Annex 1B (GATS), and Annex 1C (TRIPS); Jackson at p. 227.

[32] Articles 16–17 DSU.

[33] Ibid. The *raison d'être* of the WTO's dispute resolution is to reduce disruptions to fair trade as far as possible. In this respect, if a party's complaint is successful, recommendations of the Panel or Appellate Body will incline towards removing trade barriers and bringing 'a measure into conformity with the covered agreements', as opposed to payment of restitution or compensation (Article 22.1 DSU). The DSU provides detailed procedures regarding the implementation of rulings and recommendations once they have been adopted by the DSB, and the supervision of this implementation by the DSB (Article 21 DSU). Compliance with recommendations should occur within a 'reasonable period of time' (Article 21.3 DSU) which shall not exceed 18 months, 'unless the parties to the dispute agree that there are exceptional circumstances' (Article 21.4 DSU). In the case that a party does not comply within a satisfactory period, 'compensation and the suspension of concessions or other obligations are temporary measures available' (Article 22.1 DSU). A suspension of concessions essentially allows the prevailing party to impose tariffs against the non-complying party, equal to the economic loss that is being suffered by the winning country due to the ongoing breach of obligations under the WTO (Article 22 DSU). Such tariffs would normally be impermissible under the GATT.

the WTO General Council, that is to say, all WTO Members' representatives in Geneva, who oversee the operation of all of the constituent WTO Agreements in general. The DSB rules on actions taken under the DSU.[34]

Only States may raise complaints under the DSU.[35] When a WTO Member State brings a complaint against another WTO Member State, they must submit their dispute to a period of consultation 'with a view to reaching a mutually satisfactory solution'.[36] If no agreement is reached 'within 60 days after the date of receipt of the request for consultations',[37] the complaining State may request that the Dispute Settlement Body (DSB) (comprised of all the WTO Member States) form a Panel to hear the dispute.[38] The DSB has 'the authority to establish panels'[39] to hear particular disputes, and to make recommendations for adoption by the DSB.[40] Either side of the dispute can appeal a panel's ruling to the Appellate Body (AB),[41] which is a permanent standing body composed of seven persons, 'three of whom shall serve on any one case',[42] appointed by the DSB for four-year terms.[43] A dispute settlement recommendation to the DSB automatically becomes effective,[44] and the ruling of the Panel becomes legally effective, unless the DSB 'decides by consensus not to adopt the report'.[45] The same procedure applies to the adoption of an AB report, which the parties must unconditionally accept, 'unless the DSB decides by consensus not to adopt the Appellate Body report'.[46]

---

34 See Leal-Arcas, R. *Theory and Practice of EC External Trade Law and Policy* (London: Cameron May, 2008) at p. 418.

35 Article 1.1 DSU.

36 Article 4.3 DSU.

37 Article 4.7 DSU.

38 Article 6 DSU.

39 Article 2.1 DSU.

40 Article 16 DSU.

41 Article 17.1 DSU.

42 Ibid.

43 Article 17.2 DSU.

44 Under pre-WTO dispute settlement procedures for GATT disputes, a recommendation did not become effective unless positively adopted by consensus of all GATT Parties.

45 Article 16.4 DSU.

46 Article 17.14 DSU.

C. International Trade in Energy

The presumption is that trade liberalization will increase economic activity and therefore energy consumption.[47] All countries require energy resources, but few possess these, and thus trade in energy (primarily oil) is crucial to fulfill global energy needs.[48] Internationally, there is more trade in oil than in anything else. 'Fully half of world trade in services is intensely energy-dependent.'[49] Yet, the GATT/WTO has historically not preoccupied itself with energy trade. Very few energy-rich countries saw a need to join the GATT/WTO club, given that the reduction of import restrictions – one of the main goals of the multilateral trading system – is not an issue when it comes to energy. Saudi Arabia, the main energy-producing country in the world, only joined the WTO in 2005 and many energy-producing countries are still not WTO Members.[50]

All forms of energy should be subject to the same rules. Energy may become part of the WTO agenda in the near future.[51] Given that current WTO rules are far from addressing all the needs of energy trade today, is it necessary to have a WTO Agreement on trade in energy?[52] If so, can and should the Energy Charter Treaty be used as a model? Moreover,

---

[47] See e.g., ICTSD, 'Linking Trade, Climate Change and Energy', ICTSD, Geneva, 2006.

[48] Pauwelyn, J. 'Global Challenges at the Intersection of Trade, Energy and the Environment: An Introduction', in Pauwelyn, J. (ed.) *Global Challenges at the Intersection of Trade, Energy and the Environment* (Geneva: Centre for Trade and Economic Integration, 2010) p. 3.

[49] Gault, J. 'A World of Introduction from the Energy Industry Perspective', in Pauwelyn, J. (ed.) *Global Challenges at the Intersection of Trade, Energy and the Environment* (Geneva: Centre for Trade and Economic Integration, 2010) p. 9.

[50] For further details, see Selivanova, Y. (ed.) *Regulation of Energy in International Trade Law: WTO, NAFTA and Energy Charter* (Alphen aan den Rijn: Kluwer, 2011); Shih, W. 'Energy Security, GATT/WTO, and Regional Agreements' (2009) 49 *Nat. Resources J.* 433.

[51] Marceau, G. 'The WTO in the Emerging Energy Governance Debate' (2010) *Global Trade and Customs Journal*, Vol. 5, No. 3, pp. 83–93.

[52] On this point, see the views of Cottier, T. et al. 'Energy in WTO Law and Policy,' in Cottier, T. and Delimatsis, P. (eds) *The Prospects of International Trade Regulation: From Fragmentation to Coherence* (New York: Cambridge University Press, 2011), pp. 211–244 (arguing that, since the regulation of energy in international law is highly fragmented and largely incoherent, pertinent issues should be addressed by a future Framework Agreement on Energy in the context of WTO law).

since Russia finally joined the WTO on its own in 2012[53] (and not as a customs union along with Belarus and Kazakhstan)[54] and since energy is one of its greatest assets in economic terms, would this be the right time to include energy trade as part of the WTO Agreements? Those energy-rich Middle Eastern countries that are not yet WTO Members, but wish to become WTO Members, will most likely follow Russia.[55] These Middle Eastern countries should prioritize the conclusion of negotiations to enter the WTO in order to fully integrate into the global trading system and protect their growing interests on world markets. WTO membership will certainly help eliminate any discrimination against them in their trade and investment.

Trade in energy, *lato sensu*, encompasses various aspects and issues of transnational trade, including trade in goods, trade in services, investment matters, intellectual property, subsidies, etc. In addition, it involves different sorts of energy products, including oil, gas, coal, hydroelectricity, nuclear, and renewable energy, *inter alia*. However, the most predominant 'line' of trade in energy, both historically and currently, is trade in fossil fuels, oil and gas. In 2010, fossil fuels supply comprised more than 80% of the global energy supply.[56] Predictions are that, for many years to come, the world energy system will remain a fossil-based system.[57] That said, the various aspects of trade in energy and the different components of energy are beyond the scope of this chapter.

---

[53] WTO, 'Ministerial Conference Approves Russia's WTO Membership', 16 December 2011, available at http://www.wto.org/english/news_e/news11_e/acc_rus_16dec11_e.htm; see also 'Russia to Join WTO Alone', *The Moscow Times*, 16 April 2010, available at http://www.themoscowtimes.com/business/article/russia-to-join-wto-alone/404038.html

[54] International Centre for Trade and Sustainable Development, 'Russia Update' (June 2009) *Bridges Monthly*, Vol. 13, No. 2, available at http://ictsd.net/i/news/bridges/48583/

[55] For an analysis on the governance of global energy, see the special issue 'Global Energy Governance', *Global Policy*, Vol. 2, Issue Supplement s1, September 2011, pp. 1–154; Goldthau, A. & Witte, J.M. (eds) *Global Energy Governance: The New Rules of the Game* (Washington, DC: Brookings Institution Press, 2010).

[56] See International Energy Agency, *CO_2 Emissions from Fuel Combustion* (Paris: IEA, 2012) p. 18, available at http://www.iea.org/co2highlights/co2highlights.pdf

[57] Lesage, D., Van De Graaf, T. & Westphal, K. Global Energy Governance in a Multipolar World (Farnham, UK: Ashgate Publishing, 2010) p. 17 (where the authors cite *World Energy Outlook 2008* [Paris: OECD/IEA, 2008]).

At this initial stage and from an international trade perspective, it is worth clarifying the different statuses of countries in the energy sector, chiefly in terms of importing and exporting countries. In this respect, it has to be emphasized that not every energy-endowed country is an energy-exporting country, nor is every energy-producing country an energy-exporting country. Currently, there are two types of energy-endowed countries that produce energy: the first are energy-endowed countries that are both energy-producing and -exporting countries, such as Saudi Arabia, Russia, and Norway. In this case, the country's volume of energy production exceeds domestic demand, hence the country exports its energy surplus to the international market. The second type are energy-endowed countries that, in spite of their energy production, are considered to be energy-importing rather than energy-exporting countries, such as the US and the UK. In this case, the country's volume of energy production is less than domestic demand, and it therefore has to import energy resources from exporting countries in order to satisfy domestic consumption.[58]

The fact that trade in energy has been treated differently from other trade sectors and products stems from a combination of factors that will be addressed below. They include:

(1) the special characteristics of energy;
(2) the challenges that confront the global energy industry in general and trade in energy in particular; and
(3) ongoing legal debates and unresolved issues that emerge from the intersection between WTO law and energy trade.

Let us proceed with an analysis of each factor.

III. SPECIAL CHARACTERISTICS OF ENERGY

Energy is one of the most crucial elements of modern daily life. As a result, trade in energy constitutes, for every country, a major sector of international trade. There are a variety of reasons that make trade in energy critical and unique.

---

[58] This general classification refers to actual production vis-à-vis demand in a given country, regardless of its energy reserves or capacity.

A. Economic Aspects

Firstly, from an economic perspective, it has been known for decades that trade in energy products constitute the largest share of international trade, in terms of value and share of 'world merchandise export'.[59] According to data published by the WTO, in 2011 the value of fuel exports was USD 3,171 billion and comprised 17.8% of world merchandise exports.[60] Moreover, almost all sectors consume energy and critically rely on energy. This is in addition to the fact that the 'regularity and quality of the energy supply to economic operators' is as important as the energy prices.[61] It is also clear that low energy prices can 'boost all other sectors of the economy'.[62] The cost of energy impacts the prices of all other products and services and, as a result, affects the entire economy.[63] Additionally, the increase or decrease of energy prices in some countries leads to an increase or decrease in export prices of products and services, which then either impedes or enhances international competitiveness.[64] Energy therefore plays a crucial role in countries' economies, and heavily

---

[59] See the WTO, *International Trade Statistics 2012* (Geneva: WTO, 2012) p. 61, Table II.1, available at http://www.wto.org/english/res_e/statis_e/its2012_e/its2012_e.pdf; Y. Selivanova, 'Managing the Patchwork of Agreements in Trade and Investment', in Goldthau, A. & Witte, J.M. (eds) *Global Energy Governance: The New Rules of the Game* (Washington, DC: Brookings Institution Press, 2010) at p. 49 [hereinafter Selivanova Goldthau]; M. Desta, 'The Organization of Petroleum Exporting Countries, the World Trade Organization, and Regional Trade Agreements' (2003) *Journal of World Trade*, Vol. 37, No. 3, p. 523 [hereinafter Desta, 'World Trade'].

[60] According to WTO data, in 2011, chemical products were the second largest export after fuel, with an export value of USD 1,997 billion. Chemicals comprised 11.2% of world merchandise exports; see WTO, *International Trade Statistics 2012* (Geneva: WTO, 2012) p. 61, Table II.1, available at http://www.wto.org/english/res_e/statis_e/its2012_e/its2012_e.pdf; see also Gault, J. 'A Word of Introduction from the Energy Industry Perspective', in Pauwelyn J. (ed.) *Global Challenges at the Intersection of Trade, Energy and the Environment* (Geneva: Centre for Trade and Economic Integration, 2010) p. 9.

[61] See Energy Charter Secretariat, *Trade in Energy: WTO Rules Applying under the Energy Charter Treaty* (Brussels, 2001) at p. 11; see also C. Melly, 'Electric Power and Gas Market Reform and International Trade in Services', in UNCTAD, *Energy and Environmental Services: Negotiating Objectives and Development Priorities*, (New York & Geneva, UNCTAD, 2003) p. 164, available at http://unctad.org/en/Docs/ditctncd20033_en.pdf [hereinafter Melly UNCTAD].

[62] See Energy Charter Secretariat, *Trade in Energy: WTO Rules Applying under the Energy Charter Treaty* (Brussels, 2001) at p. 11.

[63] Ibid; see also Melly UNCTAD at p. 164.

[64] See Melly UNCTAD, p. 164.

impacts national and global economic development as well as international competitiveness.

B. Energy as an Asset of Strategic and Political Value

Secondly, since the exploration of petroleum, and particularly since the beginning of the 20th century, energy's significance is not only measured by its economic value. Rather, energy products and resources have also been recognized as strategic political assets.[65] During the 20th and 21st centuries, energy resources, markets, and trade have been the direct motives or influencing factors in several international and regional conflicts. It is worth noting some of these famous conflicts:[66] World War I (1914), World War II (1939), the Suez War (1956); the Six-Day War (1967); the oil embargo (1973); the Arab-Israel War (1973), the Iranian revolution (1979), the Iran-Iraq War (1980–1988), the invasion of Kuwait (1990), the Gulf War (1991), and the Iraq War (2003).[67] These wars and conflicts highlight the strategic importance and influence of the geopolitics of energy. Moreover, most energy products are known as scarce products, underscoring energy's importance for political stability and

---

65 See UNCTAD, *Trade Agreements, Petroleum and Energy Policies*, UNCTAD/ITCD/TSB/9 (New York and Geneva: UNCTAD, 2000), p. 14, available at http://p166.unctad.org/pluginfile.php/1839/mod_resource/content/0/31oct/itcdtsb9_en.pdf [hereinafter UNCTAD, Geneva 2003].

66 See UNCTAD, Geneva 2003, at p. 14.

67 See UNCTAD, Geneva 2003, p. 14; Bejesky, R. 'Geopolitics, Oil Law Reform, and Commodity Market Expectations' (2011) 63 *Okla. L. Rev.* 193, p. 200; Rhea, J.E. 'Privatization in the International Petroleum Industry: The Interplay Between Politics, Economics, and Reliance' (2005) 33 *Denv. J. Int'l L. & Pol'y* 609, 609–613; Venn, F. *The Oil Crisis* (London: Longman, 2002) pp. 7–8; Klare, M. *Resource Wars: The New Landscape of Global Conflict* (New York: Holt Paperbacks, 2002) at p. 25; Peters, S. 'Coercive Western Energy Security Strategies: "Resource Wars" as a New Threat to Global Security', in Le Billon P. (ed.) *The Geopolitics of Resource Wars: Resource Dependence, Governance and Violence* (London: Routledge, 2005) p. 187 at pp. 202–204; US Department of Energy, Energy Information Administration, Interagency Database and Projections Working Group (describing six major disruptions in world oil supply: the Suez War (1956); the Six-Day War (1967); the oil embargo (1973); the Iranian Revolution (1979); the Iran-Iraq War (1980); and the Gulf War (1990)); Barton, B. *Energy Security: Managing Risk in a Dynamic Legal and Regulatory Environment* (Oxford: Oxford University Press, 2004) p. 3 at p. 4 [hereinafter Barton, *Energy Security*].

national sovereignty.[68] Undoubtedly, energy resources critically impact the security and political stability of international, regional, and national regimes.

C. International Development

Thirdly, the energy sector is important for national and global development. Indeed, it played a decisive role and influenced a wide array of important developments in the aftermath of the World Wars.[69] Currently, as well as in the near and distant future, energy appears to be the most important factor for modern global development. It is also worth mentioning that the energy sector has huge importance and an increasing influence in the development of other industries, including manufacturing products and providing services.[70] In addition, the availability and affordability of energy products on international and national markets have significant impacts on 'social development and quality of life'.[71] These and other factors accentuate the importance of energy for international development.

D. Diversity of Energy Sources

Fourthly, energy trade is unique in that it involves different kinds of energy products and services that are derived from a variety of primary energy sources worldwide. Primary energy sources can be divided into two groups: conventional energy sources, known as non-renewable, and nonconventional energy sources, known as renewable. Non-renewable

---

[68] See Energy Charter Secretariat, *Trade in Energy: WTO Rules Applying under the Energy Charter Treaty* (Brussels, 2001) at p. 11.

[69] See UNCTAD, Geneva 2003, at p. 14.

[70] See Selivanova, Y. 'The WTO and Energy: WTO Rules and Agreements of Relevance to the Energy Sector', ICTSD Trade and Sustainable Energy Series Issue Paper No. 1 (Geneva, 2007), at p. 12, available at http://ictsd.org/downloads/2008/05/the20wto20and20energy.pdf; Selivanova, Y. 'Energy Challenges for International Trade Rules' (2011) *Oil, Gas and Energy Law*, Vol. 6.

[71] See Selivanova, Y. 'The WTO and Energy: WTO Rules and Agreements of Relevance to the Energy Sector', ICTSD Trade and Sustainable Energy Series Issue Paper No. 1 (Geneva, 2007) at p. 12; Melly UNCTAD at p. 164; Energy Charter Secretariat, *Trade in Energy: WTO Rules Applying under the Energy Charter Treaty* (Brussels, 2001) at p. 11 (explaining that energy is significant to everyone and has a precise social function; therefore, it is important to secure an affordable supply of energy for everyone including 'rich and poor, young and old, employed and unemployed'); Selivanova Goldthau at p. 49.

energy sources include fossil fuels (oil, coal, and natural gas) in addition to nuclear energy. Renewable energy sources encompass bio-energy, wind, solar, geothermal, and tidal energy. Although electricity is a secondary energy source that is generated through the conversion of primary sources of energy, it constitutes a crucial energy source. Indeed, all energy resources vary in terms of their features and trade-related issues, which distinguish them from other traded objects subject to the WTO regime.[72] One major distinguishing feature relates to energy's peculiar physical composition, which affects the ways energy products are stored, transported, and distributed.[73] Therefore, the distinctive features of energy resources necessitate applying appropriate treatment and trade regulations to address specific trade and investment issues pertaining to each one of the various energy resources, products, and services.

E. Finite Resources

Fifthly, the lion's share of energy trade revolves around the fossil fuel resources of oil, coal, and natural gas, which are non-renewable resources with finite amounts available within proven natural reserves.[74] Importantly, only some countries are fossil-fuel endowed and exporting countries, while the vast majority of the world is composed of energy-importing countries.[75] In this sense, energy is the largest globally traded commodity and currently global usage is composed, almost entirely, of finite and non-renewable resources upon which the modern world is thus greatly dependent. The sale of energy products is controlled only by

---

72 See Rakhmanin, V. 'Transportation and Transit of Energy and Multilateral Trade Rules: WTO and Energy Charter', in Pauwelyn, J. (ed.) *Global Challenges at the Intersection of Trade, Energy and the Environment*, (Geneva: Centre for Trade and Economic Integration, 2010) pp. 123–126, at p. 123 [hereinafter Rakhmanin]; Cossy, M. 'Energy Transport and Transit in the WTO', in Pauwelyn J. (ed.) *Global Challenges at the Intersection of Trade, Energy and the Environment* (Geneva: Centre for Trade and Economic Integration, 2010) pp. 113–121 [hereinafter Cossy] at p. 113 (arguing that the distinction rooted in the WTO rules between goods and services is not always easily applicable to trade in energy and could cause 'artificial determinations').

73 Cottier, T. et al. 'Energy in WTO Law and Policy', *NCCR Trade Regulation Working Paper* No. 2009/25, available at http://phase1.nccr-trade.org/images/stories/projects/ip6/IP6%20Working%20paper.pdf

74 See Selivanova Goldthau, p. 49 (explaining that fossil fuel resources are distributed worldwide in an 'uneven' manner, thus they are found to be 'under sovereign control of a limited number' of energy-endowed countries).

75 See Selivanova Goldthau at p. 49.

some countries, while the majority of countries are energy purchasers. Also, the multifaceted vulnerability of international trade and markets to the availability, stability, and affordability of a sustainable and steady supply of these non-renewable energy resources poses an additional challenge to the energy trade sector.

F. Energy Security

Sixthly, the significance of energy and the reliance of exporting and importing countries on energy trade emphasize national and global energy security issues.[76] Notably, the energy market is one market, thus any event that considerably impacts the supply of or demand for available energy on the market will affect energy export and import prices alike. Thus, events in any major oil importing or exporting country impact all other countries,[77] and, in fact, various historic events have given rise to deep and ongoing concerns over energy supply and demand for exporting and importing countries, respectively. This includes, *inter alia*, the era when the majority of the global oil industry was controlled by the international oil companies (IOCs) known as the 'seven sisters';[78] the oil embargo; the oil shocks; the rise of and increased concerns pertinent to climate change and carbon dioxide emissions; the financial crises; and the fluctuations of oil prices, mainly the unprecedented fluctuations of prices[79] during the last

---

[76] See Desta 'World Trade', pp. 523–524; Strange, R. 'Weaving a Tangled Web: the Intersection of Energy Policy and Broader Governmental Policies' (2009–2010) 5 *Tex. J. Oil Gas & Energy L.* 1, at p. 6 [hereinafter Strange].

[77] See Strange at p. 6.

[78] 'Seven sisters' is a term coined by Enrico Mattei to refer to the following oil companies: the Standard Oil Company of New Jersey (later Exxon), the Standard Oil Company of New York (Socony, later Mobil, which eventually merged with Exxon), the Standard Oil Company of California (Socal, later renamed Chevron), the Texas Oil Company (later renamed Texaco), Gulf Oil (which later merged with Chevron), Anglo-Persian (later British Petroleum), and Royal Dutch/Shell. See US Department of State, Office of the Historian, available at http://history.state.gov/milestones/1921-1936/RedLine

[79] During the 2008 global financial crisis, oil prices increased rapidly to record on 3 July 2008 an all-time high price of USD 145.31 a barrel (West Texas Intermediate WTI); see U.S Energy Information Administration, 'Petroleum and Other Liquids', available at http://www.eia.gov/dnav/pet/hist/leafhandler.ashx?n=pet&s=rwtc&f=d

decade.[80] Therefore, the availability and affordability of energy in the international and domestic markets affect global as well as national energy security.[81]

Moreover, global trade in energy was neither regulated by suitable rules and regulations specific to trade in energy, nor conducted *de facto* by written or transparent rules. Instead, trade in energy was managed for decades through interstate relations influenced by political and diplomatic considerations. This politicized rather than regulated way of trade lacks transparency, certainty, stability, and predictability. Furthermore, trade in non-renewable energy resources demonstrates the conflict of trade interests that exists in the intersection between the two interdependent groups of energy trading countries: the energy importing countries, that is, the vast majority of the world's countries, and the energy-endowed exporting countries, that is, a small number of countries. While the first group is interested in securing an affordable (at the 'lowest price') and steady supply of energy, the second group seeks to gain the maximum income and rent from the sale of its natural wealth for the benefit and development of its nations and economies.[82] The direct consequence is that the availability, stability, and affordability of traded energy resources in the domestic and international markets influence to a huge extent the 'political stability and economic survival'[83] of exporting and importing countries and the international community, as well as national and global energy security.

---

[80] Barton, *Energy Security*, pp. 3–5.

[81] See Yergin, D. 'Ensuring Energy Security' (March/April 2006) *Foreign Affairs*, Vol. 85, No. 2. See also Desta, 'World Trade' at pp. 523–524 (discussing the negative economic impact of high prices of oil and the role of sharp rises in oil prices in slowing down growth and causing recessions in many developed countries as well as globally, based upon data from ECOSOC, *World Economic and Social Survey, 2001*).

[82] See Selivanova, Y. 'Trade in Energy: Challenges for International Trade Regulation' (WTO: Research and Analysis), available at http://www.wto.org/english/res_e/publications_e/wtr10_11june10_e.htm#fnt3 [hereinafter Selivanova WTO]; Selivanova, Y. 'Challenges for Multilateral Energy Trade Regulation: WTO and Energy Charter', Society of International Economic Law, Second Biennial Global Conference, University of Barcelona, Working Paper No. 2010/20, available at http://papers.ssrn.com/sol3/papers.cfm?abstract_id=1632557 [hereinafter Selivanova SIEL].

[83] See Desta, 'World Trade' at p. 523.

G. Transportation of Energy

Finally, energy products are transported differently from other products. A significant share of trade in energy is network-dependent.[84] This means that trade in energy, chiefly in the cases of natural gas and electricity, does not cross borders as other products do, but rather its transportation is usually linked to a 'fixed infrastructure'.[85] In the case of natural gas, it is transported via fixed pipelines, while electric power is transported via fixed grids.[86] Because of its peculiar physical limitations, 75% of natural gas is transported internationally via fixed pipelines, and only 25%, as liquefied natural gas (LNG), is transported by sea.[87] Meanwhile, crude oil usually is transported by sea.

The dependence of natural gas trade on a fixed pipeline infrastructure could explain why the volume of international trade in gas resources is much lower than that of international trade in oil resources.[88] Moreover, given the necessity of transporting gas via pipelines and electricity via grids, trade in these energy resources has been largely restricted to regional trade between those States that are connected through adequate networks.[89] Remarkably, the network dependence of energy transportation points to the substantial capital and investment required for the construction of new pipelines and transmission grids infrastructure, as well as for the maintenance of old and new transportation networks.[90] The intrinsic reliance on fixed infrastructure of gas and electricity

---

[84] Wälde T. & Gunst, A. 'International Energy Trade and Access to Competing Networks', *Energy and Environmental Services: Negotiating Objectives and Development Priorities*, UNCTAD (New York & Geneva: UNCTAD, 2003), p. 118 (noting that trade in electricity and gas is 'as a rule network dependent', with the exception of the LNG transported via ships, and explaining, from a trade and investments perspective, that 'network dependence' means that it is not enough to eliminate import barriers for freeing trade effectively, but there have to be 'proactive measures' towards opening transportation networks for energy transit, including establishing new networks).

[85] See Rakhmanin at p. 123; see also Energy Charter Secretariat, *Trade in Energy: WTO Rules Applying under the Energy Charter Treaty* (Brussels, 2001) at p. 11.

[86] See Selivanova, Y. 'The WTO and Energy: WTO Rules and Agreements of Relevance to the Energy Sector', ICTSD Trade and Sustainable Energy Series Issue Paper No. 1 (Geneva, 2007) at p. 18.

[87] See Rakhmanin, at p. 123, footnote 122.

[88] Ibid.

[89] See Energy Charter Secretariat, *Trade in Energy: WTO Rules Applying under the Energy Charter Treaty* (Brussels, 2001) at p. 11.

[90] See Selivanova SIEL, at p. 2.

transportation stresses greatly the interdependence and complexity of energy trade, essentially the transit of energy resources, in the international market.

The significance and unique characteristics of energy mentioned above distinguish trade in energy from other sectors of trade. Thus, this predominant sector of global trade requires and necessitates a special treatment.

IV. ENERGY TRADE: CHALLENGES AND CONCERNS

The second factor that explains why trade in energy has been treated differently from other trade sectors and products has to do with the challenges that confront the global energy industry in general and trade in energy in particular.

A. Supply and Demand

The global energy system is internationally interlaced and interdependent.[91] The impacts of energy demand and supply are not limited to national borders; rather, energy supply and demand have global consequences and implications for a variety of sectors.[92] An increasingly significant example of this global interdependence is the link between trade and energy. Recently, the international trade regime has increasingly focused on energy trade,[93] and both fields interact in a variety of

[91] Leal-Arcas, R. and Filis, A. 'The Fragmented Governance of the Global Energy Economy: A Legal-Institutional Analysis' (2013) *Journal of World Energy Law and Business*, Vol. 6, No. 4, pp. 1–58; Leal-Arcas, R. and Filis, A. 'Conceptualizing EU Energy Security through an EU Constitutional Law Perspective' (2013) *Fordham International Law Journal*, Vol. 36, No. 5, pp. 1224–1300.

[92] See Westphal, K. 'Energy in an Era of Unprecedented Uncertainty: International Energy Governance in the Face of Macroeconomic, Geopolitical, and Systemic Challenges', in D. Koranyi (ed.), *Transatlantic Energy Futures: Strategic Perspectives on Energy Security, Climate Change, and New Technologies in Europe and the United States*, (Washington, DC: Center for Transatlantic Relations, 2011) pp 1–26, at p. 1 [hereinafter Westphal, 'Era of Uncertainty'].

[93] See e.g., a conference that linked these two epistemic communities (trade and energy): 'Workshop on the Role of Intergovernmental Agreements in Energy Policy', 29 April 2013, WTO Secretariat, Geneva, available at http://www.wto.org/english/tratop_e/envir_e/wksp_envir_apr13_e/wksp_envir_apr13_e.htm. Another development that links the international trade and energy fields is

ways and are becoming more and more interdependent.[94] One of the causes for this increasing interaction between trade and energy relates to the liberalization of energy markets in many countries, which subjected trade in energy products to market rules.[95]

Moreover, trade in the energy sector, as elaborated earlier, plays a very significant role in promoting both international and national economic development. However, the energy world, including trade in energy, is confronted by unprecedented concerns and challenges. The origins of these challenges are deeply rooted in the tension between expanding trade and increasing economic growth, on the one hand, and promoting efficient use of energy resources and protecting the environment, on the other hand.[96] In fact, 'the energy world faces unprecedented uncertainty',[97] according to the World Energy Outlook (2010) of the International Energy Agency (IEA).

Some of the most dominant concerns in the energy world are the concerns over energy supply and demand. These concerns are interconnected with different factors, including: the economic growth and energy consumption of developed as well as developing countries; the

---

a conference organized by the Centre for Trade and Economic Integration at the Graduate Institute of International and Development Studies in Geneva, titled 'Global Challenges at the Intersection of Trade, Energy and the Environment', WTO Secretariat, 22–23 October 2009, available at http://www.wto.org/english/res_e/reser_e/energy_oct09_e/energy_oct09_e.htm

[94] See Pauwelyn, J. 'Global Challenges at the Intersection of Trade, Energy and the Environment: An Introduction', in Pauwelyn J. (ed.) *Global Challenges at the Intersection of Trade, Energy and the Environment* (Geneva: Centre for Trade and Economic Integration, 2010) pp. 1– 8, at p. 4 [hereinafter Pauwelyn Challenges].

[95] See Pauwelyn Challenges at p. 4; Wälde T. and Gunst, A. 'International Energy Trade and Access to Competing Networks', in *Energy and Environmental Services: Negotiating Objectives and Development Priorities*, UNCTAD (New York & Geneva: UNCTAD, 2003) p. 18.

[96] See Pauwelyn Challenges at p. 1. See also Leal-Arcas, R. *Climate Change and International Trade* (Cheltenham: Edward Elgar, 2013), Chapter 3; Abu-Gosh, E. and Leal-Arcas, R. 'The Conservation of Exhaustible Natural Resources in the GATT and WTO: Implications for the Conservation of Oil Resources' (2013) *The Journal of World Investment and Trade*, Vol. 14, No. 3, pp. 480–531.

[97] See International Energy Agency, *World Energy Outlook 2010 Executive Summary* (Paris: OECD/IEA, 2010) at p. 3, available at http://www.worldenergyoutlook.org/media/weowebsite/2010/WEO2010_es_english.pdf [hereinafter IEA 2010].

availability of various energy resources; energy efficiency and sustainability; stability or fluctuations of energy prices in the international markets; financial stability or crisis; the capital of investments required for the explorations and production of energy; geopolitical matters; political stability or instability, etc. Notably, the apparent economic growth of countries worldwide is accompanied by growth in energy consumption, mainly of oil and gas resources.[98] It is worth mentioning in this respect that during the last 20 years energy consumption has increased by 45%, and over the period of 2010 to 2030 it is likely to grow by 39%.[99] Thus, the correlated high growth of economies and energy consumption in developed and developing countries, especially in emerging economies like China, Russia, and India, obviously raises the demand for energy in the long term.[100]

A similar growth, however, is not expected on the supply side. One of the reasons for this relates to the poor investment in the energy sector. Investment in this sector, mainly in exploration and production, is slow and 'lagging behind'.[101] Other reasons have to do with the 2008 global financial crisis as well as disputes between governments and investors in the energy industry, which have negative impacts and are likely to restrict investments in this sector.[102] As a consequence, energy demand will be

---

[98] See Kemfert, C. 'Global Energy Markets: Challenges and Opportunities – Energy Vision for 2050', in Herrmann C. and Terhechte, J.P. (eds), *European Yearbook of International Economic Law*, Vol. 3, 271 (2012) at pp. 272, 274 [hereinafter Kemfert]; International Energy Agency, *World Energy Outlook 2012 Executive Summary* (Paris: OECD/IEA, 2012) p. 6, available at http://www.iea.org/publications/freepublications/publication/English.pdf (explaining that in 2011 oil demand reached 87.4 mb/d, while the expectation for 2035 indicates that oil demand will reach 100 mb/d) [hereinafter IEA 2012].

[99] See British Petroleum, *BP Energy Outlook 2030* (London: BP, 2011) p. 17, available at http://www.bp.com/liveassets/bp_internet/globalbp/globalbp_uk_english/reports_and_publications/statistical_energy_review_2008/STAGING/local_assets/2010_downloads/2030_energy_outlook_booklet.pdf (last accessed 2013); see also British Petroleum, *BP Energy Outlook 2030* (London: BP, 2012) p. 11, available at http://www.bp.com/liveassets/bp_internet/globalbp/STAGING/global_assets/downloads/O/2012_2030_energy_outlook_booklet.pdf (last accessed 2013); Lesage, D., Graaf, T. & Westphal, K. *Global Energy Governance in a Multipolar World* (Farnham, UK: Ashgate Publishing, 2010) 17.

[100] See IEA 2010, p. 5; IEA 2012, p. 4; Kemfert at p. 277.

[101] See Selivanova Goldthau, at p. 50.

[102] Ibid.

higher than energy supply, which will lead to energy scarcity, high energy prices and even to global economic crises.[103]

B. Trade in Goods v. Trade in Services

An additional concern is found in the clear distinction between trade in goods and trade in services in the WTO discipline, where specific rules apply to trade in goods (the GATT) and other rules apply to trade in services (the General Agreement on Trade in Services (GATS)). But the energy sector does not apply this obvious distinction between energy products and energy services, which may result in artificial determinations and intrinsic obstacles to trade in energy.[104] Thus, this emerging debate around the dichotomy of goods and services, within trade in energy, complicates the substantial ongoing debate over the applicability and implementation of WTO rules to trade in energy.[105]

C. Transit via Fixed Networks: Pipelines and Grids

Likewise, as mentioned earlier, an important challenge to trade in energy stems from the transportation of gas and electricity through fixed infrastructures, namely pipelines for gas and grids for electricity.[106] This limitation of network usage for specific energy products entails spending huge capital and substantial investment, in addition to drafting appropriate investment rules in order to secure the transportation and flow of

---

[103] See Kemfert at pp. 274–275 (explaining that in order to satisfy the rise in global energy demand, an increase in energy supply is expected. But the traditional and low-cost oil fields are disappearing, which necessitates exploiting other oil production sites to meet demand, including deep sea drilling. This is highly risky, especially when drilling more than 1,500 meters deep, as the accident at the *Deepwater Horizon* in the Mexican Gulf in April 2010 has proven); IEA 2010 at p. 6.

[104] See Cossy at p. 113 (explaining that the distinction between goods and services is inconsistent with the daily business reality. It also has various consequences, e.g., in the investment field, where it is clear that, while the GATS contains basic investment disciplines that apply and protect trade in services, the Agreement on Trade-Related Investment Measures, which applies to trade in goods, 'does not protect investment per se').

[105] See Energy Charter Secretariat, *Trade in Energy: WTO Rules Applying under the Energy Charter Treaty* (Brussels, 2001) at p. 15.

[106] See Selivanova SIEL at p. 2; Rakhmanin, p. 123; Energy Charter Secretariat, *Trade in Energy: WTO Rules Applying under the Energy Charter Treaty* (Brussels, 2001) at p. 14.

energy products.[107] At the same time, WTO law was not designed specifically to address the crucial issues that arise from trade in energy through fixed networks. For example, WTO law includes more detailed rules regulating imports than rules relevant to exports, while, in the case of energy, countries are concerned more with rules on exports than imports in order to secure the supply of energy from exporting to importing countries.[108]

Even though Article V of the GATT addresses the freedom of transit for goods in general, its applicability to transportation of energy through fixed infrastructures is questionable.[109] Various claims surround the existing text of Article V, including: the national treatment obligation in Article V is very limited; Article V lacks the power to oblige countries to invest and construct new infrastructures needed for energy transportation; plus there is an ambiguity with respect to the applicability of Article V over energy companies, which control, by monopoly enterprises, access to energy infrastructure.[110] Therefore, although the WTO embraces basic disciplines addressing transit of goods, they are incomplete and lack substantial obligations with relevance to the specific challenges of energy trade.[111] However, the transit issue is not the only unresolved issue with relevance to the intersection between trade and energy. It appears that WTO law was not designed to address and regulate additional critical unresolved issues, which include, *inter alia*, export restrictions including export quotas and duties, subsidies, dual pricing,[112] countervailing measures on energy products, technical regulations and standards, monopolies, and state-trading enterprises.[113] The consequences are more uncertainty and more challenges to trade in energy.

---

107 See Rakhmanin at p. 123; Selivanova Challenges SIEL at p. 2.

108 See Rakhmanin at p. 124; Cossy at pp. 113–114.

109 See Cossy at pp. 114, 115.

110 See Cossy at p. 115; Rakhmanin at p. 124; Selivanova WTO; Azaria, D. 'Energy Transit under the Energy Charter Treaty and the General Agreement on Tariffs and Trade' (2009) *Journal of Energy & Natural Resources Law*, Vol. 27, No. 4, p. 559.

111 See Cossy at p. 120.

112 The dual pricing practice is a practice where countries price exported energy resources, such as natural gas, at different rates from the domestic price for the same resources.

113 See Marceau, G. 'The WTO in the Emerging Energy Governance Debate', in Pauwelyn J. (ed.) *Global Challenges at the Intersection of Trade, Energy and the Environment* (Geneva: Centre for Trade and Economic Integration, 2010) at pp. 33–36; Yannovich, A.'WTO Rules and the Energy Sector', in Selivanova, Y. (ed.), *Regulation of Energy in International Trade Law: WTO,*

D. Combating Climate Change

Moreover, one of the most pressing current challenges for all industries in general and the energy sector in particular is combating climate change.[114] Indeed, the whole energy chain involves a severe negative impact on the environment and contributes to climate change.[115] This chain includes the exploration, production, refining, storage, transportation, distribution, and consumption of energy, each of which involves the combustion of energy products. The consequence is a significant increase in greenhouse gas (GHG) emissions. In 2010, the combustion of energy resources comprised 65% of global GHG emissions.[116]

Of note in this regard is the fact that fossil fuels (oil, coal, and gas) accounted for 81% of global total primary energy supply (TPES).[117] This high fossil fuel share of TPES was addressed in an IEA report discussing global CO_2 emissions and indicating the emission quantity of each fossil fuel: coal 43%, oil 36%, and gas 20%.[118] Nonetheless, there are various measures that can help mitigate climate change: substituting fossil fuel energy sources (high GHG emissions) for green and less polluting energy sources, particularly energy derived from renewable sources; imposing energy efficiency plans and steps for both producers and consumers;

NAFTA and Energy Charter (Global Trade Law Series), (Alphen aan den Rijn: Kluwer Law International, 2011) pp. 1–74, at pp. 1-28; Selivanova, Y. 'The WTO and Energy: WTO Rules and Agreements of Relevance to the Energy Sector', ICTSD Trade and Sustainable Energy Series Issue Paper No. 1 (Geneva, 2007) pp. 15–30; Cottier, T. et al. 'Energy in WTO Law and Policy', *NCCR Trade Regulation Working Paper* No. 2009/25; Selivanova Goldthau; Marceau, G. 'The WTO in the Emerging Energy Governance Debate' (2010) *Global Trade & Customs Journal*, Vol. 5, No. 3, pp. 83–93, at pp. 88–91.

114 On the links between climate change, energy and trade, see generally Leal-Arcas, R. *Climate Change and International Trade* (Cheltenham: Edward Elgar, 2013).

115 Leal-Arcas, R. 'Linking Energy and Climate Change' (November 2012) OUTREACH, Stakeholderforum, p. 4.

116 International Energy Agency, 'CO_2 Emissions from Fuel Combustion' (Paris: IEA, 2011), p. 17, http://www.iea.org/co2highlights/co2highlights.pdf [hereinafter IEA CO_2 Emissions 2012]; Kleymeyer, A.M. 'New Rules for the Environmental Imperative: Considerations for the Energy Sector and Interaction with WTO Rules', in Pauwelyn J. (ed.) *Global Challenges at the Intersection of Trade, Energy and the Environment* (Geneva: Centre for Trade and Economic Integration, 2010) at p. 63.

117 IEA CO_2 Emissions 2012, pp. 17, 18.

118 Ibid., Figure 13, 'World primary energy supply and CO_2 emissions: shares by fuel in 2010 Percent share', p. 19.

saving consumption of energy whenever possible; increasing public awareness through various educational plans, etc.[119] In this respect, the legally binding obligations to reduce GHG emissions that countries made through the Kyoto Protocol to the UN Framework Convention on Climate Change (UNFCCC) is a significant global effort worth mentioning here.[120]

In spite of their environmental repercussions, the current demand for and consumption of fossil fuels are still high and growing constantly. Moreover, taking into account the global population and economic growth, it is expected that the demand for and consumption of fossil fuels will increase dramatically in the coming decades.[121] According to a recent report published by British Petroleum, although the OECD countries will succeed in reducing GHG emissions by 2030, the fast economic growth of non-OECD countries will cause a higher degree of emissions and outweigh the OECD countries' reduction. Therefore, in 2030 the aggregate projected increase in global emissions will be 28% (versus 2010).[122] This trend of growth in the consumption and burning of fossil fuels results in a constant growth of GHG emissions that will threaten the global climate.[123] Also, this serious, complicated and reciprocal challenge between climate change and energy constitutes part of broader challenge

---

[119] See Westphal, 'Era of Uncertainty' at p. 19; Powers, M. 'Greening the Grid: Building a Legal Framework for Carbon Neutrality' (2009) 39 *Envtl. L.* 927 at p. 927.

[120] See Kyoto Protocol to the United Nations Framework Convention on Climate Change, Dec. 10, 1997, U.N. Doc FCCC/CP/1997/7/Add.1, 37 I.L.M. 22 (1998); Energy Charter Secretariat, *Trade in Energy: WTO Rules Applying under the Energy Charter Treaty* (Brussels, 2001) p. 11. See also Leal-Arcas, R. 'Kyoto and the COPs: Lessons Learned and Looking Ahead' (2010) *Hague Yearbook of International Law*, Vol. 23, pp. 17–90. For alternative views on climate change mitigation, see Leal-Arcas, R. 'Top-down Versus Bottom-up Approaches for Climate Change Negotiations: An Analysis' (December 2011) *The IUP Journal of Governance and Public Policy*, Vol. 6, No. 4, pp. 7–52; Leal-Arcas, R. 'Climate Change Mitigation from the Bottom Up: Using Preferential Trade Agreements to Promote Climate Change Mitigation' (2013) *Carbon and Climate Law Rev*, Vol. 7, No. 1, pp. 34–42; Leal-Arcas, R. 'The BRICS and Climate Change' (2013) *International Affairs Forum*, pp. 1–5.

[121] Energy consumption is likely to grow by 39% over the period of 2010 to 2030; see BP, *Energy Outlook 2030* (2011) at p. 17; BP, *Energy Outlook 2030* (2012) at pp. 9, 11; Lesage, D. Graaf, T. & Westphal, K. *Global Energy Governance in a Multipolar World* (Farnham, UK: Ashgate Publishing, 2010) pp. 30, 31.

[122] See BP, *Energy Outlook 2030* (2012) at p. 81.

[123] See Kemfert at pp. 276–277.

to the fulfillment of global sustainable development.[124] Thus, the existing pattern of escalating energy demand, supply and consumption, accompanied by energy combustion, strengthens the threat of irreversible damage to the environment and thus to humankind and global sustainable development.

E. Energy Security

Nowadays energy security concerns are at the top of national, regional, and international agendas.[125] As mentioned above, while all countries are involved in trade and consumption of energy, most of them are energy importers, as opposed to a few energy exporters. Hence, energy security and its concerns are not determined by a single definition, but rather the definition varies and the concept of energy security means different things to different countries and regions. Attempts to conceptualize energy security and its challenges were based upon various factors including energy endowment, geographic location, economic conditions, etc. Also, critical elements and factors of energy security will vary in different countries at different times.[126] Therefore, to energy-endowed exporting countries, any disruption that threatens the stability of energy demand, production, and prices as well as the conservation of energy resources is a challenge to their economic security;[127] whereas, to energy importing countries, any factor that challenges the availability, stability, and affordability of energy products supply poses a threat to their energy security.[128] Taking into consideration the complexity and interdependency of the energy world, it is obvious that any risk to the supply or demand of energy is considered a challenge and a threat to energy security.

---

124 IEA CO_2 Emissions 2012, 19.

125 Shih, W.-C. 'Energy Security, GATT/WTO, and Regional Agreements' (2009) 49 *Nat. Resources J.* 433, at p. 434 [hereinafter Shih, 'Energy Security'].

126 Barton, *Energy Security*, 5, 9; Luft, G. *Energy Security Challenges for the 21st Century: A Reference Handbook* (Santa Barbara, CA: ABC-CLIO, 2009) pp. 5–7; Shih, 'Energy Security', 437; Martin, W.F., Imai, R. & Steeg, H. *Maintaining Energy Security in a Global Context: a Report to the Trilateral Commission*, Vol. 48 (Trilateral Commission, 1996), 4, http://www.getcited.org/pub/100130828

127 Yergin, D. 'Ensuring Energy Security' (2006) 85 *Foreign Affairs* 69, at pp. 70, 71; Winzer, C. 'Conceptualizing Energy Security' (July 2012) 46 *Energy Policy* 36, at pp. 37, 41; Luft, G. *Energy Security Challenges for the 21st Century: A Reference Handbook* (Santa Barbara, CA: ABC-CLIO, 2009), p. 6; Shih, 'Energy Security', 436.

128 Barton, *Energy Security*, 5; Shih, 'Energy Security', 435.

However, a broad variety of factors impacts the availability and affordability of steady supply and demand, namely energy security, with some of them known and predictable, and others unknown or unpredictable. In this respect, several substantial concerns around energy security should be mentioned, which include geopolitical conflicts, volatility of energy prices, disruptions of energy supply and demand, depletion of energy resources, climate change and environmental challenges, natural disasters, etc.[129] Due regard has to be given also to the monopolies that control all aspects of the energy sector in many countries, for example Russia, Saudi Arabia, and Venezuela, whose policies directly affect both national and global energy security.[130] Noticeably, a few recent events highlight some challenges to national and global energy security, such as: the global financial crises compounded by fluctuations of energy prices in 2008;[131] the accident on the *Deepwater Horizon* in 2010; the nuclear catastrophe at Fukushima Daiichi in 2011; and the ongoing revolutions in the Middle East and the North African region since 2011, known also as the Arab Spring.[132] Precisely, energy security, in its national and global concepts, is a crucial constituent that challenges the energy world. Given the expected growth in trade in energy during the coming decades, and without extreme and dramatic innovation or revolution in the energy industry, it is safe to say that the more trade in energy expands, the more the challenges to energy security will increase.

In short, several concerns indicate that the global energy sector, including trade in energy, is subject to substantial challenges, especially economic, political, and environmental. Although these challenges are very crucial in themselves, their importance is multiplied since energy influences all aspects of our daily modern life. It should be emphasized

---

[129] Redgwell, C. 'International Energy Security', in Barton, B. et al. (eds) *Energy Security: Managing Risk in a Dynamic Legal and Regulatory Environment* (Oxford: Oxford University Press, 2004), 17; Winzer, 'Conceptualizing Energy Security' 46 *Energy Policy* 36, at p. 37; Yergin, 'Ensuring Energy Security', 69.

[130] Kemfert 275; Barton, *Energy Security*, 8.

[131] Salisu A. and Fasanya, I. 'Comparative Performance of Volatility Models for Oil Price' (2012) *International Journal of Energy Economics and Policy*, Vol. 2, No. 3, pp. 167–183, at p. 182 (examining the volatility of crude oil prices from 1.2000 to 3.2012 over three periods, namely 'pre-global financial crisis, global financial crisis, and post-global financial crisis' and finding that oil prices changed most rapidly during the period of global financial crisis).

[132] Westphal, 'Era of Uncertainty', 3; Lesage, D. Graaf, T. & Westphal, K. *Global Energy Governance in a Multipolar World* (Farnham, UK: Ashgate Publishing, 2010).

in this regard that existing global energy governance is ineffective and unqualified to address and resolve the above mentioned challenges. Global energy governance suffers from critical fragmentation and lack of consistent rules.[133] Its structure includes fragmented systems across multilayered regimes such as multilateral, regional, bilateral, and national systems and treaties, in addition to a variety of international institutional governors like the IEA, the Organization of the Petroleum Exporting Countries, the UN, or the G20.[134] Therefore, the fragmentation of governance and inconsistency of rules in global energy governance will most likely cause additional tensions and uncertainties to trade in energy in particular and global energy governance in general.

V. WTO LAW AND ENERGY TRADE: SELECTED DEBATES

The third dimension that makes energy distinct from other sectors of trade is the ongoing debate and unresolved issues that emerge from the intersection between WTO law and energy trade. In principle, the trade regime embraces various sectors of trans-boundary trade with the assumption that the GATT/WTO disciplines prevail over all trade sectors. When it comes to trade in energy, however, this assumption is not entirely true. As mentioned earlier, nowadays trade in energy constitutes the largest universal constituent of trade that interacts with other sectors

---

[133] Leal-Arcas, R. & Filis, A. 'The Fragmented Governance of the Global Energy Economy: A Legal-Institutional Analysis' (2013) *Journal of World Energy Law and Business*, Vol. 6, No. 4, pp. 1–58.

[134] Ghosh, A. 'Seeking Coherence in Complexity? The Governance of Energy by Trade and Investment Institutions' (2011) *Global Policy*, Vol. 2, no. s1: 106–119, pp. 107, 117; Sovacool, B.K. & Florini, A., 'Examining the Complications of Global Energy Governance' (2012) *Journal of Energy & Natural Resources Law*, Vol. 30, No. 3, 235, 238, 252; with regard to the fragmentation of the global energy governance, see generally Florini A. & Sovacool, B.K. 'Bridging the Gaps in Global Energy Governance' (2011) *Global Governance: A Review of Multilateralism and International Organizations* 17, No. 1, pp. 57–74; Lesage, D., Graaf, T. & Westphal, K. *Global Energy Governance in a Multipolar World* (Farnham: Ashgate Publishing, 2010); Cherp, A., Jewell, J. & Goldthau, A. 'Governing Global Energy: Systems, Transitions, Complexity' (2011) *Global Policy* 2, No. 1, pp. 75–88; Marceau, G. 'The WTO in the Emerging Energy Governance Debate' (2010) *Global Trade and Customs Journal*, Vol. 5, No. 3, pp. 83–93; Florini, A. & Dubash, N.K. 'Introduction to the Special Issue: Governing Energy in a Fragmented World' (2011) *Global Policy* 2, pp. 1–5.

of trade and exerts great influence on these other sectors. Therefore, managing, fostering and securing trade in energy are on national and international agendas as a top priority for energy-importing as well as energy-exporting countries.[135] However, in spite of its high significance, trade in energy is not automatically, or by definition, included or excluded from the international trade discipline.

Notably, two major approaches have been developed in the last two decades to address the debate over the GATT/WTO disciplines and trade in energy. The first approach supports the view that the international trade discipline governs all sectors of trade including trade in energy, mainly because the energy sector was never excluded explicitly from the GATT/WTO disciplines.[136] The other approach casts doubts about the automatic governance of GATT/WTO disciplines over trade in energy and considers trade in energy a special case that was excluded *de facto*, not *de iure*, from the GATT/WTO disciplines.[137] As long as there is no conclusive decision in this debate, the divergent approaches will more

---

135 See for instance the views of Lamy, P. 'Doha Round Will Benefit Energy Trade', speech given at the 20th World Energy Congress, Rome, 15th November 2007. Available at http://www.wto.org/english/news_e/sppl_e/sppl80_e.htm

136 Jiménez-Guerra, A. 'The World Trade Organization and Oil', Oxford Institute for Energy Studies (Oxford 2001): 14, 19; Marceau, G. 'The WTO in the Emerging Energy Governance Debate', in Pauwelyn, J. *Global Challenges at the Intersection of Trade, Energy and the Environment* (Geneva: Centre for Trade and Economic Integration, 2010), 25–41, 26; Yanovich, A. 'WTO Rules and the Energy Sector', in Selivanova, Y. (ed.) *Regulation of Energy in International Trade Law: WTO, NAFTA, and Energy Charter Treaty* (Alphen aan den Rijn: Kluwer, 2011), 1–47, 2; Selivanova, Y. 'Managing the Patchwork: Challenges for Multilateral Agreements in Trade and Investment' in Goldthau, A. & Witte, J.M. (eds) *Global Energy Governance: The New Rules of the Game* (Washington, DC: Brookings Institution Press, 2010), 53.

137 The United Nations Conference on Trade and Development UNCTAD, *Trade Agreements, Petroleum and Energy Policies* (New York and Geneva: United Nations, 2000), 1–2, 14–15, available at http://p166.unctad.org/pluginfile.php/1839/mod_resource/content/0/31oct/itcdtsb9_en.pdf; Desta, M.G. 'The Organization of Petroleum Exporting Countries, the World Trade Organization, and Regional Trade Agreements' (2003) *Journal of World Trade Law*, Vol. 37, No. 3, pp. 523–552, at p. 529; Desta, M.G. 'GATT/WTO System and International Trade in Petroleum: An Overview' (2003) *Journal of Energy & Natural Resources Law*, Vol. 21, pp. 385, 387, 391; Aidelojie, K. & Makuch, Z. 'Multilateral Organizations, Fossil Fuels and Energy Law and Policy: The Tower of Babel Revisited' (2008) *European Energy and Environmental Law Review*, Vol. 17, pp. 227–255, at pp. 229, 230.

than likely be examined as a starting point in future discussions relevant to energy trade issues.

It is worth mentioning in this respect that this debate is based on a mutual significance to both sectors, namely international trade and trade in energy, and encompasses important consequences to both sectors. From the international trade system point of view, energy trade is the most significant sector of trade by virtue of being the largest trade sector in terms of share and value, as well as being crucial to other trade sectors. From the trade in energy perspective, being subject to the international trade system means being subject to a stable, agreed, and predictable set of rules. Thus, the outcome of this debate reflects the distance between the existence and non-existence of a rules-based regime to regulate the most important sector of trade, and it also entails positive or negative implications for both sectors.

A. The Applicability of WTO Law to Energy Trade

In general, the source of international economic and trade law is international treaty law, rather than international customary law.[138] Treaty law is the law formulated by the parties to a treaty. The treaty, an international contract or agreement, reflects the willingness and intention of the parties, who create the obligations of the agreement. Thus, the obligations made by the parties are the binding law that applies to the relations/transactions between the parties to the agreement. The result is that contracting parties agree between themselves which are the laws and norms that apply to them, and what is included in and excluded from this binding law.

Accordingly, in the specific case of the WTO, the founding members agreed to bind all WTO members (founders and acceding) to a set of international agreements which compose the law of the WTO and govern their trade relations. This set of agreements is known as the 'single package'. Importantly, according to WTO law, when a country joins the WTO, it must accept the single package as a binding law of the WTO. This section analyzes the chronological evolution of international trade in energy, starting with the creation of ITO and the GATT in 1947, the various rounds of GATT negotiations, the subsequent accession of energy-exporting countries to the GATT, the WTO era and energy trade, and the accession of energy-rich countries to the world trading system

---

[138] See generally Jackson, J. *The Jurisprudence of GATT and the WTO: Insights on Treaty Law and Economic Relations* (Cambridge and New York: Cambridge University Press, 2000).

since 1995, all with a view to determining whether GATT/WTO law applies to trade in energy.

1. The International Trade Organization and the GATT creation

Although energy issues were not specifically addressed during the negotiations for the establishment of the ITO and the GATT, natural resources matters in general were brought up, discussed and agreed upon.[139] During the ITO negotiations era, in parallel to the creation of the GATT, the Havana Charter addressed issues relevant to natural resources in several provisions.[140] Within these provisions, several articles warrant mention in this regard: Articles 10 and 13 of the Havana Charter, which emphasized the role that natural resources play in 'economic development and reconstruction', and Article 45 of the Havana Charter, which justified measures related to the 'conservation of exhaustible natural resources'.[141] Similar to Article 45 of the Havana Charter, Article XX(g) of the GATT granted protection to the conservation of 'exhaustible natural resources'.[142] Notably, the term 'natural resources' was understood to include 'raw material', while the term 'exhaustible natural resources' covered 'stock resources', including metal or 'oil'.[143] Hence, it can be deduced that energy trade in general was intended to be subject to the disciplines of the ITO and the GATT, unless a particular kind of energy trade was targeted by a measure aimed at conserving exhaustible natural resources, according to Article 45 of the Havana Charter and Article XX(g) of the GATT.

---

139 See Selivanova, Y. 'Managing the Patchwork of Agreements in Trade and Investment', in Goldthau, A. & Witte, J.M. (eds) *Global Energy Governance: The New Rules of the Game* (Washington, DC: Brookings Institution Press, 2010), 52.

140 See United Nations Conference on Trade and Employment, March 1948, Havana Charter for an International Trade Organization, Article 11(2), U.N. Sales No. 48.II.D.4, E/CONF.2/78 (1948) [hereinafter Havana Charter].

141 See Article 13, paragraphs 6, 7(iii) and Article 45, paragraph 1(a)(viii) of the Havana Charter; see also Selivanova, Y. 'Managing the Patchwork of Agreements in Trade and Investment', in Goldthau, A. & Witte, J.M. (eds) *Global Energy Governance: The New Rules of the Game* (Washington, DC: Brookings Institution Press, 2010) p. 52.

142 See Article XX(g) of the GATT.

143 See Charnovitz, S. 'Exploring the Environmental Exceptions in GATT Article XX' (1991) 25 *J. World Trade* 37, 45, 63.

2. Energy tradable products

Following the demise of the ITO, the GATT became the binding multilateral trade treaty, which had a general application and governed trans-boundary trade in commodities between GATT parties.[144] Generally, any product eligible as tradable, through export or import, was subject to the GATT. Thus, all tradable energy products, in principle, qualified as tradable products capable of being exported and imported. In fact, during the entire life of the GATT, since 1947, enormous volumes of energy products, specifically oil, coal, and gas, have been traded internationally. Therefore, it can be assumed that, to the extent that energy resources are tradable products, all trade in energy products, similar to other tradables, are subject to the GATT.[145]

3. Energy trade was not excluded from the GATT

One of the main reasons supporting the applicability of GATT rules to trade in energy relates to the fact that neither energy as a trade sector nor energy products as commodities were ever explicitly excluded from the application of the GATT.[146] Indeed, none of the provisions of the GATT agreements, protocols or other related legal documents approved by the contracting parties has excluded energy products from GATT coverage, unlike the case of certain products, such as agricultural goods and textiles. These commodities, which were important for some of the GATT drafters, such as the US and certain European States, were granted special treatment within the GATT regime to the extent that the general

---

[144] See the General Agreement on Tariffs and Trade, Oct. 30, 1947, 61 Stat. A-11, 55 U.N.T.S. 194; Jackson, J, Davey, W.J. & Sykes, A.O. *Legal Problems of International Economic Relations: Cases, Materials and Text on the National and International Regulation of Transnational Economic Relations* (St Paul, MN: West Publishing Co., 5th ed. 2008) pp. 215, 222.

[145] See Marceau, G. 'The WTO in the Emerging Energy Governance Debate', in Pauwelyn, J. (ed.) *Global Challenges at the Intersection of Trade, Energy and the Environment* (Geneva: Centre for Trade and Economic Integration, 2010) pp. 25–41, at p. 26.

[146] See Jiménez-Guerra, A. 'The World Trade Organization and Oil', Oxford Institute for Energy Studies SP 12 (2001), 14; Desta, M.G. 'The GATT/WTO System and International Trade in Petroleum: An Overview' (2003) *J. Energy & Nat. Resources L.,* Vol. 21, pp. 385–398, at p. 391; Waelde, T.W. & Gunst, A.J. 'International Energy Trade and Access to Energy Networks' (2002) *Journal of World Trade*, Vol. 36, No. 2, pp. 191–218.

provisions of the GATT did not apply to them.[147] Additionally, the GATT discipline granted affirmative exemptions from the coverage of its rules to certain kinds of measures, activities, or situations. These exemptions were provided to GATT contracting parties through a variety of specific as well as general GATT exceptions. According to the various exceptions, measures and activities would be exempt from compliance with general GATT rules if they met the specific requirements of whichever GATT exceptions were applicable.

Therefore, one may conclude firstly that the GATT drafters intended to apply GATT rules to all goods that were not explicitly excluded from the coverage of the GATT, and, secondly, when the GATT drafters intended to exempt an activity or a measure from compliance with GATT rules, they did so by designating certain exceptions. Accordingly, energy products were among those general non-excluded tradable products. Thus, in principle, their international trade was subject to GATT rules,[148] unless a measure related to their trade was eligible, by a party taking that measure, to invoke one of the potentially applicable GATT exceptions. However, this argument's premise relies on the questionable assumption that energy products belonged to the same pool of products as other traded products. Accordingly, as long as energy products were not explicitly left out of this pool, they, like other products, were subject to GATT rules. Nevertheless, this argument, through its inclusive interpretation of the GATT coverage, ignores the possibility that energy products might not have been intended at all to belong to the general pool of tradable products.

4. GATT negotiations

Although trade in energy in general and trade in petroleum in particular were not clearly and directly included in any of the GATT provisions,

---

[147] See generally, McPhee, J.S. 'Agriculture and Textiles: The Fare and Fabric of Current GATT Negotiations' (1992) *Indiana International & Comparative Law Review* 3, 155; Dickerson, K.G. 'Textile Trade: The GATT Exception' (1996) *St. John's Journal of Legal Commentary* 11, 393; Hathaway, D. *Agriculture and the GATT: Rewriting the Rules*, Policy Analysis in International Economics (Washington, DC: Institute for International Economics, 1996).

[148] See Selivanova, Y. 'Challenges for Multilateral Energy Trade Regulation: WTO and Energy Charter', Society of International Economic Law (SIEL), Second Biennial Global Conference, University of Barcelona, July 8–10, 2010, SSRN Scholarly Paper, June 29, 2010, available at http://papers.ssrn.com/abstract=1632557

according to GATT history, the contracting parties discussed energy-related matters during various rounds of GATT negotiations.[149] Importantly, subsequent to the wave of nationalization of the petroleum industry by several Middle East and North African countries in the early 1970s, as well as due to the oil embargo and first oil shock in 1973, the US attempted to raise the issue of energy trade export restrictions and export taxes relating to energy during the Tokyo Round (1973–1979). Ultimately, the opposition of developed and developing countries led to the failure of this initiative.[150] Despite rejecting this initiative, during the Tokyo Round several issues indirectly relevant to oil were negotiated. The Tokyo Round resulted in the creation of special agreements (Codes), which included, *inter alia*, subsidies, antidumping, and technical barriers. Notably, these agreements included new rules with potential impacts on energy products and policies applied by energy exporting countries.[151] Even though these agreements were the result of a multilateral round of the GATT, they were conceived not as binding but 'optional' agreements. However, almost two decades later, with the establishment of the WTO, the optional agreements became part of the WTO binding agreements.[152]

It is worth noting another issue relating to energy vis-à-vis the GATT, which arose directly out of the Tokyo Round, that is, the issue of the dual pricing practice. The GATT parties were required to formally discuss the dual pricing practice at the GATT Ministerial Meeting in 1982. This issue had emerged at that meeting since the GATT Council was requested to provide arrangements to serve towards the study of the dual pricing practices.[153] No substantive decision was taken in this regard and this

---

[149] See ibid. p. 4; Jiménez-Guerra, A. 'The World Trade Organization and Oil', Oxford Institute for Energy Studies SP 12, p. 14.

[150] See The United Nations Conference on Trade and Development (UNCTAD), *Trade Agreements, Petroleum and Energy Policies* (New York and Geneva: United Nations, 2000) p. 15, available at http://p166.unctad.org/pluginfile.php/1839/mod_resource/content/0/31oct/itcdtsb9_en.pdf

[151] See Leebron, D.W. 'An Overview of the Uruguay Round Results' (1996) *Columbia Journal of Transnational Law* 34, p. 18; Jiménez-Guerra, A. 'The World Trade Organization and Oil', Oxford Institute for Energy Studies SP 12, pp. 14–16 [hereinafter Jiménez-Guerra, 'WTO and Oil'].

[152] See Leebron, D.W. 'An Overview of the Uruguay Round Results' (1996) Columbia Journal of Transnational Law 34, pp. 18–25; Jiménez-Guerra, 'WTO and Oil', at p. 16 [hereinafter Jiménez-Guerra, 'WTO and Oil'].

[153] See UNCTAD, *Trade Agreements, Petroleum and Energy Policies* (New York and Geneva: United Nations, 2000), available at http://p166.unctad.org/pluginfile.php/1839/mod_resource/content/0/31oct/itcdtsb9_en.pdf [hereinafter UNCTAD, *Trade and Energy*] at p. 17, footnote 6.

specific practice continued until recently with regard to the negotiations around Russia's accession to the WTO, given Russia's practice of pricing gas exported and gas consumed domestically at different rates.[154]

5. Accession of energy-exporting countries to the GATT

During the GATT era, some energy-exporting countries became signatories to the GATT, such as Indonesia (1950), Nigeria (1960), Kuwait (1963), Mexico (1986), and Venezuela (1990).[155] Among these energy-exporting countries, it is important to focus on the accession of Mexico and Venezuela. The accession of these two countries to the GATT casts light upon the link between the GATT discipline and trade in energy. More essentially, their accession to the GATT highlights how these two energy exporting countries perceived the interplay between GATT and energy trade and the implications of their GATT accessions for their energy trade.

Mexico became a contracting party to the GATT in 1986[156] and a founding member of the WTO in 1995.[157] At the time of joining the GATT, Mexico was one of the world's most important oil producing and exporting countries. Notably, when Mexico negotiated its accession to the GATT, one of the most important energy trade issues came to the fore, that is, the issue of export restriction practices that energy producing and exporting countries used to impose over the production or exportation of energy products, essentially over crude oil.[158] In order to preserve its sovereignty and apply certain export restrictions with regard to its natural resources in general and energy products in particular, Mexico sought to

---

[154] See Selivanova, Y. *Energy Dual Pricing in WTO Law: Analysis and Prospects in the Context of Russia's Accession to the WTO* (London: Cameron May, 2008) pp. 5 and 11; Ripinsky, S. 'The System of Gas Dual Pricing in Russia: Compatibility with WTO Rules' (2004) *World Trade Review*, Vol. 3, No. 3, pp. 463–481; Selivanova, J. 'World Trade Organization Rules and Energy Pricing: Russia's Case' (2004) *Journal of World Trade*, Vol. 38, No. 4, pp. 559–602.

[155] See WTO, The 128 countries that had signed GATT by 1994, available at http://www.wto.org/english/thewto_e/gattmem_e.htm

[156] For further details, see English, R.D. 'The Mexican Accession to the General Agreement on Tariffs and Trade' (1988) *Texas International Law Journal*, Vol. 23, pp. 339–393, 340.

[157] See WTO, 'Mexico and the WTO', available at http://www.wto.org/english/thewto_e/countries_e/mexico_e.htm

[158] See UNCTAD, *Trade and Energy*, 20.

maintain its rights through Paragraph 5 of the Protocol of Accession to the GATT.[159] Paragraph 5 of Mexico's Protocol of Accession states:

> Mexico will exercise its sovereignty over natural resources, in accordance with the Political Constitution of Mexico. Mexico may *maintain certain export restrictions* related to the conservation of natural resources, *particularly in the energy sector*, on the basis of its social and development needs if those export restrictions are made effective *in conjunction with restrictions on domestic production or consumption.* (emphasis added)

On the contrary, a few years later, in 1990, Venezuela joined the GATT without retaining any right to regulate its energy trade. Venezuela is one of the leading energy producing and exporting countries and one of the five founding members of the Organization of Petroleum Exporting Countries (OPEC) in 1960.[160] With regard to the practices of production or export restriction, it is important to mention that in 1985 OPEC countries transformed their coordination practices from setting oil prices directly to imposing production ceilings or quotas.[161] Thus, at the time of becoming a contracting party to the GATT, this new practice was very relevant to Venezuela as a GATT signatory because of Article XI:1 of the GATT, which bans imposing quantitative restrictions on imports and exports. In fact, Mexico's Protocol of Accession specifically included a reservation in Paragraph 5 allowing for the retention of its ability to regulate trade in energy.

---

159 Ibid., 20 (Protocol for the Accession of Mexico to the GATT); see also Jiménez-Guerra, 'WTO and Oil', p. 22; Shih, W.-C. 'Energy Security, GATT/WTO, and Regional Agreements' (2009) 49 *Nat. Resources J.* 433, 468 [hereinafter Shih, 'Energy Security']

160 See OPEC, Member Countries, available at http://www.opec.org/opec_web/en/about_us/25.htm.

161 See OPEC, Brief History, available at http://www.opec.org/opec_web/en/about_us/24.htm; Wagner, H. *The Organization of Oil Exporting Countries* (New York: Chelsea House, 2009), pp. 54–57 (describing the events that accompanied the shift from setting oil prices to setting oil production ceilings); Gault, J., Spierer, C., Bertholet, J.-L. & Karbassioum, B. 'How Does OPEC Allocate Quotas?' (1999) *Journal of Energy Finance and Development*, Vol. 4, No. 2, pp. 137–148, at p. 137; Sandrea, R. 'OPEC's Next Challenge – Rethinking their Quota System' (2003) *Oil & Gas Journal*, Vol. 101.29, p. 2, available at http://www.ipc66.com/publications/OPEC_Nex_Challenge_quota_system.pdf; Desta, M.G. 'The Organization of Petroleum Exporting Countries, the World Trade Organization, and Regional Trade Agreements' (2003) *Journal of World Trade*, Vol. 37, No. 3, pp. 523–551.

It was expected that Venezuela would include a similar text or paragraph in its accession documents, especially bearing in mind the new quota restrictions it imposed as a member of OPEC, which could be in infringement of Article XI:1 of the GATT. However, unlike the Mexican case, it appears that Venezuela did not feel the need to incorporate any wording in its Protocol of Provisional Application (PPA), or even in the report of the Working Party, to maintain its ability to apply production or export restrictions to its oil sector. In fact, Venezuela relied on the general exception of the GATT and, in particular, on Article XX(g) of the GATT. This article provided a valid defense to measures related to the 'conservation of exhaustible natural resources'.[162] Indeed, Venezuela did not request the inclusion of any additional and specific text to the PPA for the sake of maintaining its oil production and export policies. Therefore, it is obvious that Venezuela considered the text in Paragraph 5 of Mexico's Protocol of Accession to be no different than Article XX(g) of the GATT and as not containing any particular advantage.[163] Also, it can be concluded that Venezuela considered GATT law to include an internal mechanism (i.e., Article XX(g)) that allowed regulating the exploitation of natural resources, including energy resources.

In this respect, two substantially different situations have to be addressed concerning the issue of GATT (in)applicability to energy trade issues: the first deals with excluding trade in energy initially from the GATT discipline; the second focuses on exempting energy trade from one or more GATT rules through invoking GATT methods. The first situation implies that all types of trade in energy are conducted fully outside the scope of the GATT, and both rules and exceptions have no validity over this sector of trade. Conversely, the starting point of the second situation highlights the full applicability of GATT rules to trade in energy matters. However, according to the latter situation, if a certain issue, activity or measure of energy trade meets the requirement of one of the GATT exceptions, this specific item will be exempt from the GATT discipline. All other activities, issues or measures related to energy trade will continue to be subject and bound by GATT rules.

---

[162] See Article XX(g) of the GATT; UNCTAD, *Trade and Energy*, 20; Shih, 'Energy Security', 468; Abu-Gosh, E. and Leal-Arcas, R. 'The Conservation of Exhaustible Natural Resources in the GATT and WTO: Implications for the Conservation of Oil Resources' (2013) *The Journal of World Investment and Trade*, Vol. 14, No. 3, pp. 480–531.

[163] See UNCTAD, *Trade and Energy*, 20; Jiménez-Guerra, 'WTO and Oil', pp. 22–23.

Although the approaches of Mexico and Venezuela differed in their accession to the GATT, it can be implied that both treated the GATT discipline as being applicable to trade in energy, following the second situation mentioned above. It is through the specific reservation in Paragraph 5 of its Protocol of Accession that Mexico kept 'certain export restrictions' outside the scope of GATT rules. Meanwhile, Venezuela referred to Article XX(g) of the GATT to defend a similar practice. Admittedly, the reservation within the Protocol of Accession as well as Article XX(g) of the GATT are both precisely GATT methods. These GATT methods were an inherent part of GATT law and were provided to GATT contracting parties or acceding States by GATT law. Consequently, the reliance on and the usage of GATT methods to exempt certain energy trade practices undoubtedly emphasize the coverage of the GATT discipline to all energy trade issues, except those exempted by GATT exceptions or reservations in Protocols of Accession. In other words, using GATT methods to invalidate the GATT discipline over particular energy practices means, first and foremost, accepting the applicability of this discipline to all other non-exempt energy trade issues.

6. The Uruguay Round

During the Uruguay Round (1986–1994), different groups of countries held discussions that had a clear impact on energy matters. For instance, some of the countries participating in the Negotiating Group on Natural Resources-Based Products called attention to certain problematic practices pertinent to energy products issues.[164] Among those debatable issues were dual pricing, export restrictions, and trade distortions due to governmental ownership and control practices.[165] Objecting countries claimed that these practices caused variations of energy prices, favoring domestic markets and hence resulting in trade distortion.[166]

---

[164] See Uruguay Round, Group of Negotiations on Goods, Negotiating Group on Natural Resource-Based Products, meeting of 11 February 1987, note by the GATT Secretariat, MTN.GNG/NG3/, 26 February 1987; UNCTAD, *Trade and Energy*, 15 at footnote 6, mentioning the submission of the US in MTN.GNG/NG3/W/2, MTN.GNG/NG3/W/13 and MTN.GNG/NG3/W/23, as well as the submission of the European Communities in MTN.GNG/NG3/W/37.

[165] See paras 10–11 of the Uruguay Round Meeting of 11 February 1987; UNCTAD, *Trade and Energy*, 15–16.

[166] See paras 10–11 of the Uruguay Round Meeting of 11 February 1987; UNCTAD, *Trade and Energy*, 16; Jiménez-Guerra, 'WTO and Oil', 17.

However, the opponents to this argument stressed that these practices were outside the scope of the mandate of the Negotiating Group on Natural Resources-Based Products.[167] Additionally, within the Negotiating Group on Subsidies and Countervailing Measures, attempts were made to address subsidies issues relating to energy. These attempts were also opposed for being 'outside the terms of reference of the Negotiating Group on Subsidies and Countervailing Measures'.[168] Finally, this initiative failed to incorporate energy-related texts in the Chairman's draft text of the Agreement on Subsidies and Countervailing Measures.[169]

7. The WTO coverage

The outcome of the Uruguay Round was the creation of the WTO with its set of binding agreements. Indeed, the WTO encompasses rules relevant to trade in goods, services, and intellectual property rights. Although the WTO agreements do not specify either an independent agreement addressing energy matters or any particular provisions relating to energy, the premise is that the WTO covers a multitude of energy trade issues.[170] For example, all trade in energy products is covered by GATT rules; likewise, all trade in energy services should be conducted according to GATS rules.[171]

---

[167] See para. 12 of the Uruguay Round Meeting of 11 February 1987; Cossy, M. 'Energy Trade and WTO Rules: Reflexions on Sovereignty over Natural Resources, Export Restrictions and Freedom of Transit', in Herrmann, C. & Terhechte, J.P. (eds) *European Yearbook of International Economic Law* (EYIEL) Vol. 3, 2012, pp. 281, 292; UNCTAD, *Trade and Energy*, 17.

[168] See Uruguay Round, Trade Negotiations Committee, Subsidies and Countervailing Measures, Communication from the Permanent Delegation of Mexico, MTN.TNC/W/38 (26 November 1990).

[169] Ibid. See also UNCTAD, *Trade and Energy*, pp. 18–19.

[170] See Marceau, G. 'The WTO in the Emerging Energy Governance Debate', in Pauwelyn, J. (ed.) *Global Challenges at the Intersection of Trade, Energy and the Environment* (Geneva: Centre for Trade and Economic Integration, 2010), pp. 25-41; Yanovich, A. 'WTO Rules and the Energy Sector', in Selivanova, Y. (ed.) *Regulation of Energy in International Trade Law: WTO, NAFTA, and Energy Charter Treaty* (Alphen aan den Rijn: Kluwer, 2011), 1–47, 2.

[171] See Marceau, G. 'The WTO in the Emerging Energy Governance Debate', in Pauwelyn, J. (ed.) *Global Challenges at the Intersection of Trade, Energy and the Environment* (Geneva: Centre for Trade and Economic Integration, 2010), pp. 26–30; Marceau, G. 'The WTO in the Emerging Energy Governance Debate' (2010) *Global Trade and Customs Journal*, Vol. 5, No. 3, pp. 83–93. See also the background note by the WTO Secretariat, 'Energy Services', S/C/W/311, 12 January 2010.

Moreover, the Doha Round, which began in 2001 and is an ongoing multilateral round of negotiations,[172] contains few implications for energy trade. It neither addresses energy trade as a separate or independent area of negotiations nor does it highlight its critical issues. This in spite of the fact that there are three major areas of negotiations in the Doha Round with relevance to trade in energy issues: liberalizing trade in environmental products and services (climate friendly goods and services); energy services; and trade facilitation (energy transit).[173] The fact that the Doha Round includes energy issues,[174] even if treated only as sub-matters rather than major areas of negotiation, stresses the existence of energy trade issues in the WTO.

8. Accession of energy-endowed countries to the WTO

The accession of energy-endowed countries to the WTO strengthens the argument that trade in energy is subject to the WTO discipline. In

---

[172] See WTO, Ministerial Declaration of 14 November 2001, WT/MIN(01)/DEC/1, 41 I.L.M. 746(2002). For analyses of the Doha Round (especially from a services trade perspective), see Leal-Arcas, R. 'Services as Key for the Conclusion of the Doha Round' (2008) *Legal Issues of Economic Integration*, Vol. 35, No. 4, pp. 301–321; Leal-Arcas, R. 'The Resumption of the Doha Round and the Future of Services Trade' (2007) *Loyola of Los Angeles International and Comparative Law Review*, Vol. 29, No. 3, pp. 339–461; Leal-Arcas, R. 'Bridging the Gap in the Doha Talks: A Look at Services Trade' (2007) *Journal of International Commercial Law and Technology*, Vol. 2, No. 4, pp. 241–249; Leal-Arcas, R. 'The GATS in the Doha Round: A European Perspective' in Alexander, K. & Andenas, M. (eds) *The World Trade Organization and Trade in Services* (Leiden: Brill/Nijhoff, 2008), pp. 9–104.

[173] See Lamy, P. 'Energy, Trade and Global Governance', in Pauwelyn, J. (ed.) *Global Challenges at the Intersection of Trade, Energy and the Environment* (Geneva: Centre for Trade and Economic Integration, 2010) pp. 15–18, at p. 17; Marceau, G. 'The WTO in the Emerging Energy Governance Debate', in Pauwelyn, J. (ed.) *Global Challenges at the Intersection of Trade, Energy and the Environment* (Geneva: Centre for Trade and Economic Integration, 2010), p. 31; Gibbs, M. 'Energy Services, Energy Policies and the Doha Agenda', in UNCTAD, *Energy and Environmental Services: Negotiating Objectives and Development Priorities*, UNCTAD/DITC/TNCD/ 2003/3 (Geneva: UNCTAD, 2003), p. 4, available at http://unctad.org/en/Docs/ditctncd20033_en.pdf

[174] See the reference Pascal Lamy makes to energy services in the context of the Doha Round. Lamy, P. 'Energy, Trade and Global Governance', in Pauwelyn, J. (ed.) *Global Challenges at the Intersection of Trade, Energy and the Environment* (Geneva: Centre for Trade and Economic Integration, 2010) pp. 15–18, at p. 17.

contrast to the GATT era, the WTO seems to attract more energy-endowed countries to become full members of this multilateral trade organization. The most prominent energy producing countries[175] that joined the WTO are: Qatar (1996), United Arab Emirates (1996), Angola (1996), Oman (2000), China (2001), Saudi Arabia (2005), and Russia (2012).[176] In order to properly answer the question of the applicability of GATT/WTO disciplines to trade in energy, another significant milestone should be examined, namely the accession of the energy-exporting countries to the WTO, and, particularly, the accession of the biggest energy-producing and energy-exporting countries, that is, Saudi Arabia and Russia, which joined the WTO in 2005 and 2012, respectively. Both countries have been considered for decades the biggest energy-producing and energy-exporting countries worldwide. The accession of these two countries to the WTO constitutes a landmark event in the history of the WTO in relation to trade in energy. In addition, other significant energy-endowed countries are in the process of negotiating their accession to the WTO, and in the meantime have observer status. This group of observers includes Iran, Iraq, Libya, Algeria, Kazakhstan, and Azerbaijan.[177] Accordingly, it is assumed that the dynamics of the WTO may well be changed due to the accession of energy-producing countries.[178] The more energy-endowed countries join the WTO, the more energy trade becomes subject to the WTO.

However, if the presumption was that energy trade fell outside the scope of GATT/WTO disciplines, then it may be incorrect to claim that accession of energy-producing countries to the WTO would mean the automatic application of WTO rules to energy trade. An argument based solely upon accession is weak compared to the previous arguments. In the context of applying the WTO discipline to energy trade, using the accession to the WTO of energy-producing countries entails linking this argument to other substantial aspects of accession, such as: the negotiation agenda and process; energy-related issues raised and negotiated *de*

---

[175] For an account of the major oil producing countries as of 2009, see http://aspousa.org/peak-oil-reference/peak-oil-data/production-and-peak-dates-by-country/ (last accessed 2012).

[176] See WTO, 'Members and Observers', http://www.wto.org/english/thewto_e/whatis_e/tif_e/org6_e.htm

[177] Ibid.

[178] Shih, 'Energy Security', 439–440; Richards, T.J. and Herman, L. 'Relationship between International Trade and Energy', WTO, Research and Analysis, available at http://www.wto.org/english/res_e/publications_e/wtr10_richards_herman_e.htm

facto between the negotiations' parties; notes from the WTO Working Party reports referring to energy matters; and commitments agreed between the WTO and an acceding State in the ultimate protocols of accession and whether these protocols integrated energy issues or not. Therefore, a reliance only on the mere fact and act of accession, with no clear reference to the negotiated and agreed issues pertaining to energy, would not be a sufficiently convincing argument.

B. Unresolved Energy Trade Issues

There are unresolved issues which lie at the intersection between international trade rules and trade in energy. Although WTO law applies to all other trade aspects, its application to the energy sector has been unclear.[179] Besides, WTO law, with all of its agreements, rules, obligations, and exceptions, was not originally drafted to address and tackle energy issues.[180] It should also be noted that the WTO discipline is based heavily on rules that ban WTO members from acting in certain ways.[181] Meanwhile, this discipline lacks rules imposing positive obligations on WTO members, which are necessary to regulate significant issues of trade in energy.[182]

Energy resources have always been potent geopolitical and strategic tools in the world order.[183] However, when the GATT was first negotiated in the 1940s, liberalizing global trade in energy was not considered a 'political priority'.[184] However, rising global energy needs[185] combined

---

179 See generally ICTSD, *Fostering Low Carbon Growth: The Case for a Sustainable Energy Trade Agreement* (Geneva: ICTSD, 2011).

180 See Rakhmanin at p. 123.

181 For example, the prohibition of discriminatory treatments (Articles I and III of the GATT) as well as the prohibition on imposing quantitative restrictions (Article XI:1 of the GATT); see Cossy at p. 113.

182 See Cossy at p. 114 (mentioning some of the limited or missing rules from the WTO discipline, such as rules for obliging WTO members to act and ban anticompetitive activities by monopolies, or rules pertinent to access and use of 'transport facilities' in the energy sector).

183 UNCTAD, 'Trade Agreements, Petroleum and Energy Policies' (2000) UNCTAD/ITCD/TSB/9, at 14.

184 Cottier, T. et al. 'Energy in WTO Law and Policy', Working Paper No 2009/25 (May 2009), at p. 1, available at http://phase1.nccr-trade.org/images/stories/projects/ip6/IP6%20Working%20paper.pdf; see also Selivanova, Y. 'The WTO and Energy: WTO Rules and Agreements of Relevance to the Energy Sector', Issue Paper No. 1 (August 2007), ICTSD Programme on Trade and Environment.

185 See e.g., Adelman, M.A. 'World Oil Production & Prices 1947–2000' (2002) *The Quarterly Review of Economics and Finance*, Vol. 42, No. 2, at

with factors including the recent accession to the WTO of several 'energy-significant' economies,[186] the increased centrality of energy in environmental and climate-change-related discussions,[187] and the proliferation of private-sector involvement in energy[188] have resulted in a reconsideration of this view today.[189] As a result, the role of the WTO in regulating global trade in energy goods and services has increasingly come into question.[190]

In response, this section focuses on the relationship between trade in energy and the rules currently existing under the WTO regime. It addresses the distinctive nature of trade in energy and the resulting complexities associated with its regulation under existing WTO rules; it considers whether existing WTO rules are capable of operating to cover the sector; and it concludes the discussion with a critical comment on this coverage, or lack thereof.

1. Energy vis-à-vis other goods and services

The intuitive difficulties in reasoning that the WTO agreements *ipso facto* apply to trade in energy stem from the existence of a number of features – that characterize energy trade – which are absent from trade in other goods and services. These distinctive features can broadly be grouped into two inter-related categories, based on physical features and political considerations.

In the first category falls the 'peculiar' physical form of energy goods which are volatile and often difficult to store. This means they require

p. 170; *BP Statistical Review of World Energy*, at p. 42 (June 2013), available at http://www.bp.com/content/dam/bp/pdf/statistical-review/statistical_review_of_world_energy_2013.pdf

[186] By this term, reference is made to both significant energy exporters as well as consumers (for example, Russia, a major energy exporter, joined the WTO in August 2012).

[187] UNCTAD, 'Trade Agreements, Petroleum and Energy Policies', UNCTAD/ITCD/TSB/9 at 13 (2000).

[188] See for example World Trade Organization, 'Energy Services,' S/C/W/52 (September 1998), at paragraph 6.

[189] See Cossy, M. 'Energy Transport and Transit in the WTO', in Pauwelyn, J. (ed.) *Global Challenges at the Intersection of Trade, Energy and the Environment* (Geneva: Centre for Trade and Economic Integration, 2010), at p. 113; Marceau, G. 'The WTO in the Emerging Energy Governance Debate', in ibid., at pp. 25ff.

[190] World Trade Organization, 'Energy Services', S/C/W/52 (September 1998), at p. 8; Marhold, A. 'The World Trade Organization and Energy: Fuel for Debate' (2013) *ESIL Insights*, Vol. 2, No. 8.

special infrastructure and methods to store, transport, and distribute them. Further, energy goods are naturally finite and often non-renewable,[191] form an 'essential intermediate input for almost all economic activity', and have a 'direct impact on the welfare of end-users'.[192] These distinctive 'physical' features entail a number of political and economic considerations that are not common to trade in other goods, as explained in Section III above. For instance, price, quality, availability, marketability, transport, and other conditions of purchase or sale.[193]

As for the second category, based on political considerations, a number of monopolies in exploitation exist in the sector. These result either from an unequal distribution of energy resources across countries by nature or due to the strategically motivated dominance of vertically-integrated state-controlled enterprises in the energy industry of a particular country.[194] Another distinct issue is the dependence of the sector on capital-intensive fixed infrastructures.[195] These raise dual considerations in terms of the frameworks in place to regulate investments in such infrastructures and, subsequently, the conditions of access to the same.[196] In contrast, manufactured products can be stored and distributed in settings that are not dependent on infrastructures to which access may be restricted or conditional.[197]

Thus, it becomes clear that energy products possess characteristics which evidently differentiate them from trade in other commodities and

---

[191] Selivanova, Y. 'International Energy Governance: The Role of the Energy Charter', American Society of International Law Proceedings, Vol. 106, No. 1 (March 28–31, 2012), at pp. 394–395; Cottier, T. et al., 'Energy in WTO Law and Policy', Working Paper No 2009/25 (May 2009), at p. 2.

[192] WTO, 'Communication from Venezuela, Negotiating Proposal on Energy Services', S/CSS/W/69, 29 March 2001, at p. 1; See also Selivanova, Y. 'The WTO and Energy: WTO Rules and Agreements of Relevance to the Energy Sector', Issue Paper No.1 (August 2007), ICTSD Programme on Trade and Environment, at p. 13.

[193] Article 14.d of the Subsidies and Countervailing Measures Agreement.

[194] Cottier, T. et al., 'Energy in WTO Law and Policy', Working Paper No 2009/25 (May 2009), at p. 2.

[195] Selivanova, Y. 'The WTO and Energy: WTO Rules and Agreements of Relevance to the Energy Sector', Issue Paper No.1 (August 2007), ICTSD Programme on Trade and Environment, at p. 13.

[196] Selivanova, Y. 'International Energy Governance: The Role of the Energy Charter', American Society of International Law Proceedings, Vol. 106, No. 1, at 395.

[197] Manufactured products can be stored and distributed by means such as trucks, ships or trains, which only depend on unconditionally accessible 'public' infrastructure, such as road, water or rail.

manufactured goods. The question that logically follows is whether the differentiation is substantial enough to render the WTO agreements *in limine* inapplicable to the sector.

2. Trade in energy under the existing WTO regime

Given the discussion above, a preliminary question is whether – given the uniqueness of trade in energy – the WTO agreements can at all apply to trade in energy. The traditional conception has been that the sector is one that is 'largely not covered by the WTO'[198] and did not fall within the ambit of its agreements. However, for the reasons outlined above, this assumption has, in recent times, come under enhanced scrutiny. Today, the position is rather uncontroversial with there being a broad consensus that there is nothing in the WTO framework that prevents its application to energy trade.[199] In other words, it has been for reasons that are political, strategic, and security-related, rather than legal, that states chose to address issues affecting trade in energy 'outside' the realm of the WTO.[200] Given this lack of a *de jure* exclusion of energy trade from the WTO, some of the most important issues that arise when WTO norms are made to apply to trade in energy have been outlined below.

2.1. Definitional/classification issues There are a number of unresolved issues that arise when one attempts to apply the provisions of the GATT to global energy trade. At the outset is the lack of a definitive classification of energy goods and energy services. Neither term is definitively defined – with the latter only being provisionally listed.[201] Another challenge is the difficulty associated with distinguishing clear elements of services and goods in energy trade – with most of the trade possessing elements of both.[202] Similarly, there is no unanimity on whether 'electricity' should be categorized as being either a good or a

---

[198] 'No Thanks, Geneva', *The Economist*, 18 June 2009, Moscow, available at http://www.economist.com/node/13871196.

[199] Desta, M.G. 'The GATT/WTO System and International Trade in Petroleum: an Overview' (2003) *Journal of Energy and Natural Resource Law*, Vol. 21, at p. 398; Botha, L. 'How Do the Current WTO Disciplines Apply to the Trade of Energy Goods and Services?', Discussion Paper (July 2009), at p. 3, available at http://www.internationaltradelaw.co.za/dmdocuments/LB%20Paper.pdf

[200] Botha, ibid. at 16.

[201] Marhold, A. 'The World Trade Organization and Energy: Fuel for Debate' (2013) *ESIL Insights*, Vol. 2, No. 8, p. 3.

[202] WTO, 'Energy Services', S/C/W/52 (September 1998), at p. 2.

service under WTO norms.[203] Finally, the nature of energy products brings up many questions of interpretation of specific questions, including whether different types of energy products (such as 'renewable' and 'non-renewable') can be treated as 'like products' and whether freedom of transit would apply to fixed infrastructures, such as pipelines.[204]

2.2. General Agreement on Tariffs and Trade A fundamental issue concerning the applicability of GATT Articles I and III – concerning MFN and national treatment, respectively – relates to the test of 'likeness' of energy products. An example of a potential issue is whether renewable energy goods compete with non-renewable energy goods and, therefore, whether they should be treated by law in the same manner.[205] There are additional issues regarding the interaction of these articles with prevailing practices in energy trade. For example, Article III may be violated when WTO Members grant preferential distribution network (e.g., pipeline) access to vertically-integrated state-run monopolies. The freedom to transit goods without interference through a WTO Member's territory is enshrined under Article V. While such a provision would have definite applications for cross-border energy trade, it is doubtful whether the provision covers transport through pipelines or wires under 'traffic in transit'.[206] It has also been argued that Article 7 of the ECT would offer a more robust provision for energy-related cases where applicable.[207]

---

[203] Howse, R. and Turek, E. 'The WTO Negotiations on Services: The Regulatory State Up For Grabs', Canada Watch, Vol. 9, No. 1–2, pp. 3–9, at p. 4 (September 2002): 'With respect to energy, the situation is even more complex because some WTO members view electricity as a good … while others view the generation of electricity and the operation of power plants as a service'. Others view it differently: in case C-393/92 *Almelo v Energiebedrijf IJsselmij* [1994] ECR-I-1477 [28] and case C-158/94 *Commission v Italy* [1997] ECR I-5789 [17], the European Court of Justice ruled that electricity should be treated as a good.

[204] Selivanova, Y. 'The WTO and Energy: WTO Rules and Agreements of Relevance to the Energy Sector', Issue Paper No. 1 (August 2007), ICTSD Programme on Trade and Environment, at p. 18.

[205] Marceau, G. 'The WTO in the Emerging Energy Governance Debate', in Pauwelyn, J. (ed.) *Global Challenges at the Intersection of Trade, Energy and the Environment* (Geneva: Centre for Trade and Economic Integration, 2010), at pp. 25 ff.

[206] Selivanova, Y. 'The WTO and Energy: WTO Rules and Agreements of Relevance to the Energy Sector', Issue Paper No.1 (August 2007), ICTSD Programme on Trade and Environment, at p. 18.

[207] Article 7 ECT enshrines rights relating to transit; WTO, Communication from the European Communities, 'WTO Trade Facilitation – Strengthening WTO

Article XI of the GATT prevents quantitative border restrictions. A possible issue here is the interaction of this provision with the imposition of conditions of access or licensing requirements for oil and gas pipelines of a WTO Member.

2.3. General Agreement on Trade in Services In addition to the definitional problems above, considering 'energy services' under the GATS also raises a number of unresolved issues. Article II seeks to ensure MFN status for all services of all WTO Members, without discrimination. Article VI, concerning 'domestic regulation', would be crucial to a sector that is often the subject of heavy regulatory oversight by governments. Of particular relevance to the energy sector is Article VIII, addressing 'monopolies and exclusive services suppliers'. This provision lays down specific conditions for the operation of monopolies and will have important implications for the energy sector, where state-run monopolies are not uncommon. The stricter regulations on monopolies will translate into healthy competition which, in turn, benefits energy consumers and enhances energy security globally.

2.4. Agreement on Technical Barriers to Trade The Technical Barriers to Trade Agreement is a step towards harmonization of technical regulations and product standards.[208] The Agreement would be applicable to a number of energy-trade variables, including technology efficiency requirements and standards.

2.5. Agreement on Subsidies and Countervailing Measures The application of the Subsidies and Countervailing Measures (SCM) Agreement to energy trade will raise a number of issues to be settled. Article 8 of the SCM Agreement – which expired in 1999 – deemed 'non-actionable' certain government schemes that provided 'assistance to promote adaptation of existing facilities to new environmental requirements'.[209] With the expiry of this provision, government subsidies aimed at encouraging

---

Rules on GATT Article V on Freedom of Transit', G/C/W/422 (30 September 2002), at p. 5: 'WTO members may wish to evaluate whether freedom of transit for such goods is effective and whether there is any need or scope for reassessing GATT Article V to take account of the special nature of this form of transit'. See also Azaria, D. 'Energy Transit under the Energy Charter Treaty and the General Agreement on Tariffs and Trade' (2009) *Journal of Energy and Natural Resource Law*, Vol. 27, No.4, at p. 574.

[208] Article 2.6, Agreement on Technical Barriers to Trade.

[209] Article 8.2(c) of the SCM Agreement.

the adoption of green energy technology would be called into question. Another question concerns the applicability of the SCM Agreement to the common industry practice of 'dual-pricing'.[210] If the specific conditions laid down in the SCM Agreement are met, the practice may, in fact, be illegal.

2.6. Exceptions A number of WTO agreements, including the GATT and GATS, provide for exceptions to a WTO member's obligations under WTO law. These, when implemented in accordance with the relevant rules provided therewith, would exclude a WTO member from having to respect their obligations under the respective agreement. Exceptions that may apply to the energy sector include:

(1) the necessity to protect human, animal or plant life or health;[211]
(2) measures relating to the conservation of exhaustible natural resources;[212]
(3) measures essential to the acquisition or distribution of products in general or local short supply;[213] and
(4) the national security exception – given the clubbing of energy with the national security of states.[214]

Moving forward, it will be important to evolve guidelines on the invocation of these exceptions in relation to energy trade so that WTO members do not avoid obligations based on subjective interpretations of broad provisions.

3. Final remarks

In light of the above discussion, it is clear that the existing regime under the WTO does in fact cover trade in energy. However, the status quo is far from ideal, with a number of ambiguities and uncertainties prevailing – including those detailed above. In light of these, it is important to achieve clarity in applying WTO norms to the international energy

---

[210] Marhold, A. 'The World Trade Organization and Energy: Fuel for Debate' (2013) *ESIL Insights*, Vol. 2, No. 8, p. 3.

[211] Article XX(b) of the GATT; Article XIV(b) of the GATS; Article 2.2, TBT Agreement; Article 27(2), Agreement on Trade-Related Aspects of Intellectual Property Rights (TRIPs).

[212] Article XX(g) of the GATT.

[213] Article XX(j) of the GATT.

[214] Article XXI of the GATT; Article XIV bis of the GATS; Article 73 of TRIPs.

market. This may be achieved either through a specific WTO Agreement on Energy or through *ad-hoc* interpretations of the various WTO agreements by the WTO's DSU. However, given the lack of political will in bringing in an international energy governance framework, it would seem that the latter is the most feasible model in the short and medium term. To prevent conflicting norms from developing, there is also a growing need to study the relationship between the ECT – a multilateral effort aimed at governing energy-related investments – and the existing WTO structures.

VI. CONCLUSION

WTO law governs and regulates trade relationships among WTO members. Within the scope of the WTO, energy trade is one of the most significant trade sectors, constituting the largest primary commodity of global trade in terms of volume and value.

This chapter has reviewed the treatment of energy trade in the WTO system by examining whether such type of trade deserves to be recognized as a special trade sector. The energy trade sector has been treated for decades as a distinct type of trade, mainly due to unique features attached to the energy sector in general and energy trade in particular. However, it is not only the unique features of energy that make this trade sector a special sector under the WTO regime, but there are three main factors that support this argument, as explained before. The first factor relates to the special characteristics of the energy sector that make such a sector different from other trade sectors; the second factor focuses on significant and unprecedented challenges that confront the global energy industry in general and energy trade in particular; and the third factor refers to certain ongoing debates and unresolved issues that emerge from the intersection between WTO law and energy trade.

Undoubtedly, the combination of these three main factors distinguishes energy trade from other trade sectors and contributes to presenting energy trade as a special sector under the WTO regime. Although the uniqueness of the energy trade sector becomes prominent under the WTO regime, this regime is still inadequately equipped to handle and regulate all energy trade-related issues.

Moreover, this chapter concludes that, although there are various factors which explain why international trade in energy has been treated differently from other trade sectors and products in the world trading system, no GATT/WTO provision expressly provides that energy trade is not applicable to the GATT/WTO disciplines. In fact, a combination of multiple substantial factors and arguments upholds the applicability of the GATT/WTO disciplines to trade in energy. Therefore, it can be concluded that the GATT/WTO legal regime applies to trade in energy.

3. Trade, environment, and energy: implications for the conservation of oil resources

> I believe not only that there is room for mutually beneficial negotiating trade-offs that encompass natural resources trade, but also that a failure to address these issues could be a recipe for growing tension in international trade relations. Well-designed trade rules are key to ensuring that trade is advantageous, but they are also necessary for the attainment of objectives such as environmental protection and the proper management of natural resources in a domestic setting. My final point, which will come as a surprise to no-one, is that we would greatly enhance our chances of positive action in this area if we were to come to a prompt closure of the Doha Round.[1]
>
> (Pascal Lamy, Director General WTO)

I. INTRODUCTION

The environmental significance of natural resources was explicitly recognized in the multilateral trade agreements with the establishment of the General Agreement on Tariffs and Trade (GATT) in 1947.[2] The GATT contained the general exception in its Article XX(g) justifying measures which, although deemed to be in violation of the GATT rules, aimed at conserving 'exhaustible natural resources'.[3] Since the creation of the GATT 1947, this exception has remained a central one, and still is in the context of the World Trade Organization (WTO), created in 1995.[4]

---

[1] See World Trade Organization (WTO) *World Trade Report 2010: Trade in Natural Resources* (2010) at 4, available at http://www.wto.org/english/res_e/booksp_e/anrep_e/world_trade_report10_e.pdf

[2] See General Agreement on Tariffs and Trade, Oct. 30, 1947, 61 Stat. A-11, T.I.A.S. 1700, 55 U.N.T.S. 194 [hereinafter the GATT].

[3] Ibid., Article XX(g) of the GATT.

[4] See Marrakesh Agreement Establishing the World Trade Organization, Apr. 15, 1994, The Legal Texts: The Results of the Uruguay Round of Multilateral Trade Negotiations 4 (1999), 1867 U.N.T.S. 154, 33 I.L.M. 1144 (1994), available at www.wto.org/english/docs_e/legal_e/04-wto.doc [hereinafter

The tension between trade and environment, including issues of exhaustible natural resources, has comprised an essential controversy within several important GATT and WTO decisions.[5] Importantly, neither the GATT nor the WTO agreements have defined the exact meaning and scope of the phrase 'exhaustible natural resources'. Various decisions were held pertinent to the protection of exhaustible natural resources, where different forms of natural resources were involved and a variety of interpretations and analytical approaches were utilized.

It is commonly known in the environment and trade realms that oil is a fundamental natural resource. Recently, several calls have been raised to regulate and free trade in oil and eliminate the protections regarding this resource,[6] including launching dispute settlement within the WTO mechanism[7]. Although these calls have been raised in the context of trade and

---

Marrakesh Agreement]. The WTO includes a set of agreements, of which the GATT is foundational. A clarification should be made on the relationship between GATT 1947, GATT 1994 and the WTO. The WTO replaced the GATT and became an international organization (as opposed to just an international trade agreement), but the GATT 1947 still exists as the WTO's umbrella treaty for trade in goods. It was further updated during the Uruguay Round negotiations. Trade lawyers distinguish between GATT 1994 (i.e., the updated sections of the GATT) and the GATT 1947, the original agreement which is still the basis of GATT 1994.

[5] The GATT and WTO tribunals were requested to decide on critical issues pertinent to exhaustible natural resources: whether measures that apparently aimed to conserve exhaustible natural resources were in violation of the GATT rules, and, if so, whether they were eligible for the application of the specific exception under Article XX(g).

[6] These calls include, *inter alia*; a call for new WTO round in energy, see Champion, M. & von Reppert-Bismark, J. 'Politics & Economics: EU Trade Chief Poses WTO Rules in Energy Sector' *Wall St. J.*, June 23, 2006, at A6; a collective request in energy services (submitted to the WTO), see International Forum on Globalization, Collective Request in Energy Services, available at http://www.regjeringen.no/upload/kilde/ud/nyh/2006/0078/ddd/pdfv/282776-energy.pdf; a call for a WTO Agreement pertinent to energy, see T. Cottier et al. 'Energy in WTO Law and Policy', in Cottier, T. and Delimatsis, P. (eds) *The Prospects of International Trade Regulation: From Fragmentation to Coherence* (Cambridge: Cambridge University Press, 2011), 211–44; ICTSD, 'Fostering Low Carbon Growth: The Case for a Sustainable Energy Trade Agreement' (Geneva, Switzerland 2011) http://ictsd.org/downloads/2011/12/fostering-low-carbon-growth-the-case-for-a-sustainable-energy-trade-agreement1.pdf.

[7] See the Resolution by Representative Peter DeFazio, H.R. Con. Res. 276, 106th Cong. (2000), and Office of Senator F. Lautenberg, 'Busting Up the Cartel: the WTO Case Against OPEC' (2004) available at http://lautenberg.senate.gov/documents/foreign/OPEC%20Memo.pdf (last accessed 2012).

energy, they, in addition to others, demonstrate an escalating demand leading to a considerable increase in oil consumption, which may result in its rapid exhaustion or depletion. In addition, this increase in oil consumption would result in direct negative influences on climate change. It will increase the whole cycle of, *inter alia*, the oil-manufacturing industry – the exploration, extraction, refining, storage and transportation of oil. Undoubtedly, the increase in oil production will boost carbon emissions through the various manufacturing stages, like-wise through the consumption by the final consumers. Indeed, global greenhouse gas (GHG) emissions are projected to increase by 28% in 2030 from the 2010 levels.[8] Thus, this trend in oil consumption increase will result in a remarkable GHG emissions growth that will clearly threaten the climate.

The trade dispute settlement tribunals have remarkable experience in handling debates concerning the application of Article XX(g). However, the various decisions that were held in legal debates over the relationship between trade liberalization and environmental sustainability have not yet examined the application of that exception to the interaction between trade and the conservation of oil as an exhaustible natural resource. There is a reasonable possibility that a future dispute will arise regarding the conservation of oil resources according to GATTs' provisions. This tribunal will most likely be guided or influenced by the approach of past decisions in handling natural resources, or at least will discuss and make references to these decisions.[9] Therefore, it is essential to examine the GATT and WTO cases that have so far discussed and addressed issues pertinent to the conservation of natural resources. It is also essential to demonstrate the main analytical approach or approaches and benchmarks of these decisions and their treatments regarding the various categories of natural resources as exhaustible resources.

The purpose of this chapter is to provide an explanation of how international trade and environmental law intersect when it comes to trade in natural resources. It narrates the debate on how to reconcile

---

8 See British Petroleum, *BP Energy Outlook 2030* (London: BP, 2012) at p. 81, available at http://www.bp.com/liveassets/bp_internet/globalbp/STAGING/global_assets/downloads/O/2012_2030_energy_outlook_booklet.pdf (last accessed 2013).

9 It is important to note that none of the GATT or WTO tribunals has been yet required to address oil-conserving measures, which aim to protect oil resources from exhaustion. However, the increasing demands for energy resources, mainly oil resources, along with calls for freeing trade in oil resources, will likely increase the possibility of this issue arising before WTO tribunals.

environmental and economic objectives.[10] The chapter claims that the approach of GATT and WTO case law concerning the conservation of exhaustible natural resources is complex, variable, and narrow. Current approaches limit the possibility of conserving exhaustible natural resources according to Article XX(g) and would limit the protection of any future oil-conserving measure.

Following this introduction, Section II of this chapter describes at a glance the linkage between the environment and trade in the context of the multilateral trade system, concentrating on the issue of natural resources. Section III discusses the GATT and WTO decisions pertinent to the conservation of exhaustible natural resources and the application of Article XX(g). The section examines the prominent analysis and interpretation that each tribunal has conducted in addressing the application of Article XX(g) and the conservation of natural resources. Section IV analyzes the implications of the GATT and WTO decisions for the conservation of oil resources. Section V concludes that the current approach narrows the applications of Article XX(g) to the conservation of exhaustible natural resources, and would limit the protection of any future oil-conserving measure. In the conclusion, the chapter recommends reconsidering whether Article XI:l of the GATT applies to oil-conserving measures that address oil resources in their natural state.

II. TRADE AND ENVIRONMENT

International trade and the environment have a many-sided and complicated relationship,[11] around which discussion has traditionally been

---

[10] See Schoenbaum, T. 'International Trade and Protection of the Environment: The Continuing Search for Reconciliation' (1997) *American Journal of International Law* 91, 268; Goyal, A. *The WTO and International Environmental Law: Towards a Conciliation* (Oxford: Oxford University Press, 2006); Schwartz, R. and Shaw, S. 'Trade and Environment in the WTO – State of Play' (2002) *Journal of World Trade*, Vol. 36, No. 1, pp. 129–154.

[11] See UNEP and IISD, *Environment and Trade: A Handbook* (2nd edn, 2005); Stewart, R. 'International Trade and Environment: Lessons from the Federal Experience' (1992) 49 *Wash. & Lee L. Rev.* 1329; Barrett, S. *Environment and Statecraft: The Strategy of Environmental Treaty-making* (New York: Oxford University Press, 2003) Chapter 12; Trebilcock, M. & Howse, R. *The Regulation of International Trade* (Abingdon: Routledge, 3 edn, 2005) Chapter 16; Charnovitz, S. 'The WTO's Environmental Progress' (2007) *Journal of International Economic Law* 10, 685.

'highly emotive and polarized',[12] according to Michael Trebilcock and Robert Howse. This is because many environmentalists have linked free trade with ungoverned economic growth that is damaging to the environment,[13] while many supporters of liberalized trade disregard these concerns, proclaiming them unreasonable and/or a veiled form of protection.[14] In fact, the link between trade and the environment, while admittedly posing challenges to global governance, also provides plenty of opportunity.[15] Trade mechanisms can be an effective means of achieving environmental goals.[16]

A. Environment in the GATT/WTO: Past and Present Interaction[17]

The trade and environment regimes began separately with different goals.[18] While trade rules aimed to eliminate protectionism and promote

---

[12] See Trebilcock, M. & Howse, R. *The Regulation of International Trade* (Abingdon: Routledge, 3 edn, 2005) at p. 507.

[13] See Hassoun, N. 'Free Trade and the Environment' (2009) *Environmental Ethics*, Vol. 31, pp. 51–66; Yu, D. 'Free Trade is Green, Protectionism is Not' (1994) *Conservation Biology* 8, 989–996; Ekins, P., Folke, C. & Costanza, R. 'Trade, Environment and Development: The Issues in Perspective' (1994) *Ecological Economics*, Vol. 9, No.1, pp. 1–12; Cross, F.B. 'A Syncretic Perspective on Environmental Protection and Economic Growth' (1992) *J.L & Pub. Pol'y* 53.

[14] See Esty, D.C. 'Bridging the Trade-Environment Divide' (2001) *Journal of Economic Perspectives*, Vol. 15, No. 3, pp. 113–130 (2001); Hassoun, N. 'Free Trade, Poverty and the Environment' (2008) *Public Affairs Quarterly*, Vol. 22, No. 4, pp. 353–380; Krugman, P. 'What Should Trade Negotiators Negotiate About?'(1997) *Journal of Economic Literature*, Vol. 35, No. 1, pp. 113–120 (1997); Housman, R. 'The Treatment of Labor and Environmental Issues in Future Western Hemisphere Trade Liberalization Efforts' (1994) *J. Int'l L.* 301.

[15] See Brack, D. 'Environmental Treaties and Trade: Multilateral Environmental Agreements and the Multilateral Trading System', in Sampson, G.P. & Chambers, W.B. (eds) *Trade, Environment and the Millennium* (Tokyo: United Nations University Press, 2nd edn, 2002), pp. 321–352.

[16] For further details on the link between trade and the environment, see Leal-Arcas, R. *Climate Change and International Trade* (Cheltenham: Edward Elgar, 2013) Chapter 3; Nordström, H. & Vaughan, S. 'Trade and Environment', Special Studies No. 4, World Trade Organization, 1999.

[17] See generally, Oppenheimer, M. and Stewart, R. 'Trade and the Environment: Shrimp and Turtles, Tuna and Dolphins', Global Environmental Law, Science and Governance, NYU Law School (1 April 2011, Spring 2011).

[18] For an analysis of the tension between trade and the environment, see Hufbauer, G. & Fickling, M. 'Trade and the Environment', in Narlikar, A., Daunton, M. & Stern, R.M. (eds) *The Oxford Handbook on the World Trade Organization* (Oxford: Oxford University Press, 2012), pp. 719–739; Colyer, D.

free and globalized trade, environmental measures sought to facilitate conservation or protection of the environment and its basic components.[19] However, the goals of trade and environment have clashed in many aspects: environmentalists argue that free trade will eliminate or limit the protection of the environment and cause negative environmental effects, while free traders claim that strict environmental measures will most likely restrict the market.[20] Typically, international trade law controversies appear when environmental measures – implemented either to protect an importing country's environment, or in response to the environmental policies of another State – are claimed to threaten trade liberalization under the WTO.[21] Much has been written since the early 1990s concerning this significant and ongoing interaction between trade and environment.[22]

When the GATT was drafted in 1947, environmental protection was not a major global concern for the drafters.[23] The GATT focused on the liberalization of trade, while the protection of the environment was not among its objectives.[24] However, the GATT included two exceptions that

---

Green Trade Agreements, (Houndmills: Palgrave, 2011); WTO, 'Trade and Environment at the WTO' 2004; WTO, *Trade, Development and the Environment* (Kluwer, 2000); Najam, A. et al. (eds) *Trade and Environment: A Resource Book* (IISD, 2007).

19 See Kiss, A. *International Environmental Law* (Leiden: Martinus Nijhoff, 3rd edn, 2004) at p. 776.

20 Ibid. at p. 777.

21 See Goyal, A. *The WTO and International Environmental Law: Towards a Conciliation* (Oxford: Oxford University Press, 2006); Cameron, J. et al. (eds) *Trade and the Environment: The Search for Balance* (London: Cameron May, 1994); Francioni, F. (ed.) *Environment, Human Rights, and International Trade* (Oxford: Hart 2001); Francioni, F. & Scovazzi, T. (eds) *International Responsibility for Environmental Harm* (Graham & Trotman, 1991).

22 For example, using the words 'trade, environment' & WTO while searching for literature on the Westlaw database (restricted to 'this year and last year' search) resulted in 696 articles as of February 2013.

23 See Esty, D.C. *Greening the GATT: Trade, Environment, and the Future* (Washington, DC: Institute for International Economics, 1994) at p. 9 (describing the origins of the present conflict between trade and environmental policymaking); and see Jackson, J., Davey, W.J. & Sykes, A.O. *Legal Problems of International Economic Relations: Cases, Materials and Text on the National and International Regulation of Transnational Economic Relations* (St Paul, MN: West Publishing Co, 5th ed., 2008) at p. 633.

24 See Shih, W.-C. 'Trade and Environment Linkages and Challenges Facing East Asian WTO Members' (2006) 1 *Asian J. WTO & Int'l Health L. & Pol'y* 157 at p. 159.

are relevant for environmental protection: Article XX(b) and Article XX(g).[25] It is important to note that GATT Article XX(b) provides for measures that are 'necessary to protect human, animal or plant life or health', and GATT Article XX(g) permits measures 'relating to the conservation of exhaustible natural resources' (if such measures are accompanied by corresponding restrictions on domestic production or consumption),[26] so long as these are not applied in a manner that constitutes 'a means of arbitrary or unjustifiable discrimination'[27] or 'a disguised restriction on international trade'.[28] Although the GATT text did not include the term 'environment', Article XX provides a basis for environmental protection by the two 'environmental exceptions'.[29] Notably, the clash between environmental goals and trade liberalization spans more than 20 years in the jurisprudence dealing with GATT Article XX.[30]

Compared to the GATT, the WTO has taken greater account of environmental issues. During the Uruguay Round, more attention was given to environmental matters, and certain environmental issues were included in the WTO and its cover agreements. First and foremost, the preamble of the Marrakesh Agreement highlights the importance of 'sustainable development':

> [T]heir relations in the field of trade and economic endeavor should be conducted with a view to raising standards of living … while allowing for the optimal use of the world's resources in accordance with the objective of sustainable development, seeking both to protect and preserve the environment and to enhance the means for doing so in a manner consistent with their respective needs and concerns at different levels of economic development.[31]

---

25 See Kiss, A. *International Environmental Law* (Leiden: Martinus Nijhoff, 3rd edn, 2004) at p. 779.

26 Art. XX(g) of the GATT; Alexander Kiss, *International Environmental Law* (Leiden: Martinus Nijhoff, 3rd edn, 2004), at p. 779.

27 See the chapeau of Article XX.

28 Ibid.

29 See Esty, D.C. *Greening the GATT: Trade, Environment, and the Future* (Washington, DC: Institute for International Economics, 1994) at p. 9 (discussing an explanation and interpretation of GATT Article XX).

30 On the link between WTO law and climate issues from the perspective of international distributive justice, see Armstrong, C. *Global Distributive Justice: An Introduction* (Cambridge: Cambridge University Press, 2012); Al-Tayer, A. & Maniruzzman, A. 'Addressing the Global Climate Change Problem in GATT/WTO Law: The Vision of a New International Climate Law Based on International Distributive Justice' (2011) *The Journal of World Investment and Trade*, Vol. 12, No. 5, pp. 631–670.

31 See Preamble of the Marrakesh Agreement Establishing the WTO.

Additionally, the establishment of the WTO incorporated the establishment of the Committee on Trade and Environment (CTE).[32] The goal of the CTE was to identify and understand the relationship between trade and environment in order to promote 'sustainable development'.[33] Moreover, the WTO manages several other agreements, which were added to the GATT in the 1990s to address specific topics. These agreements may also have a limiting effect on the types of measures that a State may enact for environmental reasons. The two more pertinent of these are the Agreement on Technical Barriers to Trade (the TBT Agreement)[34] and the Agreement on Sanitary and Phytosanitary Measures (the SPS Agreement).[35] Additionally, the Doha Round encompasses specific negotiations concerning various aspects of trade and the environment, emphasizing

---

[32] See the Committee on Trade and Environment (CTE), available at http://www.wto.org/english/tratop_e/envir_e/wrk_committee_e.htm; The 1994 Ministerial Decision on Trade and Environment, available at http://www.wto.org/english/docs_e/legal_e/56-dtenv_e.htm

[33] Ibid.

[34] The TBT Agreement applies to technical regulations and standards, as well as testing and certification procedures, at the same time that it ensures that such standards and procedures do not create unnecessary obstacles to trade. Technical regulations and standards set out requirements for specific characteristics of a product, such as size, shape, design, functions, and performance, or the way that it is packaged or labeled for sale. Countries are free to establish the necessary protection they deem appropriate for health, human life, or the environment. Examples include labeling requirements for tobacco products, or a requirement that fish exceed a minimum length. See The Agreement on Technical Barriers to Trade, April 15, 1994 (TBT) at http://www.wto.org/english/docs_e/legal_e/ursum_e.htm#d; see also Dröge, S. 'Ecological Labelling and the World Trade Organization', Discussion Paper No. 242, Deutsches Institute für Wirtschaftsforschung, 2001.

[35] The SPS Agreement applies to measures for the protection of food safety as well as human, animal, or plant life or health. Examples of SPS measures include requirements that products come from a disease-free area, inspection requirements, requirements for treatment or processing, and limits on allowable levels of pesticide residues. The SPS Agreement provides criteria for the assessment of risk and the determination of the correct levels of health protection. See the Agreement of the Application of Sanitary and Phytosanitary Measures, April 15, 1994 (SPS) http://www.wto.org/english/docs_e/legal_e/ursum_e.htm#bAgreement. For an explanation of the SPS Agreement in the context of biosafety, see Spreij, M. 'The SPS Agreement and Biosafety' (2007) *FAO Legal Papers Online*, No. 65.

growing importance of environmental values in the trade sphere.[36] However, all these changes that have occurred during the WTO era have not substantially influenced the ongoing interaction between trade and the environment.

B. 'Exhaustible Natural Resources' and GATT Article XX(g)[37]

The phrase 'exhaustible natural resources' is a central component of Article XX (g) of the GATT.[38] Originally, the term 'natural resources' was intended to cover 'raw material' or 'metal',[39] and the term 'exhaustible natural resources' referred to stock resources, such as metal or oil, especially since these resources are capable of being depleted or exhausted.[40] This traditional approach considered only minerals as exhaustible natural resources, while 'living resources' such as animals and plants were considered inexhaustible resources since they are renewable and can reproduce.[41]

Over time and in the context of trade and environment, several Panels and Appellate Body decisions broadly interpreted the term 'exhaustible natural resources' to cover various sorts of natural resources, both living and non-living resources.[42] For example, resources that have been termed

---

[36] For a more detailed explanation regarding negotiations on trade and the environment under the Doha Round, see http://www.wto.org/english/tratop_e/envir_e/envt_intro_e.htm

[37] For a more detailed discussion on the history and evaluation of the link between natural resources and trading systems (GATT and WTO) see World Trade Organization (WTO), World Trade Report 2010: Trade in Natural Resources (2010) at pp. 163–164, available at http://www.wto.org/english/res_e/booksp_e/anrep_e/world_trade_report10_e.pdf

[38] Article XX (g) of the GATT.

[39] See Charnovitz, S. 'Exploring the Environmental Exceptions in GATT Article XX' (1991) 25 *J. World Trade* 37, 45, 63.

[40] Ibid.

[41] See Bree, A. 'Article XX GATT – Quo Vadis? The Environmental Exception After the Shrimp-Turtle Appellate Body Report' (1998) 17 *Dick. J. Int'l L.* 99.

[42] See Schrijver, N. *Sovereignty Over Natural Resources, Balancing Rights and Duties* (Cambridge: Cambridge University Press, 2008) at p. 15 (explaining that initially the GATT referred to the term exhaustible natural resources as related to stock natural resources but, over time, the term came to cover renewable resources such as animals, plants and fish).

as 'exhaustible natural resources' include tuna,[43] salmon and herring stocks,[44] dolphins,[45] clean air,[46] migratory sea turtles,[47] and certain forms of raw material.[48]

Currently, none of the GATT or WTO dispute settlement system (DSS) decisions has directly addressed oil as a natural resource in the light of Article XX(g) in particular, nor in the light of any other rule or exception of the GATT in general. Even though oil has been recognized as an exhaustible natural resource in some of the trade literature and decisions,[49] there is neither an explicit WTO decision that determines the exhaustibility of oil resources nor an analysis of conserving oil as an exhaustible natural resource throughout Article XX(g). However, any future dispute settlement concerning oil in its natural state will first discuss the conformity or violation of the measure to the GATTs' rules. If a violation is found then it will examine the applicability of Article XX(g) by discussing the GATT and WTO significant decisions, which addressed previous cases of conserving exhaustible natural resources.

---

[43] See Panel Report, *Conciliation United States – Prohibition of Tuna and Tuna Products from Canada,* L/5198 (Feb. 22, 1982), GATT B.I.S.D. (29th Supp.) at 91–105 (1983) (*US – Tuna from Canada*).

[44] See Panel Report, *Canada – Measures Affecting Exports of Unprocessed Herring and Salmon*, L/6268 (June 1989), GATT B.I.S.D. (35th Supp.) at 98 (1988) (*Herring – Salmon* case).

[45] See Panel Report, United *States – Restrictions on Imports of Tuna*, GATT/DS29/R (June 16, 1994), reprinted in 33 I.L.M. 839 (1994) [hereinafter *Tuna-Dolphin II/Tuna II*].

[46] See Appellate Body Report, *United States – Standards for Reformulated and Conventional Gasoline*, WT/DS2/AB/R, (Apr. 29, 1996) at p. 18 [hereinafter *Gasoline* case].

[47] See Appellate Body Report, *United States – Import Prohibition of Certain Shrimp and Shrimp Products*, WT/DS58/AB/R (98-3899) (Oct. 12, 1998) [hereinafter *Shrimp-Turtle* case].

[48] See Appellate Body report, *China – Measures Related to the Exportation of Various Raw Materials*, WT/DS394/AB/R, WT/DS395/AB/R, WT/DS398/AB/R (Feb. 22, 2012) [hereinafter *China – Raw Materials* case].

[49] See Appellate Body Report, *United States – Import Prohibition of Certain Shrimp and Shrimp Products*, WT/DS58/AB/R (98-3899) (Oct. 12, 1998) para. 128; Panel Report, *United States – Taxes on Automobiles*, GATT No. DS31/R (unadopted), at para. 5.57, reprinted in (1994) 33 ILM 1399; and Charnovitz, S. 'Exploring the Environmental Exceptions in GATT Article XX' (1991) 25 *J. World Trade* 37, 45, 63.

III. THE 'CONSERVATION' OF EXHAUSTIBLE NATURAL RESOURCES UNDER GATT ARTICLE XX(G): GATT AND WTO DECISIONS

Although international trade jurisprudence principally recognizes the legitimate environmental right to restrict the extraction of exhaustible natural resources,[50] the crucial question in the context of oil resources is whether a conserving measure that limits the extraction of oil resources and violates WTO rules would be approved by the WTO dispute tribunals. This section examines treatments and analyses that were given to exhaustible natural resources in preceding cases considered by the GATT Panels and the WTO Appellate Body.[51]

The common denominator of all the GATT and WTO precedents which examined restricting measures with respect to exhaustible natural resources is that all these decisions examined the validity of the measures under one of the environmental exceptions, under Article XX(g). This Article states:

> Subject to the requirement that such measures are not applied in a manner which would constitute a means of arbitrary or unjustifiable discrimination between countries where the same conditions prevail, or a disguised restriction on international trade, nothing in this Agreement shall be construed to prevent the adoption or enforcement by any Member of measures:
>
> . . .
>
> (g) Relating to the conservation of exhaustible natural resources if such measures are made effective in conjunction with restrictions on domestic production or consumption.[52]

---

50 See Appellate Body Report, *United States – Import Prohibition of Certain Shrimp and Shrimp Products*, WT/DS58/AB/R (98-3899) (Oct. 12, 1998) para. 186, and Appellate Body Report, *United States – Standards for Reformulated and Conventional Gasoline*, WT/DS2/AB/R (Apr. 29, 1996) at p. 30.

51 It is important to note that the law surrounding Article XX(g) is dynamic where each decision either by the GATT Panels or the WTO Appellate Bodies provides a new aspect of analytical approach.

52 See Article XX of the GATT.

A. GATT Decisions

1. *US – Tuna (Canada)*[53]

This was the first GATT decision that discussed the conservation of exhaustible natural resources under the coverage of Article XX(g).[54] In this case, the US imposed prohibitions on imports of tuna and tuna products from Canada according to US law.[55] This US prohibition was pursuant to a seizure of US fishing vessels by Canada, after Canada found these vessels fishing in waters it regarded as being under Canadian jurisdiction. Canada argued that the US prohibition on import of tuna products from Canada was inconsistent with GATT rules.[56] However, the US considered its action, that is, prohibiting tuna imports from Canada, as justified according to Article XX(g).[57]

The Panel found the US prohibiting measure to be in violation of Article XI:1.[58] Then, the Panel examined the applicability of Article XX(g) according to the traditional approach, by starting with the chapeau of Article XX.[59] The Panel found that the US prohibition did not violate the chapeau of Article XX.[60] The Panel then examined subsection (g) and considered tuna stocks as exhaustible natural resources 'in need of conservation management'.[61]

However, the Panel found that the requirement in subsection (g) 'made effective in conjunction with restrictions on domestic production or consumption' was not satisfied by the US. The Panel noted that the US has not proved any domestic restrictions on consumption or production of tuna and tuna product. Therefore, the Panel found subsection (g) inapplicable to the

---

53 See GATT Panel Report, United States – Prohibition of Imports of Tuna and Tuna Products from Canada, L/5198, adopted 22 February 1982, BISD 29S/91 (US – Tuna from Canada).

54 See Panel Report, *United States – Standards for Reformulated and Conventional Gasoline*, WTO Doc. WT/DS2/R (Jan. 29, 1996).

55 The US law is the Fishery Conservation and Management Act of 1976. See Panel report in *US-Canadian Tuna*, paras 2.1–2.2 (this law authorized the US Secretary of the Treasury to conduct necessary and appropriate actions in order to ban the importation of fish from any country that seized a US vessel using the jurisdictional claim, which the US did not recognize).

56 Ibid. para. 3.1.

57 Ibid. para. 3.5.

58 Ibid. para. 4.4.

59 Ibid. para. 4.8.

60 Ibid. para. 4.8.

61 Ibid, para. 4.9.

US measure.[62] The result of this case is a violation of Article XI:1 by the US measure, meanwhile Article XX(g) was found not to be applied and the measure was not justified.[63]

2. *Canada – Herring and Salmon*[64]

In this case the GATT Panel rejected the applicability of Article XX(g) to a Canadian restricting measure. The Canadian law imposed prohibition on export of unprocessed herring or salmon from Canada.[65] Processed herring or salmon were not subject to this ban. The US argued that this prohibition and restriction on export of unprocessed herring or salmon was in violation of Article XI:1.[66] Canada's counterargument cited several GATT exceptions, particularly Article XX(g), claiming that its measure was valid under this exception since it aimed at the conservation of natural resources.[67]

The Panel found, based upon the parties' agreement, that the Canadian prohibitions on the export of unprocessed herring and salmon were in contradiction with Article XI:1.[68] Regarding the applicability of Article XX(g) to the Canadian prohibitions, the Panel dealt first with subsection (g) and not the chapeau,[69] examining the meaning of the requirement 'relating to' based on the context and purpose of Article XX.[70] The Panel found that the most appropriate interpretation of the requirement 'relating to' is that a measure must be 'primarily aimed' at the 'conservation of exhaustible natural resources'.[71] The Panel also discussed the interpretation of the condition 'in conjunction with restrictions on domestic production or consumption' in subsection (g) and again determined that a

---

62 Ibid. paras 4.10–4.12.

63 Ibid. para. 4.15.

64 See Panel Report, Canada – Measures Affecting Exports of Unprocessed Herring and Salmon, L/6268, adopted 22 March 1988, BISD 35S/98.

65 Ibid. paras 2.1–2.3. The Canadian law consists of the Canadian Fisheries Act of 1970 and two regulations: Paragraph 6 of the Regulations Respecting Commercial Fishing for Salmon in the Waters of British Columbia and Canadian Fisheries Waters in the Pacific Ocean (Pacific Commercial Salmon Fishery Regulations), and Paragraph 24 of the Regulations Respecting Fishing for Herring in Canadian Fisheries Waters on the Pacific Coast (Pacific Herring Fishery Regulations).

66 Ibid. para. 3.1.

67 Ibid. paras 3.3 and 3.6.

68 Ibid. para. 4.1.

69 Ibid. para. 4.4.

70 Ibid.

71 Ibid. para. 4.6.

measure must be 'primarily aimed' in order to be an effective measure meeting this requirement.[72]

The Panel held that herring and salmon stocks are 'exhaustible natural resources' according to subsection (g),[73] but noted that Canadian export prohibitions did not constitute a conservation measure *per se*. It found that the Canadian prohibiting measure was unnecessary to collect statistical data, since in other cases Canada had collected statistical data pertaining to a variety of fish species, including salmon, without applying any export prohibition. In addition, it found that the prohibitions restricted access to unprocessed herring and salmon supplies only for foreign processers and consumers; the restrictions did not apply domestically.[74] Therefore, the Panel held that the Canadian measure was not 'primarily aimed at the conservation of exhaustible natural resources', and was not justified by Article XX (g).[75]

3. The *Tuna-Dolphin* saga[76]

The *Tuna-Dolphin* saga is an example of the clash between trade and the environment in general, and of trade and exhaustible natural resources in particular. In order to fully appreciate the international dynamics of this case, it is important to understand the behavior of schools of tuna and dolphins in the Eastern Tropical Pacific (ETP), the strategy that was applied to harvest tuna by the US, and its repercussions on US domestic fishing policy.

The ETP extends westward from the West Coast of the Americas' central coastline, to include most of the tropical Pacific east and south of the Hawaiian Islands. It covers high sea areas, as well as the exclusive economic zones (EEZs) and territorial seas of the US, Mexico, Guatemala, El Salvador, Honduras, Nicaragua, Costa Rica, Panama, Colombia, Ecuador, Peru, Chile, and France (due to French possession of Clipperton Island). Mexico's tuna fleet fishes in the ETP, as did the US fleet until the early 1990s.

A unique phenomenon in the ETP is that mature yellowfin tuna swim underneath groups of dolphins. This has prompted fishing vessels to find schools of underwater tuna by locating and chasing dolphins on the ocean surface; they are then encircled with purse seine nets to catch the

---

72 Ibid.

73 Ibid. para. 4.4.

74 Ibid. para. 4.7.

75 Ibid. para. 4.7.

76 The Tuna-Dolphin saga refers to a trilogy of cases: two GATT cases and one WTO case.

tuna below. This technique, known as 'setting on dolphins', was first used by the US fleet in the 1950s and 1960s, and is only used in the ETP, as this link between tuna and dolphins has not been observed elsewhere.

At the height of its use, the 'setting on dolphins'/purse seine method had a grave impact on the ETP's dolphin population. At the time no controls or regulations existed, and dolphins were chased and then encircled, along with the tuna below, in large purse seine nets. The nets' bottom and top edges were then tied up like a drawstring purse, trapping both the tuna and dolphins. Many dolphins were badly injured or drowned. The situation worsened with the arrival of speedboats and helicopters in the 1960s, accompanied by nets up to a mile long and 300 feet deep. While this hugely raised the efficiency of the tuna catch, it also increased the level of incidental dolphin mortality.[77] It is estimated that the US fleet alone killed over 100,000 dolphins per year in this way,[78] and that the technique caused the deaths of around 6 million dolphins overall.[79] The technique particularly impacted the ETP's populations of the northeastern offshore spotted dolphin, the eastern spinner dolphin and the coastal spotted dolphin. Although these species are not listed under the Endangered Species Act,[80] the spotted dolphin and spinner dolphin populations in the ETP are classed as 'depleted' under the US Marine Mammal Protection Act (MMPA),[81] meaning they are below the level required to maintain a sustainable population.

In response to concerns regarding the high rate of dolphin mortality, the US Congress passed the Marine Mammal Protection Act in 1972,

---

[77] The impact of overfishing on the ocean, and perhaps on life in general, has been studied by Callum Roberts in *The Ocean of Life: The Fate of Man and the Sea* (New York: Viking, 2012).

[78] See Wahlen, B.E. 'Incidental Dolphin Mortality in the Eastern Tropical Pacific Tuna Fishery, 1973 through 1978' (1986) *Fishery Bulletin*, Vol. 84, No. 3, pp. 559–569 (1986); Boreman, S.M. 'Dolphin-Safe Tuna: What's In a Label? The Killing of Dolphins in the Eastern Tropical Pacific and the Case for an International Legal Solution' (1992) *Nat. Resources J.* 425; Pryor, K. & Norris, K. (eds) *Dolphin Societies: Discoveries and Puzzles* (Berkeley and Los Angeles: University of California Press, 1991) pp. 246 and 273.

[79] See Kelsey, E. '3.9 Degrees of Separation: A Glimpse into the Social Networks of Dolphins' (2009) *Conservation Magazine*; Joyner, C.C. and Tyler, Z. 'Marine Conservation Versus International Free Trade: Reconciling Dolphins with Tuna and Sea Turtles with Shrimp' (2000) *Ocean Development and International Law*, Vol. 31, No. 1–2, pp. 127–150.

[80] 16 U.S.C. 1531–1544 (1973).

[81] 16 U.S.C. 1361–1421 (enacted 1972, amended 1994).

which prohibited 'the taking' of marine mammals.[82] The US tuna fleet was granted an initial two-year grace period, exempting it from this prohibition, during which time it was to develop techniques to improve dolphin safety. Once the grace period expired, a decreasing quota system took effect in order to reduce the rate of dolphin deaths resulting from US tuna fishing practices, with the ultimate goal of reaching a zero mortality rate. Additionally, specific standards for fishing practices were increasingly introduced throughout the 1980s, such as the requirement for US boats to have a special panel of fine mesh netting, called a 'Medina panel', in the rear of their nets to make it easier to release dolphins.

Faced with increasingly stringent regulation of their techniques, US vessels began to drop the practice of 'setting on dolphins' with purse seine nets in the early 1990s, and started fishing outside of the ETP. Increasing consumer awareness and concern for dolphins also played a role in changing fishing practices: a consumer boycott led several major US tuna companies to adopt policies preventing the purchase or sale of tuna that had been caught by 'setting on dolphins'. The Dolphin Protection Consumer Information Act[83] was introduced, which further raised the pressure to improve fishing practices by creating a voluntary scheme to label tuna as 'dolphin safe'.[84] Ultimately, 1992 saw the introduction of the International Dolphin Conservation Act,[85] which established a five-year moratorium on the purse seine net fishing of dolphins, starting in 1994, prohibiting the US fishing fleet from chasing, capturing, and setting nets on dolphins.[86] The moratorium caused US vessels to effectively cease fishing for tuna in the ETP.

Even though the moratorium on setting on dolphins is no longer in place, US vessels overall have not resumed tuna fishing in the ETP. Instead, they fish in other areas, employing alternative methods that include:

(1) setting purse seine nets on logs and artificial fish aggregating devices. Taking advantage of the fact that tuna are often attracted to

---

[82] Marine Mammal Protection Act, Section 103.
[83] 16 U.S.C. 1385 (1990).
[84] Ibid. Section d.1.
[85] 1992 P. L. No. 102-523.
[86] Ibid. Section 302(a).

floating objects, this method uses floating devices specifically designed to attract tuna and allow them to be found more easily;[87]
(2) setting purse seine nets on free-swimming schools of tuna;
(3) long-line fishing, using trailing fishing lines up to 50 miles long, with secondary lines of baited hooks branching off them;[88] and
(4) gillnets, which consist of a netting wall kept vertical by a floatline and a weighted groundline.

Several of these methods have received criticism for being harmful to marine life,[89] with a range of species other than dolphins being captured as by-catch. In particular, long-line fishing results in high rates of mortality for sharks, seabirds, and turtles, *inter alia*. Using a purse seine net with a log or artificial fish aggregating device also leads to high levels of by-catch, as other marine life is also attracted to the floating device. These methods also tend to result in a higher level of juvenile and under-sized tuna by-catch.[90]

3.1. US – Tuna-Dolphin I (Mexico)[91] This case dealt with the US Marine Mammal Protection Act 1972 (MMPA). The MMPA prohibited the import of fish harvested with fishing methods that resulted in the incidental killing of marine mammals in excess of US standards, unless explicitly authorized.[92] In this case the relevant mammals were dolphins. Based on the MMPA and pursuant to a US court decision, the US imposed prohibitions on the import of tuna fish that had been harvested using purse seine nets in ETP, resulting in dolphin injury or death.[93] There were two embargos:

---

[87] International Seafood Sustainability Foundation, 'Fishing Method Facts' at p. 1.

[88] Ibid. at p. 3.

[89] See Sumaila, U., Guénette, S., Alder, J. & Chuenpagdee, R. 'Addressing Ecosystem Effects of Fishing Using Marine Protected Areas' (2000) *ICES Journal of Marine Science*, Vol. 57, No. 3, pp. 752–760; Tasker, M.L., Camphuysen, C.J, Cooper, J., Garthe, S., Montevecchi, W.A. & Blaber, S.J.M. 'The Impacts of Fishing on Marine Birds' (2000) *ICES Journal of Marine Science*, Vol. 57, No. 3, pp. 531–547; Islam, M.R. 'The Proposed "Driftnet-free Zone" in the South Pacific and the Law of the Sea Convention' (1991) *I.C.L.Q.*, Vol. 40, No. 1, pp. 184–198.

[90] International Seafood Sustainability Foundation, 'FAD FAQ'.

[91] See GATT Panel Report, United States – Restrictions on Imports of Tuna, DS21/R, DS21/R, 3 September 1991, unadopted, BISD 39S/155.

[92] Ibid. para. 2.5.

[93] Ibid. paras 2.5–2.7 and 5.1–5.5.

(1) the first was a 'direct embargo' on Mexico; and
(2) the second an 'intermediary-nations embargo' applied to other countries.

Mexico claimed that the US embargos stemming from the MMPA were inconsistent with various GATT rules, especially Article XI:1,[94] while the US claimed that its measures were valid under GATT exceptions, particularly Article XX(g).[95] The Panel found the US restricting measures contrary to Article XI:1,[96] and denied the applicability of Article XX(g). Importantly, the Panel noted that Article XX(g) applies to measures to restrict production or consumption only in the country's jurisdiction.[97] Since in this case the restrictions related to production and consumption located outside US jurisdiction, the Panel rejected its applicability to US measures.[98] Despite the treatment of dolphins as exhaustible natural resources, the Panel decision did not allow for the applicability of Article XX(g) to dolphins.[99] This case serves as yet another obvious denial to the protection of exhaustible natural resources under Article XX(g).[100]

3.2. US – Tuna-Dolphin II (EEC)[101] The US prohibited imports of tuna from secondary nations engaging in trade on tuna with primary nations that were prohibited from exporting tuna to the US. The exception was if

---

94 Ibid. para. 3.1.

95 Ibid. paras 3.27 and 340.

96 Ibid. paras 5.18, 5.36 and 7.1

97 Ibid. para. 5.31

98 Ibid. paras 5.31–5.34 and 5.38. In addition, the Panel stated that even if Article XX(g) could be applied extra-jurisdictionally, the US measures would not satisfy Article XX(g) conditions. The Panel found that the US restrictions on imports from Mexico were not primarily aimed at the conservation of dolphin, see para. 5.33.

99 See Neuling, B. 'The Shrimp-Turtle Case: Implications for Article XX of GATT and the Trade and Environment Debate' (1999) 22 *Loy. L.A. Int'l & Comp. L. Rev.* 1 at p. 19 (explaining that this case constituted a landmark event in the interaction between trade and environment, and resulted in continuous and broad criticisms. The author notes also that the environmentalists objected 'not only to the Panel's conclusions, but also to the restrictive way the Panel interpreted Article XX').

100 Ibid. at p. 22 (explaining that the report of the Panel was not adopted and Mexico did not seek for its adoption. It adds that various environmental groups condemned the Panel's decision, especially since it ignored the environmental protection within trade under the GATT).

101 See Panel Report, United States – Restrictions on Imports of Tuna, DS29/R, 16 June 1994, unadopted.

the secondary nation could provide 'reasonable proof' that it had 'not imported products subject to the direct prohibition within the preceding six months'.[102] Such an embargo was referred to as 'intermediary nation embargo'[103] or 'secondary embargo'.[104] The European Economic Community (EEC) and The Netherlands challenged the secondary embargo, arguing that it violated GATT rules, including Article XI:1, and that it was not valid under GATT exceptions, specifically Article XX(g).[105] The US argued that the secondary embargo was valid under Article XX(g).[106]

While examining the secondary embargo, the Panel accepted the EEC argument and found its prohibition to be in violation of Article XI:1.[107] In examining the applicability of Article XX(g) to justify the violating measure, the Panel suggested a three-step analysis to determine:

(1) whether the measure fell within the scope of conservation of exhaustible natural resources;
(2) whether the measure was 'related to' the conservation of exhaustible natural resources and was 'made effective in conjunction with restrictions on domestic production or consumption'; and
(3) whether the measure was compatible with the requirements of the chapeau.[108]

The Panel applied this three-step analysis to the US measure. As in the *Tuna-Dolphin I* case, the Panel considered dolphins to be exhaustible natural resources.[109] It also found that the US measure to protect dolphins fell within the range of policies aimed at conserving exhaustible natural resources.[110] In contrast to the *Tuna-Dolphin I* case, the *Tuna-Dolphin II* Panel rejected the argument that Article XX(g) did not apply extra-jurisdictionally, and concluded that it has an extra-jurisdictional applicability.[111]

---

[102] Ibid. paras 2.12 and 5.5.
[103] Ibid. paras 2.12 and 5.5.
[104] See Esty, D.C. *Greening the GATT: Trade, Environment, and the Future* (Washington, DC: Institute for International Economics, 1994) at p. 269.
[105] See Panel Report, *United States – Restrictions on Imports of Tuna*, DS29/R, 16 June 1994, unadopted, paras 3.1 and 3.92.
[106] Ibid. paras 3.2 and 3.7.
[107] Ibid. para. 5.10.
[108] Ibid. para. 5.12.
[109] Ibid. para. 5.13.
[110] Ibid. para. 5.13.
[111] Ibid. paras 5.15–5.20.

In the second step, the Panel examined whether the secondary embargo was 'related to' conservation according to Article XX(g), and found that the US measures forced other countries 'to change their policies, and that [they] were effective only if such changes occurred', therefore they could not be considered 'primarily aimed … at the conservation of an exhaustible natural resource'.[112] Since the measure did not satisfy the second step, the Panel did not examine the third one. Accordingly, the Panel concluded that Article XX(g) did not apply to the US import prohibitions on tuna. The *Tuna-Dolphin II* case comprises a significant GATT decision in that the GATT system invalidated again the protection of Article XX(g) to an environmental measure involving exhaustible natural resources.

B. WTO Decisions

In 1994 the WTO was created and entered into operation in January 1995 with its DSS. Article XX and its subsection (g), 'conservation of exhaustible natural resources', were central issues in the most important WTO dispute decisions: the *Gasoline*, *Shrimp-Turtle*, *Tuna-Dolphin III* and *China-Raw Materials* cases. After providing some background on these cases, this section examines the framework and complex analysis that the WTO Appellate Body applied in these significant decisions in examining the applicability of Article XX(g).

1. *US – Gasoline*[113]

The *Tuna-Dolphin II* case was the last GATT decision, and the *Gasoline* case was the first environmental case at the WTO.[114] This case dealt with the implementation of a US federal act, the Clean Air Act 1990 (CAA).[115] The CCA aimed to prevent and control 'air pollution' in the US caused by the combustion of gasoline by motor vehicles.[116] According to the authorization of the CAA, the Environmental Protection

---

112 Ibid. para. 5.27.

113 See Panel Report, United States – Standards for Reformulated and Conventional Gasoline, WTO Doc. WT/DS2/R (Jan. 29, 1996); Appellate Body Report, United States – Standards for Reformulated and Conventional Gasoline, WT/DS2/AB/R (Apr. 29, 1996).

114 See Neuling, B. 'The Shrimp-Turtle Case: Implications for Article XX of GATT and the Trade and Environment Debate' (1999) 22 *Loy. L.A. Int'l & Comp. L. Rev.* 1 at p. 24.

115 42 U.S.C. § 7401 (1994).

116 See Panel Report, *United States – Standards for Reformulated and Conventional Gasoline*, WTO Doc. WT/DS2/R (Jan. 29, 1996) para. 2.1.

Agency (EPA) determined and promulgated the Gasoline Rule aimed at reducing air pollution. This rule includes new regulations on the 'compositions and emissions effects of gasoline'. The Gasoline Rule applied to all the refiners, blenders and importers in the US.[117]

According to the Gasoline Rule, domestic refiners were required to incorporate an independent baseline that represented the quality of gasoline produced by the refiners in 1990. In this respect, the rule set three methods that were available to domestic refiners in order to determine their independent baseline.[118] In addition, the Gasoline Rule required gasoline importers to establish an independent baseline, when only the statutory baseline was available to them, with the exception of using the first method available to the domestic refiners.[119]

Notably, while the gasoline importers were automatically assigned the statutory baseline, the domestic refiners were not allowed to choose this statutory route.[120] As a result, in the context of the individual baseline, sales conditions for imported gasoline were less favorable than those of domestic gasoline. Venezuela and Brazil contended that the US Gasoline Rule derived from the CAA, violated GATT rules,[121] while the US argued that even if the Gasoline Rule was found to be in violation of GATT rules, it was still valid mainly according to Article XX(g).[122]

After finding that the Gasoline Rule did violate GATT rules, the WTO Panel discussed the applicability of Article XX(g) from the top down, by analyzing the chapeau of Article XX, and then analyzing the components of subsection (g). The Panel concluded that the methods at issue were not primarily aimed at the 'conservation of' exhaustible natural resources, therefore subsection (g) was not met and as a result Article XX(g) did not apply.[123] The Appellate Body rejected the Panel framework and analysis of Article XX(g), and rejected that subsection (g) was not satisfied, but concluded that the violation of GATT rules was not justified by Article XX(g) since the US measure was inconsistent with the chapeau of Article XX.[124]

---

[117] Ibid. paras 2.1 and 2.4– 2.6,
[118] Ibid. para. 2.6.
[119] Ibid. para. 2.8.
[120] Ibid. para. 2.6.
[121] Ibid. para. 3.1.
[122] Ibid. para. 3.4.
[123] Ibid. para. 6.40.
[124] See Appellate Body Report, *United States – Standards for Reformulated and Conventional Gasoline*, WT/DS2/AB/R, (Apr. 29, 1996) at p. 29.

Contrary to the WTO Panel, the Appellate Body conducted a different analysis concerning the assessment of Article XX(g). In what is called the 'two tiered' approach, the Appellate Body mandated a pathway that evaluated the chapeau of Article XX only after finding that the measure satisfied the elements of subsection (g).[125] Accordingly, the Appellate Body first examined subsection (g). The Panel had found in its report that 'clean air' was an 'exhaustible natural resource' within the meaning of subsection (g), mainly since clean air could be depleted.[126] The Appellate Body also treated clean air as an exhaustible natural resource,[127] and accepted the *Herring-Salmon* case interpretation that 'relating to the conservation' means 'primarily aimed at'.[128] As a result, the Appellate Body confirmed that the CAA policy to reduce the depletion of clean air as an exhaustible natural resource had a 'substantial' relationship and was 'primarily aimed at' the conservation of exhaustible natural resources.[129] Additionally, the Appellate Body concluded that a measure could be found 'in conjunction with' if its restrictions on products comprised 'even handedness' restrictions.[130] Together with restrictions on exportation or importation there should also be at least 'some' restrictions applying to domestic products.[131] The Appellate Body found that the baseline rules satisfied the 'in conjunction with' condition; therefore it concluded that the Gasoline Rule had been provisionally characterized as satisfying subsection (g) of Article XX.[132] The Appellate Body also made it clear that the party interested in utilizing the exception of Article XX(g) bears the burden of proof for both the fulfillment of the elements of subsection (g) as well the conditions of the chapeau.[133]

The Appellate Body then moved to the chapeau and examined whether the US proved the consistency of its measure with the chapeau of Article XX, and whether the baseline establishment rules in the Gasoline Rule were 'not applied in a manner which would constitute a means of

---

125 Ibid. at p. 22.

126 See Panel Report, *United States – Standards for Reformulated and Conventional Gasoline*, WTO Doc. WT/DS2/R (Jan. 29, 1996) at para. 6.37.

127 See Appellate Body Report, *United States – Standards for Reformulated and Conventional Gasoline*, WT/DS2/AB/R, (Apr. 29, 1996) at pp. 14 –16.

128 Ibid. at pp. 18–19.

129 Ibid. at p. 19.

130 Ibid. at p. 21.

131 Ibid. at p. 21 (stipulating that the condition of 'in conjunction with' did not require the 'effect test').

132 Ibid. at pp. 19–22.

133 Ibid. at pp. 22–23 (holding that the burden to demonstrate the satisfaction of the chapeau is heavier than the burden to meet the elements of subsection (g)).

arbitrary or unjustifiable discrimination between countries where the same conditions prevail, or a disguised restriction on international trade …'.[134] The Appellate Body found that there was more than one way for the US to apply regulations implementing the CAA without differentiating between domestic and imported gasoline.[135] However, it had applied the Gasoline Rule in an abusive way without considering the effects on gasoline importers. These findings led the Appellate Body to conclude that 'the baseline establishment rules in the Gasoline Rule, in their application, constitute "unjustifiable discrimination" and a "disguised restriction on international trade"'.[136] As a result, the Appellate Body concluded that although the baseline establishment rules fell under subsection (g), they were not entitled to the justifying protection of Article XX as a whole.[137]

This decision of the Appellate Body has been considered one of the most significant decisions held by WTO and GATT dispute settlement tribunals, for its analysis, reasoning, and holding. It served as an important guideline and precedent for later WTO decisions.[138] Despite its importance to the WTO DSS, and its critical implications for trade issues, the outcome of this case comprises another obvious denial and ignorance of the protection of the environment in general, and exhaustible natural resources in particular.

---

[134] Article XX of the GATT.

[135] See Appellate Body Report, *United States – Standards for Reformulated and Conventional Gasoline*, WT/DS2/AB/R, (Apr. 29, 1996) at p. 25.

[136] Ibid. at p. 29.

[137] Ibid. at p. 29.

[138] See Appellate Body Report, *European Communities – Measures Affecting Asbestos and Asbestos-Containing Products*, WT/DS135/AB/R (Mar. 12, 2001); Appellate Body Report, *United States – Import Prohibition of Certain Shrimp and Shrimp Products*, WT/DS58/AB/R (98-3899) (Oct. 12, 1998); Appellate Body Report, *United States – Measures Concerning the Importation, Marketing and Sale of Tuna and Tuna Products*, WT/DS381/AB/R (May 16, 2012); and Appellate Body Report, *China – Measures Related to the Exportation of Various Raw Materials*, WT/DS394/AB/R, WT/DS395/AB/R, WT/DS398/AB/R (Feb. 22, 2012).

2. *US – Shrimp-Turtle*[139]

The WTO *Shrimp-Turtle* dispute is arguably the most important environment-related dispute to come before the trade body tribunals.[140] The background of the *Shrimp-Turtle* case is similar to that of the *Tuna-Dolphin* cases.[141] The case stemmed from the US efforts to protect the world's endangered sea turtles.[142] To this end, seven species of sea turtles were included in the 1973 Convention on International Trade Endangered Species (CITES), and were recognized as endangered species.[143] The US act concerning endangered species is the Endangered Species Act of 1973 (ESA), which prohibited the harming of any of the seven protected species of turtles.[144] 'Turtle excluder devices' (TEDs) were invented for shrimping vessels to reduce the incidental drowning or catching of turtles in shrimp nets, and thereby killing them.[145]

Section 609 of Public Law 101-162[146] prohibited importation to the US of shrimp harvested with commercial fishing technology that may have adversely affected sea turtles.[147] In addition, Section 609 stated that countries exporting shrimp to the US had to adopt regulatory programs governing the incidental sea turtle death comparable to that of the US.[148] Moreover, Section 609 required that all imported shrimp to the US be accompanied by a declaration ('Shrimp Exporter's Declaration Form') stating that the imported shrimp was harvested in waters within the

---

[139] See Panel Report, United States – Import Prohibition of Certain Shrimp and Shrimp Products, WT/DS58/R (May 15, 1998); Appellate Body Report, United States – Import Prohibition of Certain Shrimp and Shrimp Products, WT/DS58/AB/R (98-3899) (Oct. 12, 1998).

[140] See Change, H.F. 'Toward a Greener GATT: Environmental Trade Measures and the Shrimp-Turtle Case' (2000) 74 *Southern California Law Review* 31 at p. 31.

[141] See *Tuna-Dolphin I*, *II* and *III*.

[142] See Panel Report, *United States – Import Prohibition of Certain Shrimp and Shrimp Products*, WT/DS58/R (May 15, 1998).

[143] Ibid. paras 2.1–2.3.

[144] Ibid. para. 2.4.

[145] Ibid. para. 2.5 (the 'turtle excluder devices' [TEDs] were invented by the National Marine Fishers Services [NMFS] and aimed to protect turtles and other large objects by redirecting them out of the net).

[146] Codified at 16 United States Code (U.S.C.) § 1537.

[147] Panel Report, *United States – Import Prohibition of Certain Shrimp and Shrimp Products*, WT/DS58/R (May 15, 1998), para. 2.7.

[148] Ibid. para. 2.7–2.11.

jurisdiction of a certified country, or in conditions that did not 'adversely affect sea turtles'.[149]

Several countries lodged complaints at the WTO challenging Section 609 as a violation of a number of WTO rules.[150] The US argued that Section 609 was justified according to Article XX(g).[151] The WTO Panel found that Section 609 violated Article XI:1 of the GATT[152] and, unlike the analytical framework used in the *Gasoline* case, the Panel examined Section 609 according to the chapeau of Article XX.[153] The Panel concluded that Section 609 was unjustified within the meaning of the chapeau, hence it did not address subsection (g).[154] Interestingly, although the Appellate Body reached the same conclusion to the effect that Section 609 did not comply with the chapeau of Article XX,[155] it rejected the Panel's reasoning as well as the approach used in its analysis.[156]

The Appellate Body analyzed the applicability of Article XX(g) using the 'two tiered' approach, by evaluating the elements of subsection (g) prior to the determination that the measure satisfied the elements of the chapeau.[157] The Appellate Body criticized the Panel for ignoring the analysis approach established in *Gasoline* case,[158] and ruled that:

> The task of interpreting the chapeau so as to prevent the abuse or misuse of the specific exemption … is rendered very difficult, if indeed it remains

---

149 Ibid. para. 2.11, these conditions were added in 1996 to Section 609, and the US embargo on imported shrimp was expanded to include all shrimp-exporting countries.

150 Ibid. para. 3.1 (the countries were India, Pakistan, Malaysia and Thailand).

151 Ibid. para. 3.3.

152 Ibid. para. 7.17.

153 Ibid. para. 8.1.

154 Ibid. para. 7.63 (ruling that Section 609 represented the kind of unilateral measure that 'could jeopardize the multilateral trading system', while for a measure to be valid according to Article XX it must not 'undermine the multilateral trading system').

155 See Appellate Body Report, *United States – Import Prohibition of Certain Shrimp and Shrimp Products*, WT/DS58/AB/R (98-3899) (Oct. 12, 1998).

156 Ibid. paras 186–187.

157 Ibid. paras 118–119 (ruling that the appropriate approach to analyzing the applicability of Article XX (g) is the 'two tiered' approach that was held by the Appellate Body in the *Gasoline* case, and rejecting the Panel's approach).

158 Ibid.

> possible at all, where the interpreter has not first identified and examined the specific exception threatened with abuse.[159]

According to this stated approach, the Appellate Body analyzed the applicability of Article XX(g).[160] The Appellate Body began by addressing subsection (g), and found that 'natural resources' embraced both living and non-living resources, and therefore sea turtles were considered natural resources.[161] In addition, it concluded that although living species such as sea turtles have the ability to reproduce and thus are 'renewable', they may be at risk of extinction, exhaustion or depletion.[162] Therefore, they were considered 'exhaustible' natural resources.[163]

As in the *Gasoline* case, the Appellate Body interpreted the phrase 'relating to the conservation' in subsection (g) to mean 'primarily aimed at', and its ruling affirmed the *Herring-Salmon* case interpretation.[164] Additionally, it stated that an essential examination of the requirement 'relating to the conservation' needs to address a substantial connection between the measures and the 'ends'. The Appellate Body ruled that it is not enough to state a merely incidental 'substantial relationship';[165] rather, it has to incorporate a close connection between the measures and the ends.[166] In that sense, the Appellate Body found a close and real relationship between Section 609 and the legitimate protection of endangered sea turtles as exhaustible natural resources.[167] Additionally, by implementing the *Gasoline* case ruling concerning the interpretation of 'in conjunction with', the Appellate Body found that Section 609 was made 'effective in conjunction withthe restrictions on domestic harvesting of shrimp' as required by subsection (g).[168]

---

159 Ibid. para. 120.

160 Ibid. paras 125–126.

161 Ibid. para. 131.

162 Ibid. para. 128.

163 Ibid. (reasoning that sea turtles as living resources are ' just as finite as petroleum, iron or other non-living resources are').

164 Ibid. para. 136.

165 See Appellate Body Report, *United States – Standards for Reformulated and Conventional Gasoline*, WT/DS2/AB/R (Apr. 29, 1996) at pp. 18–19.

166 See Appellate Body Report, *United States – Import Prohibition of Certain Shrimp and Shrimp Products*, WT/DS58/AB/R (98-3899) (Oct. 12, 1998) at paras 136–141.

167 Ibid. para. 141.

168 Ibid. paras 143–145. The Appellate Body found that regulations of the ESA other than Section 609 have met the 'even handedness' requirement in restricting shrimp caught by US vessels.

Pursuant to finding that Section 609 was provisionally justified under subsection (g), and according to the 'two tiered' approach, the Appellate Body turned to examine Section 609 in the light of the standards of the chapeau, in order to be justified as an exception under Article XX.[169] The Appellate Body identified three standards to determine whether a measure comprises a means of 'arbitrary or unjustifiable discrimination where the same conditions prevail':[170]

> There are three standards contained in the chapeau: first, arbitrary discrimination between countries where the same conditions prevail; second, unjustifiable discrimination between countries where the same conditions prevail; and third, a disguised restriction on international trade. In order for a measure to be applied in a manner which would constitute 'arbitrary or unjustifiable discrimination between countries where the same conditions prevail', three elements must exist'.[171]

The Appellate Body found that Section 609 constituted an 'unjustifiable discrimination' for several reasons. First and foremost, the Appellate Body found that Section 609 constituted, in effect, an embargo, which is unacceptable in international trade relations,[172] and would influence other WTO members to adopt essentially similar regulatory programs.[173] Additionally, the Appellate Body found that the regulation implemented by the US required other nations to adopt turtle conservation programs that were not merely comparable in effectiveness to those used in the US, but that had to be the same as the program applied in the US.[174] Moreover, the Appellate Body found that Section 609 was applied in a discriminatory way, since countries in the Caribbean and Western Atlantic had three years to implement the use of TEDs, while other countries (such as India, Malaysia, Thailand, and Pakistan) had only four months. The US thus failed to ensure equal treatment to all pertinent countries.[175] Furthermore, along with being considered an unjustifiable discriminatory measure, the Appellate Body found Section 609 to be an 'arbitrary

[169] Ibid. para. 147.
[170] Ibid. para. 150.
[171] Ibid.
[172] Ibid. para. 161.
[173] Ibid. para. 164.
[174] Ibid. para. 163.
[175] Ibid. para. 173.

discriminatory' measure. This was because the certification process was unclear and unpredictable, and the appellees were deprived of basic due process and had no way to appeal a decision that denied certificate.[176] It ruled that:

> The certification processes … consist principally of administrative ex parte inquiry or verification by staff … there is no formal opportunity for an applicant country to be heard, or to respond to any arguments that may be made against it, in the course of the certification process … [N]o formal written, reasoned decision, whether of acceptance or rejection, is rendered on applications for … certification … Countries whose applications are denied … do not receive notice of such denial … or of the reasons for the denial. No procedure for review of, or appeal from, a denial of an application is provided.[177]

Based upon the above findings, the Appellate Body concluded that Section 609 was applied 'in a manner which amounts to a means not just of "unjustifiable discrimination", but also of "arbitrary discrimination" between countries where the same conditions prevail, contrary to the requirements of the chapeau of Article XX'.[178] As a result, it concluded that although Section 609 met the elements of subsection (g), it was not justified under Article XX(g) since it was found to be inconsistent with the chapeau standards.[179] Interestingly, since the creation of the DSS of the WTO, the decision of the Appellate Body in the *Shrimp-Turtle* case is considered the most important WTO decision.[180] However, the outcome of this highly sophisticated decision comprises another WTO decision which is consistent with WTO and GATT decisions that did not grant exhaustible natural resources the protection of Article XX(g).

In the aftermath of the Appellate Body's decision in the *Shrimp-Turtle* case, the US revised Section 609 and the relevant guidelines in 1999.[181] A new dispute was brought before the DSS of the WTO by Malaysia,

---

176 Ibid. paras 177–188.

177 Ibid. para. 180.

178 Ibid. para. 184.

179 Ibid. para. 187.

180 See Change, H.F. 'Toward a Greener GATT: Environmental Trade Measures and the Shrimp-Turtle Case' (2000) 74 *Southern California Law Review* 31 at p. 31.

181 See Appellate Body Report, *United States – Import Prohibition of Certain Shrimp and Shrimp Products: Recourse to Article 21.5 of the DSU by Malaysia*, WT/DS58/RW (Oct. 22, 2001) para. 3.

claiming that the revised Section 609 still violates the GATT,[182] since the US did not reach an international agreement to avoid discrimination between the various nations.[183] The Appellate Body rejected this argument and held that it is sufficient for a member to meet the chapeau requirements if it made good faith efforts towards negotiations to achieve international agreements.[184] Further, it held that such negotiations 'must be comparable' in the degree of effort made to achieve an agreement, but did not need to be of identical effort.[185] As a result, the Appellate Body held that the US met the requirements of the chapeau by pursuing negotiations with Malaysia, and the revised Section 609 was not found to be an 'arbitrary or unjustifiable discrimination'.[186]

3. *US – Tuna-Dolphin III*[187]

In this section, there is no discussion of Article XX(g) since the defendant in this case did not rely on it for their defense. However, this case has been inserted because it is part of the *Tuna-Dolphin* saga and because it relates to the conservation of dolphins, which were considered exhaustible natural resources.

In March 2009, Mexico placed a Request for Establishment of a Panel under the WTO's Dispute Resolution mechanism,[188] arguing that US

---

[182] Ibid.

[183] Ibid. para. 122.

[184] Ibid.

[185] Ibid. In other words, a country has to provide all exporting/importing countries 'similar opportunities to negotiate' an international agreement. It has to make good faith efforts to reach international agreements. Good faith efforts have to be comparable from one group of negotiations to another, without discrimination. These efforts have to be comparable, but not identical.

[186] Ibid. paras 123 and 149. The Appellate Body noted also that a measure should not contain rules directly aimed at addressing the various circumstances of different countries, but should have 'sufficient flexibility to take into account the specific conditions prevailing in any exporting' country.

[187] See Panel Report, United States – Measures Concerning the Importation, Marketing and Sale of Tuna and Tuna Products, WT/DS381/R (Sept. 15, 2011); Appellate Body Report, United States – Measures Concerning the Importation, Marketing and Sale of Tuna and Tuna Products, WT/DS381/AB/R (May 16, 2012).

[188] See *United States – Measures Concerning the Importation, Marketing and Sale of Tuna and Tuna Products*, Request for the Establishment of a Panel by Mexico, WT/DS381/4, 10 March 2009.

measures violated both the GATT and the TBT Agreement.[189] The crux of Mexico's complaint was that certain provisions of the Dolphin Protection Consumer Information Act (and related regulations) had the effect of preventing Mexican tuna and tuna products from being labeled as 'dolphin-safe', even when the tuna had been harvested in compliance with the standards of the Inter-American Tropical Tuna Commission, as set out in the Agreement on the International Dolphin Conservation Program (AIDCP).[190] Mexico argued that these measures were discriminatory, and in violation of the most-favored-nation (MFN) and national-treatment requirements of Articles I.1 and III.4 of the GATT, respectively. Under the US Dolphin Protection Consumer Information Act, it is in violation of US laws against deceptive practices in commerce if any producer, importer, exporter, or seller falsely labels a product as 'dolphin safe'.[191] Mexico objected to the provision that tuna products could not be labeled 'dolphin-safe' if they contained tuna caught during a fishing trip in which purse seine nets were intentionally deployed or used to encircle dolphins, or if dolphins were killed or seriously injured in the tuna harvest.[192]

On September 15, 2011, the panel report was circulated to the WTO Members. The Panel first determined whether the US dolphin-safe labeling provisions constitute a technical regulation under the TBT Agreement. The Panel found that they do[193] and, in particular, that the measures are mandatory within the meaning of Annex 1.1 of the TBT Agreement. Moreover, the Panel rejected Mexico's first claim, finding that the US dolphin-safe labeling provisions did not discriminate against Mexican tuna products and were therefore not inconsistent with Article 2.1 of the TBT Agreement.[194] Despite finding that Mexican tuna products are like tuna products originating in the United States or any other country within the meaning of Article 2.1 of the TBT Agreement, the Panel concluded that Mexican tuna products are not afforded less

---

[189] See *United States – Measures Concerning the Importation, Marketing and Sale of Tuna and Tuna Products*, Opening Statement of Mexico at the first meeting with the Panel, 18 October 2010.

[190] See USTR 'Measures Concerning the Importation, Marketing and Sale of Tuna and Tuna Products,' available at http://www.ustr.gov/node/5714

[191] Section 5 of the Federal Trade Commission Act, 15 U.S.C. 45.

[192] US Dolphin Protection Consumer Information Act, Section (d)(3)(C)(i).

[193] See Panel Report *United States – Measures Concerning the Importation, Marketing and Sale of Tuna and Tuna Products*, WT/DS381/R (Sept. 15, 2011), para. 7.210.

[194] Ibid. para. 8.1(a).

favorable treatment than tuna products of US and other origins with respect to the US dolphin-safe labeling provisions, on the basis of their origin.[195]

With respect to Mexico's claim under Article 2.2 of the TBT Agreement, the Panel found that Mexico had demonstrated that the US dolphin-safe labeling provisions were more trade-restrictive than necessary to fulfill the legitimate objectives of:

(1) ensuring that consumers are not misled or deceived about whether tuna products contain tuna that was caught in a manner that adversely affected dolphins; and
(2) contributing to the protection of dolphins, by ensuring that the US market is not used to encourage fishing fleets to catch tuna in a manner that adversely affects dolphins.[196]

The Panel's conclusion was based on the following two findings:

(1) that the US dolphin-safe labeling provisions only partly address the legitimate objectives outlined above;[197] and
(2) that Mexico had provided the panel with a less trade-restrictive alternative capable of achieving the same level of protection as that pursued by the US dolphin-safe labeling provisions.[198]

Considering the strong commonalities between Mexico's claims under GATT Articles I.1 and III.4 and some of its claims under the TBT Agreement, the Panel held the view that it was important to examine whether it was required, for the full resolution of the dispute, to consider also the claims under GATT 1994.[199] The Panel exercised judicial economy[200] with respect to Mexico's claims under GATT Articles I.1 and III.4 and declined to rule on them.[201]

---

[195] Ibid. para. 7.374.
[196] Ibid. para. 7.620.
[197] Ibid. para. 7.599.
[198] Ibid. para. 7.619.
[199] See *United States – Measures Concerning the Importation, Marketing and Sale of Tuna and Tuna Products*, Request for the Establishment of a Panel by Mexico, WT/DS381/R, para. 7.741.
[200] Ibid. para. 7.748.
[201] The Panel noted in this respect the following determinations of the Appellate Body in relation to the completion of the analysis in the context of Peru's claims under Articles 2.1, 2.2 and 2.4 of the TBT Agreement and Article III:4 of GATT 1994 in *EC – Sardines*: 'Peru submits that, if we conclude

The new *Tuna-Dolphin* case gives rise to several questions: First, are the contested US measures in this case in violation of MFN and national treatment principles under Articles I and III of the GATT?[202] Mexico argued that the US labeling scheme led to *de facto* discrimination against Mexican exports of tuna and tuna products, in comparison to tuna and tuna products originating in the US and in other countries. Moreover, how should the panel have handled Article 2.2 of the TBT Agreement claim in this dispute? One particular concern with the panel's finding is the involvement of WTO rules in domestic policy. How could the panel have acknowledged this concern? Is there any approach to Article 2.2 of the TBT Agreement that could allow for sufficient domestic autonomy? Or is the actual provision basically lacking in this respect?

In January 2012, both the US and Mexico notified the DSB of their decision to appeal certain issues of law and legal interpretations developed by the panel.[203] Moreover, Mexico notified the DSB of its decision to appeal certain issues of law and legal interpretations developed by the panel, and the panel's failure to make an objective assessment of the matter as required by Article 11 of the DSU.

In May 2012, the Appellate Body circulated its report to WTO Members, which includes some significant changes from the findings of the Panel. Although the Appellate Body agreed with the Panel in that the

---

that the EC Regulation is consistent with Article 2.4, it would be appropriate for us to complete the Panel's analysis and resolve the dispute by making findings on those provisions of Article 2 of the *TBT Agreement* on which the Panel did not make any findings, namely Articles 2.2 and 2.1 of the *TBT Agreement*. Although Peru made a claim before the Panel under Article III:4 of the GATT 1994, Peru does not ask us to complete the analysis by addressing that provision. The European Communities objects to the completion of the analysis, expressing the view that there are not sufficient undisputed facts in the record to do so. Because we have found that the EC Regulation is *not* consistent with Article 2.4 of the *TBT Agreement*, the conditions to Peru's request have not been met, and, therefore, we do not think it is necessary for us to make a finding under Articles 2.2 and 2.1 of the *TBT Agreement* in order to resolve this dispute. Equally, we do not think it is necessary to make a finding under Article III:4 of the GATT 1994 in order to resolve this dispute. Therefore, we decline to make findings on Articles 2.2 and 2.1 of the *TBT Agreement*, or on Article III:4 of the GATT 1994' (Appellate Body Report, *EC – Sardines*, paras 312–313).

[202] See *United States – Measures Concerning the Importation, Marketing and Sale of Tuna and Tuna Products*, Opening statement of the US at the first substantive meeting of the Panel, 18 October 2010.

[203] See also the amicus curiae brief submitted to the members of the WTO Appellate Body by Professor Robert Howse on 17 February 2012, available at http://www.worldtradelaw.net/amicus/howsetunaamicus.pdf

measure at issue constitutes a 'technical regulation' within the meaning of Annex 1.1 to the TBT Agreement,[204] it reversed the Panel's finding that the US's 'dolphin-safe' labeling provisions are not inconsistent with Article 2.1 of the TBT Agreement, and found, instead, that the US measure is inconsistent with Article 2.1 of the TBT Agreement.[205] Regarding the question whether the detrimental impact from the measure stems exclusively from a legitimate regulatory distinction, the Appellate Body found that the measure at issue is not even-handed in the manner in which it addresses the risks to dolphins arising from different fishing techniques in different areas of the ocean.[206] As for Mexico's claim under Article 2.2 of the TBT Agreement, the Appellate Body reversed the Panel's finding that Mexico had demonstrated that the US's 'dolphin-safe' labeling provisions are more trade restrictive than necessary to fulfill the United States' legitimate objectives. On this basis, the Appellate Body reversed the Panel's finding that the measure is inconsistent with Article 2.2 of the TBT Agreement.[207]

The Appellate Body agreed with the Panel's conclusion that the US measure at issue is not inconsistent with Article 2.4 of the TBT Agreement.[208] However, it reversed the Panel's intermediate finding that the dolphin-safe definition and certification developed within the framework of the AIDCP is a 'relevant international standard' within the meaning of Article 2.4 of the TBT Agreement.[209] The Appellate Body concluded that the Panel erred in finding that the AIDCP, to which new parties can accede only by invitation, is 'open to the relevant body of every country and is therefore an international standardizing organization' for the purposes of Article 2.4 of the TBT Agreement.[210]

Moreover, the Appellate Body found that the Panel acted inconsistently with Article 11 of the DSU in exercising judicial economy with respect to Mexico's claims under Articles I.1 and III.4 of the GATT 1994.[211]

---

[204] See Appellate Body Report, *United States – Measures Concerning the Importation, Marketing and Sale of Tuna and Tuna Products*, WT/DS381/AB/R (May 16, 2012), para. 199.

[205] Ibid. para. 299.

[206] Ibid. para. 298.

[207] Ibid. para. 331.

[208] Ibid. para. 401.

[209] Ibid.

[210] Ibid.

[211] Ibid. para. 405. Marie Wilke has analyzed the Appellate Body's decision in *Tuna-Dolphin*, 'Tuna Labelling and the WTO: How Safe is 'Dolfin-safe'?' (2012) *ICTSD*, Vol. 6, No. 2. See also Zhou, W. '*US – Clove Cigarettes* and *US – Tuna II (Mexico)*: Implications for the Role of Regulatory Purpose under

4. *China – Raw Materials*[212]

This case is one of the most important WTO cases dealing with the intersection between trade regulation and natural resources. The case addresses export restraints that China imposed on the exportation of raw materials. When China joined the WTO in 2001, like any acceding member, it accepted the WTO 'single-package' and undertook to apply WTO rules. In addition, according to the China Protocol of Accession, Paragraph 11.3, China was obligated to eliminate all export taxes and charges, except those related to measures compatible with Article VIII of the GATT, and except for a list of raw materials that was provided in Annex 6 of its Protocol of Accession.[213] These additional commitments incorporated in the Protocol of Accession are known as WTO-plus commitments.[214] Also, in the same Protocol, China committed to eliminate and not to introduce export quotas.[215] However, from 1994 to 2010, China imposed a complex of measures that included four types of export restraints on certain raw materials:[216] (i) export duties; (ii) export quotas;

Article III:4 of the GATT' (2012) *Journal of International Economic Law*, Vol. 15, No. 4, pp. 1075–1122.

212 See Panel Report, China – Measures Related to the Exportation of Various Raw Materials, WT/DS394/R, WT/DS395/R, WT/DS398/R (July 5, 2011); Appellate Body Report, China – Measures Related to the Exportation of Various Raw Materials, WT/DS394/AB/R, WT/DS395/AB/R, WT/DS398/AB/R (Feb. 22, 2012).

213 See Protocol on the Accession of the People's Republic of China, WT/L/432, para. 11.3 & Annex 6, available at http://www.worldtradelaw.net/misc/chinaaccessionprotocol.pdf

214 For further discussion relevant to WTO-plus commitments in the *China – Raw Materials* case, see Qin, J.Y. 'The Challenge of Interpreting "WTO-PLUS" Provisions' (2010) 44 (1) *Journal of World Trade* 127; Qin, J.Y., 'The Predicament of China's "WTO-plus" Obligation to Eliminate Export Duties: A Commentary on the China-Raw Materials case', (2011) 11(2) *Chinese Journal of International Law* 237; Karapinar, B. 'China's Export Restriction Policies: Complying with "WTO plus" or Undermining Multilateralism (2011) 10(6) *World Trade Review* 389 at p. 390; Karapinar, B. 'Defining the Legal Boundaries of Export Restrictions: A Case Law Analysis' (2012) 15(2) *Journal of International Economic Law* 443.

215 See Paragraph 7.2 of the Protocol of Accession.

216 The raw materials that were subject to the export restrictions are certain forms of bauxite, coke, fluorspar, magnesium, manganese, silicon carbide, silicon metal, yellow phosphorus, and zinc. These materials are significant to daily production of items and technological products, and China is considered a leading country in producing these materials, Panel Report, *China – Measures*

(iii) minimum export price requirements; and (iv) export licensing requirements.[217]

The complainants, the US, Mexico, and the EU confronted these four types of export restrictions on raw materials through the WTO DSS.[218] They argued that China's restricting measures were in violation of WTO rules (especially Article XI:1 of the GATT), and were inconsistent with China's commitments under the Protocol of Accession (the obligation to eliminate export restrictions – duties and quotas) and Annex 6 (the exception that allows conditionally export duties).[219] The complainants argued that the application of these measures raised the prices of raw materials in the international market, whilst China's domestic market would benefit, especially through a sufficient supply of raw materials and lower prices.[220] China, however, justified its export restrictions on some raw materials by relying heavily, *inter alia*, on Article XX(g). It argued that the restricting measures related to 'the conservation of exhaustible natural resources'.[221]

This case involved a variety of issues. However, the analysis will focus on two main issues pertinent to Article XX(g):

(1) firstly, the applicability of Article XX(g) to violations of provisions undertaken in the China Protocol of Accession (WTO-plus commitments);

Related to the Exportation of Various Raw Materials, WT/DS394/R, WT/DS395/R, WT/DS398/R (July 5, 2011), para. 2.1.

[217] The Panel discussed the list of legislative and regulatory measures, see Panel Report, *China – Measures Related to the Exportation of Various Raw Materials*, WT/DS394/R, WT/DS395/R, WT/DS398/R (July 5, 2011) paras 2.3–2.5.

[218] Other WTO members, both developed and developing, have made submissions to the Panel and reserved their third party right to participate in this case. Ibid. paras 5.1–5.2.

[219] The Panel mainly addressed these issues pertinent to the Protocol of Accession: whether China has imposed restrictions through export duties on minerals that were not included in Annex 6, and whether China has imposed export duties on minerals included in the Annex 6, but which were beyond the allowed maximum level in Annex 6.

[220] See Panel Report, *China – Measures Related to the Exportation of Various Raw Materials*, WT/DS394/R, WT/DS395/R, WT/DS398/R (July 5, 2011) paras 3.2–3.3.

[221] China based its defenses on several arguments, including references to Articles XI:2, XX(b) and XX(g) of the GATT. Ibid. para. 3.5.

(2) secondly, the applicability of Article XX(g) to China's measures, which restricted the export of raw materials and violated GATT provisions.

Initially, the Panel found China's measures of imposing export duties to be in violation of Paragraph 11.3 of the Protocol of Accession.[222] The Panel was then required to decide on the first issue: whether GATT exceptions, particularly Article XX, could justify a violation of provisions under the Protocol of Accession.[223] The Panel examined the text and context of Paragraph 11.3, and found that unlike Paragraph 5.1 of the Protocol of Accession, Paragraph 11.3 does not include any reference to Article XX of the GATT. It also found that Paragraph 11.3 does not have any introductory clause that preserves China's right to invoke GATT exceptions.[224] Therefore, based upon the wording and the context of Paragraph 11.3, the Panel concluded that China does not have the right to invoke Article XX(g) as justification for the violations of Paragraph 11.3 of China's Protocol of Accession.[225]

The second issue dealt with the applicability of Article XX(g) to China's measures, which restricted the export of raw materials and violated GATT provisions. The panel found that a series of measures operated collectively (export restrictions imposed on the exportation of particular raw materials) was inconsistent with Article XI:1 of the GATT.[226] The Panel then considered whether these export restrictions were justified pursuant to GATT exceptions, including Article XX(g).[227] Notably, it was admitted between the parties of this dispute that the minerals, that is, raw materials, at issue were considered 'exhaustible natural resources'.[228]

---

[222] WT/DS394/R, WT/DS395/R, WT/DS398/R, para. 7.105.

[223] China claimed that even if its measures were inconsistent with Paragraph 11.3 of its Protocol of Accession, they were justified under Article XX(b) and (g) of the GATT, see para. 7.110 of the Panel report. The counterargument of the complainants was that Article XX is available only for GATT violations or when this article or its justifications have been incorporated through reference into another WTO agreement. According to the complainants, the Protocol of Accession is an integral part of the WTO Agreements. Ibid. para. 7.111.

[224] Ibid. para. 124.

[225] Ibid. paras 7.158–7.159.

[226] Ibid. para. 7.224.

[227] In its analysis, the Panel examined the validity of Article XX(g) according to the two-tiered approach and began by analyzing subsection (g). Ibid. para. 7.359.

[228] Ibid. para. 7.369.

Next, the Panel examined the substantial components of subsection (g). With respect to the term 'related to', the Panel, after referring to the Appellate Body in the *Gasoline* and *Shrimp-Turtle* cases,[229] defined this term as requiring 'a close and genuine relationship of ends and means'.[230] According to this interpretation, it concluded that neither the export quotas nor the export duties referred to the goal of conservation of raw materials.[231] Additionally, the Panel addressed the term 'conservation' with respect to China's sovereignty over its natural resources.[232] The Panel found that although China has sovereignty over its natural resources, once it joined the WTO it was obliged to exercise its right to regulate trade and export of natural resources according to WTO rules.[233] Hence, the fulfillment of sovereignty over natural resources is subject to the WTO rights and obligations.[234] Moreover, in interpreting the requirement of 'made effective in conjunction with restrictions on domestic production or consumption',[235] the Panel recalled the 'even handedness' test.[236] In addition to this test, the Panel required that the purpose of the restricting measures must be to ensure the effectiveness of restrictions on

---

[229] These cases ruled that the measure must be 'primarily aimed at' conservation, and that there should be a 'substantial' and 'close' relationship between the restricting measure and conservation. See the Appellate Body report in the *Gasoline* case, pp. 18–19, and the Appellate Body report in the *Shrimp-Turtle* case, paras 136–141.

[230] See Panel Report, *China – Measures Related to the Exportation of Various Raw Materials*, WT/DS394/R, WT/DS395/R, WT/DS398/R (July 5, 2011) paras 7.370–7.371. This definition was first mentioned by the Appellate Body in the *Shrimp-Turtle* case, but the Panel in *China – Raw Materials* was the one that implemented it and examined the relationship between the measures and the conservation goal according to this definition. See Appellate Body Report, *United States – Import Prohibition of Certain Shrimp and Shrimp Products*, WT/DS58/AB/R (98-3899) (Oct. 12, 1998) para. 136.

[231] See Panel Report, *China – Measures Related to the Exportation of Various Raw Materials*, WT/DS394/R, WT/DS395/R, WT/DS398/R (July 5, 2011) para. 7.418.

[232] Regarding the 'conservation of exhaustible natural resources', China argued that since it has sovereignty over its natural resources, it possesses the power to restrict exports of raw materials, which are finite and non-renewable resources. Ibid. para. 7.356.

[233] Ibid. paras 7.372–7.383.

[234] Ibid. para. 7.382.

[235] Article XX(g).

[236] See Panel Report, *China – Measures Related to the Exportation of Various Raw Materials*, WT/DS394/R, WT/DS395/R, WT/DS398/R (July 5, 2011) at paras 7.402, 7.404, 7.414, 7.462, and 7.464.

domestic production and consumption.[237] Finally, the Panel found that China's measures of restricting the export of raw materials did not satisfy the requirements of subsection (g), thus there was no need to examine the validity of the chapeau of Article XX.[238]

With regard to the issues mentioned above, the Appellate Body approved the Panel's discussion, interpretation, and consequence, except on one point. The Appellate Body upheld the Panel's decision concerning the inapplicability of Article XX(g) to justify a violation of Paragraph 11.3 of China's Protocol of Accession.[239] The Appellate Body found that Paragraph 11.3 does not have any reference to Article XX of the GATT to justify a violation of China's obligation in Paragraph 11.3 (to eliminate the export duties).[240] In discussing that issue the Appellate Body contrasted the wording of Paragraph 11.3 with other provisions from China's Protocol of Accession, which includes textual reference to the GATT exceptions.[241] Therefore, the Appellate Body concluded that the proper

---

[237] Ibid. para. 7.397; see also Karapinar, B. 'Defining the Legal Boundaries of Export Restrictions: a Case Law Analysis' (2012) 15(2) *Journal of International Economic Law* 443 at p. 468.

[238] See Panel Report, *China – Measures Related to the Exportation of Various Raw Materials*, WT/DS394/R, WT/DS395/R, WT/DS398/R (July 5, 2011) paras 7.467–7.469. The Panel found that the measures at issue did not purport to conserve the particular raw materials. It also found an increase in the domestic consumption of these raw materials, a decrease in their domestic prices and a raise in their export prices. Therefore it concluded that the measures did not satisfy the Article XX(g) requirements. See paras 7.429–7.436 of the Panel Report.

[239] See Appellate Body Report, *China – Measures Related to the Exportation of Various Raw Materials*, WT/DS394/AB/R, WT/DS395/AB/R, WT/DS398/AB/R (Feb. 22, 2012), paras 303–306.

[240] See Feld, D.S. & Switzer, S. 'Whither Article XX? Regulatory Autonomy Under Non-GATT Agreements after China – Raw Materials' (2012) 38 *Yale J. Intl. L. Online* 16 (arguing that the Appellate Body in *China – Raw Materials* ruled correctly when it created the presumption that Article XX cannot be applied outside the scope of the GATT, except if the violated provision includes specific reference to Article XX or similar text) at pp. 18 and 30.

[241] The Appellate Body found that the language of Paragraph 11.3 includes express reference to just one Article of the GATT, namely Article VIII, but it does not refer to the exceptions in Article XX. However, other provisions in the Protocol of Accession include specific or broad reference to the GATT provisions or exceptions, such as Paragraphs 5.1, 11.1 and 11.2. See paras 291–293 of the Appellate Body Report. See also the Appellate Body Report, *China – Measures Affecting Trading Rights and Distribution Services for Certain Publications and Audiovisual Entertainment Products*, WT/DS363/AB/R (Dec. 21, 2009) para. 230 (finding that GATT exceptions were applicable in the case of Paragraph 5.1

interpretation of Paragraph 11.3 does not make it possible to invoke the exception, Article XX, to justify China's violation of Paragraph 11.3.[242]

In addition, the Appellate Body upheld the Panel's interpretation and examination of the requirements in subsection (g), except with regard to one issue. The Appellate Body agreed with the Panel that, in order to examine whether China's measures were 'related to' the conservation of China's minerals, there must be 'a close and genuine relationship' between the restricting measure and the goal of conservation of raw materials.[243] Notably, the Appellate Body did not refer to the Panel's discussion of the conflict between sovereignty over natural resources and WTO law. In fact, it agreed with the Panel that China has to exercise its right to regulate trade in natural resources according to its WTO obligations.[244] In spite of approving the Panel's approach and reasoning, the Appellate Body found that the Panel erred in its interpretation of the requirement 'made effective in conjunction with' in subsection (g).[245] The Appellate Body found no additional condition in subsection (g), the

---

of China's Accession Protocol, since this paragraph includes a broad reference to the GATT, stating: 'without prejudice to China's right to regulate trade in a manner consistent with the WTO agreement'. In this case, the Appellate Body concluded that China can rely on Article XX to justify its violation of Paragraph 5.1).

[242] See Appellate Body Report, *China – Measures Related to the Exportation of Various Raw Materials,* WT/DS394/AB/R, WT/DS395/AB/R, WT/DS398/AB/R (Feb. 22, 2012) para. 307. See also Gu, B. 'Applicability of GATT Article XX in China – Raw Materials: A Clash within the WTO Agreement' (2012) *Journal of International Economic Law* 1–25 (criticizing the ruling of the Appellate Body in *China – Raw Materials*, which considered the absence of expressed reference to GATT provisions as a restriction from applying GATT exceptions. The article argues that the Appellate Body failed and erred in its interpretation and ruling, which resulted in 'inappropriateness in treaty interpretation').

[243] See Appellate Body Report, *China – Measures Related to the Exportation of Various Raw Materials*, WT/DS394/AB/R, WT/DS395/AB/R, WT/DS398/AB/R (Feb. 22, 2012) para. 355.

[244] China argued that it enjoys the 'inherent right' to regulate trade in natural resources for conservation and public health purposes. The Appellate Body limited the discussion in China's argument to the scope of Paragraph 11.3 of China's Protocol of Accession. It concluded that, unlike Paragraph 5.1, the text of Paragraph 11.3 excludes the applicability of GATT exceptions (it refers to the right to regulate trade) to justify China's violation of Paragraph 11.3. Ibid. paras 300–304.

[245] The Panel has interpreted this phrase to require that the challenged restricting-measure must ensure the effectiveness of restrictions on domestic production and consumption, Panel Report, *China – Measures Related to the*

way the Panel found, such as to ensure the effectiveness of domestic restriction upon production or consumption. It concluded that a measure can meet this requirement if its restriction imposes 'even-handedness' restrictions on the domestic production or consumption of exhaustible natural resources.[246]

Eventually the Appellate Body confirmed the Panel report and concluded that China's measures restricted the exportation of raw materials and violated its obligations to the WTO in both the Protocol of Accession and GATT rules. Additionally, the Appellate Body found that China's measures were not justified under Article XX(g): firstly, Article XX(g) had not been incorporated in Paragraph 11.3 by obvious reference; secondly, China's measures did not meet the requirements of subsection (g).

This distinctive case reiterates and highlights the consistent refusal by both the GATT and WTO to apply Article XX(g) to protect exhaustible natural resources. Moreover, it contains remarkable implications for trade and natural resources issues, including permanent sovereignty over natural resources as well as the applicability of Article XX(b) and (g) to commitments under the Protocol of Accession.[247] Undoubtedly, this case will impact future negotiations between the WTO and negotiating countries, especially pertaining to the incorporation of expressed references to the GATT rules and exceptions through the provisions of the Protocol of Accession.[248]

Exportation of Various Raw Materials, WT/DS394/R, WT/DS395/R, WT/DS398/R (July 5, 2011) para. 7.397.

[246] See Appellate Body Report, *China – Measures Related to the Exportation of Various Raw Materials*, WT/DS394/AB/R, WT/DS395/AB/R, WT/DS398/AB/R (Feb. 22, 2012) paras 356–361.

[247] This case has direct implications for a WTO dispute that the EU, Japan, and the US launched against China. The complainants in the case argue that China applies export quotas on rare earth materials. In September 2012, the DSB put together a panel to address these complaints, *China – Measures Related to the Exportation of Rare Earths, Tungsten and Molybdenum, Request for Consultations*, WT/DS431, available at http://www.wto.org/english/tratop_e/dispu_e/cases_e/ds431_e.htm. See also Liu, H.-W. & Maughan, J. 'China's Rare Earths Export Quotas: Out of the China – Raw Materials Gate, but Past the WTO's Finish Line?' (2012) *Journal of International Economic Law*, Vol. 15, No. 4, pp. 971–1005.

[248] See Karapinar, B. 'Defining the Legal Boundaries of Export Restrictions: A Case Law Analysis' (2012) 15(2) *Journal of International Economic Law*, 443, at p. 461.

IV. IMPLICATIONS FOR THE CONSERVATION OF OIL AS AN EXHAUSTIBLE NATURAL RESOURCE

This section discusses the implications of the above GATT and WTO rulings for the conservation of oil resources. At this point, there has been little public debate and scholarly work concentrating on issues of trade and oil resources under the WTO, and those that derive from the perspective of trade in energy.[249] However, the GATT and the WTO, through the prominent decisions discussed above, have created the general law, framework and rules that contain potential implications for oil-conserving measures.

Any future DS tribunal that will examine oil-conserving measures will most probably discuss these measures in the light of the above-enumerated GATT and WTO decisions. First, an elementary discussion will address the issue of whether the conserving-measures violate GATT rules or the provisions of the country's Protocol of Accession (WTO-plus commitments). Second, the conserving measures will undergo an elaborate testing under the requirements of subsection (g), that is, the first tier, to find whether such measures aim at the conservation of oil as an exhaustible natural resource. Third, fulfillment of the previous tier will shift the examination of the measures to the second tier, that is, to the chapeau. Aside from the implications above, the GATT and WTO tribunals have not questioned yet the applicability of Article XI:1 to this kind of measure. This would comprise an intrinsic issue to be considered in the context of oil-conserving measures.

---

[249] See *inter alia* a call for new WTO Round in energy, Champion M. & von Reppert-Bismark, J. 'Politics & Economics: EU Trade Chief Poses WTO Rules in Energy Sector' *Wall St. J.*, June 23, 2006, at A6; for a collective request in energy services (submitted to the WTO), see International Forum on Globalization, Collective Request in Energy Services, available at http://www.regjeringen.no/upload/kilde/ud/nyh/2006/0078/ddd/pdfv/282776-energy.pdf (last accessed 2012); for a call for a WTO Agreement pertinent to energy, see Cottier et al. T. 'Energy in WTO Law and Policy' in Cottier T. and Delimatsis P. (eds) *The Prospects of International Trade Regulation: From Fragmentation to Coherence* (Cambridge: Cambridge University Press, 2011) at pp. 211–244; ICTSD *Fostering Low Carbon Growth: The Case for a Sustainable Energy Trade Agreement* (Geneva, Switzerland: ICTSD, 2011) http://ictsd.org/downloads/2011/12/fostering-low-carbon-growth-the-case-for-a-sustainable-energy-trade-agreement 1.pdf; see also Sakmar, S.L. 'Bringing Energy Trade into the WTO: The Historical Context, Current Status and Potential Implications for the Middle East Region' (2008) 18 *Ind. Int'l & Comp. L. Rev.* 89.

A. The Conservation of Oil Resources Under GATT Article XX(g)

1. Violation of GATT or WTO-plus commitments? The applicability of Article XX(g)

Prior to any substantial discussion of the components of Article XX(g), a preliminary examination should be conducted to see whether the measure at issue violates GATT rules or breaches WTO-plus commitments (rooted in the Protocol of Accession). If the first case applies, there will be an automatic applicability of GATT exceptions, including Article XX(g). However, if WTO-plus commitments are involved, then a specific examination is necessary to examine the language of the particular provision at issue within the Protocol of Accession. If the provision's language expressly refers to the application of GATT exceptions, or a similar text, Article XX(g) will apply, subject to meeting all the requirements in this Article. If the particular provision does not contain any reference to the GATT exceptions, the result will be the inapplicability of Article XX(g).[250]

It is worth mentioning that this situation of maintaining rights, such as conserving natural resources by providing an additional text to the Protocol of Accession, is reminiscent of the accession of Mexico to the GATT. Mexico, one of the world's major oil producing and exporting countries, joined the GATT in 1986,[251] and in 1995 became a founding member of the WTO.[252] During its accession to the GATT, Mexico preserved its right to apply certain export restrictions pertinent to the conservation of natural resources in general and energy (namely oil) resources in particular.[253] This was done through paragraph 5 of Mexico's Protocol of Accession to the GATT, which states:

---

250 See Appellate Body Report, *China – Measures Related to the Exportation of Various Raw Materials*, WT/DS394/AB/R, WT/DS395/AB/R, WT/DS398/AB/R (Feb. 22, 2012) paras 303–306. Importantly, according to this case, oil producing-exporting countries that are in the process of accession to the WTO, have made WTO-plus commitments, and are willing to invoke one of the GATT exceptions to regulate their trade in oil, must incorporate express references to GATT exceptions in order to be entitled to the application of these exceptions.

251 See WTO, GATT Signatories, at http://www.wto.org/english/thewto_e/gattmem_e.htm

252 See WTO, Members and Observers, available at http://www.wto.org/english/thewto_e/countries_e/mexico_e.htm

253 See United Nation Conference on Trade and Development, *Trade Agreements, Petroleum and Energy Policies*, UNCTAD/ITCD/TSB/9 (New York and Geneva, 2000) at p. 20, available at http://p166.unctad.org/pluginfile.php/1839/mod_resource/content/0/31oct/itcdtsb9_en.pdf

> Mexico will exercise its sovereignty over natural resources, in accordance with the Political Constitution of Mexico. Mexico may maintain certain export restrictions related to the conservation of natural resources, particularly in the energy sector, on the basis of its social and development needs if those export restrictions are made effective in conjunction with restrictions on domestic production or consumption.

Given the specific reference to Article XX(g) in the various paragraphs of the Protocol of Accession, the case of Mexico provides a good example for the inclusion of paragraphs that maintain the right of the acceding country to conserve its natural resources in general, and oil in particular.[254]

When there is an applicability of Article XX(g), the next step is to analyze the substantial components of Article XX(g). The precise methodology for examining the validity of Article XX(g) follows the 'two-tier' analysis approach:[255] the first tier examines the consistency of the oil-conserving measure with subsection (g); if the measure is found consistent with the elements of subsection (g), then the second tier

---

[254] On the other hand, Venezuela is also an oil producing and exporting country and acceded to the GATT in 1990. However, unlike Mexico, Venezuela did not add to its Protocol of Provisional Application (PPA) or the final report of the Working Party any text to maintain its right to regulate Venezuela's trade in oil resources, such as the right to apply export restriction to oil exports. According to Venezuela, and in the light of Article XX(g), Paragraph 5 of Mexico's Protocol of Accession did not grant additional privilege to Venezuela. Therefore, it did not request the inclusion of any special wording to its PPA or other accession documents. See United Nations Conference on Trade and Development, *Trade Agreements, Petroleum and Energy Policies*, UNCTAD/ITCD/TSB/9 (New York and Geneva, 2000) p. 20, available at http://p166.unctad.org/pluginfile.php/1839/mod_resource/content/0/31oct/itcdtsb9_en.pdf

[255] According to the WTO decisions, the 'two tier' approach is the most used method of analysis when dealing with Article XX(g). However, as is obvious from this Article, other tribunals used different approaches when required to address the applicability of Article XX(g): the 'top down' approach, which commenced with a discussion of the chapeau and then moved to subsection (g). This approach was used in the *Canadian Tuna* case (paras 4.8–4.9), and by the Panel in the *Gasoline* case (para. 6.40); the 'three steps' approach, which focused on three issues: whether the measure fell within the scope of conservation of exhaustible natural resources; whether the measure was 'related to' the conservation of exhaustible natural resources and was 'made effective in conjunction with restrictions on domestic production or consumption'; and whether the measure was compatible with the requirements of the chapeau. This approach was used in the *Tuna-Dolphin II* case (para. 5.12).

follows, which involves examining the consistency of the oil-conserving measure with the components of the chapeau.

2. Subsection (g) – the first tier

As is obvious from the GATT and WTO case law, the elements of Article XX(g) have received diverse treatments in the various decisions of the GATT and WTO tribunals, with additional sub-requirements being imposed along with the basic requirements of Article XX(g). These requirements and sub-requirements will most probably be central to any future analysis of oil-conserving measures under Article XX(g). This section deals with the oil-conserving measure through the expressed requirements in subsection (g), and their sub-requirements, created by the GATT and WTO case law interpretation. For satisfying subsection (g), the measure has to meet three main components: firstly, that it refers to an 'exhaustible natural resource'; secondly, that it relates to 'the conservation of exhaustible natural resources'; and thirdly, that it is 'in conjunction with restrictions on domestic production or consumption'.

Firstly, oil as a natural resource is a finite, depleted and non-renewable resource.[256] It is distributed 'unevenly' worldwide.[257] This natural resource needs to be recognized as an 'exhaustible natural resource'.[258] Notably, oil resources were always considered exhaustible natural resources by both approaches: the traditional approach[259] as well as the

---

256 See Energy Charter Secretariat, *Trade in Energy: WTO Rules Applying under the ECT* (Brussels, 2001) at para. 170, p. 55 (explaining that minerals, including petroleum, are exhaustible natural resources, since they are obviously finite, non-renewable and subject to depletion).

257 See Selivanova, Y. 'The WTO and Energy: WTO Rules and Agreements of Relevance to the Energy Sector' Trade and Sustainable Energy Series, ICTSD International Centre for Trade and Sustainable Development (Geneva, 2007), p. 2, available at http://dspace.cigilibrary.org/jspui/bitstream/123456789/28428/1/The%20WTO%20and%20energy.pdf?1

258 It is apparent from the various significant GATT and WTO decisions that 'exhaustible natural resources' have been interpreted broadly to cover various sorts of natural resources, both living and non-living, see the *Gasoline* case when the Appellate Body considered 'clean air' an exhaustible natural resource, and the *Shrimp-Turtle* case, where the Appellate Body considered the sea turtles exhaustible natural resources.

259 See Charnovitz, S. 'Exploring the Environmental Exceptions in GATT Article XX' (1991) 25 *J. World Trade* 37, 45, 63; Energy Charter Secretariat, *Trade in Energy: WTO Rules Applying under the ECT* (Brussels, 2001) at para. 171, p. 55 (arguing that minerals including petroleum, which are finite and subject to exhaustion, are exhaustible natural resources and concluding that

more recent broad approach.[260] The historical facts beyond drafting the GATT, particularly Article XX(g), point out that when the GATT was drafted, the negotiators intended to include stock resources 'such as metal or oil', which are capable of being depleted, in the phrase 'exhaustible natural resources'.[261] In addition, the GATT Panel in *United States – Taxes on Automobiles*, in analyzing the scope of 'exhaustible natural resources', considered oil and petroleum as exhaustible natural resources.[262] Moreover, the Appellate Body in the *Shrimp-Turtle* case, applied the 'evolutionary' approach to achieve the appropriate interpretation of 'exhaustible natural resources', and concluded that petroleum is an exhaustible natural resource.[263]

Notably, the right of every Member State in the WTO to determine its environmental objectives is a legitimate right according to international trade jurisprudence. The Appellate Body in the *Gasoline* case approved a State's right to protect its exhaustible natural resources as part of its environmental goals. It held that 'WTO Members have a large measure of autonomy to determine their own policies on the environment (including its relationship with trade), their environmental objectives and the environmental legislation they enact and implement'.[264]

Similarly, the Appellate Body in the *Shrimp-Turtle* case recognized the autonomic right of Member States in the WTO to determine their

---

Article XX(g) was negotiated originally to allow the application of export restrictions on such minerals).

260 See GATT Panel Report, *United States – Taxes on Automobiles*, DS31/R (Oct. 11, 1994) unadopted, at para. 5.57; Appellate Body Report, *United States –- Import Prohibition of Certain Shrimp and Shrimp Products*, WT/DS58/AB/R (98-3899) (Oct. 12, 1998) at para. 128.

261 See Charnovitz, S. 'Exploring the Environmental Exceptions in GATT Article XX' (1991) 25 *J. World Trade* 37, 45, 63; Neuling, B. 'The Shrimp-Turtle Case: Implications for Article XX of GATT and the Trade and Environment Debate' (1991) 22 *Loy. L.A. Int'l & Comp. L. Rev.* 1 at p. 15.

262 See Panel Report, *United States – Taxes on Automobiles*, GATT No. DS31/R (Oct. 11, 1994) unadopted, at para. 5.57.

263 See Appellate Body Report, *United States – Import Prohibition of Certain Shrimp and Shrimp Products*, WT/DS58/AB/R (98-3899) (Oct. 12, 1998), para. 128; Energy Charter Secretariat, *Trade in Energy: WTO Rules Applying under the ECT* (Brussels, 2001) at para. 171, p. 55 (explaining that WTO case law, mainly in the *Gasoline* and *Shrimp-Turtle* cases, used the 'evolutionary interpretation' technique to consider living resources, which were threatened with depletion, as exhaustible natural resources).

264 See Appellate Body Report, *United States – Standards for Reformulated and Conventional Gasoline*, WT/DS2/AB/R (Apr. 29, 1996) at p. 30.

environmental objectives and adopt restrictions for environmental purposes including protecting exhaustible natural resources.[265] Additionally, the Appellate Body maintained the possibility for a unilateral conserving measure to satisfy the requirements and be justified under Article XX.[266]

Accordingly, oil is recognized as an exhaustible natural resource.[267] It is subject to over exploitation or exhaustion, therefore every Member State in the WTO, as part of its environmental objectives, has the legitimate right to regulate measures with respect to the conservation of oil resources.[268] Moreover, as stated in the preamble of the Marrakesh Agreement, Member States should seek to pursue 'sustainable development' and 'protect and preserve the environment'.[269] Thus, the conservation of oil as an exhaustible natural resource will likely address this objective.

Secondly, the oil-conserving measure must relate to the conservation of exhaustible natural resources. To apply the protection of subsection (g), it is essential to prove that the measure pursues the goal of conserving exhaustible oil resources. Additionally, the measure needs to be related to the conservation of oil resources, meaning that it is 'primarily aimed at' the conservation of oil resources.[270] Further, the measure must contain a 'substantial' relationship to the conservation of oil as an exhaustible natural resource, in order to meet the 'related to' or 'primarily aimed at' condition.[271] It is not sufficient, however, to show a merely incidental 'substantial relationship' between the measure and the end, but there should be a close and necessary connection between the measure and the

---

265 See Appellate Body Report, *United States – Import Prohibition of Certain Shrimp and Shrimp Products*, WT/DS58/AB/R (98-3899) (Oct. 12, 1998), at para 186, stating: 'As we emphasized in *United States – Gasoline*, WTO Members are free to adopt their own policies aimed at protecting the environment as long as, in so doing, they fulfill their obligations and respect the rights of other Members under the WTO Agreement'.

266 Ibid. para. 121.

267 Ibid. paras 128 and 130 (noting that a natural resources should be interpreted with regard to the prevailing international law at the time of the decision).

268 See Energy Charter Secretariat, *Trade in Energy: WTO Rules Applying under the ECT* (Brussels, 2001) at para. 170, p. 55 (concluding that the original negotiation pertinent to Article XX(g) aimed at allowing the application of export restrictions on minerals).

269 See the Preamble of the Marrakesh Agreement.

270 Ibid. para. 4.6.

271 See Appellate Body Report, *United States – Standards for Reformulated and Conventional Gasoline*, WT/DS2/AB/R (Apr. 29, 1996) at pp. 18–19.

sought conservation goal.[272] Actually, this substantial relationship has to comprise 'a close and genuine relationship of ends and means' between the measure at issue and the purpose of oil conservation.[273]

Thirdly, the oil-conserving measure must be made effective 'in conjunction with restriction on domestic production or consumption'. This requirement is satisfied by the oil-conserving measure if: firstly, the oil-conserving measure is applied 'together with' restrictions on domestic oil production;[274] and secondly, it involves 'even handedness', some restrictions on domestic oil production, but not necessarily 'identical' restrictions.[275] A recent attempt to import another sub-requirement that would change the interpretation of this requirement was rejected by the Appellate Body.[276]

Consequently, an oil-conserving measure that satisfies all the above requirements and sub-requirements, would provisionally be considered consistent with subsection (g), and proceed to the second tier. On the contrary, an oil-conserving measure that does not meet the elements of

---

[272] See Appellate Body Report, *United States – Import Prohibition of Certain Shrimp and Shrimp Products*, WT/DS58/AB/R (98-3899) (Oct. 12, 1998) at paras 138–141.

[273] See paras 7.370–7.371 of the Panel Report and para. 355 of the Appellate Body Report in the *China – Raw Materials* case.

[274] See Appellate Body Report, *United States – Standards for Reformulated and Conventional Gasoline*, WT/DS2/AB/R (Apr. 29, 1996) at p. 21; Appellate Body Report, *China – Measures Related to the Exportation of Various Raw Materials*, WT/DS394/AB/R, WT/DS395/AB/R, WT/DS398/AB/R (Feb. 22, 2012), paras 356–361.

[275] See Appellate Body Report, *United States – Standards for Reformulated and Conventional Gasoline*, WT/DS2/AB/R (Apr. 29, 1996) at p. 21, and Appellate Body Report, *United States – Import Prohibition of Certain Shrimp and Shrimp Products*, WT/DS58/AB/R (98-3899) (Oct. 12, 1998) at paras 143–145.

[276] The Panel in *China – Raw Materials* required that the purpose of the restricting measures must be to ensure the effectiveness of restrictions on domestic production and consumption, Panel Report, *China – Measures Related to the Exportation of Various Raw Materials*, WT/DS394/R, WT/DS395/R, WT/DS398/R (July 5, 2011), para. 7.397. The Appellate Body rejected this interpretation and found no additional condition in subsection (g) to ensure the effectiveness of domestic restriction upon production or consumption. See Appellate Body Report, *China – Measures Related to the Exportation of Various Raw Materials*, WT/DS394/AB/R, WT/DS395/AB/R, WT/DS398/AB/R (Feb. 22, 2012) paras 356–361.

subsection (g) cannot be justified under Article XX, and will therefore fail and receive no further analysis of the chapeau.[277]

3. The chapeau – the second tier

The examination of an oil-conserving measure in the light of the chapeau requires that the application of the measure does not result in either 'arbitrary or unjustifiable discrimination between countries where the same conditions prevail' or 'a disguised restriction on international trade'.[278] Importantly, a country that invokes the justification of an oil-conserving measure under Article XX bears a dual burden of proof: to demonstrate its consistency with subsection (g); and to demonstrate that the chapeau is not violated.[279] This twofold burden of proof thus includes the heavier task of demonstrating consistency with the chapeau's conditions, as opposed to only demonstrating the satisfaction of subsection (g).[280]

According to the analysis of the GATT and WTO decisions, the task of showing that an oil-conserving measure does not constitute 'arbitrary or unjustifiable discrimination' includes:

(1) proving the granting of equal and not different treatment to countries where the same conditions prevail;[281]
(2) pursuing good faith efforts and negotiations to reach international agreement with respect to the application of the measure;[282]
(3) avoiding conducting, in effect, an embargo which is unacceptable in global trade relations;[283] and

---

277 See Appellate Body Report, *United States – Import Prohibition of Certain Shrimp and Shrimp Products*, WT/DS58/AB/R (98-3899) (Oct. 12, 1998) paras 118–119.

278 See the chapeau of Article XX of the GATT.

279 See Appellate Body Report, *United States – Standards for Reformulated and Conventional Gasoline*, WT/DS2/AB/R, (Apr. 29, 1996) at pp. 22–23.

280 Ibid. at pp. 22–23.

281 See Appellate Body Report, *United States – Import Prohibition of Certain Shrimp and Shrimp Products*, WT/DS58/AB/R (98-3899) (Oct. 12, 1998) paras. 172–173.

282 See Appellate Body Report, *United States – Import Prohibition of Certain Shrimp and Shrimp Products: Recourse to Article 21.5 of the DSU by Malaysia*, para 3, WT/DS58/RW (Oct. 22, 2001) para. 122.

283 See Appellate Body Report, *United States – Import Prohibition of Certain Shrimp and Shrimp Products*, WT/DS58/AB/R (98-3899) (Oct. 12, 1998) para. 161.

(4) if a process of certification is involved through the application of the measure, then it should be a clear process which grants due process to the applicants.[284]

These aspects do not constitute all the required elements under the chapeau and they do not comprise a closed list of considerations. By meeting all the elements of both tiers, subsection (g) as well as the chapeau, an oil-conserving measure will qualify under Article XX(g).

4. GATT Article XX(g): narrow application

The obvious consequence of the GATT and WTO decisions is a careful, narrow and conservative approach in invoking the exception of Article XX(g).[285] With the exception of one WTO case,[286] all the decisions involving natural resources and Article XX(g) have consistently rejected the invocation of Article XX(g) to justify different measures, which apparently aimed at conserving exhaustible natural resources. Each decision applied its own analytical approach in reviewing the conserving measure at issue. In spite of upholding some former decisions' interpretations or reasoning by recent tribunals, the clear outcome of all these decisions stresses the lack of a unified and consistent approach in addressing the application of Article XX(g).

Therefore, it appears that the GATT and WTO decisions have implemented various interpretations and analytical approaches to examine the justification of measures under Article XX(g). The outcome is a plethora of requirements and sub-requirements that need to be satisfied. This places clear impediments before any future oil-conserving measure under Article XX(g), and results in a diversity of legal and factual requirements that the measure must meet. As a consequence, a narrow and variable interpretation, complex analysis, and heavy burden of proof will confront any endeavor to utilize Article XX(g) to justify an oil-conserving measure.

---

[284] Ibid. paras 177–188.

[285] See Wirth, D.A. 'International Trade Agreements: Vehicles for Regulatory Reform?' (1997) U. Chi. Legal F. 331 at p. 336 (arguing that both subsections (b) and (g) of Article XX were 'interpreted rather restrictively'); Gaines, S. 'The WTO's Reading of the GATT Article XX Chapeau: A Disguised Restriction on Environmental Measures' (2001) 22 *U. Pa. J. Int'l Econ. L.* 739 at pp. 743–744 (explaining the ineffective applicability of Article XX(g) to environmental measures).

[286] See Appellate Body Report, *United States – Import Prohibition of Certain Shrimp and Shrimp Products: Recourse to Article 21.5 of the DSU by Malaysia*, WT/DS58/RW (Oct. 22, 2001) para. 3.

B. The Scope of Article XI:1 with Regard to Conserving Natural Resources

Admittedly, no legal examination will discuss the applicability of Article XX(g), or any other exception, without finding a provisional violation of one of the GATT rules. If a future measure conserves natural resources such as raw materials, crude oil or metal in the ground, raw timber in forests, or freshwater in lakes, rivers or aquifers, etc., by imposing a limitation or restriction that affects their extraction, then the question arises as to whether it constitutes a violation of the prohibition on quantitative restrictions, in accordance with Article XI:1. Notably, and due to recent challenges, there is a possibility that a WTO tribunal would address the restriction of crude-oil extraction in the light of GATT provisions, particularly Article XI:1.[287] However, no international case law or legislation has yet determined or examined explicitly whether Article XI:1 applies to restricting the extraction of natural resources from their natural state. Nor have they discussed whether natural resources in their natural state constitute 'products'. Article XI:1 includes the rule of 'prohibition on quantitative restriction' pertaining to import or export of products. It dictates:

> No prohibitions or restrictions other than duties, taxes or other charges, whether made effective through quotas, import or export licenses or other measures, shall be instituted or maintained by any contracting party on the importation of any product of the territory of any other contracting party or on the exportation or sale for export of any product destined for the territory of any other contracting party.[288]

Any future WTO tribunal that is expected to examine oil-conserving measures will first address the applicability of Article XI:1 to the case before analyzing the application of Article XX(g) and its components.[289]

---

287 See the Resolution by Representative Peter DeFazio, H.R. Con. Res. 276, 106th Cong. (2000). See also Office of Senator F. Lautenberg, 'Busting Up the Cartel: The WTO Case Against OPEC' (2004) available at http://lautenberg.senate.gov/documents/foreign/OPEC%20Memo.pdf (last accessed 2012).

288 Article XI:1 of the GATT.

289 Notably concerning the type of governmental measure that is covered by Article XI:1, a GATT Panel discussed the interpretation of 'measure' that falls under Article XI:1. The Panel gave the term 'measures' a broad interpretation to include a wide array of governmental measures where their effect constituted *de facto* restrictions on exports and imports, irrespective of the legal status of the

It is obvious that Article XI:1 deals with restrictions on activities of 'importation', 'exportation', or 'sale for export'. It is equally clear that this provision does not deal with the limitation or restriction of 'extraction' activity. Additionally, 'extraction' and other similar activities were not mentioned at all within the text of Article XI:1, either as explicit conditions of the prohibition or as implicit components of the substantial principles of this Article.[290] Therefore, it is obvious that Article XI:1 adheres to the quantitative prohibition of 'importation' or 'exportation' activities without reference to 'extraction' or similar activities.[291]

Moreover, Article XI:1 describes 'exportation' as the shipment of product from one country to another, which comprises a crucial component of the Article's validity. Unlike 'exportation', 'extraction' is conducted in the territory of one country and mostly in the same location, and this activity is not considered a material or even incidental component of Article XI:1.[292] In accordance with the intrinsic disparity and distinction between the prohibited restriction on 'exportation' and the non-prohibited limitation on 'extraction', it is likely that any limitation on the extraction of natural resources in their natural state would not violate Article XI:1.

Furthermore, the proper interpretation of the term 'product' describes 'something that is produced'.[293] In order for raw materials to reach the

---

measure. However, the Panel did not discuss the interpretation of the other components of Article XI:1; see Panel Report, *Japan – Trade in Semiconductors*, L/6309 (May 4, 1988), GATT B.I.S.D. (35th Supp.) (1989) at pp. 152–153.

[290] Article XI:1 of the GATT does not apply to any activity other than exportation, importation or sale for export. Other activities, such as extraction, refining, or production, which relate to the transforming of natural resources into products for commerce, are not part of this provision.

[291] Ibid. See also Broome, S. 'Conflicting Obligations for Oil Exporting Nations? Satisfying Membership Requirements of Both OPEC and The WTO' (2005) 38 *Geo. Wash. Int'l L. Rev.* 409 (2005) at p. 414.

[292] Ibid.

[293] See World Trade Organization (WTO), *World Trade Report 2010: Trade in Natural Resources* (2010) at p. 162, available at http://www.wto.org/english/res_e/booksp_e/anrep_e/world_trade_report10_e.pdf (pointing out the difference between the applicability of WTO law on natural resources that may be traded, such as: 'extracted coal and oil, lumber that has been cut down or marine species that have been caught' and inapplicability of WTO rules on natural resources 'before they are extracted or harvested'); see also Johnson, J.R. *The North American Free Trade Agreement: A Comprehensive Guide* (Canada Law Book, 1994) at pp. 109–110; Broome, S. 'Conflicting Obligations for Oil Exporting Nations? Satisfying Membership Requirements of Both OPEC and The WTO' (2005) 38 *Geo. Wash. Int'l L. Rev.* 409 at p. 416.

status of being a 'product', they have to pass through a production process.[294] This obvious definition refers to various natural resources and raw materials.[295] According to this interpretation of the term 'product', a natural resource could become a 'product' within the meaning of Article XI:1 after being extracted, refined, processed or somehow 'transformed into an article of commerce'.[296] Conversely, a natural resource in its natural state, such as in the ground, that has not been involved in production processes or 'produced' within the literal meaning of the word, does not comprise a 'product' under Article XI:1.[297] As a feasible

---

[294] See Johnson, J.R. *The North American Free Trade Agreement: A Comprehensive Guide* (Canada Law Book, 1994) at pp. 109–110 (explaining that, in order to treat a product as a tradable product, it must be 'extracted, harvested, collected, stored, graded, transported, refined, processed, assembled, packaged, or somehow transformed into an article of commerce … unexploited resources such as oil or gas in the ground or water in lakes, rivers or aquifers are not "products"').

[295] See International Joint Commission, *Protection of the Waters of the Great Lakes: Final Report to the Governments of Canada and the United States* (2000), available at http://www.ijc.org/php/publications/html/finalreport.html. The International Joint Commission, which included members from Canada and the United States, dealt with the issue of Canadian restrictions on the amount of Canadian freshwater that can be exploited for commercial purposes within the definition of tradable 'product'. The Commission observed that 'it is unlikely that water in its natural state (e.g., in a lake, river, or aquifer) is included within the scope of [NAFTA or any of the WTO agreements, including GATT]'. The Commission mentioned that pursuant to signing NAFTA, the three parties of NAFTA issued a joint declaration that 'creates no rights to the natural water resources of any party; that unless water, in any form has entered into commerce and has become a good or product for commerce, it is not covered by any trade agreement, including NAFTA'; see Johnson, J.R. *The North American Free Trade Agreement: A Comprehensive Guide* (Canada Law Book, 1994) at p. 110; see also Brown Weiss, E. et al. (eds) *Water Transfers and International Trade Law, in Fresh Water and International Economic Law* (Oxford: Oxford University Press, 2005) pp. 61, 83.

[296] See World Trade Organization (WTO), *World Trade Report 2010: Trade in Natural Resources* (2010) at p. 166, available at http://www.wto.org/english/res_e/publications_e/wtr10_e.htm; Dufour, S. 'The Legal Impact of the Canada-United States Free Trade Agreement on Canadian Water Exports' (1993) *Les Cahiers de Droit*, Vol. 34, No. 2, pp. 705–762, at pp. 741–742; Johnson, J.R. *The North American Free Trade Agreement: A Comprehensive Guide* (Canada Law Book, 1994) at pp. 109–110.

[297] See Dufour, S. 'The Legal Impact of the Canada-United States Free Trade Agreement on Canadian Water Exports' (1993) *Les Cahiers de Droit*, Vol. 34, No. 2, pp. 705–762 at pp. 741–742.

result, Article XI:1 embraces the term 'product' as a finished product for commerce that is eligible to be subject to exportation and importation. However, a natural resource that is still in its natural state in the ground, lake or forest, etc., does not have the characteristics of a finished product for commerce, and most likely does not constitute a tradable 'product' under Article XI:1.

Consequently, the core of Article XI:1, seemingly, has questionable applicability to the limitation on natural resources. When observing the applicability of Article XI:1 to an oil-restricting measure, the following crucial issues should be addressed: whether the measure is being mandated on crude oil in its natural state, or on oil as a finished product for commerce; whether the measure restricts the activity of exportation of oil products from one country to another, or whether it restricts the extraction or transformation of oil from its natural state to a final product. If the factual findings demonstrate that the measure restricts the extraction of crude oil, then most probably the measure will not be covered by the scope of Article XI:1, and there will be no need to examine the measure in the light of Article XX(g). On the contrary, if the measure restricts the exportation of oil as a product, this would be considered a violation of Article XI:1. The violation of Article XI:1 is a provisional violation, and if the oil-restricting measure satisfies the requirements of one of the GATT exceptions, it could finally be justified. This approach of analysis applies equally to crude oil and metal in the ground, to freshwater in rivers, lakes or aquifers, and to timber in forests.

V. CONCLUSION

It is very clear that the conservation of exhaustible natural resources has been a critical debate and central issue within the GATT and WTO decisions. The conformity of the various environmental measures to the multilateral trade provisions has been examined by several GATT Panels and WTO tribunals. Notably, this examination concentrated on analyzing the legality of the measures in accordance with Article XX(g), and whether the measures were justified under this provision. Further, the various decisions limited the conservation of exhaustible natural resources under Article XX(g), by utilizing different frameworks, benchmarks and complex analytical approaches.

Indeed, there has been no unified and consistent approach in determining whether a measure satisfies the elements of Article XX(g). The examination of Article XX(g) started with distinguishing between a principle applicability in cases involving a violation of GATT rules, versus a questioned applicability in cases dealing with WTO-plus commitments. Where Article XX(g) applied, the analysis was divided in most of the cases into two stages, with the exception of one case (the *Tuna-Dolphin II* case), which was divided into three stages. These two stages are the chapeau and subsection (g). While some tribunals began their discussion with the chapeau, others stressed the need to start the analysis with subsection (g) and turn to the chapeau only after meeting the elements of this subsection. Moreover, the analysis of the two parts of Article XX(g) contained interpretations of the core elements and components of this exception. These core elements were interpreted in various or inconsistent ways, and even though a tribunal may have followed previous decisions in interpreting one of Article XX(g) elements, it added its own contribution to the interpretation of the specific element. The consequence of these multi-approach decisions is that currently there is no single, precise, and fixed pathway towards applying Article XX(g) to conserve exhaustible natural resources.

In any future dispute settlement, the various GATT and WTO decisions will directly influence the conservation of oil as an exhaustible natural resource. The analytical approaches and the inconsistency in the interpretations would demand the satisfaction of many requirements. Additionally, they would place a heavy burden of proof on the party that is interested in invoking Article XX(g). In spite of the apparent narrow approach, any future dispute settlement tribunal that would handle an oil-conserving measure should consider commencing its discussion by examining the applicability of Article XI:1 to the oil-conserving measure. If the tribunal finds that the measure limits the extraction of oil in its natural state, then most probably it will not be recognized as a violation of Article XI:1. However, if it finds that the measure restricts the exportation of oil as a product, this will constitute a provisional violation of Article XI:1, and the validity of the measure will be examined in accordance with GATT exceptions, particularly Article XX(g).

4. Energy and law of the sea: Eastern Mediterranean Basin scenarios

I. INTRODUCTION

Energy is a matter that touches upon almost every aspect of human endeavor in the modern era. It sustains levels of modernity and fuels further industrialization and economic development. Achieving a steady and reliable supply of energy is a principal concern of all States not endowed with sufficient energy resources to meet their energy demands. In short, energy is highly desirable. On the other hand, global energy consumption draws heavily from primary energy resources that are patchily distributed, finite, and highly polluting. The fact that the mainstay of global energy derives from resources that are finite and unequally distributed across the globe is worrying, given that it makes traditional energy resources acutely desirable. In turn, this acute desirability drives competition for access and control over energy resources to such lengths that this competition often escalates into armed conflict with grave humanitarian consequences.

This persistence to mainly draw energy from finite polluting energy resources[1] – particularly hydrocarbons such as oil, gas, and coal – means that discoveries of energy reserves in parts of the globe already marred by political tension and armed conflict could contribute to further regional precariousness. One such region is the Eastern Mediterranean

1 The overwhelming majority of the global primary energy supply continues to derive from hydrocarbons, despite the no longer disputed great environmental cost. In 2009, 80.9% of the 12,150 million tons of oil equivalent (Mtoe) of global primary energy supply came from petroleum, natural gas and coal; a slight decrease from 1973 levels. In 1973 86.6% of the total global primary energy supply of 6,111 Mtoe derived from this unholy trinity. Although the share of coal and gas has increased at the cost of oil within the hydrocarbon mix of primary energy supply over that period, oil continues to be the most dominant primary energy source, e.g. 46% during 1973 and 32.8% during 2009 (source: International Energy Agency, *Key World Energy Statistics Report* (2011) at p. 6).

Basin (EMB),[2] which includes the following entities: Cyprus, Egypt, Greece, Israel, the Palestinian Occupied Territories[3] (namely, in the case of the EMB, the Gaza Strip), Lebanon, Syria, and Turkey. It is often unclear, within a global order that continues to be predicated on the basis of the nation-state, whether energy resource endowments are a blessing or a curse. The fault-lines for conflict have long existed in the EMB. Amongst other things, the 1974 Turkish invasion of the Republic of Cyprus and the lasting occupation of a substantial part of its territory,[4] the 2006 Israeli aggression towards Lebanon,[5] the recent souring of Israeli-Turkish relations (made more evident with the 2010 Israeli

---

[2] The Eastern Mediterranean Basin/Levant Basin Province – over which extend the exclusive economic zones (EEZs) of Israel, Lebanon, Syria, Cyprus, and the Gaza Strip – spans roughly over 83,000 km^2 of territory. The 2010 US Geological Survey estimates it to contain 122 trillion cubic feet of recoverable gas and 1.7 billion barrels of recoverable oil. See World Petroleum Resources Project, 'US Geological Survey Fact Sheet: Assessment of Undiscovered Oil and Gas Reserves of the Levant Basin Province, Eastern Mediterranean', March 2010, available at http://pubs.usgs.gov/fs/2010/3014/pdf/FS10-3014.pdf

[3] Israel and the Palestinian Authority (PA) have concluded an Agreement-in-Principle for energy exploration off the coast of Gaza. The status of a territory under occupation means that there are special conditions on how the territory and its resources are administered. See http://www.mfa.gov.il/MFA/HumanitarianAid/Palestinians/Economic_situation_West_Bank_Gaza_Israeli_measures_PA_Aug_2012.htm for information on Israel–PA relations. It is worth noting that this nexus ought not be seen as one between two ordinary parties, but one which involves, on the one hand, an entity that represents an occupied people – namely, the PA and the Palestinians – and on the other, a fully constituted, albeit with undefined international borders, sovereign State – namely Israel. Incidentally, in terms of the delimitation of the Israeli territorial borders with its neighbors, see D'Amato, A. 'Israel's Borders under International Law', Northwestern University School of Law Public Law and Legal Theory Series No. 06-34, in which D'Amato cogently asserts that, according to how international law currently stands, Israel's lawful borders can never exceed those contemplated in the 1947 UN General Assembly Resolution No. 181, given that international law, and the entire UN system, prohibits the acquisition of territory through conquest.

[4] See Darbouche, H. et al. 'East Mediterranean Gas: What Kind of a Game-Changer?', Oxford Institute of Energy Studies (OIES), December 2012 report (at pp. 7–8) for some background information on this. See also Georgiou, G. 'Cyprus: Economic Consequences of Reunification', *Mediterranean Quarterly* Summer 2009, where it is stated that 40% of the island's territory remains under occupation (at p. 51).

[5] See the following BBC 'Facts and Figures' page on the 2006 Middle East Crisis: http://news.bbc.co.uk/1/hi/world/middle_east/5257128.stm, leading to up to 1,152 civilian fatalities (1,109 in Lebanon, and 43 in Israel), causing the

interception of the Turkish-flagged *Mavi Marmara* aid vessel[6] destined for the Gaza Strip), and the longstanding dispute between Turkey and Greece in relation to the delimitation of their maritime boundaries point towards the political difficulties that could turn the EMB into another Pandora's Box of the early 21st century. This may not be that alarmist an assertion if one considers the enduring financial crisis that has blighted the global economy for the last five years.[7] And in times of scarcity, conflict for control can become an increasingly appealing policy option.

What is more, the region presents competing claims involving a variety of states and matters, including the delimitation of territorial sea, the continental shelf, and of exclusive economic zones (EEZ) in the Aegean Sea and the EMB between Greece and Turkey, EEZ delimitation between Cyprus and Lebanon, Cyprus and Turkey, and between Israel and Lebanon.[8] In addition, the EEZ delimitation agreement between Cyprus and Egypt met with Turkish protest, and the EEZ delimitation agreement between Cyprus and Israel met with Lebanese protest.

The changing geopolitics of the region – including the rise of the AKP[9] in Turkey and its loosening-up of the historic *entente* with Israel, the

destruction of Lebanese infrastructure, and displacing hundreds of thousands on both sides.

[6] See the following BBC FAQ website for details of this incident that had resulted in the deaths of nine people and the wounding of dozens: http://www.bbc.co.uk/news/10203726

[7] The global financial crisis is considered the worst since the Great Depression that followed the 1929 Wall Street Crash. See http://www.reuters.com/article/2009/02/27/idUS193520+27-Feb-2009+BW20090227, where three leading economists assert this.

[8] Nasrallah, the leader of Hezbollah, has publicly alluded to the threat of force against Israel should Israeli EMB exploration in disputed territory take place before the demarcation of their respective EEZs has been agreed with Lebanon. See the Lebanese Army's website news-item http://www.lebarmy.gov.lb/article.asp?ln=en&id=29445 and the following article: 'Nasrallah: Hands Off Our Waters', *The Daily Star*, 27 July 2011, available at http://www.dailystar.com.lb/News/Politics/2011/Jul-27/Nasrallah-Hands-off-our-waters.ashx#axzz2O01cifUP

[9] See Abramowitz, M. & Barkey, H.J. 'Turkey's Transformers' (November/December 2009) *Foreign Affairs*, in which the authors discuss the more 'energetic and confident' diplomacy of Turkey following the rise of the AKP (the Justice and Development Party). In this article, the authors refer to incidents such as the high-level reprimand of Israel by Turkey over the 2008/09 Gaza Massacre.

emergence of a Cyprus-Greece-Israel strategic relationship,[10] the recent Arab Spring events that led to the toppling of the Mubarak regime in Egypt,[11] the on-going humanitarian crisis in Syria,[12] the growing dependence of Greece and Cyprus on extraneous bailouts with neoliberal strings attached[13] – suggest that often there is much more that may come to bear on the resolution of claims and disputes than the applicable norms of particular and general international law.

What is more, EU energy security interests are also implicated, as are US energy sector interests. For instance, EU energy supply diversification is a key element in the EU's energy security policy for the coming decades.[14] In that sense, the sooner maritime delimitation disputes in the EMB region are resolved, the sooner its energy-related mineral wealth could be explored and exploited to the evident benefit of EU energy markets. In relation to the US, it is not only strong US commercial

---

[10] In relation to energy exploration and defense, see the August 2011 http://www.upi.com/Business_News/Energy-Resources/2011/08/26/Cyprus-Israel-move-closer-on-East-Med-gas/UPI-62821314382019. See also the German Marshall Fund of the US Mediterranean Policy Program, East Mediterranean Energy Project, June 2012 Policy Brief article by Jeffrey Mankoff 'Resource Rivalry in the Eastern Mediterranean: The View from Washington' (at p. 2).

[11] Two-fifths of Israeli gas needs came from Egypt through a preferential arrangement. See Daly, J. 'Egyptian-Israeli Natural Gas Contract Casualty of Arab Spring?' *Oilprice.com*, March 13, 2012, at http://oilprice.com/Energy/Natural-Gas/Egyptian-Israeli-Natural-Gas-Contract-Casualty-of-Arab-spring.html

[12] See the US Energy Information Administration's report containing a full analysis of the implications for energy of the popular uprising and conflict in Syria (updated in February 2013) http://www.eia.gov/countries/cab.cfm?fips=SY

[13] See the following BBC News link with Q&A on the Greek economic crisis: http://www.bbc.co.uk/news/business-13798000. See also the following link in relation to the March 2013 Cyprus bank meltdown, which led the Cypriot parliament to reject a set of conditions attached to a bailout plan involving the International Monetary Fund and the EU: http://www.bbc.co.uk/news/world-europe-21817197. Both states are Eurozone members with a common currency – the Euro – and have relinquished monetary sovereignty to a supranational institution of the EU, namely the European Central Bank.

[14] See the Communication from the Commission to the European Parliament, the Council, the European Economic and Social Committee, and the Committee of the Regions, *Energy Roadmap 2050*, Brussels, 15 December 2011 (COM(2011) 885 final), where it is stated that: 'New gas infrastructures for interconnecting the internal market along the North-South axis and linking Europe to new diversified supplies through the Southern Corridor will be vital to foster the creation of well- functioning gas wholesale markets in the whole EU' (at p. 15).

interests that are present in the region,[15] but also complex US geostrategic interests. EU dependence on Russian energy supplies is a concern for the US.[16] The resolution of outstanding maritime delimitation disputes in the EMB region could potentially translate into more regional (to the EU) energy supplies becoming available. A consequential reduction in EU dependence on Russian energy imports would also dovetail with US geostrategic interests.

Whilst there shall be reference to particular disputes in the EMB, this would be for illustrative purposes rather than a full exposition of the disputes themselves,[17] given that the purpose of this chapter is to outline

---

[15] See Darbouche, H. et al., 'East Mediterranean Gas: What Kind of a Game-Changer?' Oxford Institute of Energy Studies (OIES), December 2012 report, where it appears that Noble Energy, a US energy company, has substantial stakes in several exploration projects in the EMB (at p. 5).

[16] See a December 2012 report entitled 'Energy and Security from the Caspian to Europe' by the Foreign Affairs Committee of the US Senate which contains a series of recommendations for the US Government to implement to ensure the energy security of NATO members and their progressive energy independence from Russia. The Committee goes on to call for NATO involvement, given that the decades to come are likely to involve armed conflict over scarcity of energy resources and related disputes (at p. 55) (report available at http://www.foreign.senate.gov/publications/download/energy-and-security-from-the-caspian-to-europe). In relation to EU energy dependence on Russia, during 2009, 33% of EU oil imports and 34% of EU gas imports came from Russia (European Commission, 'Key Figures', Market Observatory for Energy, June 2011 (at p. 7)).

[17] For analyses of the geopolitical context of the region, see amongst others Darbouche, H. et al. 'East Mediterranean Gas: What Kind of a Game-Changer?', Oxford Institute of Energy Studies (OIES), December 2012; 'The Geopolitical Impacts of the Discovery of Natural Gas in the Eastern Mediterranean Basin', Arab Center for Research and Policy Studies, December 2012; Natali, D. 'The East Mediterranean Basin: A New Energy Corridor?', Institute for National Strategic Studies, Centre for Strategic Research (www.dtic.mil/cgi-bin/GetTRDoc?AD=ADA570233), July 2012; and the German Marshall Fund of the US Mediterranean Policy Program, East Mediterranean Energy Project June 2012 Policy Brief article by Jeffrey Mankoff titled: 'Resource Rivalry in the Eastern Mediterranean: The View from Washington'. Furthermore, see the Harvard Kennedy School of Government's The Geopolitics of Energy Project 2nd Annual Case Competition (April 2012) titled 'New Finds of Energy in the Eastern Mediterranean: Cause for Conflict or Cooperation?', which contains a wealth of energy-related data and information about the geopolitical context for the purposes of the School of Government's 2nd Annual Case Competition (NB: the 'Goliath field' cited in this paper is hypothetical for the purposes of this case competition; therefore, all references and data associated with this hypothetical

the principal contours of the normative framework at the interstate level that may come to bear on questions of delimitation of the territorial sea, the continental shelf, and of the EEZ of the coastal States in the EMB region. We focus on these three matters given the fact that the EMB contains no maritime area outside either the territorial sea or the EEZ of coastal States in the region.[18]

Moreover, whilst the United Nations 1982 Convention on the Law of the Sea (UNCLOS)[19] is a sophisticated comprehensive international treaty that has codified and brought into existence many a great norm that has come to bear on legal disputes connected to maritime delimitations, some coastal States such as Israel, Turkey, Syria, and Venezuela are not parties; the first three are regionally significant coastal States in relation to the EMB. Turkey has repeatedly rejected the view that certain UNCLOS norms have crystallized in customary international law, despite asserting in other areas (namely the Black Sea) maritime boundaries reflecting norms equivalent to those contained in UNCLOS.[20] This leaves us with the task of having to identify the norms that apply in cases where UNCLOS norms are not applicable, or where it is not conclusively held that the content of UNCLOS norms is mirrored in customary international law. In other words, we would need to identify the relevant

---

area ought to be ignored). Further analyses about historical events in the region with implications for energy (e.g. resource nationalism, the rise of National Oil Companies (NOCs), and the implications of conflict for energy flows) could be assessed in Fattouh, B. 'How Secure Are Middle East Oil Supplies?' (Chapter 4) in Wenger et al. (eds) *Energy and the Transformation of International Relations: Toward A New Producer-Consumer Framework*, Oxford Institute for Energy Studies (Oxford: Oxford University Press, 2009); and Stevens, P. 'Oil Wars: Resource Nationalism and the Middle East' (Chapter 2) in Andrews-Speed, P. (ed.) *International Competition for Resources: The Role of Law, the State, and of Markets*, Centre for Energy, Petroleum, and Mineral Law and Policy (Dundee: Dundee University Press, 2008).

18 For a full exposition of the relevant provisions on maritime delimitation, see Antunes, Nuno Sergio Marques (2002) 'Towards the Conceptualisation of Maritime Delimitation: Legal and Technical Aspects of a Political Process', doctoral thesis, Durham University (available at Durham E-Theses Online http://etheses.dur.ac.uk/4186).

19 1833 UNTS 3. UNCLOS was finalized on 10 December 1982 in Montego Bay, and came into force on 16 November 1994. One hundred and sixty-five parties (one being the European Union *sui juris*) have ratified UNCLOS. See http://www.un.org/Depts/los/reference_files/chronological_lists_of_ratifications.htm.

20 See Kariotis, T. 'A Greek Exclusive Economic Zone in the Aegean Sea', *Mediterranean Quarterly*, Summer 2007 (at p. 66).

tenets of general international law and/or any particular international law – for example, a particular bilateral treaty or instances of regional custom relevant to the States in question – that may be relevant to questions of the delimitation of their maritime boundary.

II. THE NORMATIVE FRAMEWORK

Oceans cover about 66% of the planet's surface.[21] Maritime trade is no new phenomenon as there was extensive maritime trade between the city-states and empires during ancient times. Yet, for a variety of reasons,[22] the crystallization of an international maritime law that is more widely accepted is a relatively recent phenomenon.[23] What is more, it is one that has not been entirely concluded. This has implications for maritime delimitations in cases where the post-World-War-II international conventions (discussed below) do not apply – that is to say, in disputes in which not all actors are parties to those conventions. In such cases, what is invariably in contention is the nature and precise content of the norms applicable to a maritime boundary delimitation dispute. This is not aided by the fact that State practice that predates the advent of the post-World-War-II international conventions is patchy and inconsistent.

For the purposes of this chapter, we shall not be exploring issues such as the regime and norms applicable to areas of the oceans and seas[24] that lie beyond those maritime areas within the sphere of sovereign control. The maritime areas within the sphere of sovereign control examined below are: the territorial sea; the continental shelf; and the EEZ of littoral States. In relation to the last two, whilst one might be able to trace some

---

[21] Based on the following figures: 510,066,000 km^2 and 335,258,000 km^2 relating, respectively, to the surface area of the planet and of the oceans. See http://www.worldatlas.com/aatlas/infopage/oceans.htm.

[22] An example would be persistent perceptions in the pre-modernity eras that the oceans were vast and infinite, and that, therefore, there was little need to declare *dominium* over them.

[23] See Schrijver, N. *Sovereignty Over Natural Resources: Balancing Rights and Duties* (Cambridge: Cambridge University Press, 1997) pp. 203–207 for a historical account of the notion of territorial sea.

[24] Such areas are international waters/the high seas over which no State or group of States may assert sovereignty; rather, these areas are for common use and their resources – including the mineral resources in the seabed underneath – are deemed the 'common heritage of mankind' (see Article 136 UNCLOS). There are special regimes under the UNCLOS that govern how such resources may be utilized (see Part XI UNCLOS).

conceptual precursors in legal history, they are recent innovations in modern international maritime law. The effect of this is that we are denied an important aid – namely, the historical dimension – in attempting to deduce the relevant customary international law norms that may come to apply to questions involving continental shelf and EEZ delimitation in disputes where the post-World-War-II international conventions are inapplicable.

A. The Territorial Sea

When we refer to territorial sea, we mean the part of the sea adjacent to the territory of a coastal State that is considered for the purposes of international law to form part of the territory over which territorial sovereignty, and its legal corollaries, extend. There was widely divergent State practice before the advent of the post-World-War-II international conventions and their relevant provisions. In fact, some instances of practice – e.g., the *cannon-shot* measure[25] – appear, from a 21st-century standpoint, rather amusing in their simplicity. Other instances are held to less intuitive measures, such as a fixed distance of about four nautical miles (nm) from the baseline of coastal States; however, these two measures seem to have merged into a fixed 3 nm limit for a State's territorial sea.[26]

In 1930 there were attempts within the context of the League of Nations (LN) during the Hague Codification Conference to adopt a mutually acceptable limit. Twenty out of 36 states were in favor of the 3 nm limit, 12 States asserted their territorial sea to extend to up to 6 nm, and the three Scandinavian States continued to claim the Scandinavian league (i.e., 4 nm).[27] These attempts resulted in no agreement.

Following negotiations during the 1958 and 1960 UN Conferences on the Law of the Sea, no fixed territorial sea limit was adopted. States continued to apply different limits. What is more, the 1958 Convention

---

25 Schrijver, N. *Sovereignty Over Natural Resources: Balancing Rights and Duties* (Cambridge: Cambridge University Press, 1997), where Schrijver states that: 'Sovereignty was only recognized for a narrow belt of sea along the coast: more or less three [nautical] miles, as far as one could see or fire a cannon from ashore' (at p. 202). This was a position advocated in 1693 by Van Bynjershoek (as cited by Schrijver).

26 Scandinavian states claimed up to one Scandinavian league (namely 4 nm) as their maritime *dominium*. See Schrijver, N. *Sovereignty Over Natural Resources: Balancing Rights and Duties* (Cambridge: Cambridge University Press, 1997) at p. 203.

27 Ibid. at p. 204.

on the Territorial Sea and Contiguous Zone, whilst affirming the sovereign right of coastal States over their territorial sea, failed to define the precise length.[28] This failure on the part of the international community of States to adopt some definitive framework resulted in further inconsistency. State practice became further divergent. For instance, many Western States would claim a 3 nm territorial sea, whilst Chile, El Salvador, and Panama claimed a 200 nm coastal belt to be their territorial sea. Incidentally, it should be noted that none of the EMB States in question – namely Cyprus, Egypt, Greece, Israel, Lebanon, Turkey, and Syria – are parties to the 1958 Convention.

Schrijver claims that between the 1930 Hague Conference and the time of the first UN Conference on the Law of the Sea (1958), what appeared to be more popular amongst States was a wider limit than the 3 nm that had once been preferred by the majority of the LN States in 1930. He attributes this development to changing priorities. Whilst once it was important to promote open seas and unencumbered avenues of 'transportation and communication', by 1958 priorities had shifted due to the implications of developments in science and technology for resource exploitation, and the need, on the part of States, to secure control over more sources of mineral wealth. This led to coastal States preferring a wider field of control over waters adjacent to their land territories.[29]

The advent of UNCLOS, however, has revolutionized the state of international maritime law in many areas including the territorial sea claims of its parties. UNCLOS stipulates that the Parties that are coastal States may delimitate the boundaries of their territorial sea up to 12 nm[30]

---

[28] 516 UNTS 205, signed in Geneva on 29 April 1958, and came into force on 10 September 1964. Article 1 states that: 'the sovereignty of a state extends, beyond its land territory and its internal waters, to *a belt of sea* adjacent to its coast, described as the territorial sea'. Article 2 states that this sovereignty extends to: 'the air space over the territorial sea *as well as to its bed and subsoil*' (emphasis added). Given the title of Section II of the 1958 Convention, namely 'Limits of the Territorial Sea', one would be forgiven for expecting a figure to be stipulated in this treaty. Rather, no such figure exists in this instrument to guide states in their claims to their territorial sea.

[29] See Schrijver, N. *Sovereignty Over Natural Resources: Balancing Rights and Duties* (Cambridge: Cambridge University Press, 1997) at p. 204.

[30] See Article 3 UNCLOS, which states that the territorial sea proclaimed by a state should not exceed 12 nm.

from their baselines.[31] The majority of State Parties to UNCLOS have proclaimed territorial seas in line with UNCLOS.[32]

UNCLOS also contains provisions that acknowledge that island territories of coastal States – so long as they can 'sustain human habitation or economic life of their own'[33] – are treated equally to mainland coastal land territories. In any event, whether they can or cannot sustain human habitation or economic life of their own, such island formations belonging to a coastal State are entitled to their 12 nm territorial sea limit from their baseline.[34] Moreover, in cases where groups of islands form archipelagic States, Part IV (Articles 46–54) regulates the delimitation of their baselines in an exceptional manner to other coastal States and, in turn, this has implications for the delimitation of their territorial waters, alongside their continental shelves and EEZs.

In addition, UNCLOS recognizes that enclosed or semi-enclosed seas may warrant a special mention. However, this special mention – namely Part IX (Articles 122–123) – does not suggest that the ordinary UNCLOS regime regarding the territorial waters, continental shelf, and EEZ delimitation is displaced by some other regime. Rather, these provisions place a special responsibility on States bordering on such seas to cooperate in relation to the preservation of the marine environment.[35]

In the EMB, Israel, Turkey and Syria are coastal States that are not bound by the strictures of UNCLOS. Rather, the applicable norms are those that are found elsewhere in general and particular international law.

---

31 That is to say, the low – non-tidal – point to which their land territories extend. See UNCLOS Section II 'Limits of Territorial Seas'. Also see Article 14 in relation to baseline determinations. There is International Court of Justice (ICJ) – an Article 7 UN Charter organ of the UN – jurisprudence in relation to baselines. In the 1951 ICJ *Anglo-Norwegian Fisheries case* (ICJ *Reports* (1951)), it was held that the fact that the Norwegian coast was acutely indented warranted the use of a straight line, rather than a highly indented line, to function as the baseline. Admittedly, this is before the advent of UNCLOS, and Article 7 UNCLOS regulates in relation to disputes between UNCLOS parties.

32 By late 1996, out of 151 coastal states that existed at the time, 130 – the overwhelming majority – had proclaimed territorial seas up to the 12 nm limit. Interestingly, at that time, 10 Latin American and African States held to their claims of territorial seas extending up to 200 nm. For both sets of data, see Schrijver, N. *Sovereignty Over Natural Resources: Balancing Rights and Duties* (Cambridge: Cambridge University Press, 1997) at p. 205.

33 See Article 121§3 UNCLOS, which states that: 'Rocks which cannot sustain human habitation or economic life of their own shall have no exclusive economic zone or continental shelf'.

34 See Part VIII Article 121 UNCLOS on the regime of islands.

35 Article 123 UNCLOS.

Greece – although an UNCLOS party – has refrained from declaring its 12 nm territorial sea for diplomatic reasons and adheres to a 6 nm limit. It has not helped that Turkey has asserted that any unilateral declaration on the part of Greece of a 12 nm territorial sea limit would be treated as *casus belli*.[36] Whilst Turkey is not a party to UNCLOS, it is worth noting that UNCLOS Article 15 contemplates delimitation of the territorial sea of opposite or adjacent coastal States on the basis of equidistance line. The 1958 Convention on the Territorial Sea and Contiguous Zone also contemplates this method.[37]

B. The Continental Shelf

A shift took place whereby previously – around the time of the 1930 Hague Conference – coastal States, members of the League of Nations, mostly seemed content with limiting their territorial sea to around the 3 nm mark, mainly to keep the oceans free from transit and communication restrictions.[38] It was a very different world by the time the first UN Conference on the Law of the Sea (1958) was convened. Further industrialization, the decolonization process, and other world events all contributed to coastal States now looking at the maritime areas adjacent to their land territories as further fields of economic exploitation. Technological advancements made the economic exploitation of these areas more feasible. By 1940, the legal notion of the continental shelf – as distinct to its geological peer – began to emerge.

The 1945 Truman Proclamation brought this notion squarely onto the scene.[39] President Truman asserted that: 'the United States regards the

---

[36] See Kariotis, T. 'A Greek Exclusive Economic Zone in the Aegean Sea', *Mediterranean Quarterly:* Summer 2007, p. 63. See also Melakopides, C. 'Implications of the Accession of Cyprus to the European Union', *Mediterranean Quarterly*, Winter 2006 (*passim*). The use or threat of use of force, is, of course, prohibited under the UN Charter (see Article 2§4) unless in line with Chapter VII UN Charter (e.g., under Article 51 for individual and collective self-defense purposes).

[37] See Article 12 of the 1958 Convention on the Territorial Sea and Contiguous Zone.

[38] See Lauterpacht, E. 'Freedom of Transit in International Law' (1958) *Transactions of the Grotius Society,* Vol. 44, Problems of Public and Private International Law, Transactions for the Year 1958–59 pp. 313–356 for a full exposition of the concept of freedom of transit in legal history.

[39] However, an earlier instance may have been the 1942 UK–Venezuela Agreement that equally delimited the common shelf under the Gulf of Paria between Trinidad and Venezuela. See Schrijver, N. *Sovereignty Over Natural*

natural resources of the subsoil and sea bed of the continental shelf beneath the high seas but contiguous to the coasts of the United States as appertaining to the United States, subject to its jurisdiction and control'.[40] What followed was the 1958 Convention on the Continental Shelf[41] that enshrined a coastal State's sovereign right to exploit its continental shelf to the exclusion of other States.[42] However, what the continental shelf consists of in legal terms lacks the precise content it has in geological terms. The 1958 Convention defines the continental shelf as the seabed and subsoil part of the underwater area that is adjacent to a State's territorial waters up to a depth of 200 meters or beyond that limit if it is possible to access and exploit the natural resources present.[43] One may identify how this imprecise definition lent itself to controversy: by making the delimitation of the continental shelf open-ended to the extent that a maritime area was accessible for exploitation, coastal States, and their extractive and other relevant industries, would push to extend their

---

Resources: Balancing Rights and Duties (Cambridge: Cambridge University Press, 1997) at p. 208.

[40] See the Truman Proclamation of 28 September 1945, available at http://www.presidency.ucsb.edu/ws/index.php?pid=12332

[41] 499 UNTS 311, signed in Geneva on 29 April 1958 and came into force on 10 June 1964. As of March 2013, there were 43 signatories and 58 parties to this convention.

[42] More specifically, see the language of Article 2 of the 1958 Continental Shelf Convention, which states that: '1. The coastal State exercises over the continental shelf *sovereign rights* for the purpose of exploring it and exploiting its natural resources. 2. The rights referred to in paragraph 1 of this article are *exclusive* in the sense that if the coastal State does not explore the continental shelf or exploit its natural resources, *no one may undertake these activities, or make a claim to the continental shelf, without the express consent of the coastal State*. 3. The rights of the coastal State over the continental shelf do not depend on occupation, effective or notional, or on any express proclamation. 4. The natural resources referred to in these articles consist of the mineral and other non-living resources of the seabed and subsoil together with living organisms belonging to sedentary species, that is to say, organisms which, at the harvestable stage, either are immobile on or under the seabed or are unable to move except in constant physical contact with the seabed or the subsoil' (emphasis added). What is more, in the *North Sea Continental Shelf Case* (1969) (*ICJ Reports (*1969)), the ICJ asserted the rights of coastal States to their continental shelf. The ICJ referred to this right to be *ispo facto*, *ab initio*, and inherent, flowing from the coastal State's sovereignty over the land adjacent to the maritime area in question (at p. 122).

[43] Article 1 of the 1958 Continental Shelf Convention.

sovereign control over wider maritime areas to the degree that technological developments made possible.[44]

The advent of UNCLOS has also had significant implications for the legal notion of continental shelf. More specifically, Part VI UNCLOS (Articles 76–85), whilst encapsulating the provisions of the 1958 Continental Shelf Convention, expressly refers to limits of the continental shelf of coastal States up to a possible 350 nm in certain cases where the seabed formation is indeed a natural prolongation of the land territory.[45] That said, even in such cases in which a coastal State lacks a natural prolongation of its land territory, it is possible to claim a continental shelf area up to 200 nm from its baseline.[46]

The implications for the EMB region are the following: Turkey is a party to neither the 1958 Convention on the Continental Shelf nor to UNCLOS; Israel is a party to the former but not the latter; and Cyprus, Greece, Lebanon, and Egypt are parties to both agreements. The continental shelves of Greece and Turkey remain in dispute and therefore not definitely delineated.[47] This is a longstanding matter that makes the relationship between these two States particularly mercurial. Turkey recently issued exploration licenses in parts of the Aegean Sea claimed by Greece as its continental shelf that provoked a protest to the UN on the part of Greece.[48] More than three decades ago, before the advent of UNCLOS, Greece had sought recourse to the International Court of

---

[44] It is interesting to note that, out of the EMB coastal States in scope, only Cyprus, Greece, Israel, and Lebanon are parties to the 1958 Continental Shelf Convention (Egypt, Turkey, and Syria are not).

[45] See Article 76.5 & 6 UNCLOS.

[46] See Article 76 UNCLOS, which states that: '1. The continental shelf of a coastal State comprises the seabed and subsoil of the submarine areas that extend beyond its territorial sea *throughout the natural prolongation of its land territory to the outer edge of the continental margin, or to a distance of 200 nautical miles from the baselines from which the breadth of the territorial sea is measured where the outer edge of the continental margin does not extend up to that distance*' (emphasis added).

[47] See Kariotis, T., 'Hydrocarbons and the Law of the Sea', *Mediterranean Quarterly*, Spring 2011; and Kariotis, T. 'A Greek Exclusive Economic Zone in the Aegean Sea', *Mediterranean Quarterly*, Summer 2007, where it is stated (*passim*) that Greece's continental shelf has yet to be declared.

[48] See the following news item on the Greek Ministry of Foreign Affairs' (MFA) website, which states that on 20 February 2013, the Greek Minister of Foreign Affairs, Dimitris Avramopoulos, instructed for a *note verbale* to be communicated to the UN. In this announcement, the MFA refers to the maritime areas at issue pertaining to the Greek continental shelf'. See http://www.mfa.gr/

Justice (ICJ) for a determination on its continental shelf. However, that case foundered on jurisdictional grounds[49] and its substantive aspects were never examined by the ICJ.[50]

Although Turkey is party to neither international agreement, it is worth mentioning how delimitations of continental shelves between parties with maritime boundaries are contemplated by these agreements. The 1958 Continental Shelf Convention, in its Article 6, stipulates that this be done on the equidistance line basis. For its part, UNCLOS Article 83 stipulates no substantive basis for the delimitation of the continental shelf between coastal States *per se* with opposite or adjacent coasts other than to set out, at some length, the delimitation procedures, placing much emphasis on agreement.[51] Failing that, UNCLOS holds that the matter should be handled through processes under Part XV (Articles 279–299) of UNCLOS, which promotes collaborative approaches to dispute resolution before mentioning the option of taking the matter to a forum such as the International Tribunal on the Law of the Sea (ITLOS), the ICJ or an arbitration panel for a binding resolution.

C. The Exclusive Economic Zone (EEZ)

The 1930 Hague Conference and the first UN Conference on the Law of the Sea failed to result in fixed widths for the territorial seas of coastal States. States continued to claim disparate spans of the sea adjacent to

---

en/current-affairs/news-announcements/foreign-ministry-announcement-regarding-the-sending-of-note-verbale-to-the-united-nations-on-the-safeguarding-of-greeces-sovereign-rights-on-the-continental-shelf.html. This was met soon afterwards with a *note verbale* on the part of the Turkish government. See news-item: http://www.ekathimerini.com/4dcgi/_w_articles_wsite1_1_13/03/2013_487564.

49 *Aegean Sea Continental Shelf Case*, 1978 (*ICJ Reports* 1978). Judgment of 19 December 1978 on jurisdiction.

50 Turkey officially refers to the ICJ's rejection of Greece's petition on jurisdictional grounds to be a rejection of Greece's 'contentions and claims'. See the information available on the Turkish Ministry of Foreign Affairs website: http://www.mfa.gov.tr/the-delimitation-of-the-aegean-continental-shelf.en.mfa.

51 The wording of Article 83.1 & 2 UNCLOS: '1. The delimitation of the continental shelf between States with opposite or adjacent coasts *shall be effected by agreement* on the basis of international law, as referred to in Article 38 of the Statute of the International Court of Justice, in order to achieve an equitable solution. 2. If no agreement can be reached within a reasonable period of time, the States concerned shall resort to *the procedures provided for in Part XV*' (emphasis added).

their land territories as their territorial sea. Moreover, States further claimed an area of sea beyond their territorial sea to amount to a zone in which they had exclusive rights to conserve and harvest fishery resources. In 1958, Iceland declared a 12 nm exclusive fishery zone, and other States appear to have espoused this practice of asserting a claim over a stretch of sea that was adjacent to their territorial sea – in other words, a stretch of sea that was beyond the limit of their territorial sea, whatever the stretch of their territorial sea had been at the time.[52] In 1974, the ICJ confirmed the 12 nm exclusive fishery zone to reflect customary law. However, in its judgment, it described this zone as being up to a maximum of 12 nm from the baseline of coastal States.[53] In that sense, a State that was claiming, say, X nm as its territorial sea and then a further 12 nm as its exclusive fishery zone would have been claiming X nm in excess of what customary law would have sanctioned.

The advent of UNCLOS revolutionized practice in relation to zones beyond the territorial sea. This concept was called exclusive economic zone (EEZ).[54] Article 57 makes clear that the EEZ is 'an area beyond and adjacent to the territorial sea … [which] shall not extend beyond 200 nm from the baselines from which the breadth of the territorial sea is measured'. Island territories, not just mainland territories, of a coastal State are afforded an EEZ.[55] Article 56 spells out what this entitlement contains: an EEZ entails the sovereign right of a coastal State to exploit to the exclusion of others the resources – including energy resources – of the waters, seabed and subsoil of its EEZ, and to use the currents, winds, and waters for the production of energy to the exclusion of others.

---

[52] Let us be reminded that by 1974 – that is to say before the advent of UNCLOS – coastal States, for the most part, claimed a territorial sea of up to 3 nm.

[53] See the *Fisheries Jurisdiction Cases* (merit) (Germany v Iceland) (*ICJ Reports* (1974)) (at p. 192).

[54] See Part V (Articles 55–75) UNCLOS. Article 57 UNCLOS defines EEZ as 'an area beyond and adjacent to the territorial sea … [which] shall not extend beyond 200 nm from the baselines from which the breadth of the territorial sea is measured'.

[55] But, again, as discussed above, according to Part VIII (Regime for Islands) Article 121§3: 'Rocks which cannot sustain human habitation or economic life *of their own shall have no exclusive economic zone* or continental shelf' (emphasis added).

As we have pointed out, Israel, Turkey, and Syria are the only EMB coastal States that are not parties to UNCLOS.[56] In that respect, given the novelty of the EEZ, in the absence of any specific, or otherwise applicable, norms in bilateral or regional agreements that involve these States, to deduce what may be the customary law norms on delimiting these maritime boundaries becomes a fraught affair, not least because it is bereft of a historical dimension from which to draw. That said, there is ICJ jurisprudence that supports the view that modern international maritime law has moved to the extent that EEZ norms along the lines of

---

[56] The Palestinian Occupied Territories and the part of northern Cyprus that has been outside the Republic of Cyprus's effective control and under Turkish occupation since 1974 (also known as the self-proclaimed 'Turkish Republic of Northern Cyprus') are not recognized by the international community to be *de jure* States for the purposes of the UN. Also, for the purposes of this chapter, which is mainly concerned with delineating sovereign rights in the EMB, those two administrative entities have been kept outside the scope of this chapter. That said, setting aside the imperialist realities for both those territories and their diplomatic and legal consequences, we affirm that the peoples of these territories *ought to be entitled* to equitable shares of the wealth that resources in waters adjacent to their lands may yield. The same goes for the populations of the other EMB coastal states. Sovereignty over such resources should be popular and not accrue to economic elites. In both territories in question (Palestinian and North Cyprus), the living standards are substantially below the global median level, not least because of the economic consequences of occupation and isolation, whatever their particular circumstances may be. See the US Central Intelligence Agency (CIA) Factbook entry for Cyprus (containing information for the occupied territories) https://www.cia.gov/library/publications/the-world-factbook/geos/cy.html and for Israel (containing information for the Palestinian territories under its occupation) https://www.cia.gov/library/publications/the-world-factbook/geos/is.html. For economic indicators of the economy administered by the Turkish Cypriot administration, see https://www.cia.gov/library/publications/the-world-factbook/geos/cy.html#Econ (scroll down to the relevant section). For indicators in relation to the Occupied Palestinian Territories, see https://www.cia.gov/library/publications/the-world-factbook/geos/we.html#Econ in relation to the West Bank and https://www.cia.gov/library/publications/the-world-factbook/geos/gz.html#Econ in relation to the Gaza Strip. For illustrative purposes, *per capita* figures for GDP, depending on where one finds oneself, are: for Turkish Cypriots USD 11,700 (2007 estimate), whilst for the Republic of Cyprus citizens this is USD 26,900 (2012 estimate); and for Palestinians in the Occupied Territories USD 2,900 (2008 estimate), whilst for their Israeli peers *per capita* GDP is USD 32,200 (2012 estimate) (NB: data sourced from the particular entries at the US CIA Factbook).

UNCLOS have come to exist in customary international law.[57] See Figure 4.1 for an idea of how the EMB would look were all concerned coastal States to delimit their EEZs on the basis of UNCLOS norms.

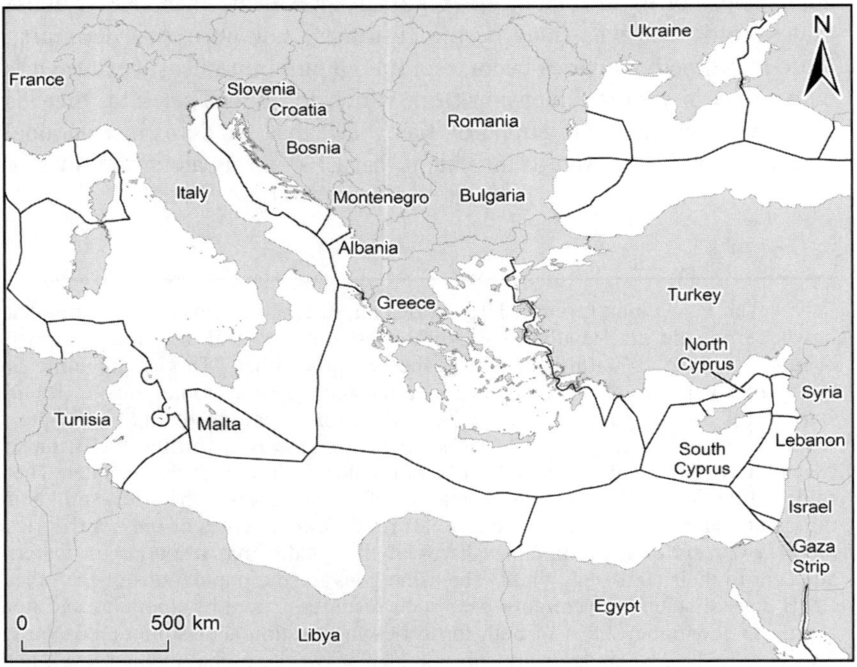

Source: *Sea Around Us*, http://www.seaaroundus.org

Figure 4.1 Putative EEZ delimitation in the EMB under UNCLOS

We include Table 4.1 to help visualize the relationship between the international agreements in place and their relation to coastal States in the EMB region.

[57] See the dicta in the ICJ *Libya v Tunisia 1985 Case* (on the delimitation of the continental shelf) (at para. 34, p. 24). See also the *1982 Libya v Tunisia Case* (again on the continental shelf) (at para. 100, p. 60). A more recent case is the *1993 Denmark v Norway Case* (at paras 47–48, p. 25).

Table 4.1 List of international agreements in place in the EMB region

EMB States	International legal agreements		
	1958 Convention on the Territorial Sea and Contiguous Zone	1958 Convention on the Continental Shelf	1982 Convention on the Law of the Sea
Cyprus	No	Yes	Yes
Egypt	No	No	Yes
Greece	No	Yes	Yes
Lebanon	No	Yes	Yes
Israel	Yes	Yes	No
Syria	No	No	No
Turkey	No	No	No

III. THE PRINCIPAL LEGAL IMPLICATIONS FOR EMB COASTAL STATES

Assessing the interstate legal aspects of the pending delimitations of maritime boundaries in the EMB requires a closer focus on the particular nexus between the States involved. In this respect, this section examines the Cyprus–Turkey nexus, the Greece–Turkey nexus, as well as the Lebanon–Israel nexus.

A. The Cyprus–Turkey Nexus

Whilst Cyprus may draw on UNCLOS to assert its EEZ and continental shelf claims in the region – and whilst it would be unlikely for this to be opposed by fellow EMB peers that are UNCLOS parties (namely Egypt, Lebanon, and Greece), or by Israel, which, although not party to UNCLOS, has agreed to delimitate its EEZ with Cyprus[58] – this becomes a less straightforward affair where it concerns Turkey. Not only because Turkey is not a party to the treaties discussed, but also for the following reasons:

[58] Agreement between the Government of the State of Israel and the Government of the Republic of Cyprus on the Delimitation of the Exclusive Economic Zone, signed in Nicosia on 17 December 2010 (entry into force on 25 February 2011).

- Cyprus became independent from British rule in 1960 – therefore before the 1958 Conventions[59] entered into force – and its sovereign existence is founded on the quadrilateral international agreement to which the United Kingdom (being the sovereign State that relinquishes *dominium* over its colonial possession), Cyprus, Greece, and Turkey are parties;[60] and
- Turkey asserts patronage over the Turkish-Cypriot communities in the northern part of the island of Cyprus occupied since 1974.

In that respect, the delimitation of maritime boundaries between Cyprus and Turkey cannot be lastingly and meaningfully concluded if conducted in isolation from the situation of (what is for the purposes of international law) the illegal Turkish occupation of the northern territory of the island of Cyprus.[61]

According to UN records, Turkey's practice in relation to its territorial waters is twofold: 12 nm in the Black Sea and 6 nm in the Aegean Sea. What is more, Turkey delimits its EEZ in the Black Sea to 200 nm – no delimitation of its EEZ in the Aegean Sea appears officially recorded.[62] Cyprus, for its part, asserts its claims to the extent possible under UNCLOS – that is, it delimits its territorial sea to 12 nm, its EEZ to 200 nm, and its continental shelf to the maximum limit that exploitability is possible.[63] Turkey's maritime delimitation with Bulgaria, Romania, and what had been the Soviet Union appears to be in line with principles

---

[59] Namely the 1958 Convention on the Territorial Sea and Contiguous Zone and the 1958 Convention on the Continental Shelf.

[60] See the Treaty between the United Kingdom of Great Britain and Northern Ireland, the Hellenic Republic, and the Republic of Turkey, and the Republic of Cyprus concerning the Establishment of the Republic of Cyprus of 16 August 1960. Section 1 of this agreement restricts territorial sea claims on the part of Cyprus to those in compliance with its contents. The agreement neither refers to EEZ – which, naturally, is unsurprising given that EEZ is an UNCLOS concept that had yet to appear – nor to the continental shelf.

[61] See, amongst others, Macdonald, R. 'International Law and the Conflict in Cyprus', *Canadian Yearbook of International Law: 1981* (London, Ontario: Queens University, 1981), 15.

[62] See the following UN Maritime Claims record (NB: search document for 'Turkey') http://www.un.org/Depts/los/LEGISLATIONANDTREATIES/PDFFILES/table_summary_of_claims.pdf.

[63] See the following UN Maritime Claims record (NB: search document for 'Cyprus'). http://www.un.org/Depts/los/LEGISLATIONANDTREATIES/PDFFILES/table_summary_of_claims.pdf.

as contained in UNCLOS.[64] Cyprus has delimited its EEZ with Egypt[65] and Israel.[66] Lebanon and Turkey have registered their objections to these bilaterals. Turkey, for its part, objects to the competence of the government of Cyprus to negotiate with Egypt a matter that affects its interests and the interests of the Turkish-Cypriot population it purports to defend within the international order. Lebanon, for its part, considers that no delimitation that involves maritime boundaries disputed between itself and Israel can be the subject of another bilateral.[67] Greece has supported Cyprus against the Turkish objection to Cyprus's EEZ delimitation agreement with Egypt.[68]

---

[64] See Kariotis, T. 'Hydrocarbons and the Law of the Sea', *Mediterranean Quarterly*, Spring 2011, p. 55. In that sense, the delimitation of Turkey's EEZ was entirely in line with UNCLOS (particularly Article 74 UNCLOS) in that it was based on agreement between the parties concerned.

[65] See Agreement between the Republic of Cyprus and the Arab Republic of Egypt on the Delimitation of the Exclusive Economic Zone of 17 February 2003. Article 1(a) states that: 'The delimitation of the exclusive economic zone between the two Parties is effected by the median line of which every point is equidistant from the nearest point on the baseline of the two Parties'. Note Turkey's declaration/objection in relation to the subject matter of this bilateral to which it is not a party at the following link: http://www.un.org/Depts/los/LEGISLATIONANDTREATIES/STATEFILES/CYP.htm

[66] Agreement between the Government of the State of Israel and the Government of the Republic of Cyprus on the Delimitation of the Exclusive Economic Zone, signed in Nicosia on 17 December 2010 (entry into force on 25 February 2011).

[67] For both these objections, see http://www.un.org/Depts/los/LEGISLATIONANDTREATIES/STATEFILES/CYP.htm for further information. Turkey objects to the delimitation as it considers that its rights to its continental shelf and EEZ are infringed upon. See the Law of the Sea Bulletin No. 54 (at p. 127), where it is stated that: 'It is the considered opinion of the Republic of Turkey that the delimitation of the EEZ and the continental shelf beyond the western parts of the 1ongitude 32°16'18″ should be effected by agreement between the related states at the region based on the principle of equity'. See http://www.un.org/Depts/los/doalos_publications/LOSBulletins/bulletinpdf/bulletin54e.pdf. Turkey also raises the issue of legitimacy on the part of the government of Cyprus to conclude such agreements. In Law of the Sea Bulletin No. 59, Turkey states in a separate 2005 *note verbale* that it 'wishes to reiterate that there is no single authority which in law or in fact is competent to represent jointly the Turkish Cypriots and the Greek Cypriots, consequently Cyprus as a whole'. See http://www.un.org/Depts/los/doalos_publications/LOSBulletins/bulletinpdf/bulletin59e.pdf.

[68] See the *note verbale* by the Greek government to the UN, in which it opposes the Turkish objection and asserts that the delimitation between coastal

B. The Greece–Turkey Nexus

The chronic impasse in relation to maritime boundary delimitation between Greece and Turkey is as old as the hills.[69] According to UN records of maritime claims, there is only a claim to a territorial sea of up to 6 nm from both States in relation to the Aegean Sea and a 12 nm Turkish claim to its territorial sea in the Black Sea. What is more, no EEZ is registered on the part of Greece, whilst Turkey asserts a 200 nm EEZ in the Black Sea. Greece, however, appears to register a continental shelf of up to 200 meters depth or to the extent that the maritime area is exploitable.[70]

The situation between these neighboring coastal States is not made any easier with Turkey disputing the sovereignty of Greece over islets[71] in the

---

states opposite or neighboring states ought to be in line with the equidistance principle according to the strictures of international law and not in accordance to that proposed by Turkey. See Law of the Sea Bulletin No. 57 (at p. 129): – http://www.un.org/Depts/los/doalos_publications/LOSBulletins/bulletinpdf/bulletin57e.pdf.

[69] For a rundown of Greek-Turkish diplomatic relations from the Greek State perspective, see the following link: http://www.mfa.gr/en/issues-of-greek-turkish-relations/. Equally, the official position of the Turkish State on the Aegean Sea dispute is set out at the following link: http://www.mfa.gov.tr/sub.en.mfa?deb1dc4c-926f-45bd-9a7c-27b45654c0e4. For a third-party account of the matters at issue, see the International Crisis Group's, July 2011*Turkey and Greece: Time to Settle the Aegean Dispute*, Policy Briefing (Europe Briefing No. 64), available at http://www.crisisgroup.org/~/media/Files/europe/turkey-cyprus/turkey/B64-%20Turkey%20and%20Greece-%20Time%20to%20Settle%20the%20Aegean%20Dispute.pdf

[70] See the following UN Maritime Claims record (NB: search the document for 'Greece' and for 'Turkey' for their respective claims in the region): http://www.un.org/Depts/los/LEGISLATIONANDTREATIES/PDFFILES/table_summary_of_claims.pdf (NB: this table-summary of claims is, according to the *caveat* that the UN attaches to it, an unofficial enumeration of the respective claims that does not amount to an official endorsement on the part of the UN).

[71] See the following statement on the webpage of the Turkish MFA, which asserts that: 'There are numerous small islets and rocks in the Aegean ownership of which is not determined by international treaties'. See http://www.mfa.gov.tr/background-note-on-aegean-dispute.en.mfa. See also the International Crisis Group's, July 2011*Turkey and Greece: Time to Settle the Aegean Dispute*, Policy Briefing (Europe Briefing No. 64), which refers to the 'grey zones' in the Aegean Sea over which Turkey disputes Greek sovereignty. Available at http://www.crisisgroup.org/~/media/Files/europe/turkey-cyprus/turkey/B64-%20Turkey%20and%20Greece-%20Time%20to%20Settle%20the%20Aegean%20Dispute.pdf

Aegean Sea, in contravention to the 1923 Lausanne Peace Treaty.[72] The implications are that, by opposing Greek territorial sea limits around those islets, Turkey restricts Greek control over maritime areas that Turkey, for its own part, consequently claims become international waters.[73] Whilst Greece is a party to UNCLOS and the 1958 Convention on the Continental Shelf, Turkey is not. Turkey has repeatedly objected to the application of UNCLOS norms to the Aegean. Turkey asserts a 6 nm territorial sea in the Aegean Sea and a 12 nm in the Black Sea. Greece has yet to declare its continental shelf or EEZ, whilst Turkey has declared a 200 nm EEZ in the Black Sea. Turkey insists that the Aegean Sea is exceptional and so delimitation ought to be conducted on grounds mutually acceptable to the coastal States affected – that is, itself and Greece – on the basis of equity. Greece insists that its delimitation ought to be conducted in accordance to international law. It has refrained from declaring a 12 nm territorial sea limit.[74]

For any coastal State to assert an EEZ outside the context of UNCLOS is difficult, given that the EEZ is an UNCLOS concept. To be sure, during the pre-UNCLOS era, States asserted exclusive fishery zones in maritime areas beyond their territorial sea limits. As was endorsed by the ICJ in 1974, the view is that an exclusive fishing zone of up to 12 nm from the baselines of coastal States had at the time become customary law.[75] Regarding the Greece–Turkey nexus, there is little particular international law on delimitation, other than the 1923 Lausanne Treaty.

Turkey, however, is a party to bilaterals concerned with maritime delimitation with Bulgaria, Georgia, the Russian Federation, and

---

[72] The 1923 Lausanne Treaty (the 1923 Treaty of Peace with Turkey signed at Lausanne on 24 July 1923), which was forced on Turkey by the then British Empire, France, Italy, Japan, Greece, Romania, and the then Serb-Croat-Slovene State, expressly provides that all islands and islets within 3 nm from the coast of the Anatolian peninsula (see Article 6) – alongside the islands of Imbros and Tenedos, and the Rabbit Islands, belong to Turkey (see Article 12), and that Greece acquires sovereignty over all other islands in the Eastern Mediterranean and Aegean Sea, with the exception of those in the Aegean Sea under Italian control (see Articles 12–15).

[73] See the content of the following webpage of the Turkish MFA for an exposition of the Turkish position http://www.mfa.gov.tr/background-note-on-aegean-dispute.en.mfa

[74] For fuller analyses on the putative reasons behind Greek hesitations, see Kariotis, T. 'A Greek Exclusive Economic Zone in the Aegean Sea', *Mediterranean Quarterly*, Summer 2007.

[75] *Fisheries Jurisdiction cases* (merit) (*Germany v. Iceland*) (*ICJ Reports* (1974)).

Ukraine, and a party to multilaterals concerning the establishment of Cyprus, with Cyprus, Greece, and the United Kingdom.[76] Turkey has sought to present the Aegean Sea to be a *sui generis* case within the context of the UN Conferences on the Law of the Sea (leading to the adoption of UNCLOS), though this was successfully opposed by Greece.[77] In sum, were Greece to claim the optimum under UNCLOS for its territorial sea, save for areas where Greece must limit its territorial sea according to the equidistance principle,[78] much of the Aegean Sea would be subject to the 12 nm territorial sea limit, including from the baseline of its mainland, its islands, and its uninhabited rocks (see Figure 4.2).

Were Greece to claim its EEZ from the baselines of its mainland and island territories,[79] there would be very little, if any, maritime territory to delimit with Turkey. We say this given the size of the Aegean Sea and the fact that much of the maritime area would be within the 12 nm territorial sea limits of Greece, were Greece to claim a 12 nm territorial sea limit from all the baselines of all its mainland and island territories.

Finally, it is worth noting that the European Council, at its 1999 Helsinki Summit, reaffirmed the need for EU candidates to resolve their outstanding border disputes with EU members peacefully and, failing resolution, to submit their disputes to the ICJ.[80]

C. The Lebanon–Israel Nexus

In the last few years, large energy reserves, such as gas and oil, have been discovered in the Eastern Mediterranean Sea, particularly in the Levant Basin province (see Figure 4.3), which stretches from the Jordan

---

[76] See the following webpage for a run-down of the relevant domestic law provisions and treaties in connection to Turkey's maritime delimitation: http://www.un.org/Depts/los/LEGISLATIONANDTREATIES/STATEFILES/TUR.htm. For a run-down of international treaties concerned with maritime delimitation to which Greece is a party, see the following: http://www.un.org/Depts/los/LEGISLATIONANDTREATIES/STATEFILES/GRC.htm.

[77] See Kariotis, T. 'A Greek Exclusive Economic Zone in the Aegean Sea', *Mediterranean Quarterly*, Summer 2007, at pp. 60–61.

[78] See Article 15 UNCLOS in relation to territorial sea limits, where there are opposing or neighboring coastal states.

[79] As discussed earlier, uninhabited and uninhabitable rocks and islets do not qualify under Article 121§3 UNCLOS for sovereign claims to EEZ from their baselines.

[80] See the Helsinki European Council Summit Presidency's Conclusions at http://www.consilium.europa.eu/uedocs/cms_data/docs/pressdata/en/ec/ACFA4C.htm

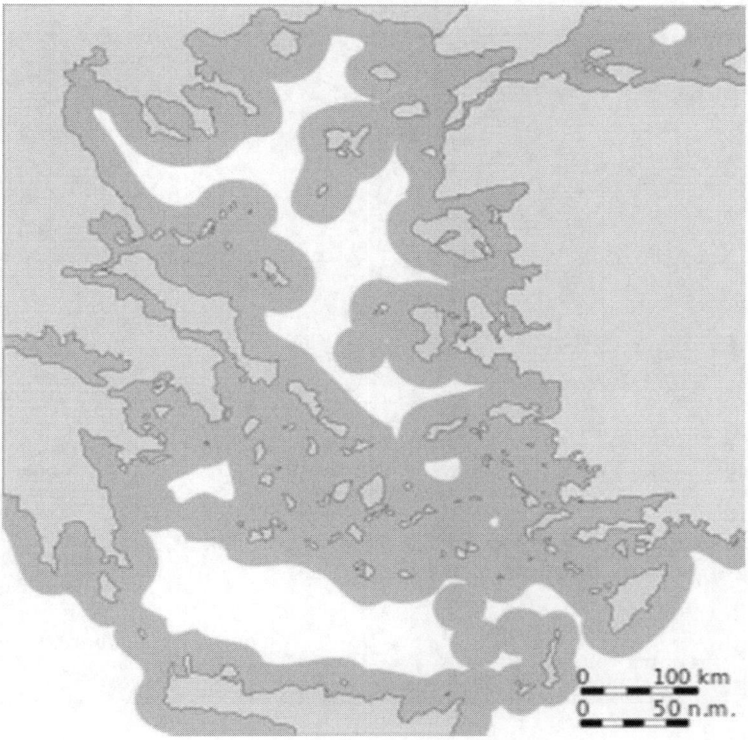

Source: http://www.geostrategicforecasting.com/the-recent-visit-of-the-turkish-foreign-minister-to-athens-another-lost-opportunity-for-the-delimitation-of-a-greek-exclusive-economic-zone-eez-in-the-aegean-sea/

Figure 4.2 Were Greece to claim 12 nm territorial sea

River to the Mediterranean Sea, covering the lands and maritime territories of Israel, the West Bank, the Gaza Strip, Lebanon, Cyprus, and Syria. The main part of the discovered energy reserves was found in the EEZ of different countries, including Israel, Lebanon, and Cyprus. These oil and gas reserves could amount to significant sources of revenue and energy security for the countries in the region, especially Lebanon and Israel.

Apparently, part of the crucial energy discoveries of the Levant Basin exists in a contested maritime area between the northern part of Israel's maritime boundaries and the southern part of Lebanon's maritime boundaries. Ordinarily, maritime disputes concerning boundaries demarcation have risen in regions where sovereignty and borders are contested by

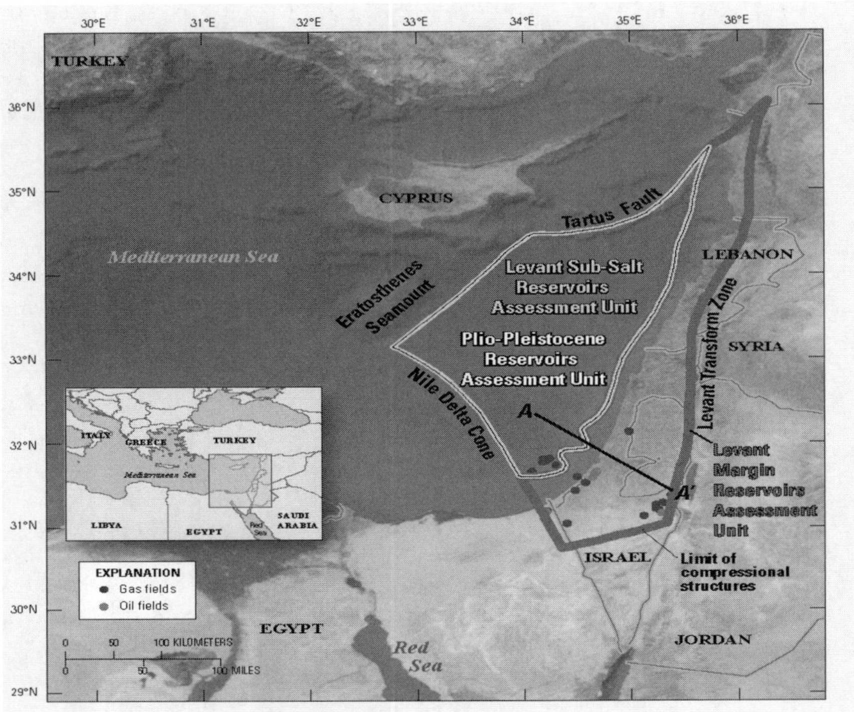

Source: US Geological Survey, http://pubs.usgs.gov/fs/2010/3014/pdf/FS10-3014.pdf

Figure 4.3 Map of the Levant Basin province in the Eastern Mediterranean

more than one country. A political conflict, based upon a maritime boundary dispute, has emerged between Israel and Lebanon pertinent to the delimitation of their respective EEZs. In recent years, a variation and a series of events occurred with implications for the delimitation of Lebanon's and Israel's EEZs. The most relevant of these include: the Lebanon–Cyprus Agreement on the delimitation of their EEZs (2007);[81]

[81] See Agreement between the Government of the State of Lebanon and the Government of the Republic of Cyprus on the Delimitation of the Exclusive Economic Zone, signed on January 17, 2007, available exclusively to Middle East Economic Survey at Editor's Note, 'Cyprus–Lebanon, Cyprus–Israel Offshore Delimitation', Middle East Economic Survey, October 1, 2012, http://

the Israel–Cyprus Agreement on the delimitation of their EEZs (2010);[82] a unilateral proclamation submitted to the UN by Lebanon containing lists and charts of geographical coordinates to delimit Lebanon's EEZ (2010);[83] a unilateral proclamation embracing a list of geographical coordinates submitted to the UN by Israel to delimit its EEZ (2011);[84] a complaint submitted to the UN by Lebanon rejecting the Israel–Cyprus Agreement;[85] and another protest submitted by Lebanon contesting the Israeli proclamation of its EEZ boundaries.[86] In fact, Lebanon treats the delimitation of Israel's and Cyprus's EEZs as an infringement upon part of its southern EEZ.

---

www.mees.com/en/articles/6015-cyprus-lebanon-cyprus-israel-ofshore-delimitation (last accessed 2013) [hereinafter: the Lebanon–Cyprus Agreement, 2007].

[82] See Agreement between the Government of the State of Israel and the Government of the Republic of Cyprus on the Delimitation of the Exclusive Economic Zone, signed in Nicosia on 17 December 2010 (entry into Force: 25 February 2011); Registration #: I-48387; Registration Date: 9 March 2011, http://www.un.org/depts/los/LEGISLATIONANDTREATIES/PDFFILES/TREATIES/cyp_isr_eez_2010.pdf [hereinafter, The Israel–Cyprus Agreement 2010].

[83] See List of Geographical Coordinates for the Delimitation of Exclusive Economic Zone of Lebanon in WGS84 (submitted to the UN by the Permanent Mission of Lebanon on July 14, 2010), http://www.un.org/Depts/los/LEGISLATIONANDTREATIES/PDFFILES/DEPOSIT/lbn_mzn79_2010.pdf [hereinafter, the Lebanese List of Geographical Coordinates].

[84] See List of Geographical Coordinates for the Delimitation of the Northern Limits of the Territorial Sea and Exclusive Economic Zone of the State of Israel in WGS84 (submitted to the UN by the Permanent Mission of Israel on July 12th, 2011), http://www.un.org/Depts/los/LEGISLATIONANDTREATIES/PDFFILES/isr_eez_northernlimit2011.pdf [hereinafter, the Israeli List of Geographical Coordinates].

[85] See a letter dated 20 June 2011 from the Minister for Foreign Affairs and Emigrants of Lebanon Addressed to the Secretary-General of the United Nations Concerning the Agreement Between the Government of the State of Israel and the Government of the Republic of Cyprus on the Delimitation of the Exclusive Economic Zone, signed in Nicosia on 17 December 2010, http://www.un.org/Depts/los/LEGISLATIONANDTREATIES/PDFFILES/communications/lbn_re_cyp_isr_agreement2010.pdf

[86] See a letter dated 3 September 2011 from the Minister for Foreign Affairs and Emigrants of Lebanon Addressed to the Secretary-General of the United Nations Concerning the Geographical Coordinates of the Northern Limit of the Territorial Sea and the Exclusive Economic Zone Transmitted by Israel, http://www.un.org/Depts/los/LEGISLATIONANDTREATIES/PDFFILES/communications/lbn_re_isr__listofcoordinates_e.pdf

The variety of bilateral agreements and unilateral proclamations on the delimitation of each country's EEZ gives rise to contrasting and overlapping claims over the same maritime area. For example, as illustrated in Figure 4.4, there is a maritime dispute between Lebanon and Israel over the same EEZ area.[87] This disputed maritime area between Lebanon and Israel is expected to contain considerable energy resources, particularly natural gas. Thus, although it is seemingly a conflict over the delimitation of the EEZ, in effect it is a complicated dispute relating to sovereignty and ownership rights over the most predominant natural resources, namely oil and gas.

In spite of the promising economic opportunities and energy security that may be derived from these energy discoveries in the Levant Basin, a complex conflict has emerged between Lebanon and Israel pertaining to the delimitation of their EEZ boundaries, namely a specific overlapped EEZ area. Its settlement to delimit the maritime boundaries presents a variety of complications. This section addresses the currently most topical maritime dispute in the Levant Basin, namely between Lebanon and Israel. Specifically, it examines the complications that challenge the settlement of this maritime dispute and the delimitation of the maritime boundaries and that are crippling the exploitation of the energy reserves situated within the disputed EEZ area. Although a lot of gas has been found in the EMB region, which will certainly enhance the EU's energy security, it remains to be seen whether these discoveries will make a dramatic difference in EU energy security.

This section offers an overview of the gas and oil discoveries in the Levant Basin, and the economic opportunities embodied in these explorations for Lebanon and Israel. It then focuses on the political conflict during the recent years between Lebanon and Israel due to the energy discoveries and as a result of contrasting maritime delimitations' proclamations. It also addresses the maritime dispute in depth and examines the major complications that challenge the settlement of the Lebanon–Israel maritime dispute, including the legal complications. Finally, it concludes that in the current state of affairs, the Lebanon–Israel maritime dispute is unlikely to be settled without a dramatic shift in attitudes at the highest political/diplomatic level in both countries.

---

[87] See Figure 4.4, illustrating the disputed maritime area between Israel and Lebanon.

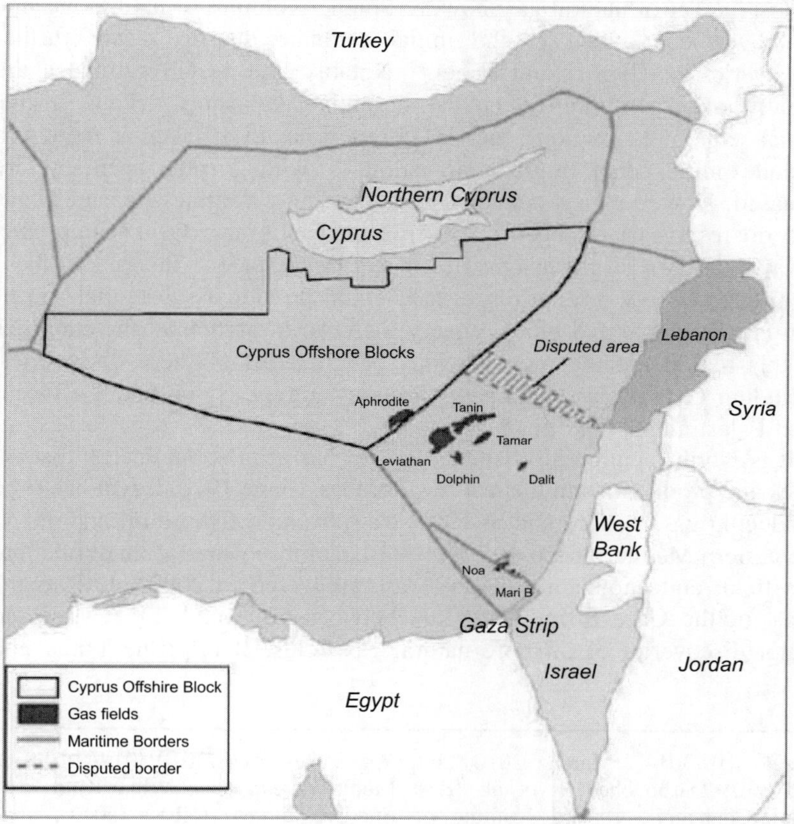

Source: PFC Energy, 'Memo Petroleum Risk Manager', June 2012, http://www.gmfus.org/wp- content/blogs.dir/1/files_mf/1339170753Leigh_SummaryDocument_Jun12_maps.pdf

Figure 4.4 Map of the disputed maritime area between Israel and Lebanon

1. Oil and gas explorations: energy and economic opportunities

In March 2010, the US Geological Survey (USGS) published a report estimating that the Levant Basin province contains 122 trillion cubic feet (Tcf) of recoverable natural gas as well as 1.7 billion barrels of recoverable oil.[88] In fact, the Levant Basin was estimated to contain

[88] See United States Geological Survey, 'Assessment of Undiscovered Oil and Gas Resources of the Levant Basin Province, Eastern Mediterranean', Fact

almost 77 Tcf of natural gas; however, higher volumes of natural gas and oil have been added to the initial estimate due to recent further discoveries in Cyprus and Israel.[89] Notably, the USGS estimates are usually taken as initial, rather than definitive, indicators.[90] Thus, in this initial stage of estimations, the USGS report has to be taken as merely to include initial data, until new estimates with greater accuracy are released. However, it is acknowledged that huge volumes of natural gas and oil reserves have been discovered in the Levant Basin, comprising the world's largest gas discoveries in the last decade.[91] In general, these significant energy reserve discoveries could provide a substantial contribution to regional and global energy markets. In particular, the countries in this region are the most obvious beneficiaries of these discoveries, including Cyprus, Israel, Lebanon, Turkey, Egypt, Syria, and the Occupied Palestinian Territories.[92]

It is worth mentioning that, this region has seen some energy discoveries and productions in the last few decades. Since 1970, Egypt has been producing gas onshore and in 1997 it discovered offshore oil and gas in the eastern Mediterranean Sea. In 1993 Israel discovered a small offshore gas field, and another small one was discovered in 2000, close to the coast of the Gaza Strip. The years between 2009 and 2011 witnessed major discoveries of offshore natural gas fields, chiefly: the Tamar and

---

Sheet 010-3014, March 2010, http://pubs.usgs.gov/fs/2010/3014/pdf/FS10-3014.pdf; Darbouche, H. et al. 'East Mediterranean Gas: What Kind of a Game-Changer?', Oxford Institute of Energy Studies (OIES) (2012), at 4 [herinafter, Darbouche, 'East Mediterranean Gas'].

[89] See Shaffer, B. 'Energy Resources and Markets in the Eastern Mediterranean Region', *The German Marshall Fund of the US*, Policy Brief (2012): 2, http://www.gmfus.org/wp-content/blogs.dir/1/files_mf/1339172423Shaffer_Energy MarketProspects_Jun12.pdf [hereinafter, Shaffer, 'Energy Resources'].

[90] Ibid.

[91] See Wählisch, M. 'Israel-Lebanon Offshore Oil & Gas Dispute – Rules of International Maritime Law' (2011) American Society of International Law, Vol. 15, No. 31, http://www.asil.org/insights/volume/15/issue/31/israel-lebanon-offshore-oil-gas-dispute-%E2%80%93-rules-international-maritime [hereinafter Wählisch, 'Israel-Lebanon Offshore']

[92] For a detailed review pertinent to the various interested parties, see Leigh, M. & Charlotte Brandsma, C. 'Energy Resources in the Eastern Mediterranean: Source for Cooperation or Fuel for Tension', Brussels Forum Paper Series (March 2012), http://www.gmfus.org/archives/energy-resources-in-the-eastern-mediterranean-source-for-cooperation-or-fuel-for-tension/ [hereinafter, Leigh and Brandsma, 'Energy in the Eastern Mediterranean'].

Dalit fields off Israel in 2009; the Leviathan field off Israel in 2010; and the Aphrodite field off Cyprus in 2011.[93]

Focusing on the case of Lebanon and Israel, it is evident that the natural gas and oil discoveries have enormous benefits for each country in terms of their energy security as well as economic development. For decades, both countries relied on imported oil and gas, hence they are considered energy dependent and net energy importing countries. For example, the lion's share of Israel's imported natural gas came from Egypt.[94] This natural gas supply from Egypt to Israel suffered recently from regular supply disruptions, following the Egyptian Revolution of January 2011.[95] The situation deteriorated in May 2012 when Egypt's national gas company announced the cancelation of the natural gas deal with Israel.[96]

In the case of Lebanon, it has an even greater energy reliance on other countries than Israel. Lebanon does not produce any oil or gas and, until now, it has had no proven oil and gas discoveries. In its energy consumption, Lebanon depends on small volumes of imported gas from Egypt (transported through Jordan and Syria via the Arab Gas Pipeline), while its oil consumption is supplied by Syria.[97] In addition to its enormous dependence on foreign oil and gas, Lebanon has been suffering for many years from a fatal electricity crisis and shortage of electricity supply.

Given these circumstances, there is no doubt that the recent discoveries of substantial natural gas and oil reserves will provide both countries with considerable energy security and stabilize their energy situation,

---

93 See Shaffer, 'Energy Resources', at 2.

94 See Shaffer, B. 'Natural Gas Supply Stability and Foreign Policy' (2013) *Energy Policy*, Vol. 56, pp. 114–125 [herinafter Shaffer, 'Natural Gas Supply'].

95 See Shaffer, 'Energy Resources', at 5; For more discussion on Israeli gas reserves, energy policy and future options, see Shaffer, B. 'Israel – New Natural Gas Producer in the Mediterranean', The German Marshall Fund of the US, (2011) 39 *Energy Policy* 5379–5387; Ratner, M. 'Israel's Offshore Natural Gas Discoveries Enhance Its Economic and Energy Outlook', Congressional Research Servic*e* (January 31, 2011), http://www.fas.org/sgp/crs/mideast/R41618.pdf.

96 See Shaffer, 'Natural Gas Supply Stability and Foreign Policy', at 9; Bar-Eli, A. 'Egypt Cancels Natural Gas Deal with Israel' *Haaretz* (Apr. 22, 2012), http://www.haaretz.com/news/diplomacy-defense/egypt-cancels-natural-gas-deal-with-israel-1.425883

97 See Shaffer, 'Energy Resources', at 8; Stonaker, M.E. 'Energy Infrastructure as a Diplomatic Tool: The Arab Gas Pipeline', *Journal of Energy Security*, December 14, 2010, http://www.ensec.org/index.php?option=com_content&view=article&id=270:energy-infrastructure-as-a-diplomatic-tool-the-arab-gas-pipeline-in-perspective&catid=112:energysecuritycontent&Itemid=367.

despite the fact that both countries are officially at war, which complicates matters. The foreseen utilization and production of the discovered gas and oil will likely transform these countries from being dependent on foreign energy sources to consuming a vast amount of their own energy resources and become much less energy-dependent on foreign supply. In fact, in the optimist scenario, it is estimated that both countries may achieve energy independence.[98] Out of the two countries, Israel has a much more developed energy industry, and the Tamar field commenced gas production operations in 2013.[99] Hence, predictably, in the coming years Israel will become a gas exporting country.[100] It is worth mentioning that the Israeli government decided to establish a sovereign wealth fund in order 'to contribute to a fair intergenerational distribution of gas revenue' and which will invest gas levy receipts abroad.[101] It is also worth mentioning that the apparent potential markets for Israeli gas are Jordan and European countries.[102] Therefore, this dramatic change in the energy landscape of both countries could contribute effectively to promoting these countries' economies as well as their social development.

2. Political conflict

In spite of their economic importance to Lebanon and Israel, these energy discoveries also pose a risk in terms of escalating political tension in the region. Indeed, in addition to the great opportunities for both countries, and mainly for their energy sectors and their social and economic modernization and development, these discoveries could lead to geopolitical and security crises that could, at worst, result in armed conflict. A state of war already shadows the Lebanon–Israel relationship, namely the 2006 Israel–Lebanon War (Israel-Hezbollah War).[103]

---

[98] See Leigh and Brandsma, 'Energy in the Eastern Mediterranean', at 1.

[99] Reed, J. 'Israel Begins Offshore Gas Production', *Financial Times*, 31 March 2013, available at http://www.ft.com/cms/s/0/3de8b0ca-99ea-11e2-83ca-00144feabdc0.html#axzz2PHYJE69W

[100] See Darbouche, 'East Mediterranean Gas', at 2.

[101] See Bank of Israel Annual Report, 2012, p. 24, available at http://www.boi.org.il/en/NewsAndPublications/RegularPublications/Documents/Doch2012/chap-1.pdf.

[102] See Wählisch, 'Israel-Lebanon Offshore'; Bunter, M. 'The Mediterranean Basin: A Strategic Component of a European Energy and Defense Area?' *Oil, Gas & Energy Law Journal (OGEL)*, Vol. 2, No. 1 (February 1, 2004), http://www.ogel.org/article.asp?key=1020.

[103] See Inbar, E.'How Israel Bungled the Second Lebanon War', Middle East Quarterly (June 1, 2007), http://www.meforum.org/1686/how-israel-bungled-the-second-lebanon-war

Lebanon and Israel are neighboring countries with adjacent territories and coasts. They share land and maritime borders. Lebanon's southern land borders constitute the majority of Israel's northern borders, where the remaining part of Israel's northern borders is shared with Syria. Furthermore, Lebanon's southern maritime borders intersect the Israeli northern maritime borders. The maritime borders between Lebanon and Israel were never agreed upon or delimited officially by both countries. Importantly, the existing escalating dispute between Lebanon and Israel focuses on the delimitation of the EEZs of both countries, the maritime boundaries. It is a specific dispute pertaining to an overlapped EEZ area that is likely to contain substantial gas and oil reserves.

From Lebanon's perspective, these energy resources located in the contested EEZ area are part of Lebanon's territorial waters and EEZ. Accordingly, Lebanon declared that it will not remain silent if any aggression occurs towards its oil and gas resources. This unambiguous position was expressed clearly by Lebanon's President Michel Suleiman:

> On the other hand, we reaffirm that we are strongly attached to our full sovereign and economic rights over our territorial waters and exclusive economic zone and our freedom of exploitation of our natural resources, be they on land or deep in the sea, away from any designs or threats.[104]

In addition, Lebanon's Energy and Water Resources Minister Jibran Bassil affirmed that Lebanon is determined to defend its oil and gas resources within its EEZ.[105] Moreover, Hassan Nasrallah, the leader of Hezbollah (the Lebanese resistance group) expressed an official threat toward Israel: 'Those who harm our installations will have their own installations harmed … we warn Israel not to touch this area or try to steal Lebanon's resources'.[106]

For its part, Israel claims exclusive sovereign rights over the gas and oil resources within the disputed EEZ area. On this basis Israel announced expressly its readiness to utilize military force to protect the

---

[104] See H.E. General Michel Sleiman, 'President of the Republic of Lebanon, at the Sixty-Sixth Session of the General Assembly of the United Nations' (New York, September 21, 2011), at 4, http://gadebate.un.org/sites/default/files/gastatements/66/LB_en.pdf

[105] See Mroueh, W. 'Lebanon to Fight Israel at U.N.', *The Daily Star Newspaper – Lebanon*, July 11, 2011, http://www.dailystar.com.lb/News/Politics/2011/Jul-11/Lebanon-to-fight-Israel-at-UN.ashx

[106] See Karam, Z. 'Hezbollah Warns Israel Against "Stealing" Gas', World News, The Guardian, January 23, 2008, http://www.guardian.co.uk/world/feedarticle/9765255

energy resources from any attack. For instance, Israel's Minister of National Infrastructures, Uzi Landau, warned Lebanon that Israel would not hesitate to use military force to protect Israel's gas fields.[107] Following this announcement, the Prime Minister of Israel Benjamin Netanyahu emphasized that the oil and gas resources are a 'strategic objective that Israel's enemies will try to undermine' and affirmed that 'Israel will defend its resources'.[108] Based upon both sides' warning statements, if the dispute over the delimitation of maritime boundaries is not soon settled peacefully, the threat of military force may materialize.

Importantly, the Israel–Lebanon conflict is not the only threat that undermines the effective exploitation of the energy discoveries in the Levant Basin. In fact, the Levant Basin is part of broader globally significant region that is the Middle East and North Africa (MENA) area. The MENA region constitutes a globally well-known geographical region fraught with various historical conflicts and tensions. The most predominant conflicts in this region include the Israeli–Arab conflict broadly defined; the Israeli–Palestinian conflict;[109] the Israeli–Syrian conflict; the Israeli–Lebanese conflict; the Turkish–Kurdish conflict; the Turkish–Greek conflict and the Turkey–Cyprus dispute; the Sudan conflict; the Iranian nuclear program; and the multifaceted conflict in Iraq, including the US invasion, the civil war, the Sunni-Shia conflict, and the Kurdish issue. In this context, a further reference has to be made to the ongoing Arab revolutions in several MENA countries, specifically Tunisia, Libya, Egypt, Yemen, Bahrain, and in Syria.

These current and historic conflicts, as well as creating instability and the region's complicated geopolitical atmosphere, all contribute, directly or indirectly, to hindering the optimal exploitation of the energy discoveries. Undoubtedly, the Lebanon–Israel dispute over the overlapped maritime area and the delimitation of the EEZ contributes more fuel to the existing variety of political and historical disputes and conflicts in the

---

[107] See *Haaretz* 'Infrastructure Minister Warns Hezbollah: Israel Will Fight for Its Gas Fields', *Haaretz.com*, June 24, 2010, http://www.haaretz.com/news/diplomacy-defense/infrastructure-minister-warns-hezbollah-israel-will-fight-for-its-gas-fields-1.298077

[108] See Blanford, N. 'The Next Big Lebanon-Israel Flare-Up: Gas', *Time*, April 6, 2011, http://www.time.com/time/world/article/0,8599,2061187,00.html

[109] Despite the political tension between Israel and Palestine, in early 2014 both parties agreed to have a gas deal for 20 years. See 'Palestinians to be first buyers of Israeli natural gas,' *Times of Israel*, 6 January 2014, available at http://www.timesofisrael.com/palestinians-to-be-first-buyers-of-israeli-natural-gas/

MENA region. If the political instability and tension between Lebanon and Israel are not alleviated, and, more particularly, if the maritime dispute is not resolved peacefully between them, the discovered energy reserves in the Levant Basin could comprise a great loss of economic and social development opportunities for Lebanon and Israel. The worst scenario would encompass the translation of both sides' threats into acts, which would mean launching another war between Lebanon and Israel, with disastrous consequences for the populations of both countries. The metaphorical words of Lebanon's Parliament Speaker Nabih Berri, describe neatly the complicated political challenges restraining the development of energy resources in the Levant Basin: 'Oil exploration is the victim of the current political vacuum'.[110]

Based upon the above, it is safe to say as a fundamental premise that the Lebanon–Israel maritime dispute should be settled soon and peacefully. The pressing necessity for achieving an optimal and effective exploitation of the new energy discoveries confers on both countries the burden to exert huge diplomatic efforts to attain a lasting settlement of this dispute. However, as elaborated in the following sections, in addition to the obstacles highlighted above, a variety of issues impedes the resolution of Lebanon–Israel maritime dispute. As a result, the utilization of the energy discoveries in the disputed maritime area remains unattained.

3. Complications for the delimitation of the disputed EEZ area

The Lebanon–Israel maritime dispute is unlikely to be resolved smoothly. This is not only due to the political issues that obscure the economic opportunities that offshore energy discoveries present. Rather, the Lebanon–Israel maritime conflict entails various internal complications, including legal challenges, which impede the possibility of a lasting resolution of this maritime delimitation dispute.[111] This section sheds light on the major complications confronting the delimitation of Lebanon's and Israel's EEZs.

---

[110] See Blanford, N., *supra* note 108.

[111] See generally the analysis of international maritime law issues relating to various maritime delimitation disputes in the Eastern Mediterranean Sea by Tullio Scovazzi, 'Maritime Boundaries in the Eastern Mediterranean Sea', The German Marshall Fund of the US, Policy Brief (June 2012), at 1–2, available at http://www.gmfus.org/wp-content/blogs.dir/1/files_mf/1339504227Scovazzi_MaritimeBoundaries_Jun12.pdf [hereinafter, Scovazzi, 'Maritime Boundaries'].

3.1. Contrasting maritime proclamations: the disputed EEZ area In accordance with Article 75 of UNCLOS, Lebanon and Israel, each through a unilateral step, launched an initiative for the demarcation of their EEZs. In 2010 Lebanon proclaimed its EEZ by submitting to the UN charts and lists of geographical coordinates to define its EEZ's southern boundaries. According to Lebanon's submission to the UN (as illustrated in Tables 4.2 and 4.3), its southern EEZ – its maritime boundary with Israel – extends from Ras Al-Naqurah (coastal borders), indicated as Point 18 (coordinates 33° 5' 38.94" N Latitude and 35° 6' 11.84" E Longitude), to Point 23 (coordinates 33° 31' 51.17" N Latitude and 33° 46' 8.78" E Longitude).[112] Also, according to Lebanon's submission, Point 23 reflects the maritime 'equidistant tripoint' between Lebanon, Israel, and Cyprus. On the other hand, in 2011 Israel submitted a list of geographical coordinates to the UN (see Table 4.4), proclaiming its EEZ's northern boundaries. Based upon Israel's submission to the UN, Israel delimited its EEZ's northern boundaries to extend from Ras Al-Naqurah, indicated as Point 31 (coordinates 33° 5' 39.5" N Latitude and 31° 35' 6" E Longitude) to Point 1 (coordinates 33° 38' 40" N Latitude and 33° 35' 40" E Longitude).[113] The Israeli position recognizes Point 1 to represent the tripoint between the three countries: Lebanon, Cyprus, and Israel.[114]

Table 4.2 List of Lebanese geographical coordinates submitted to the UN for the southern median line between Lebanon and Palestine (Israel)

Points	Degrees	Minutes	Seconds		Degrees	Minutes	Seconds	
18	35	6	11.84	E	33	5	38.94	N
19	35	4	46.14	E	33	5	45.79	N
20	35	2	58.12	E	33	6	35.15	N
21	35	2	13.86	E	33	6	52.73	N
22	34	52	57.24	E	33	10	19.33	N
23	33	46	8.78	E	33	31	51.17	N

[112] See The Lebanese Lists of Geographical Coordinates submitted to the UN in Tables 4.2 and 4.3.
[113] Ibid.
[114] See the Israel–Cyprus Agreement, 2010.

Source: The Division for Ocean Affairs and the Law of the Sea of the Office of Legal Affairs of the United Nations, Lebanon's List of Geographical Coordinates for the Delimitation of the Exclusive Economic Zone in WGS84, 14 July 2010.

Table 4.3 List of Lebanese geographical coordinates submitted to the UN for the southern part of the western median line between Lebanon and Cyprus

Points	Degrees	Minutes	Seconds		Degrees	Minutes	Seconds	
23	33	46	8.78	E	33	31	51.17	N
24	33	51	30.31	E	33	37	13.10	N
25	33	50	25.30	E	33	36	8.01	N
1	33	53	40.00	E	33	38	40.00	N

Source: The Division for Ocean Affairs and the Law of the Sea of the Office of Legal Affairs of the United Nations, Lebanon's List of Geographical Coordinates for the Delimitation of the Exclusive Economic Zone in WGS84, 19 October 2010.

Table 4.4 List of the Israeli geographical coordinates submitted to the UN

Points	Degrees	Minutes	Seconds		Degrees	Minutes	Seconds	
31	35	6	13.0	E	33	5	39.5	N
32	35	4	10.0	E	33	6	23.0	N
33	35	3	3.0	E	33	6	39.0	N
34	34	53	11	E	33	10	33.5	N
35	34	46	38.0	E	33	13	9.0	N
1	33	53	40.0	E	33	38	40.0	N

Source: The Division for Ocean Affairs and the Law of the Sea of the Office of Legal Affairs of the United Nations, Israel's List of Geographical Coordinates for the Delimitation of the Northern Limit of the Territorial Sea and Exclusive Economic Zone of the State of Israel in WGS84, 12 July 2011, http://www.un.org/Depts/los/LEGISLATIONANDTREATIES/PDFFILES/isr_eez_northernlimit2011.pdf

Based upon the positions of both countries through the lists of geographical coordinates submitted to the UN, it is obvious that Point 1 of the Israeli list of geographical coordinates is different from Point 23 of the

Lebanese list of geographical coordinates.[115] Meanwhile, according to the same lists of geographical coordinates of both countries, the coastal borders point between Lebanon and Israel, which was determined as Point 18 in the Lebanese list and Point 31 in the Israeli list, is almost the same point.[116] The outcome is in clear contrast to the proclamations submitted by Lebanon and Israel to the UN. This contrast of proclamations resulted in an overlapped area in the EEZs, which is the disputed triangular maritime area.[117]

Neither submission constitutes a bilateral agreement. In fact, both submissions comprise only unilateral proclamations, where each proclamation represents each country's proposal for the delimitation of its EEZ. The interim conclusion from the declared positions of Lebanon and Israel highlights the clear EEZ maritime dispute between these two countries. This EEZ maritime dispute is concentrated on the delimitation of the tripoint between Lebanon, Cyprus, and Israel. Based upon the lists submitted by Lebanon and Israel, the difference between Lebanon's Point 23 (south of the Israeli tripoint) and Israel's Point 1 (north of the Lebanese tripoint) is 17 kilometers long.[118] In fact, the EEZs proclamations of Lebanon and Israel clash over an overlapped EEZ area of almost 850 square kilometers. In other words, contrasting proclamations overlap over the same triangular EEZ area, namely over the same gas and oil resources.

3.2. The applicability of UNCLOS With respect to maritime boundaries, including the delimitation of EEZs and the identification of States' rights to exploit undersea resources, the developed international governing law is UNCLOS to the extent that States are parties to this instrument. With regard to the delimitation of EEZs of costal countries, Article 74(1) of UNCLOS states that the delimitation of EEZs between 'States with opposite or adjacent coasts shall be effected by agreement on the basis of international law ... in order to achieve an equitable

---

[115] See Point 23 in Tables 4.2 and 4.3 (the Lebanese proclamation submitted to the UN) compared with Point 1 in Table 4.4 (the Israeli proclamation deposited with the UN).

[116] See Table 4.2 (the Lebanese proclamation) and Table 4.4 (the Israeli proclamation).

[117] See Figure 4.4, illustrating the disputed maritime area between Israel and Lebanon.

[118] See Abdel-Kader, N. 'Potential Conflict between Lebanon and Israel over Oil and Gas Resources – A Lebanese Perspective', *Defense Magazine*, http://www.lebarmy.gov.lb/article.asp?ln=en&id=29445

solution'.[119] The primary rules for the delimitation of maritime boundaries are the delimitations by agreement based upon international law.[120] Moreover, Article 75 of UNCLOS provides that any State interested in delimiting its EEZ has to deposit with the Secretary-General of the UN a copy of charts or lists of 'geographical coordinates', which proclaim its EEZ. Besides, UNCLOS embraces many other developed and important governing norms that are relevant to the demarcation of maritime boundaries and delimitation of a country's EEZ.

Significantly, according to UNCLOS, a prerequisite to apply UNCLOS and to utilize its compulsory dispute resolution system to settle a maritime dispute between two or more States in disputed maritime boundaries is that the parties to the dispute have to be 'State Parties'.[121] The term 'State Parties' was defined in Article 1, paragraph 2(1) of UNCLOS to include those States that have expressed their consent to be bound by UNCLOS and for which UNCLOS is in force. In other words, according to UNCLOS, in order to activate UNCLOS to delimit maritime borders and settle maritime disputes, the parties to the dispute have to be State Parties to UNCLOS.

Consequently, a particular challenge contests the applicability of UNCLOS to delimit the EEZs and to settle the maritime dispute between Lebanon and Israel. While Lebanon has ratified UNCLOS and became a State Party to this Convention on January 5, 1995, Israel is not a State Party to UNCLOS.[122] Even though Israel is not a State Party to

---

119 Article 74(1) UNCLOS.

120 See Dundua, N. 'Delimitation of Maritime Boundaries Between Adjacent States' (2006) at 3 and 83, available at http://www.un.org/Depts/los/nippon/unnff_programme_home/fellows_pages/fellows_papers/dundua_0607_georgia.pdf

121 Ibid, see Part XV of UNCLOS in general, and Section 2 of Part XV in particular. For example, Article 287(1) UNCLOS, which regulates the 'Choice of Procedure', points out the importance of being a State Party to UNCLOS in order to activate its dispute settlement procedure: 'When signing, ratifying or acceding to this Convention or at any time thereafter, a State shall be free to choose, by means of a written declaration, one or more of the following means for the settlement of disputes concerning the interpretation or application of this Convention …'.

122 See UN, Oceans and the Law of the Sea: Division for Ocean Affairs and the Law of the Sea, Chronological lists of ratifications of, accession and successions to the convention and the related agreements as at 23 January 2013) at http://www.un.org/Depts/los/reference_files/chronological_lists_of_ratifications.htm.

UNCLOS, the rules of international maritime law relating to the delimitation of the EEZ can be applied to Israel for the settlement of this dispute, based mainly upon two foundations:

(1) UNCLOS provisions and rules concerning maritime boundaries, including the EEZ areas and other provisions pertaining to undersea resources, are recognized as part of customary international law.[123] The rules regulate the delimitation of EEZs, as reflected in UNCLOS, and can be applied to the Lebanon–Israel dispute as customary international law.[124] Thus, these rules are likely to bind Lebanon and Israel in the delimitation of their EEZs, even if Israel has not acceded to UNCLOS.
(2) On December 17, 2010, Israel and Cyprus signed an agreement on the delimitation of their EEZs.[125] In the preamble of this agreement, both countries recognized the importance of the delimitation of their EEZ and, for this purpose, they agreed to recall the 'provisions of the United Nations Convention on the Law of the Sea of 10 December 1982, relating to the Exclusive Economic Zone'. Furthermore, Israel and Cyprus were based on the 'rules and principles of the international law of the sea applicable to the matter'.[126] This clear recognition provides strong evidence that Israel behaves internationally in a manner that may suggest its willingness to be bound by UNCLOS provisions and international law relating to the delimitation of the EEZ with third parties. Notably, in the bilateral relation between Israel and Cyprus, Israel

---

[123] See Emerson, M. 'Fishing for Gas in Cypriot Waters' (2012) *Policy Brief* 2, http://www.iai.it/pdf/GTE/GTE_PB_02.pdf; pertaining to the recognition of UNCLOS rules as customary international law with regard to maritime boundaries, specifically the EEZ and continental shelf areas, see ICJ judgments in *Case Concerning Continental Shelf (Libyan Arab Jarnahiriya/Malta), Judgment*, I.C.J. Reports 1985, p. 13, para. 34 at p. 33, http://www.icj-cij.org/docket/files/68/6415.pdf; *Case Concerning the Continental Shelf (Tunisia/Libyan Arab Jamahiriya)*, Judgment, I.C.J. Reports 1982, p. 18, at para. 100 p. 60, http://www.icj-cij.org/docket/files/63/6267.pdf; *Maritime Delimitation in the Area between Greenland and Jan Mayen (Denmark v. Norway)*, Judgment, I.C.J. Reports 1993, p. 38, at paras 47–48, p. 59, http://www.icj-cij.org/docket/files/78/6743.pdf.

[124] See ASDEAM, 'The Legal Framework of Lebanon's Maritime Boundaries: The Exclusive Economic Zone and Offshore Hydrocarbon Resources', *Association Suisse Pour Le Dialogue Euro-Arabo-Musulman* (November 2012), at 10; Wählisch, 'Israel-Lebanon Offshore'.

[125] See Israel–Cyprus Agreement, 2010.

[126] See Preamble of the Israel–Cyprus Agreement, 2010.

> agreed to apply UNCLOS to the delimitation of its EEZ boundaries that includes Point 1 – the disputed tripoint with Lebanon. Thus, it can be concluded that Israel has accepted – through the Israel–Cyprus Agreement – to apply UNCLOS for the delimitation of Israel's and Cyprus's EEZ boundaries, including the tripoint intersect with a third country. It can also be concluded that Israel has accepted applying UNCLOS, in particular, to the trilateral relation between Lebanon, Cyprus, and Israel, to delimit the tripoint between them, which is also the disputed tripoint between Lebanon and Israel. Alternatively, it can be implied from the preamble of the Israel–Cyprus Agreement that Israel agreed to be bound by the provisions of UNCLOS through customary international law in the delimitation of its EEZ boundaries with other countries.

There is no precise applicable discipline, such as UNCLOS or general international law. This lack of a precise applicable law constitutes a complicated challenge to the settlement of the Lebanon–Israel dispute. It also poses a challenge to the activation of a legally binding law as well as to conferring jurisdiction on a dispute settlement procedure. Additionally, although the Israel–Cyprus Agreement contains a reference to UNCLOS and to international law of the sea relating to the delimitation of the EEZ, it can be argued that only in this particular agreement has Israel agreed to apply UNCLOS provisions. Thus it cannot be implied from this specific bilateral agreement that Israel agreed to apply the Convention on other matters, including its maritime dispute with Lebanon.

3.3. The absence of a bilateral agreement between Lebanon and Israel

Article 74 of UNCLOS addresses the delimitation of the EEZ between States with 'opposite or adjacent coasts'. Article 74(4) of UNCLOS provides that: 'Where there is an agreement in force between the States concerned, questions relating to the delimitation of the exclusive economic zone shall be determined in accordance with the provisions of that agreement'.[127] In the ICJ case *Maritime Delimitation in the Black Sea*

---

[127] See Article 74(4) UNCLOS. A similar rule exists in Article 83(4) UNCLOS. Article 83(4) deals with the continental shelf and provides that, if there is an agreement that binds the States concerned, questions 'relating to the delimitation of the continental shelf shall be determined in accordance with the provinces of the agreement'.

(Romania v. Ukraine),[128] the ICJ referred to Article 74(4) of UNCLOS and interpreted the term 'agreement' in Paragraph 4 to refer to an agreement 'delimiting the exclusive economic zone'.[129] The ICJ explained that, in practice, such a case occurs when the delimitation of a maritime zone between States is effected by a boundary agreed between the same States, which delimited another maritime zone.[130] An example is when applying an agreement on the delimitation of the continental shelf boundary for the delimitation of an EEZ.[131]

However, the relationship between Lebanon and Israel is distinguished by the absence of a valid and binding bilateral agreement delimiting any of their maritime zones, continental shelf or EEZs. A history of hostility prevails over the relationship between Lebanon and Israel, where Lebanon does not recognize the State of Israel, but it considers Palestine to be its neighbor State.[132] Indeed, there is no formal binding bilateral agreement between Lebanon and Israel recognizing the borderline drawn on land by the UN between these two countries. Nor is there a bilateral agreement between Lebanon and Israel with relevance to the delimitation of maritime boundaries in particular.[133]

---

[128] See *Maritime Delimitation in the Black Sea (Romania v. Ukraine)*, Judgment, I.C.J. Reports 2009, p. 61, http://www.icj-cij.org/docket/files/132/14987.pdf

[129] Ibid. at p. 87. In the case of Article 83(4) UNCLOS, the judgment interpreted the word 'agreement' to refer to an agreement delimiting the continental shelf.

[130] Ibid. at 87.

[131] The example that the ICJ indicated in its interpretation in *Romania v. Ukraine* is the agreement between Turkey and the USSR, where both parties applied their continental shelf agreed-boundary to their EEZ boundary. Ibid. at 87.

[132] See The Lebanese List of Geographical Coordinates submitted to the UN; ASDEAM, 'Lebanon's Maritime Boundaries', at 19.

[133] See Henderson, S. 'Energy Discoveries in the Eastern Mediterranean: Source for Cooperation or Fuel for Tension? The Case of Israel', The German Marshall Fund of the US, Policy Brief (2012): 7, http://www.europarl.europa.eu/meetdocs/2009_2014/documents/d-il/dv/henderson_energydiscoveries_jun12_/henderson_energydiscoveries_jun12_en.pdf. In this respect it has to be mentioned that in 1949 Israel signed a set of Armistice Agreements with its neighboring countries including Lebanon, to end the Arab-Israeli War (1949). The Lebanese-Israeli Armistice Agreement was signed on 23 March 1949, where its provisions were influenced by military considerations and did not relate to the delimitation of Lebanon's and Israel's maritime boundaries; see Lebanese-Israeli General Armistice Agreement, UN Doc. S/1293, March 23, 1949, http://unispal.un.org/UNISPAL.NSF/0/71260B776D62FA6E852564420059C4FE

Pursuant to the recent exploration of energy reserves in the Levant Basin – which possess a unique geological structure and straddle the EEZs of several countries, including Lebanon, Cyprus, and Israel – and given the absence of an agreed bilateral agreement between Lebanon and Israel on the delimitation of their EEZ or their continental shelf, both countries have to exert substantial efforts to delimit their EEZ peacefully. Article 74(3) of UNCLOS provides that, until an agreement is reached according to Article 74(1), 'the States concerned, in a spirit of understanding and cooperation, shall make every effort to enter into provisional arrangements of a practical nature and, during this transitional period, not to jeopardize or hamper the reaching of the final agreement. Such arrangements shall be without prejudice to the final delimitation'. Neither a bilateral agreement nor any efforts and 'provisional arrangements' exist between Lebanon and Israel. The present situation lacks any effort even to negotiate a bilateral arrangement, whether provisional or permanent.

Therefore, the existing situation, where there is no bilateral relationship between Lebanon and Israel, hinders progress towards achieving an agreed delimitation of EEZs and of peacefully settling the escalating dispute. Additionally, it impedes the exploitation of the discovered energy resources in the disputed EEZ. *De facto*, although Israel currently controls the disputed EEZ, the political tension and maritime dispute accompanied by absence of negotiation and cooperation between Lebanon and Israel cripples any exploration activities in this disputed maritime area.[134]

3.4. The Lebanon–Cyprus Agreement The controversial tripoint, Point 1 according to the Israeli proclamation and Point 23 according to the Lebanese proclamation, relates to two important agreements on the delimitation of EEZs: the Lebanon–Cyprus Agreement (2007) and the Israel–Cyprus Agreement (2010). The Lebanon–Cyprus Agreement, on the delimitation of their EEZs, was signed on January 17, 2007.[135] This agreement aimed at delimiting most of the EEZ boundaries of Lebanon and Cyprus as countries with opposite coasts. As shown in Table 4.5, with regard to delimiting the southern EEZ borders of Lebanon and Cyprus, particularly the tripoint between Lebanon, Cyprus, and Israel, the agreement determined the tripoint as Point 1 (coordinates

---

[134] See Scovazzi, 'Maritime Boundaries' at 9.
[135] See the Lebanon–Cyprus Agreement, 2007.

33° 38' 40" N Latitude and 33° 35' 40" E Longitude).[136] In fact, it is the same tripoint that Israel proclaimed through its submission to the UN in 2011.[137]

Table 4.5 Annex I to the Lebanon–Cyprus Agreement (2007), list of geographical coordinates

Number of points	Latitude (North)	Longitude (East)
1	33° 38' 40"	33° 53' 40"
2	33° 51' 30"	34° 02' 50"
3	33° 59' 40"	34° 18' 00"
4	34° 23' 20"	34° 44' 00"
5	34° 39' 30"	34° 53' 50"
6	34° 45' 00"	34° 56' 00"

Source: the Lebanon–Cyprus Agreement (January 17, 2007), Editor's Note, 'Cyprus-Lebanon, Cyprus-Israel Offshore Delimitation', *Middle East Economic Survey*, October 1, 2012, http://www.mees.com/en/articles/6015-cyprus-lebanon-cyprus-israel-ofshore-delimitation (last accessed 2013).

However, it could be argued that no dispute was supposed to rise between Lebanon and Israel over the delimitation of the tripoint that constitutes the converging point of Lebanon's, Cyprus's, and Israel's EEZs. This argument is derived from the Lebanon–Cyprus Agreement. According to this agreement, Lebanon delimited its EEZ in 2007 with the same tripoint, that is, Point 1, which was proclaimed by Israel in 2011.[138] If that was the case, most probably there should be no dispute or debate over the tripoint between Lebanon and Israel. *De facto*, there is an existing dispute, where two main issues complicate the situation: the first is the validity of the agreement between Lebanon and Cyprus, and the second is the reasoning behind the delimitation of the tripoint.

Firstly, given the legal status of the bilateral agreement between Lebanon and Cyprus, it can be argued that this agreement is legally invalid. Although both countries signed the agreement on January 17,

[136] See Table 4.5, which lists the geographical coordinates in Annex I to the Lebanon–Cyprus Agreement (2007); ASDEAM, 'Lebanon's Maritime Boundaries', 16–17.

[137] See Table 4.4, The Israeli List of Geographical Coordinates Submitted to the UN.

[138] See ASDEAM, 'Lebanon's Maritime Boundaries', 17.

2007, Cyprus ratified the agreement, while Lebanon has not ratified it yet. Within the agreement itself, both countries agreed that the legal validity of the agreement is subject to 'ratification according to the constitutional procedures in each country'.[139] Likewise, it was agreed that the agreement would not enter into force until the 'exchange of the instruments of ratification'.[140] Accordingly, the Lebanon–Cyprus Agreement requires its ratification to express the consent of the parties to be bound by it, as well as the exchange of the 'instruments of ratification' to enter into force. Since only one party ratified the agreement and, as a result, no exchange of instruments of ratifications occurred, the Lebanon–Israel Agreement is an unratified agreement with no legally binding validity.[141] On that ground, neither country can claim rights or definitively delimit its EEZ on the basis of this agreement.

Secondly, in accordance with the Lebanese position, the delimitation of the EEZ of Lebanon and Cyprus, in principle, has to be conducted based on the agreed guiding principle of 'median line' (equidistant line) between both countries.[142] Article 1(a) of the Lebanon–Cyprus Agreement provides that the delimitation of the EEZ between both countries is effected by 'the median line of which every point along the length of it is equidistant from the nearest point on the baselines of the two parties'.[143] Nevertheless, in its agreement with Cyprus, Lebanon did not delimit its southern EEZ tripoint with Cyprus and Israel as exact median lines or equidistant tripoints. Likewise, and in the same agreement with Cyprus, Lebanon did not designate its northern EEZ tripoint with Cyprus and Syria as exact median lines or equidistant tripoints. Moreover, in this agreement, Lebanon did not delimit its northern and southern tripoints like the equidistant tripoints it proclaimed through its submissions to the

---

139 Article 5(1) of the Lebanon–Cyprus Agreement, 2007; ASDEAM, 'Lebanon's Maritime Boundaries', 16.

140 Article 5(2) of the Lebanon–Cyprus Agreement, 2007.

141 Article 14(1)(a) of the United Nations Vienna Convention on the Law of Treaties states that when a treaty requires that the consent of countries to be bound by the treaty has to be expressed through ratification, then the ratification is the means that the parties have to use in order to express their consent to be bound by the treaty. United Nations, Vienna Convention on the Law of Treaties, 23 May 1969, United Nations, Treaty Series, Vol. 1155, p. 331, http://www.unhcr.org/refworld/docid/3ae6b3a10.htm. Even though Lebanon and Israel are not parties to the Vienna Convention on the Law of Treaties, customary international law applies to the unratified treaties in this regard.

142 Article 1(e) of the Lebanon–Cyprus Agreement, 2007.

143 See Article 1(a) of the Lebanon–Cyprus Agreement, 2007.

UN.[144] In fact, in its bilateral agreement with Cyprus, Lebanon left margins in the determination of the southern and northern borders tripoints, Point 1 and Point 6 respectively. In the southern borders, Lebanon delimited its EEZ boundaries with Cyprus and Palestine (Israel) at Point 1, which falls to the north of the equidistant tripoint between Lebanon, Israel, and Cyprus.[145] In the northern borders, Lebanon delimited its EEZ boundaries with Cyprus and Syria at Point 6, which falls to the south of the equidistant tripoint between Lebanon, Syria, and Cyprus.[146]

In doing so, Lebanon has followed a frequently witnessed international practice used in bilateral agreements on maritime delimitation. This practice provides that, when a third party State, a concerned State, is not a party to a bilateral agreement, the parties to the bilateral agreement stop the maritime boundaries short before reaching the tripoints with the third country concerned.[147] By doing so, the door would be open to delimit the tripoints by future participation of all countries concerned. Hence, Lebanon explains that the delimitation of Point 1 in the Lebanon–Cyprus Agreement was not a final delimitation of the southern maritime tripoint, but a provisional one, following the consuetudinary practice of maritime boundaries delimitation.[148] Additionally, Lebanon's intention to set the southern border tripoint as a provisional delimitation until the final delimitation with the 'neighboring States concerned' is done can be implied also from Article 1(e) of the Lebanon–Cyprus Agreement, which states that the geographical coordinates could be reviewed or modified 'in the light of future delimitation of the exclusive economic zones with other neighboring States concerned in accordance with an agreement that may be reached regarding this matter with the neighboring States concerned'.[149] Thus, according to Lebanon's position, the Lebanese delimitation of the southern tripoint shared with Cyprus and Israel cannot

[144] See Table 4.5, which lists the geographical coordinates in Annex I to the Lebanon–Cyprus Agreement, 2007, compared with Tables 4.2 and 4.3, which are the Lebanese lists of geographical coordinates submitted to the UN.

[145] See ASDEAM, 'Lebanon's Maritime Boundaries', at 17.

[146] Ibid.

[147] See Colson, D. 'The Legal Regime Of Maritime Boundary Agreements' In Charney, J.I & Alexander, L.M. (Eds) *International Maritime Boundaries*, Vol. I (Leiden: Martinus Nijhoff Publishers, 1993), p. 43.

[148] See ASDEAM, 'Lebanon's Maritime Boundaries', at 17.

[149] Article 1(e) of the Lebanon–Cyprus Agreement, 2007; ASDEAM, 'Lebanon's Maritime Boundaries', at 17.

bind Lebanon, since it was temporarily delimited until an agreed tripoint is settled upon with the other neighboring countries concerned.

Consequently, the agreement between Lebanon and Cyprus on the delimitation of the EEZs of both countries does not provide a decisive solution to the disputed tripoint between Lebanon and Israel. On the one hand, there is a clear contradiction between what Lebanon has agreed as the southern tripoint with Cyprus in this agreement (Point 1) and what Lebanon proclaimed later on through the proclamation it deposited with the UN (Point 23). Likewise, Lebanon's delimitation of the southern tripoint in this agreement is compatible with Israel's EEZ proclamation to the UN (Point 1). On the other hand, this agreement was never ratified by Lebanon, which gives rise to the invalidation of the agreement. Moreover, Lebanon's delimitation of the southern tripoint was not considered by Lebanon to become a final binding delimitation, but a provisional one, following a widespread international practice. For these reasons, the Lebanon–Cyprus Agreement contributes more complications than options for a solution to settle the maritime dispute between Lebanon and Israel.

3.5. The Israel–Cyprus Agreement[150] The Israel–Cyprus Agreement on the Delimitation of the EEZ was signed on December 17, 2010. It purported to delimit the EEZ boundaries of Israel and Cyprus. The agreement was ratified by Israel[151] and Cyprus[152] in February 2011. While Cyprus ratified by law the Israel–Cyprus Agreement on the delimitation of the EEZ, Israel submitted this agreement to the Israeli Parliament on 22 December 2010, and it was ratified by the Israeli government through a governmental decision on 3 February 2011.[153] Israel relies on this agreement as a binding international agreement. This

---

150 See Agreement Between the Government of the State of Israel and the Government of the Republic of Cyprus on the Delimitation of the Exclusive Economic Zone, signed in Nicosia on 17 December 2010 (entry into force 25 February 2011; Registration #:I-48387; Registration Date: 9 March 2011, http://www.un.org/depts/los/LEGISLATIONANDTREATIES/PDFFILES/TREATIES/cyp_isr_eez_2010.pdf).

151 See The Government of Israel, Decision 2794 (3.2.2011): Ratification of the Israel–Cyprus Agreement on the Delimitation of the EEZ, http://www.pm.gov.il/PMO/Archive/Decisions/2011/02/des2794.htm

152 See The Government of Cyprus: Ministry of Commerce, Industry and Tourism, http://www.mcit.gov.cy/mcit/mcit.nsf/All/A6D222B09D72E659C2257441002EE9BE?OpenDocument

153 See the Israeli Parliament, session 195 of the 18th Knesset, 27 December 2010 (in Hebrew) at www.knesset.gov.il/plenum/data/04885210.doc

appears chiefly from its proclamation submitted to the UN, where, through the list of geographical coordinates, in Note 1, Israel noted that Point 1 of its proclamation 'is derived from Point 1 of the Agreement between the State of Israel and the Republic of Cyprus on the Delimitation of the Exclusive Economic Zone, dated December 17, 2010'.[154] So, for both countries, it is most likely a legally binding international agreement. As mentioned above, even though Israel is not a party to UNCLOS, both parties to the agreement agreed to apply the rules of UNCLOS and international law to the delimitation of their EEZs.[155]

In addition, in Article 1(a) of the agreement, Israel and Cyprus have agreed that the delimitation of the EEZ boundaries between the two States is 'effected by the median line'.[156] Article 1(b) defines the median line between the two States and assigns its limits according to points 1–12 and their geographical coordinates. These points and geographical coordinates were identified by Annex I of the Israel–Cyprus Agreement.[157] As seen in Table 4.6, according to Annex I of the Israel–Cyprus Agreement, Point 1 is the intersection point of three countries' EEZs: Lebanon, Cyprus and Israel. Its coordinates are 33° 38' 40" N Latitude and 33° 53' 40" E Longitude.[158] Importantly, Point 1, with its coordinates, is the same tripoint that was proclaimed by Israel on the delimitation of its EEZ, as indicated in the Israeli proclamation deposited with the UN in 2011.[159] Moreover, Point 1 in the Israel–Cyprus Agreement is similar to Point 1 in the Lebanon–Cyprus Agreement (2007).[160] As pointed out earlier, Point 1 in the Lebanon–Cyprus Agreement represented the tripoint where the three EEZs of Lebanon, Cyprus, and Israel intersect.

---

154 See the Israeli List of Geographical Coordinates submitted to the UN.

155 See the Preamble of the Israel–Cyprus Agreement, 2010.

156 Ibid. Article 1(a).

157 Ibid. Article 1(b).

158 Ibid. Annex I.

159 See Table 4.4, The Israeli List of Geographical Coordinates to the UN.

160 See Tables 4.5 and 4.6; see also ASDEAM, 'Lebanon's Maritime Boundaries', 18.

Table 4.6 Annex I to the Israel–Cyprus Agreement (2010), list of geographical coordinates

Point	Latitude	Longitude
1	33° 38' 40"	33° 53' 40"
2	33° 37' 24"	33° 52' 06"
3	33° 32' 59"	33° 46' 42"
4	33° 30' 00"	33° 43' 05"
5	33° 24' 27"	33° 36' 15"
6	33° 16' 56"	33° 27' 02"
7	33° 09' 25"	33° 17' 50"
8	33° 03' 22"	33° 10' 28"
9	32° 59' 37"	33° 05' 56"
10	32° 56' 03"	33° 01' 36"
11	32° 54' 35"	32° 59' 50"
12	32° 53' 20"	32° 58' 20"

Source: the Israel–Cyprus Agreement (17 December 2010), http://www.un.org/Depts/los/LEGISLATIONANDTREATIES/PDFFILES/TREATIES/cyp_isr_eez_2010.pdf

One of the complications with this agreement is that it contradicts the Lebanese proclamation to the UN. Although Point 1 in the Israel–Cyprus Agreement is the same as Point 1 in the Lebanon–Cyprus Agreement, in its submission to the UN, Lebanon proclaimed a different tripoint. As mentioned, Lebanon proclaimed Point 23 as the southern tripoint, that is 17 kilometers south of the Israel–Cyprus tripoint, Point 1. Based on the EEZ delimitation according to the Israel–Cyprus Agreement, particularly Point 1, in June 2011 Lebanon objected to this agreement and complained to the UN against it.[161] Similarly, in September 2011 Lebanon protested to the UN against the Israeli proclamation, which had been submitted to the UN in July 2011 to delimit Israel's southern EEZ.[162] In these protests, Lebanon rejected the EEZ demarcation suggested by Israel and Cyprus. It explained that Point 1 does not reflect the southern end point of the median line between Lebanon and Cyprus. According to Lebanon's position, Point 1 is viewed only as 'a point shared by Lebanon and Cyprus. It is not a terminal point and therefore may not be taken as a starting point between Cyprus and any other country, particularly given

[161] See Lebanon's Letter to the UN, June 2011.
[162] See Lebanon's Letter to the UN, September 2011.

the fact that it is just one point like any of the others on this line'.[163] Lebanon stressed that:

> Israel has adopted point 1 as the point that separates the exclusive economic zones of Cyprus, Israel and Lebanon, while it is point 23, which is equidistant between those three countries … [o]n the basis of the foregoing, it is clear that the geographical coordinates that were deposited with you by Israel violate the sovereign and economic rights of Lebanon over its territorial waters and exclusive economic zone.[164]

On the other hand, Israel rejected Lebanon's position. Israel's Prime Minister Benjamin Netanyahu made an announcement which reflects the Israeli position pertaining to the contradiction and complications of the EEZs demarcation:

> The [maritime] line that Lebanon presented to the UN is significantly south of the Israeli line … It contradicts the line Israel has agreed upon with Cyprus, and what is more significant to me is that it contradicts the line that Lebanon itself concluded with Cyprus in 2007. Our goal is to establish the position of Israel regarding its maritime boundary, according to international maritime law.[165]

An additional complication can be distinguished in this agreement with respect to the delimitation of the Point 1. Seemingly, when Israel and Cyprus bilaterally delimited the tripoint between the three countries, they did not take into account through the delimitation of Point 1 the concerns and interests of Lebanon as the third party concerned, and ignored the margin left in the Lebanon–Cyprus Agreement.[166] Israel and Cyprus did not stop the maritime boundaries short before reaching the equidistant tripoint with Lebanon as the country concerned.

It is clear that the dominant contradiction between the Israel–Cyprus Agreement and the Lebanese proclamation deposited to the UN highlights the disputed EEZ area between Lebanon and Israel. Moreover, it complicates the delimitation of the EEZs of Lebanon and Israel and, as a result, obstructs the exploitation of the energy resources in these EEZs. Consequently, this unresolved and ongoing maritime dispute between Lebanon and Israel is likely to generate more legal, political, and

---

[163] See Lebanon's Letter to the UN, June 2011.

[164] See Lebanon's Letter to the UN, September 2011.

[165] See Keinon, H. 'Cabinet Approves Northern Maritime Border', *Jerusalem Post* (July 10, 2011) http://www.jpost.com/LandedPages/PrintArticle.aspx?id=228666

[166] See ASDEAM, 'Lebanon's Maritime Boundaries', 18.

diplomatic unilateral steps and statements by both countries disregarding a bilateral agreement or collaborative efforts to settle the current dispute.

Despite the complications derived from the Israel–Cyprus Agreement or the circumstances surrounding it, three provisions should be recalled from this agreement that might be useful in any future negotiation or dispute settlement procedure. The first two provisions are Article 1(a) and 1(b) of this agreement, which are similar to Article 1(a) of the Lebanon-Cyprus Agreement.[167] According to these provisions, Israel and Cyprus agreed that the delimitation of the EEZ boundaries is effected by the 'median line' principle. The third provision is Article 1(e) of the Israel–Cyprus Agreement, which is similar to Article 1(e) of the Lebanon–Cyprus Agreement. Article 1(e) of the Israel–Cyprus Agreement provides:

> Taking into consideration the principles of customary international law relating to the delimitation of the Exclusive Economic Zone between States, the geographical coordinates of points 1 or 12 could be reviewed and/or modified as necessary in light of a future agreement regarding the delimitation of the Exclusive Economic Zone to be reached by the three States concerned with respect to each of the said points.[168]

Two points can be extracted from these provisions of the Israel–Cyprus Agreement:

(1) The borders' points 1 and 12 were not delimited to be decisive or conclusive demarcations. In essence, they were intended to be subject to review or modification in any future agreement that would involve the three countries concerned in the delimitation of the EEZ boundaries;

(2) The median line is the guiding rule in setting the EEZ boundaries, including the tripoints where the three EEZs converge.

Accordingly, while Article 1(e) of the Israel–Cyprus Agreement provides the mechanism for re-negotiating Point 1 or the accurate tripoint between the three concerned countries, that is, Lebanon, Cyprus, and Israel, Article 1(a) and 1(b) of the same agreement provides the guiding

---

[167] See Article 1(a) and 1(b) of the Israel–Cyprus Agreement, 2010, and Article 1(a) of the Lebanon–Cyprus Agreement, 2007; ASDEAM, 'Lebanon's Maritime Boundaries', 16.

[168] See Article 1(e) of the Israel–Cyprus Agreement, 2010, and Article 1(e) of the Lebanon–Cyprus Agreement, 2007; ASDEAM, 'Lebanon's Maritime Boundaries', 17.

substantial rule for the delimitation of the tripoint. Thus, in spite of the complications and the unilateral approaches, some common ground exists that could serve as a basis for any future efforts or attempts to reach a lasting agreement settling this EEZ delimitation dispute.

3.6. Resolving the dispute through dispute settlement procedures Under the existing circumstances, given that Lebanon and Israel submitted to the UN their EEZs' unilateral proclamations, and as long as no bilateral negotiations are taking place to resolve the Israel–Lebanon dispute, this maritime dispute may reach a formal international dispute settlement procedure. However, the path of invoking an international tribunal to settle this maritime dispute involves further complications.

As mentioned earlier, UNCLOS constitutes a developed framework of international law that governs maritime issues, including delimiting maritime boundaries in general and EEZs in particular. Article 59 of UNCLOS provides that in cases where conflict between the interests of coastal States arises, such conflict 'should be resolved on the basis of equity and in the light of all the relevant circumstances'. In addition, Article 74(1) of UNCLOS provides that the EEZ delimitation of coastal countries has to be obtained through agreement between the concerned parties 'on the basis of international law'. If no agreement can be reached within a reasonable time, Article 74(2) of UNCLOS states that 'the States concerned shall resort to the procedures provided for in Part XV'. In this respect, a central reason that makes UNCLOS one of the most significant constitutive methods of international law is its inclusion of a compulsory dispute settlement system.[169] Notably, UNCLOS refers to a compulsory dispute settlement procedure and jurisdiction. In order to settle a dispute and delimit maritime boundaries, Article 287(1) of UNCLOS provides the parties with the right to choose an agreed dispute mechanism from a set of dispute settlement institutions:

> When signing, ratifying or acceding to this Convention or at any time thereafter, a State shall be free to choose, by means of a written declaration, one or more of the following means for the settlement of disputes concerning the interpretation or application of this Convention:
>
> (a) the International Tribunal for the Law of the Sea established in accordance with Annex VI;
> (b) the International Court of Justice;
> (c) an arbitral tribunal constituted in accordance with Annex VII;

[169] See Klein, N. *Dispute Settlement in the UN Convention on the Law of the Sea* (Cambridge: Cambridge University Press, 2004), at 349.

(d) a special arbitral tribunal constituted in accordance with Annex VIII for one or more of the categories of disputes specified therein.

Subsequently, after choosing an agreed dispute settlement procedure from the abovementioned institutions, the chosen tribunal with the jurisdiction to settle the maritime dispute shall apply UNCLOS rules and other international law rules compatible with UNCLOS.[170]

The question is: which tribunal is likely to be the agreed, authorized, and appropriate one to settle the dispute between Lebanon and Israel? In the first stage of the compulsory procedure, the parties are free to choose from one of two judicial branches, that is, the International Tribunal for the Law of the Sea (ITLOS) and the International Court of Justice (ICJ), or the arbitration procedure.[171] However, according to Article 287(5) of UNCLOS, if the same procedure for settling the dispute has not been accepted by the parties to the dispute, the dispute may be settled only by arbitration. Arbitration is held to be the obligatory dispute settlement choice, except if the parties agree otherwise. It is worth noting that, in line with Article 280 of UNCLOS, choosing any of the settlement procedure options does not derogate from the fundamental right of the parties to settle the dispute between them, at any time, by any 'peaceful means of their own choice'.[172]

One of the initial challenges confronting the reference to, or the activation of, the compulsory dispute settlement procedure according to UNCLOS is the absence of the full consent of all the parties to the dispute in respect to the applicability of UNCLOS. In general, one of the most established and predominant principles of international law focuses on the jurisdiction of international courts. This principle dictates that the jurisdiction of international courts shall be based on the clear consent of

---

170 Article 293(1) UNCLOS. In parallel, the chosen tribunal has the power to decide, if the parties agree, what it considers to be fair and equitable in a particular case. Ibid., Article 293(2).

171 Regarding conflicts that might develop between the ITLOS, ICJ, and arbitrations pertaining to settling maritime disputes according to UNCLOS, see in general Treves, T. 'Conflicts Between the International Tribunal for the Law of the Sea and the International Court of Justice' (1999 1998) *New York University Journal of International Law and Politics* 31, 809; Zekos, G.I. 'Competition or Conflict in the Dispute Settlement Mechanism of the Law of the Sea Convention' (2003) *Revue Hellenique de Droit International*, Vol. 56, No. 1, pp. 153–166; Fleisschhaur, C.-A. 'Relationship Between the International Court of Justice and the Newly Created International Tribunal for the Law of the Sea in Hamburg' (1997) 1 *Max Planck Y.B. U.N. L.* pp. 327–334, 345.

172 Article 280 UNCLOS.

the countries concerned.[173] In particular, in the context of the dispute settlement mechanism of UNCLOS, it should be emphasized again that a prerequisite for the application of UNCLOS is the consent of the States that are in dispute to be bound by UNCLOS provisions. Lebanon acceded to UNCLOS in 1995 and Cyprus in 1988. Israel, however, is not a party to this convention. Therefore, since Israel, as a pivotal party to this dispute, is not a party to UNCLOS, this has significant implications for the resolution of the maritime dispute between Lebanon and Israel and for delimiting the tripoint between Lebanon, Cyprus, and Israel.

Assuming *arguendo* UNCLOS is applicable, not only the applicability of its rules for the delimitation of the EEZ boundaries as customary international law, but also the applicability of the provisions with regard to the dispute settlement procedures, according to Article 287(1) of UNCLOS, Lebanon and Israel have to choose a dispute settlement institution. This choice of procedure out of the listed dispute settlement institutions, that is, ITLOS, the ICJ, or arbitration, has to be agreed upon by Lebanon and Israel; otherwise, the arbitration procedure will be imposed on them.[174] At this point, when the Lebanon–Israel dispute requires any bilateral agreement or consent, the complications to settling the dispute that were discussed above may rise again.

3.6.1. The International Tribunal for the Law of the Sea (ITLOS)

The ITLOS was established in accordance with Annex VI of UNCLOS.[175] UNCLOS provides the State Parties with the option of settling maritime disputes, including delimiting EEZs, via the ITLOS. The option to settle the current dispute between Israel and Lebanon through adjudication before one of the proposed tribunals by UNCLOS is unlikely to be accomplished. Article 20(1) of the ITLOS Statute provides that the ITLOS is open to State Parties to UNCLOS, whereas Israel is still not a State Party to this convention. Article 20(2) of the ITLOS Statute provides that the ITLOS is open not only to State Parties to UNCLOS, but also to other entities. This additional access to the ITLOS jurisdiction occurs in cases expressly provided for either in Part XI of

---

173 See Greenwood, C. 'Some Challenges of International Litigation' (2012) *Cambridge Journal of International and Comparative Law*, Vol. 1, No 1, pp. 7–22, at pp. 14–15.

174 Article 287(5) UNCLOS.

175 UNCLOS, Annex VI; Seymour, J. 'The International Tribunal for the Law of the Sea: A Great Mistake?' (2006) *Indiana Journal of Global Legal Studies*, Vol. 13, No. 1, pp. 1–35 [hereinafter, Seymour, 'The International Tribunal for the Law of the Sea'].

UNCLOS or 'in any case submitted pursuant to any other agreement conferring jurisdiction on the Tribunal which is accepted by all the parties to that case'.[176] This track, which provides additional access to the ITLOS, requires the consent of the parties to the dispute.

Consequently, the Statute of the ITLOS stresses the importance of the State Party status as well as the consent of all parties to a dispute for the sake of conferring jurisdiction on the ITLOS to settle a particular dispute. Yet, neither Lebanon nor Israel expressed their consent to submit their maritime dispute to the ITLOS jurisdiction. Israel is neither a State Party to UNCLOS nor has it agreed with Lebanon that they will submit their EEZ dispute to the ITLOS. Without fulfilling one of these prerequisites, ITLOS cannot establish its jurisdiction over the Lebanon–Israel maritime dispute. In other words, unless Israel becomes a State Party to UNCLOS or both Lebanon and Israel expressly consent by agreement to submit their maritime dispute to ITLOS jurisdiction, ITLOS will not be authorized to address and settle the Lebanon–Israel dispute and, as a result, delimit their EEZ boundaries.

A mention must be made with respect to the ITLOS experience of settling maritime disputes involving delimitation of maritime boundaries. In comparison with the ICJ and arbitration procedures, the ITLOS has very little experience in addressing cases concerning delimitation of maritime boundaries. In fact, the first maritime delimitation judgment of the ITLOS was delivered in 2012, relating to the delimitation of the maritime boundary between Bangladesh and Myanmar.[177]

3.6.2. THE INTERNATIONAL COURT OF JUSTICE (ICJ) Article 7(1) of the UN Charter determines the principal organs of the UN to include: 'a General Assembly, a Security Council, an Economic and Social Council, a Trusteeship Council, an International Court of Justice, and a Secretariat'.[178] Additionally, Article 92 of the UN Charter defines the ICJ as the 'principal judicial organ of the United Nations'.[179] The ICJ, as the

---

176 Seymour, 'The International Tribunal for the Law of the Sea', 7–8.

177 See *Dispute Concerning Delimitation of the Maritime Boundary between Bangladesh and Myanmar in the Bay of Bengal (Bangladesh/Myanmar)*, Judgment of 14 March 2012, http://www.itlos.org/fileadmin/itlos/documents/cases/case_no_16/C16_Judgment_14_03_2012_rev.pdf

178 See Article 7(1) of the Charter of the United Nations, 24 October 1945, 1 UNTS XVI, http://www.unhcr.org/refworld/docid/3ae6b3930.html

179 Ibid., Article 92; United Nations, *Statute of the International Court of Justice*, 18 April 1946, Article 1, http://www.unhcr.org/refworld/docid/3deb4b9c0.html

most ostensibly important international court, has a proven record in and experience of settling maritime disputes between countries.[180] Interestingly, apart from the requisite consent in order to be bound by UNCLOS, the jurisdiction of the ICJ to settle disputes is based also upon the consent of the States concerned (save for in exceptional circumstances under international law). Article 36(1) of the ICJ Statute provides that '[t]he jurisdiction of the Court comprises all cases which the parties refer to it and all matters specially provided for in the Charter of the United Nations or in treaties and conventions in force'.[181] Whatever the form of the consent might be, it must serve as a precondition to invoke the ICJ jurisdiction.[182] In this regard, the ICJ has stressed the significance of consent expressed by the concerned States in order to confer jurisdiction upon the ICJ: 'The Court recalls in this respect that one of the fundamental principles of its Statute is that it cannot decide a dispute between States without the consent of those States to its jurisdiction'.[183]

Since the ICJ acquires jurisdiction only after the disputed parties have accepted its jurisdiction, conferring jurisdiction on the ICJ in the Lebanon–Israel dispute is not possible without acquiring the consent of Lebanon and Israel. As mentioned earlier, based on the Israel–Cyprus

---

[180] See *Case Concerning the Continental Shelf (Tunisia/Libyan Arab Jamahiriya)*, Judgment, I.C.J. Reports 1982, p. 18, http://www.icj-cij.org/docket/files/63/6267.pdf; *Case Concerning Continental Shelf (Libyan Arab Jarnahiriya/Malta)*, Judgment, I.C.J. Reports 1985, p. 13, http://www.icj-cij.org/docket/files/68/6415.pdf; *Maritime Delimitation and Territorial Questions between Qatar and Bahrain, Merits*, Judgment, I.C. J. Reports 2001, p. 40, http://www.icj-cij.org/docket/files/87/7027.pdf; *Territorial and Maritime Dispute between Nicaragua and Honduras in the Caribbean Sea (Nicaragua v. Honduras)*, Judgment, I.C.J. Reports 2007, p. 659, http://www.icj-cij.org/docket/files/120/14075.pdf; *Maritime Delimitation in the Black Sea (Romania v. Ukraine)*, Judgment, I.C.J. Reports 2009, p. 61, http://www.icj-cij.org/docket/files/132/14987.pdf; *Land and Maritime Boundary between Cameroon and Nigeria, Preliminary Objections, Judgment*, I.C. J. Reports 1998, p. 275, http://www.icj-cij.org/docket/files/94/7473.pdf; Shi Jiuyong, 'Maritime Delimitation in the Jurisprudence of the International Court of Justice' (2010) *Chinese Journal of International Law* 9, 271.

[181] See Statute of the ICJ, Article 36(1); International Court of Justice website: Basis of the Court's Jurisdiction, http://www.icj-cij.org/jurisdiction/index.php?p1=5&p2=1&p3=2#1

[182] See Gozie Ogbodo, S. 'Overview of the Challenges Facing the International Court of Justice in the 21st Century', *Annual Survey of International & Comparative Law* 18 (2012): 93, 101–102.

[183] See *East Timor (Portugal v. Australia)*, Judgment, I.C.J. Reports 1995, p. 101, para. 26, http://www.icj-cij.org/docket/files/84/6949.pdf

Agreement (2010), which was followed by Israel's EEZ proclamation being submitted to the UN in 2011, Lebanon submitted a complaint against Israel's unilateral EEZ's delimitation. In such a situation, with the ICJ being requested to address the Lebanese compliant against Israel, it will require Israel's consent to invoke jurisdiction over the Lebanon–Israel case. Hence, if Israel does not agree to the ICJ to adjudicating upon the disputed EEZ area with Lebanon, or if it opposes the ICJ's jurisdiction, the ICJ will lack the jurisdictional basis to address this dispute.[184] In the present situation, given that a state of war prevails between Lebanon and Israel, and given the unilateral proclamations to the UN regarding the disputed and overlapped EEZ area, as well as the various political statements, including reciprocal official threats, obtaining such consent from both parties of the dispute, or at least from Israel, appears to be unlikely.

Therefore, the consent to confer jurisdiction upon the ICJ would also be a crucial precondition for an eventual adjudication of the Lebanon–Israel maritime dispute before the ICJ. As a consequence, the lack of consent and agreement between Lebanon and Israel is a substantial complication that bans the demarcation of their EEZ boundaries through the ICJ.

3.6.3. ARBITRATION In principle, UNCLOS provides the disputed parties with a choice of procedure. Accordingly, the parties to the maritime dispute have the right to choose one of the dispute settlement procedures available under Article 287(1) of UNCLOS, namely the ITLOS, ICJ, arbitration in accordance with Annex VII, or a special arbitral procedure constituted according to Annex VIII of UNCLOS. However, following Article 287(1) of UNCLOS, failure to agree upon dispute resolution methods leads to UNCLOS imposing an obligatory procedure on the disputed parties. It is the arbitration procedure that is in

---

184 The ICJ did not exercise its jurisdiction in a number of cases where the opposing parties have not accepted the ICJ jurisdiction: *Treatment in Hungary of Aircraft and Crew of the United States of America (United States of America v. Hungary)*; *Treatment in Hungary of Aircraft and Crew of the United States of America (United States of America v. USSR)*; *Aerial Incident of 10 March 1953 (United States of America v. Czechoslovakia)*; *Antarctica (United Kingdom v. Argentina)*; *Antarctica (United Kingdom v. Chile)*; *Aerial Incident of 7 October 1952 (United States of America v. USSR)*; *Aerial Incident of 4 September 1954 (United States of America v. USSR)*; and *Aerial Incident of 7 November 1954 (United States of America v. USSR)*.

conformity with Annex VII of UNCLOS.[185] That is to say, when one of the dispute settlement procedures has not been designated by consensus between the disputed parties, UNCLOS will impose arbitration as the default procedure for the resolution of maritime disputes. Since UNCLOS entered into force in 1994,[186] the arbitration procedure plays a pivotal role in the resolution of disputes according to Annex VII of UNCLOS. In effect, several arbitral proceedings were conducted according to Annex VII of UNCLOS, three of which addressed the delimitation of maritime boundaries.[187]

With relevance to the delimitation of the maritime boundaries of Lebanon and Israel, namely their disputed EEZ boundaries, the two bilateral agreements examined above have recourse to an arbitration procedure. According to Article 4(1) of the Lebanon–Cyprus Agreement, both countries have agreed to settle any dispute which arises from the implementation of their agreement through 'diplomatic channels'. If the dispute is not settled through diplomatic channels within a reasonable period of time, according to Article 4(b) of this agreement, 'the dispute will be referred to arbitration'. Equally, the Israel–Cyprus Agreement urges the parties to seek settlement for any dispute through diplomatic channels.[188] Article 4(b) of the Israel–Cyprus Agreement states that in any case where both countries cannot settle a dispute escalated between them through diplomatic channels and within a reasonable period of time, 'the dispute will be referred to arbitration'.[189] From these two separate bilateral agreements, one can infer that, in the bilateral relations between Lebanon and Cyprus as well as Israel and Cyprus, they have made clear reference to arbitration to be the agreed and appropriate forum to settle any dispute that may arise between the parties of each agreement.

One would think that arbitration is likely to be the suitable method to settle the Lebanon–Israel maritime dispute. However, the Lebanon–

---

185 Article 287(5) UNCLOS.

186 Article 308 UNCLOS; United Nations Convention on the Law of the Sea of 10 December 1982: Overview and full text, http://www.un.org/Depts/los/convention_agreements/convention_overview_convention.htm

187 See *Barbados v. Trinidad and Tobago* (2006) 139 ILR 449; *Guyana v. Suriname* (2007) 139 ILR 566. See also the pending case of *Bangladesh v. India* (Permanent Court of Arbitration).

188 See Article 4(a) of the Israel–Cyprus Agreement, 2010.

189 Ibid., Article 4(b). The parties did not determine the terms of reference and the procedure of the arbitration, but they agreed to determine these issues through a mutual agreement, prior to launching into arbitration.

Cyprus Agreement is an unratified agreement, has no legal binding power and needs to be ratified by Lebanon first in order to obtain the required international legal validity. Moreover, both agreements are bilateral agreements and bind only the parties to the agreements. Furthermore, these bilateral agreements bind in those matters and disputes arising from the 'interpretation or implementation' of each one of the agreements separately. Additionally, let us assume, for the sake of the argument, that Lebanon ratified the agreement with Cyprus and that it is due to an agreed modification that preserves Lebanon's right over its maritime boundaries, particularly the boundaries with Israel. In such a case, and in spite of the ratification, the Lebanon–Cyprus Agreement is not binding. Firstly, the agreed arbitration clause in the Lebanon–Cyprus Agreement binds only the parties to the agreement, Lebanon and Cyprus; additionally, it binds them only to issues relevant to the agreement. Thus, despite the assumed ratification of the Lebanon–Cyprus Agreement, this agreement does not bind a third party to the agreement, including Israel, and has no applicability over the Lebanon–Israel dispute.

The same analysis applies to the Israel–Cyprus Agreement. In this agreement the arbitration clause binds the two parties only to the agreement and to matters arising from the agreement itself. Hence, the arbitration clause in the Israel–Cyprus Agreement neither binds Lebanon as a third party nor applies to the Lebanon–Israel dispute. Given the limited applicability of the arbitration clauses in each bilateral agreement, and given that there is no binding bilateral agreement between Lebanon and Israel with relevance to the delimitation of EEZs, no arbitration clause obliges Lebanon and Israel to launch an arbitration procedure, or any other dispute resolution procedure, to resolve their maritime dispute and delimit their EEZ boundaries.

Consequently, Lebanon and Israel have never agreed to settle their maritime dispute or delimit their EEZ boundaries through arbitration. However, if Israel accepts and ratifies UNCLOS, only in this case will the arbitration procedure be imposed as a default compulsory dispute resolution to settle the Lebanon–Israel maritime dispute. Certainly, and similar to the previously discussed tribunals, that is, the ITLOS and the ICJ, in the context of the Lebanon–Israel case, without the express consent of Lebanon and Israel, the arbitration procedure is unlikely to be imposed as a default obligatory procedure, notwithstanding the foregoing default obligatory prevalence.

IV. CONCLUSION

Law of the sea is another legal aspect of interstate energy governance. A clear example of the link between maritime delimitation (regulated by law of the sea) and interstate energy governance is the energy reserves discoveries in the EMB. As we have briefly discussed, what had been a firmer geopolitical situation in the EMB is now becoming more fluid. The fairly recent souring of hitherto amiable Israeli–Turkish relations has recast the possibilities for strategic partnerships in the region in a way that potentially excludes Turkey. Israel now joins Cyprus and Greece – both embroiled in longstanding unresolved disputes with Turkey – in cooperation efforts over energy in the EMB. The exploration of energy reserves in the EMB region is not straightforward. The state of affairs between the coastal States – Cyprus, Egypt, Greece, Israel, Lebanon, Syria, Turkey – and the other entities in the region (namely the Palestinian Occupied Territories and the Turkish-Cypriot administration) presents persistent obstacles. We have also alluded above to the EU energy security interests and the US commercial and geostrategic interests at play in the EMB region.

The desire on the part of Cyprus, Israel, and Greece to collaborate to bring gas and oil from the region to EU markets makes this contentious, given the conflicting claims existing in the region. Turkey, for instance, considers that the government of Cyprus – the internationally recognized entity – lacks the legitimacy to engage with third States in defining the maritime boundaries of the entire island, given that the government of Cyprus does not represent the interests of the Turkish-Cypriot population. These disputes – however, politicized – remain matters to which legal principles may apply. The issue is, as in many interstate disputes, how to subject the dispute to an adjudicative agency where the jurisdiction of the ICJ is not automatic or capable of being established via other means – for example, through a bilateral or multilateral treaty provision involving the States that are parties to a dispute.

The entire body of public international law has been developed over the course of centuries to regulate the relations between *imperia*, and, in modern times, between nation-states. Following the advent of the UN system, disputes between sovereign actors are amenable to peaceful resolution processes and subject to compliance with the UN Charter.[190] Whilst the advent of UNCLOS has revolutionized and modernized

[190] See Chapter VI UN Charter in relation to State obligations to settle disputes peacefully and Article 103 UN Charter, which states that, in the case of

international maritime law, the fact that two important regional actors are not parties to it may have implications on delimitation attempts of their maritime boundaries. What is more, UNCLOS cannot in its entirety be held to reflect customary law, given the state of maritime law at the time of the negotiation and conclusion of UNCLOS. However, UNCLOS introduces concepts – for example, the EEZ – which did not exist in that form prior to its advent. The coastal States with disputes pending are all energy dependent. Turkey is an important energy transit State. The cooperation on energy between the nexus Cyprus–Israel–Greece could also enhance the EU's energy security. So would more integrated energy relations with Turkey.

Moreover, the energy discoveries in the Levant Basin, by virtue of the circumstances and facts discussed above, may not constitute the beginning of a new golden energy era for Lebanon and Israel. Although there are economic and development opportunities embodied in these discoveries, in parallel, political conflict is escalating, and the maritime dispute has intensified and become more complex. There is a pressing necessity to settle the maritime dispute between Lebanon and Israel in order to achieve two crucial goals. Firstly, to avoid slipping into any utilization of military force against each other, leading, as a consequence, to another tragic war between both countries; secondly, to allow the most effective exploitation of the energy discoveries in the Levant Basin.

As mentioned, coastal countries, with opposite or adjacent coasts, are required to delimit the boundaries of their maritime zones by reaching agreements based on an equitable solution. However, in the Lebanon–Israel case, a variety of aspects have to be taken into account, which comprise real challenges and complications towards reaching an equitable solution to the settlement of this EEZ dispute. The Lebanon–Israel maritime dispute over the delimitation of the EEZ boundaries will not be settled easily without the cooperation of both countries. Undoubtedly, these complications do not restrain only the resolution of the Lebanon–Israel dispute. The prevalence of these complications cripples any exploitation of the significant energy resources discovered in the disputed EEZ area.

The preferred primary mechanism for the delimitation of maritime boundaries or resolution of maritime disputes is negotiation between the concerned States. The alternative mechanism is the dispute resolution procedures provided by UNCLOS. In the first stage of the dispute resolution procedure, the parties are free to choose one of the procedures

---

conflict between provisions in interstate agreements and the UN Charter, the provisions of the latter shall prevail.

provided by UNCLOS. If the parties cannot agree on the same procedure, they will be assigned an arbitration procedure as a compulsory dispute settlement procedure. In the case of the Lebanon–Israel dispute, so far, no bilateral negotiation has been held between the countries either to delimit the maritime boundaries or to resolve the maritime dispute. In addition, with respect to the dispute resolution procedure, without both countries satisfying the prerequisite and without their express consent to the same settlement procedure, it is most likely that either procedure derived from Part XV of UNCLOS will be imposed to settle the Lebanon–Israel dispute.

In this present state of affairs, the Lebanon–Israel dispute is unlikely to be resolved without a shift in attitudes at the highest political and diplomatic levels of both countries in order to overcome these complications. As long as this dispute continues to remain unsettled, besides its negative implications for Lebanon and Israel, it deters interested third parties, particularly international gas and oil companies. These international gas and oil companies will be concerned with the security of their operations in this politically disputed maritime area between two countries fraught with a history of hostility and wars. Such companies will also feel insecure in investing a high level of capital in this disputed maritime area in order to utilize energy operations, regardless of which State, Lebanon or Israel, is the licensor State. As a result, the discovered energy resources in the disputed maritime area are unlikely to be effectively exploited, if exploited at all.

The history of hostility between Lebanon and Israel demonstrates that both countries have wasted energy resources on war and deadly conflicts, destroying the welfare and damaging the standard of life in each country. The great potential of the recent energy discoveries in the Levant Basin imposes on Lebanon and Israel the need to exploit these resources for the sake of their peace and development. With effective exploitation of recently discovered gas and oil resources in the Levant Basin, the landscape of both countries will most probably be changed.

In short, it is in the interests of the coastal States to resolve their maritime boundary disputes sooner rather than later. Naturally, against the backdrop of longstanding grievances, energy security is not the sole determinant of their respective foreign relation policies with one another. It may be that these disputes ultimately become resolved through diplomatic means outside the strictures, yet in the shadow, of international law in a manner that takes the interests of the regional unrepresented/under-represented (e.g., the Palestinian and Turkish-Cypriot) populations into earnest consideration.

PART II

EU energy governance: selected legal aspects

5. EU energy security

I. INTRODUCTION

The principal aim of this chapter is to provide the reader with an overview of the key legal considerations at play in relation to European Union (EU) energy security. As part of that process, we explore the complexities that contribute to the contentiousness of EU action in relation to certain aspects of energy. We also provide some background information on key facts and figures regarding energy in the EU.

While extensive literature exists on discrete aspects of the EU–energy nexus, there is a lack of research contextualizing EU energy security through a constitutional/public law prism. We therefore intentionally take a broad view of the subject. Such an approach is relevant because of the very nature, on the one hand, of the EU, and on the other, of energy, both of which are highly complex. For instance, the EU is a complex *sui generis* example of interstate cooperation. For its part, energy – due to inherent and contingent reasons explored below – is highly politicized. Combining these two fields makes for potentially very contentious politics. It follows, therefore, that a public law approach in relation to the competences of the supranational aspects of the EU – in other words, a clear delineation of the competences of the EU and of its member states[1] – would be highly pertinent towards understanding energy within the EU context.

We also aim to highlight in our present work the inescapable diplomatic overtones of energy in international relations. Although our focus is on the legal aspects of EU energy security, we consider it necessary to outline what may be the principal contours of the broader geostrategic dynamics at play, including EU efforts to secure its energy supply. In that respect, we support a view of international law as only an aspect – albeit an important one – of the international rules-based system that seeks to discipline interstate relations to the extent that is politically acceptable to

---

[1] On supranationalism in the European Union, see for instance Leal-Arcas, R. 'Theories of Supranationalism in the EU' (2007) *Journal of Law in Society*, Vol. 8, No. 1, pp. 88–113.

the State actors concerned. That is to say that international law and its normative effect ought not be seen as functioning in some geostrategic vacuum.

The EU extensively engages with the world that is external to it. We see its *sui juris* and observer-status participation in various international fora. This can encourage perceptions that overestimate the EU's actual competence to speak and act with one voice on all policy matters.[2] In that sense, the question of the EU's actorness within the broader international environment is part of its complexity. Whilst the EU certainly possesses the institutional capacity to speak and act with one voice on behalf of its Member States, it lacks the absolute discretion to do so in all fields of policy. What is more, a complex policy matter such as energy needs to be broken down into its various aspects in order for the EU to determine what action might be acceptable in relation to each aspect. This shall be explored more fully in this chapter.

The EU is essentially about the common economic area between 28 sovereign States.[3] The main features of that common economic area are its customs union and internal market. In matters directly linked to the customs union and the competition rules of the internal market, EU members have expressly endowed the EU with powers to exclusively handle such matters on their behalf.[4] In other words, the EU acts to the

---

2 There is a large amount of literature on the EU acting with one voice on the international stage. See for instance Leal-Arcas, R. *Theory and Practice of EC External Trade Law and Policy* (London: Cameron May, 2008) Chapters 2, 4 and 5; Leal-Arcas, R. 'Unitary Character of EC External Trade Relations' (Fall 2001) *Columbia Journal of European Law*, Vol. 7, No. 3, pp. 355–383; Leal-Arcas, R. 'United We Stand, Divided We Fall – The European Community and its Member States in the WTO Forum: Towards Greater Cooperation on Issues of Shared Competence?' (Spring 2003) *European Political Economy Review*, Vol. 1, No. 1, pp. 65–79, http://aei.pitt.edu/632/1/LEAL.PDF; Leal-Arcas, R. 'The EC in the GATT/WTO Negotiations: From Rome to Nice – Have EC Trade Policy Reforms Been Good Enough for a Coherent EC Trade Policy in the WTO?' (March 2004) *European Integration Online Papers*, Vol. 8, No. 1, pp. 1–29, http://eiop.or.at/eiop/texte/2004-001.htm; Leal-Arcas, R. 'Polycephalous Anatomy of the EC in the WTO: An Analysis of Law and Practice' (2007) *Florida Journal of International Law*, Vol. 19, No.3, pp. 569–670.

3 The EU and the members (minus Switzerland) of the European Free Trade Association (EFTA) form the European Economic Area (EEA). As a consequence, this expanded free-trade area applies the entire EU internal market *acquis communautaire* – save for that on fisheries and agriculture. (See Agreement on the European Economic Area, 1994 O.J. L 1/3.)

4 See Article 3 of the Treaty on the Functioning of the European Union (TFEU) and Article 6 TFEU.

exclusion of Member States. Member States foresaw that certain other matters – supplementary to the EU project – made it necessary for the EU to have a degree of competence to act. These are considered shared competence areas.[5] Generally, any policy matter for which the treaties make no express provision remains the sovereign preserve of Member States.[6] That said, notably, the treaties foresee cases where, while no EU competences exist, EU institutions may have to act, albeit to the extent that Member States unanimously consent to this.[7] Of course, there are matters over which both sets of actors – namely EU institutions and EU Member States – may act. And in relation to such matters, there are treaty-based solutions that promote an efficient use of coexistent competences whilst discouraging the unjustifiable sidelining of Member States by EU institutions.[8]

---

[5] See Article 4 TFEU.

[6] Also, in accordance with the interpretative principle of *expressio unius est exclusio alterius*, that is to say, that the express mention of a matter or circumstance has the effect of excluding those not mentioned. This is an interpretative principle to assist in deducing the scope of any given norm where textually this is unclear. The Vienna Convention on the Law of Treaties 1969 (VCLT) – drafted by the International Law Commission pursuant to Article 13 of the United Nations Charter to codify a complex area of international law – signed and ratified by most of the 28 EU Member States, codifies norms concerned, amongst other things, with interpretative matters. See Part III (Articles 26–38) VCLT. However, the fact that France and Romania – both EU members and parties to EU constitutive treaties – have neither signed nor ratified the VCLT means that any interpretative dispute submitted to adjudication cannot be resolved on the basis of the VCLT. Rather, it would need to be resolved on the basis of customary law. That said, for the most part, as expressed *passim* in the commentary to the draft version of the VCLT, the VCLT is deemed to mirror customary norms. In that respect, the customary norms that were thought to exist are mirrored in Articles 26–38 VCLT. Article 31, and its mirror norm in custom, focuses on the ordinary meaning of the wording in question. In that respect, to read broader powers into a treaty provision in dispute would be unjustifiable save for where some other legally significant event or circumstance permits this to happen. An example would be subsequent state practice or international agreements that indicate that there is state consent to reading broader powers into a treaty. See e.g., Article 30 VCLT on successive international agreements and Article 31(3)(a) & (b) on subsequent agreement or practice on the part of the states concerned, respectively.

[7] See Article 352§1 TFEU.

[8] See Article 5 of the Treaty on European Union (TEU), which limits the actions of the EU to the extent that the EU has been conferred express treaty-derived powers to act and to the extent that EU action is proportionate to the intended objective. In relation to shared competences, Article 5 TEU

Returning to energy in its wide sense, what becomes evident is that it is a multidimensional matter. The centrality of energy – by which we mean its significance to almost every field of human endeavor in modern times – is what makes it multidimensional. For instance, the production, transport, distribution, sale, and consumption of energy engage several policy areas. It is possible, therefore, that certain aspects of energy within the EU context are a field where the EU has exclusive, shared or even no competence. This shall be explored further below. What is more, once a policy matter transcends the EU border, it becomes internationalized. Here, too, the question in relation to the EU's actorness – inextricable from that of its competences – comes sharply into focus. Most energy-related policy matters have become internationalized in the post-World-War-II era increasingly globalized world economy. In that respect, one could sensibly segregate aspects of EU energy-related policy matters into internal and external. This too shall be explored at greater length below.

The chapter is divided into six sections. After the introduction, Section II contextualizes EU energy security by providing facts and figures regarding EU energy consumption and production. Section III analyzes the legal aspects of EU energy policy, focusing on the changes brought by the Treaty of Lisbon and the challenges the EU faces when aiming for a common energy security policy, while Section IV provides an analysis of the Internal Energy Market and the Energy Community. Section V presents the geostrategic context of the nexus between the EU and energy security. Section VI concludes the chapter.

II. ENERGY AND THE EU: CONTEXTUALIZATION, FACTS AND FIGURES

A. Contextualizing EU Energy Security

1. The traditional EU energy position: dependent and undiversified

Traditionally, the EU has been strongly dependent on imports to fulfill its internal energy requirements.[9] To illustrate, between 2007 and 2011, the

---

conditions EU action according to the subsidiarity principle – i.e., to the extent that action is more effective at the supranational level in order to achieve what cannot be similarly achieved at a local, regional, or national level.

[9] Haghighi, S. *Energy Security: The External Legal Relations of the European Union with Major Oil and Gas Supplying Countries* (Oxford: Hart Publishing, 2007) 9; Voutilainen, P. 'Developing Energy Policy For Europe: A

EU relied on non-EU Member States to supply around 53.5% of its total energy[10] – a statistic which included imports of 41% of its solid fuels, 25% of its petroleum, and 67% of its gas supplies as of 2011.[11] Such a high level of energy dependence has resulted in a concerning paradox, where the EU – consuming one-fifth of the world's energy supply – is the world's largest importer of energy.[12] This positional incongruity is further accentuated by the lack of diversity within the EU's primary energy suppliers (namely Russia, Norway, and Algeria), who account for 85% of the EU's natural gas imports and almost 50% of its crude oil imports.[13]

Such an undiversified reliance on external energy sources places the EU in a position that is vulnerable 'to energy price shocks or energy supply disruptions, which may translate into significant losses to competitiveness and GDP, inflationary pressures and trade balance deterioration'.[14] This was most visible in relation to the energy supply disruptions due to the 2006 and 2009 Russia–Ukraine gas disputes, which had significant deleterious consequences for infrastructure and quality of life in a number of EU Member States.[15] Given the continuation of this trend of energy dependence in recent times,[16] the forecast of

---

Finnish Perspective on Energy Cooperation in The European Union' (2008) 29 *Energy L.J.* 121, 123.

10 European Commission Statistics (Eurostat), 'Eurostat Data for 2011, Energy Dependence', last update of data: 08.01.2014, available at http://epp.eurostat.ec.europa.eu/tgm/table.do?tab=table&init=1&language=en&pcode=tsdcc310&plugin=1.

11 European Commission, 'EU Energy in Figures: Statistical Pocketbook 2013' (2013) 24.

12 European Commission, 'The European Union Explained: Energy – Sustainable, Secure and Affordable Energy for Europeans' (2012) 3.

13 European Commission, 'Renewable Energy: A Major Player in the European Energy Market' SWD (2012) 149 final, 8.

14 European Commission Directorate-General for Economic and Financial Affairs, 'Member States' Energy Dependence: An Indicator-Based Assessment', Occasional Papers 145 (April 2013) 5.

15 Stern, J. 'The Russian-Ukrainian Gas Crisis of January 2006' (2006, Oxford Institute for Energy Studies) 8; Kovacevic, A. 'The Impact of the Russia–Ukraine Gas Crisis in South Eastern Europe' (March 2009, Oxford Institute for Energy Studies) 1.

16 European Commission, 'Renewable Energy: A Major Player in the European Energy Market' SWD (2012) 149 final, 8.

its significant increase[17] to 70% by 2030,[18] and the rise of competition for energy supplies from emerging economies,[19] there are important implications for the continued economic stability and security of European energy supplies.

2. Energy security: definitions

The majority of concerns generated by the challenges outlined above can be grouped under the umbrella term of those that impact the 'energy security' of the EU. In terms of the concept of *energy security*, the literature is diverse. Energy security itself is a nebulous concept, with competing approaches to defining its meaning and scope.[20] These approaches differ not only in their general conceptual understandings of the term, but also in its application to the different forms of energy resources such as oil and gas.[21] One approach emphasizes the continuity of energy supplies,[22] while another also factors in the absence of price volatility above a given price,[23] and a third approach extends this definition to the impacts on 'the economy and in some cases the

---

[17] European Commission, 'A European Strategy for Sustainable, Competitive and Secure Energy, Commission of the European Communities', COM(2006) 105 final 3, 9, 10.

[18] European Commission, 'Renewable Energy: A Major Player in the European Energy Market' SWD (2012) 149 final, 11; also see generally Haghighi, S. *Energy Security: The External Legal Relations of the European Union with Major Oil and Gas Supplying Countries* (Oxford: Hart Publishing, 2007) 10–11, citing *International Energy Outlook 2006* (at p. 43).

[19] In the context of natural gas supplies, see Ratner, M. 'Europe's Energy Security: Options and Challenges to Natural Gas Supply Diversification' (August 2013, Congressional Research Service) 1–2.

[20] Winzer, C. 'Conceptualising Energy Security' (EPRG Working Paper 1123, University of Cambridge Electricity Policy Working Group, July 2011) 4.

[21] Haghighi, S. *Energy Security: The External Legal Relations of the European Union with Major Oil and Gas Supplying Countries* (Oxford: Hart Publishing, 2007) 14.

[22] UK Department of Energy & Climate Change, 'Energy Markets Outlook Report' (2009) 19: 'Secure energy means that the risks of interruption to energy supply, are low'.

[23] The International Energy Agency provides the following definition: 'Energy security is defined in terms of the physical availability of supplies to satisfy demand at a given price'. See IEA, *Towards a Sustainable Energy Future* (Paris, 2001).

environment'.[24] The European Commission's definition of the term falls into this last category:

> The European Union's long-term strategy for energy supply security must be geared to ensuring, for the well-being of its citizens and the proper functioning of the economy, the uninterrupted physical availability of energy products on the market, at a price which is affordable for all consumers (private and industrial), while respecting environmental concerns and looking towards sustainable development, as enshrined in Articles 2 and 6 of the Treaty on European Union.[25]

As the Commission in the same paper acknowledged, the path to EU energy security is one that takes into account the undiversified energy dependence of the EU economy and aims at reducing the risks associated with such dependence by diversifying sources of supply, both by product and geographically.[26] This path to energy security is, however, not as linear as it first seems, there being a multitude of factors that exert strong influences. Examples include the EU's own clean energy commitments, the proposed Trans-Adriatic pipeline, and the ongoing shale revolution in the United States.

Some regard energy security as an economic and even a security matter. From the EU perspective, unsurprisingly given the EU's energy-dependency, energy security is perceived from a *supply* security point of view. This is the notion we have espoused for the purposes of this chapter.[27] In relation to EU *energy security*, this seems to engender all that could make EU energy policy complex, given that energy security is a matter that relies on several factors for it to be achieved.[28]

Firstly, however, we must be clear on what we mean by *energy security*. To answer this, we need to understand to whom the benefits of energy security accrue. For instance, if we were to answer this in

---

24 Winzer, C. 'Conceptualising Energy Security' (EPRG Working Paper 1123, University of Cambridge Electricity Policy Working Group, July 2011) 5.

25 European Commission, 'Towards a European Strategy for the Security of Energy Supply', COM(2000) 769 final, p. 2.

26 Ibid. at p. 10.

27 See Korkmaz, D. 'Internal and External Dynamics of European Energy Security' (2010) (paper based on a chapter of Korkmaz's PhD thesis) available at http://www.jhubc.it/ecpr-porto/virtualpaperroom/034.pdf (at pp. 5–6) for a review of the relevant literature.

28 See Baumann, F. 'Europe's Way to Energy Security. The Outer Dimensions of Energy Security: From Power Politics to Energy Governance'(2010) *European Foreign Affairs Review* 15, at p. 87.

connection to the EU, we would claim that energy security means the steady and secure access to energy supplies to meet the energy needs of all 28 EU Member States.[29] It is also worth noting early on that the EU's origins partly lie in matters connected to energy security.[30]

If we were then to supplement the question of what energy security is within the EU context by asking who might be a responsible or influential agent in fulfilling the objective of EU energy security, we enter the complexity of energy within the EU context. This is because to ask who is responsible engages the question of competences (e.g., who does what and to what extent); and to ask who is influential engages the question of competences *plus* who possesses the diplomatic clout. The latter becomes even more pronounced when we take into consideration the disparate levels of influence between EU Member States. Again, these are issues we explore in the present chapter. Furthermore, within the EU context, energy security has come to be heavily conditioned by

[29] In fact, this is what the initial set of ministers from six European states (namely the Federal Republic of Germany, Belgium, France, Italy, Luxembourg and the Netherlands) had in mind when they promulgated the Messina Declaration in 1955, in which they stated: '*Putting more abundant energy at a cheaper price at the disposal of the European economies constitutes* a fundamental element of economic progress. That is why all arrangements should be made to develop sufficient exchanges of gas and electric power capable of increasing the profitability of investments and reducing the supply costs. Studies will be undertaken of methods to co-ordinate development prospects for the production and consumption of energy, and to draw up general guidelines for an overall policy …' (emphasis added) (cf. point 2 of the 1955 Messina Declaration, available at http://www.eurotreaties.com/messina.pdf). Clearly, the initial set of European governments was well attuned to the importance of energy security to the economic reconstruction of European economies in the postwar period.

[30] Let us be reminded that the initial instances of European interstate cooperation which eventually resulted in the remarkable international entity that is the EU revolved around locking together French and German coal and steel resources. See e.g., the 1952 Coal and Steel Community Treaty and the 1957 Euratom Treaty. See the 2007 Commission Communication to the European Parliament and the Council, where the Commission reminds members and EU institutions to be faithful to the EU's roots: 'Europe needs to act now, together, to deliver sustainable, secure and competitive energy. In doing so the EU would return to its roots … the founding Member States saw the need for a common approach to energy'. Communication from the Commission to the European Council and the European Parliament, *An Energy Policy for Europe*, Brussels, 10 January 2007 (COM(2007) 1 final) (at p. 3).

environmental objectives with the addition of 'sustainable' to the notion of EU energy security.[31]

As stated above, energy security relies on a variety of factors – including efficient infrastructure and consumption, and diversity of primary energy mix and supply – that, again, illustrate how EU energy security may rely on action across the EU policy spectrum, and that engages the internal-external cleavage. As we shall explore below, much *has been done* at the intra-EU level to rationalize the energy market to the extent that the Internal Energy Market (IEM) is heading towards coherence.[32] As we shall also explore below, much *has been said* to make possible more cohesive external energy action. We conclude, however, that so long as the constitutive treaties that spell out EU competence are not substantively amended, the furthest the EU could go in relation to EU energy security is to act to the extent that the treaties make possible – that is to say, to the extent that the EU has powers to address some, albeit not all, key factors upon which energy security relies. That said, it is our view that EU institutions appear to be making full and very competent use of the means at their disposal. For instance, the EU Commission makes good use of its capacity to make recommendations to the Council and the Parliament, and to also propose legislation focused on enhancing EU energy relations and ultimately energy security.

---

31 This is a relatively novel development. See The 2010 Commission Communication: *Europe 2020: A Strategy for Smart, Sustainable and Inclusive Growth*, Brussels, 3 March 2010 (COM(2010) 2020 final) where economic growth, climate change, and energy objectives have been presented as interlinked and mutually conditional.

32 The EU is committed to fully integrating the electricity and gas markets of the 28 Member States by 2014 into the Internal Energy Market (IEM). See Communication from the Commission to the European Parliament, the Council, the European Economic and Social Committee, and the Committee of the Regions, *Energy Roadmap 2050*, Brussels, 15 December 2011 (COM(2011) 885 final), p. 19. For a useful historical analysis of the IEM and the integration of the US markets and an examination of the regulatory regimes in the EU and the US, see Bellantuono, G. 'Contract law, Regulation, and Competition in Energy Markets' (2009) 10 *Competition & Reg. Network Indus*. 159–188. According to Bellantuono, EU and US energy markets have shifted from being monopolistic towards a competitive approach. The EU energy markets started shifting towards integration in earnest from around the beginning of the 2000s, whilst this happened around the 1980s in the US. A further interstate treaty-based organization to which the EU is a party along with several neighboring states is the Energy Community (EnC), which essentially seeks to extend the IEM to those states as a means of EU energy interests.

In sum, therefore, it is useful to conceptualize EU energy security primarily in relation to the structural challenges – namely the question of *vires* – that the EU faces when compared to other prominent players on the international plane, for example sovereign actors such as China and the US. The energy markets of the 28 EU Member States vary widely in terms of, amongst other things, infrastructure, investment, and pricing. The IEM is not fully integrated; however, it is not far from achieving this in relation to electricity and gas. What is more, the EU has strategically promoted the integration of energy markets and regulatory convergence with bordering third-party States, through the medium of rational markets, to the end of its own energy security. This is also explored below. In that respect, perhaps what has so far been achieved in terms of the promotion of EU energy security is optimal, given the circumstances.

B. Energy Consumption in the EU

In 2009, EU consumption stood at 1,703 Mtoe, 37% of which was produced from oil, 24% from gas, 16% from coal, 14% from nuclear energy and only 9% (almost a tenth) from renewable energy sources.[33] These figures indicate that 77% of EU energy consumption derives from traditional energy sources – namely hydrocarbons/fossil fuels – that are highly polluting. In that sense, the current EU energy supply draws heavily from sources that are highly politicized. Competition for control over these resources has often led to great human suffering and loss. Simply put, the EU is 77% energy-dependent on these controversial hydrocarbons.[34]

This is a reality with significant implications, as it poses dilemmas for the EU in terms of balancing its energy security objectives against its aspirations to robustly protect the environment.[35] Although this figure (namely 77%) is marginally lower than the global figure,[36] it remains

---

33 European Commission, 'Key Figures', Market Observatory for Energy, Directorate-General for Energy, June 2011, at p. 11. Based on 2009 figures.

34 Ibid.

35 For an earlier study on the broader link between energy and the environment, see Guruswamy, L. 'Energy and Environment Security: The Need for Action' (1991) 3 *J Entvtl L* 209.

36 During 2011, c.81% of global energy consumption came from hydrocarbons/fossil fuels. This figure represents 10,689 Mtoe out of a total 12,274 Mtoe. The actual breakdown is 4,059 Mtoe/c.33% from oil, 2905.6 Mtoe/c.24% from gas, and 2,724.3 Mtoe/c.30% from coal. See BP Statistical Review of World Energy, June 2012, at pp. 40–41, available at www.bp.com/statisticalreview

problematic, given the urgency with which the degradation of the ecosystem ought to be handled by the international community, including the EU. Currently, just 9% of EU energy consumption derives from renewable energy sources.[37] The EU has committed to increasing the share of renewables in the EU's final energy consumption to 20% by 2020,[38] and it is not clear whether it would be able to meet this goal within the timeframe. Given the pressing realities of climate change, and their implications for human populations[39] and the ecosystem at large, it would be most unfortunate for the EU to miss this target.[40] Incidentally, in 2009 EU investments in renewables dropped by 10% whilst they rose by 50% in China. Still, the EU remains the investor *par excellence* in renewables given that during 2009 there were EU investments of around USD 43 billion in renewables, whilst investments in China stood at around USD 24 billion.[41] Currently, the EU renewable energy industry

---

[37] European Commission, 'Key Figures', Market Observatory for Energy, Directorate-General for Energy, June 2011, at p. 11.

[38] European Commission Communication, 'Europe 2020: A Strategy for Smart, Sustainable, and Inclusive Growth' Brussels, 2010 (COM (2010) 2020 final), Annex I (at p. 32). See also Directive 2009/28/EC (*of the European Parliament and the Council of 23 April 2009 on the promotion of the use of energy from renewable sources and amending and subsequently repealing Directives 2001/77/EC and 2003/30/EC*), Article 3 of which mandates minimum national targets that ought to be met in order for the EU to achieve its target, namely to derive 20% of its final energy consumption from renewable energy sources (RES) by 2020. Annex I of Directive 2009/28/EC expressly states the national targets with regard to the energy realities that each Member State faces. See e.g., Belgium is bound to increase its RES from 2.2% in 2005 to 13% by 2020, whilst Sweden is bound to increase this from 39.8% to 49%.

[39] See e.g., Leal-Arcas, R. 'On Climate Migration and International Trade'(2012) *Vienna Journal of International Constitutional Law*, Vol. 6, Nos 3 and 4, pp. 410–440.

[40] On the role of the EU in climate change negotiations, see Leal-Arcas, R. 'The Role of the EU, the US, and China in Addressing Climate Change', in Larsen, F. (ed.) *The EU and the Political Economy of Transatlantic Relations* (Brussels: PIE Peter Lang) pp. 221–260; Leal-Arcas, R. 'The Role of the European Union and China in Global Climate Change Negotiations: A Critical Analysis' (2012) *Journal of European Integration History*, Vol. 18, No. 1, pp. 67–81.

[41] European Commission, 'Key Figures', Market Observatory for Energy, Directorate-General for Energy, June 2011, at p. 30.

has a €20 billion turnover and employs about 300,000 people, amounting to roughly 60% of the global market share.[42]

Whilst the EU consumes about 1,703 Mtoe of energy, during 2009 only 48% (818 Mtoe) of its total energy needs were produced within the EU. Consequently, it relies on energy imports to meet 52% of its energy needs – in that respect, it is *energy dependent* by 52%.[43] The specific realities of each Member State's energy dependency are hugely disparate, as we see below. What is more, EU energy dependency varies depending on the energy resource in question. For example the EU imports 83.5% of its oil, 64% of its gas, and circa 38% of its coal.[44] Furthermore, as shown in Table 5.1 about 50% and 80% of EU oil and gas imports, respectively, come from only four countries: namely Algeria, Libya, Norway, and Russia.[45] One third of those gas imports – 34% – comes from Russia.[46] The fact that at the EU level, the 28 Member States are collectively 52% energy-dependent should not mask the EU Member States' individual energy realities. At the Member-State level, the degree of energy dependency varies hugely, as it is contingent upon their particular energy endowments, energy efficiency, respective market access to the energy resources/markets of third-party States, and on whatever their other relevant energy-related particularities might be.

---

[42] See Communication from the Commission to the European Council and the European Parliament, *An Energy Policy for Europe*, Brussels, 10 January 2007 (COM(2007) 1 final) (at p. 4). For further details on funding renewable energy in the Euro-Mediterranean region, see Tagliapietra, S. *The Geoeconomics of Sovereign Wealth Funds and Renewable Energy: Towards a New Energy Paradigm in the Euro-Mediterranean Region* (Deventer, the Netherlands: Claeys & Casteels, 2012).

[43] European Commission, 'Key Figures', Market Observatory for Energy, Directorate-General for Energy, June 2011, at p. 5.

[44] Ibid. at p. 6.

[45] European Commission, 'Statistical Pocketbook 2009. EU Energy in Figures (Part 2)', Directorate-General for Energy and Transport, Jan. 2009, at p. 14.

[46] Based on calculations on 2009 figures available in European Commission, 'Key Figures', Market Observatory for Energy, Directorate-General for Energy, June 2011, at p. 11.

Table 5.1 Origin of EU oil and gas imports during 2009

Oil	Gas
35% OPEC	34% Russia
33% Russia	31% Norway
15% Norway	14% Algeria
17% others (including Kazakhstan 5%, Azerbaijan 4%)	21% others (including Qatar 5%, Libya 3%)

Source: European Commission, 'Key Figures', Market Observatory for Energy, June 2011 (at p. 7).

Also, it is helpful to understand EU energy consumption against the backdrop of global consumption figures. The EU has steadily consumed roughly circa 1,700 Mtoe of energy since 1990, and projections suggest that its annual consumption is likely to stay at that level over the next two decades.[47] EU energy consumption composes about 14% of global consumption.[48] However, given that its rate of consumption is held to remain static over the next two decades, whilst global demand is set to rise significantly, the share of EU consumption in relation to global energy consumption is set to drop to circa 10% by 2035.[49] The rest of the Organisation for Economic Co-operation and Development (OECD) – that is to say, the other States in the OECD that are not EU members – is also set to consume at the same rate it has done historically, whilst the greatest increase in global energy demand between now and 2035 (namely from circa 12,000 Mtoe to 18,000 Mtoe) will happen due to the increasing energy needs of China, India, and the rest of the world

[47] See projections up to 2035 as cited in European Commission, 'Key Figures', Market Observatory for Energy, Directorate-General for Energy, June 2011, at p. 3.

[48] Based on calculations of data (namely 12,274 Mtoe, representing global total energy consumption and 1690.7 Mtoe, representing EU total energy consumption). BP Statistical Review of World Energy, June 2012, at p. 40, available at www.bp.com/statisticalreview

[49] This is based on the assumption that global energy demand is set to rise to circa 18,000 Mtoe by 2035, by which time EU energy demand is likely to remain static at around the 1,700 Mtoe mark. See data that appear in European Commission, 'Key Figures', Market Observatory for Energy, Directorate-General for Energy, June 2011, at p. 3.

consequent to their further industrialization.[50] Based on these figures, by 2035, the EU and the rest of its OECD peers are likely to collectively account for about 30% of global energy demand, whilst China and the rest of the world for about 70%.[51] What these dwindling figures might also reflect is the waning influence of the EU over the coming decades in relation to its environmental agenda. To say the least, this would be unfortunate, given the EU's more robust approach to environmental protection.[52] If the EU's voice in the global arena were to be further weakened, it seems unlikely that any other State, or bloc of States,[53] would take on the responsibility in earnest to call for more robust action to protect the ecosystem.

As briefly mentioned above, whilst overall EU energy dependency across its primary energy mix stands at around 52%, the situation varies widely in relation to each EU Member State. For instance, Denmark is entirely energy import independent whilst Malta is entirely energy import

---

[50] Ibid. Further, in relation to China and India, the International Energy Agency (IEA) projects that India and China would account for roughly 45% of the anticipated increase in global energy consumption between 2005 and 2035. See the Executive Summary to the 2007 IEA World Energy Outlook: China and India Insights report (at p. 3).

[51] The EU and the rest of the OECD are likely to account for just under 6,000 Mtoe out of the global energy demand figure of 18,000 Mtoe by 2035. See European Commission, 'Key Figures', Market Observatory for Energy, Directorate-General for Energy, June 2011, at p. 3.

[52] This shall be explored in a separate part of this chapter; however, it is worth briefly mentioning the EU's Emissions Trading System and its expanding application over all major polluting industries within EU territory. Also, it is worth mentioning that the EU appears to constrain its pursuit of energy security by environmental objectives, which, when compared to other players internationally – namely China, India, Japan, and the US – might in the long-run place the EU in an economically disadvantaged position. These concerns were echoed by Saryusz-Wolski, the European Parliament's Committee for Foreign Affairs (AFET) Rapporteur, in his concluding address during a November 2012 workshop on the EU's '2050 Energy Roadmap' organized by the European Parliament's Directorate-General for External Policies, in which he also stated that: 'Energy policy should be viewed as a policy on its own, and not as a by-product of climate policy' (EXPO/B/AFET/FWC/2009-01/Lot1/42 at p. 14).

[53] With the exception of the Alliance of Small Island States (AOSIS) and those other States especially affected by further environmental degradation such as desertification, and so on. However, such States fail to garner the level of influence that the EU currently has and that it is likely to have in the future despite its potentially waning influence.

dependent.[54] In terms of oil, Denmark is entirely oil independent, given that it is the only EU member state that is a net oil exporter. The next comparatively better off EU member is the United Kingdom (UK) as it is 9% oil dependent, followed by a very distant third, Romania, which is circa 50% oil dependent. All other EU members' oil dependency ranges from circa 63% to 100%.[55] Predictably, such acute disparities, along with other differences between EU Member States, have implications for cohesive EU action. This shall be explored more fully in the next chapter, where we explore the various attitudes of EU Member States towards energy cooperation with partners such as Russia, and how differences affect the chances for cohesive EU action regarding energy.[56]

In terms of how total EU energy consumption is broken down, roughly 33% goes on transport, 27% on households, 24% on industry, 12% on services, and 2% on agriculture.[57] From this breakdown we can deduce that energy price volatility coupled with weather-induced increased energy consumption could have considerable implications for the economy and human welfare. For instance, higher energy prices add to industry costs that, in turn, may lead to EU-produced services and goods becoming less competitive in relation to like products produced in economies where energy costs are lower.[58] Furthermore, as households account for 27% of EU energy consumption, price increases would eat into household disposable income that, in turn, could, potentially depress consumption rates and thus affect the entire EU economy.[59] In that

---

[54] European Commission, 'Key Figures', Market Observatory for Energy, Directorate-General for Energy, June 2011, at p. 8.

[55] Ibid. at p. 9.

[56] The concern regarding a cohesive energy infrastructure has been studied by Leibert, R.A. 'The War on Energy: Why the United States and the International Community need Cohesive Energy Infrastructure Security Policy' (2007) 29 *Hous J Int'l Law* 453.

[57] European Commission, 'Key Figures', Market Observatory for Energy, Directorate-General for Energy, June 2011, at p. 14.

[58] See e.g., Pogoretskyy, V. & Behn, D. 'The Tension between Trade Liberalization and Resource Sovereignty: Russia–EU Energy Relations and the Problem of Natural Gas Dual Pricing' (2011) *Oil, Gas and Energy Law*, Vol. 6, in which the authors analyze Russia's dual pricing practice of gas against the strictures of the WTO and in relation to the tension between sovereignty prerogatives and trade liberalization objectives. In the article, the authors refer to EU commission countervailing action in response to what it considers to be energy subsidies on the part of the Russian state to its domestic industries.

[59] Energy costs are likely to increase so that households end up spending up to 16% of income on energy – including transport-related energy – by 2030. This

respect, setting aside the environmental imperatives, promoting a paradigm shift from hydrocarbons – on which the EU is hugely externally dependent – to renewables could potentially immunize the EU considerably from such shocks.

It is interesting to read the above breakdown of EU energy consumption against the backdrop of overall EU CO_2 emissions. The energy industries produce 35% of EU CO_2 emissions, closely followed by transport at 30%, industry and construction at 18%, and residential use at 11% of EU CO_2 emissions.[60] In that respect, one could argue that action be largely targeted at the most polluting sectors. However, as we shall see below, given that the situation is disparate between EU Member States, a more variegated approach would be necessary when, for instance, we look at the energy industries across the EU. Electricity is produced in a more environmentally damaging way in Malta, Cyprus, Estonia, and Poland than it is, say, in Sweden and the Netherlands.

C. Energy Production in the EU

As briefly mentioned above, during 2009 the EU met 48% of its energy needs from its own energy production. That is 818 Mtoe out of the 1,703 consumed that year. Sixty-six percent of EU energy production comes from just five EU Members States: namely the UK, France, Germany, Poland, and the Netherlands.[61] The breakdown in relation to the 818 Mtoe figure, which represents the amount of EU-produced energy during 2009, is as follows: 28% from nuclear power, 19% from gas, 13% from oil, 20% from coal, and 18% from renewables. When comparing these figures to those of 1990, we witness that the share of coal in EU energy production dropped from 39% to 20%, the share of nuclear power increased from 22% to 28%, and reliance on renewables also increased from 7% to 18%.[62] However, this should be understood against the fact that EU energy production in 1990 was higher – namely 943 Mtoe – largely due to greater use of coal back then.[63] This illustrates the current

figure is likely to drop to 15% by 2050. Communication from the Commission to the European Parliament, the Council, the European Economic and Social Committee, and the Committee of the Regions, *Energy Roadmap 2050*, Brussels, 15 December 2011 (COM(2011) 885 final).

[60] European Commission, 'Key Figures', Market Observatory for Energy, Directorate-General for Energy, June 2011, at p. 25.

[61] Ibid. at p. 18.

[62] Ibid. at p. 16.

[63] Ibid.

trade-off between, on the one hand, environmental protection objectives and, on the other, the pursuit of energy security that, for the most part, relies on hydrocarbons.

As we have stated, the situation between EU members is disparate not least in relation to their reliance on renewable energy. For instance, the most exemplary are Austria, Latvia, and Sweden in that 68%, 65% and 58% of their respective electricity needs in 2009 came from renewables at a time when the EU average was circa 18%.[64]

When it comes to nuclear power – which, whilst less polluting than hydrocarbons in terms of CO_2 and other greenhouse gas (GHG) emissions, is also harmful to the ecosystem – the situation is also disparate between EU members. France leads with 76% of its electricity derived from nuclear power, followed by Lithuania and Slovakia at 70% and 55% respectively, whilst the Netherlands derives less than 4% of its electricity from nuclear power.[65]

Several EU states derive more than 50% of their electricity production from gas. For instance, Luxembourg produces 74% of its electricity from gas, the Netherlands about 63%, Ireland about 57%, and Italy about 53%, whilst Sweden, Slovenia, and Poland produce about 2%, 3%, and 4%, respectively.[66]

At the most polluting end of the spectrum is electricity generated by coal and oil. Poland and Estonia derive about 87% and 86%, respectively, of their electricity from coal. The Czech Republic, Greece, Bulgaria, and Denmark derive approximately 57%, 56%, 48%, and 47% of their respective electricity production from coal.[67] In terms of electricity produced by oil, Malta and Cyprus derive almost 100% of their electricity from oil, whilst the rest of the EU members derive between circa 17% and 1% of their electricity needs from this energy source.[68]

D. Energy Pricing in the EU

In terms of energy prices and taxation, again, the situation is quite uneven.[69] For instance, pricing and taxation may vary along several cleavages – for example, according to energy source and from sector to

---

64 Ibid. at p. 20.
65 Ibid. at p. 21.
66 Ibid. at p. 22.
67 Ibid. at p. 23.
68 Ibid. at p. 24.
69 See the official EU website for energy facts and figures across the EU at http://www.energy.eu/

sector within a national economy, and across the EU membership. For instance, during the second semester of 2010 the highest electricity prices for households were in Austria, Belgium, Cyprus, the Czech Republic, Denmark, Germany, Italy, Luxembourg, the Netherlands, Spain, and Sweden, whilst the highest electricity prices for industry were in Denmark, Germany, Ireland, Italy, Spain, and Sweden.[70] In terms of taxation for household-destined electricity, it is around the 15% mark in Ireland, Malta, and the UK, whilst it is around the 35% mark in Denmark, Germany, and Portugal. Taxation for industry-destined electricity is around the 15% mark in Ireland, Luxembourg, Malta, and Portugal, whilst it is around the 35% mark in Denmark and Germany.[71]

E. Overall Energy Challenges in the EU

The purpose of this section is to provide insights into how disparate energy realities are across the bloc of 28 States. These realities are important given that considerations specific to a particular EU member might be the driving factors behind the policies that said member would want to promote at the EU level. It might be more difficult to persuade EU Member States that heavily rely on energy sources other than gas and oil to support a common EU position aimed at more institutionalized relations with gas and oil behemoths such as Russia, other members of the Commonwealth of Independent States (CIS), and of States across the Middle East and North Africa (MENA) region. For instance, States that derive a large share of their electricity from coal might be indifferent, or in some cases, opposed to deeper EU–Russia economic integration. In the case of Poland and the Baltic States, for example, this could be compounded by historic animosity towards a State they regard as the successor to Imperial Russia and the Soviet Union rather than the most important EU energy partner. On the other hand, it might be in the national interest of those highly reliant on gas imports for their electricity, for example Luxembourg and the Netherlands, to promote a more strategic approach.[72]

---

70 European Commission, 'Key Figures', Market Observatory for Energy, Directorate-General for Energy, June 2011, at pp. 34–35.

71 Ibid. at p. 38.

72 See e.g., Benelux's 'Position Paper on Energy Security and Foreign Policy', March 2006, in which this tripartite bloc of EU States urges the European Council to provide the steer for more cohesive EU common external relations that enhance the EU's energy security through a multiplicity of approaches, including encouraging Russia to ratify the Energy Charter Treaty.

All the above instances of divergence between EU Member States present a situation that makes cohesive policymaking more difficult than it would be in a fully confederated system charged with the external relations of the whole (e.g., Germany, Switzerland, and the US), not simply due to EU structural/*vires* issues but also due to the highly divergent infrastructural, economic, regulatory, and diplomatic climates that exist from EU Member State to Member State.

In this respect, it may be helpful to think of the EU as:

(1) a fully federated entity *solely* in relation to policy areas in which it has exclusive competence;[73]
(2) a loosely federated entity for shared competence policy fields in which the central authority (the EU institutions) must ensure that it develops policy to the extent acceptable to the constituent elements (the Member States) of the federated entity (the EU);[74]
(3) an association of States for policy areas that fall outside both exclusive and shared competence EU remits.[75]

This shall also be explored in Section III concerned with the legal aspects of the EU and its energy policy capacity.

An EU member's position essentially seeks to capture the interplay of considerations at the national level that arise in relation to each EU member's economic, political, and historical tradition. An EU member's position, in turn, interplays with those of its peers before, if ever, an EU common position is finally adopted.[76] All this makes a cohesive EU energy security policy particularly sticky to achieve.

---

[73] See Article 3 TFEU for a list of areas where the EU has exclusive competence.

[74] Article 4 TFEU.

[75] For a closer look at the anatomical structure of the EU, see Leal-Arcas, R. *Theory and Practice of EC External Trade Law and Policy* (London: Cameron May, 2008) pp. 86–89.

[76] Such *modus operandi* reminds us of EU trade policymaking in the pre-Lisbon Treaty era. For further details, see Leal-Arcas, R. *Theory and Practice of EC External Trade Law and Policy* (London: Cameron May, 2008) Chapters 3–6; Leal-Arcas, R. 'The EU Decision-Making Process in EC Trade Policy: The Three Internal Tensions', in Astengo, F. & Neuwahl, N. (eds) *A Constitution for Europe? Governance and Policy-Making in the European Union*, Vol. II, Collection 'Etudes Européennes', Chaire Jean Monnet, Université de Montreal, 2004, pp. 132–156; Leal-Arcas, R. 'The EU Constitutional Treaty and International Trade', in Laursen, F. (ed.) *The Rise and Fall of the EU's Constitutional Treaty* (Leiden: Brill/Nijhoff, 2008) pp. 25–50; Leal-Arcas, R.

In sum, the EU faces structural limitations in *sui juris* promulgating a comprehensive energy strategy, quite unlike how a sovereign actor would. This is due to the multifaceted nature of energy that leads to certain aspects of energy falling within the exclusive or shared competence remit of the EU whilst other aspects of energy sit squarely with Member States. Even where matters sit with the EU, there are other issues – for example, how a decision might be adopted – that are capable of complicating or even stalling the adoption of a common position.

III. LEGAL ASPECTS OF EU ENERGY POLICY

Although apt historical precedents do not seem to exist,[77] some parallels have been drawn between the EU and Germany, Italy, and the US during,

---

'Exclusive or Shared Competence in the Common Commercial Policy: From Amsterdam to Nice' (2003) *Legal Issues of Economic Integration*, Vol. 30, No.1, pp. 3–14; Leal-Arcas, R. 'The State of Play of the EC's Common Commercial Policy: A Legal And Policy Analysis' (2003) *Tilburg Foreign Law Review*, Vol. 11, No. 2, 537–559; Leal-Arcas, R. 'The EC in the WTO: The Three-Level Game of Decision-Making. What Multilateralism Can Learn from Regionalism' (September 2004) *European Integration Online Papers*, Vol. 8, No. 14, pp. 1–43, http://eiop.or.at/eiop/texte/2004-014.htm; Leal-Arcas, R. 'The EU Institutions and their *Modus Operandi* in the World Trading System' (Winter 2005/2006) *Columbia Journal of European Law*, Vol. 12, No. 1, pp. 125–197; Leal-Arcas, R. 'Is EC Trade Policy Up to Par?: A Legal Analysis Over Time – Rome, Marrakesh, Amsterdam, Nice, and the Constitutional Treaty' (Spring 2007) *Columbia Journal of European Law*, Vol. 13, No. 2, pp. 305–399; Leal-Arcas, R. 'Will EU Member States Play Any Role at the WTO after the EU Reform Treaty?' (2007) *Vienna Journal of International Constitutional Law*, Vol. 1, No. 2, pp. 75–90; Leal-Arcas, R. '50 Years of Trade Policy: Good Enough or as Good as it Gets?' (2008) *Irish Journal of European Law*, Vol. 15, Nos 1 and 2, pp. 157–182; Leal-Arcas, R. 'Reflections on EU International Trade Law: An Introspective View' (2012) *Frontiers of Law in China*, Vol. 7, No. 1, pp. 1–20.

[77] The EU is quite unlike any other structure that historically has ever existed. See Sands, P. *Lawless World: The Whistle-Blowing Account of how Bush and Blair are Taking the Law into their own Hands* (London: Penguin, 2006), in which Philippe Sands informs us that: 'The most highly integrated regional system is that between the EU's twenty-five [at that time] members. [The EU] … originally intended to remove barriers to trade, it soon became clear that creating a common market necessarily meant addressing other standards which would affect flows of goods and services and the free movement of people. Gradually standards were developed on everything from labour to the environment, from agriculture to competition rules. The original six became the nine … the nine became ten and then twelve, and then fifteen [and so on]' (at p. 101).

in the case of the first two their unificatory/nationalist geneses, and in the case of the latter its secessionist genesis.[78] Also, parallels have been drawn to the Canadian model in terms of how EU Member States seem to interact with the overarching EU order.[79] What the EU has achieved is to create a core of States that had historically – in their previous configurations – been belligerent towards each other. This core, in turn, attracted the polities of smaller States at the periphery into an economic order within which it is unimaginable for armed conflict to break out. In that respect, this order of sovereign equals – deeply tied together economically through buy-in rather than military force – has been quite unlike any other historical precedents of empire, and comes the closest to the Kantian ideal of a peaceful universalism.[80]

What ought to surely set the EU apart from all confederated examples is its limited capacity to represent – though its institutions – its Member States across the entire policy spectrum. In other words, its limited *vires* – as opposed to institutional – capacity to handle the foreign relations of EU members to their exclusion. That said, the EU is endowed with powers to act in its own right and to the exclusion of EU members – including to contract with third-party States and other international organizations[81] – in matters that fall squarely within its exclusive, yet

---

[78] See Goldsmith, J. & Posner, E. *The Limits of International Law* (Oxford: Oxford University Press, 2005), where they state that: 'Many scholars view European Union integration as a possible model for a more ambitious public international law. Although the EU project is in some respects constituted by international law, we think it is more usefully viewed as an example of multi-state unification akin to pre-twentieth century unification efforts in the United States (which, during its Articles of Confederation period, was viewed by some as a federation governed by international law), Germany, and Italy' (at p. 5).

[79] Within the EU context, states have been likened to Canadian Provinces vis-à-vis their relationship with the federal order. See for instance Sands, P. *Lawless World: The Whistle-Blowing Account of how Bush and Blair are Taking the Law into their own Hands* (London: Penguin, 2006) at p. 102, who deduces this view from the pleadings of the UK government in the 2003 Permanent Court of Arbitration 'MOX PLANT' case between Ireland and the UK.

[80] Immanuel Kant laid out the case for an international league of democracies governed by the rule of law in his essays *Perpetual Peace: A Philosophical Sketch* as well as *An Idea for A Universal History with a Cosmopolitan Purpose*. Kant, I. *Political Writings* (Cambridge: Cambridge University Press, 1970).

[81] See Weiler, J. *The Constitution of Europe: Do the New Clothes have an Emperor?* (Cambridge: Cambridge University Press, 1999) (providing a full exposition of the legal position in relation to the possibility of the concurrent

limited, competence remit.[82] However, it should be borne in mind that these powers derive from treaties contracted by sovereign actors who, at any time, may potentially withdraw in accordance with international law, and, consequently, re-assume full sovereign control over such aspects of policy that are currently within the EU's exclusive competence remit.

A. The EU's Structure Regarding Competences in Energy Policy

The EU is a *sui generis* interstate organization composed of 28 sovereign states that has certain intergovernmental and – most pertinently, for the purposes of this chapter – supranational/federal-like features. As part of this brief introduction to the EU, it is worth noting the general parameters of competence allocation between the EU and its Member States. Broadly, EU Member States – through the founding treaties – have expressly endowed the EU with exclusive competence (that is to say, to the exclusion of its constituent Member States) to handle such matters that are directly linked to principally the achievement and completion of the customs union and internal market, the competition rules of the internal market, and the administration of the monetary union for those EU Member States that have adopted the euro as their currency.[83]

In relation to certain other matters that, although important, had not been deemed to be indispensable to the achievement of the principal aims of the EU, the original EU Member States involved in drafting the founding treaties of the 1950s have extended a degree of competence to the EU to act *alongside* Member States. Competence over such matters is therefore shared.[84] 'Energy', in its broad sense, could be seen as one such matter, although there are aspects of energy, such as customs policy on energy imports into the EU, which are clearly a matter over which the EU is competent to develop policy to the exclusion of Member States.

Equally, there are other features of energy that may sensibly be considered to be within the sovereign preserve of EU Member States. An example would be, for instance, German diplomatic efforts with Russia to promote the interests of German energy downstream companies (over those of other EU Member States' energy companies) by having EU

---

international treaty-making capacities of two different agents such as a central authority – e.g., the EU – and its constituent parts – e.g., EU Member States).

[82] Article 3 TFEU.

[83] See Article 3 TFEU. See also Article 6 TFEU for areas where the EU will have competence to carry out actions to support EU Member States' actions.

[84] See Article 4 TFEU.

energy imports from Russia arrive into Germany.[85] Generally, it can reasonably be assumed that all other matters over which the treaties are silent (by containing no express provision) remain the sovereign preserve of EU Member States. Fundamental tenets of treaty interpretation would support this view.[86] In that sense, assessing the appropriate level of EU action initially requires the identification of the various policy matters implicated in order to subsequently assess what could be done at the EU level without the EU institutions unjustifiably infringing upon whatever prerogatives have been preserved by the 28 sovereign actors that make up the EU.[87] It is also important to bear in mind that the challenges the EU faces in developing and promoting a coherent energy policy are not limited to inherent and systemic limitations, but stem from the grossly disparate energy realities among its 28 Member States.

That said, EU Member States are obligated to refrain from acting in ways that would undermine EU *external and security* policy action.[88] This is a provision with a potentially restrictive effect on Member States'

---

[85] See Korkmaz, D. 'Internal and External Dynamics of European Energy Security' (2010) 5–6, available at http://www.jhubc.it/ecpr-porto/virtualpaperroom/034.pdf, where he discusses energy diplomacy between Russia and Germany, and the latter's pledge to underwrite the Nord Stream gas-pipe project.

[86] Namely the notion that States are, save for exceptional cases (e.g., arguably, under the operation of United Nations Charter provisions around Security Council prerogatives, or in the case of *jus cogens*), normatively bound to the extent that they consent to the norm in question through treaty-making (or the operation of custom). It would be improper from an interpretative point of view to aggrandize EU competences where no competence has expressly been granted in those treaties by the sovereign actors involved, or where such a possibility is not contemplated in the relevant treaties. In this context, see also what Takis Tridimas calls 'dormant EU competence' to refer to situations 'where, although the EU cannot pass legislation, the discretion of the national governments to do so is constrained by EU law', Tridimas, T. 'Competence after Lisbon: The Elusive Search for Bright Lines', in Ashiagbor, D., Countouris, N. & Lianos, I. (eds) *The European Union after the Treaty of Lisbon* (Cambridge: Cambridge University Press, 2012) pp. 47–76, at 75.

[87] For a fuller analysis on the EU constitutional aspects of, and considerations in, EU energy policy development and EU energy security, see Leal-Arcas, R. & Filis, A. 'Conceptualizing EU Energy Security through an EU Constitutional Law Perspective' (2013) *Fordham International Law Journal*, Vol. 36, No. 5, pp. 1225–1301. See also Johnston, A. and van der Marel, E. '*Ad Lucem*? Interpreting the New EU Energy Provision, and in particular the Meaning of Article 194(2) TFEU' (2013) *European Energy and Environmental Law Review*, Vol. 22, No. 5, pp. 181–199.

[88] See Article 24§3 TEU.

policy space, given that it is not unusual for their energy policies to contain features that affect EU interests in the EU's external action. On the other hand, safeguard provisions exist that aim at the *containment* of EU competences to the limits prescribed in the founding treaties, that promote proportionality in EU action, and that promote efficient use of shared competences.

Additionally, the founding treaties further contemplate the possibility that there may be cases in which, while the EU has no express competence (i.e., neither shared nor exclusive competence) to act, it may be appropriate for it to do so, so long as Member States expressly and unanimously consent to this via the appropriate EU deliberative and decision-making bodies.[89]

The foregoing has been included in order to outline the high-level EU constitutional coordinates within which to understand the question of competences. It is important to bear in mind that, because of energy's multifaceted nature, different levels of EU competence apply to different energy-related issues. This makes it difficult to identify the relevant EU competence without having first identified which energy-related issues will be engaged.[90] Finally, in relation to the aspects of the EU constitutional framework that may affect energy, the advent of the Lisbon Treaty has had certain implications for EU competences over energy. However, importantly, this has not been in a manner that erodes Member State prerogatives. In relation to energy, the Lisbon Treaty provides some degree of streamlining, while boosting the EU's environmental protection objectives by giving these a more prominent role in EU energy policy development. This has been expressed in legislative backing for renewable energy within EU policy as a means of making good on the EU's commitment to environmental protection and to achieving a more *sustainable* energy reality.[91]

Returning to the question of EU powers to handle external energy relations, it may be helpful to approach this through a series of assessments: firstly, it would be necessary to assess whether an energy-related proposal in question falls within the exclusive or the shared competence remit of the EU. Should it unequivocally fall within the

---

[89] See Article 352§1 TFEU.

[90] For further details on EU law and competences regarding energy matters, see Leal-Arcas, R. & Filis, A. 'Conceptualizing EU Energy Security through an EU Constitutional Law Perspective' (2013) *Fordham International Law Journal*, Vol. 36, No. 5, pp. 1225–1301.

[91] See Title XXI TFEU, which relates to energy and has only one article, Article 194 TFEU.

former category, the EU would enjoy unbridled powers to pursue the external aspects of the energy-related policy proposal in question. Should the energy-related policy fall within the latter category, it would then be necessary to assess how the proposal ought to be decided at the EU level – that is to say, whether it engages such matters that the Council of the European Union[92] may have to decide unanimously or by majority in order for an EU policy to be adopted.

Article 192§2(c) of the Treaty on the Functioning of the European Union (TFEU) refers to the *vires* of the Council to seek to legislate or take measures that *significantly affect* a Member State's choice between different energy sources and the general structure of its energy supply. We witness a high degree of incursion by the supranational into the national sphere. However, Article 192§2 introduces safeguards by making clear that decision-making by the Council under Article 192§2(c) must be reached in the Council on the basis of unanimity and not by qualified majority.[93]

What this might indicate is that, in the final analysis, crucial energy-security-related measures with strong diplomatic overtones – such as measures that, if taken, affect rather significantly a Member State's choice between what energy sources it may use, or what the general structure of its energy supply ought to be – remain firmly with Member States, given the unanimity requirement in such cases. In effect, this preserves certain sovereign prerogatives of Member States.

---

[92] This is a key institution of the EU composed of 28 ministers whose composition alters according to the policy matter at hand; e.g., ministers with responsibility for agriculture meet within the EU context to decide a particular EU-wide agricultural policy. This is an important institution in that, alongside the EU Parliament through a co-decision process, it may adopt legislation. Hereinafter we shall refer to it as the 'Council'. It should not be confused with the European Council (i.e., the configuration of the 28 heads of State/government), which is the supreme political body within the EU. The European Council – technically, in its *alter ego*, namely the *ad hoc* summit gathering of heads of State/government – is the body that contracts the treaties upon which the EU rests.

[93] Council decision-making based on the qualified majority voting procedure is the norm, unless stated to the contrary, under Articles 238 of the TFEU. See also Article 16 TEU. From November 2014, qualified majority shall mean at least 55% of Council members representing at least 65% of the EU population or 72% of Council members representing at least 65%, depending on the circumstances. See Article 16§4 TEU and Articles 238§2 and 238§3 TFEU.

If we take as an example Directive 2009/28/EC,[94] we note in its preamble that this instrument was adopted in accordance with Articles 95, 175§1, and 251 of the Treaty Establishing the European Community (TEEC).[95] Having regard to Articles 175§1 and 251, which are cited in this Directive, decisions were adopted within the Council on the qualified majority decision-making procedure. This is interesting, given that Directive 2009/28/EC sets, amongst other things, mandatory national targets for the overall share of renewables in a Member State's final consumption[96] which could be interpreted as *significantly affecting* a Member State's choice of energy sources. However, it might have been the view of Council members that the interference was not so significant as to invoke the unanimity-based decision-making process.[97]

As we shall see below, EU energy policy is multifaceted. Its introspective aspects have been adopted to, amongst other things, integrate the IEM in terms of gas and electricity, and to promote energy efficiency and the use of renewables. There is sufficient legal basis within the treaties – namely the TFEU – for the EU to take action, for example by promulgating policy, to handle aspects of the IEM. Conceivably, creating an effective IEM also rests on a degree of regulatory convergence across the EU. Under the TFEU,[98] the EU may legislate to such an end. However, whether either the qualified majority vote or the unanimity-based Council decision-making process applies depends on which matters are being considered for convergence. The language of the relevant provisions do

---

[94] Directive 2009/28/EC (*of the European Parliament and the Council of 23 April 2009 on the promotion of the use of energy from renewable sources and amending and subsequently repealing Directives 2001/77/EC and 2003/30/EC*).

[95] The TEEC was amended by the Treaty of Lisbon, which was signed on 13 December 2007 in Lisbon and which entered into force on 1 December 2009, embracing a revised Treaty on European Union (TEU) and a revised Treaty Establishing the European Community, which would be called a Treaty on the Functioning of the European Union (TFEU). Consequently, Articles 95, 175, and 251 TEEC became Articles 114, 192, and 294 TFEU. Do note, however, that when Directive 2009/28/EC was concluded (April 2009), it was done on the basis of the TEEC, which was applicable at the time. Furthermore, this Directive also cites the Kyoto Protocol to the UNFCCC in relation to the EU's international obligations, and those of its Member States, under that instrument.

[96] Article 1 of Directive 2009/28/EC.

[97] This seems to be the case when one notices that the national targets are calculated on factors that take into account national figures around energy consumption, thus applying a variegated regime rather than seeking to enforce a uniform target on all members alike. See Article 5 of Directive 2009/28/EC.

[98] Namely Chapter 3 (Articles 114–118) TFEU on the approximation of laws.

not make it an easy task to ascertain which decision-making process applies, given how nuanced it appears to be. To make this clear, let us look at Articles 114 and 115 TFEU. Article 115 states that the Council in unanimity may adopt such measures for the approximation of laws across the EU in relation to matters that *directly affect* the establishment or functioning of the internal market, whilst, under Article 114, the Council may decide on the qualified-majority basis for measures for the approximation of laws that *have as their object* the establishment or functioning of the internal market. Here we witness the cleavage in EU law and policy making in relation to Council decision-making procedures. Furthermore, the TFEU contains the legal basis for the integration of energy infrastructure and the development of EU-wide energy infrastructure.[99]

The evolution of the EU involves two directions: the widening (enlargement) and the deepening (greater integration) of the Union. The institutional challenges that this phenomenon engenders have eventually pushed EU Member States to seriously consider ways of consolidating and rationalizing the EU processes. To that end, the Treaty Establishing a Constitution for Europe[100] was proposed but eventually defeated in France and the Netherlands by popular *referenda* in 2005, despite having been ratified by more than 15 EU Member States.

The Treaty of Lisbon (ToL)[101] is a replacement for the EU Constitutional Treaty,[102] since the latter failed ratification. Because the EU Constitutional Treaty did not enter into force,[103] and after a political

---

[99] See Article 170 TFEU dealing with the Trans-European networks (TEN), including for energy (TEN-E).

[100] This proposed Treaty, commonly referred to as the European Constitution, is an unimplemented Treaty which was signed in Rome in 2004 by the representatives of the 25 (at the time) EU Member States, but failed to be unanimously ratified as the populations of France whilst the Netherlands rejected the Treaty in *referenda*. Following a period of reflection given this initial defeat, the European Council met again in June 2007 and initiated negotiations on a draft to replace the failed form of the Constitutional Treaty. A revised and substantially reduced version of that Treaty (from then on referred to as the Reform Treaty or Lisbon Treaty) was signed in Lisbon in December 2007 and entered into force on 1 December 2009.

[101] Official Journal C 306 of 17 December 2007.

[102] Official Journal C 310 of 16 December 2004.

[103] Before the European Council of June 2007, the idea was that when the EU Constitutional Treaty would enter into force, the EC Treaty, the EU Treaty, as well as acts and Treaties which have supplemented or amended them, would have been repealed, as laid down in the general and final provisions in Part IV of the EU Constitutional Treaty. The EU Constitutional Treaty was supposed to

agreement was reached at the European Council meeting of June 2007, the Portuguese Presidency of the EU launched an intergovernmental conference for the negotiation of a fall-back revision treaty, that is, the Treaty of Lisbon, on 23 July 2007, embracing a revised Treaty on European Union (TEU) and a revised European Community Treaty, which would be called a Treaty on the Functioning of the European Union (TFEU).[104] Much if not all of the content of the new Treaties was agreed at the European Council meeting in Brussels in June 2007. In theory therefore, this intergovernmental conference was meant to be less controversial than its predecessors, which led to the Single European Act and the Maastricht, Amsterdam, and Nice Treaties,[105] as well as the abandoned EU Constitutional Treaty. The European Council decided that the intergovernmental conference would conclude before the end of 2007, so that the ToL could be ratified by all the then 27 EU Member States before the European Parliament elections in June 2009, which did not happen.

Unlike the abandoned EU Constitutional Treaty – which would have replaced all previous Treaties with a single text – the Treaty of Lisbon

---

enter into force after ratification by all EU Member States. It was also provided for that the Union would succeed to all the rights and obligations, whether internal or resulting from international agreements, which arose before the entry into force of the EU Constitutional Treaty. The case law of the Court of Justice of the EU would have been maintained as a source of Union law interpretation. As stated in Article I-6 of the EU Constitutional Treaty, the Constitution and law adopted by the Union's institutions in exercising competences conferred on it would have had primacy over the law of the Member States.

[104] The intergovernmental conference (IGC) mandate also provided in its paragraph 22 that 'a Protocol annexed to the Reform Treaty will amend the existing Protocols, as agreed in the 2004 IGC' (including the deletion of 10 of them). See Presidency Conclusions of the Brussels European Council, 21–22 June 2007, 11177/07, CONCL 2, Annex I, para. 22.

[105] EU leaders intended to replace the EU's basic treaties with a single, shorter, simpler document spelling out the EU's purposes and aims and stating clearly who does what. This document (technically known as the Constitutional Treaty) would have been rather similar to the constitution of a country – even though the EU is not, and does not aim to be, a single country. The text of the EU Constitution was agreed in June 2004 and signed by all the Member State governments in October 2004 in Rome. It was due to come into force in 2006, but it failed to be ratified by all the national parliaments and, in some countries, be approved by referendum. Vernon Bogdanor, however, argues that it would make more sense to have a Europe-wide referendum with a double and qualified majority of Member States and population required in order to ratify any proposed Treaty amendment.

adds to – but does not replace or consolidate – the TEU and EC Treaty, including the Acts of Accession. This means that there is now another layer of Treaty law with the ToL. On the positive side however, the ToL is a substantive legal document, introducing significant legal, procedural, and institutional changes. It draws heavily on the EU Constitutional Treaty, confirms much of the substance of the EU Constitutional Treaty, and includes, *inter alia*, provisions relating to the EU's capacity to formulate a common foreign policy and to enjoy a single legal personality[106] for it to conclude international agreements and to join international organizations. It is somewhat paradoxical that, in the period since the collapse of the Berlin Wall, at precisely the time in which there were few credible alternatives to liberal democracy, there have been growing doubts about the capacity of the structures and institutions of liberal democracy to respond to contemporary problems.[107]

The advent of the Lisbon Treaty did not affect EU competences in any *substantive* way. In relation to the EU's external relations, including those linked to its external energy policy, the impact of the Lisbon Treaty has been to streamline and rationalize existing processes and competences that are linked to the various EU institutional actors.[108] Most ostensibly, the Lisbon Treaty streamlines processes related to the EU's common foreign and security policy.[109] It has amended the role of the High

---

106 Article 47 TEU as amended by the Lisbon Treaty. See also Leal-Arcas, R. 'EU Legal Personality in Foreign Policy?' (2006) *Boston University International Law Journal*, Vol. 24, No. 2, pp. 165–212.

107 Laursen, F. 'The Post-Nice Agenda: Towards a New "Constitutional" Treaty?' in Laursen, F. (ed.) *The Treaty of Nice: Actor Preferences, Bargaining and Institutional Choice* (Leiden, the Netherlands: Martinus Nijhoff Publishers, 2006) pp. 543–560.

108 In some cases, the Lisbon Treaty has enhanced the role of existing office holders – e.g., of what had previously been the High Representative of the Common Foreign and Security Policy (now the High Representative for Foreign Affairs and Security Policy) – to be involved in more EU processes with the aim of promoting cohesion across the EU external policy spectrum. This office has not been granted competences to take decisions on behalf of the 28 Member States. Rather, its competences focus on executing EU decisions and representing EU common positions that have already been reached by the Council and other bodies of the EU. For further details, see Leal-Arcas, R. 'The European Union's New Common Commercial Policy after the Treaty of Lisbon', in Trybus, M. & Rubini, L. *The Treaty of Lisbon and the Future of European Law and Policy* (Cheltenham: Edward Elgar, 2012) pp. 262–284.

109 Amongst other things, the Lisbon Treaty has created the office of the President of the European Council who is a high level official of the EU, carrying out essentially an administrative role in relation to the work of the

Representative of the EU of the Common Foreign and Security Policy to now become the High Representative of the EU for Foreign Affairs and Security Policy[110] (High Representative). The High Representative is supported in their work by the EU's External Action Service.

How decisions at the EU level might be taken on the basis of the TEU has remained unaffected by the Lisbon Treaty. Article 16§3 TEU stipulates that the Council may adopt measures on the basis of the qualified majority decision-making procedure. However, as is the case with Article 192§2(c) TFEU,[111] this is without prejudice to specific provisions in EU treaties which stipulate that Council decisions be based on the unanimity decision-making procedure.

The Lisbon Treaty amended the Treaty on European Union (TEU)[112] and the Treaty Establishing the European Community[113] (TEEC), the latter consequently becoming the TFEU. Title V, Chapter I (Article 21) of the TEU stipulates in very clear terms how the EU's external action might be conducted. From a public law point of view, Article 21 TEU heavily constrains how EU external relations may be conducted. The language is enlightened in that it makes EU external action subject to such guiding principles as: 'democracy, the rule of law, the universality and indivisibility of human rights and fundamental freedoms, respect for human dignity, the principles of equality and solidarity, and respect for the principles of the United Nations Charter and international law'.

B. Energy Governance and the Treaty of Lisbon

1. Pre-Lisbon Treaty

Until the entry into force of the landmark Lisbon Treaty in 2009, there was no express provision for the development of a common energy

---

European Council and also representing the EU on the world stage alongside other EU officials (namely the High Representative and the President of the EU Commission).

110 Articles 17 to 24 TEU, and elsewhere, in relation to the High Representative's role and powers.

111 Article 192§2 (c) TFEU stipulates that measures that, if adopted, would *significantly affect* Member States' choice between different energy sources and the general structure of their energy supply, ought to be taken on the basis of the unanimity decision-making procedure. Note that this provision pre-existed the amendments introduced by the Lisbon Treaty, namely as Article 175 TEEC.

112 Also known as the Maastricht Treaty, signed on 7 February 1992 and in force since 1 November 1993.

113 Also known as the Treaty of Rome, signed on 25 March 1957 and in force since 1 January 1958.

policy at the EU level.[114] While numerous false starts were made towards this objective, consensus was elusive.[115] As a result, the pre-Lisbon Treaty period was characterized by EU-level energy policy developments which were an incidental function of the EU's 'environmental protection' and 'internal market' mandates.[116] During this period, energy policy was primarily formulated and implemented at national levels.[117] This position gradually shifted in the new millennium as a number of factors such as the increasing dependence on external energy sources, the lack of EU influence on the energy supply side and the potential failure of the EU to meet its climate change obligations under the Kyoto Protocol led to the recognition of the need for a pan-EU policy aimed at ensuring long-term energy security.[118] This recognition first manifested in a European Commission Green Paper on the 'Security of Energy Supply'[119] in 2000 and was subsequently followed up in a number of similar documents and accords, all of which were slow but steady steps towards a pan-EU energy policy that ultimately came into force through the Lisbon Treaty.

2. The Lisbon Treaty

The entry into force of the Lisbon Treaty in 2009 represented a turning point in the structure of EU energy policy governance. Firstly, it marked

---

114 See e.g., Groome, F. 'From Contradiction to Cooperation: A New Legal and Diplomatic Foundation for Energy Policy in the EU' April 2012, *Journal of Energy Security*, available at http://www.ensec.org/index.php?option=com_content&view=article&id=343:from-contradiction-to-cooperation-a-new-legal-and-diplomatic-foundation-for-energy-policy-in-the-eu&catid=123:content&Itemid=389

115 An example of this was the attempt to include an energy chapter in the 1992 Treaty of Maastricht. This move was opposed by a number of EU Member States, especially those with high reserves, 'as they did not want to give away autonomy in that field', Susanne Langsdorf, 'EU Energy Policy: From the ECSC to the Energy Roadmap 2050' (December 2011, Green European Foundation) 5.

116 European Commission, 'Towards A European Strategy for the Security of Energy Supply', COM(2000) 769 final, 11: 'As a result, the energy problems which have inevitably cropped up since the Treaty of Rome was adopted, more particularly after the first oil crises, have been approached either through the mechanism of the internal market, or from the angle of harmonisation, environmental policy or taxation'.

117 Voutilainen, P. 'Developing Energy Policy for Europe: A Finnish Perspective on Energy Cooperation in The European Union' (2008) 29 *Energy L.J.* 121, 122–123.

118 COM(2000) 769 final 12.

119 http://ec.europa.eu/energy/green-paper-energy-supply/doc/green_paper_energy_supply_en.pdf

the shift of energy policy from being an exclusive EU Member State subject to one upon which EU Member States and the EU possess 'shared' legislative competence.[120] This means that both the Union and its Member States can 'legislate and adopt legally binding acts' in the area of energy policy.[121] However, EU Member States' competence is limited to the extent that the Union has not exercised or has decided to cease exercising its competence.[122]

Secondly, and more crucially, a separate section in the TFEU (Title XXI) on energy was included in the form of Article 194. This provided that the Union would act in a 'spirit of solidarity' between EU Member States to: '(a) ensure the functioning of the energy market; (b) ensure security of energy supply in the Union; (c) promote energy efficiency and energy saving and the development of new and renewable forms of energy; and (d) promote the interconnection of energy networks'.[123] While the same provision allows EU Member States to retain decision-making autonomy in matters concerning the mix of energy sources, the conditions for exploiting its energy resources and the structure of its energy supply,[124] this approach has signified a marked departure from the earlier approach in the pre-Lisbon Treaty era of EU Member States retaining complete control over policy decisions in the energy sector.

Article 194 TFEU sets out the proclaimed objectives of EU energy policy and their principal procedural aspects. Notably, under Title XXI, EU energy policy is unequivocally linked to the EU's environmental objectives. In particular, Article 194 TFEU expressly refers to the need for EU energy policy to preserve and improve the environment and to promote energy efficiency and the development of renewable sources. However, Article 194§2 states that EU measures 'shall not affect a Member State's right to determine the conditions for exploiting its energy resources, its choice between different energy sources and the general structure of its energy supply, without prejudice to Article 192(2)(c)'.

---

[120] Article 4.2(i) TFEU. The case of energy is, however, much more complex than just stating what the TFEU says in Article 4.2(i). For a constitutional analysis, see Leal-Arcas, R. & Filis, A. 'Conceptualizing EU Energy Security through an EU Constitutional Law Perspective' (2013) *Fordham International Law Journal*, Vol. 36, No. 5, pp. 1225–1301. See also Lilliestam, J. & Patt, A., 'Conceptualising Energy Security in the European Context: A Policy Perspective Bottom-up Approach to the Cases of the EU, UK and Sweden' (SEFEP Working Paper 2012-4, June 2012) 9.

[121] Article 2.2 TFEU.

[122] Ibid.

[123] Article 194(1) TFEU.

[124] Article 194(2) TFEU.

In that respect, the impact of the Lisbon Treaty – whilst significant in that it has streamlined and clarified EU processes – has been, most importantly, to craftily preserve Member States' prerogatives over sensitive policy areas such as energy security. Article 194 TFEU also refers to one of the prescribed aims of EU energy policy as being to ensure security of energy supplies in the EU.[125] Naturally, an objective such as that could be effectively pursued with the appropriate legislative support, which in this case seems to be lacking. Whilst Article 194 proclaims EU energy security as an EU objective for the first time, it does not supplement the supranational EU bodies with further competences to facilitate the pursuit of a common EU energy security policy. Again, this is not surprising given how sensitive this policy area is, and given the challenges of garnering the requisite political will amongst Member States to endow the EU with powers to act to their exclusion in energy security matters. However, Article 352 TFEU makes it possible for the Council to make decisions necessary to attain treaty objectives even when the treaties grant no express powers. However, action pursuant to Article 352 TFEU can only be based on unanimity in the Council.

Article 21§2 TEU provides another example of the impact of the Treaty of Lisbon on EU external relations, including those that engage energy resources. It states that the EU shall define and pursue common policies and actions, and shall work for a high degree of cooperation in all fields of international relations, in order to, amongst other things, help develop international measures to preserve and improve the quality of the environment and the sustainable management of global natural resources, in order to ensure sustainable development (at Article 21§2(f)).[126] This is

---

125 See Article 194§1(b) TFEU.

126 Literature on the link between governance and sustainable development is abundant. For instance, Kaufmann, D., Kraay, A. & Zoido-Lobatón, P. 'Governance Matters: From Measurement to Action' (2000) 37(2) *Finance and Development* 10; Rivera-Batiz, F.L. 'Democracy, Governance, and Economic Growth: Theory and Evidence' (2002) 6(2) *Review of Development Economics* 225; Stiglitz, J.E. 'Participation and Development: Perspectives from the Comprehensive Development Paradigm' (2002) 6(2) *Review of Development Economics* 163; Grindle, M.S. 'Good Enough Governance: Poverty Reduction and Reform in Developing Countries' (2004) 17(4) *Governance* 525; van Kersbergen, K. & van Waarden, F. '"Governance" as a Bridge between Disciplines: Cross-Disciplinary Inspiration Regarding Shifts in Governance and Problems of Governability, Accountability and Legitimacy' (2004) 43(2) *European Journal of Political Research* 143; Kishor, N. & Belle, A. 'Does Improved Governance Contribute to Sustainable Forest Management?' (2004) 19(1–3) *Journal of Sustainable Forestry* 55; Hope, K.R. 'Toward Good Governance and Sustainable Development:

relevant to the EU's external relations that engage, amongst other things, energy resources. What we may conclude from the above is that, constitutionally, EU external action, including in relation to its energy policy, is heavily constrained by Article 21 and the enlightened principles enshrined therein.

However, under Article 4§1(i) TFEU, 'energy', in its wide sense, is expressly referred to as a matter of shared competence. Let us be reminded that shared competence matters may be handled by the EU in accordance to the 'subsidiarity'[127] and proportionality principles,[128] that is to say, should action be considered more effective at the supranational level, EU action may justifiably take precedence over Member States. Certain energy-related matters, though, are deemed exclusive to the EU under Article 3 TFEU; for instance, the competitive conditions of energy trade within the internal market, or the question of tariffs when third country energy commodities cross an EU border (in other words a common commercial policy when commodities enter the customs union) appear to fall squarely within the exclusive competence of the EU.[129] It is worth noting that for matters that do not fall within the EU competence remit, it is still possible for the EU to act in that the Council may make decisions in order to attain the objectives of the EU as set out in the EU treaties.[130]

Thus, the Lisbon Treaty is an important stepping-stone for the EU to emerge as an entity with one voice in the international energy setting.[131] While questions exist about the method of policy formulation and implementation[132] – most notably the unanimity requirement, which

---

The African Peer Review Mechanism' (2005) 18(2) *Governance* 283; Goldsmith, A.A. 'Is Governance Reform a Catalyst for Development?' (2007) 20(2) *Governance* 165; and Andrews, M. 'Good Government Means Different Things in Different Countries' (2010) 23(1) *Governance* 7.

[127] Article 5§3 TEU.

[128] Article 5§4 TEU.

[129] For further details on the trade policy front, see Leal-Arcas, R. 'Is Lisbon the Answer or the Anathema to EC Trade Law and Policy?' (2009) *International Journal of Liability & Scientific Enquiry*, Vol. 2, No. 2, pp. 125–146.

[130] See Article 352.1 TFEU.

[131] Groome, F. 'From Contradiction to Cooperation: A New Legal and Diplomatic Foundation for Energy Policy in the EU' *Journal of Energy Security* (April 2012) 1.

[132] For example, whether the Lisbon Treaty actually changed the way the EU approached energy issues. See Falkner, G. 'EU Policies in the Lisbon Treaty: A Comparative Analysis' (Working Paper No. 03/2008, Institute for European Integration Research) 59.

effectively allows each EU Member State a veto on decisions – there is no doubt that the Lisbon Treaty is a solid manifestation of not just the recognition of the EU's precarious energy position, but also of the general agreement that the way forward lies through concerted and unified action by EU Member States. Whether the Lisbon Treaty is an effective or even appropriate framework for the fulfillment of this long-standing objective, however, is a matter that remains to be seen.[133]

C. Challenges to Achieving a Common EU Energy Security Policy

As we shall examine in Section V, the geostrategic context and the disparate energy security capabilities of each Member State appear to explain why it might be unrealistic to have a common EU energy security as a matter of exclusive EU competence. Furthermore, achieving a common position on matters of EU external action has never been easy.[134] That said, there is scope for the EU to enhance its members' energy security in a number of smaller yet significant ways. For instance, by streamlining and rationalizing EU processes, and thus removing any inconsistencies or contradictions in EU action, the EU becomes a better, more efficient, actor. Also, Article 122 TFEU refers to the possibility of cross-EU solidarity in cases where a Member State is facing *severe difficulties* in, amongst other things, the energy supply.

Article 21 TEU imposes major obstacles to achieving EU energy security that are not encountered by other sizeable energy consumers such as China, India, Japan, and the US, who are free to pursue any energy security policy that they find most expedient.[135] Again, this illustrates the challenges faced by groups of States that are not fully federalized across the policy spectrum. However, Article 21 TEU places

133 For a number of potential challenges that the implementation of the Treaty of Lisbon may be faced with, see generally Braun, J.F. 'EU Energy Policy under the Treaty of Lisbon Rules: Between a New Policy and Business As Usual' (Working Paper No. 31/February 2011, European Policy Institute Network).

134 See generally the analysis by Leal-Arcas, R. *Theory and Practice of EC External Trade Law and Policy* (London: Cameron May, 2008) Chapter 2.

135 Note that the Gulf Cooperation Council (GCC) refused EU overtures for energy cooperation because the latter wanted energy relations with GCC on a pro-market regulatory basis whereas the GCC wanted relations on the basis of strategic partnerships. The GCC viewed with suspicion EU calls for GCC market liberalization as potentially disruptive of the social order in those States. See Korkmaz, D. 'Internal and External Dynamics of European Energy Security' (2010) (paper based on a chapter of Korkmaz's PhD thesis) available at http://www.jhubc.it/ecpr-porto/virtualpaperroom/034.pdf (at p. 25).

no constraints on how EU Member States might, in their own right, pursue their respective energy security needs, for which they could conceivably pursue the same *realpolitik* as any other State.

Article 22 TEU makes it clear that the European Council[136] – in its capacity as the highest agenda-setting EU institution[137] – may identify the EU's strategic interests on the basis of the principles of Article 21 TEU and on the basis of unanimity (as per Article 22§1 TEU). Again, Articles 21 and 22 TEU make clear that there is no legally endorsed scope for *realpolitik* within the EU.

However, it is worth noting that the EU extensively engages with third-party States – namely those of MENA, Russia, Central Asia, and the Caspian States – some of whose respect for the humanist principles set out under Article 21 TEU is, at best, doubtful. In such cases, we should be asking: to which extent does EU external energy policy, necessitated by the EU's economic imperatives, contradict the dictates of Articles 21 and 22 TEU, and how are any such contradictions resolved?

Energy is multidimensional in that it cuts across several fields of policy, including foreign policy, international trade, human rights, security issues, and economics, among others. This complicates matters, given that EU competences are uneven, depending on what is at issue. When we discuss energy within the context of the EU and its external relations with third-party States, a multiplicity of EU offices and institutions may be at play: namely the EU Commissioner for Energy; the European Council's President; the High Representative – who is also a vice-president of the Commission – assisted by the EU External Action Service; and the Foreign Affairs Council – which is a sub-committee of the Council. Numerous provisions across the TEU and TFEU spell out their powers and duties.

For instance, the European Council's President's role is, *inter alia*, to ensure the external representation of the EU's common foreign and security policy without prejudice to the High Representative's mandate of representing the EU abroad in foreign and security policy.[138] The High

---

136 The European Council is an EU institution comprised of the heads of government or State of the 28 EU Member States.

137 As opposed to an *ad hoc* summit of heads of State/government who are otherwise only bound by general international law and their own respective constitutions in how they behave.

138 Article 15§6 TEU.

Representative's role is more comprehensive in order to promote cohesion of EU external action.[139] To that end, the High Representative has access to relevant Council sessions and to those of the Commission. The role of the EU's Foreign Affairs Council – a subcommittee of the Council – is to develop EU external action in line with strategic guidance provided beforehand by the European Council.[140] In that respect we witness how external relations, given their sensitive nature, are deferred to the EU institutions in which Member States participate in their own right and are thus able to fully defend their interests, rather than to supranational institutions such as the EU Commission. Article 15§4 TEU emphasizes that a consensus decision-making process applies, unless there is express provision in the treaties for decisions to be taken differently. Also, Article 31(1–3) TEU makes clear that proposals by the High Representative in relation to the common foreign and security policy put to the European Council and the Council are subject to the unanimity decision-making procedure in those intergovernmental fora.[141] However, as the European Council is an EU body – albeit an intergovernmental rather than supranational one – all action flowing from it must be in compliance with the guiding principles of the EU mentioned above.[142] Therefore, whilst warmer or fully institutionalized relations with authoritarian energy-rich third-party States are clearly matters of strategic interest for the EU, their potential conflict with Article 21 TEU could potentially present complications for cohesive action.

Furthermore, Article 22(1) TEU promotes consistency and conditions the decision-making capacity of the European Council by stating that European Council decisions on the EU's strategic interests and objectives must be in accordance with its common foreign and security policy and with other areas of EU external action. In that respect, the European Council – in its capacity as an EU institution – does not have free reign to promulgate policy in a manner that is inconsistent with the entire EU project. Thus, as the treaties stand, even the most supreme political body

---

[139] See Articles 21, 22, 24, and 26 TEU regarding consistency, and Article 329 TFEU, which provides for the High Representative to make pronouncements on consistency of EU action.

[140] According to Article 26 TEU, the European Council is charged with identifying the EU's strategic interests, along with determining the objectives of and defining the general guidelines for the common foreign and security policy, including for matters with defense implications.

[141] Article 22 TEU.

[142] Article 21§1 TEU.

of the EU – the European Council[143] – cannot sanction EU energy policy that contradicts Article 21 TEU. Of course, this obstacle could be overcome were Member States to take the necessary legislative steps to remove the Article 21 TEU constraints, such as concluding a subsequent treaty that amends or supersedes its effect, or, more controversially, were they to condone Article 21 TEU non-compliant EU action by not opposing or challenging it in the relevant EU fora. Naturally, these are politically difficult options that are unlikely to be supported by Member States other than those willing to accept the trade-offs between enlightened ideals and economic exigencies. Conceivably, Member States with strong liberal traditions and a politically active civil society might be less likely to support such significant ontological changes to the EU. Again, law follows political changes, and shifts in the political direction are good portends of the legislative changes that may potentially follow.

Whilst the EU lacks the powers of a sovereign actor in relation to diplomatically pursuing its energy security, it does possess a comprehensive energy policy that is multifaceted and that makes the most of the powers that lie within its remit of competences. Moreover, whilst its energy policy focuses mainly on the IEM, it strategically contains outward aspects that focus on promoting the EU's energy interests regionally and globally. Again, this happens to the extent that the EU may act in unison in such matters. Whilst it cannot *sui juris* assume EU Member States' competences over the entire diplomatic policy spectrum, it is not prohibited from taking action globally that, as a consequence, enhances the EU's energy security. As we shall see, this may take the form of the EU promoting greater energy-market liberalization in the belief that more fluid energy markets would benefit energy consumers such as itself that are reliant on regional and international markets for their energy needs. It may also take the form of promoting regional

[143] Throughout the EU treaties, we witness a logical deference towards the European Council. Under Article 15 TEU, the European Council is charged with: 'provid[ing] the necessary impetus for its development and shall define the general political direction and priorities thereof'. It also makes clear at Article 15§1 that the European Council does not exercise legislative functions. Strictly speaking, therefore, any subsequent treaties contracted between the 28 heads of State/government are done so outside the context of the EU institution of the European Council – in that respect, although it is the same configuration of individual national office holders, they do not function within the public law aspects of EU, rather, in their capacity to conclude international conventions, they function within the context of the area of public international law relating to the law of treaties and to the extent permitted by their respective national laws.

integration in that the EU has set up and promoted the Energy Community (EnC) that involves several neighboring States with a view to integrating their energy markets to the IEM.[144] These actions, while soft approaches, may potentially have a cumulative effect towards achieving energy security.

IV. DIVERSITY OF EU ENERGY POLICY

As we have briefly discussed above, EU energy policy is a composite affair that reflects the complexities of energy in its wide sense. To be more precise, EU energy policy is essentially a bundle of policies that target or engage various aspects of energy, both internal and external. For instance, several EU policies aim at the progressive integration chiefly of the gas and electricity energy landscapes of Member States and the consequent formation of the IEM. There is a raft of EU legislation to this end.[145] In that respect, such policies are internally focused. However, many of these policies also contain externally focused aspects. For instance, policies linked to the IEM also seek to draw third-party States into the IEM through the creation and development of the Energy Community. In that respect, the IEM itself contains internal and external aspects that are inherent to it.

Other instances of EU policy aim at promoting greater liquidity of energy markets on the assumption that more voluminous trade flows towards global markets are ultimately in the interests of net energy consumers – such as the EU – who depend on the outside world for their energy security, chiefly on markets.[146] This aim (greater liquidity of energy markets), in turn, is pursued through a variety of strategies (e.g.,

---

[144] http://www.energy-community.org/portal/page/portal/ENC_HOME

[145] See Europa, Summaries of EU Legislation: Energy, http://europa.eu/legislation_summaries/energy/index_en.htm (summarizing EU legislation in relation to energy). The purpose of the present chapter is to highlight the comprehensive nature of EU energy policy rather than provide an account of its finer aspects. In that respect, we do not intend to list and discuss all legislation. Section III of this chapter (on the legal aspects of EU energy policy) aims at providing an overview of the constitutional aspects of energy policy within the EU by highlighting the complexities of energy in terms of how it may engage separate spheres of competences.

[146] Naturally, this does not preclude the EU from seeking closer, strategic, relations with energy producers in the MENA and Caspian regions and with Russia. This illustrates the diversified approach to energy security that the EU pursues.

through the promotion of the Energy Charter Treaty and of pro-market practices abroad).

A. Types of EU Energy Policy

It might be helpful, therefore, to regard EU energy policy as actually being a wide range of policies that could broadly be aggregated into the following two categories:

(1) policies that relate to energy markets and energy use within the EU; and
(2) policies that promote EU energy security interests with third-party States and in international organizations.

Policies that seek to draw third-party neighboring States into the IEM – for example, through the EnC – although concerned with the IEM, clearly sit in the second category in that their ultimate aim is the promotion of EU energy interests abroad. Policies that set targets for more efficient and sustainable use of energy within the EU fall within the first category, whilst policies that seek to promote efficient use of energy abroad sit in the second category, as, arguably, it is ultimately in the EU's energy security interests to promote energy efficiency abroad. There may also be policies that relate to energy markets and energy use in the EU which make it necessary for the EU to engage with the outside world; such policies also fall within the second category, given that they are ultimately connected with furthering EU energy interests. What is also becoming increasingly clear is that there is little point to a fully integrated IEM and Trans-European Network for energy (TEN-EN) when there are insufficient energy supplies flowing into it.

In that sense, a fully integrated IEM and TEN-EN risks becoming somewhat redundant when there are insufficient inward energy flows.[147]

---

[147] See 2011 EU Commission Communication to the European Parliament, the Council, the European Economic and Social Committee, and the Committee of the Regions, 'On Security of Energy Supply and International Cooperation – "The EU Energy Policy: Engaging with Partners beyond Our Borders"', 7 September 2011 (COM(2011) 539 final), where it is stated that: '*The EU energy market depends on high levels of imports to function, and therefore depends on free and transparent markets. In their absence, the EU is vulnerable to political and price volatility.* Supply security in one part depends on security across the market as a whole. External energy policy needs to reflect the interconnectedness of the internal market and the interdependence of the EU Member States' (at p. 4, emphasis added).

In that sense, a fully integrated and functional yet energy-starved TEN-EN might end up a tragic reminder – such as ghost towns or decommissioned rail-tracks – of what might have been. A weak long-term EU external energy strategy that is not integrated and unified could lead to EU failure to address its security needs. Again, as we mention throughout this chapter, the EU is 52% energy dependent on the outside world. If too much effort and resource on the part of the EU is being diverted into the development of the IEM and TEN-EN without there being proportionately effective EU action to address the external aspects of EU security, the EU may have squandered precious resources that could have been usefully diverted into making the EU less hydrocarbon dependent by, amongst other things, greater promotion and subsidization of low-carbon and renewable energy research and development. However, again, as we have analyzed above, the treaties upon which the EU rests, in their current form, present structural constraints that restrict the deployment of a more effective comprehensive EU external energy policy.[148]

As discussed above, the integration of the IEM is considered an important element of EU energy policy in that a more efficient internal system enhances energy security. To that end, there is regulatory convergence that is taking place across the EU. Currently, the regulatory situation across the EU is not fully harmonized.[149] The IEM has also been promoted through the Energy Community (EnC) in order to also achieve regulatory convergence with a view to integrating the electricity and gas markets of neighboring States with the IEM.

The EnC was set up further to the Energy Community Treaty between the EU and several third-party States. It currently involves 10 parties – the EU, Albania, Bosnia & Herzegovina, Croatia, Kosovo, Macedonia, Moldova, Montenegro, Serbia, and Ukraine.[150] It has been promoted by the EU to engage its neighbors on the basis that energy market and network integration is in the EU's energy security interests.[151]

---

[148] Ibid. at 2.

[149] Mizulin, N. 'EC Experience in Creating an Internal Energy Market: Lessons for the WTO' in Pauwelyn, J. (ed.) *Global Challenges at the Intersection of Trade, Energy, and the Environment* (Geneva: Centre for Trade and Economic Integration (CTEI), 2010) pp. 67–74.

[150] http://www.energy-community.org/portal/page/portal/ENC_HOME/ENERGY_COMMUNITY/Stakeholders/Parties

[151] Note that the EU Commission states that the EnC should be promoted with third-party States who are negotiating or concluding an FTA with the EU. See Communication from the Commission to the European Parliament, the

The EnC could be seen as a uni-sectoral 'integration without membership'[152] arrangement. The effect of the EnC is that parties are legally obligated to apply the EU energy *acquis*[153] with the aim of creating a legal and economic framework in relation to the EU's *Network Energy*[154] in order to

> create a stable regulatory and market framework capable of attracting investment in gas networks, power generation, and transmission and distributions networks, … create a single regulatory space for trade …, enhance the security of supply of the single regulatory space …, improve the environmental situation … and related energy efficiency, foster the use of renewable energy, and set out the conditions for energy trade in the single regulatory space, [and] develop … market competition … and exploit economies of scale.[155]

The key features of the EnC could be understood as regulatory convergence towards achieving a common regulatory and more predictable investment space as a means towards more integrated energy markets.[156] Georgia, Turkey, Armenia, and Norway have observer status.[157]

Many EU Member States engage in other fora to promote their energy interests; for instance through, amongst others, the Energy Charter Treaty

---

Council, the European Economic and Social Committee, and the Committee of the Regions, On Security of Energy Supply and International Cooperation, *The EU Energy Policy: Engaging with Partners Beyond Our Borders,* Brussels, 7 August 2011, COM(2011) 539 final (at p. 7).

[152] See Petrov, R. 'Energy Community as a Promoter of the European Union's "Energy Acquis" to Its Neighbourhood' (2012) *Legal Issues of Economic Integration*, Vol. 38, No. 3.

[153] However, it does allow for staggered implementation. For instance, Moldova is doing so in four successive waves, whilst Ukraine is doing so in five.

[154] See Article 2§2 of the Treaty establishing the Energy Community (EnCT).

[155] See Article 2§1 EnCT.

[156] The EnC is governed by a Ministerial Council which is the supreme political forum within its structures. There is a dispute settlement body that legal persons affected by some EnC measures may petition.

[157] This is possible under Article 96 EnCT, though all EnC members must consent to this through the Ministerial Council which governs the EnC. It is also possible for EU Member States to 'join' this organization as 'participants' rather than members (as is the EU) as per Articles 1§2 and 95 EnCT. Presently, Austria, Bulgaria, Cyprus, Greece, and the UK, conceivably due to their bordering and energy-transit significant geographic positioning, participate in EnC meetings with this status.

(ECT), the EnC, the North Atlantic Treaty Organization (NATO)[158] and the Organisation for Economic Cooperation and Development's International Energy Agency (IEA).[159] Consequently, the benefits of multilateralism might also accrue at the EU collective level.

---

[158] NATO is not concerned with energy security *per se*. It is concerned with the collective defense interests of its members. That said, there have been suggestions that it could expand its remit to address the defense of its members' key energy infrastructures and the security of their energy supply chain against 'terrorist' acts. In that sense, its work could potentially enhance its members' energy security from potential shocks linked to hostilities. How exactly this could take form in relation to installations that are outside the territories of NATO members in a manner consistent with international law and the principle of non-intervention is far from clear. Also, see Baumann, F. 'Europe's Way to Energy Security. The Outer Dimension of Energy Security: From Power Politics to Energy Governance' (2010) *European Foreign Affairs Review* 15, 77–95 (at p. 84). Moreover, note a December 2012 report entitled 'Energy and Security from the Caspian to Europe' by the Foreign Affairs Committee of the US Senate, which contains a series of recommendations for the US Government to implement to ensure the energy security of NATO members and their progressive energy independence from Russia. The Committee goes on to call for NATO involvement, given that the decades to come are likely to involve armed conflict over scarcity of energy resources and related disputes (at p. 55) (Report available at http://www.foreign.senate.gov/publications/download/energy-and-security-from-the-caspian-to-europe). That said, see Bejesky, R. 'Geopolitics, Oil Law Reform, and Commodity Market Expectations' (2011) 63 *Okla. L. Rev*. 276, for a useful analysis of the geopolitics at play around national security anxieties that in the post-Cold War world have mutated into anxieties around energy security. We are inclined to agree with Bejesky's conclusions: 'If consumption reduces due to technological progress, then demand and global market prices drop ceteris paribus. So, too, should the "national security" anxiety, articulated by some as manifesting into a post-Cold War Pentagon mission to "protect" global oil supply, dissipate. The argument that global military hegemony breeds stability – including for markets – out of what would otherwise be chaos, lacks substantial foundation' (at pp. 276–277).

[159] Note that the IEA obligates its members to hold oil reserves worth 90 days of their oil consumption under its Coordinated Emergency Response Mechanism. See http://www.iea.org/topics/energysecurity/. The EU, however, also has similar energy reserve requirements to those of the IEA. Council Directive 98/93/EC that mandates EU Member States to hold 90 days' worth of their average consumption of petroleum products (Article 1). In effect, this Directive inducts the IEA requirement into EU law by mandating that all EU Member States – not just IEA members – hold 90 days' worth of internal consumption of petroleum products.

B. Factors Affecting EU Energy Policy

In listing a few aspects of EU energy policy, we want to illustrate how multifaceted EU energy policy is:

(1) It focuses on integrating the domestic gas and electricity markets of EU Member States into the IEM.
(2) It promotes the IEM's integration with the energy markets and networks of neighboring third-party States;
(3) It sets minimum targets in relation to energy efficiency, GHG emissions reduction, and energy source diversification for Member States to implement.
(4) It outlines the general features of the EU's approach to external energy relations.

In relation to the last point, the EU's external energy policy is itself a highly composite affair given that there are several policy objectives to be promoted. Amongst others, such objectives are:

(1) the promotion of emissions reduction abroad to ensure that the EU's industries operate competitively against foreign industries;
(2) a more efficient use of energy abroad to ensure that energy consumers such as the EU benefit from lasting supplies; and
(3) further liberalization and integration of energy markets abroad to ensure that more energy flows reach global markets on which large consumers such as the EU rely, in order to meet a considerable part of their energy needs.

Successive EU Commission communications highlight the purported desire to achieve cohesion and consistency across the EU policy spectrum. We have also seen how the post of High Representative has been amended to, amongst other things, ensure cohesion and consistency in the EU's external action. This leads us to conclude that EU energy policy may not only be conditioned by the multiplicity of energy-related EU policy objectives but may further be conditioned by EU objectives in policy fields other than energy. This means that the development of EU energy policy is contingent upon seemingly extraneous objectives, such as those concerned with environmental protection and economic growth. We witness this in energy policies aimed at containing CO_2 emissions, for example the EU's policy that sets targets for 20% of its overall energy consumption to come from renewable energy. Let us take Directive

2009/28/EC[160] (briefly mentioned earlier) as an example: it is concerned with the promotion of renewables. According to Article 1 (subject matter and scope), the directive establishes:

> … a common framework for the promotion of energy from renewable energy sources. It sets mandatory national targets for the overall share of energy from renewable energy sources in gross final energy consumption and for the share of renewable energy for transport. It lays down rules relating to statistical transfers between member states, joint projects between member states and third countries, guarantees of origin, administrative procedures, information and training, and access to the electricity grid for energy from RES. It also establishes sustainability criteria for biofuels and bio-liquids.

It is clear that this legislative instrument promotes policies that impact a number of other EU policy fields and fields of action, including the internal market, investment, external relations, energy, environmental protection, and trade. Clearly, policy fields do not exist in isolation from one another. What is more, in this sense, 'external relations' is no stand-alone field of action; rather, it is one that could potentially engage any policy field of the EU in so far it has an ultra-EU dimension. For instance, to promote joint-projects between Member States and third-party States that take place outside the EU, the EU must engage in the promotion of investment protection outside the EU.

To take another example, in the EU Commission's *Energy Roadmap 2050* (the 2050 Roadmap),[161] the Commission – an EU institution with executive powers tasked with defending the entire EU project and the general EU interest in line with the treaties[162] – proposes a comprehensive strategy for the EU's energy needs. In this policy document, the

---

[160] Directive 2009/28/EC *of the European Parliament and of the Council of 23 April 2009 on the promotion of the use of energy from renewable sources and amending and subsequently repealing Directives 2001/77/EC and 2003/30/EC.* NB: 'Directive 2001/77/EC (27 September 2001) on the promotion of electricity produced from renewable energy sources in the internal electricity market' and 'Directive 2003/30/EC (8 May 2003) on the promotion of the use of biofuels or other renewable fuels for transport' both established definitions for different types of energy from renewable energy sources.

[161] Communication from the Commission to the European Parliament, the Council, the European Economic and Social Committee, and the Committee of the Regions, *Energy Roadmap 2050*, Brussels, 15 December 2011 (COM(2011) 885 final).

[162] See Article 17 TEU. Note also that under Article 17§2 TEU, the EU Commission has the exclusive right, save for where the treaties provide for otherwise, to propose EU legislation for adoption. In relation to EU energy

EU's energy security and environmental protection objectives are inextricably linked. The proposals focus on promoting renewables, energy efficiency, and the decarbonization of the EU economy at the EU, national, and regional levels.[163]

Also, the Commission acknowledges that the more interdependent and globalized the energy market becomes, the more the EU energy situation becomes vulnerable to global trends such as supply shocks and price fluctuations. Whilst therefore it may be in the EU's interests to pursue strategic bilateral and regional relations with energy producers in order to lock energy flows towards the EU, it is also in its interests to promote energy market liberalization for all energy flows outside its strategic relationships in the hope that more energy on global markets will ultimately serve the interests of energy importers such as the EU.[164]

The Commission sees in Russia an important partner, despite EU objectives to move towards a low-carbon economy and away from

---

policy, the Commission has been heralded as a progressive force ready to take on strong German and French interests in pushing for the unbundling of the energy markets of Germany and France and of the EU in order to allow more market actors to participate in the belief that this leads to better conditions of competition, that, in turn, would benefit EU consumers. See Korkmaz, D. *Internal and External Dynamics of European Energy Security* (2010) (paper based on a chapter of Korkmaz's PhD thesis) available at http://www.jhubc.it/ecpr-porto/virtualpaperroom/034.pdf (at p. 19).

163 Key features of the Roadmap are the diversification of the primary energy mix through supportive policies so that 55–75% of energy consumption comes from renewable sources, with about 97% of electricity from renewables. These are very ambitious targets to be met by 2050. It contains the goal of reducing CO_2 emissions by 80–95% of pre-1990 levels by 2050. Given that 35% of CO_2 emissions in the EU arise from the production of energy, achieving this goal will put the energy industries under considerable pressure. See Roadmap (at p. 4). See also Glachant, J.-M., Ahner, N. & Meeus, L. (eds) *EU Energy Innovation Policy Towards 2050* (Deventer, the Netherlands: Claeys & Casteels, 2012).

164 Note for instance that roughly 50% of global oil supplies are made available on global markets with no restrictions on who ends up being the purchaser. See Goldthau, A. & and Witte, J.M. 'The Role of Rules and Institutions in Global Energy: An Introduction', in Goldthau A. & Witte, J.M. (eds) *Global Energy Governance: The New Rules of the Game* (Washington, DC: Brookings Institution Press, 2010) at pp. 4–5. Whilst the EU would want to preserve its strategic relationships with energy suppliers, it would be in EU interests to promote energy market liberalization for the rest of the world, hoping that more energy commodities would reach the market for it – along with the other energy consumers – to meet needs not met by preferential deals. See also Luciani, G. *Security of Oil Supplies: Issues & Remedies* (Deventer, the Netherlands: Claeys & Casteels, 2013).

hydrocarbons. For instance, Russia and Ukraine are important regional producers of biofuels that could assist the EU in its move towards a low-carbon economy. What is more, conventionally extracted natural gas[165] is less polluting than coal and oil; so access to a secure supply of Russian gas, through Ukraine[166] or other routes, also contributes to the EU's efforts to produce energy in a less polluting way than energy derived from coal and oil.

The 2050 Roadmap acknowledges the importance of international cooperation in the pursuit of EU energy interests abroad. For example, the EU must also ensure that it pushes for greater environmental protection abroad for economic reasons alongside environmental concerns: namely to ensure that EU-based industries do not become uncompetitive in relation to goods and services produced by industries based in other economies which are not under similar constraints.[167]

However, the fusion of environmental and energy security objectives within the EU's energy policy in the 2050 Energy Roadmap has attracted criticism for harming the EU's energy security by making it conditional on, rather than unfettered by, environmental objectives.[168] Successive Commission communications emphasize the need to shift the energy mix

---

[165] We draw a distinction between conventionally extracted gas and that through fracking, given that shale gas extracted through fracking is environmentally harmful. See the British Geological Survey's (BGS) website, where the BGS lists its concerns (e.g., degradation of water bodies, methane leakage, increasing seismic volatility, etc.) in relation to shale gas extraction http://www.bgs.ac.uk/research/energy/shaleGas/environmentalImpacts.html.

[166] According to the EU web page on EU–Ukraine relations: 'The EU has negotiated a Deep and Comprehensive Free Trade Agreement (DCFTA). The negotiations were launched in 2008 and they have now been concluded. The DCFTA will be part of a future Association Agreement, which will replace the present Partnership and Cooperation Agreement between the EU and Ukraine (which dates from 1998). The initialing of the EU-Ukraine Association Agreement took place in Brussels in March 2012, except for the DCFTA which was initialed on 19th July 2012. Since the entire Agreement has now been initialed, the next step will be the signature of the Agreement by the Council when the conditions are met'. See http://ec.europa.eu/trade/creating-opportunities/bilateral-relations/countries/ukraine

[167] See *the Energy Roadmap 2050* at p. 16 in relation to carbon-leakage concerns.

[168] At a 5 November 2012 workshop organized by the European Parliament's external policy committee to discuss the implications of the *Energy Roadmap 2050* (EXPO/B/AFET/FWC/2009-01/Lot1/42), various criticisms were raised on the assumption that the EU's quest for energy security, which is simultaneously environmentally friendly, places the EU at a disadvantage when compared with

composition to one that is more *sustainable* in terms of supply but also in terms of less harmful environmental impacts.

Renewables provide the obvious solution; however, the financial cost of developing such energy resources makes them less economically competitive than hydrocarbons. This has important implications for investments. The EU Commission places great expectations on markets to provide the necessary solutions, not least because the capital amounts necessary would place great strain on Member States' and the EU's budgets.[169] What remains feasible at the EU and Member State policy-development levels is the use of various policy tools to encourage investments in the renewable energy sector.

On the other hand, we should also point out that the EU is not shifting towards a more *sustainable* or low-carbon energy mix anytime soon, or at least, is doing so at a slower rate than circumstances demand. Scientists have overwhelmingly agreed that natural and anthropogenic climate change is a reality, and that it may be irreversible. In its Synthesis Report of 2007,[170] the Intergovernmental Panel on Climate Change (IPCC)[171]

---

other energy consumers – e.g., China and India – which pursue a harder energy security.

[169] The EU would have to invest €900 billion in new electricity generation alone over the next 25 years or so. See Communication from the Commission to the European Council and the European Parliament, *An Energy Policy for Europe*, Brussels, 10 January 2007 (COM(2007) 1 final) (at p. 9). See also Communication from the Commission to the European Council, *A European Economic Recovery Plan*, Brussels, 26 November 2008 (COM(2008) 800 final), where the Commission states that the European Investment Bank (EIB) will significantly increase its financing of climate change, energy security and infrastructure investments by up to €6 bn per year (at p. 14).

[170] See the Intergovernmental Panel on Climate Change (IPCC) report entitled *Climate Change 2007: Synthesis Report. An Assessment of the Intergovernmental Panel on Climate Change* (available at http://www.ipcc.ch/pdf/assessment-report/ar4/syr/ar4_syr.pdf). This document consists of the underlying report, adopted section by section at IPCC Plenary XXVII (Valencia, Spain, 12–17 November 2007) that represents the formally agreed statement of the IPCC concerning key findings and uncertainties contained in the Working Group contributions to the Fourth Assessment Report. Also, in the Fourth Assessment Report, the IPCC has referred to the 'unequivocal heating of the planet'.

[171] The Intergovernmental Panel on Climate Change is the international corpus of scientists *par excellence* formed, ultimately, under the auspices of the United Nations. According to its website, 'The Intergovernmental Panel on Climate Change (IPCC) is the leading international body for the assessment of climate change. It was established … to provide the world with a clear scientific view on the current state of knowledge in climate change and its potential

stated that: 'Anthropogenic warming could lead to some impacts that are *abrupt or irreversible*, depending upon the rate and magnitude of the climate change' (emphasis added).[172]

At the global level, colossal capital investments are necessary to upgrade and expand the extraction and distribution infrastructure for hydrocarbons.[173] Such upgrading must also happen to EU-based or -linked infrastructure, and the cost of that is likely to be high. However, investments do not materialize when all costs alongside projected profits cannot be recouped for a certain period of time. Investing such vast sums

---

environmental and socio-economic impacts. The IPCC is a scientific body. It reviews and assesses the most recent scientific, technical and socio-economic information produced worldwide relevant to the understanding of climate change. *It does not conduct any research nor does it monitor climate related data or parameters*. … Currently 195 countries are members of the IPCC. *Governments participate in the review process* and the plenary Sessions, where main decisions about the IPCC work programme are taken and reports are accepted, adopted and approved. The IPCC Bureau Members, including the Chair, are also elected during the plenary Sessions. Because of its scientific and intergovernmental nature, the IPCC embodies a unique opportunity to provide rigorous and balanced scientific information to decision makers. By endorsing the IPCC reports, governments acknowledge the authority of their scientific content. *The work of the organization is therefore policy-relevant and yet policy-neutral, never policy-prescriptive*' (emphasis added) (available at http://www.ipcc.ch/organization/organization.shtml).

[172] See IPCC *Climate Change 2007: Synthesis Report. An Assessment of the Intergovernmental Panel on Climate Change* (available at http://www.ipcc.ch/pdf/assessment-report/ar4/syr/ar4_syr.pdf) at p. 53.

[173] This is not to be dismissed lightly given that IEA projections call for investments of at least USD 6.3 *trillion* by 2030 for the oil sector alone to meet growing global energy demand. (See International Energy Agency 2008 World Energy Outlook report (at p. 89).) For the entire energy sector, the IEA calls for investments of USD 33 trillion by 2035 (see the International Energy Agency's 2010 World Energy Outlook report, where it is stated, at p. 93, that: 'Cumulative investment of $33 trillion (year-2009 dollars) over 2010–2035 is needed in energy-supply infrastructure. … This investment enables the replacement of reserves and production facilities that are retired, as well as the expansion of production and transport capacity to meet demand growth'). Note also that regarding the IEA projects that are on a global level, for each USD 1 not spent on such infrastructure before 2020 an additional USD 4.3 would need to be spent after 2020 so as to compensate for the increased costs associated with emissions. See IEA 2011 World Energy Outlook report (as cited in the Commission Communication to the European Parliament, the Council, the European Economic and Social Committee, and the Committee of the Regions, *Energy Roadmap 2050*, Brussels, 15 November 2011 (COM(2011) 885 final) (at p. 16)).

towards hydrocarbon-related infrastructure seems to, if not pull in the opposite direction of sustainability, have a disincentivizing effect on efforts to shift economies towards more '*sustainable*' and low-carbon energy mixes any time soon.

V. GEOSTRATEGIC CONTEXT REGARDING THE NEXUS OF EU AND ENERGY SECURITY

As we have alluded to so far, the EU is quite unlike other actors in the international arena in that it is neither a sovereign State – entailing the legal consequences stemming from such a status – nor is it merely an international organization. In that respect, there are structural obstacles in the EU's path towards energy security that are not met by sovereign States that are fully federated, where the central/federal authority has fewer or no obstacles in deploying a comprehensive external energy security strategy. These obstacles have implications for an *optimum* EU energy security. That is not to say that that EU efforts undermine EU Member States' efforts, nor do we mean to suggest that the combined effect of the *individual* energy security efforts of each EU member would have amounted to a more enhanced collective EU energy security. Rather, that it is more probable that each Member State's individual energy security may be better addressed were action to be orchestrated by some central supranational authority[174] – even more so were the EU to be a fully federalized entity with an unrestrained remit for external action on all aspects, including diplomatic, of energy.

In certain policy areas (including the customs union among its 28 members), the EU is fully federalized, whereas in others, no *sui juris* EU competence exists.[175] Energy itself is no unitary policy matter; rather, it

---

[174] Naturally, this is an assumption contingent on the *doxa* that integration leads to economies of scale and that there are inherent benefits to such a phenomenon. See Communication from the Commission to the European Council, *A European Economic Recovery Plan*, Brussels, 26 November 2008 (COM(2008) 800 final), where the Commission states that: Member States should again take advantage of the strengths of the EU – effective coordination, credible frameworks offered by the Stability and Growth Pact and the Lisbon Strategy, as well as the benefits of scale offered by the euro and the largest single market in the world. The interplay of national and EU action can help all Member States weather the worst of the global economic storms and emerge stronger from the crisis' (at p. 4).

[175] See Korkmaz, D. 'Internal and External Dynamics of European Energy Security' (2010) (paper based on a chapter of Korkmaz's PhD thesis [hereinafter,

is a multi-dimensional composite matter that cuts across numerous policy fields, some of which sit chiefly with the EU – for example, the IEM in electricity and gas – whilst others are the sovereign preserve of member states – for example, the hard diplomatic aspects of energy.

A. Nexus of EU Energy Policy and Foreign Policy

In the case of the nexus between energy and foreign policy, what we witness is the watershed between hard sovereignty matters and other, softer, matters that are more amenable to being assigned to the EU. It would be misleading to regard energy as a strict economic matter that may be assigned to some supranational body when, actually, a sovereign actor – in this case, any EU Member State – may consider itself better placed than some supranational body to pursue its energy needs. To make

---

Korkmaz, 'Internal and External Dynamics'), available at http://www.jhubc.it/ecpr-porto/virtualpaperroom/034.pdf (at pp. 8–11) for an interesting taxonomy of interstate collective energy security arrangements based on international relations theory. For instance, interstate energy relations could be based on energy societies that are:

- *asocial*, that is to say, societies in which State X forcefully occupies State Y and exploits, amongst other things, its energy resources (hence the 'asocial' tag);
- *coexistent*, in that sovereign actors are each after their own needs through peaceful means;
- *cooperative*, by cooperation through bilateral and multilateral means;
- *converging*, in that parties seek to harmonize aspects of their energy landscapes;
- *confederative*, in that parties pool some sovereignty together on specific internal and external aspects of energy to address some – not all – aspects of their collective energy needs; or, lastly
- *federative*, where there is total integration whereby each party becomes a province of the federal system and all competence in relation to energy is pooled at the federal level.

Korkmaz concludes that there is no transfer of competence from EU Member States to the EU over external energy matters. Member States preserve this aspect of their sovereignty. What is more, the lack of absolute convergence between their internal energy markets means that the EU is disqualified from being considered a *convergence* energy security society. (Note that the IEM is restricted to predominantly the regulatory aspects of the internal gas and electricity EU Member State markets). In that respect, it remains a *cooperative* one. Notably, Korkmaz states that the EU: 'lacks the ability to guarantee companies the right to sell electricity and gas in member states on equal terms with national companies' (Korkmaz, 'Internal and External Dynamics' p. 28).

this clearer, let us imagine that Germany's energy relations with Russia are more privileged than, say, Latvian relations with Russia. German energy interests might therefore be better served in that its energy industry and national economy benefit from the consequent energy trade to a greater extent than those of another Member State. Conceivably, preserving that specific energy reality within the EU would be in Germany's national interests.[176] Let us look at a more concrete example: the *Nord Stream* is a pipeline installation that goes under the North Sea and, therefore, bypasses the most geographically straightforward route – that is to say, the territories of EU Member States whose relations with Russia are somewhat strained (namely the Baltic States and Poland).[177] Other EU states – namely Hungary and Italy – may want to promote the Nabucco pipeline,[178] in the case of Italy, possibly, on account of its energy industry's interests, and in the case of Hungary, as a means towards decreased EU gas dependence on Russia.[179] In this example we

---

[176] Note the German Chancellor Angela Merkel's call at a 2007 European Parliament session, for more 'institutionalized energy relations' with Russia in order to discipline Russian energy relations, which she felt, after citing some controversial incidents, were too susceptible to the whims of the Kremlin. The EU meets some competition by, amongst others, China and India for access to Russia's abundant energy resources. This places Russia in a particularly strong position. Germany has been promoting a strong EU–Russia energy partnership. See Dolata-Kreutzkamp, P. 'Canada-Germany-EU: Energy Security and Climate Change' (2008) *Int'l J.*, Vol. 63, No. 3, pp. 665–681, at p. 669. It is also interesting to note Dolata-Kreutzkamp's views on changing perceptions on energy policy in Germany. Since the late 1950s, energy policy was an economics rather than strategic matter for western Germany's government; a matter for the ministry for the economy rather than for defence or foreign affairs. This led to the historical development of energy policy along the lines of the promotion of markets and market regulation. This approach was inadequate in the face of the geostrategic realities at play. In that sense, energy had been somewhat depoliticized for Germany which consequently suffered the consequences of few energy strategic relationships. However, Germany seems to have made up for lost time recently.

[177] See Korkmaz, 'Internal and External Dynamics' (pp. 14–15) in relation to German–Russian bilateralism in energy matters and Germany's pledge to underwrite the Nord Stream project to the tune of 1 billion euros.

[178] The natural gas pipeline called Nabucco is supposed to bring gas from the Middle East and Central Asia to Europe via Turkey, Bulgaria, Romania, Hungary, and Austria. The project is geopolitically significant on energy-security grounds because it will bypass Russia.

[179] See http://en.trend.az/capital/energy/2095611.html for more on this. See also Glachant, J.-M. et al. *A New Architecture for EU Gas Security of Supply* (Deventer, the Netherlands: Claeys & Casteels, 2012).

see the disparity between interests, or rather between the rationales that may underpin the external energy strategy that each Member State may want to promote to be adopted at the EU level.[180]

As we have alluded to so far, the EU faces geostrategic challenges quite unlike its comparatively similar economic peer – the US. There are geological and geostrategic, along with structural reasons for this – geological and geostrategic in that the US is likely to become energy independent by 2030;[181] structural in that whilst the US is a fully federalized entity in certain respects, the EU is constrained by competence issues when it comes to pursuing external energy relations. Whilst the US is 20% energy dependent and moving closer to energy independence,[182] the EU is far from ever reaching such a privileged position. As we mentioned earlier, the EU is 52% energy dependent.[183] In other words, it relies for just over half of its entire energy needs on the outside world. This relative weakness is compounded by the fact that the largest part of its primary energy mix comes from just four providers (Norway, Russia, Algeria, and Libya).[184] It also competes for energy with the rest of the world, including with those energy-poor behemoths of energy consumption that are the 'emerging' economies of China and India,[185] that are likely to amount to more than 45% of the increase in

---

[180] As a previous EU Commissioner for trade, Peter Mandelson, rather tellingly has said: 'No one country reveals our differences as does Russia'. See *International Herald Tribune*, 21–22 April 2007 (at p. 3).

[181] See the Executive Summary to the IEA's 2012 World Energy Outlook report, pp. 1–2, available at http://www.iea.org/Textbase/npsum/weo2012sum.pdf

[182] Ibid.

[183] European Commission, 'Key Figures', Market Observatory for Energy, Directorate-General for Energy, June 2011, at p. 5.

[184] Serious concerns were raised when attacks on oil and gas facilities took place in Algeria in January 2013. See for instance Faucon, B. 'BP Report Warned of Risks in Algeria', *The Wall Street Journal*, 14 February 2013, available at http://online.wsj.com/article/SB10001424127887324162304578301982286838010.html

[185] Brazil, Indonesia, and Russia possess their own energy supply and so we have not listed them along with China and India in relation to consumer competitors of the EU. Brazil, Russia, India, and China are commonly aggregated and referred to as the 'BRIC' countries – a term coined by Jim O'Neill, an economist at Goldman Sachs. The expansion of this term has been witnessed as 'BRIICS' so as to include Indonesia and South Africa. For an exposition of trade relations between the EU and major emerging economies, see Leal-Arcas, R. 'The European Union and New Leading Powers: Towards Partnership in Strategic Trade Policy Areas' (2009) *Fordham International Law Journal*, Vol. 32, No. 2, pp. 345–416; Leal-Arcas, R. 'The European Union and the BRIC

global energy consumption by 2035.[186] However, the EU's total energy needs are only a fragment of global energy needs. As we mentioned earlier, the EU's energy consumption has been fairly static since 1990 and is projected to be so until 2035 at an annual figure not exceeding 2,000 Mtoe.[187] And it may be that competition from China and India, alongside other net consumers such as Japan, is not too great a concern, given that:

(1) The EU is shifting towards a lower carbon and a more energy efficient economy – a fact that, logically, could lead to reduced energy consumption.
(2) The existing suppliers of the EU – particularly Russia – are endowed with sufficient energy reserves to continue to meet the needs of multiple consumers.[188]

As it currently stands, the EU is surrounded by energy significant States – Russia, Norway, those in the MENA region, the Caspian region, and the CIS – that all, presumably, see a lucrative energy export market in the EU. Also, developments in the storage and transportation of natural gas – namely its conversion into liquefied form (LNG) – could potentially lead to the globalization of the gas markets that are currently highly regionalized due to the challenges around storage and transportation.[189] The

Countries: Unilateralism, Bilateralism, and Multilateralism', in Laursen, F. (ed.) *The EU in the Global Political Economy* (Brussels: PIE Peter Lang, 2009) pp. 91–118.

186 The IEA projects that India and China are likely to be responsible for roughly 45% of the increase in global energy consumption between 2005 and 2035. See the Executive Summary to the 2007 IEA World Energy Outlook: China and India Insights report (at p. 3) (available at http://www.iea.org/Textbase/npsum/WEO2007SUM.pdf).

187 European Commission, 'Key Figures', Market Observatory for Energy, Directorate-General for Energy, June 2011, at p. 3.

188 In relation to this point, see an interview with Professor Jonathan Stern where, in relation to EU–Asian competition for Russian gas, he states that: 'I've never thought that was an argument worth talking about. Russia has vast amounts of gas in Asia, very far away from Europe that wouldn't be economic to transport to Europe. At the same time, they've got a huge amount of gas in eastern Siberia and far east provinces which is stranded and not going anywhere, so for me there's no real competition between Europe and Asia for Russian gas'. Interview on 3 December 2012, available at http://www.naturalgaseurope.com/europes-biggest-gas-supplier-no-bluffing?goback=%2Egde_1808658_member_191862754

189 See de Jong, D. et al. 'The Evolving Role of LNG in the Gas Market', in Goldthau, A. & Witte, J.M. (eds) *Global Energy Governance: The New Rules of*

implications of this for EU energy security could be positive, as a more globalized gas market may lead to greater energy flows becoming available on global markets.

What is more, the EU – through Denmark (specifically, its control over Greenland), Finland, and Sweden – borders an increasingly energy significant region, that is, the Arctic. Denmark, Finland, and Sweden – rather than the EU in any *sui juris* capacity – are involved in ongoing negotiations with the group of States that has interests in that region. However, energy exploration and exploitation is far from straightforward given the presence of competing claims in the region. The five States with immediate borders who could potentially claim exclusive economic zone interests up to 200 miles from their coastlines – namely Canada, Denmark, Norway, Russia, and the US – have not reached any resolution so far. What the Arctic issue also brings to the surface are questions as to what ought to be the EU's stance. Whilst the EU does not participate *sui juris* in the Arctic Council – unlike the above five states – developing a common approach is complicated, not least because not all 28 Member States are affected in the same way.[190] Should EU resources be pursued to represent an EU common position when it is a handful of Member States that are likely to benefit? Should the EU espouse Denmark's interests in the Arctic region and potentially come into opposition with what has been a reliable energy partner, that is, Russia? Is it accurate to say that this would be in the energy interests of the entire EU? These are the types of questions that EU policymakers are possibly examining in considering how to approach this matter. Once the EU resolves to take a common position, it is then confronted with questions around competences. Conceivably, different aspects of the Arctic question would have to be examined to ascertain the level of EU competences. A hard diplomatic matter such as this seems to fall outside the competence remit

---

the Game (Washington, DC: Brookings Institution Press, 2010) at pp. 221–246, in relation to developments in the gas markets.

[190] See Pieper, M., Winter, M., et al. 'The European Union as an Actor in Arctic Governance' (2011) *European Foreign Affairs Review* 16, 227–242, for a full exposition of EU action in relation to the Arctic. The EU is unlike traditional Arctic actors – namely Canada, Denmark, Russia, Norway, Sweden, Iceland, Finland and the US – which are States with rights and obligations that flow from that status. They all have Arctic strategies. The Arctic has been on the agenda of the EU since 2008. It is relevant to the EU's energy security, environmental protection, and maritime policy objectives. See also the Commission's 2008 Communication to the European Parliament and the Council, *The European Union and the Arctic Region*, Brussels, 20 November 2008, (COM(2008) 763 final) in relation to EU action.

of the EU. However, as we have seen earlier, even in such cases where there is no EU competence, it is possible for the EU to take a common position so long as it is done on a unanimity basis between Member States in the Council.[191]

Again, setting aside the structural obstacles – that is to say, the competence issues – to the EU pursuing a unified external energy security policy, the EU further faces inherent restrictions to whatever competences exist for it to pursue such a policy on behalf of the collective EU interest. Namely, as we discussed above, the guiding principles of the EU as enshrined in Article 21.1 TEU.[192] These principles form the broader normative parameters outside which all EU external action, consequently, appears *ultra vires*.

Let us take as an example, cited by Korkmaz,[193] the relations between the Gulf Cooperation Council (GCC) and the EU. The EU sought closer energy relations through the promotion of pro-market regulatory norms. The GCC, however, preferred strategic partnerships rather than energy relations that were conditional on market liberalization. Presumably, third-party States – such as the GCC – would be loath to contract such international agreements with the EU that, incidentally or intentionally, seek to depoliticize energy and promote integrated or more rational market models. Korkmaz also cites further instances where the inescapable politics of energy at the interstate level impact EU interests.[194] For instance, Central Asian States have shunned the EU 'neighborhood' like integration of energy markets and prefer hard contracts. Also, see how Spanish support of Moroccan interests in Western Sahara[195] led to the cancelation of concessions for Spain's Repsol by Algeria, the latter being a long-term supporter of the independence movement for Western Sahara.

---

[191] See Article 352§1 TFEU. In this respect, the Council is the final arbiter on whether to espouse a Commission recommendation, thus preserving the primacy of the inter-governmental/diplomatic EU institutions (e.g., the Council) over that of EU supranational institutions (e.g., the Commission) in matters where no express powers have been granted to EU institutions by the EU treaties.

[192] Article 21.1 TEU mandates that all EU external action complies with the following 'guiding principles': 'democracy, the rule of law, the universality and indivisibility of human rights and fundamental freedoms, respect for human dignity, the principles of equality and solidarity, and respect for the principles of the United Nations Charter and international law'.

[193] Korkmaz, 'Internal and External Dynamics' at p. 25.

[194] Ibid. at pp. 25–26.

[195] Currently, largely under Moroccan administration. See the CIA World Factbook https://www.cia.gov/library/publications/the-world-factbook/geos/wi.html

Also, the Algerian regime relies on oil deals with local tribes as a means of remaining in power.[196]

These are just a few instances where political and diplomatic considerations – which some might view or even dismiss as externalities – may actually drive third-party States' attitudes towards pursuing energy relations with the EU or any other partner. In short, energy-related national strategies are developed against complex backdrops, rather than solely within market/regulatory contexts. While energy-poor State actors and groups of States (e.g., the EU) cannot use energy as a diplomacy tool or weapon to either encourage or coerce behavior of other States, they can, however, use their tariffs, and generally, their trade policies as a stick or a carrot in their external relations with third-party States in a manner that may not be available to energy-rich States. This is particularly the case for energy-rich exporter states, whose economies rely principally on energy revenues due to their being insufficiently diversified or due to their lack of any other comparative advantage on account of geological and other factors relevant to their economies. Such states instead capitalize on their energy relevance, using it as either a stick or carrot in their foreign relations. This is at odds with the agenda of the EU and conceivably other significant energy consumer economies who wish to promote the de-politicization of energy. The 'international community' is thus made up of sovereign actors who, whilst legally equal vis-à-vis one another within the context of Westphalian sovereignty and the post-World-War-II international legal order,[197] actually amount to an aggregation of disparate parties rather than a cohesive community *per se*. Internationally, state actors possess interests, strengths, and levels of influence that are highly disparate *inter se*.

We have seen some of the matters that may push third-party States to prefer strategic partnerships with hard contracts, rather than regulatory

---

[196] See *La rente pétrolière ne garantit plus la paix sociale*, *Le Monde Economie*, 15 March 2011, available at http://lemonde-emploi.blog.lemonde.fr/2011/03/15/«-la-rente-petroliere-ne-garantit-plus-la-paix-sociale-»-dans-«-le-monde-economie-»/

[197] Namely of the United Nations (UN) and of any other legal orders based on multilateral arrangements to which States are parties and to the extent that such agreements provide; with the exception of those States that have a privileged position within the UN by having a *sui juris* seat in the UN Security Council which places them apart from the overwhelming majority of sovereign States. Also, inequality between sovereign States exists within other fora – e.g., the International Monetary Fund (IMF), where influence is linked to the extent of a State's voting rights, which, in turn, are determined by its fiscal contributions to the IMF.

and market convergence with the EU. On the other hand, as we have also mentioned, the EU is restricted in its external actions not only by competence issues but also by inherent limitations on how it may pursue external relations for matters where competence exists. To be more precise, a proper application of Article 21 TEU on all instances of EU external relations – including all consequent EU energy-related agreements with third-party States that have poor human rights records, such as some States in the Caspian and MENA – must comply with, if not promote, the EU's guiding principles. In that respect, whilst the EU's strategic energy partners may want a straightforward partner in their energy dealings with the EU, the EU is inherently constrained in meeting such expectations. That is not to say that EU Member States' energy needs remain unaddressed; EU Member States continue to engage with the outside world through their strategic partnerships and through the operation of regional and global energy markets. At the general international law level, a plethora of agreements exist between various configurations of State parties (including EU States in their own right) – for example, the ECT, bilateral and multilateral investment treaties (BITs/MITs) – that establish the fundamental conditions that facilitate interstate investment, trade, and the operation of markets. As we mentioned earlier, Article 21 TEU does not, on its own strength, restrict external action pursued by EU Member States *qua* sovereign entities in their own right.[198]

[198] That said, under international law (namely under rules of customary international law on state responsibility), EU Member States in their capacity *qua* subjects of international law with treaty-making capacity may be committing an international wrong by breaching or otherwise not honoring any of their international obligations owed to other subjects of international law, including to international organizations. This is a complex field of customary law that, amongst other things, is concerned with aspects of an obligation at issue – e.g. whether it flows from *jus cogens* or from elsewhere, to whom it is owed, and so on in order to establish who may raise legal complaints, what action is legally feasible, and what form such action may take. For the purposes of the present chapter, we do not intend to analyze this in any further detail. However, EU Member States have freely consented to be bound by the TEU. At Article 24§3 TEU, it is stated that: 'The Member States shall support the Union's external and security policy actively and unreservedly in a spirit of loyalty and mutual solidarity and shall comply with the Union's action in this area. The Member States shall work together to enhance and develop their mutual political solidarity. *They shall refrain from any action which is contrary to the interests of the Union or likely to impair its effectiveness as a cohesive force in international relations*' (emphasis added). The implication of this provision is that, potentially, any *sui juris* activity on the part of an EU Member State that is deemed 'contrary

Another element to take into account in relation to EU preference for market liberalization over strategic relations based on hard contracts of supply is the EU's commitment to competitive markets. For instance, the EU Commission – as we said earlier, theoretically the vanguard of the EU collective interest – has been critical of long-term energy contracts in the EU and their implications for competition.[199] Contracts often tied prices and energy trade volumes, and often excluded other players from the market by placing conditions on final use. For the EU Commission, and undoubtedly for many others, such matters have distortive effects on trade and competition. Although long-term contracts are not on their face illegal within the EU context, they are to be scrutinized on a case-by-case basis to assess their impact on the overall market context. The implications of this are that provisions in long-term contracts between energy actors based in an EU Member State and third-party supplier states may be set aside if found to be in breach of EU competition rules. This may

---

to the interests' of the EU could be the subject of objections including legal proceedings instigated by the Commission in its role as vanguard of EU collective interest. In effect, Article 24 TEU becomes a further – supranational – limitation to each Member State's capacity to engage in external affairs. Setting aside whether a Member State's legal system is monist or dualist in terms of its international agreements, in that sense, Article 24 TEU could be regarded a restriction present in all EU Member States' constitutional landscape by way of their adoption of the TEU.

[199] According to Bellantuono, the EU Commission found that the IEM was structurally characterized by long-term contracts that foreclosed supply and had other restrictions or distribution clauses. The Commission scrutinized contracts for their effects on the IEM. The Commission then took a dim view of these practices and became more interventionist on account of its remit to promote/restore competitive conditions in the IEM. This was intensified when it was granted powers by Council Regulation (EC) No 1/2003 of 16 December 2002 *on the implementation of the rules on competition laid down in Articles 81 and 82 of the Treaty*. There had also been EU determinations on alleged anti-competitive practices in the energy markets of EU Member States; for instance, the 2007 Commission's Hearing Officer's determination in the *Distrigas* case, where a dominant Belgian gas operator had made certain contractual commitments that disfavored other operators in Belgian markets (available at http://ec.europa.eu/competition/antitrust/cases/dec_docs/37966/37966_594_7.pdf). See also case C-17/03 of 7 June 2005, VEMW [2005 ECR I- 4983] in relation to priority rights for reserving transport capacity for energy goods. Again, an energy actor was forced to make changes to allow other actors a share of the market. See Bellantuono, G. 'Contract Law, Regulation, and Competition in Energy Markets' (2009) 10 *Competition & Reg. Network Indus*. 159–188, at pp. 167–175.

affect how desirable long-term contracts with EU Member States might be to third-party supplier States.

B. Rise in Shale Gas Extraction and its Effect on EU Energy Security

There are also other developments internationally that have implications for EU energy security. A fairly recent one is the rise in shale gas extraction that could potentially translate into larger volumes of gas becoming available on gas markets.[200] This development has assisted the US on its path towards energy independence and makes it a potential competitor of Russia as a supplier of gas to the EU. In what has been lauded as a positive consequence of the rise of shale gas fracking, gas reserves that had been too difficult to extract now reach markets. This is a development that could lead to the reduction or even displacement of coal as a primary input resource for the production of energy. Moreover, the shale gas boom in the US, seen simply from a supply security point of view, is therefore a chance for the EU to diversify its world market position as a gas consumer and possibly reduce its dependence on Russian conventional gas.

The EU could also make use of its own shale gas reserves. That said, there are reasons that still make shale gas extraction in the EU rather difficult: (1) there is no harmonized EU-level legislation regarding its extraction (namely in some EU Member States, it is banned; in others, it is allowed; and in others, it is allowed and permits are issued); (2) public opinion seems to be against the idea in some EU jurisdictions; and (3) there is a lack of drilling and exploration kit.[201] So the EU could explore its domestic shale gas reserves, where necessary with test drilling and, if the appropriate technology can be found, protecting the local environment, with commercially viable extraction.

All of this is important, given the need to lower the GHG footprint of energy production. Whilst gas is not emissions-free, it is less polluting

---

200 It is worth noting that gas is chiefly traded regionally. Gas markets are largely more regional than global. That said, the prospect of more gas reserves – be it through shale fracking or conventional extraction processes – becoming accessible and exploitable, alongside technological developments around gas storage and transfer, may pave the way towards the integration of gas markets into a global gas market. See de Jong, D. et al. 'The Evolving Role of LNG in the Gas Market', in Goldthau, A. & Witte, J.M. (eds) *Global Energy Governance: The New Rules of the Game* (Washington, DC: Brookings Institution Press, 2010) at pp. 221–245, about developments in gas markets globally.

201 *The Economist* 'Conscious Uncoupling' 5 April 2014, p. 30.

than coal. That said, shale gas, due to the intensiveness of fracking – the extraction process used – is environmentally harmful in other ways.[202] In that respect, the evangelism that surrounds shale gas may be unjustified given that this energy source is not in the final analysis necessarily 'greener'.[203] The geostrategic implications are that greater use of shale gas could potentially undermine the environmental objectives of the EU and of the international community, whilst also leading to environmental – including geological – deterioration in the regions where extraction is taking place.

Naturally, environmental degradation is indifferent towards territorial boundaries. Often, environmental disasters transcend boundaries and wreak havoc on adjacent territory – for example through oil spills, land subsidence, and so on – or even on territory considerably further afield, as is the case with rising sea levels, tsunami reverberations, and other climatic disasters. This is important to bear in mind when risk-assessing and also establishing obligations owed to other rights holders under general and particular international law. For instance trade-related measures taken by the EU to discourage highly polluting processes elsewhere in the globe[204] could be justified under general international law and

---

[202] See the British Geological Survey's web page, where it lists its concerns – including the degradation of water bodies, methane leakage into the atmosphere, and increasing seismic volatility – associated with shale gas extraction. Available at http://www.bgs.ac.uk/research/energy/shaleGas/environmentalImpacts.html.

[203] Most astonishing has been Professor Riley's evangelism of shale gas in his address at the November 2012 workshop on the EU's '2050 Energy Roadmap' organized by the European Parliament's Directorate-General for External Policies, in which he asserted that the US moved from a position where in 2005 it was using coal for 50% of energy production to the current 30% due to shale gas, and that the US was set on becoming energy self-sufficient. In the US, gas now costs as low as USD 3 per British Thermal Unit (BTU), whereas the EU price is around USD 10–14 per BTU. What is more, the US has or may have overtaken Russia in gas and could compete with it for gas sales. Professor Riley ended by advising that the EU ought to adopt policies that de-link its energy security from its environmental protection commitments (EXPO/B/AFET/FWC/2009-01/Lot1/42) (*passim* and at p. 7).

[204] A case in point is an earlier dispute between Canada and the EU in relation to oil extracted from the tar sand-fields in Alberta, Canada. This tar oil is highly polluting when compared to conventionally extracted crude oil. The EU Commission had proposed to the EU membership to agree on labeling such oil 'highly polluting' as a first step towards introducing measures to discourage its importation and therefore use of this extraction process. This appears to have not been unanimously endorsed by EU Member States and therefore the proposal

under particular international law (e.g., within the justifications possible to invoke in the WTO system).

Despite the warm reception that the rise of shale gas may meet with, other projections indicate that there may be a regression towards greater coal reliance. Rising consumption rates, inadequate investment in upstream and downstream oil and gas infrastructure, wildly inadequate investment in renewables, diminishing peak oil and peak gas reserves, and energy security concerns may all coalesce to push economies back to coal. Energy production may get a lot dirtier.[205] Also, the IEA considers it likely that by 2017 global coal consumption is to stand at 4.32 billion tons of oil equivalent (btoe), versus around 4.40 btoe for oil.[206] Naturally, this is most disconcerting, given that more meaningful action is needed to avert the likelihood of climate change that is both irreversible and catastrophic. In this respect, how can the EU take meaningful action globally?[207]

---

was abandoned. Canada's earlier response is telling however, as it threatened action within the WTO. See the International Centre for Trade and Sustainable Development's (ICTSD), 'Trade Tensions Soar as EU Prepares to Vote on Canadian Oil' *Bridges Weekly Trade News Digest*, No. 7, 22 February 2012, http://ictsd.org/i/news/bridgesweekly/126262/. See also the following link for a fuller analysis http://foreignaffairsreview.co.uk/2012/10/oil-eu-canada/, in which it is suggested that Canada thought of acting proactively, given that it does not export such oil to the EU.

[205] See the University of Amsterdam's International Institute for Asian Studies' Newsletter No. 62 (Winter 2012) and in particular its 'The Focus Pullout' supplement (at p. 22), available at http://www.iias.nl/sites/default/files/IIAS_NL62_FULL.pdf.

[206] This is based on IEA medium-term projections announced in a news item published on 17 December 2012. See http://www.iea.org/newsroomandevents/pressreleases/2012/december/name,34441,en.html. Nineteen percent of the current global energy mix derives from alternative and renewable energy sources; however, only 3% comes from renewables, presumably the balance comes from nuclear and other alternatives that are neither renewable nor environmentally safe. By 2030, no significant changes are anticipated to take place. Renewables are likely to remain marginal to the global energy mix.

[207] For alternative views to the current system on how to tackle climate change from the bottom up, see Leal-Arcas, R. *Climate Change and International Trade* (Cheltenham: Edward Elgar, 2013); Leal-Arcas, R. 'Kyoto and the COPs: Lessons Learned and Looking Ahead' (2011) *Hague Yearbook of International Law*, Vol. 23, pp. 17–90; Leal-Arcas, R. 'A Bottom-up Approach for Climate Change: The Trade Experience' (2011) *Asian Journal of Law and Economics*, Vol. 2, No. 4, pp. 1–54; Leal-Arcas, R. 'Top-down Versus Bottom-up Approaches for Climate Change Negotiations: An Analysis' (December 2011) *The IUP Journal of Governance and Public Policy*, Vol. 6, No. 4, pp. 7–52;

C. Environmental Protection

In relation to its environmental protection efforts, the EU has, amongst other things, set up a sophisticated intra-EU emissions trading system (EU ETS) into which it is progressively drawing all major polluting industries, including aviation and prospectively the shipping industry.[208] In the case of aviation, this has rattled many a third-party State, given that the EU ETS regime had been extended to all airline operators with flights that enter or depart from EU territory.[209] What is more, the inclusion of aviation was also opposed by the EU aviation industry. Following sustained opposition, the EU caved in and announced a year-long moratorium on 12 November 2012 that suspends the application of the EU ETS on flights that are not entirely limited to EU territory.[210] Whilst, rather self-servingly, various industries would want the EU ETS to fail, it is an example of environmentally minded action that ought to be supported and replicated globally. We say this because the EU ETS goes way beyond any other instance of interstate cooperation on the protection of the environment within the context of the UNFCCC, the WTO, or elsewhere.[211] The EU ETS has proven worthwhile in that during 2011, of the 8,081 million tons of CO_2e that were globally traded through emission credits, 7,853 were traded through the EU ETS – in

Leal-Arcas, R. 'Combining Top-down and Bottom-up Approaches for Climate Change Negotiations' (December 2011) *OUTREACH*, Stakeholderforum, pp. 4–5; Leal-Arcas, R. 'Alternative Architecture for Climate Change: Major Economies' (2011) *European Journal of Legal Studies*, Vol. 4, Issue 1, pp. 25–56; Leal-Arcas, R. 'Is the Kyoto Protocol an Adequate Environmental Agreement to Solve the Climate Change Problem?' (Winter 2001) *European Environmental Law Review*, Vol. 10, No. 10, pp. 282–294.

208 Fuller background information on the EU ETS is available at http://ec.europa.eu/clima/policies/ets/index_en.htm. See also Leal-Arcas, R. 'Unilateral Trade-related Climate Change Measures' (2012) *The Journal of World Investment and Trade*, Vol. 13, No. 6, pp. 875–927.

209 China, India, and Saudi Arabia, amongst others, have instructed their airlines not to comply. For a collection of ICTSD Bridges articles on this matter, see http://lawonglobaltradeinenergyandfoodcommodities.wordpress.com/2012/04/14/eu-ets/

210 See http://ictsd.org/i/news/bridgesweekly/134007/.

211 See World Bank, *State and Trends of the Carbon Market* (May 2012), pp. 73–104 (in relation to initiatives elsewhere including Australia, South Korea, and the USA).

other words, the value of EU ETS transactions stood at USD 147.8 billion whilst the value of global transactions stood at USD 148.8 billion.[212]

In this respect, the EU ETS is an example of EU action that has implications for third-party States. Conceivably, discontent on the part of third-party States in relation to what they may regard as EU unilateral action could lead to their taking hostile action against the EU's interests abroad, including in connection with its energy security efforts. Whether this is a risk worth taking really depends on the effect of EU action. Whilst measures aimed at the protection of the environment – such as the EU ETS, whose inherent value is that it seeks to contain emissions within EU territory – are always worth encouragement in the grander scheme of things, it may be that their benefit is disproportionate to the consequential cost – for example, to the economic damage by likely retaliatory responses on the part of third-party States. To make this clear, let us list some figures around global emitters: The greatest GHG emitting economies globally, in terms of absolute volumes of emissions during 2007 were: China (c. 6,538 million tons of CO_2), the US (c. 6,094 $mtCO_2$), the EU (c. 4,200 $mtCO_2$), India (c. 1,610 $mtCO_2$), Russia (c 1,580 $mtCO_2$), Japan (c. 1,303 $mtCO_2$), Canada (c. 590 $mtCO_2$), South Korea (c. 503 $mtCO_2$), Iran (c. 495 $mtCO_2$), Mexico (471.46 $mtCO_2$) Saudi Arabia (c. 402 $mtCO_2$), Indonesia (c. 397 $mtCO_2$), Australia (c 396 $mtCO_2$), and Brazil (368.32 $mtCO_2$).[213] In terms of CO_2 emissions per capita or per territorial span (measured in square kilometers), a different picture emerges.[214] However, the point we wish to make is this: whilst it is a

---

212 Ibid. at p. 10.

213 These figures are based on 2007 data available from the United Nations Statistics Division. In the case of the EU, the global figure cited by the authors is based on the individual figures for all 27 EU Member States (before the accession of Croatia to the EU on 1 July 2008 as the 28th EU Member State) excluding their overseas territories. We have done this in order to get a figure regarding man-made emissions that would correspond to the territorial reach of the EU ETS. See http://unstats.un.org/unsd/ENVIRONMENT/air_co2_emissions.htm

214 The highest polluting economies in terms of tons of CO_2 per capita during 2007 were: Qatar (c. 55.4 tCO_2), Dutch Antilles (c. 32 tCO_2), the United Arab Emirates (c. 31 tCO_2), Kuwait (c. 30 tCO_2), Bahrain (c. 29 tCO_2), Luxembourg (c. 25 tCO_2), Aruba (c. 23 tCO_2), Brunei (c. 19.8 tCO_2), the US (c. 19.7 tCO_2), the Falkland Islands (c. 19.6 tCO_2), Australia (c.19 tCO_2), and Canada (c. 18 tCO_2). We have no global figure for the EU average given that the figure per EU Member State would have a different weighting on the EU average due to the disparate population sizes. However, if we were to discount the

laudable move on the part of the EU to act responsibly in terms of its highly polluting global impact in implementing the EU ETS territorially, it is less clear how proportionate it is for the EU to seek to extend the scope of the EU ETS to foreign industries – in the way that the EU had attempted to do regarding foreign aviation industries that operated flights with portions within EU territory – when, potentially, it could face retaliatory action on the part of third-party States.

D. Energy Trade and Transit

The WTO system handles the trade aspects of energy to the extent that its norms extend to energy commodities – be they goods or services – that are traded between WTO members. It is important to note that these norms do not extend to the pre-extraction stage. In that sense, they too preserve the notion of sovereignty over natural resources.[215] However, once natural resources have been extracted and are being traded, WTO members must comply with WTO norms, including the prohibition of quantitative restrictions[216] on trade flows that are otherwise inconsistent with the specific commitments each WTO member had, at the time of accession, contracted with the WTO. This has important implications, say, for energy-resource-endowed WTO members who may want to restrict energy or other types of exports or imports in ways that the various WTO agreements do not allow.[217] For instance, Russia, which

---

highest EU Member State figure – namely Luxembourg (c. 25 tCO_2 per capita) – the next offenders in the EU are: Estonia (c. 14 tCO_2), the Czech Republic (c. 12.6 tCO_2), and Finland (c. 12.5 tCO_2). The remaining EU Member States vary from around 3.7 to 11.4 tCO_2 per capita. Ibid. Eurostat figures from 2009 suggest that the EU figure per capita for CO_2 emissions from fuel combustion stood at around c. 7 tCO_2 per capita. Also according to this set of figures, Russia stood at 10.8 tCO_2, China at circa 5 tCO_2, India at 1.3 tCO_2, and Brazil at 1.7 tCO_2 per capita. See the 2012 Eurostat Pocketbook on *The European Union and the BRIC Countries* (at p. 108), available at http://epp.eurostat.ec.europa.eu/cache/ITY_OFFPUB/KS-31-11-414/EN/KS-31-11-414-EN.PDF

[215] For further details on the link between the WTO and natural resources, see Abu-Gosh, E. and Leal-Arcas, R. 'The Conservation of Exhaustible Natural Resources in the GATT and WTO: Implications for the Conservation of Oil Resources' (2013) *The Journal of World Investment and Trade* Vol. 14, No. 3, pp. 480–531.

[216] Article XI GATT.

[217] There had been three recent complaints (namely complaints WT/DS431/6, WT/DS432/6 and WT/DS433/6) against China and a measure that restricted exports of rare earth minerals. See http://www.wto.org/english/news_e/news12_e/dsb_23jul12_e.htm for more background information.

became a WTO Member in August 2012, might conceivably have views on the WTO implications for its energy endowments that are at odds with those of energy net importing WTO members.

One measure that has been a source of contention is Russia's practice of maintaining different prices for gas sold domestically and that destined for foreign markets. This issue has concerned the Commission to the extent that it took unilateral action, irrespective of whether it was proven that any WTO norms had been breached. The Commission did this by raising duties on imports that it had deemed had benefited from cheaper production costs due to lower domestic gas prices.[218]

The recent gas disputes between Ukraine and Russia, which led to EU energy flow disruptions, had negative implications for EU energy security. EU Member States acted unilaterally – in this case, with German Chancellor Angela Merkel holding discussions with Russian President Vladimir Putin. This approach has been criticized as another missed opportunity for the EU to speak with one voice.[219] In 2011, the EU

[218] See Pogoretskyy, V. & Behn, D. 'The Tension between Trade Liberalization and Resource Sovereignty: Russia-EU Energy Relations and the Problem of Natural Gas Dual Pricing' (2011) *Oil, Gas & Energy Law*, Vol. 6, at p. 10 (for an analysis of the relationship between Russia's dual pricing practice and the various WTO provisions that may be engaged). Pogoretskyy and Behn inform us that the International Bank for Reconstruction and Development (i.e., the World Bank) advised that Russian domestic gas prices ought to rise at least to a level that meets production costs. This is incrementally happening. Pogoretskyy and Behn also believe that Russia is likely to reach a point where there would be total harmony between both gas prices by 2014. They also feel that this will not be due to external pressure, rather, due to economic reasons – namely so that the Russian State would be able to fund the enormous capital investments necessary to modernize and further develop its energy infrastructure. See also Selivanova, J. *Energy Dual Pricing in WTO Law: Analysis and Prospects in the Context of Russia's Accession to the WTO* (London: Cameron May, 2008) Chapter 2.

[219] See Baumann, F. 'Europe's Way to Energy Security. The Outer Dimensions of Energy Security: From Power Politics to Energy Governance' (2010) *European Foreign Affairs Review* 15, where Baumann states that: '... it took the EU quite some time to understand what was really happening. Soon after Brussels recognized that this was not simply a trade dispute, a common EU approach was challenged by several bilateral moves, including Germany's Chancellor Angela Merkel meeting independently with Russian Prime Minister Vladimir Putin. Thus, the Union had once again missed an opportunity to "speak with one voice". NATO, for its part, did not show any public reaction at all. However, this crisis in particular revealed not only how import-dependent countries suffer from such a dispute but also how exporters who are reliant on the revenue from energy trade are negatively affected' (at p. 78).

Commission made a series of policy recommendations to the EU Council and Parliament that included measures to speed up the integration of the Ukraine into the EnC by instituting political and administrative tri-partite cooperation involving the EU, Russia, and Ukraine to ensure steady gas supplies from Russia through Ukraine.[220] Evidence shows that tension between Russia and Ukraine has remained high over gas transit disputes, and as recently as January 2013 Ukraine received a $7bn bill from Russia's Gazprom for taking less gas than originally contracted[221] whilst Gazprom rejected an appeal by Ukraine to renegotiate its gas supply contract.[222]

This is an example of how reliant the functioning of the IEM is on external action aimed at supply security. The Russia–Ukraine gas dispute brought to the fore energy transit issues.[223] The EU, its constituent members, Russia, and Ukraine are all WTO members. Article V GATT relates to goods that temporarily enter the territory of a member and that are destined for consumption outside that territory. Article V mandates that such goods be exempt from customs duties and other encumbrances. It that respect, it enshrines the *freedom of transit* of commodities across the territories of the WTO membership.[224] This duty requires that the most convenient route be made available to such traffic and that transit be free from unjustified restrictions.[225] There is debate as to whether this

---

220 See the 2011 EU Commission Communication to the European Parliament, the Council, the European Economic and Social Committee, and the Committee of the Regions, *On security of energy supply and international cooperation – 'The EU Energy Policy: Engaging with Partners beyond Our Borders'*, 7 September 2011 (COM(2011) 539 final) (at p. 5).

221 See Olearchyk, R. 'Russia and Ukraine Adopt Poker Faces as Questions Loom Over USD7bn Gas Bill', *Financial Times*, 8 February 2013, available at http://blogs.ft.com/beyond-brics/2013/02/08/russia-and-ukraine-adopt-poker-faces-as-questions-loom-over-7bn-gas-bill/#axzz2Kxsfj9im

222 Chazan, G. 'Gazprom Rejects Kiev Gas Contract Plea', *Financial Times*, 14 February 2013, available at http://www.ft.com/intl/cms/s/0/49f8ce1c-75d8-11e2-9891-00144feabdc0.html#axzz2KxsYtfgo.

223 For further analysis on energy transit issues, see Rakhmanin, V. 'Transportation and Transit of Energy and Multilateral Trade Rules: WTO and Energy Charter', in Pauwelyn, J. (ed.) *Global Challenges at the Intersection of Trade, Energy, and the Environment* (Geneva: Centre for Trade and Economic Integration (CTEI), 2010) pp. 123–127.

224 Article V:2 GATT.

225 What is more, Article V:2 expressly requires that the 'most convenient' route for international transit be made available to such goods. See the determination by the WTO Panel in its report on the *Colombia – Indicative Prices and Restrictions on Ports of Entry* case (29 April 2009) WTO/DS366/R, where the

right extends to transit through infrastructures that are fixed to the territory of WTO members.[226] Russian gas imports into the EU flow principally through fixed infrastructure in Ukraine. Fixed infrastructure is

---

Panel held that restrictions on the number of Colombian ports permitted to receive certain imports amounted to a restriction unjustified under Article XI given that it had had a 'limiting effect' on trade. What is 'most convenient' under Article V:2 is far from clear. Presumably, this means whatever route is most convenient to the interests of international trade actors, rather than to the interests of the host-transit State. See Azaria, D. 'Energy Transit under the Energy Charter Treaty and the General Agreement on Tariffs and Trade' (2009) *Journal of Energy & Natural Resources Law*, Vol. 27, No. 4, pp. 559–596 (at pp. 570–574), who highlights this ambiguity. Azaria – quoting Lauterpacht – refers to the notion of *freedom to transit* – be it found in treaty or custom – as part of a broader *law of peace*/public international law concept relating to freedom of transit and to communication (at p. 561). Ehring, L. and Selivanova, Y. 'Energy Transit', in Selivanova, Y. (ed.) *Regulation of Energy in International Trade Law: WTO, NAFTA, and Energy Charter* (Alphen aan den Rijn: Wolters Kluwer, 2012) refer to freedom of transit as a controversial notion that cannot be held to reflect customary law. They argue this is because States have frequently included transit provisions in their bilateral treaties, which suggests the absence of a freedom of transit provision in customary law (at pp. 51–52).

226 Cossy argues that there is nothing in the wording to suggest that transportation via fixed structures is excluded under Article V. She refers to the express exclusion in Article V of aircraft in transit and therefore seeks to argue – presumably, along the lines of the interpretative notion of *expressio unius est exclusio alterius* – that transit through fixed structures is within the scope of Article V. See Cossy, M., 'Energy Transport and Transit in the WTO', in Pauwelyn, J. (ed.) *Global Challenges at the Intersection of Trade, Energy, and the Environment* (Geneva: Centre for Trade and Economic Integration (CTEI), 2010). However, Azaria argues more persuasively in Azaria, D. 'Energy Transit under the Energy Charter Treaty and the General Agreement on Tariffs and Trade' (2009) *Journal of Energy & Natural Resources Law*, Vol. 27, No. 4 that, whilst Article 7 ECT applies to such structures, Article V GATT does not. Article 7 ECT, on its own strength, mandates ECT contracting parties – who incidentally are also GATT/WTO parties – to facilitate transit including via fixed pipes (See Article 7§10 (b)). The fact that all ECT parties are also WTO members does not mean that the later ECT is capable alone of influencing the interpretation of the earlier GATT; nor does it mean that the interpretation of Article V GATT is static: the law of treaties governs interpretation of legal obligations flowing from interstate agreements, and there is an elaborate set of applicable rules and principles that may be at play (see Article 31 VCLT that largely codifies customary law relating to treaty interpretation). Conversely, the earlier GATT influences the interpretation of the later ECT given that there is express systemic reference in ECT (Article 4 ECT and *passim*) mandating non-derogation from GATT. Incidentally, there are 100 mentions of the GATT in the ECT.

quite unlike mobile means of transportation for obvious reasons and we consider that, on balance, it is currently outside the scope of Article V GATT. Freedom of transit under Article 7 ECT, however, includes transit through fixed infrastructures.[227] The EU and its members along with Ukraine are parties to the ECT, while Russia had signed – but not ratified – and has now withdrawn from the ECT. A transit state is obligated to facilitate transit of commodities originating from and/or destined to its WTO and ECT peers, including, in the case of ECT peers, through fixed infrastructure. However, whilst it is one thing to assert that Ukraine – or any other state under ECT obligations – is legally obligated to facilitate transit and to refrain from placing restrictions on it, it is quite another, to say that transit/transportation operators – for example fixed infrastructure private operators – are obligated to perform their contractual duties and to continue facilitating energy flows in cases where a dispute arises between the private actors involved and where their contractual agreements do not otherwise mandate.[228]

The Kremlin clearly views the exploration of its energy endowments as beneficial for Russia on its path to its development[229] and possibly as a means to its return to being a *machtpolitik* global player. In this respect, put simply, the EU's interests lie in getting more goods to markets. It does this by, amongst other things, promoting measures such as encouraging market liberalization and foreign investment protection, globally and regionally, and by supporting calls for energy subsidies[230] to be

---

[227] See Article 7§10(b) ECT. The ECT's more detailed approach to energy transit than that found in the WTO system is not surprising as the ECT could be viewed as the energy-specific agreement that arose out of the aborted attempt to get an energy-specific agreement concluded within the auspices of the WTO.

[228] We make this point because we feel it is important to bear in mind that many operators in the global energy markets are also private law subjects, be they private international energy companies or State energy companies, and that price and service-related disputes, whilst potentially harmful to the energy security of States by causing energy supply disruptions, could originate in disputes between private actors.

[229] An interesting fact cited in Pogoretskyy, V. & Behn, D. 'The Tension between Trade Liberalization and Resource Sovereignty: Russia-EU Energy Relations and the Problem of Natural Gas Dual Pricing' (2011) *Oil, Gas and Energy Law*, Vol. 6, is that Putin's doctoral thesis mentioned the importance of using the energy sector as a State monopoly with a view to fueling the economic development of Russia and returning it to the position of a global superpower.

[230] In terms of energy subsidies in the EU and abroad, the EU Commission recommends that EU action, including external action, also seek to discourage energy subsidies which it deems as contributing to inefficient energy use. See the

rolled back (given that these could be seen as potentially encouraging inefficient energy use and as creating anticompetitive conditions). On the other hand, Russia's interests lie in retaining as much control over all aspects of its enormous energy endowments as possible, whilst also securing the export markets it relies on to obtain the constant flow of hard currency necessary to update and develop further its upstream and downstream infrastructure and capacity.[231]

We have discussed the polarizing effect that the prospect of closer – more institutionalized – relations between the EU and Russia has on the EU membership. Some EU members may see in Russia a capricious partner, whilst others see a reliable energy supplier. As mentioned above, about a third of EU gas comes from Russia. The Nord Stream pipeline would allow for this to come under the North Sea whilst the South Stream would allow this to come under the Black Sea to Bulgaria and beyond. Other gas pipelines are being constructed to establish the EU's southern gas corridor – including the Trans-Anatolian (TANAP) pipeline

---

2011 EU Commission Communication to the European Parliament, the Council, the European Economic and Social Committee, and the Committee of the Regions, *On security of energy supply and international cooperation – 'The EU Energy Policy: Engaging with Partners beyond Our Borders'*, 7 September 2011 (COM(2011) 539 final) at pp. 2, 10 and 17. This is consistent with the efforts of the G-8 and the G-20 that have set energy policy priorities, including in relation to hydrocarbon subsidies. See http://www.g20.org/images/stories/docs/g20/conclu/Policy_Commitments_By_G20_Members.pdf (last accessed 2013) for a list of commitments, where, amongst others, Argentina pledges to reduce household energy subsidies (presumably to make more oil available on global markets). See also the 2009 G-20 leaders' Communiqué, which suggests their desire to rationalize and phase out *inefficient* fossil fuel subsidies. See Joint Report by IEA, OPEC, OECD, and World Bank, *Analysis of the Scope of Energy Subsidies and Suggestions for the G-20 Initiative* 16 June 2010 (at p. 6), available at http://www.iea.org/weo/docs/G20_Subsidy_Joint_Report.pdf (last accessed 2013).

[231] At an EU-Russia summit (21 December 2012), President Putin of Russia defended Russia's practice of linking the price of gas to oil, and its opposition to extending market liberalization norms to its fixed infrastructure through the inclusion of specific terms in the renewed EU–Russia Partnership and Cooperation Agreement. See http://www.euractiv.com/energy/putin-barroso-right-guilty-news-516827?utm_source=EurActiv%20Newsletter&utm_campaign=bc497ce398-newsletter_energy&utm_medium=email. See also http://www.consilium.europa.eu/uedocs/cms_Data/docs/pressdata/en/ec/134546.pdf for a brief summary statement of the President of the European Council on the EU-Russia Summit of 21 December 2012.

crossing Turkey, and pipelines between Turkey and Austria (Nabucco),[232] and Greece and Italy (ITIG) – to support EU security of supply and to increase import volumes. However, in spite of diversifying supply, it is unlikely that EU dependency on Russian gas imports will lessen.[233]

The geostrategic considerations in relation to the global energy economy, its governance, and global energy security are complex.[234] We have neither attempted nor intended to provide a full rundown of these

---

[232] A slight variation of the Nabucco project excludes Turkey. It is called Nabucco-West and connects to TANAP. See Socor, V. 'Nabucco-West in Synergy with Trans-Anatolia Project', *Eurasia Daily Monitor* 9 (90), 11 May 2012.

[233] See excerpts from an interview with Professor Jonathan Stern with analyses in relation to EU and Russia gas relations that seem to support this view. On the South Stream, Stern states that: 'Across much of Europe, including the European Commission, the South Stream [i.e., the pipeline constructed by Russia to bring gas into the EU market via the Black Sea and Bulgaria] was always regarded as a bluff in order to keep the Nabucco [the pipeline intended to carry Caspian State gas imports into the EU to also weaken EU dependence on Russia] from being built. I've never regarded it as a bluff, because the Russians do not play poker, they play chess'. On the reliability of Russia, Stern states that: 'There are many reasons why these pipelines [i.e., those built to bring non-Russian gas into the EU market] have taken a long time to happen and haven't happened yet, but if you're in Central & Eastern Europe, your question is "Look, I'm tired of talking about this – I want something to happen". By contrast the Russians are going to build their pipeline and it looks like they're going to build it now'. On the non-feasibility of a Southern Corridor, Stern states that: 'The problem that all the Caspian Southern Corridor pipelines have had is, there is not enough gas for those pipelines. There are huge gas reserves in a range of Caspian and Central Asian countries and we know all about them, but reserves don't make deliverable gas. The only deliverable gas we have from the Southern Corridor before 2020 is 10 billion cubic metres (and maybe less) of Shah Deniz gas from Azerbaijan – that's not enough to build a brand new, large scale pipeline. It's enough for the scaled down Nabucco or the TAP lines, but it's not enough gas on which to base a major new pipeline system'. See the entire interview at http://www.naturalgaseurope.com/europes-biggest-gas-supplier-no-bluffing?goback=%2Egde_1808658_member_191862754.

[234] For a thorough analysis, see Bhattacharyya, S. *Energy Economics: Concepts, Issues, Markets, and Governance* (London: Springer, 2011); Florini, A. & Sovacool, B.K. 'Who Governs Energy? The Challenges Facing Global Energy Governance' (2009) 37 *Energy Policy* 5239–5298; Florini, A. & Sovacool, B.K. 'Bridging the Gaps in Global Energy Governance' (2011) 17 *Global Governance* 57–74; Ghosh, A. 'Seeking Coherence in Complexity? The Governance of Energy by Trade & Investment Institutions' (2011) *Global Policy* 2; Sovacool, B. & Florini, A. 'Examining the Complications of Global Energy Governance' (2012) *Journal of Energy and Natural Resources Law*, Vol. 30, No. 3.

considerations. However, what we have sought to do is provide some insights into the sort of considerations and realities that impact the energy interests and security of the EU and its Member States.

VI. CONCLUSION

In modern times, energy impacts almost every field of human endeavor. This 'centrality' has implications for policymaking given that it cuts across a range of matters. Developing an energy policy that is cohesive and sympathetic to a wide range of policy objectives is hard enough for unitary actors, let alone for the EU that must mediate between the interests of its 28 Member States. As energy cuts across a numerous policy fields – some of which fall within the existing EU competence remit – the complexities of EU energy policymaking become ever more apparent. Setting aside questions of EU competence, energy within the EU context complicates EU policy development due to the hugely disparate energy realities between Member States. These differences make the adoption of common positions and policies particularly sticky.

A further factor that compounds EU energy policy development is the inescapable politics of energy. Energy resources are highly desirable due to their scarcity, exhaustibility, and highly patchy global distribution. Scarcity coupled with desirability leads to intense competition, and armed conflict even, for control. All economies rely on a steady and secure supply of energy, and disruptions can have considerable human and economic implications. In that sense, the very nature of energy resources politicizes energy and energy relations. In the case of the EU, the legacy of the past has also compounded the difficulties surrounding consensus building. For instance, whilst some States regard more integrated relations with an important energy partner such as Russia to be desirable, others would baulk at this prospect.

As we have said, certain matters that energy engages currently fall within the EU competence remit. Others do not. Again, even for matters that fall within the EU competence remit, some may be matters on which the EU is exclusively competent, whilst others are matters on which the EU shares competence with its Member States. Other energy-related matters outside the EU competence remit are the sole preserve of EU Member States by virtue of their being sovereign entities. This arrangement seems to preserve the most acute political/diplomatic aspects of energy within the discretion of EU Member States, to delegate the less acute political aspects of energy to a process which involves intensified systematized cooperation between the EU Member States through EU institutions, and to entirely assign the least acute political aspects of energy to the EU institutions to the exclusion of EU Member States. We have also seen that where there is sufficient political will between the 28 members to legislate or otherwise develop policy that engages matters outside the EU competence framework, this must be done on the basis of unanimity. What is more, as we have seen in Section III of this chapter, the more acute a matter for which the EU has competence (be it shared or exclusive), the more likely it is that related decisions must be reached on the basis of unanimity between the EU Member States in the EU institutions.

Whilst some might tend to view the EU – in terms of the size of its economy, its energy needs, and its industrialization levels – as similar to comparable net energy importing economies, for example the US, in reality, the EU is geologically, structurally, and geo-strategically quite unlike the US and other economies. The EU lacks what the other actors might take for granted: namely actorship flowing from sovereign state status. That is to say, whilst it possesses the necessary international legal personality[235] to contract certain international agreements[236] and pursue certain external relations, it can only do so to the extent that it has expressly been granted powers by EU Member States to do so.[237] That said, however, we have also seen that in the absence of such powers, the EU may take action so long as there is sufficient political will between its entire membership to unanimously sanction use of Article 352 TFEU to pursue some common approach that is not otherwise expressly sanctioned by the treaties upon which the EU rests.

A further factor that conditions EU energy-related action is the requirement that action be in line with the guiding principles contained in Article 21§1 TEU. We have briefly referred to calls to delink EU energy security from other considerations, including those relating to environmental and human rights. Conceivably, hard economic matters could

---

[235] Article 47 TEU as amended by the Treaty of Lisbon endows the EU with legal personality. See also Leal-Arcas, R. 'EU Legal Personality in Foreign Policy?'(2006) *Boston University International Law Journal*, Vol. 24, No. 2, pp. 165–212.

[236] Title V (Articles 216–219) TFEU provisions delineate general EU capacity to contract international agreements. Article 8 TEU relates to international agreements between the EU and third-party States, aiming to 'establish an area of prosperity and good neighbourliness', and Article 37 TEU relates to international agreements between the EU and third-party States in relation to matters regarding the EU Common Foreign and Security Policy.

[237] Namely by Articles 3 and 4 TFEU.

push the respective economic and political elites in EU Member States to consider what we deem to be regressive steps, such as reforming the EU to focus on the hard economic matters of cooperation and to shed its more enlightened aspects underpinned by the EU's humanist ideals. A 2010 Commission communication included three scenarios for economic growth by 2020, two of which made less sanguine predictions: the second scenario foresaw a sluggish recovery, whilst the third scenario foresaw a lost decade for economic growth.[238] The prospect of these scenarios could give rise to anti-EU sentiments and harden anti-EU attitudes on the assumption that 'Brussels red tape' economically stifles the EU. Foreseeably, this could lead to all sorts of developments such as the weakening or, even, the collapse of the Eurozone,[239] and the downgrading or abandonment of more humanist and idealistic aspects, so that the EU is stripped down to its EEA fundamentals. We have seen calls from high-profile UK politicians for the UK to seek a relationship with the EU similar to that of Norway and Switzerland.[240] The EnC illustrates how single-sector integration – minus the softer, more enlightened EU desiderata around civil, social, and political rights – could be the way forward for those who want to preserve the common market and customs union whilst shedding what they might deem the softer, less necessary bits of the EU project. This would be particularly appealing to an EU polity that may want to engage in energy diplomacy without the conditionality posed by the EU's 'guiding principles' under Article 21 TEU and other provisions that promote consistency and cohesion across the EU policy spectrum. This, of course, would be a tremendously regressive step if it were to happen. However, the persistent global economic crisis has had budgetary implications in that public services are being scaled back across a number of EU Member States. At the EU

---

[238] See The 2010 Commission Communication, *Europe 2020: A Strategy for Smart, Sustainable and Inclusive Growth*, Brussels, 3 March 2010 (COM(2010) 2020 final) (at p. 9), which posits three scenarios for Europe by 2020. Scenario 1 (sustainable recovery) envisages the EU to be able to make a full return to the earlier growth path and to raise its potential to go beyond that. Scenario 2 (sluggish recovery) envisages that the EU will have suffered a permanent loss in wealth and start growing again from this eroded basis. Scenario 3 (lost decade) predicts the EU will have suffered a permanent loss in wealth and potential for future growth. See also p. 20, where the Commission warns against the risks of economic nationalism.

[239] That is to say, the Economic and Monetary Union among 18 EU Member States (as of 1 January 2014).

[240] See BBC, 'Boris Johnson Calls for "Pared Down" EU Relationship', 4 December 2012, available at http://www.bbc.co.uk/news/uk-politics-20592596

level, this dynamic might find expression in the paring down of the EU to its strict economic essentials.

Finally, our intention has been, on the one hand, to present the limitations at play when the EU seeks to move in unison in relation to the collective energy security of its members, whilst, on the other, to highlight the dynamism with which the EU functions when there is sufficient political will to do so. We conclude that, whilst the EU is restricted from acting the way a sovereign actor such as China or the US would in promoting their energy security, it makes good and full use of its existing competences by handling its energy needs comprehensively. We say this because the EU has a comprehensive energy policy that seeks to address internal and external aspects of energy security whilst also taking energy and its implications – for example, on the environment, on the economy, etc. – as being interlinked and therefore as meriting a cohesive response. We have also sought to provide insights into the breadth of EU energy-related policy and to use this as an example to highlight how questions around competences are invariably most pertinent when we consider energy security within the EU context.

6. The EU and its systemic relationship to the Energy Community and the Energy Charter Treaty

I. INTRODUCTION

This chapter relates to European Union (EU) energy security and two special and important multilateral regimes (namely the Energy Charter Treaty (ECT) and the Energy Community (EnC)) regarding the promotion of EU energy security interests at the extra-EU level. EU energy security often takes place through the propagation of energy-related norms among third-party States via, among other things, hard-law means (e.g., international legal agreements). In this context, we home in on the normative frameworks in relation to the ECT and the Energy Community Treaty (EnCT), examine their systemic relationship to the EU, and offer an account of their respective dispute settlement arrangements.

The EU is, for its most part, dependent on the world outside its borders for a steady and secure energy supply. The EU borders, or is close to, areas rich in energy-related natural resource endowments – such as Russia, the Caspian Sea, the Middle East and North Africa regions, and Norway – from where the bulk of energy imports into the EU are sourced. The collapse of the Soviet Union and of the bureaucratic regimes in Central and Eastern Europe – which precipitated the opening up of those economies to globalization and its attendant processes – has increasingly made their energy-related natural resource endowments available on global markets. Developed, yet energy-poor, Western economies – many of which have galvanized behind the EU – saw opportunities to enhance their energy security through those economies on the brink of collapse. To that end, the EU has sought to entangle those energy-rich (or otherwise 'energy-significant' states, e.g., regarding energy transit) areas into multilateral regimes – such as those based on the Energy Charter Treaty and the Energy Community. While both these special regimes count among their numbers several parties that are not EU Member States, they are not neutral in their ontology, given that these regimes, since their inception, are inherently linked to the energy interests of EU economies.

After this introduction, Section II provides some background information on EU energy policy. Section III presents some aspects of EU external energy relations with the outside world. Section IV provides an overview of the systemic links between the EU and the two multilateral systems within scope (the ECT and the EnC). Section V examines the dispute settlement arrangements of the ECT and the EnC. Section VI comments on issues concerning concurrent legal obligations in order to further situate the topic within the broader international legal system. Section VII concludes the chapter.

II. EU ENERGY POLICY AND ITS COMPLICATIONS

A number of authors predict that the wars of the future will not be fought over religion or freedom, but over resources and energy.[1] While these predictions may seem overly drastic, the fact remains that global energy consumption demands are growing at rates that are far from sustainable, given the current sources of energy. A crucial component of this equation is the concept of 'energy security', which deals with the ability of a state to sustainably provide for its energy demands.

This section seeks to analyze the case of the EU – a major economic bloc – in the context of the governance frameworks that ostensibly contribute, and are likely to contribute, to its energy security. This discussion assumes significance, given the weak energy position the EU has traditionally possessed and the steps taken by it to mitigate the effects thereof. The journey towards an energy-secure EU requires the presence and functioning of strong governance mechanisms and structures that are not only able to ensure that internal EU policy be undeterred from its energy security objectives, but that externalities such as the effects of a changing global energy environment be carefully studied and accounted for. It is within such a context that this section seeks to examine the existing EU energy governance framework and the effects that are likely to result from developments in global energy trade. It will survey the existing EU governance frameworks and institutions that exist in relation

---

[1] See e.g., Klare, M.T. *Resource Wars: The New Landscape of Global Conflict* (New York: Henry Holt, 2001) xi; Glover, P.C. & Economides, M.J. *Energy and Climate Wars: How Naive Politicians, Green Ideologues, and Media Elites are Undermining the Truth about Energy and Climate* (New York: Continuum, 2010) 228.

to energy and energy security, and will take a deeper normative look at these frameworks in light of recent international developments.

The nature of EU energy policy has previously been examined.[2] We notice that EU energy policy is comprehensive and multifaceted. Multiple EU Commission communications testify to this. EU energy policy extends over a wide range of policy matters that relate to energy, and we note that EU energy policy encompasses inwardly and outwardly facing aspects. For instance, EU energy policy aims at, among other things:

- the integration of the intra-EU electricity and gas markets through the 'Internal Energy Market' (IEM);
- the promotion of energy efficiency within the EU;[3] and
- the decarbonization of EU economies.

Much of this relates to the internal EU reality and applies to the intra-EU territory. However, the advancement of EU energy interests cannot be, and – as we shall see – is clearly not, restricted to introspective EU measures.[4]

---

[2] See for instance Leal-Arcas, R. & Filis, A. 'Conceptualizing EU Energy Security through an EU Constitutional Law Perspective' (2013) *Fordham International Law Journal*, Vol. 36, No. 5, pp. 1225–1301.

[3] There is a raft of EU policies and legislation aimed at the promotion of the efficient use of energy across the EU membership. See http://europa.eu/legislation_summaries/energy/energy_efficiency/index_en.htm for more details. In relation to primary legislation, see Article 194.1(c) of the Treaty on the Functioning of the European Union (TFEU), which promotes the efficient use of energy as an objective of the establishment and functioning of the internal market among the EU Member States.

[4] See 2011 EU Commission Communication to the European Parliament, the Council, the European Economic and Social Committee, and the Committee of the Regions, *On security of energy supply and international cooperation – 'The EU Energy Policy: Engaging with Partners beyond Our Borders'*, 7 September 2011 (COM(2011) 539 final). Here the Commission cites the EU's heavy energy dependency on imports (c. 60% of its gas and c. 80% of its oil) and the growing competition the EU is likely to face in relation to rising future energy demand. All these matters necessitate a comprehensive external energy policy. The Commission emphasizes how an EU external energy policy is central to achieving an IEM. Noting that the rise in global energy demand will not be due to the EU and other developed economies, the EU Commission recommends that the EU engage in activity aimed at encouraging less and least developed countries to access sustainable energy and to adopt more sustainable processes to ensure that global energy use becomes more prudent. See pp. 14ff.

The EU also directs efforts outwardly by engaging with third-party States in order to encourage, outside its borders, a range of practices such as more efficient and sustainable energy use, energy sector liberalization and investment protection, and pro-market processes that, arguably, contribute to the promotion of EU energy interests by enhancing the volume of energy commodities that eventually reach global markets and/or protect EU energy investments abroad. We could call such efforts directed outside the EU, and principally concerned with energy, the EU's external energy policy.

Although the EU faces challenges (be they inherent, systemic or incidental) in going about addressing its energy interests in the manner that, say, China, India, Japan, or the US may, it makes full and effective use of whatever competences it is afforded. For instance, the EU (or, to be more accurate, its predecessor, i.e., the European Communities (EC)) had been the prime mover behind the ECT. Moreover, the EU played a major role in setting up the EnC, which draws in surrounding energy-significant states.[5] For instance, through the EnC, an isolated Greece – at the most southeastern extremity of the EU – has finally been territorially linked to the rest of the EU, thus territorially integrating the entire IEM into one cohesive area. The ECT, for its part, creates, among other things, important energy transit rights for ECT parties, which, crucially, also extend to fixed energy-related infrastructure,[6] thus enhancing energy trade flows between ECT parties and flows into the EU.

It is also the case that institutions such as the EnC allow the EU to maximize its interests in cases where it is perhaps politically challenging (or naïve to expect the EU) to attract energy-significant neighboring states with EU membership. In the immediate aftermath of the collapse of the bureaucratic regimes across Eurasia – in what had been lauded as the *end of history*[7] – it may have been more realistic to think that those economies on the brink of collapse might have been willing to join on whatever terms the developed Western European states may have imposed. This may have changed significantly nowadays, what with the protracted global economic slump. Market failure may have given rise to

---

[5] Significant in terms of their energy-related natural resource endowments and/or their significance to the transit of energy flows into the EU.

[6] Article 7 ECT.

[7] This is the notion that large-scale conflicts between economic models during the Cold War had been resolved with the collapse of the Soviet Union, and that the result of human progress was the triumph of the purportedly inherently superior capitalist model. See Fukuyama, F. *The End of History and the Last Man* (London: Penguin, 1992) at p. 67.

skepticism regarding globalized markets and economic integration as being unquestionably safer paths towards modernization and economic development. Consequently, those states may be less willing to seek EU membership proper.

Within this context, we could perhaps understand a realization on the part of EU members' polities that it is best to focus on the core economic relations *per se* and to draw in third-party States, particularly energy-significant States, into EU membership-*lite* arrangements. In that respect, while it is politically naïve for the EU to expect states such as Moldova and Ukraine to be joining the EU as fully fledged EU members any time soon, drawing these states into more institutionalized energy relations is a less maximalist way of achieving EU energy security ends.[8]

In relation to EU energy needs, let us briefly examine some aspects of EU external energy relations with the outside world.

III. EU EXTERNAL ENERGY RELATIONS

The EU has been engaging in energy diplomacy with various states. These efforts have either resulted in international agreements or the creation of specialized bodies to facilitate energy relations. Some of them have major repercussions for the EU's energy security moving forward. Below is a non-exhaustive group of countries with which the EU has energy relations.

A. The BRIC Countries

The EU has strategic partnerships with all BRIC (Brazil, Russia, India and China) countries.[9] Whilst the EU does not deal with the BRICs as a single group, it does so bilaterally.[10] Whilst the BRIC countries have

---

[8] See also the EU neighborhood policy, which draws into relations with the EU Member States to its south and east. See http://ec.europa.eu/world/enp/policy_en.htm

[9] This is the case beyond the field of energy. In the field of trade, see for instance Leal-Arcas, R. 'The European Union and New Leading Powers: Towards Partnership in Strategic Trade Policy Areas'(2009) *Fordham International Law Journal*, Vol. 32, No. 2, pp. 345–416; Leal-Arcas, R. 'How Will the EU Approach the BRIC Countries? Future Trade Challenges' (2008) *Vienna Journal of International Constitutional Law*, Vol. 2, No. 4, pp. 235–271.

[10] See for instance Leal-Arcas, R. 'The European Union vis-à-vis Brazil and India: Future Avenues in Selected Trade Policy Areas' (2009) *International Journal of Private Law*, Vol. 2, No. 2, pp. 109–134; Leal-Arcas, R. 'The EU and

certain aspects in common – including large populations, wide territorial span, and rapid economic growth – they are also separated from each other, and from the EU, by significant economic, social and political differences. Brazil and Russia are major energy-significant economies in that they are net energy exporters *par excellence*, whilst the opposite is the case for China and India. Out of the BRICs, China and India are the ones that rely on energy imports for their economic growth. However, the emergence of the BRICs has been powered by the prodigious use of highly polluting hydrocarbons. The fast pace of development has caused unprecedented environmental impacts in those economies, and globally, in terms of hydrocarbon combustion-related emission increases. Nevertheless, whilst China remains the highest GHG emitting economy in absolute terms, it is taking a lead in investment in renewables and reforestation. In that respect, China appears to be an environmentally responsible energy consumer.[11]

In relation to Chinese and EU relations, there has been bilateral activity.[12] The EU and China currently amount to about a third of global energy consumption, with the share of China projected to rise over the

Brazil: Trading Partners in Different Fora', *The Jean Monnet/Robert Schuman Paper Series*, Vol. 8, No. 11, June 2008, pp. 1–12.

[11] However, this is not the case in terms of the implications that Chinese energy diplomacy has on global human security. China is involved in aid-for-oil relations with African States. This is problematic when it involves States such as Sudan (before the secession of South Sudan) and Zimbabwe, and has implications for human security in those States. For instance, China may have opposed UN Security Council action in relation to the massacre in Sudan possibly due to its energy interests in the region. This sort of horse-trading is sadly the order of the day in diplomatic circles. It is not specific to China. Taking the post-World-War-II era alone, the US and other Western states have also promoted their economic – including their energy – interests at a great human cost to their societies and to the societies of other States – e.g., in relation to the two Iraq wars, support for the 1953 Iranian *coup d'état* in the aftermath of oil nationalizations, and so on. Western geostrategic interests in various regions – including the MENA, Caspian, Latin American, and Sub-Saharan regions – have aided, and consequently benefited from installing, repressive regimes.

[12] On the EU's breadth of external action with China, see http://eeas.europa.eu/delegations/china/eu_china/political_relations/index_en.htm; in relation to EU–China energy relations, see http://ec.europa.eu/energy/international/bilateral_cooperation/china/china_en.htm. On EU–China trade relations, see Leal-Arcas, R. 'European Union-China Trade Relations' (2010) *Trade, Law and Development*, Vol. 2, No. 2, pp. 224–251.

next two decades.[13] In May 2012 the EU and China issued joint declarations in relation to energy, including energy security.[14] In December 2012 a high-level conference was held in Beijing in connection to one of those declarations – namely the EU–China *Joint Declaration on Energy Security* – to look at ways to cooperate on energy-related matters. Areas of cooperation include nuclear safety (in light of Fukushima), energy security, and the promotion of environmental policies including greater use of renewables.[15] What is more, the EU and China have shared interests in the MENA region given that energy transit States such as Yemen and Egypt are of critical importance to their security of supply. Again, to whatever extent EU competences permit, the EU and China could coordinate responses to events that disrupt their energy supplies.[16]

---

[13] European Commission, 'Key Figures', Market Observatory for Energy, Directorate-General for Energy, June 2011, at p. 3.

[14] The three Joint Declarations signed on 3 May 2012 in Brussels are the Joint Statement for Enhanced Cooperation on Electricity Markets between the European Commission and the State Electricity Regulatory Commission of China, the EU–China Partnership on Urbanisation, and the EU–China Joint Declaration on Energy Security. See http://eeas.europa.eu/delegations/china/press_corner/all_news/news/2012/20121213_01_en.htm

[15] See the information sheet on the high-level conference on 'Cooperation on Energy Security: China-EU Government and Business Perspectives', held on 13 December 2012 in Beijing, China, organized by the Europe-China Clean Energy Centre, available at http://ec.europa.eu/euraxess/links/china/docs/20121213_Cooperation_on_energy_security_background.pdf. The Europe-China Clean Energy Centre (EC2) annual high-level conference was held in Beijing on 13 December 2012.

[16] China and EU Member States currently cooperate in various fora. For instance, in the Major Economies Forum on Energy and Climate Change (MEF), which brings together 17 major economies – namely Australia, Brazil, Canada, China, the EU, France, Germany, India, Indonesia, Italy, Japan, Korea, Mexico, Russia, South Africa, the UK, and the US – with net energy importer economies such as the EU, India, China and the US, alongside net energy exporters such as Brazil, Russia, and Mexico. It was set up at the instance of the US – as the 'Major Economies Meeting on Energy Security and Climate Change' – to act as a negotiations anteroom for the most emissions-significant economies in relation to wider UN negotiations on climate change that were taking place. Purportedly, the MEF is also concerned with: '… advanc[ing] the exploration of concrete initiatives and joint ventures that increase the supply of clean energy while cutting greenhouse gas emissions'. See http://www.majoreconomiesforum.org/about.html for more information. Also, China participates in the International Energy Forum – which brings together OPEC and IEA members – in the G8+5 forum, the G20, and also on a more informal footing directly with the IEA (see http://www.iea.org/countries/non-membercountries/).

In relation to Russia and its relations with the EU,[17] it is pertinent to mention that Russia is a key EU energy partner in terms of its oil, gas, and biofuels exports.[18] As mentioned earlier, a steady supply of gas – which is less polluting than oil and coal for the production of energy – alongside biofuel imports could considerably enhance EU efforts towards a low-carbon economy.

Also, the fact that there may be rising demand competition for the EU by China and India is perhaps less of a concern when one considers the vast Russian reserves and their wide distribution across Russian territory. The implication of this is that Russia needs a healthy EU energy market as much as the EU needs a steady supply of energy from Russia. However, as we have also alluded to, relations are complicated in that EU Member States, due to historical and economic reasons, have very different attitudes towards EU energy dependence on Russia. The much publicized, and perhaps somewhat misunderstood, recent gas disputes between Russia and Ukraine also compounded these attitudes when several EU states consequently experienced energy shortages.[19]

---

[17] See http://ec.europa.eu/trade/creating-opportunities/bilateral-relations/countries/russia for a run-down on EU-Russia trade relations.

[18] See generally Kuzemko, C. (ed.) *Dynamics of Energy Governance in Europe and Russia* (Basingstoke: Palgrave Macmillan, 2012).

[19] Ukraine has historically enjoyed prices for Russian gas exports that were lower than the prices for gas exports destined for EU markets. It appears that some sort of agreement had been in place between Russian and Ukrainian energy operators, and their respective governments, that involved transit for subsidized gas prices. Presumably, the pro-Western stance of a section of the Ukrainian political establishment, which had previously sought NATO membership, antagonized Russia into using its energy advantage as a political tool by announcing increases to the subsidized gas prices destined for Ukraine for domestic consumption. Consequently, Ukraine attempted to reserve gas for its own needs at the previous prices, which meant that Russian gas intended for EU markets was held in Ukraine. This resulted in several EU states experiencing energy shortages. See a rundown of the dispute at http://news.bbc.co.uk/1/hi/world/europe/7240462.stm. Tension between Russian gas company Gazprom and Ukraine continues because Ukraine failed to import agreed natural gas in 2012, which, in turn, has meant disruption of gas supply to the EU in the past. See Shiryaevskaya, A. & Daryna Krasnolutska, D. 'Gazprom Sends Ukraine $7 Billion Bill as Gas Dispute Deepens,' *Bloomberg*, 28 January 2013, available at http://www.bloomberg.com/news/2013-01-27/gazprom-sends-7-billion-bill-to-naftogaz-as-gas-dispute-deepens.html. For background information on Ukraine–NATO relations, see http://www.nato.int/cps/en/SID-E2280ADF-B6517611/natolive/topics_37750.htm

There is a constitutionally entrenched need for EU external action to be consistent across the EU policy spectrum. Often this means that bilateral legal relations between the EU and third-party States, including Russia, are not strictly *realpolitik* in that they involve enlightened conditionalities (e.g., in relation to the promotion of the rule of law, human rights, and civil liberties).[20] This can be problematic as, understandably, the Kremlin may balk at what may appear to it as hypocritical lecturing on the part of the West. However, it is helpful for Russian policymakers to understand that in their dealings with the outside world, EU institutions *per se* do not have a free hand in how they engage, but must do so within the existing competence parameters. Again, as we have said, this leaves EU Member States largely able to pursue closer bilateral/multilateral relations outside the EU context. That said, the EU and Russia have had a Partnership and Cooperation Agreement (PCA) in place since 1994. Whilst this PCA has expired (namely in 2007, ten years after being ratified in 1997), this has not inhibited mutual trade and investment flows.[21] However, a new PCA has yet to be concluded.[22] Conceivably, energy and social reform matters might have made for complicated negotiations.

Furthermore, the exceptionally large energy resource endowments of Russia mean that its interests in energy-related multilateralism and, consequently, its stance towards it, can be very different from those of net energy importing states. For instance, Russia, whilst initially having signed it, had not ratified the Energy Charter Treaty (ECT) when it informed the ECT Secretariat of its decision to withdraw.[23] It is helpful

---

[20] For a fuller exposition of EU–Russia trade relations, see Leal-Arcas, R. 'The EU and Russia as Energy Trading Partners: Friends or Foes?' (2009) 14 *EFA Rev*. pp. 337–366.

[21] On EU–Russia trade relations, see Leal-Arcas, R. 'EU Relations with China and Russia: How to Approach new Superpowers in Trade Matters' (2009) *Journal of International Commercial Law and Technology*, Vol. 4, No. 1, pp. 22–52.

[22] For more details, see http://eeas.europa.eu/russia/index_en.htm.

[23] The ECT currently has 54 Members of which 49 have ratified (see http://www.encharter.org/index.php?id=61&L=0). Parties that have ratified may withdraw after the conclusion of the first five years after ratification. What is more, parties remain bound by ECT investment protection obligations for 20 years post-withdrawal (see Article 47 ECT). For those parties who have signed but not ratified, it is possible to withdraw within a shorter timeframe – namely 60 calendar days (see Article 45(3)(a)) – as was the case of Russia, which had not ratified the ECT before its notification to withdraw. We mentioned in a previous footnote that the Benelux states, in their March 2006 joint 'Position Paper on

to think of the ECT as Plan B to what had been Plan A of Western net energy importing states – namely to conclude an energy-specific agreement within the context of the General Agreement on Tariffs and Trade (GATT)/WTO system.[24] As an aside, it is worth pointing out that the ECT does not obligate its parties to liberalize their energy markets, to permit inward flows of foreign investment, or to provide energy exploitation contracts to all ECT parties on a non-discriminatory basis. Broadly, what it does is provide disciplines for energy-sector foreign investment once this has been welcomed in the territory of an ECT party.

In sum, once investments take place within ECT party territories, ECT parties must provide indiscriminate treatment between foreign investors, and among foreign investors and domestic investors (on the Most-Favored-Nation (MFN) and National Treatment bases). Incidentally, on 23 November 2012, the ECT parties agreed to begin the process of updating the ECT during successive rounds of negotiations – known as the *Warsaw Process* – to take place in Warsaw, Poland. This has been argued as necessary to meet current demands and to also draw in membership from regions outside those initially anticipated at the time of the ECT's adoption.[25] Despite the situation concerning Russia's withdrawal from the ECT, it is interesting to note that the EU is the largest foreign investor in Russia, with investments worth around €120 billion in 2010. Russian investments in the EU amounted to €42 billion in 2010.[26]

B. The Euro-Mediterranean Partnership

The Mediterranean has always held significant strategic importance for the EU and its energy supplies.[27] This is emphasized by the fact that

---

Energy Security and Foreign Policy', addressed to the European Council, had recommended that the EU should push Russia to ratify the ECT.

24 See Wälde, T. *The Energy Charter Treaty: An East-West Gateway for Investment and Trade* (London: Kluwer Law International, 1996) for a fuller analysis of the ECT and its history, and for a more critical perspective.

25 See http://www.encharter.org/index.php?id=21&id_article=334&L=0

26 See http://ec.europa.eu/trade/creating-opportunities/bilateral-relations/countries/russia

27 EU Neighbourhood Info Centre, 'Euro-Mediterranean Energy Co-operation: Working Together for Secure and Sustainable Energy', where it is stated: 'The Euro-Mediterranean Partnership agreed as far back as 1998 that work on energy issues should cover the following priorities: Security of supply; Energy industry competitiveness; Environmental protection and sustainable development'. Available at http://www.enpi-info.eu/mainmed.php?id=286&id_type=3

around 65% per cent of the oil and natural gas consumed in Western Europe originates or passes through the region every year.[28] Given that these figures are likely to escalate as the EU seeks to diversify its energy sources amidst a declining internal production capacity,[29] the importance of the region is set to grow enormously.[30] To this effect, EU-Mediterranean relations have, for a long time, contained energy-specific policies and commitments. These are primarily oriented towards two distinct objectives.

The first pertains to the objective of building a stable and more integrated Mediterranean energy supply grid through which energy can be routed to the EU.[31] In this regard, a number of initiatives such as the MED-REG (energy regulators), MED-EMIP (energy cooperation), MED-ENEC II (energy efficiency in construction), EAMGM II (Euro-Arab Mashreq gas market project) and the electricity market integration project have all been taken under the Euro-Mediterranean Partnership as well as other regional cooperation agreements.[32]

---

[28] North Atlantic Treaty Organization, 'NATO's Role in Energy Security', available at http://www.nato.int/cps/en/natolive/topics_49208.htm; see also Weissenbacher, M. 'Energy Security in the Euro-Mediterranean Region', in Calleya, S. & Wohlfeld, M. (eds) *Change and Opportunities in the Emerging Mediterranean* (Malta: MEDAC, 2012), pp. 452–469, at 458.

[29] Market Observatory for Energy, 'Europe's Energy Position – Markets and Supply' (Publication Office of the EU, 2010) 16. The oil output of Norway and the UK – the largest and second largest European oil producers, respectively – has been in the decline since production in both countries peaked early in the 21st century. See 'Memorandum submitted by the Department of Energy and Climate Change', in *UK Offshore Oil and Gas: first Report of Session 2008–09, Vol. 2: Oral and Written Evidence* (House of Commons: Energy and Climate Change Committee, 2009) 68; see also Höök, M. & Aleklett, K. 'A Decline Rate Study of Norwegian Oil Production' (2008) *Energy Policy*, Vol. 36, No. 11, pp. 4262–4271.

[30] European Commission, *On Security of Energy Supply and International Cooperation – 'The EU Energy Policy: Engaging with Partners beyond Our Borders'* COM(2011) 539 final, p. 5.

[31] The Africa-EU Partnership, 'Completing the circuit – interconnecting the energy grids of the Mediterranean' available at http://www.africa-eu-partnership.org/success-stories/completing-circuit-interconnecting-electricity-grids-mediterranean

[32] Weissenbacher, M. 'Energy Security in the Euro-Mediterranean Region', in Calleya, S. & Wohlfeld, M. (eds) *Change and Opportunities in the Emerging Mediterranean* (Malta: MEDAC, 2012) pp. 452–469, at 464.

The second closely-related objective pertains to the EU's renewable energy commitments such as the '20-20-20' plan.[33] One of the options for EU Member States to meet their obligations under the commitments is to support the installation of renewable energy sites in third countries with the energy being produced to be used within the EU.[34] The Mediterranean, with its vast potential for the generation of renewable energy, presents a feasible option for states seeking to exploit this avenue.[35] One initiative thus oriented is the Mediterranean Solar Plan under which the EU provides financial and capacity-building assistance to States seeking to exploit solar power.

C. The Africa-EU Energy Partnership

The Africa-EU Energy Partnership (AEEP) is a 'long-term framework for structured political dialogue and cooperation between Africa and the EU'[36] on energy issues of mutual strategic importance. The objective of the AEEP is to ensure 'improved access to reliable, secure, affordable, cost-effective, climate friendly and sustainable energy services for both continents, with a special focus on achieving the MDGs [Millennium Development Goals] in Africa'.[37] To this effect, the First High Level Ministerial Meeting of the AEEP agreed on a set of goals to be achieved by 2020.[38]

These were centered on six primary focus areas, namely:

---

33 See European Commission, *Communication from the Commission, Europe 2020: A Strategy for Smart, Sustainable, and Inclusive Growth*, Brussels 3.3.2010, COM(2010) 2020 final.

34 Varouxakis, S. 'Renewable Energy in the Euro-Mediterranean Framework' (Instituto Europeo del Mediterráneo, 2013) 263–264.

35 Ibid.

36 Africa-EU Partnership, '2nd Joint Africa-EU Strategy Action Plan 2011–2013', p. 55, available at http://www.africa-eu-partnership.org/sites/default/files/documents/doc_energy_action_plan_2011-2013_en.pdf

37 See e.g., Africa-EU Energy Partnership, 'AEEP Moving with Full Steam Ahead' (EU Energy Initiative – Partnership Dialogue Facility, 2012).

38 High-Level Meeting of the Africa-EU Energy Partnership Bulletin (International Institute for Sustainable Development (IISD) in collaboration with the German Agency for Technical Cooperation (GTZ) GmbH, September 2010) Volume 181, Issue 1.

(1) energy access targets, including bringing access to energy to at least an additional 100 million Africans;[39]
(2) energy security targets, including doubling interconnections within Africa and between Africa and the EU, and doubling the African gas exports to Europe;[40]
(3) renewable energy targets, including increasing the generation and use of renewable energy in Africa;[41]
(4) capacity building targets, involving training and financing;[42]
(5) investment targets aimed at stimulating the flow of investment into the energy sector in Africa;[43] and
(6) dialogue goals targeted at continuing the ongoing dialogue on the sector.[44]

D. Persian Gulf-EU Partnerships

The geographical scope of the Persian Gulf encompasses the six members of the Gulf Cooperation Council (GCC) (namely Saudi Arabia, Oman, the United Arab Emirates, Qatar, Bahrain, and Kuwait), plus Iran and Iraq. According to British Petroleum, proven oil reserves in the Persian Gulf countries (without counting Bahrain) accounted for more than 60% of the global proved oil resources as of 2007[45] and more than 40% of the proved gas reserves at the end of the same year.[46] When this is taken in conjunction with the fact that less than 30% of these resources are currently being exploited,[47] it becomes clear that any energy security policy must target deep cooperative links with this region. This need was realized as early as the late 1980s, when the EU and the GCC states

---

[39] Africa-EU Partnership, '2nd Joint Africa-EU Strategy Action Plan 2011–2013', p. 56, available at http://www.africa-eu-partnership.org/sites/default/files/documents/doc_energy_action_plan_2011-2013_en.pdf,.

[40] Ibid. p. 57.

[41] Ibid. at p. 58.

[42] Ibid. at p. 59.

[43] Ibid.

[44] Ibid. at p. 60.

[45] BP Statistical Review of World Energy, June 2008, p. 6, available at http://www.bp.com/liveassets/bp_internet/globalbp/globalbp_uk_english/reports_and_publications/statistical_energy_review_2008/STAGING/local_assets/downloads/pdf/statistical_review_of_world_energy_full_review_2008.pdf (last accessed 2013).

[46] Ibid. at p. 22.

[47] Economist Intelligence Unit, 'The GCC in 2020: Resources for the Future' (*The Economist*, 2010) pp. 3–4.

entered into a Cooperation Agreement which aimed to promote cooperation on 'mutually advantageous terms in all spheres'.[48] Specific to the field of energy, the Agreement sought to further cooperation through a number of processes: cooperation between energy undertakings in the two regions, joint analyses and studies of the energy trade and clean energy between the two regions, and the exchange of information between the regions on energy issues.[49] Furthermore, the Agreement led to the establishment of two bodies, namely an annual Joint Council and Ministerial Meeting on the strategic level, and an Energy Experts Group on the operational level.[50]

However, it would seem that the EU-GCC Cooperation Agreement has not been able precipitate cooperation to the extent initially contemplated. This fact was recognized and sought to be altered by the signing of a Joint Action Program for the execution of the Cooperation Agreement for the period 2010–2013, which contained specific sections devoted to oil and gas issues, energy efficiency, and clean energy.[51] This move is illustrative of the potential benefits that cooperation between the two parties can bring – fulfilling the EU's need for diverse and secure energy sources while, at the same time, accounting for the GCC states' desires to secure a sustainable demand for its oil and gas, and to foster internal capital injections and inflows from capital surplus states.[52]

Energy relations between the EU and the other two Persian Gulf countries (Iran and Iraq) have not developed as efficiently as with the GCC states.

---

48 Preamble, Cooperation Agreement between the European Economic Community and the Gulf Cooperation Council ('EU-GCC Cooperation Agreement'); Article 1(1)(b) of the EU-GCC Cooperation Agreement.

49 Article 6, paras 1–5 of the EU-GCC Cooperation Agreement.

50 Papadopoulou, A. et al. 'Tools and Mechanisms Fostering EU GCC Cooperation on Energy Efficiency' (World Renewable Energy Congress, Policy Issues, 2011), p. 2309.

51 See generally, Al-Shalabi, A., Cottret, N. & Menichetti, E. 'EU-GCC Cooperation on Energy – Technical Report' (Sharaka Research Paper No. 3, June 2013) 57.

52 Al-Sahlawi, M. 'Energy Security in the EU from GCC Perspective' in Ramady, M.A. (ed.) *The GCC Economies: Stepping Up to Future Challenges* (New York: Springer, 2012) 57.

IV. LINKING THE EUROPEAN UNION TO THE ENERGY CHARTER TREATY AND THE ENERGY COMMUNITY

It is well known that Europe has many years of experience in integrating markets. The EU can be seen as a regional model for the judicialization and juridification of energy relations. In this section, we provide an analysis of the EU relationship with both the ECT and the Energy Community.

A. The Energy Charter Treaty and its Relationship to the EU

The Energy Charter Treaty (ECT) is an international agreement which aims to provide a 'multilateral framework for energy cooperation' based on the principles of 'open, competitive markets and sustainable development'.[53] By binding governments to commitments that guarantee open markets, non-discrimination and access for foreign investment,[54] the ECT aims to strengthen the global rule of law on energy issues and thereby reduce the risks associated with energy-related investments and trade.[55] The ECT itself rests on five primary areas: investment protection,[56] trade,[57] transit,[58] environmental protection,[59] and dispute settlement,[60] while there are optional protocols on various topics, including energy efficiency and the environment.[61]

In 1990, at a European Council meeting in Dublin, Ruud Lubbers, the Dutch Prime Minister, who, at the time, presided over the Council, called for more institutionalized relations with the energy-rich economies in

---

[53] *The Energy Charter Treaty and Related Documents: A Legal Framework for International Energy Cooperation* (Brussels: Energy Charter Secretariat, 2004) p. 13.

[54] McGowan, F. 'Can the European Union's Market Liberalism Ensure Energy Security in a Time of "Economic Nationalism"?' (2008) *Journal of Contemporary European Research*, Vol. 4, No.2, pp. 90–106, at 97.

[55] *The Energy Charter Treaty and Related Documents: A Legal Framework for International Energy Cooperation* (Brussels: Energy Charter Secretariat, 2004) at 14.

[56] Part III of the ECT.

[57] Part II of the ECT.

[58] Article 7 of the ECT.

[59] Article 19 of the ECT.

[60] Part V of the ECT.

[61] Protocol on Energy Efficiency and Related Environmental Aspects (PEERA), 1994.

Eurasia following their collapse in order to benefit from their consequent opening-up and orientation towards the global market-based economic order. This led to the adoption of the 1991 European Energy Charter, which is a non-legally binding political declaration embodying key principles of international energy cooperation. The 1991 European Energy Charter paved the way for the negotiation and eventual adoption of the ECT[62] and the Energy Charter Process.[63] Prior to the advent of the ECT, Western industrialized states attempted to have an energy-sector specific agreement adopted within the context of the General Agreement on Tariffs and Trade (GATT), but this effort ultimately foundered.[64] In that sense, the advent of the ECT was a success for multilateralism, given the political difficulties in having such an agreement adopted within the multilateral trade system.

The ECT's fundamental purpose was to promote open energy markets, predicated on, chiefly, investment protection, in the energy-significant yet economically depressed Eurasian economies following the geopolitical and geo-economic re-shuffle in Eurasia as a result of the collapse of the Soviet Union. A more critical reading of the ECT and the events that led to its adoption would suggest that, beyond the official rhetoric, its actual aim was to enhance the energy security of developed European economies by, amongst other things, laying down norms to promote the eventual opening-up of those economies, and their energy sectors, to external exploitation, and to thus promote access for the industries of the developed European economies to the energy resources in those economies.[65] In that sense, with such ostensible foundational links to the EU, the ECT regime presents an inherent bias towards EU industrial and energy interests.[66] Whilst there is legal equality between ECT parties, the fact that their economies are so disparate means that the benefits of ECT

---

[62] 34 ILM 360 (1995). The official historiography is contained in the *Final Act of the European Energy Charter Conference*. For the official account, see *Final Act of the European Energy Charter Conference (Lisbon, 1994*) in *The Energy Charter Treaty and Related Documents: A Legal Framework for International Energy Cooperation* (Brussels: Energy Charter Secretariat, 2004) at pp. 23–24.

[63] The Energy Charter Process is a forum to exchange best practices with third parties and refers to all Energy-Charter-related activities.

[64] See Wälde, T. *The Energy Charter Treaty: An East-West Gateway for Investment and Trade* (London: Kluwer Law International, 1996) for a fuller analysis on the ECT, its history, and for a more critical perspective.

[65] Ibid.

[66] For an account of the European Energy Charter, the Energy Charter Treaty, and its relationship to the EU from an EU perspective, see http://

membership – such as investment protection in the energy sectors – are likely to accrue in an asymmetric manner that favors those economies with developed energy exploration (upstream) sectors. The European Communities is a foundational *sui juris* party to the ECT, as are those EU Member States that were part of the European Communities at the time of the ECT's adoption.[67]

Currently, there are 54 ECT signatories (including each EU Member State and the EU in its own right), out of which four ratifications are still pending (Australia, Belarus, Iceland, and Norway).[68] Russia signed the ECT and was applying it provisionally until 18 October 2009, but has not ratified it, arguably because it was concerned about the potential loss of its monopoly access to its vast domestic pipeline network that ratification – and thereby subjection to the non-discrimination principle – would entail.[69] Russia notified the Energy Charter Secretariat that it would withdraw from the ECT's provisional application from that date.[70] This has implications for EU energy interests, given the volume of EU-bound energy flows from Russia. Russia's unwillingness to ratify the ECT, combined with the non-participation of other major economies such as the United States and China, arguably significantly undercuts the ECT's effectiveness in a globally accepted energy framework, from an EU standpoint and from the standpoint of other Western energy-importing economies.[71]

---

europa.eu/legislation_summaries/energy/external_dimension_enlargement/l27028_en.htm

67 See for background, http://eur-lex.europa.eu/LexUriServ/LexUriServ.do?uri=CELEX:31998D0181:EN:HTML

68 Energy Charter Secretariat, 'Members and Observers, available at http://www.encharter.org/index.php?id=61

69 Talseth, L.-C. U. 'The EU-Russia Energy Dialogue: Travelling Without Moving' (Working Paper FG 5, German Institute for International and Security Affairs, April 2012) 8; for the exact order by which Russia expressed its intention to discontinue its observance of the ECT, see Government Ordinance 1055-r issued by Prime Minister Putin on July 30 2009; see also generally Belyi, A. 'Russia's Position on the Energy Charter' (Chatham House, April 2012).

70 See http://www.encharter.org/index.php?id=61 in relation to membership, pending ratifications, and the Russian position, and http://www.encharter.org/fileadmin/user_upload/document/ECT_ratification_status.pdf for details of ratification.

71 Belyi, A. 'Energy Charter Treaty: Attempting Multilateralism in Energy' (e-International Relations, July 2013), http://www.e-ir.info/2013/07/02/energy-charter-treaty-attempting-multilateralism-in-energy-2/

ECT parties that have ratified may withdraw after the conclusion of the first five years following ratification.[72] Additionally, ECT parties that had ratified before communicating their intention to withdraw from the ECT remain bound by ECT investment protection obligations for a further 20 years following withdrawal.[73] For those parties who have signed but not ratified the ECT – as in the case of Russia – it is possible to withdraw within a shorter timeframe – namely 60 calendar days.[74]

Whilst the ECT expressly asserts state sovereignty over natural resources[75] – itself a *truism* under international law[76] – it provides robust protection for investor interests in the territories of ECT parties.[77] It does so by entrenching a legal right to compensation in cases where an ECT party carries out an expropriation or otherwise compromises investor interests in some legally significant manner. The ECT does not necessarily obligate its parties to liberalize their energy markets, it does not mandate inward flows of foreign investment, and it does not obligate its parties to provide energy exploitation contracts to *all* ECT parties on a non-discriminatory basis.[78] However, it does provide disciplines that

---

72 Article 47 ECT.

73 Ibid.

74 Article 45(3)(a) ECT.

75 Article 18 ECT.

76 See Sornarajah, M. *The International Law on Foreign Investment* (Cambridge: Cambridge University Press, 2nd ed., 2004), where Sornarajah refers to the notion of permanent sovereignty over natural resources (PSNR) as: '[merely] assert[ing] *a truism* in international law that the sovereignty of a State includes control over all persons, incidents, and substances within a State unless such control has been removed by treaty' (at p. 43, emphasis added) – in other words, there must be previous State consent for any erosion of PSNR.

77 See Part III ECT (Articles 10 to 17), which exclusively deals with obligations to protect foreign investment, thus elevating investor *interests* to legally protected *rights* flowing from the ECT. These include the right to compensation (Article 12(2) ECT), which embeds the *Hull formula* of compensation – i.e., that it be 'prompt, adequate, and efficient', named after Cordell Hull, the US Secretary of State in 1938, who articulated the US's position in relation to the expropriations carried out by the Mexican State during the Mexican Revolution of 1910. The ECT also heavily restricts sovereign rights of expropriation so that expropriations may be permissible to the extent they are ECT-compliant (Article 13 ECT).

78 See *Final Act of the European Energy Charter Conference (Lisbon, 1994)*, Part IV (Understandings), in *The Energy Charter Treaty and Related Documents: A Legal Framework for International Energy Cooperation* (Brussels: Energy Charter Secretariat, 2004) at p. 25.

benefit energy-sector investment interests once these have been welcomed by ECT parties into their territory. In sum, once investments take place within ECT party territories, ECT parties must provide indiscriminate treatment to foreign investors (in other words, they must treat all as if they were investors from their 'most favored nation'), and must not discriminate between foreign and domestic investors (in other words, they must provide 'national treatment' to foreign investors).

B. The Energy Community and its Relationship to the EU

The Energy Community (EnC) is a treaty-based regime set up under the Energy Community Treaty (EnCT) whose signatories include the EU and several third-party States. It is not an EU institution, despite the fact that it inducts various parts of the EU's *acquis communautaire* into the EnC's legal order. Unlike the Energy Charter, which is an independent, international organization, the EnC is a regional EU platform oriented at the creation of an integrated energy market in South-East Europe (SEE).[79] The Treaty establishing the Energy Community was signed in October 2005 by the European Community and nine countries from SEE,[80] with the objective of creating 'a single energy market, including the coordination of mutual assistance in case of serious disturbances to the energy network or external disruptions, and which may include the achievement of a common external energy trade policy'.[81] This was to be achieved by the Contracting Parties in two primary ways. First, the Parties were to adopt the *acquis communitaire* in a number of areas,[82] including energy, environment, competition, electricity, gas, oil, and renewables.[83] And

---

[79] Council Decision (2006/500/EC) on the conclusion by the European Community of the Energy Community Treaty (2006), at p. 15.

[80] Energy Community, 'About the Treaty', available at http://www.energy-community.org/portal/page/portal/ENC_HOME/ENERGY_COMMUNITY/Legal/About_the_Treaty

[81] Karova, R. 'Energy Community for South Eastern Europe: Rationale Behind and Implementation to Date' (EUI Working Papers RSCAS 2009/12, Robert Schuman Centre for Advanced Studies, 2009) 10.

[82] European Commission, 'Report from the Commission to the European Parliament and the Council under Article 7 of Decision 2006/500/EC (Energy Community Treaty)' COM(2011) 105 final.

[83] For details, see European Community, 'Energy Community Acquis', available at http://www.energy-community.org/portal/page/portal/ENC_HOME/ENERGY_COMMUNITY/Legal/EU_Legislation

second, the Parties were to ensure compliance with a set of 'generally acceptable standards' of the EU.[84]

Currently, the EnC extends to nine parties – the EU, on the one hand, and Albania, Bosnia & Herzegovina, Kosovo,[85] the Former Yugoslav Republic of Macedonia, Moldova, Montenegro, Serbia, and Ukraine,[86] on the other. Georgia, Turkey, Armenia, and Norway have EnC observer status.[87] The EnC came into existence in 2006 and has initially been designed to last for ten years – up to its expiry in 2016.[88] Following the EnC's expiry, parties to the EnCT may unanimously extend its duration

---

[84] Title II, Chapter VI of the Treaty establishing the Energy Community.

[85] Kosovo's status under international law is unsettled. The administrative region commonly referred to as Kosovo has been a territory within the Yugoslav Republic and, subsequently, within Serbia. The United Nations' (UN) Security Council, under Resolution 1244 of 10 June 1999, established the UN Interim Administration Mission in Kosovo (UNMIK) in order to provide an interim administration for Kosovo under which its people could enjoy substantial autonomy. The UN Security Council vested UNMIK with authority over the territory and people of Kosovo, including all legislative and executive powers and administration of the judiciary. Since then, Kosovo authorities declared independence (15 June 2008), which was recognized by a majority of UN members. However, this move was not unanimously endorsed by the UN Security Council, which leaves the status of Kosovo unsettled under international law. Currently, Kosovo is listed as neither a UN permanent member nor as a UN observer.

[86] Ukraine is a highly energy-significant state regarding EU energy inflows from Russia. In 2011, the EU Commission made a series of policy recommendations to the EU Council and Parliament aimed at the speedy integration of Ukraine into the EnC, including through tripartite political and administrative cooperation between the EU, Russia, and Ukraine, to ensure steady relations in light of gas price and supply disputes between Russia and Ukraine, which had implications for EU energy security. See the 2011 EU Commission Communication to the European Parliament, the Council, the European Economic and Social Committee, and the Committee of the Regions, *On Security of Energy Supply and International Cooperation – 'The EU Energy Policy: Engaging with Partners Beyond Our Borders'*, 7 September 2011 (COM(2011) 539 final) (at p. 5).

[87] This is possible under Article 96 EnCT, although all EnC members must consent to this through the Ministerial Council, which governs the EnC. It is also possible for EU Member States to participate in this organization as 'participants' rather than members (as is the EU) as per Articles 1§2 and 95 EnCT. Presently, Austria, Bulgaria, Cyprus, Greece, and the UK, conceivably due to their bordering and energy-transit significant geographic positioning, participate in EnC meetings with this status.

[88] For an EU account of the EnC, see http://europa.eu/legislation_summaries/energy/external_dimension_enlargement/l27074_en.htm

or, where there is no unanimity, may extend it for those parties that are in favor of doing so, so long as two-thirds of the parties support this.[89]

The EnC could be seen as a uni-sectoral 'integration without membership'[90] arrangement. The effect of the EnC is that parties are legally obligated to apply certain areas of the EU *acquis communautaire*[91] as a means of setting up an institutional, legal, and economic framework aimed at integrating the energy landscapes across the territories to which the EnC extends.[92] Regulatory convergence and investment protection seem to be key features of the EnC, which aims at integrating the gas and electricity markets among EnC parties to whatever extent may be politically possible. In this manner, the EnC can be seen as extending the EU's IEM with those EnC members that have not become EU members.

The EU, for its part, is inextricably linked to the EnC.[93] It was the EU – an original signatory – who proposed the EnC. EU interests are represented in both of the EnC decision-making bodies set up under the EnCT (namely the 'Ministerial Council'[94] and the 'Permanent High Level Group')[95] at a higher rate than those of ordinary EnC members.

The EnC could be used to further promote EU energy interests with third-party (i.e., non-EU members) States. One means of doing so is through the EU's trade relations. For instance, the EU Commission has

---

[89] Ibid.

[90] See Petrov, R. 'Energy Community as a Promoter of the European Union's "Energy Acquis" to its Neighbourhood' (2012) *Legal Issues of Economic Integration*, Vol. 38, No. 3.

[91] See Title II of the EnCT. The EU energy *acquis* and the EU environment *acquis* are inducted into the EnCT legal order (see Chapters II and III, respectively), whilst Chapters IV and V of the EnCT contain provisions on the effect of the EU renewable energy *acquis* and EU competition *acquis*, respectively, on the EnCT legal order. The EnC permits staggered implementation. For instance, Moldova is doing so in four successive stages, Ukraine in five.

[92] Article 2 EnCT.

[93] See Council Decision of 29 May 2006 on the conclusion by the European Community of the Energy Community Treaty (2006/500/EC), which spells out the level of the EU's involvement and influence in the EnC.

[94] Article 48 EnCT: 'The Ministerial Council shall consist of one representative of each Contracting Party and *two representatives of the European Community*. One non-voting representative of each Participant may participate in its meetings' (emphasis added).

[95] Article 54 EnCT: 'The Permanent High Level Group shall consist of one representative of each Contracting Party *and two representatives of the European Community*' (emphasis added).

recommended that free trade agreements with third-party States neighboring the EU be used as a means of promoting EU energy interests.[96] What is more, the EU Commission has stated that the EnC should be promoted with geographically proximate and energy-significant third-party States that are currently negotiating or concluding an FTA with the EU.[97]

The advent of the EnC could also be seen as a less idealistic way of integrating neighboring states into the EU's sphere of economic influence, without the conditionality and strings that come with full EU membership; conditionality regarding minimum standards for EU Member States in relation to civil, political, and social rights. All these issues are generally bypassed – despite arguably a very clear mandate in primary EU legislation against this[98] – by drawing neighboring States into economic relations via means such as the EnC that advance EU energy interests without alienating the economic and political elites in

---

[96] See Communication from the Commission to the European Parliament, the Council, the European Economic and Social Committee, and the Committee of the Regions, *On Security of Energy Supply and International Cooperation – 'The EU Energy Policy: Engaging with Partners Beyond Our Borders'*, Brussels, 7 September 2011 (COM(2011) 539 final) (at p. 7). Note also that the EU already has a series of complementary and targeted frameworks, ranging from specific energy provisions in bilateral agreements with third countries (Free Trade Agreements, Partnership and Cooperation Agreements, Association Agreements, etc.) to Memoranda of Understanding on energy cooperation. The EU is currently negotiating new agreements with several third-party States, which will contain important energy provisions. See Communication from the Commission to the European Parliament, the Council, the European Economic and Social Committee, and the Committee of the Regions, 'Energy 2020: A Strategy for Competitive, Sustainable and Secure Energy', Brussels, 10 November 2010 (COM(2010) 639 final) (p. 19). See also a list of energy-related treaties concluded between the EU and third-party states at http://ec.europa.eu/world/agreements/searchByActivity.do?parent=8512&xmlname=751&actName=Energy&printAcrivity=

[97] Communication from the Commission to the European Parliament, the Council, the European Economic and Social Committee, and the Committee of the Regions, *On Security of Energy Supply and International Cooperation – 'The EU Energy Policy: Engaging with Partners Beyond Our Borders'*, Brussels, 7 September 2011, COM(2011) 539 final (at p. 7).

[98] See Article 21.1 of the Treaty on European Union (TEU), which refers to the guiding principles that must frame EU action. According to Article 21 TEU, EU external action is subject to guiding principles such as: 'democracy, the rule of law, the universality and indivisibility of human rights and fundamental freedoms, respect for human dignity, the principles of equality and solidarity, and respect for the principles of the United Nations Charter and international law'.

those third-party States through any EU demands for social reform in their territories.

Despite the Energy Community being lauded as a 'success story'[99] by the European Commission, numerous challenges have been identified. The most significant of these relate to the failure of many Contracting Parties to fully implement the *acquis* and ensure the enforcement of the rules thereof.[100] Another concern has been the lack of sufficient investment to foster the infrastructure modernization required for the proper implementation of a number of EU directives and policies.[101] In other terms, there has been a discernible discord between the not unimpressive form and content of the Energy Community Treaty and its actual implementation at the national level. Thus, while there has been limited progress for the Contracting Parties of the Energy Community, it has been far below expectations at the time of formation. Even the European Commission acknowledged in a 2011 report that the Energy Community's 'ultimate ambition – integration into the EU's internal energy market – seems, for the time being, just a long-term objective'.[102]

V. DISPUTE SETTLEMENT IN THE ENERGY CHARTER TREATY AND IN THE ENERGY COMMUNITY

A. Dispute Settlement in the Energy Charter Treaty

Dispute resolution within the ECT regime would vary depending on the nexus of parties to a particular dispute and/or the subject matter of the dispute. In relation to the nexus of disputants, dispute resolution is differentiated depending on whether the dispute involves a State against another State or an investor against a State. There are separate dispute resolution regimes for interstate disputes and investor-State disputes, as there are for disputes over investment, trade, transit, or environmental or competition matters.

---

99 COM(2011) 105 final, p. 3.

100 Ibid. pp. 5–6.

101 Ibid. Also see e.g. World Bank, 'Lights Out? The Outlook for Energy in Eastern Europe and the Former Soviet Union' (World Bank, 2010), available at http://siteresources.worldbank.org/ECAEXT/Resources/258598-1268240913359/Full_report.pdf

102 COM(2011) 105 final 5.

In relation to *interstate* disputes, Article 27 ECT provides for an arbitration procedure for disputes regarding the interpretation or application of the Treaty (except for competition and environmental issues). In relation to *State-investor/investor-State* disputes,[103] Article 26 ECT provides various options at the discretion of *investors* on how to seek redress, including the option of taking host governments to international arbitration in relation to complaints about investment protection.[104] In relation to *trade-related* disputes, Article 29 and Annex D of the ECT include a mechanism – closely based on the World Trade Organization's (WTO) Dispute Settlement System – for settling trade disputes between ECT parties, where at least one of them is not a WTO member; otherwise, the ECT defers to the WTO's dispute resolution regime all trade-related disputes between ECT parties who are also WTO members. The fact of deferring disputes to other more appropriate fora – in this case the WTO's dispute settlement mechanism – is an important element of dispute resolution within the ECT order.[105] In relation to disputes involving *transit matters*, Article 7 ECT provides for a specialized conciliation mechanism (Article 7(7) ECT) which aims to expedite dispute resolution and to make the process less formal.

Finally, in relation to competition and environmental issues, these engage Articles 6 and 19 ECT, respectively, which contain sub-clauses promoting dispute resolution through diplomatic processes. Article 6(7) makes clear that complaints based on competition matters are to be

---

[103] Traditionally, disputes have been investor-State, where the State was the defendant. However, more recently, we are seeing State-investor disputes, where the State is the plaintiff. For a list of disputes registered at the International Center for the Settlement of Investment Disputes (ICSID), see https://icsid.worldbank.org/ICSID/FrontServlet

[104] Investor-State disputes under Part III of the ECT are governed by Article 26 ECT, which gives the choice to investors, following a three-month cooling-off period, to initiate resolution proceedings by submitting the dispute: (a) to the courts or administrative tribunals of the host state party to the dispute; (b) in accordance with a previously agreed dispute settlement procedure; or (c) to international arbitration. If the investor opts for international arbitration, the investor has the further choice between arbitration under the rules of the ICSID, the United Nations Commission on International Trade Law (UNCITRAL), or the Arbitration Institute of the Stockholm Chamber of Commerce. In effect, therefore, States give their unconditional consent under Article 26(3) ECT to the submission of a dispute to international arbitration, given that the choice lies with investors.

[105] See Article 4 ECT, which prohibits derogation from the GATT, while Annex G of the ECT conditions how WTO rules are discharged between ECT parties.

resolved diplomatically wherever possible, according to Articles 6(5) and 27(1) ECT, rather than through international arbitration or some other binding adjudicative process. Regarding complaints based on environmental issues, Article 19(2) ECT defers their resolution to whatever applicable international fora may exist and, in the absence of such fora, the complaint may be referred to the ECT diplomatic body, namely the Charter Conference.

In sum, *interstate* disputes are outside the remit of binding adjudicative processes, as there is a clear preference for bilateral solutions and for conciliation based on multilateral practices, thus underlying the need for international standards and multilateralism. It is not surprising that diplomatic – as opposed to independent adjudicative – means of resolving interstate disputes are popular among states, given that these preserve important sovereign prerogatives and are also more amenable to the promotion of voluntarist multilateralism. In that sense, an adjudicative-*lite* ECT may be more legitimate in the minds of its parties and, consequently, more enduring than some other special regime with a more robust supranational adjudicative agency. That said, however, complaints brought by investors are dealt with in a more robust – from an investor standpoint – manner given that, as we have seen above, it is within the prerogative of investors to choose how an *investor-State* dispute should be addressed.[106]

Under Article 26 ECT, unconditional state consent to international arbitration-based resolution appears to be the norm, despite the two exceptions to a State's unconditional consent to arbitration under Article 26(3)(a) ECT.[107] In fact, there are about 30 investor-State international

---

[106] See Article 26 ECT.

[107] Annex ID-related exception: States listed under Annex ID of the ECT do not give unconditional consent to international arbitration in cases where the investor has already submitted the dispute to a national court or tribunal (cf., Article 26.2.a ECT) or to a previously agreed mechanism (cf., Article 26.2.b ECT). States listed under Annex ID must provide a written statement of policies, practices and conditions to the ECT Secretariat. Annex ID States are: Australia, Azerbaijan, Bulgaria, Canada, Croatia, Cyprus, the Czech Republic, the EU, Finland, Greece, Hungary, Ireland, Italy, Japan, Kazakhstan, Mongolia, Norway, Poland, Portugal, Romania, Russia, Slovenia, Spain, Sweden, Macedonia, Turkey, and the USA. Note, however, that neither Canada nor the USA has signed the ECT. Annex IA-related exceptions: States listed under Annex IA do not give unconditional consent with respect to a dispute arising under the last sentence of Article 10(1) ('umbrella clause'). Annex IA States are: Australia, Canada, Hungary, and Norway.

arbitration cases[108] under the ECT of which the Energy Charter Secretariat is aware, whilst there is one *interstate* case known (to the Energy Charter Secretariat) that was ultimately resolved diplomatically.[109]

Finally, there is no inherent (to the ECT special regime) adjudicative agency in the sense that one exists within the EU legal order (cf., the Court of Justice of the European Union (CJEU)), or which, to an extent, exists within the WTO with its Dispute Settlement Body (DSB). What the ECT provides for, however – particularly in *investor-State* disputes – is, among other things, recourse to international arbitration – that is to say, to an agency extraneous to the ECT-related institutional framework that has been invested with adjudicative competence. That said, the ECT-related bodies such as the Energy Charter Secretariat do not, in any way, manage or handle disputes.[110]

B. Dispute Settlement in the Energy Community

The Treaty Establishing the Energy Community (EnCT) sets up a dispute settlement mechanism (DSM) under Articles 90 to 93. This DSM is closely modeled on the EU's 'infringement procedure', that is to say, the process to challenge and to ultimately correct EU law infringements committed by EU Member States.[111] However, the EnC dispute settlement process and the EU's infringement procedure diverge on an

---

[108] See http://www.encharter.org/index.php?id=213 for a list of the investor-State arbitration cases known to the Energy Charter Secretariat.

[109] See http://www.encharter.org/index.php?id=269

[110] See the following link http://www.encharter.org/index.php?id=213&L=0, where the Energy Charter Secretariat states that: '… there is no requirement that such disputes be notified to the Secretariat, nor is the Secretariat involved in the administration of the investor-state dispute settlement procedure. The information below was compiled from various public sources, and includes links to publicly available documents; while the Secretariat has made efforts to ensure that this information is reliable, its accuracy and completeness cannot be guaranteed'.

[111] EU Member States are responsible for applying EU law. This responsibility involves the adoption of domestic measures by a specified deadline in order to incorporate EU law into their respective legal systems. Where a Member State fails to do this correctly or in time, this is deemed an EU law *infringement*, be it due to an action or an omission on the part of an EU Member State. Under the relevant Treaties (Article 258 TFEU and Article 106a of the Treaty establishing the European Atomic Energy Community), the EU Commission is responsible for ensuring that EU law is correctly applied and has powers to mandate EU Member States to take corrective action. The EU Commission also has powers to refer an EU Member State's infringement to the CJEU. For a fuller exposition of

important point: there is no recourse to a traditional *adjudicative* agency that could lead to a *judicial* decision within the EnC's dispute settlement regime. Instead, what we have within the EnC's DSM is recourse to a diplomatic forum to render what appears to ultimately remain a diplomatic decision. This forum is the EnC's 'Ministerial Council,' a body charged with finding whether there has been a breach of the EnCT and with deciding on how such a breach ought to be rectified.[112]

Furthermore, an Advisory Committee (a team of three lawyers) exists as an adjunct to the Ministerial Council whose role is to prepare reasoned opinions on alleged breaches of EnC obligations (similar to how, within the context of the EU, the Advocates-General discharge their duties towards the CJEU). Moreover, the Ministerial Council has a quasi-judicial role in relation to issues of interpretation in certain circumstances.[113] Those who may petition the Ministerial Council for a determination are: any party to the EnCT, the EnC's 'Regulatory Board', and its 'Secretariat'.[114] Serious and persistent breaches of EnCT obligations may incur penalties such as the suspension of EnC member rights. A 2008 Decision[115] by the (EnC) Ministerial Council further added flesh

---

the infringement procedure and the role of the EU Commission, see http://ec.europa.eu/eu_law/infringements/infringements_en.htm

[112] See generally TITLE VII of the EnCT, Implementation of Decisions and Dispute Settlement, Articles 89–93.

[113] Under Article 94 EnCT, the 'Ministerial Council' and, on occasion, the 'Permanent High Level Group' exercise quasi-judicial functions in interpreting terms or concepts in the EnCT where there is no EU jurisprudence to assist with interpreting these.

[114] See Articles 90 and 92 EnCT.

[115] See Procedural Act No. 2008/01/MG-EnC of the Ministerial Council of the Energy Community, 27 June 2008, on the Rules of Procedure for Dispute Settlement under the Treaty, available at http://www.energy-community.org/pls/portal/docs/296193.PDF. This preliminary procedure is normally handled by the Secretariat as 'an independent institution being in a position to clarify the factual and legal circumstances of each case'. Under such circumstances, the Secretariat will initiate a case by way of an *Opening Letter* (see Article 12, 2008 Ministerial Council Decision) to be followed, as the case may be, by a *Reasoned Opinion* (Article 13, 2008 Ministerial Council Decision) and a *Reasoned Request* to the Ministerial Council. In the course of this three-step procedure, the offending party is given the opportunity to argue its case and to justify its measure or, to 'comply of its own accord with the requirements of the Treaty' before the complaint is submitted to the Ministerial Council (under Article 14, 2008 Ministerial Council Decision). As the Secretariat may be approached by private bodies for it to espouse their complaints, the procedural rules introduced by the 2008 Ministerial Council Decision also contain provisions that govern that

to the bones of the somewhat minimal provisions of the EnC's DSM regime by elaborating more detailed rules. The contribution of these rules has been to introduce preliminary procedures before complaints reach the Ministerial Council.

From a comparative perspective, the EnC's diplomatic element, as reflected in the Ministerial Council, stands in for the adjudicative element often encountered in other legal orders – such as in the EU (with the possibility, say, of recourse to the CJEU) or even in the WTO system (where, despite its own DSB's diplomatic-judicial hybrid character, there are adjudicative organs that make judicial determinations).[116] That said, certain areas of the EU's *acquis communautaire* are also the *acquis* of the EnC.[117] Therefore, we see the induction of discreet *corpora* of law from an extraneous legal order – namely from that of the EU – into another particular legal order – namely into the EnC's. Whilst this allows no *systemic* role for the CJEU *per se* in the EnC legal order, by directly inducting its energy (and parts of other) *acquis* jurisprudence, the CJEU becomes, in effect, an influential adjudicative agency *for* the EnC, albeit one that is extraneous and whose activity is restricted to other jurisdictional realms.[118]

---

avenue for complaints. For a summary of the EnC's DSM, see http://www.energy-community.org/portal/page/portal/ENC_HOME/AREAS_OF_WORK/Dispute_Settlement.

116 Namely the 'Panel' and, if Panel findings are appealed, the 'Appellate Body', which is charged with making determinations that are then issued in reports to be ultimately considered for adoption by the WTO's DSB.

117 See Title II of the EnCT. The EU energy *acquis* and the EU environment *acquis* are inducted into the EnCT legal order (see Chapters II and III, respectively), whilst Chapters IV and V EnCT contain provisions on the effect of the EU competition *acquis* and EU renewable energy *acquis*, respectively, to the EnCT legal order.

118 Namely to the jurisdictions of the EU and the European Atomic Energy Community (Euratom). The CJEU is the adjudicative institution of the EU (see Articles 13 and 19 TEU; Article 251 TFEU) and Euratom (see Article 144 of the Consolidated version of the Euratom Treaty). The CJEU is also an adjudicative institution for the European Economic Area (EEA) in relation to the EU Member States involved in the EEA, *but not* for Iceland, Liechtenstein, and Norway (which, while EEA parties, are not EU Member States), for whom the European Free Trade Agreement (EFTA) Court has jurisdiction in relation to cases involving any of those three countries. In relation to the EFTA Court, see Articles 105–108 of the Agreement on the European Economic Area.

VI. CERTAIN ISSUES RELATING TO CONCURRENT SPECIAL LEGAL REGIMES

A. General Remarks

The EU foundational treaties, the ECT and the EnCT create legal relations between their respective sovereign State parties and, in the case of the EU treaties and the EnCT, between the parties *inter se* and between each party and the EU, and between each party and the EnC; to the exclusion of third-party States. All three regimes – the EU, the ECT, and the EnC – are instances of particular international law predicated on general international law in order to function.[119] They depend on the broader normative framework that is general international law, given that the latter is dispositive of a wide range of State acts and interstate situations, including the contracting of interstate agreements that create legal relations (or that have other legal implications) and the setting-up of supranational legal orders. We could understand the relevance of general international law to such interstate and supra-State processes through viewing public international law as an institution that initially arose due to the necessity to regulate the inter-action between *imperia*,[120] and, as such, it persists in recent history to be dispositive of legal questions engaging state sovereignty and state responsibility.

Here we shall focus on the ECT and EnCT. Both these instruments involve parties that, for the most part, are also United Nations (UN) members and that – setting aside their other incidental *inter se* diplomatic relations – are already involved with each other in all manner of legal relations, be these treaty-based or otherwise. In that sense, a broader normative context comes to apply to all these states, both jointly and severally. Unsurprisingly, normative conflicts (that is to say, conflicts between concurrent norms, be these in relation to rules or principles, within a single legal regime but flowing from different instruments, or between norms flowing from different legal regimes) and/or conflicts of

---

[119] Should all parties concerned in contracting an interstate legal agreement have previously ratified the Vienna Convention on the Law of Treaties (VCLT) 1969, then the functioning of any such agreement would also be predicated on the provisions of the VCLT 1969.

[120] See, among others, Anghie, A. *Imperialism, Sovereignty, and the Making of International Law* (Cambridge: Cambridge University Press, 2007); and Mieville, C. *Between Equal Rights: A Marxist Theory of International Law* (Leiden: Brill, 2005).

jurisdiction are neither uncommon nor unheard of in complex networks of international obligation.[121]

1. Fragmentation of international law as it relates to normative conflicts

'International' law *per se* is not a phenomenon that is necessarily conceptualized, applied, or otherwise countenanced, in a consistent and coherent manner, not least due to the fact that international law itself is not some homogenous monolithic entity. Rather, it is a broad construct/artifact encompassing instances of 'law' that cannot be appositely paralleled to 'law' as it is encountered and perhaps understood to function within domestic legal orders. International law encompasses instances of 'law' ranging from those which are cumbersomely enforceable and/or patchily enforced, to those that operate as part of special legal regimes, aided by appropriate agencies of adjudication and enforcement (cf., the EU legal order). However, this is certainly not to say that international law is some random or inconsequential collection of rules. As we shall see below, there are important interrelationships at play between norms,[122] and it is the task of jurists and practitioners to tease these out effectively.

In that respect, there is a catalogue of such issues present in the international legal system – including the lack of universal/central adjudicative and enforcement agencies, the disparity among perceptions over the content, bindingness, and application of norms, as well as the expanding diversity of areas of modern international law – that have contributed to the perception that the modern international legal system is becoming increasingly fragmented.[123] This fragmentation is essentially a

---

[121] See UN General Assembly, International Law Commission (ILC), 58th session, Geneva (1 May–9 June and 3 July–11 August 2006), Report of the Study Group of the International Law Commission, *Fragmentation of International Law: Difficulties Arising from the Diversification and Expansion of International Law* (A/CN.4/L.682) (13 April 2006), §484, p. 245 and §486, p. 246.

[122] See Conclusion 1, International Law Commission Study Group on fragmentation, as it appears in the General Assembly, Official Records, Sixty-first session Supplement No. 10 (A/61/10), *Report of the International Law Commission, Fifty-eighth Session* (1 May–9 June and 3 July–11 August 2006) (at §251, p. 400).

[123] In fact, fragmentation is such a concern that the International Law Commission, at its fifty-fourth session (2002), decided to include the topic 'Risks ensuing from fragmentation of international law' in its program of work and to establish a Study Group to examine this. For an introduction to the ILC's program of work in relation to fragmentation, see General Assembly, Official

corollary of interstate cooperation in the modern era. While this high degree of specialization in the modern international legal system is, on the one hand, necessary to handle specific issues, it may, on the other hand, cause efforts focused on specific issues to diverge from one another, thus leading to persistent perceptions and instances of incoherence.[124] Given that this degree of specialization and consequent fragmentation seems to be an artifact of the successive development of international law, the desire for coherence across the international legal system may appear somewhat idealistic.[125]

Notwithstanding whatever fragmentation may exist, there is a tool-kit of juridical techniques at the disposal of jurists and law practitioners to help overcome normative conflicts, or at least resolve them in such a way that there is juridical integrity. Such techniques and tools can be found at both the *general international law* level and, often, when provision has been made, at the *particular international law* level within the special legal regimes themselves. These tools, by helping address normative conflicts, contribute towards greater coherence among the 'impressive federation of special areas'[126] that is the modern system of international law.

For the most part, ECT and EnCT parties are UN members. The UN legal order contains a most helpful tool to address such normative conflicts that engage a norm flowing from the UN legal order or the UN legal order *per se*: namely Article 103 of the UN Charter, which promotes obligations owed by UN members under the Charter over their other international obligations, should a conflict arise. From an international law (and UN) standpoint, where a dispute involves a State that is

---

Records, Sixty-first Session Supplement No. 10 (A/61/10), *Report of the International Law Commission, Fifty-eighth Session* (1 May–9 June and 3 July–11 August 2006) (at p. 400).

[124] See the ILC Report of the Study Group, *Fragmentation of International Law: Difficulties Arising from the Diversification and Expansion of International Law* (A/CN.4/L.682) (13 April 2006). Also see, Jenks, C.W. 'The Conflict of Law-Making Treaties' (1953) *British Yearbook of International Law*, Vol. 30, at p. 403.

[125] For an exposition of the phenomenon of fragmentation and the risks it poses, see Kuijper, P.-J. 'Conflicting Rules and Clashing Courts: The Case of Multilateral Environmental Agreements, Free Trade Agreements and the WTO', Issue Paper No. 10 (2010) (Geneva: International Centre for Trade and Sustainable Development).

[126] See Brownlie, I. 'The Rights of Peoples in Modern International Law', in Crawford, J. (ed.) *The Rights of Peoples* (Oxford: Clarendon Press, 1988) at p. 14.

also a UN member, any potential deadlock between, on the one hand, a UN Charter-based obligation, and, on the other, an obligation owed, say, under ECT or EnCT, would have to be resolved in favor of the former. Also, another feature of the international legal system is the notion that when any given norm comes into conflict with some peremptory norm (*jus cogens*), the latter shall always prevail.

2. Legal hierarchies in addressing normative conflicts

Such degree of practicability and straightforwardness (as expressed through Article 103 of the UN Charter and the paramountcy of *jus cogens* norms) is not necessarily encountered in every instance of normative conflict, which is often why we must resort to the most universal setting – namely general international law – to identify the key features of the meta-normative regime, and what kind of tie-breaking features this meta-normative regime may contain. Thus, the question remains: what happens where there is no tie-breaker, such as Article 103 of the UN Charter, or no conflict with a peremptory norm within a particular international law order, such as a special legal regime (as are the EU, the EnC, and the ECT) to help unlock normative tensions of this nature?

Evidently, a useful response to a similar question that involves a *known* nexus of identifiable states (or other relevant entities for the purposes of international law) would begin by identifying the applicable normative context(s) linked to those states or entities; normative contexts founded on an interplay between norms flowing from peremptory or other norms of general international law, from norms flowing from relevant (to the nexus of entities) international conventions, or from other sources of international law.[127] In that sense, invariably, recourse to broader normative frameworks would be necessary, given that the normative conflict (or

---

[127] For an illustrative list of the sources of norms to be taken into consideration from a UN legal order standpoint, see the Statute of the International Court of Justice (ICJ), and in particular Article 38. Article 38 states the ICJ *shall* apply: international legal instruments – be they general or particular – that establish rules expressly recognized by the States in question to have a binding effect on them; the imprecise field of international custom as illustrative of what may be considered – erroneously or not – by States to be general practice mandated by law under the circular notion of *opinio juris sive necessitatis*; and the general principles of law recognized by *civilized* nations – a further imprecise and controversial normative context. The ICJ may also have regard to, but is not bound by, its previous decisions (and of its predecessor, the Permanent Court of International Justice) given that *stare decisis* is expressly excluded under Article 59, ICJ Statute. It may also have regard to: 'the teachings of the most highly qualified publicists of the various nations …' which potentially injects some

conflict of jurisdictions) may involve norms that flow from peremptory (*jus cogens*) or other *erga omnes* norms of general international law. This inherent hierarchy in the international legal system[128] means that, where such peremptory or other *erga omnes* norms exist at the general level, such norms may operate to resolve an otherwise intractable normative conflict. The point is to identify the types of universal *erga omnes* norms that apply in such cases in the absence of applicable particular international law conflict-resolving norms or in the event that such norms do indeed exist but where reliance upon these would lead to an unfair and solipsistic outcome not in line with international law.

While we shall outline below the sort of juridical tools and techniques that help unlock normative conflicts, we posit that it is neither a lack nor ignorance of these tools that is at the center of intractable normative conflicts; rather, it is the fact that legal disputes among States (or between States and other international entities) are rarely addressed before an adjudicative agent invested with the necessary breadth of authority/jurisdiction, or that possesses an all-encompassing omniscient gaze to make such a body likely to reach the kind of coherent determinations that draw from *all* relevant elements of the entire *corpus* of international law.[129] The closest we come to that is probably when interstate disputes come before the International Court of Justice (ICJ)

---

dynamism in the adjudicative process given the potential for a plurality of juristic opinion to contribute to the dynamic development of the normative context and for its interpretation. However, previous decisions and the teachings of highly qualified publicists are subsidiary means of identifying legal norms. Furthermore, under Article 38(2), the ICJ may decide a case on an *ex aequo et bono* basis, i.e., according to what it deems to be an equitable outcome, so long as the parties to a dispute before the ICJ expressly agree to such an elastic normative context being deployed in their situation.

[128] No hierarchy exists in relation to the sources of law – e.g., by pitching, say, general principles against norms flowing from some legal agreement. That said, a hierarchy exists between norms – be they found in custom, convention, or elsewhere. A clear example is how peremptory norms (*jus cogens*), UN Charter norms, other *erga omnes* obligations, or acts of the UN Security Council may trump norms flowing from contracted international legal agreements. In that sense, there is no formal hierarchy of normative sources *per se*; rather, there is a substantive hierarchy based on the content of the norms, irrespective of their source provenance. See ILC Report of the Study Group, *Fragmentation of International Law: Difficulties Arising from the Diversification and Expansion of International Law* (A/CN.4/L.682) (13 April 2006), at §85, p. 47.

[129] The independence and the expansiveness-of-purview of the arbiter is a fundamental issue in cohesively resolving normative conflicts involving norms flowing from other regimes. See General Assembly, Official Records, Sixty-first

for a determination.[130] Another example of such a universal omniscient *juristic/scholarly* – albeit not *adjudicative* – gaze would be that of the International Law Commission (ILC).[131] Rather, what we have are determinations – say, within the WTO or the EU – that are based, for the most part, on the objectives of the particular legal agreements that those legal regimes are founded upon. However, there are exceptions where we witness legally coherent determinations that go beyond the objectives of those legal agreements to include norms flowing from other legal agreements that exist in other legal systems, or generally from other normative sources.

When we talk about normative conflicts, we need to begin by making clear where a conflict may arise and what it may involve. Are all the seemingly conflicting norms valid and relevant to the matter in hand and, if so, what is the relationship between the norms in conflict? For instance, this relationship can be one of complementarity or exclusivity. Also, normative conflicts may arise between norms from within one legal instrument, from within different instruments but one legal order, or from within distinct legal orders. However, as we shall see below, no legal order is ever isolated from the broader normative context that an interstate act, event, or situation may engage.

The area of normative conflicts is as complex as the question of fragmentation. In 2006, the ILC Study Group on fragmentation issued its report to the UN General Assembly.[132] This report outlines the various aspects of the complexities surrounding the fragmentation of international law and of normative conflicts, without necessarily being dispositive of these matters. That said, the 2006 ILC report clearly provides an indispensable facility by authoritatively mapping out the conceptual juridical framework with which legal scholars and practitioners may *begin* to understand the phenomena of normative conflicts

---

Session Supplement No. 10 (A/61/10), *Report of the International Law Commission, Fifty-eighth Session* (1 May–9 June and 3 July–11 August 2006), at § 28, pp. 417–418.

[130] However, such an eventuality would likely be due to the operation of particular international law, given that it would likely take place within the context of, and would be pursuant to, the UN Charter and to the Statute of the ICJ.

[131] See ILC Report of the Study Group, *Fragmentation of International Law: Difficulties Arising from the Diversification and Expansion of International Law* (A/CN.4/L.682) (13 April 2006), at p. 255.

[132] ILC Report of the Study Group, *Fragmentation of International Law: Difficulties Arising from the Diversification and Expansion of International Law* (A/CN.4/L.682) (13 April 2006).

and fragmentation in the international legal system. Rather than providing definitive answers, the 2006 ILC report outlines the principal legal techniques that could be enlisted in addressing normative conflicts. In that sense, it provides a *tour d'horizon* of such meta-norms that address the *validity* and *primacy* of conflicting norms and that, generally, promote integration across the international legal system.

The two *inter-normative* relationships (namely the validity of each norm in conflict and the primacy between equally valid conflicting norms) to consider in relation to normative conflicts are: (1) what is the interplay by which one norm modifies another?; and (2) what is the interplay by which one norm trumps another: The Vienna Convention on the Law of Treaties 1969 (VCLT) – an incidence of particular international law, given that it is a treaty-based regime binding *sui juris* only on its signatories – is widely held, for the most part,[133] to mirror analogous norms thought to exist in general international law, namely in custom. This is particularly so in relation to those norms concerned with the interpretation of treaties and their norms. The treaty interpretation provisions of VCLT (Articles 31–33) and, most importantly, their *analogous* in content customary norms, may usefully be enlisted to address questions relating to the interplay of norms and normative conflicts.

3. Principle of harmonization in treaty interpretation

The norms described above (be they situated in VCLT or in custom) require that the interpretation of treaties be done in a manner that promotes integration/harmonization so as to give effect to all relevant aspects of the *broader* normative context that may be at play in relation to the parties in question and the matters at issue; and certainly not in a manner that treats a treaty as if it were in some sort of 'clinical isolation to international law'.[134] In that sense, in relying upon these meta-norms to interpret a norm situated in a treaty, regard must be had to all valid norms that form the broader normative framework applicable to whatever the situation under examination may be. This principle (of *harmonization/systemic integration*) is a fundamental tenet of treaty

[133] This is certainly the view of the ILC's Study Group on fragmentation, particularly with regard to the interpretative rules of VCLT. See Ibid. at § 168, p. 89 and at §198, p. 100. See also the ILC report to the UN General Assembly, *Draft Articles on the Law of Treaties with Commentaries* (1966), for a clause-by-clause analysis.

[134] See the Appellate Body of the WTO's dispute settlement system in *United States – Standards of Reformulated and Conventional Gasoline* (20 May 1996) WT/DS2/AB/R (at pp. 16–17).

interpretation in general international law and has been reflected in instances of particular international law (namely Article 31(3)(c) VCLT). Essentially, it is concerned with giving effect to all normative elements in conflict by seeking to adjust their respective effect to whatever point may *juridically* permit all relevant normative elements to be accommodated.[135]

In fact, the meta-normative principle of systemic integration/ harmonization could be viewed as enshrining the objective of the international legal system for coherence in that it seeks to integrate – not seclude – its various aspects towards coherence. It does this by admitting other parts of international law (applicable to the matter in hand, be these other particular international law instances or general international law) into special regimes to fill in the gaps, provide coherence, and be dispositive or clarificatory of issues that can be settled neither entirely nor appropriately were one to rely solely on the express norms of the special regime in question to resolve arising conflicts. Campbell McLaughlin cites an apposite analogy: namely that the principle of systemic integration functions in the way that a 'master-key' is capable of opening separate chambers in a building.[136] In that sense, the building is the entire normative context and, potentially, the entire *corpus* of international law. Naturally, there are limits to the use of such a principle when, for instance, the conflict involves norms that flow from legal instruments or among legal orders predicated on very different objectives/ policy settings, and where there are no other pointers to how to harmonize/integrate these conflicting norms in a manner that is diplomatically acceptable and, for the purposes of the law, in a manner that does not sacrifice its juridical integrity.

Having recourse to other aspects of the *broader* normative context via the principle of systemic integration is not to say that one has recourse to *extraneous* aspects *per se*. To say such a thing would be to reinforce the misperception that any given treaty is a 'self-contained' isolate, and that when recourse is had to the broader normative framework, somehow one is looking at things *outside* that particular legal regime *per se*. Such a

---

[135] In fact, the ILC Study Group considers that there is a strong preference in interpretative exercises for the avoidance of conflict. See ILC Report of the Study Group, *Fragmentation of International Law: Difficulties Arising from the Diversification and Expansion of International Law* (A/CN.4/L.682) (13 April 2006), at §37, p. 25.

[136] McLachlan, C. 'The Principle of Systemic Integration and Article 31(3)(c) of the Vienna Convention' (2005) *International and Comparative Law Quarterly*, Vol. 54, No. 2, pp. 279–320, at p. 281.

perception is erroneous, not least because all 'self-contained' *particular international law* orders are predicated on general international law and the international legal system in order to function. This, in turn, inducts all relevant (to the parties and the issues at hand) norms so that they are actually part of an integrated normative context which is applicable.

Furthermore, in relation to the question of the *validity* of seemingly conflicting norms, there are other principles at the general international law level (which are also reflected in instances of particular international law) that are concerned with the specificity of norms and with their temporal relationship. Namely those in relation to the maxims *lex specialis derogat legi generali* – i.e., the more particular legal regime trumps the more general legal regime – and *lex posterior derogat legi prior* – i.e., the most recent legal regime trumps the chronologically earlier one. There may be situations where a combination of these two principles is applicable.

In relation to the temporality-related aspects of norms, again, this is an important aspect of the meta-normative framework. There are principles that govern the validity of acts or events that were consistent with norms as these had existed at the time the acts or events took place, but that would now be normatively invalid under the existing normative framework, were these acts or events to take place today. There are also norms that relate to how terms must be interpreted, were one to adjudge acts, events, or other situations that took place in the past. Suffice it to say that normative conflicts could involve such complex questions alongside others.[137]

However, we should stress that these are *general* principles and, as such, the actual facts of a particular normative conflict, or conflict of jurisdiction, may restrict their application. In fact, the ILC Study Group on fragmentation has highlighted a range of circumstances in which the above principles may be legitimately modified or even set aside.[138] It is

---

[137] The general rule is to apply the principle of contemporaneity – that is to say, that an act or event be assessed according to the existing normative context of the time. That is not to say, however, that some norm – e.g., related to the slave trading aspects of a 17th-century treaty – must be upheld when this would be insufferable within the modern international legal system, given that it would conflict with its evolving *jus cogens*/peremptory norms; themselves supreme in the context of, say, a normative hierarchy within international law. See D'Amato, A. 'International Law, Intertemporal Problems', entry in *Encyclopedia of Public International Law* (Amsterdam: North-Holland, 1992). See also Article 28 VCLT.

[138] For a full analysis of the relationship between *lex specialis* and *lex generalis*, see ILC Report of the Study Group, *Fragmentation of International*

beyond the scope of this chapter to drill down to a deeper level of analysis, given that the purpose of this section is to offer a general overview of the meta-normative framework as it may exist in the international legal system.

What is more, it is important to bear in mind that the international legal system is dynamic. Norms do not necessarily have everlasting effect nor is their content static. A highly dialectical relationship exists between norms and events in that norms both influence State behavior and are shaped by, or evolve according to, State behavior.[139] It is essentially the task of jurists to take snapshots in time to determine the validity and content of norms. This dynamism is reflected in the interpretative norms as they exist in custom and as they are deemed to be enshrined in the VCLT.[140]

While conflicts between the ECT, the EnCT, and the EU regimes are, admittedly, not commonplace, they are not entirely unlikely. Nor is speculation about the interplay between these regimes redundant. In this section, we offer an overview of a rather complex area of international law in order to situate the phenomenon of normative conflict, and/or jurisdictional conflicts, within the context of the broader international legal system, and to outline its main features.

Law: Difficulties Arising from the Diversification and Expansion of International Law (A/CN.4/L.682) (13 April 2006), at pp. 30–114. For a full analysis of the relationship between *lex posterior* and *lex prior*, see the same report at pp. 115–165.

[139] A special legal regime example that illustrates how there has been recourse to non-inherent norms (to that regime) involves the WTO's adjudicative structures. See *United States – Import Prohibition of Certain Shrimp and Shrimp Products* (6 November 1998) WT/DS58/AB/R (at § 151, p. 2755). The instruments cited by the adjudicative agency in that WTO dispute were not relevant to all WTO parties and, on their strength alone, could not be relied upon within the meaning of Article 31(3)(c) VCLT (and its analogous customary norm). However, the adjudicative agency considered external (non-WTO) instruments as illustrative of how the matters at hand were deemed in such instruments, and, therefore, as indicative of evolving practice, rather than as binding and directly relevant to the dispute at hand.

[140] An example would be subsequent state practice or practice in subsequent international legal agreements that may point towards evolving textual meanings or evolving perceptions of obligation (*opinio juris*). See e.g. Article 30 VCLT on successive international agreements and Article 31(3)(a)&(b) VCLT on subsequent agreement or practice on the part of the States concerned. These norms are held to reflect custom.

B. Normative Conflicts and the EU Legal Order

Within the EU legal order, there are express *quasi*-meta-norms that consider normative conflicts and provide for their resolution. Namely Article 351 TFEU, which states that the TFEU takes precedence over previous treaties (i.e., treaties to which a current EU Member State is a party and that came into force when that EU Member State had yet to accede to the EU) involving EU Member States, without affecting their legal relations with third-party States.

C. Normative Conflicts and the Energy Charter Treaty

Within the ECT legal order, the interplay of ECT norms may also assist with normative conflicts. Article 16 ECT makes clear what the effect shall be of previous or subsequent legal agreements on the disposition of obligations under the ECT. The wording reflects general principles of international law in relation to the interpretation and interplay of concurrent yet competing international obligations – in sum, that subsequent international obligations involving a particular nexus of States are discharged contingent and without prejudice to earlier international obligations involving that particular nexus of States.

A case in point of a jurisdictional and normative conflict involving the EU and the ECT is the *Electrabel v. Hungary* arbitration case within the context of the International Centre for the Settlement of Investment Disputes (ICSID).[141] This case illustrates the legal fault-lines involving clashes among special regimes. Whilst the ECT involves a distinct legal regime to that of the EU, the EU is also implicated in that there are ECT provisions that show deference towards regional supranational organizations, such as the EU. Also, the EU is implicated in that it is a fundamental proponent of the ECT multilateral system.

This *Electrabel v. Hungary* arbitration case concerned concessions given through a power purchase agreement (PPA) by the Hungarian State to an energy production company which was later privatized. With the accession of Hungary to the EU and the consequent application of the *acquis communautaire* – including the EU's competition *acquis* – to its territory, the EU Commission reviewed various preferential agreements that Hungary had in place and advised Hungary to nullify those in breach of EU competition rules. Consequently, the PPA in question had to be set aside by Hungary. Unsurprisingly, this had implications for the PPA

---

141 *Electrabel S.A. v. the Republic of Hungary* (ICSID Case No. Arb/07/19), available at http://www.italaw.com/cases/documents/1624

rights holders, who subsequently issued arbitration tribunal proceedings under the ECT citing the investment protection rules in the ECT, which Hungary had ratified in 1998, before its EU entry in 2004. The complaint hinged principally on the ECT requirement to treat investors fairly and equitably.

The tribunal examined both questions of jurisdiction and applicable law, given the seeming normative conflict between Hungary's ECT obligations and its EU obligations. Whilst neither party objected to the tribunal's jurisdiction, the EU Commission (not a party *per se* to the proceedings, but clearly an important actor given its vanguard role in the EU project) raised *amicus curiae* jurisdictional objections on the basis that the matter was within the exclusive jurisdiction of the CJEU. As the proceedings were brought under the ECT, and in line with the admissibility provisions of the ICSID Convention, the tribunal was ultimately satisfied that it could establish jurisdiction to examine the complaint. The tribunal found in favor of Hungary on the particular relationship between EU law and the ECT to that case. While it held that the dispute could be considered on the basis of the ECT, regard would have to be had to the broader normative context, which in this case included the EU *acquis* and general international law, in order to resolve the normative tensions at play.

Ultimately, the case turned on the distinct facts of the case, including the timing of Hungary's accessions to the ECT and the EU, and the investors' home state, which in this case had been Belgium, that is, another EU Member State and not some (non-EU) third-party state, which undoubtedly would have led to a very different argumentation and outcome. However, what we have witnessed with this case is the assertion of the notion that it is possible for as many fora as are implicated by a matter and nexus of States to be legitimately simultaneously seized of a case, with no hierarchy of legal regime or forum *per se*. In this case, we clearly witness that, although the arbitration tribunal asserted the legitimacy of the ECT endorsed resolution process, given that jurisdiction was established and not estopped by some inherent fact relevant to the ECT special regime, the tribunal's examination of the dispute – having admitted recourse to EU law as part of the broader normative context that governed the matter at issue – ultimately led to the upholding of EU norms, rather than to their relegation as secondary vis-à-vis ECT norms.

D. Normative Conflicts and the Energy Community

The EnC also contains provisions that contemplate the interplay of concurrent international obligations. Articles 101–103 EnCT make clear that obligations flowing from the EnCT are without prejudice to chronologically earlier obligations and to obligations owed in relation to the WTO system.

E. Other Conflict-Related Matters Relevant to the European Union–Energy Charter Treaty–Energy Community Nexus

1. Concurrent jurisdictions

Conflicts between special regimes are not limited to substantive normative conflicts, but may also relate to questions of forum admissibility and jurisdiction. Unsurprisingly, it may be in the interests of parties to a dispute to have it examined by a particular forum. As the *Electrabel v. Hungary* arbitration case attests, there often is no dispositive norm to promote one forum over another, given that there is no necessary hierarchy among special regimes when considered against the backdrop of general international law. Under the autonomous jurisdiction rules of each regime, their respective adjudicative agencies may legitimately be able to exercise jurisdiction.[142] When all competing elements claim

[142] A case in point is the *Mox Plant* dispute between Ireland and the UK, in which three distinct special regimes were engaged – namely the EU, the tribunal under the UN Convention on the Law of the Sea (UNCLOS), and the arbitration provisions under the 1992 Convention for the Protection of the Marine Environment of the North East Atlantic (OSPAR Convention) – which brought four decisions. See Dispute Concerning Access to Information Under Article 9 of the OSPAR Convention, Final Award (*Ireland v. the United Kingdom*) (2 July 2003), Permanent Court of Arbitration, ILM Vol. 42 (2003) p. 1118. The other *Mox Plant* cases are: *The MOX Plant Case, Request for Provisional Measures Order (Ireland v. the United Kingdom)* (3 December 2001), International Tribunal for the Law of the Sea (ITLS), ILM Vol. 41 (2002); and *The MOX Plant Case, Order No. 3* (*Ireland v. the United Kingdom*) (24 June 2003), Permanent Court of Arbitration, ILM Vol. 42 (2003), p. 1187. Regarding the *MOX Plant* case in the context of the EU legal order, the EU Commission brought a legal action against Ireland before the European Court of Justice for having brought this case against the UK before the ITLS under UNCLOS. See Case C-459/03, ECR 2006, p. I-4635. For a fuller analysis of the relationship between special regimes from a general international law perspective, see ILC Report of the Study Group, *Fragmentation of International Law: Difficulties Arising from the Diversification and Expansion of International Law* (A/CN.4/L.682) (13 April 2006), at pp. 65–83 and 97–99.

exclusivity, questions about jurisdiction can be handled through reasoned legal arguments along the lines of the principles discussed earlier with regard to the relationship between *lex specialis*, *lex generalis*, *lex posterior, and lex prior*, aided by other norms of general international law.

In cases, say, that involve a trade-related dispute between two WTO members, the terms of the WTO system prohibit parties from seeking determinations from other fora, should such disputes involve matters that fall within their WTO membership.[143] Similarly, under EU law, an EU Member State may be restricted, by operation of EU law, in its recourse to the fora of other special regimes to which it is party, so long as the subject matter falls within the scope of its EU membership and where the CJEU purportedly has exclusive jurisdiction.[144] Consequently, how and to which end interpretative norms – be they flowing from applicable VCLT or customary law norms – are applied depends largely on the specific adjudicative forum considering the dispute. That said, States are not automatically estopped from taking matters to other fora, should this be, among other things, permissible under the admissibility rules specific to those fora. In that respect, although certain special legal regimes may obligate parties, on a contractual (therefore 'voluntarist') basis, to *opt out* from whatever benefits are afforded under other special legal orders, they neither, on their own strength, invalidate *per se* the legal obligations owed by parties under other special regimes, nor do they invalidate whatever *erga omnes* (or otherwise) obligations those parties owe or are owed under general international law.[145]

---

143 See Article 23.1 of the Dispute Settlement Understanding (DSU), which obligates members to refer their disputes to the DSS to the exclusion of self-determination or other fora. Furthermore, under Article IX:2 of the WTO Agreement, the WTO Ministerial Conference and the General Council have the exclusive authority on a three-fourths majority basis to adopt interpretations. Again, we witness the elevation of the political/diplomatic mechanisms of the WTO over the adjudicative mechanism. In this manner, it may be better equipped to contain intractable interstate disputes and prevent them from resulting in other fora.

144 The CJEU has exclusive jurisdiction over EU institutions acts and over certain aspects of intra-EU relations. See Section 5 (Article 264) TFEU, whereby the CJEU has exclusive jurisdiction over cases issued by EU Member States against the European Parliament and certain actions against the Council or brought by EU institutions *inter se*, and may declare measures by EU bodies void.

145 The fulfillment of international obligation is governed by norms of general international law pertaining to State responsibility. Draft Articles on

It is also worth pointing out that at the particular international law level – that is to say, at the level of regional custom and at the level of special legal regimes[146] based on a theme or geographical region – other than operative general law principles flowing from general international law, we may also have conflict resolving norms (e.g., conflict clauses) that have been inscribed into the constitutive instruments of those orders. Such provisions express an acknowledgement on the part of State parties of the existence of broader enveloping or parallel normative contexts/ frameworks by which State parties are obligated to abide. For instance, we see this in EU treaties, in the ECT and in the EnCT, alongside other special legal regimes based on particular international law (e.g., the WTO system).[147]

Responsibility of States for Internationally Wrongful Acts ('Draft Articles') exist (available at http://www.refworld.org/docid/3ddb8f804.html), which provide some indication as to how issues around State responsibility for an international wrong, including a breach of an international obligation, may be considered under international law. As of August 2012, the Draft Articles had yet to be adopted in the form of a legal instrument by the international community. For a historical run-down of the development of the Draft Articles, see http:// untreaty.un.org/ilc/summaries/9_6.htm (last accessed August 2012). In that respect, the breach of an international, say, treaty-based obligation is not governed only by the treaty in question, but also by the operation of rules of general international law that deal with obligations that pertain to State responsibility at the interstate level.

[146] Sometimes these special legal orders are erroneously referred to as 'self-contained' orders. This is misleading as it reinforces the misperception that these exist in isolation to the broader normative context that governs the relationship between a particular nexus of States and/or that is engaged by the circumstance at issue. See ILC Report of the Study Group, *Fragmentation of International Law: Difficulties Arising from the Diversification and Expansion of International Law* (A/CN.4/L.682) (13 April 2006), at §193, p. 100.

[147] The DSU stipulates the exclusive jurisdiction of the DSB over WTO disputes. Although WTO Panels and the Appellate Body have considered international agreements outside the WTO-covered agreements in interpreting provisions – discussed *passim* – and although Article 3.2 DSU refers to 'customary rules of interpretation of public international law', it is less clear that this creates sufficient scope for the DSB to widen its purview from interpreting WTO rules to interpreting these in an *intra vires* manner sympathetic to extraneous international legal agreements and custom. There have been instances where interpretations of terms have been given in relation to extraneous agreements (see *US – Shrimp/Turtle* discussed *passim*); however, arguably, these have not added to or diminished the rights and duties of WTO members. Under Article IX:2 of the WTO Agreement, only the Ministerial Council – i.e., the

2. *'Inter se'* legal agreements

The EU sets up its own legal order, which is both thematic (ostensibly about a customs union and internal market) and geographical (extending over the territories of 28 European States). The ECT sets up a special regime along thematic lines (namely, for the most part, energy-sector investment protection) and quasi-geographical lines (mainly concerned with east–west energy flows) among its signatories. The EnCT sets up an order that is both geographical (the EU and its periphery) and thematic (gas and electricity market regulatory convergence and integration). What we often encounter in such regimes is an *inter partes* strengthening of legal (and other) relations to the exclusion of third-party states, while, at the same time, the initial set of states (involved in the *inter se* agreements in question) maintains its independent legal relations with third-party States. In such situations, it is important to note that normative conflicts may arise in relation to obligations owed under different arrangements.

These sort of *inter se* legal agreements often may affect the rights of third-party States. An example is where, say, WTO members set up an *inter se* union – for example, the EU. In such an event, this may not be to the detriment of their WTO peers, nor may this diminish the rights held by third-party States under whatever multilateral or bilateral legal agreements may have been in place at the time. In the example of the WTO, this is not simply by operation of Article XXIV of the GATT, which mandates that the setting up of free-trade areas or customs unions involving a WTO member may not diminish the existing trade concessions towards those WTO members that are excluded. It is also because other concurrent legal obligations owed to those third-party States which are excluded (that is to say, States that are not party to those free-trade areas or customs unions) may not be docked, given that they too involve valid norms and obligations that also have to be discharged.

It is also worth noting that under the ECT regime, Article 25.1 makes clear that *inter se* agreements between States that happen to be ECT parties may also be contracted even if these exclude other ECT parties. This, however, is not to say that any such agreements may diminish the rights owed under the ECT between ECT parties *per se*. With respect to Article 25 ECT, the EU and its Member States declared in the Final Act of the European Energy Charter Conference that, while the effect of Article 25 ECT is to uphold EU legislation that discriminates in favor of companies incorporated in any EU Member State, Article 25 ECT seems

utmost diplomatic and legislative WTO organ – and the General Council may adopt authoritative interpretations of WTO rules.

not to uphold EU legislation, which makes it possible for the EU to extend the preferential treatment resulting from the wider process of economic integration to companies in other (third-party) States, unless this is done in a manner that is in line with Article 25 ECT[148] – presumably through the contracting of an Economic Integration Agreement, rather than a mere extension of EU law *per se*. There may be inherent rules in particular legal orders – for example, conflict clauses – on how this ought to be avoided. A case in point is Article 351 TFEU, which expressly states that international legal agreements between any EU Member State, in its own right, and any third-party State contracted before 1958, or for acceding States before the date of their accession to the EU, are unaffected by the TFEU (and its predecessor) so that the rights of third-party States are not diminished and their obligations are not made more onerous.

However, where no such inherent express rules exist, there are techniques to resolve these tensions, mainly by having regard to general principles of law at the general international law level. One such principle is *pacta sunt servanda* (i.e., legal agreements must be upheld).[149] In relation to legal consequences for third-party States, another fundamental principle is that which seeks to shield third-party States from legal effects arising from legal agreements to which they are not party, as per Article 34 VCLT and its analogous norm existing in custom. These principles are important to bear in mind when we consider the legal implications that the EU, the ECT, and the EnC special orders may have for third-party States.

VII. CONCLUSION

The EU engages with the world outside the territory of its constituent Member States in a diverse manner in order to promote its energy security. For instance, the EU does this in various fora where it co-exists with third-party States, including through special regimes relating to energy, such as the ECT and the EnC. We have seen how the EU has been the prime mover behind both the ECT and the EnC. The ECT was a timely response to significant geostrategic events – namely the collapse of the bureaucratic regimes in the eastern and central part of Europe and

---

[148] See *The Energy Charter Treaty and Related Documents: A Legal Framework for International Energy Cooperation* (Brussels: Energy Charter Secretariat, 2004) p. 32.

[149] Article 26 VCLT.

the re-casting of *machtpolitik* regionally – that had enhanced opportunities for the industries of the developed Western states to access energy resources in those regions, whilst the EnC came a few years later to place on a more institutionalized footing the EU energy interests in those regions by promoting the integration of energy markets – chiefly gas and oil – through regulatory convergence across EnC members. In the case of the EnC, the EU is afforded a more prominent position in that, among other things, certain areas of its *acquis* are inducted into the EnC's legal order, the EU has more influence than its EnC peers in the highest decision-making bodies of the EnC,[150] and the EnC is essentially the realization of EU external energy policy with those States between it (i.e., the EU) and its energy supplier *par excellence*, namely Russia.

The EU's pursuit of closer energy relations with its neighbors along single-sector lines – as is the case with the EnC – could also be understood as a less maximalist approach of EU Member States' polities to promoting their interests with neighboring energy-significant states (without the conditionality of EU membership) in terms that are politically acceptable to the polities in those neighboring states.

The dispute settlement arrangements for both the ECT and EnC legal orders contain a considerable degree of deference towards the diplomatic process. In the ECT, in instances involving purely interstate disputes there is a clear preference for diplomatic solutions. Moreover, in the ECT, irrespective of the nexus of parties, for disputes engaging matters such as competition and the environment, there is a preference for diplomatic solutions and, in the case of environmental matters, for multilateralism. For trade, the ECT system defers to the WTO normative framework to which the majority of ECT parties are also subject. Where we see the possibility for adjudicative-like processes within the ECT is in State-investor disputes, where investors are given first dibs in relation to *their* preferred method of dispute resolution, including arbitration.

With the EnC, there is no traditional adjudicative agency *per se*; however, there is an omnipotent Ministerial Council – the highest EnC decision-making body – which has powers to make determinations and, in some cases, adopt its own definitive interpretations (where none exist within the applicable *acquis* by the CJEU). This shows a preference for diplomacy over supranational independent adjudicative structures, as we see in the EU and, to a limited extent, in the WTO legal order.

---

[150] As mentioned earlier, in the EnC's Ministerial Council and the Permanent High Level Group, the EU is afforded two representatives, whilst the other EnC members are afforded one.

While within the modern international legal system there is fragmentation along law fields across various cleavages – namely between public and private law, and between different themes (e.g., humanitarian, environmental, and economic), and between public and private law within each theme[151] – the modern international legal system generally possesses the juridical tools to help unlock normative conflicts arising within or between legal orders. This is certainly so at the general international law level, what with interpretative principles that exist at the universal level. However, it is not a lack of juridical tools that is the issue; rather, it is the implausibility for normative conflicts to be addressed by a competent adjudicative omniscient agency.

What is more, when we assess the international legal system through the prism of 'coherence' do we not expect too much from the system as we, perhaps, make more allowances for social reality? In other words, is it not perhaps a tall order to expect coherence to be reflected in the international legal system and in international law when this is not to be found in interstate social reality?[152] Ultimately, incoherence at the international law level is merely reflective of incoherence in interstate interaction, which itself, in turn, is reflective of the plurality and disparity of interests and clout that exist among States and other actors at the international level. In that sense, should the international 'community' – itself a motley crew of States – be sufficiently concerned about this, incoherence ought to, more appositely, be addressed politically, rather than be seen to flow from reasons inherent to the international legal system.[153]

---

[151] For instance, 'international' 'investment' law, 'international' 'energy' law, which, in our view – particularly, in relation to interstate and supra-State law relating to interstate *economic* matters – are essentially *ad hoc* artifacts coming into existence in the eye of the beholder (in our case, that of jurists, legal analysts, and practitioners).

[152] See ILC Report of the Study Group, *Fragmentation of International Law: Difficulties Arising from the Diversification and Expansion of International Law* (A/CN.4/L.682) (13 April 2006), where it is stated that: '*Special rules and rule-complexes are undoubtedly necessary – somewhat in the sense that different sovereignties are. The world is irreducibly pluralistic.* … Public international law does not contain rules in which a global society's problems are, as it were, already resolved. *Developing these is a political task*' (at §488, p. 247, emphasis added).

[153] As the ILC Study Group on fragmentation states: 'But it may also be rationalized in terms of a political obligation on law-appliers to make their decisions cohere with the preferences and expectations of the community whose law they administer'. See ILC Report of the Study Group, *Fragmentation of*

Returning to the ECT and EnC and how they relate to the EU legal order and between one another, we note that fragmentation *per se* and normative conflict are actually less of an issue, given the high degree of kinship and provenance between the legal orders involved. In relation to the ECT, the *Electrabel v. Hungary* arbitration case – albeit an arbitration case binding on the parties concerned and with very limited normative effect for the purposes of international law – illustrates how conflicts may be resolved when the EU legal order is focused upon. This is not to say that the EU and/or States burdened by EU-related obligations have a free hand to renege on ECT obligations; rather, it is to say that the EU is taken as one entity and that ECT breach allegations between EU Member States are deferred to the EU's legal order for resolution. We witness this preference to defer a dispute to a more *specific* or *chronologically recent* order in the way the International Tribunal for the Law of the Sea has deferred disputes between EU Member States to the CJEU on the basis that a more appropriate forum seems to exist, to whose jurisdiction both parties were subject due to their common EU membership and, crucially, due to the fact that the subject-matter of the dispute fell within the scope of their EU relationship. In the EnC legal order, the fact that its law stems from certain areas of the EU's *acquis* restricts the possibility for conflicts with the EU legal order, or with other orders, given the primacy of the EU *acquis* within the EnC.

International Law: Difficulties Arising from the Diversification and Expansion of International Law (A/CN.4/L.682) (13 April 2006), at §35, p. 24.

PART III

Renewable energy in the WTO and EU: selected legal aspects

7. Renewable energy in the World Trade Organization

I. INTRODUCTION

The argument of Part III of this book is that the use of renewable energy will help towards energy security regionally and climate change mitigation globally. This chapter examines selected legal aspects of the multilateral trade system regarding renewable energy promotion. It argues that the WTO rules are capable of promoting environmental protection objectives. The multilateral trade system aims at the eventual total liberalization of cross-border trade through the removal of as many trade barriers – such as tariffs, quantitative restrictions, and trade-distortive practices – as may be politically acceptable to the economic areas involved.

For their part, the governing structures of the economic areas concerned – for the most part, the governments of sovereign states – are faced with the task of addressing a much broader set of interests than those pertaining to trade. However, the accession of sovereign actors and regional economic unions (such as the EU) to international treaty-based organizations (such as the WTO), and their acceptance of the relevant international obligations often commensurately condition their policy-making. In that respect, it is not uncommon for, say, certain measures that WTO members take in order to address some subjective policy objective that is, on the face of it, extraneous to cross-border trade, to infringe upon their international obligations – for instance, such measures may infringe upon obligations owed by WTO members under their WTO membership in a manner that is not in line with WTO rules.

This chapter is principally concerned with how the existing multilateral trade system, based on the WTO, countenances the promotion of renewables. We carry out this examination by discussing certain WTO norms that have, or may, come to bear on measures that WTO members take which have a distortive or restrictive effect on cross-border intra-WTO trade and which have been argued in connection with environmental protection and/or with renewable energy,[1] and by reviewing the relevant WTO jurisprudence. This contribution is therefore part of the so-called 'trade and …' debate, which relates to concerns surrounding the fragmentation of the international legal system, and of international law, along thematic or other lines that lead to artifacts such as 'international' 'economic' law and 'energy' law.

The International Law Commission set up a Study Group on fragmentation which issued its report to the United Nations General Assembly in 2006. In that report, the Study Group referred to the reasons that fragmentation of the international legal system has arisen and identified the advent of special regimes – including not only legal orders, but also fields of law such as 'international' 'trade' law – which reinforced perceptions that these were 'self-contained', itself a fallacy when, among other things, any special legal regime set up further to interstate contracting is predicated upon general international law to function.[2] Starting from the premise that the world's ecosystems, their preservation, and

[1] While the WTO and its norms apply to intra-WTO trade, they may also have implications for trade flows involving a nexus between States where at least one party is a WTO member. For instance, the requirement under Article I GATT (regarding the principle that WTO members ought to treat all their WTO peers as they would their 'most-favored nation') makes clear that any trade privilege that a WTO member affords to any other State must, in effect, be unconditionally extended to all of its WTO peers. Naturally, this does not create obligations for non-WTO members.

[2] See the International Law Commission, Report of the Study Group, *Fragmentation of International Law: Difficulties Arising from the Diversification and Expansion of International Law* (A/CN.4/L.682) (13 April 2006), §15, at p. 14, where it is stated that: 'The rationale for the Commission's treatment of fragmentation is that the emergence of new and special types of law, "self-contained regimes" and geographically or functionally limited treaty-systems creates problems of coherence in international law. New types of specialized law do not emerge accidentally but seek to respond to new technical and functional requirements. The emergence of "environmental law" is a response to growing concern over the state of the international environment. "Trade law" develops as an instrument to regulate international economic relations. "Human rights law" aims to protect the interests of individuals and "international criminal law" gives legal expression to the "fight against impunity". Each rule-complex or "regime" comes with its own principles, its own form of expertise and its own "ethos", not necessarily identical to the ethos of neighbouring specialization. "Trade law" and "environmental law", for example, have highly specific objectives and rely on principles that may often point in different directions. In order for the new law to be efficient, it often includes new types of treaty clauses or practices that may not be compatible with old general law or the law of some other specialized branch. Very often new rules or regimes develop precisely in order to deviate

climate change mitigation are global public goods, there is a nexus between energy and climate change which encompasses a range of issues such as clean energy subsidies and emission-related levies (e.g., carbon taxes, and border adjustment taxes for carbon emissions). International law is threatened by incoherence due to its fragmentation, and there is a need to bring greater coherence not least for the promotion of environmental protection through the entire normative context that is international law.[3] One would need to look at various special regimes (such as the WTO, the EU, the NAFTA) and institutions (such as civil society and markets) for resolving disputes that pitch environmental objectives against other (say, investment protection, market liberalization) objectives in a manner that sufficiently promotes environmental objectives so that we come closer to achieving more coherent global environmental governance.

After the introduction, Section II provides some background for context purposes. We shall then briefly refer to some general global energy data and to some data that are more specific to renewable energy in Section III. In Section IV, we shall sum up arguments in relation to the suitability of the existing multilateral system to sufficiently balance the interstate environmental objectives with those relating to interstate trade liberalization objectives. Section V advocates implementing stronger governance of energy trade and provides an analysis of the WTO's treatment of renewable energy. It also discusses the impact of subsidies on different forms of energy and whether feed-in tariffs count as subsidies in the WTO context. Section VI concludes the chapter.

II. SETTING THE SCENE

Environmental degradation occurs due to a variety of reasons, including processes that are entirely inherent to nature.[4] However, in recent history,

---

from what was earlier provided by the general law. When such deviations or [sic] become general and frequent, the unity of the law suffers'.

[3] On the fragmentation of international law, see the work of the International Law Commission, 58th Session, *Final Report of the Study Group on Fragmentation*, UN Doc. A/CN.4/L.682, and the conclusions of the Study Group on fragmentation, UN Doc. A/CN.4/L.702. On the specific case of international trade law, see also Leal-Arcas, R. 'The Fragmentation of International Trade Law: Is Now the Time for Variable Geometry?' (2011) *The Journal of World Investment and Trade*, Vol. 12, No. 2, pp. 145–195.

[4] For further explanation, see Leal-Arcas, R. *Climate Change and International Trade* (Cheltenham: Edward Elgar, 2013) Chapter 2.

the rate of environmental degradation has been ostensibly more rapid than during the previous millennia of organized human society.[5] What is more, we are fast approaching the tipping point after which environmental degradation may become irreversible.[6] This excessiveness in 'climate change' has largely been anthropogenic in that it flows from the effects of human activity. Moreover, environmental degradation operates dynamically in that the anthropogenic effects on the environment may themselves cause or contribute to further environmental degradation.

To illustrate this point, let us take the example of atmospheric greenhouse gases (GHGs),[7] which are almost entirely human-caused.[8] The concentration of GHGs in the atmosphere not only degrades the atmosphere, but also creates the 'greenhouse effect', thus trapping a significant part of the Earth's energy and heat that would otherwise be

---

[5] See the executive summary to the IEA 2013 report, *Redrawing the Energy-Climate Map*, World Energy Outlook Special Report, at p. 1.

[6] See the Intergovernmental Panel on Climate Change report, *Climate Change 2007: Synthesis Report* (2007), where it is stated that: 'Anthropogenic warming could lead to some impacts that are abrupt or irreversible, depending upon the rate and magnitude of the climate change' (at p. 53).

[7] Article 1 of the UN Framework Convention on Climate Change (UNFCCC) defines greenhouse gases as 'those gaseous constituents of the atmosphere, both natural and anthropogenic, that absorb and re-emit infrared radiation'.

[8] During 2004, the breakdown of global GHG emissions was the following: 26% regarding the energy supply, 19% regarding industry, 17% regarding gases released from land-use change and forestry, 14% from agriculture, 13% regarding transport, 8% regarding residential, commercial, and service sectors, and 3% regarding waste. See IPCC, 2007 [Metz, B., Davidson, O.R., Bosch, P.R., Dave, R. & Meyer, L.A. (eds)], *Climate Change 2007: Mitigation. Contribution of Working Group III to the Fourth Assessment Report of the Inter-governmental Panel on Climate Change* (Cambridge and New York: Cambridge University Press) at pp. 27 and 104. NB: This appears to be the latest illustrative compilation of global GHG emission figures. It is worth noting that the breakdown of GHG indicates that the overwhelming majority of GHG emissions relates to CO_2. The breakdown is: 57% from CO_2 (produced due to fossil-fuel use), 17% from CO_2 (related to biomass and deforestation), 14% from methane, 8% from nitrous oxide, and 8% from various fluorinated gases. These figures have been calculated by the US Environmental Protection Agency (EPA) based on data in the IPCC, 2007 [Metz, B., Davidson, O.R., Bosch, P.R., Dave, R. & Meyer, L.A. (eds)], *Climate Change 2007: Mitigation. Contribution of Working Group III to the Fourth Assessment Report of the Inter-governmental Panel on Climate Change* (Cambridge and New York: Cambridge University Press). (See http://www.epa.gov/climatechange/ghgemissions/global.html for the EPA's calculations.)

reflected back into space. The effect of this phenomenon is the rise of the Earth's temperature, which, in turn, has far-reaching consequences – including severe weather events, desertification and the melting of polar water-bodies and territories – for ecosystems and the human, animal, and plant populations they sustain.

In light of the above, it is unsurprising that climate change is a concern to many a State and interstate actor. What is surprising, however, are the underwhelming efforts on the part of the international 'community' to meaningfully address climate change.[9] While a *gathering* – for lack of a better word – of State actors indeed exists, in our view this does not possess the characteristics of a community with equal interests. References to an *international community* often disguise the fact that what we are dealing with is, essentially, a collection of sovereign entities that, while formally enjoying the legal equality flowing from their sovereign status, in reality are as highly disparate amongst themselves as their interests. How this may translate at the interstate cooperation level is that meaningful efforts to address climate change might founder on the fact that certain States – including those with significant hydrocarbon/fossil fuel[10] endowments and those whose privately- and/or State-owned enterprises have considerable interests in the conventional energy sector, along with highly polluting States with heavy industries – do not share the same sense of urgency as those States who seek to spearhead collective interstate efforts aimed at climate change mitigation (e.g., such as the group of small island developing States[11] that face existential threats by

[9] The 1992 UNFCCC and its 1997 Kyoto Protocol may have laid the foundations for a nigh-universal climate change mitigation regime that is predicated, amongst other things, on the principle of *equity* (see Article 3.1 UNFCCC) that differentiates the climate change mitigation duties owed by the industrialized States from those owed by less- and least-developed States, according to their emitting history and their current capabilities. The UNFCCC and its Kyoto Protocol are significant multilateral steps for the cause of environmental protection; however, in the grander scheme of things, they may have been of little consequence. We say this as we are astonished to note that, while the strength of the Kyoto Protocol lies in the fact that 191 out of 192 of its parties have ratified it (with the notable exception of the US), its Clean Development Mechanism (CDM) (pursuant to Article 12 of the Kyoto Protocol) has only resulted in a 1% containment of global CO_2 levels. See Goldthau, A. & Witte, J.M. (eds) *Global Energy Governance: The New Rules of the Game* (Washington, DC: Brookings Institution Press, 2010) at p. 146.

[10] We shall be referring to fossil fuel/hydrocarbon-based fuel as 'conventional' energy sources throughout the present chapter.

[11] See www.un.org/special-rep/ohrlls/sid/list.htm (last accessed 2013).

rising sea levels).[12] In this respect, we shall be avoiding the term *international community* and shall be utilizing references to *interstate cooperation*.

We see some instances of unilateralism with respect to measures taken on the basis of the need to address climate change; however, these are not enough. The EU's emissions trading system (ETS) is a case in point, where an economic area – namely the EU – that is also a WTO member in its own right, had unilaterally, and much to the ire of several other States and WTO peers,[13] sought to include within its ETS all commercial aviation industry actors whose flight operations engaged EU territory. The EU finally suspended this policy under the pressure of the reaction that ensued, which could be seen as EU deference towards multilateralism.[14] Unsurprisingly, the EU had argued that such instances of unilateralism were necessary, if not justified, given the urgency associated with climate change and given the rather inadequate efforts of the international 'community' through its various relevant organizations, including the International Civil Aviation Organization.[15]

---

[12] For a call to change the current approach to climate change mitigation and the suggestion that major economies be more active in the fight against climate change, see Leal-Arcas, R. 'Top-down Versus Bottom-up Approaches for Climate Change Negotiations: An Analysis' (December 2011) *The IUP Journal of Governance and Public Policy*, Vol. 6, No. 4, pp. 7–52; Leal-Arcas, R. 'The BRICS and Climate Change' (2013) *International Affairs Forum*, pp. 1–5.

[13] See 'India Joins China in EU Aviation Emissions Scheme Boycott' (22 March 2012) *Bridges Trade BioRes*, Vol. 12, No. 6, International Center for Trade and Sustainable Development, where it is stated that 20 countries met in Moscow, Russia, in February 2012 to discuss the possible adoption of countermeasures (available at http://ictsd.org/i/news/biores/129175/).

[14] The inclusion of the aviation industry in the EU's ETS was suspended on 30 April 2013 on the basis that multilateral negotiations on aviation industry emission containment are currently taking place in other organizations (see: http://ictsd.org/i/news/bridgesweekly/158472/). For information regarding this temporary suspension, see European Parliament, 'CO_2: MEPs want ETS exception for intercontinental flights and progress in ICAO', Press Release, 26 February 2013, available at http://www.europarl.europa.eu/sides/getDoc.do?pubRef=-%2f%2fEP%2f%2fTEXT%2bIM-PRESS%2b20130225IPR06039%2b0%2bDOC%2bXML%2bV0%2f%2fEN&language=EN. For an analysis of the inclusion of aviation in the EU's ETS, see Leal-Arcas, R. 'Unilateral Trade-related Climate Change Measures' (2012) *The Journal of World Investment and Trade*, Vol. 13, No. 6, pp. 875–927.

[15] On this issue, see http://ec.europa.eu/clima/policies/transport/aviation/index_en.htm, where it is stated that the EU had been pressing the International Civil Aviation Organization (ICAO) for more than 15 years to take meaningful

Having accepted that the threat of irreversible environmental degradation is real rather than imagined, and having understood that the political realities of interstate cooperation – namely the disparity of interests at play – are, to say the least, partly to blame for the lack of meaningful interstate action, it seems reasonable to expect that measures – be they unilateral or collective – aimed at climate change mitigation and adaptation ought to be systemically encouraged and supported. Such measures may be schemes at the domestic, regional, and/or interstate levels aimed at promoting the development and use of energy sources that are less polluting.[16] We have seen how the lion's share of GHG emissions derives from CO_2 emissions that, in turn, are caused by, or linked to, the energy supply through the combustion of fossil fuels.

---

action in relation to GHG emissions. Also at the same link, read the official EU narrative on this issue. The EU holds to the view, further to a December 2011 Court of Justice of the European Union case brought by some US airlines, that the inclusion of aviation in the EU ETS is compatible with the EU's international obligations (see case C-366/10).

16 We shall be referring throughout this chapter to such sources as renewable energy/renewables/renewable energy sources. In terms of what this term includes, we draw from how this concept is handled by the International Energy Agency (IEA) in its publications and periodical reports. See the FAQ page of the IEA, where it is stated that renewable energy is 'Energy derived from natural processes (e.g. sunlight and wind) that are replenished at a faster rate than they are consumed. Solar, wind, geothermal, hydro, and some forms of biomass are common sources of renewable energy' (available at http://www.iea.org/aboutus/faqs/renewableenergy/). See also the 2012 IEA report, where the sort of energy sources that, for the purposes of this chapter, we could aggregate together as 'renewable energy' are those that yield energy through the processing of: 'biofuels & waste', 'hydro', 'geothermal', 'solar', 'wind', and 'heat'. See International Energy Agency, 2012 Key World Energy Statistics, OECD/IEA, 2012 (at 6, in the legend to the 2010 pie chart). Moreover, Article III of the International Renewable Energy Agency (IRENA) statute defines renewables to be: '… all forms of energy produced from renewable sources in a sustainable manner, which include, inter alia: bioenergy; geothermal energy; hydropower; ocean energy, including inter alia tidal, wave and ocean thermal energy; solar energy; and wind energy'. In our view, certain energy sources that are more environmentally friendly due to their lower CO_2 emissions when compared with fossil fuels – namely, biomass/biofuels – are rightly considered non-conventional energy sources. That said, given that they are produced by mainly processing plants that need to be replanted, strictly speaking these sources are not *renewable* in the way that wind, solar, hydro, and geothermal forms of energy are renewable. Despite this, we have followed the practice of the IEA and IRENA to aggregate these too as *renewables*.

Energy-related CO_2 emissions reached 31.6 Gigatons (Gts) in 2012 – that is 31.6 billion tons of CO_2.[17]

Diversifying the global energy supply mix in a manner that increasingly draws from renewable sources could have far-reaching geo-economic and geo-strategic implications,[18] including: the containment of GHG emissions to levels that would avert more costly future redress; the conservation of ecosystems and safeguarding the human, animal, and plant populations they sustain; more enhanced energy security for those States and groups of States that are net energy importers; and foreign relations that are less skewed by energy considerations. The scope of this chapter relates to the implications of renewable energy for the environment, and how, therefore, measures taken to promote the development and take-up of renewable energy may engage the rules of the multilateral trade system.[19]

III. FACTS AND FIGURES ON RENEWABLE ENERGY AND ITS GOVERNANCE

The latest readily available global data compiled by the International Energy Agency (IEA) indicate that renewable energy sources made up 13.2% of the global energy supply mix in 2010, while conventional energy sources (oil, natural gas, and coal) made up 81.1% of the mix.[20] The figures for 1973 – the year used in successive IEA reports as a basis

[17] See the executive summary to the IEA 2013 *Redrawing the Energy-Climate Map*, World Energy Outlook Special report (at p. 1).

[18] See IPCC, 2011: 'Summary for Policymakers', in [Edenhofer, O., Pichs-Madruga, R., Sokona, Y., Seyboth, K., Matschoss, P., Kadner, S., Zwickel, T., Eickemeier, P., Hansen, G., Schlömer, S. & von Stechow, C. (eds)], *IPCC Special Report on Renewable Energy Sources and Climate Change Mitigation* (Cambridge and New York: Cambridge University Press) at pp. 4–26 for an exposition of the potential benefits of increasing the proportion of renewables in the global supply energy mix. See also Ghosh, A. & Gangania, H. (2012) 'Governing Clean Energy Subsidies: What, Why and How Legal?', International Centre for Trade and Sustainable Development (pp. 11–18) for an exposition of the various arguments for the promotion of renewable energy.

[19] A similar line of thought is to be found in Leal-Arcas, R. 'Climate Change Mitigation from the Bottom Up: Using Preferential Trade Agreements to Promote Climate Change Mitigation' (2013) *Carbon and Climate Law Rev*, Vol. 7, No. 1, pp. 34–42 (discussing how to promote climate change mitigation by using preferential trade agreements).

[20] Figures calculated based on data as these appear in International Energy Agency, 2012. Key World Energy Statistics, OECD/IEA, 2012 (at p. 6). During

for comparison – were 12.4% and 86.7%, respectively.[21] In almost forty years, the composition of the global primary energy supply has changed very little. Any reduction in the proportion of conventional energy sources has largely been replaced by the rise in the proportion of nuclear energy from 0.9% in 1973 to 5.7% by 2010.[22] While nuclear energy is an alternative energy source, it is far from environmentally friendly. As the disasters at the nuclear power plants of Chernobyl (Ukraine) in 1986 and Fukushima Dai-ichi (Japan) in 2011 tragically testify, nuclear energy presents nigh-apocalyptic consequences for human safety and the environment.

We fleetingly alluded to political realities (i.e., the disparate interests of States in preserving the *status quo* in relation to the primacy of conventional energy sources) that, generally, seem to undermine meaningful action to protect the environment. In relation to the global energy mix, there are other factors that stack the odds against the proliferation of renewables, such as pervasive fuel subsidies,[23] which have implications for conventional energy demand and, consequently, retard the move towards a more environmentally friendly global energy supply mix.[24] It should be noted that such conventional energy subsidies have been tolerated within the WTO system.[25]

In recent years, there has been an increase in subsidies directed at the promotion of renewable energy. The global figures for subsidies in the

---

2010, the global primary energy supply was 12,717 million tons of oil equivalent (Mtoe). During 1973, it stood at 6,107 Mtoe.

[21] Ibid.

[22] Ibid.

[23] According to the IEA 2012 World Energy Outlook factsheet, '[e]nergy subsidies – government measures that artificially lower the price of energy paid by consumers, raise the price received by producers or lower the cost of production – are large and pervasive. When they are well-designed, subsidies to renewables and low-carbon energy technologies can bring long-term economic and environmental benefits. However, when they are directed at fossil fuels, the costs generally outweigh the benefits' (at p. 6) (http://www.worldenergyoutlook.org/media/weowebsite/2012/factsheets.pdf).

[24] Howse, R. 'World Trade Law and Renewable Energy: The Case of Non-Tariff Barriers' (UNCTAD, 2009) at p. 17; and Pershing, J. & Mackenzie, J. 'Removing Subsidies: Leveling the Playing Field for Renewable Energy Technologies' (2004), available at http://www.ren21.net/Portals/0/documents/irecs/renew2004/Removing%20subsidies.pdf

[25] See Thomas Cottier's comments at the 2011 WTO public forum discussions on International Governance of Energy Trade: WTO and Energy Charter Treaty, available at http://www.wto.org/english/forums_e/public_forum11_e/programme_e.htm#session40

renewable energy sector increased from USD 39 billion in 2007 to USD 66 billion by 2010.[26] While this increase is laudable, the figures are eclipsed by the enormity of fossil-fuel-related subsidies, which in 2010 stood at USD 409 billion.[27] The IEA projects that by 2035, a variety of positive developments could take place under its various policy scenarios, should renewables subsidies rise to USD 250 billion. For example, onshore wind could become competitive by 2020 in the EU and by 2030 in China,[28] and up to 3.4 gigatons – that is, 3.4 billion tons – of energy-related CO_2 could be contained.[29]

At the interstate level, there are various initiatives that concern renewable energy. There are several intergovernmental organizations (IGOs) and/or supranational organizations – including the IEA, the EU, and the United Nations (UN) – whose remits to varying degrees concern renewable energy. What is more, there are numerous instances of interstate cooperation along the lines of transnational policy networks and discussions at summit meetings.[30]

The most ostensibly renewables-related IGO is the International Renewable Energy Agency (IRENA),[31] which counts 116 Member States (plus the EU in its own right) and another 44 in accession talks.[32] The

---

[26] IEA 2012 World Energy Outlook factsheet at p. 6, available at http://www.worldenergyoutlook.org/media/weowebsite/2012/factsheets.pdf

[27] Ibid.

[28] Ibid.

[29] Ibid.

[30] See Sovacool, B. & Florini, A. 'Examining the Complications of Global Energy Governance' (2012) *Journal of Energy and Natural Resources Law*, Vol. 30, No. 3; and Steiner, A., Wälde, T., Bradbrook, A. & Schutyser, F. 'International Institutional Arrangements in Support of Renewable Energy', in Abmann, D., Laumanns, U. & Uh, D. (eds), *Renewable Energy: A Global Review of Technologies, Policies, and Markets* (London: Earthscan, 2006) at pp. 152–165 for a rundown of such organizations and instances concerning renewable energy at the interstate governance/cooperation level. Some relevant examples are the Organización Latinoamericana de Energía, the World Council for Renewable Energies (the precursor to IRENA), the Inter-American Development Bank, the Organization of the Black Sea Economic Cooperation, the South Asian Association for Regional Cooperation, the Renewable Energy and Energy Efficiency Partnership, the Global Network on Energy for Sustainable Development, the International Institute for Energy Conservation, and the Global Energy Efficiency and Renewable Energy Fund (an EU associated scheme).

[31] See http://www.irena.org/menu/index.aspx?mnu=cat&PriMenuID=13&CatID=30

[32] See http://www.irena.org/Menu/Index.aspx?mnu=Cat&PriMenuID=46&CatID=67

declared purpose of IRENA is to promote the adoption and sustainable use of all forms of renewables in a manner that takes into account 'national priorities'.[33] IRENA lacks the power to make binding recommendations on its members and its members are under no obligation[34] to implement the advice they periodically receive from IRENA.

Having briefly referred to the instances of interstate cooperation concerned with renewables, we turn to another instance of interstate cooperation, albeit one with a very different mandate from those mentioned above, and with a much stronger normative effect – namely, the WTO. The WTO is the main component of the multilateral trade system since 1995. It evolved from the 1947 General Agreement on Tariffs and Trade (GATT), which it entirely incorporated. The WTO provides degrees of governance over the trade flows between its members to the extent that their policies and practices may engage WTO norms. We should also like to add that the WTO system is neither *expressly* concerned with energy trade in general, nor with renewables trade in particular. Unless expressly stated (for instance, there is a degree of divergence from standard WTO rules in the field of agricultural trade,[35] trade in services,[36] and, up to 2005, for clothing and textiles),[37] WTO norms could potentially apply, and habitually apply, evenhandedly to all cross-border trade involving WTO members, including energy-related trade.[38] Consequently, cross-border trade in renewable energy goods and

---

[33] See Article II of the IRENA Statute.

[34] See Article IV(1)(a) of the IRENA Statute.

[35] See http://www.wto.org/english/thewto_e/whatis_e/tif_e/agrm3_e.htm for a rundown of the issues

[36] WTO members are under no obligation to liberalize their services sectors. However, they are obligated to provide the same treatment to all WTO peers indiscriminately in relation to those sectors which they have previously liberalized in their respective Schedules of Commitments (see Articles II and XVI of the General Agreement on Trade in Services (GATS). What is more, WTO members are obligated, in relation to those sectors previously liberalized, to not discriminate between domestic service providers and those of their WTO peers (see Article XVII of the GATS).

[37] The Agreement on Textiles and Clothing (ATC), which permitted departures from the general WTO rules, terminated on 1 January 2005. Its expiry means that trade in textile and clothing products is no longer subject to quotas under a special regime outside normal WTO rules, but is now governed by the general WTO rules and disciplines.

[38] See Leal-Arcas, R. & Filis, A. 'The Fragmented Governance of the Global Energy Economy: A Legal-Institutional Analysis' (2013) *Journal of World Energy Law and Business*, Vol. 6, No. 4, pp. 1–58 (at pp. 21–22 and *passim*) and

services that involve at least one WTO member is potentially within the WTO ambit.

The following section provides a *tour d'horizon* of the sort of WTO norms that have been, and might be, engaged by measures linked to the promotion of renewables, and a commentary on how the WTO system may generally countenance the promotion of renewables.

IV. THE WTO AND RENEWABLES

A. Initial Remarks

The WTO system is inherently biased towards the objective of trade liberalization primarily through promoting market access.[39] Moreover, WTO jurisprudence has been effective in clarifying the content and application of WTO rules and, arguably, in discouraging unjustifiably discriminatory and/or non *bona-fide* trade-restrictive measures. Since the advent of the WTO, the multilateral trade system has been increasingly capable of balancing, among other things, environmental protection objectives against those of trade liberalization in cases where tension arises.[40]

The WTO system does not handle general energy trade, or particular renewables trade, any differently from any other trade sector that is within its scope. In that respect, WTO norms apply to disputes or questions raised in connection with renewable energy. That said, the key objective that underpins the promotion of renewable energy – namely environmental protection – could amount to grounds that regulate how WTO norms are applied and/or, in certain cases, to grounds that displace those norms. For instance, the core obligations under the WTO system

WTO, 'World Trade Report 2010: Trade in Natural Resources' (2010), for a more thorough exposition of the relationship between the WTO and energy trade.

[39] See for instance the quintessence of the General Agreement on Tariffs and Trade 1994, the principal multilateral agreement of the WTO.

[40] See Leal-Arcas, R. & Filis, A. 'Certain Legal Aspects of the Multilateral Trade System and the Promotion of Renewable Energy', in Lim, C.L. & Mercurio, B. (eds) *International Economic Law after the Crisis: A Tale of Fragmented Disciplines* (Cambridge: Cambridge University Press, forthcoming); also published as Queen Mary School of Law Legal Studies Research Paper No. 166/2014, pp. 1–37. See also Marceau, G. & Wyatt, J. 'The WTO's Efforts to Balance Economic Development and Environmental Protection: A Short Review of Appellate Body Jurisprudence' (2013) *Latin American Journal of International Trade Law*, Vol. 1, No. 1, pp. 291–314.

relate to the principle of non-discrimination, which is a fundamental pillar of the multilateral trade system, given that the system is predicated on the necessity for trade liberalization.[41]

While there have been calls for an energy-specific multilateral agreement to be adopted within the WTO auspices,[42] these have yet to result in a WTO agreement that is energy-specific. Arguably, the Energy Charter Treaty (ECT) – an international treaty relating to various aspects,

---

[41] See the preamble to the Marrakesh Agreement Establishing the World Trade Organization (WTO Agreement), which states that: 'The Parties to this Agreement, Recognizing that their relations in the field of trade and economic endeavour should be conducted with a view to raising standards of living, ensuring full employment and a large and steadily growing volume of real income and effective demand, *and expanding the production of and trade in goods and services*, while allowing for the optimal use of the world's resources in accordance with the objective of sustainable development, seeking both to protect and preserve the environment and to enhance the means for doing so in a manner consistent with their respective needs and concerns at different levels of economic development; … Being desirous of contributing to these objectives *by entering into reciprocal and mutually advantageous arrangements directed to the substantial reduction of tariffs and other barriers to trade and to the elimination of discriminatory treatment in international trade relations* …' (emphasis added).

[42] See Cottier T. et al. 'Energy in WTO Law and Policy', in Cottier T. & Delimatsis, P. (eds) *The Prospects of International Trade Regulation: From Fragmentation to Coherence* (Cambridge: Cambridge University Press, 2011) at pp. 211–244; in relation to a speculative proposal for a Sustainable Energy Trade Agreement (SETA), see Kennedy, M. (2012), 'Legal Options for a Sustainable Energy Trade Agreement', International Centre for Trade and Sustainable Development (ICTSD). Furthermore, see the following May 2013 ICTSD news item: http://ictsd.org/i/news/bridgesweekly/162166/, reporting proceedings from a workshop held at the WTO Headquarters in Geneva, where several attendees commented on the need for the WTO system to better accommodate the promotion of renewables and energy particularities. We would add that such statements generally support the misperception that the current normative framework may be woefully inadequate. While we believe that guidelines based on the WTO rules and jurisprudence would be helpful to WTO members – imaginably, these could be drafted by the WTO legal division in cooperation with the WTO's Committee on Trade and the Environment, and any other relevant WTO organ – the rules and jurisprudence, as they currently stand, do not obstruct measures taken to promote renewable energy, so long as such measures are, generally, *bona fide,* not unduly discriminatory, and not unduly restrictive. It is therefore one thing to call for far-reaching – through, e.g., guidelines and clarifications – systemic encouragement of the scaling-up and taking-up of renewables, and quite another to attempt to do away with the existing safeguards in WTO rules and jurisprudence that seek to prevent abuse (e.g., discriminatory treatment and/or protectionism).

including trade, investment, and environmental protection, of its parties' respective energy sectors – may fit that bill. The ECT could appropriately be regarded as an interstate arrangement that arose out of the GATT/WTO system, given that the ECT was concluded as an alternative to previously unsuccessful efforts on the part of several developed net energy-importing WTO members to have an energy-specific agreement adopted within the WTO.[43]

In the absence of a specific energy-trade agreement, the WTO system and its multilaterally covered agreements are the principal structures that provide governance in cross-border energy trade, including cross-border renewable energy trade, to the extent that such trade flows involve a WTO member.[44] In addition, the multilateral trade rules that come to bear on such trade flows may further be enhanced by the rules contained in the WTO's *plurilateral* agreements so long as the WTO member(s) concerned have acceded to these and have, therefore, assumed that further layer of WTO obligation. An example of one such plurilateral agreement would be the Agreement on Government Procurement (GPA), to which a minority of WTO members are party,[45] and which may be relevant in instances, say, where a WTO member which is a party to the GPA takes some trade-distortive measure connected to government procurement.

---

43 See Wälde, T. *The Energy Charter Treaty: An East-West Gateway for Investment and Trade* (London: Kluwer Law International, 1996).

44 The Agreement Establishing the WTO, signed in Marrakesh on 15 April 1994, sets the WTO's terms of reference. Annexes to this Agreement specify which the covered agreements are. The GATT is the principal multilateral trade agreement under the WTO concerning tradable goods. See the Agreement Establishing the WTO's Annex 1A. Note that Annexes 1 & 4 to the Agreement Establishing the WTO distinguish between 'multilateral' and 'plurilateral' WTO agreements, with the former binding upon the entire WTO membership, while the normative effect of the latter set relies on WTO members having specifically acceded to this class of international agreements. The entire WTO system is predicated on the core principle of non-discrimination by prohibiting discrimination along the following two axes: among WTO peers (Article I of the GATT) and among domestic and imported tradables (Article III of the GATT). Certain trade-distortive measures argued to have been taken to promote renewables may, and often do, engage any, or both, of these twin aspects of the non-discrimination principle.

45 Currently there are 41 parties to the GPA, including all 28 EU members (with the Netherlands in its own right and on account of Aruba). Note that the EU is not a party in its own right to the GPA (see http://www.wto.org/english/tratop_e/gproc_e/memobs_e.htm#parties).

For their part, measures aimed at the promotion of renewable energy can be highly varied[46] and, consequently, might each engage a variety of WTO norms; norms, however, that are not necessarily all applicable in every single case that involves a measure claiming to promote renewables. In that respect, any assessment of a measure's WTO compatibility would have to be performed on a case-by-case basis and in relation to the facts of each case. For instance, policy elements that encourage the use of locally sourced or assembled components (known in WTO parlance as based on *local content requirements*/LCRs) as a condition for, say, a renewables-related subsidy, may engage Article III GATT[47] and the Agreement on Trade-Related Investment Measures (the TRIMs Agreement)[48] in terms of the WTO agreements that bind all WTO members automatically by virtue of their WTO membership.[49] In fact, this has been the principal ground upon which an aspect of a Canadian pro-renewables policy was struck down as an unjustifiable breach of WTO rules.[50] Therefore, the issues that arise at the juncture of renewables-related policy and WTO obligations often engage questions on the treatment of imports.

Moreover, certain measures may rely on the subsidization of the renewables generation industry through financial incentives for market actors, by, say, subsidizing partly or entirely the cost of technologies for

---

46 In terms of the diverse typology of policy tools to promote renewables, see Ghosh, A. & Gangania, H. (2012) 'Governing Clean Energy Subsidies: What, Why and How Legal?', International Centre for Trade and Sustainable Development, at pp. 20–26.

47 However, there are exceptions to this when, for instance, the LCR relates to government procurement of which there is no subsequent commercial resale or other commercial use. Such a LCR would be in line with WTO rules. (See Article III:1 and Article III:8 GATT.)

48 The TRIMs Agreement is also an Annex 1A (to the Agreement Establishing the WTO) covered multilateral agreement, and, therefore, binding on all WTO members. Paragraph 1(a) of the Annex to the TRIMs Agreement makes clear that trade-related investment measures requiring the use or purchase of domestic products are inconsistent with Article III GATT.

49 That is to say, to the 'multilateral' agreements, as opposed to the 'plurilateral' WTO agreements that only bind those parties that opt in.

50 See *Canada – Certain Measures Affecting the Renewable Energy Generation Sector* (WT/DS412/AB/R), and *Canada – Measures Relating to the Feed-in Tariff Program* (WT/DS426/AB/R). In the circumstances, the regional government of Ontario – for which Canada was responsible vis-à-vis the WTO – had a pro-renewables policy in place, which made the benefits of that policy conditional upon the use of locally sourced or assembled equipment on the part of the beneficiaries under that policy.

households to generate renewable electricity. Those examples alone could illustrate how different WTO norms might be engaged; while there is little in the WTO rules to obstruct a government from assuming or otherwise supporting, say, the cost of renewable technologies for *households* to generate their own electricity, this is, generally, not the case were a government to subsidize a specific sector in a manner that, by conferring a benefit to that sector, consequently, injures the domestic industry of another WTO member. Again, it would be necessary to examine all relevant aspects of a measure and its effect to establish whether imports are indeed injured and whether this may be justified under WTO rules. The Agreement on Subsidies and Countervailing Measures (SCM Agreement) defines what may be a subsidy, provides a typology of subsidies to list those that are *prohibited*, *actionable*, and *non-actionable*, and lists the available remedies.[51]

Building on the previous example involving households, another brief example of WTO incompatibility would be where a government financially supports only such households that install, say, domestically manufactured and/or assembled renewable energy technologies, given that, amongst other things, such a measure would clearly favor domestic producers/market actors, and thus disadvantage identical or substitutable imported goods vis-à-vis domestically produced goods. Such a measure would, at face value, offend a principal tenet of the WTO system that *like* products, once over the border, be treated in a non-discriminatory manner, irrespective of whether they are imports or domestically produced.[52] Such measures are unlikely to be permitted under the general exceptions (cf., Article XX of the GATT), given that, should imported goods do as good a job as those domestically sourced, the consequent discrimination may actually be mercantilist protectionism veiled by environmental protection pretexts.[53]

---

[51] The SCM Agreement is also a covered agreement listed in Annex 1A of the Agreement Establishing the WTO. Article 1 defines subsidies; Article 3 defines which subsidies are prohibited; Article 4 relates to remedies for prohibited subsidies; Article 5 relates to actionable subsidies; Article 7 to remedies for actionable subsidies; and Article 8 defines what type of subsidies may be non-actionable. For further details on how WTO subsidies provisions apply to renewable energy, see Leal-Arcas, R. *Climate Change and International Trade* (Cheltenham: Edward Elgar, 2013) pp. 136–150.

[52] See Article III of the GATT.

[53] The Article XX general exceptions, if applicable, could allow WTO members to derogate from their core obligations under the GATT and potentially other covered agreements. Articles XX(b) and (g) are the exceptions evidently related to the ecosystem. Article XX(b) contemplates that trade-restrictive

What is more, what often defines the outcome of a dispute before the WTO Dispute Settlement Body's (DSB) adjudicative organs – namely, at first instance, the Panel, and, on final appeal, the Appellate Body – are the issues that parties choose to raise along with how they choose to argue these, thus somewhat restricting the ability of the adjudicative bodies concerned to approach the dispute in a more autonomously coherent manner.[54]

B. Environmental Protection Objectives and the WTO

Throughout Section IV, we shall be looking at the specific WTO norms that have been, and are likely to be, engaged by trade-distortive measures that WTO members may seek to argue have been taken to promote renewables. Before doing so, it may be helpful to briefly consider how environmental concerns have been handled within the GATT/WTO system since the beginning. Essentially, the GATT/WTO system is concerned with trade liberalization. It came in shortly after the end of World War II as part of broader efforts to formalize interstate cooperation along pro-market development lines during the Cold War. The GATT was agreed within the context of the 1944 United Nations Monetary and Financial Conference at Bretton Woods, New Hampshire (United States), along with the other 'Bretton Woods' institutions – namely, the International Monetary Fund and the International Bank of Reconstruction and Development (commonly known as the World Bank). In that sense, its pro-market/pro-trade liberalization bias is inherent and systemic.[55] For

---

measures necessary to protect human, animal, or plant health or life could potentially be justified, and Article XX(g) contemplates that trade-restrictive measures taken to conserve exhaustible natural resources could potentially be justified. There is a wealth of WTO jurisprudence that further articulates the application of these two grounds. We shall refer to the relevant cases elsewhere in this chapter. What is more, it is worth noting that the chapeau to Article XX conditions the application of the general exceptions to ensure that it is not used to offer protection to domestic industry or to discriminate between trade partners. Thus, the chapeau reiterates the non-discriminatory dual principle upon which the WTO system is predicated, namely Article I (most-favored nation treatment) and Article III (national treatment) of the GATT.

[54] See the Understanding on Rules and Procedures Governing the Settlement of Disputes (being Annex 2 of the Agreement Establishing the WTO), where Articles 7 and 17.6 suggest that the terms of reference of the Panel and Appellate Body, respectively, unless otherwise agreed by the parties in dispute, ought to follow the issues and pleadings of the parties.

[55] See the preamble to the GATT 1947.

the purposes of the GATT, all other policy objectives, while not unimportant, were relegated as systemically *external* considerations.

Within the GATT regime, the principal vehicle to accommodate other policy objectives – including environmental protection – has been Article XX of the GATT. This provision contains *general exceptions* to GATT/WTO obligations that, if applicable, may justify derogation on the part of WTO members. The grounds of derogation pertinent to the ecosystem are: Article XX(b), concerning measures *necessary* for the protection of human, animal and plant life or health; and Article XX(g), regarding measures *in relation* to the conservation of exhaustible natural resources.[56] During the GATT era (i.e., in the pre-WTO era, before the conclusion of the Uruguay Round of trade negotiations, which resulted in the Agreement on the Establishment of the WTO in 1994), interpretations of Article XX had been very scarce.[57] This, however, changed with the advent of the WTO system.

The advent of the WTO system in 1995 also saw the inclusion of the notion of 'sustainable development' in the preamble of the Agreement Establishing the WTO (to which the GATT 1994 and all other covered agreements are annexed). Furthermore, in 2001, WTO members issued the Doha Ministerial statement, in which they affirmed the importance of 'sustainable development'[58] to the multilateral trade system. This is not an inconsiderable addition for the purposes of interpreting treaty obligations; the principle of effective treaty interpretation presumes that all relevant textual elements ought to be afforded what may be their appropriate weight in the circumstances.

---

[56] For an analysis, see Abu-Gosh, E. & Leal-Arcas, R. 'The Conservation of Exhaustible Natural Resources in the GATT and WTO: Implications for the Conservation of Oil Resources' (2013) *The Journal of World Investment and Trade*, Vol. 14, No. 3, pp. 480–531.

[57] See Marceau, G. & Wyatt, J. 'The WTO's Efforts to Balance Economic Development and Environmental Protection: A Short Review of Appellate Body Jurisprudence' (2013) *Latin American Journal of International Trade Law*, Vol. 1, No. 1, pp. 291–314, at p. 293.

[58] WT/MIN(01)/DEC/1, (20 November 2001), at point 6 of the Declaration. See http://www.wto.org/english/thewto_e/minist_e/min01_e/mindecl_e.htm

1. *US – Shrimp*

The WTO's Appellate Body, in its determination of the *US – Shrimp* case,[59] expressly referred to the need to utilize the addition of 'sustainable development' in its determinations.[60] Gabrielle Marceau goes further to refer to this interpretative development, which has paid heed to the 'sustainable development' objective, as the: 'consecration of WTO Members' fundamental right to take measures to protect the environment … at a level *they* consider appropriate' (emphasis added).[61]

A further development during the WTO years has been the establishment of the Committee on Trade and Environment (CTE)[62] – a deliberative and advisory body set up to examine the interplay between trade and the environment – created under the 1994 Ministerial Decision on Trade and Environment.[63]

In fact, in the WTO era, there have also been disputes resolved by the WTO's DSB adjudicative bodies that, in effect, have extended the level of environmental protection acceptable within the WTO. In the *US – Shrimp Turtle* case, it was confirmed that the meaning of the GATT Article XX(g) notion of *exhaustible natural resources* had evolved to encompass living beings (in that specific case, these being sea turtle populations). The Appellate Body did this by taking an evolutionary-teleological approach to interpreting that notion. What is more, the interpretation of this notion was, to an extent, colored by extraneous considerations, given that the Appellate Body examined other international agreements to which not all WTO members had been parties. This allowed the Appellate Body, in interpreting the obligations of WTO members, to take into account contemporary concerns expressed at the level of interstate cooperation.[64]

---

59 *United States – Import Prohibition of Certain Shrimp and Shrimp Products* (12 October 1998) (WT/DS58/AB/R).

60 See the Appellate Body report, at §153–155.

61 Marceau, G. & Wyatt, J. 'The WTO's Efforts to Balance Economic Development and Environmental Protection: A Short Review of Appellate Body Jurisprudence' (2013) *Latin American Journal of International Trade Law*, Vol. 1, No. 1, 291–314, at p. 294.

62 See http://www.wto.org/english/tratop_e/envir_e/wrk_committee_e.htm for background information on the CTE.

63 Accessible at http://www.wto.org/english/docs_e/legal_e/56-dtenv.pdf

64 See the Appellate Body report in the *US – Shrimp* dispute, where it is stated that: 'The words of Article XX(g) … must be read in the light of contemporary concerns of the community of nations about the protection and conservation of the environment' (at §129). This is a fine example of *systemic integration*, where the entire international law edifice is approached cohesively

It is worth stating that the WTO adjudicative agencies have, on balance, adhered to the general international law rules on interpretation in a manner that has been consistent with general international law so as to give appropriate weight to agreements that are outside the WTO's scope. The Appellate Body has corrected interpretative errors at the lower adjudicative level,[65] thus not ceasing to regard treaty-based systems – such as the WTO – as being operative against the backdrop of general international law, and, might we add, thus not ceasing to regard the treaties themselves as anything other than *creatures*[66] of public international law.

2. *US – Gasoline*

The *US – Gasoline* case[67] is another seminal case illustrating the extent to which the WTO system may be amenable to environmental protection. While the case was resolved against the party who sought to rely on an Article XX(g) ground to derogate – namely, the US[68] – the case has important implications for environmental protection, given that the Panel in that case held that 'clean air' may, for the purposes of Article XX(g) be considered an *exhaustible natural resource*;[69] a finding subsequently upheld by the Appellate Body on appeal. It is an important development for environmental protection within the WTO system and jurisprudence. In fact, the Panel had drawn from previous (GATT era) jurisprudence,

---

and its elements sympathetically to one another. This systemically integrative approach had previously been confirmed by the Appellate Body in *United States – Standards for Reformulated and Conventional Gasoline*, 29 April 1996 (WT/DS2/AB/R), where the Appellate Body had stated that the GATT ought not be considered 'in clinical isolation of public international law' (see p. 17 of the *US – Gasoline* Appellate Body report).

[65] See Fitzmaurice, M. & Merkouris, P. 'Canons of Treaty Interpretation: Selected Case Studies from the World Trade Organization and the North American Free Trade Agreement', in Fitzmaurice, M. et al. (eds) *Treaty Interpretation and the Vienna Convention on the Law of Treaties: 30 Years On* (Leiden: Martinus Nijhoff Publishers, 2010) at pp. 234–237.

[66] See McLachlan, C. 'The Principle of Systemic Integration and Article 31(3)(C) of the Vienna Convention' (April 2005) *ICLQ* Vol. 54, pp. 279–320, at p. 280.

[67] *United States – Standards for Reformulated and Conventional Gasoline* (WT/DS2/AB/R).

[68] The Appellate Body found that the measure in question discriminated unjustifiably against imports and therefore did not satisfy the non-discrimination requirements of the chapeau of Article XX and of the remaining part of Article XX(g).

[69] See Panel Report, §6.37.

where resources capable of renewal – such as air and living organisms – had been considered *exhaustible natural resources* within the meaning of Article XX(g) of the GATT and, thus, that trade-restrictive measures in relation to their conservation or in order to protect the life or health of human, animal, or plant populations may be justified under Article XX(g).[70]

What is more, in the *US – Gasoline* case, in finding against the US measure and thus disallowing its justification under Article XX(g), the Appellate Body clearly felt the need to reiterate that the specific finding does not compromise in any way the *autonomy* of WTO members to take environmental protection measures that may be trade-restrictive/distortive so long as they are WTO consistent, which largely means they are *bona fide* and non-discriminatory.[71]

---

[70] In *US – Gasoline*, the Panel stated that: 'the fact that a resource was renewable could not be an objection. A past panel had accepted that renewable stocks of salmon could constitute an exhaustible natural resource' (see §6.37, at p. 44 of the Panel report). The case cited by the Panel had been a GATT-era dispute, namely, the *Canada – Measures Affecting Exports of Unprocessed Herring and Salmon* (BISD 35S/98) (adopted on 22 March 1988) dispute in which herring and salmon were considered exhaustible natural resources for the purposes of Article XX(g). In that case, however, Canada could not cite Article XX given that it applied the measure in question discriminatorily in favor of the domestic fisheries processing industry. Note also that dolphins were considered exhaustible natural resources for the purposes of Article XX(g) as per the Panel report (not adopted) in the *United States – Restrictions on Imports of Tuna* dispute (DS29/R) (see §5.13).

[71] In *US – Gasoline*, the Appellate Body stated that: 'It is of some importance that the Appellate Body point out what this does not mean. *It does not mean, or imply, that the ability of any WTO Member to take measures to control air pollution or, more generally, to protect the environment, is at issue. That would be to ignore the fact that Article XX of the General Agreement contains provisions designed to permit important state interests – including the protection of human health, as well as the conservation of exhaustible natural resources – to find expression*. The provisions of Article XX were not changed as a result of the Uruguay Round of Multilateral Trade Negotiations. Indeed, in the preamble to the WTO Agreement and in the [1994 Ministerial] Decision on Trade and Environment *there is specific acknowledgement to be found about the importance of coordinating policies on trade and the environment. WTO Members have a large measure of autonomy to determine their own policies on the environment (including its relationship with trade), their environmental objectives and the environmental legislation they enact and implement*. So far as concerns the WTO, that autonomy is circumscribed only by the need to respect the requirements of the General Agreement and the other covered agreements' (WT/DS2/AB/R, at pp. 29–30, emphasis added).

It is worth noting at this point that, while, undoubtedly, there is a preference within the WTO system for multilateralism[72] in trade-restrictive measures taken in pursuit of legitimate objectives – including environmental protection – as the Appellate Body's comments in *US – Gasoline* suggest, this does not negate WTO members' right to autonomously – that is, unilaterally – take such measures.[73]

3. The SPS Agreement

The Agreement on the Application of Sanitary and Phytosanitary Measures (SPS Agreement)[74] further contemplates the relationship between WTO trade obligations and environmental protection. It acknowledges that it may be appropriate for WTO members to take such trade-restrictive measures that seek to protect the life or health of human, animal, and plant populations within their territory (Article 2.1). The SPS Agreement tightly conditions recourse to justificatory grounds in order to prohibit its discriminatory application (Article 2.3), and to ensure that there is *some* scientific basis to such trade-restrictive measures (Articles 3.2 and 3.3). That said, it affords discretion to members to take measures that seek to offer a higher degree of protection than what may be

---

[72] See Articles 1.1 & 2.4 of the Agreement on Technical Barriers to Trade (TBT Agreement). The TBT Agreement is also in the Annex 1A to the Agreement Establishing the WTO and, therefore, binding on all WTO members. See also the 1994 Ministerial Decision on Trade and Environment, where it is stated that there should be: '... adherence to effective multilateral disciplines to ensure responsiveness of the multilateral trading system to environmental objectives set forth in Agenda 21 and the Rio Declaration, in particular Principle 12'. In relation to Principle 12 of the Rio Declaration, it relates to the 1992 UN Conference on Environment and Development, where participants declared their commitment: 'Unilateral actions to deal with environmental challenges outside the jurisdiction of the importing country should be avoided. Environmental measures addressing transboundary or global problems should, as far as possible, be based on an international consensus'.

[73] Comments as appear in the previous footnote. What is more, in the *US – Shrimp* case, the Appellate Body, while citing a list of WTO documents and other agreements in which a preference for multilateralism is articulated, stated that: 'WTO Members are free to adopt their own policies aimed at protecting the environment as long as, in so doing, they fulfill their obligations and respect the rights of other Members under the *WTO Agreement* ...' (at p. 71, Appellate Body report).

[74] The SPS Agreement is an Annex 1A (to the Agreement Establishing the WTO) multilateral WTO covered agreement, binding on the entire WTO membership.

possible, say, under international standards.[75] In other words, it is for members to determine the level of risk they are willing to assume. In the *European Communities – Measures Affecting Asbestos and Asbestos-containing Products* case,[76] the Appellate Body reiterated the prerogative of WTO members to determine the level of risk[77] so long as this exercise, predictably, is *bona fide* and not unjustifiably discriminatory in relation to the treatment of trade partners and of imports vis-à-vis domestic products.

4. The TBT Agreement

Another relevant aspect of the WTO system and measures taken in relation to a wide range of policy objectives is the Agreement on Technical Barriers to Trade (TBT Agreement). The general obligation under the TBT Agreement is that technical regulations taken on the part of members in pursuit of certain legitimate policy objectives are not unduly restrictive, discriminatorily applied, or otherwise improperly used. The TBT Agreement does not provide derogation grounds *per se* in the sense that Article XX of the GATT does. What it does is allude to a non-exhaustive list of legitimate objectives that may be behind a WTO member's technical regulation.[78] That said, in one recital in the preamble, it is made clear that WTO members preserve their rights in relation to, amongst other things, environmental protection.[79] What is more, the TBT Agreement systemically defers to the SPS Agreement for measures that may more appropriately fall within the scope of the latter.[80] Gabrielle Marceau considers that the TBT Agreement could potentially be more accommodative than Article XX of the GATT.[81]

---

[75] See Article 3.3 SPS Agreement.

[76] WT/DS135/AB/R.

[77] Ibid. at §168.

[78] Article 2.2 TBT Agreement.

[79] 'Recognizing that *no country should be prevented from taking measures necessary to ensure the quality of its exports, or for the protection of human, animal or plant life or health, of the environment, or for the prevention of deceptive practices, at the levels it considers appropriate*, subject to the requirement that they are not applied in a manner which would constitute a means of arbitrary or unjustifiable discrimination between countries where the same conditions prevail or a disguised restriction on international trade, and are otherwise in accordance with the provisions of this Agreement' (emphasis added).

[80] See Article 1.5 TBT Agreement.

[81] Marceau persuasively argues that: 'TBT Article 2.2 "provides a non-exhaustive, open list of legitimate objectives" and the complaining Member bears

5. The SCM Agreement

A further pro-environment aspect of the WTO system is contained in the SCM Agreement, which permits, as non-actionable, such subsidies that are directly related to making existing industrial facilities more environmentally friendly.[82] Furthermore, under Article 8 of the SCM Agreement, government subsidies for, say, renewables research could potentially be acceptable so long as certain conditions are met to ensure it is not protectionism under the veneer of environmentalism.[83] Article 8, however, expired in 1999[84] and no new list of non-actionable subsidies appears to have been agreed upon.[85]

6. Discussion

All the above developments point towards a multilateral trade system that has evolved to its current WTO form to better and more meaningfully integrate non-core objectives – for example, environmental protection –

---

the burden of proving that the responding Member's objective is not legitimate. The practical effect of this difference is that some policy objectives that would not be permissible to justify a prima facie GATT breach through GATT Article XX will be admitted under TBT Article 2.2 as legitimate objectives capable of justifying technical regulations that create obstacles to trade. Already in the US – COOL dispute [i.e., United States – Certain Country of Origin Labelling (COOL) Requirements, (WT/DS384/DS386)], an objective that would most probably not have come within any of the sub-paragraphs of GATT Article XX[,] the US objective of providing consumers with information on the countries in which the livestock from which the meat they purchase is produced were born, raised, and slaughtered, was considered legitimate for the purposes of TBT Article 2.2', Marceau, G. & Wyatt, J. 'The WTO's Efforts to Balance Economic Development and Environmental Protection: A Short Review of Appellate Body Jurisprudence' (2013) *Latin American Journal of International Trade Law*, Vol. 1, No. 1, pp. 291–314, at p. 311.

[82] See Article 8.2(c) of the SCM Agreement, which lays down the conditions for non-actionable subsidies, including that the environmental protection levels an existing facility seeks to meet be prescribed by law and that the subsidy not exceed 20% of the total cost of adaptation.

[83] See Article 8.2(a) of the SCM Agreement in relation to the conditions that emphasize the need for the benefit of any such subsidy to accrue to the beneficiary during the pre-competitive stage.

[84] See Article 31 of the SCM Agreement, which states that the provisions of Article 8 of the SCM Agreement, amongst others, shall apply not more than five years after the date that the Agreement on the Establishment of the WTO comes into force.

[85] See Ghosh, A. & Gangania, H. (2012) 'Governing Clean Energy Subsidies: What, Why and How Legal?', International Centre for Trade and Sustainable Development, at p. 39.

with its core trade liberalization objectives. And towards a system that affords, if not preserves, the necessary policy space for WTO members to continue to pursue a wider range of policy objectives, including those linked to environmental protection.

While it is evident from the above that the multilateral trade system has evolved to better accommodate environmental protection objectives, we have also witnessed a significant development in WTO jurisprudence to strengthen the safeguards against abuse.[86] This has happened to ensure that trade restrictive measures remain *bona fide* and that the multilateral trade system remains credible. There is a raft of cases relating to Article XX of the GATT derogatory grounds, where recourse to it has been disciplined to ensure that it is not abused. The adjudicative bodies of the WTO have sought to articulate what ought to be the relationship between a trade restrictive measure at issue and the GATT Article XX derogatory grounds cited. While such an exercise would depend on the actual Article XX paragraph(s) that a WTO member chooses to cite,[87] the chapeau to

---

[86] There is a wealth of cases that contain findings which, in effect, regulate reliance on GATT Article XX. For the purposes of this chapter, however, we are not drilling down to such a level in this subsection as we are mainly concerned with presenting aspects of the WTO system that are amenable to environmental protection objectives. Such cases are aspects of the *US – Gasoline*, which articulates the relationship between the measure and the policy objective it seeks to advance (the *means* and *ends* relationship); *Brazil – Measures Affecting Imports of Retreaded Tyres* (WT/DS332) and *Korea – Measures Affecting Imports of Fresh, Chilled and Frozen Beef* (WT/DS161/WT/DS169), which are concerned, amongst other things, with the necessary degree of proximity between the means and ends; and *China – Measures Related to the Exportation of Various Raw Materials* (WT/DS394/WT/DS 395/WT/DS398) in relation to analyzing the relationship between the means and ends to also examine when the measure in question was likely to have any positive impact on the objective cited by a State defending its trade-restrictive measure. See Marceau, G. & Wyatt, J. 'The WTO's Efforts to Balance Economic Development and Environmental Protection: A Short Review of Appellate Body Jurisprudence' (2013) *Latin American Journal of International Trade Law*, Vol. 1, No. 1, pp. 291–314, at pp. 297–300, for a recent rundown of the relevant cases.

[87] Note that the wording between groups of Article XX grounds (namely, the use of 'necessary' in paragraphs (a), (b), and (d); 'relating to' in paragraphs (c), (e), and (g); 'in pursuance of' in paragraph (h); 'essential' in paragraph (j); 'for the protection of' in paragraph (f); and 'involving' in paragraph (i)) varies, which suggests that its effect on the required degree of relationship between the objective behind the trade-restrictive measure and the measure taken may vary. See the Appellate Body's comments in the *US – Gasoline* dispute, where it refers to the significance of textual nuances (at pp. 17–19).

Article XX makes clear that such measures that are arbitrary and unjustifiable discrimination between WTO peers and/or disguised restriction on international trade may not be justified under Article XX.

While the purpose of the present chapter is to discuss pro-renewable energy measures and their relationship to WTO rules, we have included this section about environmental protection in relation to WTO rules,[88] as these are issues that we see frequently arising in disputes involving such measures.

C. The Promotion of Renewables and the WTO

This section makes reference to disputes at the WTO over subsidies for renewable energy.[89]

1. The Canada Renewables cases

Government measures connected to the promotion of renewables may be highly divergent. In the recent WTO disputes in which Canada responded to complaints raised by the EU[90] and Japan,[91] the pro-renewables measures that could be teased out of the facts of these cases were: the offer on the part of the provincial government of Ontario of financial support for those who fed energy that was derived from renewable sources into the electricity grid, and the favoring of local renewables technology manufacturing and/or

---

[88] See http://www.wto.org/english/tratop_e/envir_e/climate_change_e.pdf for a WTO take on the intersection between the WTO system and climate change. For a more general discussion on the link between trade and climate change, see Leal-Arcas, R. *Climate Change and International Trade* (Cheltenham: Edward Elgar, 2013).

[89] On renewable energy and the WTO, see Rubini, L. '*Ain't Wastin' Time no More*: Subsidies for Renewable Energy, The SCM Agreement, Policy Space, and Law Reform', *Journal of International Economic Law*, advance access published 25 April 2012; Howse, R. 'World Trade Law and Renewable Energy: The Case of Non-Tariff Barriers' (2009) UNCTAD/DITC/TED/2008/5; Howse, R. & Eliason, A. 'Domestic and International Strategies to Address Climate Change: An Overview of the WTO Legal Issues', in Cottier, T. et al. (eds) *International Trade Regulation and the Mitigation of Climate Change* (Cambridge: Cambridge University Press, 2009) pp. 48–93.

[90] *Canada – Measures Relating to the Feed-in Tariff Program* (WT/DS426/AB/R). Appellate Body report published *in tandem* with *Canada – Certain Measures Affecting the Renewable Energy Generation Sector* (*Canada – Renewable Energy*) (WT/DS412/AB/R).

[91] *Canada – Certain Measures Affecting the Renewable Energy Generation Sector* (WT/DS412/AB/R). Appellate Body report published *in tandem* with *Canada – Measures Relating to the Feed-in Tariff Program* (WT/DS426/AB/R).

assembling industries. In relation to the latter, we say this because the offer of financial support[92] to those generating electricity through renewable sources (wind and solar means, in these particular cases) was contingent upon their drawing a substantial part (50–60%)[93] of the technological components from domestic manufacturers or assemblers. In that sense, these two distinct, yet linked, measures engage different aspects of the WTO. While the former measure may immediately call into question the consistency of a subsidy-like measure with WTO rules and, more broadly, of appropriate levels of government support and market intervention, the latter, most crucially, engages several WTO rules that relate to local content requirements (LCR).

The pleadings and findings in the *Canada – Renewable Energy* and *Canada – Feed-in Tariff [FIT] Program* disputes brought to the fore a catalogue of matters engaged, including the WTO's core non-discrimination provisions (Articles I and III of the GATT) as well as provisions in the SCM Agreement, the GPA,[94] and in the Agreement on Trade-Related Investment Measures (TRIMs Agreement).[95]

The production of electricity through renewable means is less regular than through the combustion of hydrocarbons or through nuclear fission. Energy production through the harnessing of, say, solar and wind power is contingent upon weather conditions. There can be no steady production outside the vagaries of the weather. What is more, the cost of the necessary infrastructure makes this field of the renewables industry uncompetitive when compared with conventional energy production.[96] The gist of it in relation to these cases is that the Appellate Body – having upheld some and having nullified other earlier findings by the Panel – ended up recommending that Canada abandon the LCR component of its measure as it found this to be, amongst other things, an

---

[92] Let us refer to this as the feed-in tariff and micro feed-in tariff contracts, as well as by the shorter 'FITs and micro-FITs contracts.'

[93] There are various figures ranging from 25% to 60%. However, from 2012, the range has been 50%–60%. See joint Appellate Report (at p. 18).

[94] As stated earlier, the GPA is a plurilateral agreement annexed to the Agreement Establishing the WTO. Canada and Japan are parties to the GPA. The EU is listed as a party 'with respect to its 28 member states', which suggests it is not a party in its own right. See http://www.wto.org/english/tratop_e/gproc_e/memobs_e.htm. In any event, the GPA has been cited in the Appellate Body report in side comments (pp. 50 and 58).

[95] The TRIMs Agreement is also an Annex 1A (to the Agreement Establishing the WTO) covered multilateral agreement and, therefore, binding on all WTO members.

[96] See §5.174 (at p. 124) of the Appellate Body joint report.

unjustifiable breach of Article III of the GATT in relation to the non-discrimination principle that imported products be treated similarly to *like* domestic products (i.e., the 'national treatment' aspect of the non-discrimination principle that underpins the multilateral trade system).

The complainants had sought to have the measure examined primarily under the specific provisions in the SCM and TRIMs Agreements as they considered these to be the *lex specialis* applicable to the measure in question. Article 3.1(b) of the SCM Agreement expressly places subsidies contingent on LCRs in the prohibited category[97] and paragraph 1(a) in the Annex to the TRIMs Agreement makes clear that trade-related investment measures requiring the use or purchase of domestic products are inconsistent with Article III of the GATT. In that sense, both Agreements condemn LCRs. While no loophole exists in the SCM Agreement for measures containing LCRs, the TRIMs Agreement admits some departure by its reference to Article III of the GATT. We say this because, while Article III of the GATT prohibits discriminatory treatment of imports vis-à-vis domestic products[98] and prohibits the use of LCRs,[99] it permits derogation in relation to government procurement so long as there is no subsequent commercial dimension to this procurement.[100] The Appellate Body rejected the argument that both of these instruments were somehow more specific to the measure and considered that the measure could appropriately be examined under Article III of the GATT. Also, the Appellate Body rejected the view that, when confronted with claims engaging all three instruments (namely the GATT, the SCM and TRIMs Agreements), it ought take into consideration and examine these in a sequence that promoted the last two.[101]

As one may expect, the Appellate Body report contains several nuanced interpretations over various matters, including terms from the GATT, the SCM and TRIMs Agreements and their respective jurisprudence.[102] It is outside the immediate scope of this chapter to review these

---

97 Readily we see the prohibition of any subsidy that seeks to boost exports or substitute imports.

98 Article III:4 GATT.

99 Article III:1 GATT.

100 Article III:8 GATT.

101 See §5.5, p. 84, of the Appellate Body joint report.

102 Issues examined were, amongst others, the extent to which the measure amounted to government purchases, whether it had been for government purposes (NB: there was recourse to the French and Spanish version of the text of GATT 1994 to establish the meaning of 'purposes'), and what the conditions were which governed the government procurement.

here. However, what we want to emphasize is that this report *does not* condemn pro-renewables policies or measures *per se*. What it does condemn are unnecessarily discriminatory practices that favor domestic commercial production. The measure was ultimately found to be inconsistent because it unjustifiably discriminated between domestic and imported products (under Article III of the GATT and, as a trade-related investment measure, also under Article 2.1 of the TRIMs Agreement); and not because preferential rates were paid to Ontario's renewable energy producers under their FIT and micro-FIT contracts.[103]

The Panel and the Appellate Body attempted to carry out an analysis under the SCM Agreement. The Appellate Body upheld the Panel's earlier finding that the payment of higher rates for renewables-derived electricity under the FIT and micro-FIT contracts had been a 'purchase of goods' for the purposes of Article 1.1(a)(1)(iii) of the SCM Agreement. However, in relation to satisfying the other aspect indicating that a subsidy exists – namely, that there is a 'benefit' that may accrue to another (as per Article 1.1(b) of the SCM Agreement) – the Appellate Body was unable to carry out an assessment of 'benefit', given, in this case, the complexities of establishing what is the likely market benchmark that ought to be used to assess what the 'benefit' had been in that particular case. Also, in assessing what may have been the 'subsidy' and its 'benefit,' the parties were concerned with those who benefited from the higher tariffs under the FIT and micro-FIT contracts – that is to say, the renewable energy producers – rather than the domestic producers and/or assemblers of the renewables' technology who, despite their being third parties, clearly benefited under the LCRs of the FIT and micro-FIT contracts vis-à-vis foreign producers and/or assemblers of such technologies. Eventually, there were sufficient grounds to find against Canada under Article III of the GATT.

Finally, the political reasons behind Canada's insistence to defend the LCR aspect of its measure – namely, regional job-creation – is a trade-restrictive 'externality' for the purposes of WTO rules that cannot be accommodated when it exceeds the limits afforded to WTO members under, amongst other measures, Article XX of the GATT, Article III:8 of the GATT, and Article 8 of the SCM Agreement. However, the objectives of job creation and of environmental protection are inherently different and, while the multilateral trade system has evolved to better accommodate environmental protection, this is not so in relation to job creation.

---

103 See §5.84, at p. 103, of the Appellate Body joint report.

In *Canada – Renewable Energy* and *Canada – Feed-in Tariff Program*, the EU successfully complained against a renewables-related measure that offended its trade interests. In this joint case, the WTO rejected those aspects of a measure that were wholly unnecessary for the renewables cause *per se*. The LCR aspect of the policy favored domestic producers and disadvantaged importers in a manner that was protectionist, without substantially enhancing the renewables cause *per se*. For the party taking the pro-renewables measure in question, the negative outcome in that case cannot be said to be a defeat for the renewables cause, given that it neither discourages FITs nor does it discourage the take-up of renewables. Consequently, any accusation against the EU as applying double standards would be misinformed and unfair, given that the specific aspects of the EU policies that are the subject of complaints are qualitatively different, do not amount to protectionism of EU domestic production *per se*, are arguably far from being capricious, and, in the final analysis, are taken in a disinterested manner on the part of the EU and in the face of unabated environmental degradation.

2. Other WTO cases connected to renewable energy[104]

2.1. China – Wind Power[105] In December 2010, the US requested consultations with China concerning certain measures it alleged benefited wind-power technology manufacturers in China.[106] The US contended, amongst other things, that such measures appeared to be contingent upon the use of domestically produced goods and, therefore, inconsistent with Article 3 of the SCM Agreement. The US argued that, as these measures appear to be subsidies that had not been notified to the WTO, they also breached, amongst other measures, Article XVI of the GATT regarding subsidies and Article 25 of the SCM Agreement regarding the duty to notify.[107]

---

[104] This section refers to other renewable-energy-related complaints that have engaged the WTO dispute settlement processes; however, not all cases necessarily resulted in determinations.

[105] WT/DS419.

[106] *China – Measures Concerning Wind Power Equipment*, Request for Consultations by the United States, January 6, 2011 (WT/DS419/1); see also Office of the United States Trade Representative, 'United States Requests WTO Dispute Settlement Consultations on China's Subsidies for Wind Power Equipment Manufacturers', Press Release, December 2010, available at http://www.ustr.gov/about-us/press-office/press-releases/2010/december/united-states-requests-wto-dispute-settlement-con

[107] See http://www.wto.org/english/tratop_e/dispu_e/cases_e/ds419_e.htm

2.1.1. A RECOUNTAL OF THE CASE[108] Although *China – Measures Concerning Wind Power Equipment* was amicably settled between the US and China,[109] it is nevertheless relevant to discuss the merits of this case. In December 2010, the US filed a complaint against China before the WTO regarding certain measures providing public funds, grants, or awards to enterprises that manufacture wind power equipment. The US argued that certain measures undertaken by the Chinese government in support of its wind power industry are contrary to Article 3 of the SCM Agreement. The US complaint was based on a petition that was filed with the Office of the US Trade Representative by the Steelworkers Union in September 2010 pursuant to Section 301 of the Trade Act of 1974.[110] In that petition, the Steelworkers Union complained of a wide range of policies undertaken by China to 'stimulate and protect its domestic producers of green technology, from wind and solar energy products to advanced batteries and energy-efficient vehicles'.[111] Their petition argued that these policies have permitted China to become the dominant global supplier of green technology, and have 'drained manufacturing investment from the US to China, transferred valuable technology and research and development activities to China, cost American workers the high-skilled green jobs of the future, and increased the US trade deficit'.[112]

The Steelworkers' petition identified five categories of China's policies that, in their view, are contrary to WTO rules:

(1) restrictions on access by foreign nations and firms to critical materials necessary for the manufacture of green technologies.[113] These include solar panels, wind turbines, advanced batteries, and energy efficient lighting. According to the petition, 'China produces

---

[108] This section draws from Leal-Arcas, R. Climate Change and International Trade (Cheltenham: Edward Elgar, 2013) pp. 147–150.

[109] See Office of the United States Trade Representative, 'China Ends Wind Power Equipment Subsidies Challenged by the Unites States in WTO Dispute', Press Release (June 2011), available at http://www.ustr.gov/about-us/press-office/press-releases/2011/june/china-ends-wind-power-equipment-subsidies-challenged

[110] Petition for Relief under Section 301 of the Trade Act of 1974, as Amended: China's Policies Affecting Trade and Investment in Green Technology, September 9, 2010, available at http://www.ustr.gov/sites/default/files/09-09-2010%20Petition.pdf

[111] Ibid. p. 1.

[112] Ibid. pp. 1–2.

[113] Ibid. p. 2.

more than 90 percent of the world's supply of [the] minerals'[114] necessary for the production of these technologies, and 'uses a variety of means to restrict exports of these materials to users in the US and other countries';[115]

(2) the use of subsidies contingent on export or domestic content, such as subsidies for the manufacture and development of green technology that are conditioned on the use of domestic over imported inputs;[116]

(3) discrimination against foreign firms and goods in bidding out the construction of wind farms and solar power plants;[117]

(4) requirements for foreign companies to transfer technology, even though when China joined the WTO in 2001 it committed not to ask foreign firms to transfer technology as a condition of making investment agreements with Chinese state-owned enterprises or financial institutions, or granting technology licenses to Chinese partners;[118] and

(5) the provision of domestic subsidies alleged to be trade-distorting, 'including in the solar, wind, biomass, geothermal, hydropower, nuclear, advanced battery, alternative vehicle, and energy-efficient consumer product, sectors'.[119]

The US complaint addressed only category number 2, that is, the provision of subsidies contingent on export or domestic content.[120] It targeted measures which appear in regulations[121] that establish a special fund to support the wind power equipment manufacturing sector in China.[122] This fund is stated to be for the purpose of 'encouraging corporate R&D activities on market demanded products',[123] and it is

---

114 Ibid.

115 Ibid. pp. 2–3.

116 Ibid. p. 3.

117 Ibid. pp. 3–4.

118 Ibid. p. 4.

119 Ibid. p. 5.

120 USTR, 'United States Requests WTO Dispute Settlement Consultations on China's Subsidies for Wind Power Equipment Manufacturers', available at http://www.ustr.gov/about-us/press-office/press-releases/2010/december/united-states-requests-wto-dispute-settlement-con

121 Ministry of Finance Document [2008] No. 476, 'Management Regulations on Special Fund for Wind Power Manufacturing Sector in China' available at http://www.cresp.org.cn/uploadfiles/2/981/mof_476_eng.pdf

122 Ibid. Appendix, Article 1.

123 Ibid. Appendix, Article 2.

purported that it will be allocated as 'incentives instead of subsidies'.[124] The US complaint appears to focus, in particular, on the qualifications of wind power manufacturing companies applying for a grant from the fund, which are set out in Article 6(4) of the Appendix of the Management Regulations on Special Fund for Wind Power Manufacturing Sector in China, which requires that 'the wind turbine component of blades, gearboxes and generators must be manufactured by Chinese companies or Chinese-controlled stock companies. Converters and bearings manufacturing are encouraged'.

The US complaint alleged that the subsidies appear to be 'prohibited subsidies' according to Article 3 of the SCM Agreement.[125] The complaint also alleged breaches of a number of provisions of the SCM Agreement (namely Articles 25.1, 25.2, 25.3, and 25.4) as well as Article XVI.1 of the GATT 1994 requiring the notification of subsidies.[126] Moreover, the US also argued that China had breached the terms on which it acceded to the WTO which required translation of measures into one or more of the official languages of the WTO, thereby failing to comply with its obligation under Part I, paragraph 1.2 of its Protocol of Accession.[127]

The US–China consultations took place in February 2011, when the Chinese government agreed to put an end to the special fund.[128] The dispute therefore concluded amicably. It is reasonable to say that the US complaint seems relatively narrow, given that it dealt only with one of the many policies that the Steelworkers Union brought forward in its petition.

2.2. *US – Countervailing Measures (China)*[129] In May 2012, China requested consultations with the US concerning countervailing duties that the US was levying on certain Chinese products, including renewable energy technologies, on the basis that they are State-owned enterprise products with subsidized inputs on the part of the Chinese government.

---

[124] Ibid.

[125] *China – Measures Concerning Wind Power Equipment* (WT/DS419/1), p. 1.

[126] Ibid.

[127] Ibid.

[128] Drajem, M. 'China Agrees to End Wind-Power Subsidies After WTO Case, Trade Office Says', *Bloomberg* News, 7 June 2011, available at http://www.bloomberg.com/news/2011-06-07/china-agrees-to-end-wind-power-subsidies-after-wto-case-trade-office-says.html

[129] WT/DS437.

China also challenged the US Department of Commerce's presumption that enterprises with majority government ownership ought to be treated as *public bodies* for the purposes of WTO rules.[130] China claimed that the measures in question infringed upon the following provisions: Article VI of the GATT; Articles 1, 2, 11, 12, and 14 of the SCM Agreement; and Article 15 of the Protocol of Accession of China to the WTO. A Panel was established in September 2012 and its composition was determined in November 2012. At the time of writing this chapter, the Panel was expected to issue its report by May 2014.[131]

2.3. EU and a Member State – Importation of Biodiesels[132] In August 2012, Argentina requested consultations with the EU and Spain concerning certain measures affecting biofuel imports into the EU and how related data collection practices discriminated against certain biofuel imports. Argentina claimed the measure was inconsistent with, amongst others, Articles III and XI of the GATT as well as Article 2 of the TRIMs Agreement. In December 2012, Argentina requested a panel be established, which was then deferred by the DSB.

2.4. US – Countervailing and Anti-Dumping Measures (China)[133] In September 2012, China requested consultations with the US in relation to US measures that affected, amongst other Chinese exports, wind-power technologies. These measures related to the following: US legislation that permitted the application of countervailing measures (i.e., a type of trade-balancing remedy permissible, subject to conditions, under WTO law) to tradables from 'non-market' economies; the countervailing duties pursuant to that legislation; and to countermeasures taken by the US in relation to its subjective findings of dumping practices on the part of China. China claimed that the measures in question are inconsistent with the following provisions: Articles 10, 15, 19, 21, and 32 of the SCM

[130] This is despite an earlier (NB: the report was circulated in March 2011) Appellate Body determination in a case brought by China against the US, where the Appellate Body reversed the Panel's interpretation of the term 'public body' in Article 1.1(a)(1) of the SCM Agreement and found that a public body is an entity that possesses, exercises, or is vested with, governmental authority, and where it found that the US had acted inconsistently with Articles 1.1(a)(1), 10, and 32.1 of the SCM Agreement, in finding that certain State-owned enterprises constituted public bodies. See *United States – Definitive Anti-Dumping and Countervailing Duties on Certain Products from China* (WT/DS379).

[131] See https://www.wto.org/english/tratop_e/dispu_e/cases_e/ds437_e.htm

[132] WT/DS443.

[133] WT/DS449.

Agreement; Articles VI, and X of the GATT; and Article 9 of the Anti-Dumping Agreement (ADA).[134] The DSB established a Panel in December 2012, which the WTO Director-General composed in March 2013. In March 2014, the Panel report was issued.

2.5. EU and Certain Member States – Renewable Energy Measures[135] In November 2012, China requested consultations with the EU, Greece and Italy in relation to certain measures, including domestic content restrictions that affect the renewable energy generation sector relating to the feed-in tariff (FIT) programs of EU Member States, including Italy and Greece. China cited ten separate pieces of EU and Member State legislation that it claimed affected its trade interests. Amongst the WTO rules cited by China are the following: Articles I and III of the GATT; Article 3.1(b) of the SCM Agreement; and Article 2 of the TRIMs Agreement.

2.6. India – Solar Cells Measures[136] In February 2013, the US requested consultations with India in relation to certain measures linked to renewable energy generation in India that contained a local content requirement for solar energy technologies. On the face of it, this measure would injure *like* imports as it encouraged the use of domestic components. The US claims that this is inconsistent with: Article III of the GATT; Article 2 of the TRIMs Agreement; Articles 3, 6, and 25 of the SCM Agreement, and that it directly or indirectly nullifies or impairs the benefits that accrue to the US due to India's and its own WTO membership.

2.7. Recurring issues in renewables-related WTO cases An overview of the above complaints suggests that the commonest issue complainants raise is that some LCR aspect of a measure has been harmful to their industries and is unjustified under WTO rules. Other issues appear to be whether countermeasures taken to address dumping concerns have been justified in the circumstances, and whether some technical barrier exists – such as a definition employed by a WTO member – that leads to less favorable treatment for imports. As we have stated, the above listed disputes, for the most part, are at the early stages of the dispute

---

[134] The ADA is officially listed as the *Agreement on Implementation of Article VI of the GATT 1994* and is an Annex 1A (to the Agreement Establishing the WTO) multilateral agreement binding on all WTO members.

[135] WT/DS452.

[136] WT/DS456.

resolution process. However, there is WTO jurisprudence that, although not directly concerned with renewables, has implications for renewables within the WTO.

The issues that arise in the list of complaints above often hinge on whether *like* products are treated evenhandedly. Articles III:2 and III:4 of the GATT refer to the obligation to treat *like* products in a non-discriminatory manner. Therefore, the first step in assessing whether less favorable treatment indeed exists is itself complicated by the need to establish that there is sufficient *likeness* between the products for an allegation to be legally relevant. What establishes *likeness* is determined on a case-by-case basis. While the competitive relationship between the products in question is clearly material to a determination of *likeness*, it is not the sole determinant, nor are all products in a strong competitive relationship with one another necessarily *like* products under the WTO rules.[137]

Likeness could potentially depend on a wide range of issues, including the physical characteristics of the products, end uses, consumer habits and sensibilities,[138] with the possibility that other factors may, in certain cases, also be relevant for establishing whether there is *likeness*. Once likeness has been established, the question is to then establish whether imports have been treated less favorably than domestic products.[139] In that sense, Article III of the GATT is aimed at preventing against protectionism,[140] and, therefore, determinations of *likeness* cannot be restricted to an inflexible array of issues to be taken into consideration. *Likeness* considerations could be relevant to, say, complaints alleging that electricity produced through renewable means is treated more favorably than other products that exist in a competitive relationship and, on a number of parameters – including substitutability, physical likeness, and others – are sufficiently *alike.*

---

137 See §99 (at p. 37) of the Appellate Body Report, *European Communities – Measures Affecting Asbestos and Asbestos-Containing Products* (WT/DS135/AB/R), adopted 5 April 2001.

138 For instance, consumer sensibilities around the use of asbestos were held to be sufficiently material in establishing likeness in *EC – Asbestos* (WT/DS135/AB/R).

139 See the report by the United Nations Conference on Trade and Development, *World Trade Law and Renewable Energy: The Case of Non-Tariff Barriers* (New York and Geneva, 2009) for a fuller analysis on this two-step test in the relevant WTO jurisprudence (at pp. 5–7, and *passim*).

140 See Appellate Body report, *Japan – Taxation on Alcoholic Beverages* (WT/DS8/AB/R), at p. 16.

Potentially, an importer of electricity may argue that the higher tariffs paid to, or preferential price levels set by government for, renewable-energy domestic producers breach Article III of the GATT. Here there is a series of questions that would have to be addressed. For instance, are the electricity imports, which are alleged to be treated less favorably, *like* products for the purposes of Article III of the GATT? A determination of *likeness* could foreseeably focus on how this electricity has been produced. While a single unit of electricity is identical to any other unit of electricity – and, therefore, while the physical aspects of electricity may make electricity derived from different energy sources (e.g., conventional (fossil fuel), nuclear, or renewables) a *like* product – their production method may well make these sufficiently *unlike*.[141]

It is worth noting that in the Canada cases, the Appellate Body – albeit for the purposes of assessing what might be the appropriate market benchmark for an assessment of 'benefit' under Article 1.1(b) of the SCM Agreement – contemplated the differences between the electricity generation industries drawing from conventional sources and those drawing from renewables, as being rather distinct.[142] In that respect, less favorable treatment for electricity produced by conventional or nuclear means than for electricity produced by renewables may be entirely justified under WTO rules if they are determined to be *unlike*, *so long as* domestically produced electricity derived by conventional or nuclear means is also treated in an evenhanded manner. Otherwise, the complaint by foreign electricity producers could be structured on the less favorable treatment accorded to those *like* products – namely, imported electricity produced by conventional or nuclear means vis-à-vi*s* domestically produced electricity produced by conventional or nuclear means, given that discriminatory treatment could then be said to exist between *like* products.

Other issues that appear repeatedly in the renewables-related complaints we have listed earlier relate to whether a particular measure actually amounts to a prohibited or otherwise actionable subsidy within the context of the SCM Agreement. Again, making such a determination relies on a thorough review of all relevant aspects of a measure. Does the measure involve some sort of material support on the part of a government to its domestic industry in a manner that is trade-distortive? In that sense, 'government' or 'public body' (or even a 'private body' where it is

---

141 Howse, R. 'World Trade Law and Renewable Energy: The Case of Non-Tariff Barriers' (UNCTAD, 2009) at p. 3.

142 See Appellate Body joint report, §5.174, at p. 124.

clear or imputed that it exercises some government-like functions)[143] and 'subsidy' have a specific meaning within the SCM Agreement. Regarding a subsidy: there must be some sort of 'financial contribution'[144] *or* price or income support;[145] it must confer a 'benefit' on the recipient;[146] and, unless it involves a subsidy that on its face is prohibited,[147] in order for it to be actionable, it would be necessary to establish that the subsidy is 'specific',[148] that it has 'adverse effects'[149] on the trade interests of another WTO member, and that the level of support is above the permissible limits of Article 8 of the SCM Agreement.

Findings as to whether the above elements are present in a measure that is the subject of a complaint are not without their complexities. There would be little doubt that a measure aimed at the development of the renewables industries – for example, by providing interest-free or low-interest loans to the domestic renewable energy technology industry – would be a clear case of a financial contribution that confers a benefit and that is specific to a particular industry. It is less clear on first inspection whether it would be inconsistent with WTO rules. While such a measure would appear less likely, on the face of it, to amount to a prohibited subsidy aimed at export stimulation or import substitution *per se*, it is likely to be actionable under Article 5 of the SCM Agreement, should it have adverse effects on the trade interests of other WTO members; and should the level of support conferred by it be outside the permissible limits stipulated in Article 8 of the SCM Agreement.

We acknowledge that there may be various measures connected to the promotion of renewables that may infringe upon WTO rules; not only those measures that are linked to feed-in tariff (FIT) renewables schemes.

---

143 See Article 1.1(a)(1)(i) & (iii) of the SCM Agreement.

144 Article 1.1(a)(1) of the SCM Agreement.

145 Article 1.1(a)(2) of the SCM Agreement. In relation to findings as to whether a financial contribution exists, it is not necessary for a State to be financially burdened or forego, say, tax income, given that the material support it gives may be indirect and, at the same time, fulfill the requirement of Article 1 of the SCM Agreement. See Jerjian, A. 'The Feed-in Tariff Controversy: Renewable Energy Challenges in WTO Law' for a review of the relevant WTO jurisprudence relating to Article 1 of the SCM Agreement (at pp. 5–8), available at http://www.sielnet.org/Resources/Documents/SIEL%20CUP%202012%20highly%20comended%20%20-%20article%20by%20Jerjian.doc

146 Article 1.1(b) of the SCM Agreement.

147 See e.g., such subsidies designed to boost export performance or import substitution as per Article 3 of the SCM Agreement.

148 Article 2 of the SCM Agreement.

149 Article 5 of the SCM Agreement.

However, the relationship between FIT schemes and WTO rules seems to have attracted a fair amount of scholarly attention and scrutiny.[150] The purpose of this chapter has been to present sufficient high-level background in relation to environmental protection and the WTO system in which to then situate the relationship between renewables promotion and the WTO system. The rules and jurisprudence appear to suggest that *bona fide* non-discriminatory measures linked to environmental protection objectives – including the promotion of renewable energy – are not actually blocked or otherwise discouraged within the multilateral trade system, particularly since the advent of the WTO.

V. ENERGIZING THE DISCUSSION

No discussion of climate change and sustainable development can fail to address energy, which plays a crucial role both in climate change mitigation as well as in achieving sustainable development goals. In this context, our world faces two major challenges when it comes to energy. For one thing, almost one person in five on the planet still lacks access to electricity,[151] and almost three billion people still use wood, coal, charcoal or animal waste – none of which are 'clean' fuels – for cooking and heating.[152] Not only are such traditional energy sources inefficient and unreliable, they also have serious consequences for people's health. Combined with the fact that they mainly use three-stone fires and traditional mud stoves with no functioning chimneys, the resulting pollution levels are dangerous.

According to the World Energy Outlook, 'As a consequence of the pollutants emitted by these devices, pollution levels inside households cooking with biomass are often many times higher than typical outdoor levels, even those in highly polluted cities'.[153] The World Health Organization estimates that

---

150 See, amongst others, Jerjian, A. 'The Feed-in Tariff Controversy: Renewable Energy Challenges in WTO Law'. Jerjian carries out an extensive analysis of how FIT schemes for renewables engage WTO rules. See also Wilke, M. (2011) 'Feed-in Tariffs for Renewable Energy and WTO Subsidy Rules: An Initial Legal Review', Trade and Sustainable Energy Series, Issue Paper No. 4, International Centre for Trade and Sustainable Development.

151 See http://www.se4all.org/our-vision/our-objectives/universal-energy/

152 See http://www.who.int/mediacentre/factsheets/fs292/en/

153 See http://www.worldenergyoutlook.org/resources/energydevelopment/energypovertyhealthwhocollaboration/

> nearly 2 million people die prematurely from illness attributable to indoor air pollution from household solid fuel use; Nearly 50% of pneumonia deaths among children under five are due to particulate matter inhaled from indoor air pollution; More than 1 million people a year die from chronic obstructive respiratory disease (COPD) that develop [sic] due to exposure to such indoor air pollution.[154]

In fact, the number of premature deaths from household air pollution is greater than the number of premature deaths from malaria or tuberculosis.[155] With such serious repercussions for human health and the environment, it is no wonder that the lack of modern energy services poses a major obstacle to sustainable development, and, according to the United Nations (UN), it 'is a major barrier to eradicating poverty and building shared prosperity'.[156]

The other main global energy challenge is that, in places with access to modern energy services, the lion's share of energy usage stems from fossil fuels. In fact, the latest available data compiled by the International Energy Agency (IEA) indicate that conventional energy sources (fossil fuels such as oil, natural gas, and coal) made up 81.1% of the mix, while renewable energy sources made up only 13.2% of the global energy supply mix in 2010.[157] Burning fossil fuels, of course, results in emissions of GHGs such as carbon dioxide, and this contributes to global warming. Exploring alternative energy options – energy that is clean and efficient – is crucial.

In this sense, the two major energy challenges in the world today are closely tied, and the only way forward is to increase access to energy for all – but energy that is clean, efficient, and renewable. Continuing in the current vein is not an option. The UN is calling for *sustainable energy for all*, a vision based on three interlinked objectives:

(1) Ensure universal access to modern energy services.
(2) Double the global rate of improvement in energy efficiency.
(3) Double the share of renewable energy in the global energy mix.[158]

---

[154] See http://www.who.int/mediacentre/factsheets/fs292/en/

[155] See www.worldenergyoutlook.org/resources/energydevelopment/energypovertyhealthwhocollaboration/

[156] See http://www.se4all.org/our-vision/

[157] Figures calculated based on data as these appear in International Energy Agency, 2012, Key World Energy Statistics, OECD/IEA, 2012 (at p. 6). During 2010, the global primary energy supply was 12,717 million tons of oil equivalent (Mtoe). During 1973, it stood at 6,107 Mtoe.

[158] See http://www.un.org/millenniumgoals/pdf/SEFA.pdf

This section examines two trade-related mechanisms for achieving these energy goals: (i) better governance of global energy trade – governance that promotes equitable access to resources and streamlined, efficient processes in the energy trading system; and (ii) strong trade support for green energy options such as renewable energy. The section examines the potential of both avenues for moving the climate mitigation agenda forward overall.

A. Stronger Governance of Energy Trade

The nexus between energy and climate change encompasses a range of trade issues such as clean energy subsidies, carbon taxes, and border adjustment for carbon emissions. Thus far, the overall approach towards addressing the role of energy in climate change mitigation has involved finding incentives to reduce fossil fuel emissions. However, a more holistic approach towards achieving greener energy may prove more effective in the long run. In other words, arguably, we need more cohesive energy trade governance. International trade in energy spans a number of key policy areas, including trade, investment, economic development, and environmental protection, and, currently, the international community does not provide cohesive governance over it.[159]

On the contrary, governance of energy trade arises by default, rather than design, through the *ad hoc* interplay of different aspects of the international economic system. This fragmented and multi-layered trade in energy governance regime for energy trade is perhaps not conducive to global energy security. Moreover, a more cohesive global governance system for energy trade would facilitate energy flows, avoid unnecessary legal disputes and provide predictability. This will require a thorough assessment of the elements, workings, and evolution of the current global energy trade governance regime.

At the international level, there is a patchwork of institutions that may have implications for cross-border energy trade, for example, the WTO, which provides governance over trade within its scope, including over energy trade. The WTO does not handle energy commodities any differently from other tradable commodities within its scope. In that sense, it provides energy trade governance by default. Another example is the EU. While the EU lacks the powers of a sovereign actor to diplomatically pursue its energy security in the manner that, say, China

---

159 See generally Leal-Arcas, R. & Filis, A. 'The Fragmented Governance of the Global Energy Economy: A Legal-Institutional Analysis' (2013) *Journal of World Energy Law and Business*, Vol. 6, No. 4, pp. 1–58.

or the US may do, it does possess a comprehensive energy policy that is multifaceted and that makes good use of the powers that lie within its competences. Another such institution is the Energy Charter Treaty (ECT), whose principal concerns surround the investment protection and trade aspects of energy between contracting States.[160] Many other institutions exist that provide degrees of governance over aspects of trade in energy at the interstate level. This patchwork of institutions and regimes amounts to a sort of 'accidental' energy trade governance, and presents some areas of overlap. For instance, both the WTO and the ECT have rules that apply to the trade, investment, and environmental protection aspects of energy. These overlaps, however, in no way amount to cohesive governance of energy trade.

One explanation for the current fragmentation of the global energy trade regime, perhaps, is that it is developing progressively. For instance, in 1947 a number of sovereign actors came together to lay down arrangements for the General Agreement on Tariffs and Trade to provide multilateral trade governance. Some decades later, others came together to adopt the ECT to provide multilateral disciplines mainly for energy investments and, to a lesser extent, for energy trade.

Furthermore, sovereign States engage with one another to the extent that it is in their national interest to do so. Efforts within the EU, for example, to promote its collective energy security may be undermined by disparate energy realities between its members and also by exogenous factors such as global energy market conditions and competition by other global actors. In other words, a number of international institutions and global actors affect the global energy economies. There is an obvious diversity of interests, including conflicts of interests, at both national and international levels, and this plurality of actors and the diversity of energy interests illustrate the complexity present in energy trade governance.

The role of trade in promoting energy efficiency and raising the share of renewable energy in the global energy mix cannot be overestimated. For example, there is potential to incorporate energy-efficient provisions within regional and multilateral trade agreements; there are trade incentives to better manage competition and invest in technologies such as up-to-date energy grids; and possibilities for importing/exporting cutting-edge technologies through trade and bilateral cooperation agreements.

---

[160] See generally Selivanova, Y. (ed.) *Regulation of Energy in International Trade Law: WTO, NAFTA, and Energy Charter* (Alphen aan den Rijn: Kluwer, 2011); and Wälde, T. *The Energy Charter Treaty: An East-West Gateway for Investment and Trade* (London: Kluwer Law International, 1996).

In this context, numerous bilateral arrangements on energy and climate exist. In fact, since the faltering of a global climate treaty, bilateral agreements aimed at reducing GHG emissions have increased exponentially. Examples of such agreements are the US–Mexico Bilateral Framework on Clean Energy and Climate Change or the Australia–EU Partnership Framework. These bilateral arrangements promote trade relations between parties, while incorporating approaches to clean energy promotion and climate change mitigation. One significant bilateral agreement in this regard is the Transatlantic Trade and Investment Partnership (TTIP). An initial EU position paper on raw materials and energy acknowledges that the multilateral trade system would 'benefit from a stronger set of rules in the area of energy and raw materials', and suggests that the TTIP could make an important contribution to the development of this process. Areas where specific raw material and energy provisions could be developed include transparency, market access and non-discrimination, trade in sustainable energy, competitiveness, as well as energy security.[161]

It is worth determining to what extent such bilateral arrangements, as well as current energy trade rules (at WTO, Energy Charter Treaty, and UNFCCC levels, for example), enhance sustainable energy, and therefore climate change mitigation goals. If the TTIP or the Trans-Pacific Partnership (TPP) proves successful in enhancing trade relations while promoting sustainable energy, could their provisions be applied to a multilateral agreement on energy trade? Might an overarching General Agreement on Trade in Energy, or a Sustainable Energy Trade Agreement, be the next logical step?[162] Any such agreement would need to have a strong 'environmental voice' so as to avoid merely facilitating energy flows without factoring in environmental impacts and promotion of more efficient and renewable energy. In other words, to quote Pascal Lamy, 'trade regulations are not, and cannot be, a substitute for environmental regulations'.[163] Any global energy trade agreement aiming at enhancing

---

161 European Commission, 'EU-US Transatlantic Trade and Investment Partnership – Raw Materials and Energy', Initial EU Position Paper, EU Directorate-General for Trade (2013).

162 For more information on proposals regarding a Sustainable Energy Trade Agreement and Sustainable Energy Trade Initiatives, see ICTSD, 'Fostering Low Carbon Growth: The Case for a Sustainable Energy Trade Agreement', International Centre for Trade and Sustainable Development (Geneva, 2011).

163 WTO, 'Lamy: Doha Could Deliver Double-Win for Environment and Trade' (2007), available at http://www.wto.org/english/news_e/sppl_e/sppl83_e.htm

energy security along with environmental protection would need strong input from a major environmental forum such as the UNFCCC.

B. WTO's Treatment of Renewable Energy

As mentioned earlier, the majority of our world's energy consumption is derived from fossil fuels. Diversifying the global energy supply mix in order to make greater use of renewable sources could have far-reaching geo-economic and geo-strategic implications,[164] including: the containment of GHG emissions to levels that could prevent more costly future damage; the conservation of our planet's ecosystems and protecting the welfare of the human, animal, and plant populations they sustain; greater energy security for those States and groups of States that are net energy importers; and foreign relations that are less influenced by energy considerations. Trade can play a crucial role in this context, given that trade policy can be designed to promote and support renewable technology. However, such policies have also caused an increasing number of disputes at the WTO. Arguably, therefore, there is a need to examine WTO rules and work towards removing any systemic 'obstacles' to the scale-up and take-up of renewable energy.

Certain measures, such as feed-in tariff schemes for renewable energy, have been the subject of dispute at the WTO, with their consistency with the Subsidies and Countervailing Measures Agreement, as well as national treatment obligations under the General Agreement on Tariffs and Trade and the Agreement on Trade-Related Investment Measures being called into question. With the share of renewable energy close to 20% of global final consumption,[165] investment and innovation in the renewables sector are only set to increase. Is the WTO's 'nature as a

---

164 See IPCC, '2011: Summary for Policymakers', in [Edenhofer, O., Pichs-Madruga, R., Sokona, Y., Seyboth, K., Matschoss, P., Kadner, S., Zwickel, T., Eickemeier, P., Hansen, G., Schlömer, S. & von Stechow, C. (eds)] *IPCC Special Report on Renewable Energy Sources and Climate Change Mitigation* (Cambridge and New York: Cambridge University Press, 2011), at pp. 4–26, for an exposition of the potential benefits of increasing the proportion of renewables in the global supply energy mix. See also Ghosh, A. & Gangania, H. 'Governing Clean Energy Subsidies: What, Why and How Legal?' International Centre for Trade and Sustainable Development (2012), pp. 11–18, for an exposition of the various arguments for the promotion of renewable energy.

165 UNEP, 'Renewable Energy – Trends, Challenges and Opportunities', United Nations Environment Programme (2013), available at www.unep.org/greeneconomy/Portals/88/GETReport/pdf/Chapitre%206%20Renewable%20Energy.pdf

body focused on negotiated outcomes'[166] a plausible or effective mechanism for addressing disputes that are likely to arise with increasing frequency?

In spite of the associated controversy, in recent years, there has been an increase in subsidies aimed at promoting renewable energy. The global figures for subsidies in the renewable energy sector increased from USD 39 billion in 2007 to USD 66 billion by 2010.[167] While this increase is a positive sign, the figures are eclipsed by the enormity of fossil-fuel-related subsidies that stood at USD 409 billion in 2010.[168] The IEA projects that by 2035, under its various policy scenarios, should renewables subsidies rise to USD 250 billion, a variety of positive developments could take place, such as onshore wind becoming competitive by 2020 in the EU and by 2030 in China,[169] and the containment of up to 3.4 gigatons – that is, 3.4 billion tons – of energy-related carbon dioxide when compared with the current total energy supply fuel mix.[170]

In the fragmented world of renewable energy governance, the WTO has an important role to play, as complying with WTO policies can be a game changer in promoting a shift to renewables. The WTO is also one of the few truly effective multilateral institutions when it comes to the enforcement of its legal mandate, thanks to an efficient dispute resolution system. Further, energy is not comparable to merely any tradable commodity; it is acutely needed and a source of great geopolitical tension and insecurity. The dynamics within which the WTO operates help it to address this crucial political issue to a great extent. While trade is one of the many cards in global energy governance, the incentive it creates across the board has broad implications for global energy security and governance.

Trade in renewable energy entails both production and transmission aspects and therefore involves the regulation of both goods and services.[171] The technology demands of the energy sector also make

---

166 Wilke, M. 'Feed-in Tariffs for Renewable Energy and WTO Subsidy Rules', ICTSD Trade and Environment Papers, Issue Paper No. 4 (2011).

167 IEA 2012 World Energy Outlook factsheet (at p. 6).

168 Ibid.

169 Ibid.

170 Ibid.

171 While energy-containing resources such as coal, wind, etc., can be classified as goods, the treatment of 'energy' is debatable. For example, Gabrielle Marceau states that 'we define energy as the action (product and process) through which energy-containing natural resources are transformed and consumed in response to a series of societal and individual human requirements for

intellectual property issues vital, which are a component of the WTO system under the Agreement on Trade-related Aspects of Intellectual Property Rights (TRIPS). Therefore, the institutional mechanism of the WTO has a great role to play in securing global green energy governance.

1. Trade policy shapes green energy governance

Energy demands have rapidly increased since the time that the General Agreement on Tariffs and Trade (GATT) was concluded in 1947, and the same is true for energy prices. For example, a barrel of crude oil was as cheap as US$20 at present prices.[172] In spite of this, there continues to be an absence of a trade agreement specific to the energy sector.[173] However, while the WTO's role in conventional energy security[174] is considered 'incidental, though not inconsiderable',[175] it has a substantial role to play in the context of renewable energy. Considered against the background of an established framework (for example, most energy distribution systems are catered to conventional energy sources such as gas and oil) and a well-supported framework (for instance, through

---

heat and power', see Marceau, G. 'The World Trade Organisation in the Emerging Energy Governance Debate', World Trade Report 2010, available at http://www.wto.org/english/res_e/publications_e/wtr10_forum_e/wtr10_marceau_e.htm. However, energy can exist in various forms such as electricity or nuclear power. Electricity, for example, is classified as a good under the Harmonized System Nomenclature (Cottier, T. et al. 'Energy in WTO Law and Policy', available at http://www.wto.org/english/res_e/publications_e/wtr10_forum_e/wtr10_7may10_e.pdf) and so is the generation of electricity (Voigt, C. *Sustainable Development as a Principle of International Law: Resolving Conflicts between Climate Measures and WTO Law* (Leiden: Martinus Neijhoff, 2009), p. 218).

[172] Lamy, P. 'Doha Round Will Benefit Energy Trade', Speech at the 20th World Energy Congress, Rome, Italy, (15 November 2007), available at http://www.wto.org/english/news_e/sppl_e/sppl80_e.htm

[173] Pascal Lamy has emphasized the need for considering energy a separate sector; ibid.

[174] Conventional energy refers to all forms of fossil-fuel based energy, as opposed to renewable sources of energy.

[175] Leal-Arcas, R. & Filis, A. (2013) 'The Fragmented Governance of the Global Energy Economy: A Legal-institutional Analysis', *Journal of World Energy Law and Business*, Vol. 6, No. 4, pp. 1–58.

subsidies) within which conventional energies operate, shifting to renewable energy requires high incentives, which can be provided by WTO-compatible policies for renewables.[176]

The need to shift focus from fossil-based fuels and divert attention to green and sustainable forms of energy has been in vogue for some time.[177] The United Nations Framework Convention on Climate Change (UNFCCC) and its Kyoto Protocol established the requirement of reducing greenhouse gas (GHG) emissions for sustainable environmental protection 'in accordance with ... common but differentiated responsibilities'.[178] The policy tools to achieve this include enhancing energy efficiency; the promotion of renewable energy, carbon sequestration and green technology; and promoting sectoral reforms to encourage GHG emissions reduction.[179] At the national level, countries have set in place various mechanisms to achieve these objectives and move towards renewable energies.[180]

Two common initiatives undertaken at the national level to fulfill GHG emission responsibilities are the internalization of carbon emission costs and the introduction of green energy production support policies. However, as Peter Mandelson points out, a key imperative behind the Kyoto Protocol is the creation of an open global market and greater investment in green technologies,[181] which cannot happen in isolation. This has also

---

[176] According to Yvo de Boer, if one takes into account the broader environmental costs of using energy from fossil fuels, generating energy from renewables is actually cheaper in the long run. Information gathered from de Boer, Y. 'Can the International Climate Policy Impasse Be Broken?', University College London Institute for Sustainable Resources Public Lecture, London, United Kingdom (2 December 2013).

[177] Leahy, J. 'Brazil: Wind Gathers Force in Mix of Renewable Sources' (May 15, 2013), available at http://www.ft.com/cms/s/0/e1cd2bf0-b0d6-11e2-9f24-00144feabdc0.html#axzz2mjExW3q.

[178] Article 3.1 of the UNFCCC.

[179] Article 2.1(a) of the Kyoto Protocol.

[180] Hübner, N. 'Brazil's Wind Power Auction Spurs More Clean Energy Development' (29 December, 2009), available at http://www.renewableenergyworld.com/rea/news/article/2009/12/brazils-wind-power-auction-spurs-more-clean-energy-development; See also 'Government Applauded over £40bn Renewable Energy Support Plans' (4 December 2013), available at http://www.clickgreen.org.uk/news/national-news/124070-government-supported-over-40bn-renewable-energy-support-plans.html

[181] Mandelson, P. 'Energy Security and Climate Change – What Role for Trade Policy?' (9 February 2007), available at http://www.google.co.uk/url?sa=t&rct=j&q=&esrc=s&source=web&cd=3&cad=rja&ved=0CEUQFjAC&url=http%3A%2F%2Feuropa.eu%2Frapid%2Fpress-release_SPEECH-07-73_en.pdf&ei

been highlighted in the Rio+20 outcome document, 'The Future We Want', which highlights 'the role of foreign direct investment, international trade and international cooperation in the transfer of environmentally sound technologies'.[182]

A clear set of rules in energy trade at the multilateral level (and also, realistically, at a bilateral level) will help energy-producing countries to find newer markets and help energy-consuming countries to find cross-border resources, thus creating greater energy efficiency, interdependence and stability. Implementing such measures within the WTO, therefore, is important firstly to promote national energy security and, more importantly, to create a uniform approach towards achieving global green energy security.

2. Renewable subsidies: changing the playing field

Renewable energy forms a small component of the global energy mix. However, considering the environmental repercussions of using energy derived from fossil fuels, as well as the volatility of the conventional energy market, it makes sense to reduce the consumption of fossil fuels and redirect efforts towards deriving energy from renewable sources. Current high production costs, however, are an impediment and, in the absence of support mechanisms, renewable energy production is unprofitable. Further, fossil fuels enjoy more than one-sixth the level of renewable energy subsidies,[183] which makes a robust subsidy system for renewables increasingly important.

In an effort to address these challenges, governments across the world have introduced renewable energy feed-in tariffs (FITs) to improve green energy efficiency, increase production, and advance research and development in green technologies. Also, by supporting and promoting renewable energy technology, new markets are created, along with new and sustainable jobs.

This begs the question: what are FITs? In a sense, they can be explained as a premium, generally above the market rate, provided to

---

=KZ3JUq7XEMyZhQeVuIDYBg&usg=AFQjCNHhiMuj80z97833ytNveMBBdGu22w&sig2=1GaRs0h-8unlHcmdAsUUjg

182 UN General Assembly, Resolution adopted by the General Assembly on 27 July 2012, 'The Future We Want', A/RERS/66/288, 11 September 2012, at para. 271.

183 International Energy Agency (IEA), World Energy Outlook 2012 (12 November 2013), available at http://www.worldenergyoutlook.org/resources/energysubsidies/

green energy generators, with an assurance to purchase electricity.[184] They are essentially a purchase guarantee agreement between the government and the energy producers. Therefore, FITs may be deemed as a government subsidy under Article 1 of the Agreement on Subsidies and Countervailing Measures (SCM) due to their providing a 'financial contribution'. However, the issue of subsidies under the SCM Agreement is not that simple and requires the fulfillment of complex conditions set out in the SCM Agreement.

3. Are feed-in tariffs subsidies?

To be classified as a subsidy, firstly the scheme must be a 'financial contribution' under Article 1.1(a)(1) of the SCM Agreement. Willkie identifies three ways in which FITs qualify as subsidies under Article 1 of the SCM Agreement.[185] When the 'financial contribution' is in the form of public funds directed to execute the FIT, it is a subsidy under Article 1.1(a)(1)(iii) of the SCM Agreement; where a program is financed by government but executed by a private body, it classifies as a subsidy under Article 1.1(a)(1)(iv,) first clause of the SCM Agreement; and where the private body executes the FIT and the government raises resources through reallocation of different costs, it is a subsidy under Article 1.1(a)(1)(iv), second clause of the SCM Agreement.[186]

Further, a subsidy under the SCM Agreement can be provided by either a public body or a private body performing functions 'normally … vested in the government' and implementing 'practices normally followed by governments'.[187] As the Appellate Body in the *US – Anti-Dumping and Countervailing Duties* case[188] clarifies, it is not just 'control' but exercise of 'relevant authority and responsibility'[189] that determines whether a body is public.[190] Therefore, private bodies deemed public are limited to the ones empowered to direct and entrust in a

---

[184] Available at http://www.investopedia.com/terms/f/feed-in-tariff.asp

[185] Wilke, M. 'Feed-in Tariffs for Renewable Energy and WTO Subsidy Rules: An Initial Legal Analysis', Trade and Sustainable Energy Series, Issue Paper No. 4, International Centre for Trade and Sustainable Development, November 2011.

[186] Ibid.

[187] Article 1.1(a)(1)(iv) of the SCM Agreement.

[188] *United States – Definitive Anti-Dumping and Countervailing Duties on Certain Products from China* (WT/DS379/AB/R).

[189] Ibid. para. 294.

[190] Ibid.

similar capacity as the government, subject to what qualifies as 'normal'.[191] This differentiation becomes important when one considers, for example, the *Canada – Renewables* cases.[192] In these jointly decided cases, the Ontario Power Authority (OPA), acting under the mandate of the Ontario Ministry of Energy and Infrastructure,[193] was entrusted with the responsibility of administering the FIT program through a standard set of rules, standard contracts and standard pricing.[194] However, it did not have the power to structure the program or direct private bodies. Moreover, OPA was neither a crown corporation,[195] nor a part of the Ministry of Energy or a public body as per the Ontario Ministry of the Environment,[196] even though most of the public regards OPA as a public body.[197] Therefore, in spite of retaining the control feature associated with earlier definitions of public bodies, the crucial element of authority was missing. Although OPA was considered a public body in this case, it creates a potentially dicey situation for the future.

The second requirement for considering a measure a subsidy is the occurrence of a 'benefit',[198] which implies any treatment that is more favorable than would be offered under normal conditions.[199] FITs guarantee electricity purchase with prices above market standards and unnaturally long contractual durations; both of these guarantees go beyond normal market conditions and therefore count as benefits. However, it is worth bearing in mind that the market may already be distorted in the

---

[191] Robert Howse argues that this 'normal' function is not a delegation of governmental power, but a regulation of market behavior and transactions. See Howse, R. 'Climate Mitigation Subsidies and the WTO Legal Framework: A Policy Analysis', International Institute for Sustainable Development, May 2010, available at http://www.iisd.org/pdf/2009/bali_2_copenhagen_subsidies_legal.pdf

[192] *Canada – Measures Relating to the Feed-in Tariff Program* (WT/DS426/AB/R) and *Canada – Certain Measures Affecting the Renewable Energy Generation Sector* (*Canada – Renewable Energy*) (WT/DS412/AB/R). The Appellate Body report contains both cases *in tandem.*

[193] Ontario Energy and Infrastructure Directive, 24 September 2009, FIT Direction.

[194] *Canada – Measures Relating to the Feed-in Tariff Program* (WT/DS426/AB/R) and *Canada – Certain Measures Affecting the Renewable Energy Generation Sector* (WT/DS412/R; WT/DS426/R) para 7.67.

[195] Ontario Electricity Restructuring Act, 2004, Part II.1, Section 25.3.

[196] Annual Report of the Environmental Commissioner of Ontario 2006–2007 Supplement, 'Reconciling Our Priorities', p. 148, available at http://www.eco.on.ca/uploads/Reports%20-%20Annual/2006_07/2007su.pdf

[197] Ibid.

[198] Article 1.1(b) of the SCM Agreement.

[199] Article 14 of the SCM Agreement.

industry where the subsidy is offered. Fossil-fuel markets traditionally have been highly subsidized, so, in a sense, renewable-energy subsidies offset these existing market distortions.[200] Additionally, the advantage of conventional electricity is that the electricity grid is modelled to its nature, and integrating renewables into the existing electricity grid is a challenge in terms of cost and technological updates.[201]

The *Canada – Renewables* cases also provide an interesting pointer in this regard. The Appellate Body (AB) emphasized the need for a market benchmark in determining a 'benefit'. The AB stated that both the demand and supply sides had to be considered in determining the relevant market against which such a benefit benchmark is to be decided.[202] Pointing to the specific case, the AB stated that the governmental action led to the creation of a renewable market and thus the governmental action was not a subsidy, as, without such intervention, the renewable energy market would not exist in the first place.[203] The AB acknowledged the sovereign right to create an energy mix in reflection of long-term energy security policies.[204] While this decision potentially acknowledges energy security as an acceptable policy consideration, it simultaneously opens other trapdoors. Considering the demand side, if renewable and conventional energies are considered substitutable products, this may create new demands for subsidizing harmful conventional forms of energy other than oil and gas (e.g., shale gas) that may be deemed to require governmental support, considering the high initial operational costs. This situation would be detrimental to renewable energy security in the long run, as the introduction of environmentally harmful subsidies for conventional, polluting forms of energy over subsidies for clean energy would reduce the level of renewables in the energy mix. A better outcome would have been to introduce cleaner energy targets and thus be in line with the sustainable development objective found in the preamble of the Marrakesh Agreement.

---

200 See e.g. Alan Sykes, 'The Questionable Case for Subsidies Regulation: A Comparative Perspective', Stanford Law and Economics Olin Working Paper No. 380, p. 24.

201 World Nuclear Association, 'Renewable Energy and Electricity', available at http://www.world-nuclear.org/info/Energy-and-Environment/Renewable-Energy-and-Electricity/

202 *Canada – Measures Relating to the Feed-in Tariff Program* (WT/DS426/AB/R) and *Canada – Certain Measures Affecting the Renewable Energy Generation Sector* (*Canada – Renewable Energy*) (WT/DS412/AB/R), para. 5.185.

203 Ibid. para. 5.188.

204 Ibid. para. 5.175.

Under the SCM Agreement, three forms of subsidies exist: prohibited,[205] actionable,[206] and non-actionable.[207] Subsidies are prohibited if they fall within any of the two conditions provided under Article 3 of the SCM Agreement. According to Article 5 of the SCM Agreement, actionable subsidies are subsidies which are not prohibited, but cause adverse effects to the interests of other WTO members. Further, Article 8 of the SCM Agreement considers the case of non-actionable subsidies.[208] While prohibited subsidies are automatically 'specific' as they contain a local content requirement or export requirement, for a measure to qualify as an actionable subsidy under the SCM Agreement it has to be specifically targeted to particular enterprises or industries and cannot be based on objective criteria.[209] In a plethora of recent cases, protectionist FITs with local content requirements have been prohibited under Article 3 of the SCM Agreement. However, the question remains whether FIT programs without local content can still be classified as subsidies; the AB has not clarified the situation, which creates problems for a transition to a greener energy economy under the WTO, as will be explained later.

Regarding specificity under Article 2 of the SCM Agreement, the language of the FITs assumes importance. Where the FIT scheme is extended to 'all' electricity producers who use green energy, it would not be a subsidy as, in this case, it would be extended without differentiating between two sectors: one releasing more GHG emissions due to the use of fossil fuels, and the other being the renewable sector, where emissions are negligent or low. This is opposed to the scheme's benefit being extended to 'only' green source users. Therefore, inclusionary or exclusionary language would play a vital role in determining a 'subsidy'.

---

[205] Part II of the SCM Agreement.

[206] Part III of the SCM Agreement.

[207] Part IV of the SCM Agreement.

[208] Although the SCM Agreement, as originally entered into force, had non-actionable subsidies as one of three categories of subsidies, this category was provisional for five years until December 1999, with the possibility of extending its application for a further period (see Article 31 of the SCM Agreement). As of 31 December 1999, no consensus had been reached in the WTO's SCM Committee for such an extension, which means that non-actionable subsidies have been phased out. For further explanation of the SCM Agreement, see http://www.wto.org/english/tratop_e/scm_e/subs_e.htm

[209] The word 'objective' has a special connotation under the SCM Agreement. Article 2.1(b), footnote 2 reads: 'Objective criteria or conditions, as used herein, mean criteria or conditions which are neutral, which do not favour certain enterprises over others, and which are economic in nature and horizontal in application, such as number of employees or size of enterprise'.

However, the *US – Softwood Lumber IV* case[210] assumes importance in this context. In this case, the Panel noted that 'the availability of a subsidy which is limited by the inherent characteristics of the good cannot be considered to have been limited by 'objective' criteria …'.[211] While the amount and type of GHG emissions from 'traditional' and 'renewable' energy may be different, it is not clear whether this suffices for their being treated as different industries under WTO jurisprudence. Indeed, in the *Canada – Renewables* cases, the Appellate Body concluded that, in the retail electricity market, conventional and renewable energies are substitutable products.[212] However, considering not only the product itself, but also ancillary concerns like distribution networks, which are distinct for each of these forms of energy, a different conclusion could easily be drawn by another Panel or the Appellate Body. Marie Wilke draws on the decision of the panel in the *US – Upland Cotton* case to state that the determination of specificity is case-specific, which leaves uncertainty in the debate.[213]

In the case of actionable subsidies, an adverse effect of the subsidies must finally be demonstrated. Where the complaint is a traditional energy supplier, an adverse effect on the industry would have to be proven. Ironically, the fossil-fuel market is highly distorted, making it a difficult task to demonstrate an adverse effect on prices based on the operation of the FIT program. A detailed factual data analysis is required under Article 6.3 of the SCM Agreement for a reasoned conclusion where a serious prejudice is claimed.[214] In this sense, the FIT is saved by the very evil that it fights.

Therefore, the answer to the question whether FITs qualify as subsidies under Article 1 of the SCM Agreement is not straightforward and largely dependent on the structure of the FIT in question, unless, of course, the benefits under it are subject to a local content requirement or export restrictions requirement. However, some clarity as to whether they indeed qualify as subsidies may be helpful for policy considerations. If they are subsidies, it may be possible to negotiate a different treatment

---

210 *United States – Final Countervailing Duty Determination with Respect to Certain Softwood Lumber from Canada* (*US – Softwood Lumber IV*).

211 Ibid., Panel report (WT/DS257/R), para. 7.116, footnote 179.

212 *Canada – Measures Relating to the Feed-in Tariff Program* (WT/DS426/AB/R) and *Canada – Certain Measures Affecting the Renewable Energy Generation Sector* (*Canada – Renewable Energy*) (WT/DS412/AB/R), para. 4.3.

213 *US – Subsidies on Upland Cotton* (WT/DS267/R), para. 7.1142.

214 *United States – Subsidies on Upland Cotton*, Appellate Body Report (WT/DS267/AB/R).

for sustainable energy subsidies as opposed to environmentally harmful subsidies. Or if indeed they are not subsidies, increasing renewable energy within the global energy mix can bring the goals of the Kyoto Protocol and the WTO into greater alignment.

4. The case of local contents

It is interesting to note that recent disputes before the WTO involve the requirement of local contents in FIT schemes. The first WTO decision on the matter, the *Canada – Renewables* cases,[215] did not rule on whether the FIT program was a subsidy; instead, it decided that the local content requirement was discriminatory against imports. Following on its heels, the US initiated a consultation with India.[216] India prescribed domestic origin requirements in its Jawaharlal Nehru National Solar Mission program in order for producers to qualify for the benefits of long-term tariff rates.[217] The US consultation provoked retaliation from India, which questioned the local content requirement in at least five of the US's state legislations.[218]

These disputes followed US action against Chinese wind power equipment in 2011, in which the US initiated consultation with China for requiring the use of local equipment in order to be eligible for benefits under its FIT.[219] While the measure in question was rolled back, the US brought anti-dumping charges against Chinese solar and wind products benefiting from domestic subsidies.[220] Political and national concerns over the development of domestic markets have, to a large extent, prevailed over genuine environmental considerations and the promotion

---

215 *Canada – Certain Measures Affecting the Renewable Energy Generation* Sector (WT/DS412/AB/R) and *Canada – Measures Relating to the Feed-in Tariff Program* (WT/DS426/AB/R).

216 *India – Certain Measures Relating to Solar Cells and Solar Modules* (WT/DS456).

217 For further details about the case, see http://www.wto.org/english/tratop_e/dispu_e/cases_e/ds456_e.htm

218 Miles, T. 'India Questions US Green Energy Incentives at WTO', *Reuters* (17 April 2013), available at http://uk.reuters.com/article/2013/04/17/us-india-usa-trade-idUKBRE93G11U20130417

219 WT/DS419.

220 Crystalline Silicon Photovoltaic Cells and Modules from China, Investigation Nos 701-TA-481 & 731-TA-1190 (Final), USITC Publication 4360 (November 2012) and Utility Scale Wind Towers from China and Vietnam, Investigation Nos 701-TA-486 & 731-TA-1195-1196 (Final)] USITC Publication 4372 (Feb 2013), available at http://www.usitc.gov/trade_remedy/publications/opinions_index.htm#u

of global energy security. However, it can be argued that local content does build local energy security and attracts wide public support based on perceived nationalistic policies and job creation. These aspects are crucial if we consider how FIT schemes can hit a snag where consumers are the final bill payers of renewable energy costs. For example, Germany announced proposals to reduce energy subsidies, prompting fears of loss of competiveness due to the shale gas industry boom in the US.[221] Germany's energy bills are among the highest in the world.[222]

In developing countries, where the common man has to make ends meet, a lack of social incentives can make it very difficult for a government to push the case for renewables. Regarding China's case in its dispute with the US, it has been argued that, considering China's alarming air quality and its huge energy demands, it is imperative that China develop a strong domestic industry in renewable goods.[223] This, however, is a fact-specific case, as only a few other major emerging economies (such as the so-called BRICs, namely Brazil, Russia, India, and China) will have the potential for such surging economic growth or actually meet their annual economic growth targets with such fortitude. Indeed, besides being trade-distortive, it is debatable to what extent local content requirements are effective in building domestic industry as compared to a competitive global open market. Of the 99 jurisdictions throughout the world which use FITs as of 2013, most do not have a local content requirement.[224] Considered in this context, FITs with local content requirements must indeed be dismissed as anomalies and trade-distortive attempts in an otherwise grand scheme.

5. Green Subsidy Fund

While FITs face SCM-compatibility issues, an alternative in the form of a WTO waiver system has been proposed.[225] Under this system, a Green

---

[221] Hromadko, J. & Kissler, A. 'Germany Plans to Cap Renewable Subsidies', *The Wall Street Journal*, 29 January 2013, available at http://online.wsj.com/news/articles/SB10001424127887323375204578269934082438240

[222] Ibid.

[223] Howse, R. 'Climate Change, China and the WTO', Speech at Columbia University Law School (30 March 2011), available at http://media.law.columbia.edu/specialevents/Climate_Change_Panel_110330_Gerrard.mp3

[224] Casier, L. & Moerenhout, T. 'WTO Members, Not the Appellate Body, Need to Clarify Boundaries in Renewable Energy Support', International Institute for Sustainable Development (July 2013) p. 2, available at http://www.iisd.org/pdf/2013/wto_members_renewable_energy_support.pdf

[225] Howse, R. 'Climate Mitigation Subsidies and the WTO Legal Framework: A Policy Analysis', International Institute for Sustainable Development (May

Subsidy Fund under the UNFCCC system can be set up. Unless they are blatantly discriminatory, any subsidy reported to the Fund may be granted a full waiver from WTO rules. A continuous monitoring of the subsidies reported must be in place, with signatories benefiting from technology transfers and support systems.

6. Funding energy security through GHG emissions control

Joseph Stiglitz[226] considers the failure to penalize carbon emission costs a 'hidden subsidy'.[227] The atmosphere within a State's boundary is its resource over which it has proprietary rights. The State has a duty to implement various initiatives to protect it, including GHG emissions control and related taxes. Any failure to do so can be treated as a 'financial contribution' under Article 1.1(a)(1)(iii) of the SCM Agreement. Further, where the government was considered to be providing goods or services, any failure to charge for such resources where the State had proprietary right could be a violation of Article 1.1(a)(1)(i) of the SCM Agreement. The revenue generated from such negative subsidies can fund a shift to renewable energy. Even if such inaction is not considered a subsidy within the SCM Agreement, national governments can indirectly achieve GHG emissions control by redirecting valuable resources from fossil subsidies towards FIT schemes and developing renewable energy technology. The potential for such a measure can be appreciated when we consider that the bill for fossil fuels subsidies globally was USD 1.9 trillion in 2011.[228]

Former WTO Director-General Pascal Lamy acknowledged the potential for such a move when he proclaimed the reformation of fossil-fuel subsidies and trade-related aspects of renewable energy as the most crucial, but under-addressed, issue at the WTO.[229] Dale Andrew of the Organisation for Economic Co-operation and Development also points

---

2010), available at http://www.iisd.org/pdf/2009/bali_2_copenhagen_subsidies_legal.pdf

[226] Ibid. at p. 6.

[227] That said, Stiglitz has been criticized by eminent commentators like Jagdish Bhagwati, who calls such hidden costs irrelevant under the SCM Agreement. See Bhagwati, J. & Mavroidis, P. 'Is Action Against US Exports for Failure to sign Kyoto Protocol WTO-Legal?' (2007) *World Trade Review*, Vol. 6, No. 2, pp. 299–310, p. 300, footnote 3, and p. 302.

[228] International Monetary Fund, 'Energy Subsidy Reform: Lessons and Implications' (28 January 2013), p. 13, available at http://www.imf.org/external/np/pp/eng/2013/012813.pdf

[229] Lamy, P. 'Energy Policy and the WTO' (29 April 2013), available at http://www.wto.org/english/news_e/sppl_e/sppl279_e.htm

out that full payment on fossil fuels will invariably create a competitive playing field for renewables and will foster energy security.[230] In this regard, an agreement in the energy sector may just be the missing piece of the puzzle for the WTO to help secure global energy accessibility.

7. General exceptions under GATT Article XX

The GATT's general exceptions under Article XX also present opportunities to develop renewable energy security. The 2006 World Trade Report of the WTO Secretariat recognized the 'in principle' application of Article XX to subsidies.[231] Considering that the SCM Agreement is a *lex specialis* to Article XVI of the GATT, this is not surprising. There is ample support that can be drawn for such a position.

Article II.2 of the Marrakesh Agreement states that all multilateral trade agreements are an integral part of the WTO. In this sense, the SCM Agreement and the GATT are agreements within Annex 1 of the Marrakesh Agreement. In *Korea – Dairy*, the Appellate Body recognized that the WTO is a single undertaking requiring simultaneous compliance.[232] Further, we should take into account former Article 8 of the SCM Agreement regarding non-actionable subsidies, which contained a list of non-actionable subsidies, including those related to environmental protection. Commentators have stated that, in spite of its non-renewal, there is an agreement among WTO members that certain subsidies are better not challenged.[233] Therefore, there is an indication that subsidies for good causes are permissible for certain grounds. Instead of other cumbersome exceptions on free trade being introduced in a *lex specialis* agreement, it is much better if such 'good' subsidies are made permissible and trade-compliant within the nuances of Article XX of the GATT.

Still, there has been some criticism of this approach. Commentators have noted that, while the Sanitary and Phytosanitary Measures (SPS) Agreement makes specific reference to GATT Article XX, no such

---

[230] 'Energy Subsidies and the WTO' (30 April 2013), available at http://www.iisd.org/gsi/news/energy-subsidies-and-wto

[231] *World Trade Report 2006*, Section II.D, pp. 65ff., available at http://www.wto.org/english/res_e/booksp_e/anrep_e/world_trade_report06_e.pdf

[232] *Korea – Definitive Safeguard Measure on Imports of Certain Dairy Products*, Appellate Body report (WT/DS98/AB/R), para. 74.

[233] Wilke, M. 'Feed-in Tariffs for Renewable Energy and WTO Subsidy Rules: An Initial Legal Review', Trade and Sustainable Energy Series, Issue Paper No. 4, International Centre for Trade and Sustainable Development, November 2011, p. 31.

pointers lie in the SCM Agreement.[234] The issue of Article 3.1 of the SCM Agreement is even more interesting. It creates an exception for certain prohibited subsidies under the Agreement on Agriculture, but fails to mention GATT Article XX. However, considering the strong position for an integrated treatment of Annex 1 multilateral agreements in the Marrakesh Agreement, the spirit of Article XX is embedded in all *lex specialis* agreements and, therefore, it can be argued that a specific reference is not mandatory.

However, as seen in recent decisions of the WTO's Dispute Settlement system, there appears to be an anomaly. In *China – Publications and Audiovisual Products*, the Appellate Body ruled on the applicability of GATT Article XX to non-GATT Agreements on the basis of a specific mention in China's Accession Protocol to the WTO.[235] The AB ruled that China had the right to regulate trade using GATT Article XX if it was done 'in a manner consistent with the WTO Agreement'.[236] However, in *China – Raw Materials*, the Appellate Body decided that, since the Accession Protocol had no reference to GATT Article XX, it would not be applicable.[237] Therefore, the jurisprudence surrounding the applicability of GATT Art XX to non-GATT disputes provides no clear pattern or answers. While environmental concerns in a predominantly trade-related agreement seem secondary, the above decisions provide some confidence that future WTO Dispute Settlement tribunals (panels and the Appellate Body) may give some consideration for sustainable development when ruling on the institutional framework of the Marrakesh Agreement.

The importance of GATT Article XX in protecting renewable subsidies where compelling environmental reasons exist cannot be overemphasized.[238] Considering the nascent development of renewable energy technologies, coverage by the exception under GATT Article XX would provide uniformity in decision-making as well as stability and assurance

---

[234] Ibid. p. 30.

[235] WT/L/432, available at http://www.worldtradelaw.net/misc/chinaaccessionprotocol.pdf

[236] *China – Measures Affecting Trading Rights and Distribution Services for Certain Publications and Audiovisual Entertainment Products* (WT/DS363/AB/R), para. 233.

[237] *China – Measures Related to the Exportation of Various Raw Materials* (WT/DS394/AB/R; WT/DS395/AB/R; WT/DS398/AB/R), para. 77.

[238] See International Economic Law and Policy Blog, 'GATT Article XX and Domestic Production of Environmental Goods', posted by Simon Lester (3 April 2011), available at http://worldtradelaw.typepad.com/ielpblog/2011/04/article-xx-domestic-production-of-environmental-goods.html

to investors. The applicability of GATT Article XX can be extended to both local content requirements under the FITs of least developed countries which want to finance the development of renewable technologies, as well as to cases of actionable subsidies. In either case, it has to satisfy either the GATT Article XX(b) or (g) conditions, along with the chapeau of GATT Article XX.

Since renewables ensure cleaner emissions than conventional energy, they help maintain clean air, which is an 'exhaustible natural resource' as per the Panel decision in *US – Gasoline*, and they are within the scope of GATT Article XX(g). Further, as opposed to fossil fuels with their high volumes of toxic emissions, renewables help protect human, animal and plant life, which makes them a 'necessity' under Article XX(b). Moreover, although alternative measures can be implemented for environmental protection, as per *Brazil – Retreaded Tyres*,[239] justifiable quantitative and qualitative evidence is sufficient for the existing measure to be 'necessary,' even if immediate impact is not visible. In addition, in *Korea – Various Measures on Beef*, the AB emphasized that WTO members 'have the right to determine for themselves the level of enforcement of their WTO-consistent laws and regulations'.[240] This can be in consideration of cost, feasibility and efficiency. Therefore, the exceptions under GATT Article XX can be a useful tool in securing accessible renewable energy.

The long-term effectiveness of subsidies has been disputed at times. This issue is, however, beyond the scope of the WTO. The use of subsidies may not address long-term incentives for energy efficiency, which is vital for energy security. For example, State aid for US corn-based ethanol production is less efficient than for production of alternative biofuels such as sugarcane, as corn-based ethanol production is more costly and leaves a larger carbon footprint. However, all these issues are secondary to the question of whether FITs are subsidies.

VI. CONCLUSION

The main barriers to the scaling-up and proliferation of renewables relate to the infrastructural costs that make energy production uncompetitive when compared with energy production based on conventional energy

---

[239] *Brazil – Measures Affecting Imports of Retreaded Tyres* (WT/DS332/AB/R), para. 151.

[240] *Korea – Measures Affecting Imports of Fresh, Chilled and Frozen Beef* (WT/DS161/AB/R; WT/DS169/AB/R, p. 54), para 176.

sources. This is a barrier that is certainly compounded by the long-standing subsidization of conventional energy sources. What is more, conventional energy source-related subsidies – amounting to up to 90% of energy subsidies – which, incidentally, negatively impact the eco-system, are actually tolerated within the WTO system. Predictably, these are unlikely to be addressed in WTO litigation, given that these are popular measures among States, but also because demand for conventional energy sources exists to a large extent due to the distortive effects of such subsidization. For instance, if there were fewer conventional energy subsidies, at best, renewable energy may have been more competitive and therefore more viable; however, at worst, perhaps a larger part of the human population would have been denied access to affordable energy and would have been condemned to pre-modern standards of life.[241]

Our conclusion is that the main obstacles to the scale-up and take-up of renewable energy are not normative/institutional *per se*. Rather, they are economic. The only systemic 'obstacle' that the WTO presents is its requirement that measures not be disguised mercantilism and that they be applied evenhandedly. The WTO system, as it stands, could, and does, accommodate *bona fide* non-discriminatory measures that promote the scale-up and take-up of renewable energy. After all, we see that it tolerates conventional energy subsidies, which certainly are not predicated on the general exceptions to WTO rules or other dispensations, as these appear in the covered agreements. That said, while the system, as it stands, is considerably flexible towards externalities such as environmental protection objectives, further trade liberalization remains the system's principal objective. This, however, does not happen in a policy-value vacuum, given that the cause of trade liberalization is increasingly conditioned by environmental protection objectives.

Having said that, we acknowledge that confusion about how the WTO system may accommodate measures aimed at the promotion of renewable energy could strengthen the case for a separate specific agreement.

---

[241] Almost two billion people currently live without modern forms of energy such as electricity. That is nearly more than 1 in 4 people globally. See the World Bank Report *Meeting the Challenge for Rural Energy and Development for Two Billion People*, at cover page 3, available at http://siteresources.worldbank.org/INTENERGY/Resources/Rural_Energy_Development_Paper_Improving_Energy_Supplies.pdf. Note that this report draws from a previous World Bank report (No. 16002, published on 30 September 1996) entitled *Rural Energy and Development: Improving Energy Supplies for Two Billion People, Volume 1*, available at http://go.worldbank.org/G6ZXYV3ER0

However, such an agreement is likely to contain clarifications of, or even replicate the policy space that we believe currently exists within, the existing normative framework. As such, we believe it may be an unnecessary legislative step when its objectives (e.g., legal certainty) could be addressed by the adoption of an explanatory note containing clarificatory guidelines issued by the WTO Ministerial Conference[242] under its existing mandate and powers.[243] Such a note could contain an illustrative index/table with a series of examples of pro-renewables measures and their classification as *WTO-consistent* or *-inconsistent*, according to the policy motivation behind these (given that there may be a variety of policy objectives hidden behind these), their adverse effects, and the specific WTO rules that are engaged.[244]

In the meantime, one solution, as proposed by Nielsen, is to cover only those subsidies in the SCM Agreement that support renewable energy and green technology.[245] According to Nielsen, such an arrangement

> would naturally have to include a limit on the magnitude of the subsidy so that the prices would not get overly distorted, but some minimal subsidisation could be allowed. The subsidies should of course not be linked to WTO-inconsistent local content measures or import substituting measures – so the subsidies to, for example, feed-in tariffs would not be actionable provided they were granted equally to green technologies irrespectively of where they are produced.[246]

As we have attempted to outline in this chapter, the policy space appears to be preserved for WTO members to take measures to support environmental goals, including the promotion of renewables. This is particularly the case in the WTO era. Rather than finding fault with the existing

---

[242] Article IV.1 of the Agreement Establishing the WTO.

[243] See Articles III, IV, IX, and X of the Agreement Establishing the WTO, which relate to the competences of the Ministerial Conference. The Ministerial Conference may either consensually or on the basis of a three-fourths majority – whichever may be required under the specific requirements of these provisions – adopt amendments to the agreements or interpretations of terms within the agreements.

[244] In fact, an excellent example, albeit one that considers these from a subsidies point of view, appears in Ghosh, A. & Gangania, H. (2012) 'Governing Clean Energy Subsidies: What, Why and How Legal?', International Centre for Trade and Sustainable Development, at p. 41.

[245] Nielsen, L. 'Trade and Climate Change – Establishing Coherence', in Evenett, S. & Jara, A. (eds) *Building on Bali – A Work Programme for the WTO* (London: Centre for Economic Policy Research, 2013) p. 151.

[246] Ibid.

normative framework of the multilateral trade system in relation to the further development and proliferation of renewables, we believe the obstacles to the promotion of renewables do not flow from some normative failure, but from the economics that underlie energy.

8. Renewable energy in the European Union

I. INTRODUCTION

The principal aim of this chapter is to present the issue of renewable energy policy development at the EU level against the backdrop of EU law and, more importantly, against the backdrop of the EU's obligations owed to third-party States and organizations, and the international community at large. Both energy and the EU, albeit for different reasons inherent to them, are complex affairs. EU renewable energy policy encompasses several practices, ranging from EU Member State obligations to increase the overall share of renewables in their energy mix, to the obligation to prioritize electricity from renewable sources in the grid infrastructure, the obligation to increase the share of biofuels in the transport sector, the requirement that emitting industries purchase emission credits through the EU Emissions Trading System, the obligation to use energy more efficiently, and, to sum up, the obligation to promote renewables both at the intra-EU and extra-EU levels. The EU's renewable energy policy is further conditioned by the EU and its Member States' obligations owed to third-party States and organizations (for instance, relating to trade, investment, and environmental protection).

EU renewable energy policy is not only framed by the normative context at the intra-EU level, but also by a broader normative context, comprising other instances of international law. EU renewable energy policy must not only never involve any arbitrary and unjustifiable encroachment on EU Member State sovereign prerogatives, but it must also be in line with the EU and Member States' obligations to the outside world. At the juncture between EU renewable energy policy and WTO rules, a number of issues have trade-restrictive effects, which may be justified under environmental protection objectives, including the propagation of renewable energy. Striking the balance between multiple objectives is key for a functional multilateral system. In recent years, the WTO system has evolved to better accommodate environmental protection objectives. However, questions remain around unilateral measures that do not necessarily flow from international practice or from international standards, as well as the differential treatment between tradables, depending on their process and production methods.

All 28 EU Member States are WTO members, as is the EU in its own right.[1] This is also the case in relation to the United Nations Framework Convention on Climate Change (UNFCCC)[2] and its Kyoto Protocol ('the Protocol').[3] As we shall see below, this has important implications for EU renewable energy policy development, given that the breadth of supporting policies invariably leads to situations where some multilateral trade rule or another is potentially engaged. This – in and of itself – is far from suggesting that any such rule is necessarily infringed or, should there be an infringement, that this is necessarily legally unjustifiable. Moreover, the EU has been quick to point out fault in the policies of other WTO members when it has deemed these to have harmed its own renewables-related industries, and – as we shall see in Section III, where we discuss the interplay between EU renewable energy policy and WTO rules – it has also found itself in the position of the respondent to renewables-related complaints by its WTO peers.

The EU has certainly not shied away from its UNFCCC obligations. In fact, while its Kyoto Protocol commitments (regarding the Kyoto Protocol's first commitment period, namely from 2008 to 2012) require that the then 15 EU Member States[4] that decided to fulfill their obligations jointly at the time of their adoption of the Kyoto Protocol reduce their overall greenhouse gas (GHG) emissions by 8% vis-à-vis 1990 levels,[5] the EU unilaterally has committed to reducing its overall GHG emissions by 20% by 2020 compared to 1990 levels.[6] The EU has also indicated that it would be willing to commit to a 30% reduction by 2020, so long

---

1 See http://www.wto.org/english/thewto_e/whatis_e/tif_e/org6_e.htm

2 See http://unfccc.int/parties_and_observers/items/2704.php

3 See http://unfccc.int/kyoto_protocol/status_of_ratification/items/2613.php

4 Namely Austria, Belgium, Denmark, Finland, France, Germany, Greece, Ireland, Italy, Luxembourg, the Netherlands, Portugal, Spain, Sweden, and the United Kingdom.

5 For a summary of the EU's Kyoto Protocol commitments, see http://ec.europa.eu/clima/policies/g-gas/kyoto/index_en.htm

6 See Danish Presidency of the Council of the European Union 2012, 'Information on the Quantified Emission Limitation or Reduction Objectives (QELROs) for the Second Commitment Period under the Kyoto Protocol', 19 April 2012, p. 2, available at http://unfccc.int/files/meetings/ad_hoc_working_groups/kp/application/pdf/awgkp_eu_19042012.pdf

as other parties follow suit by taking meaningful steps towards emission abatement.[7]

This is an example of meaningful global leadership that ought to be applauded, given that climate change is a real threat to the life and health of human, animal, and plant populations globally. This instance of EU leadership casts into unfavorable light that of the Unites States ('the US'),[8] the only country which has not ratified the Kyoto Protocol.[9] What is more, the EU's unilateral 20% GHG emissions reduction target by 2020 is part of a wider '20:20:20' set of targets, which also contains the EU's aim of increasing EU energy efficiency by 20% by 2020, and, most pertinently to this chapter, the EU's aim to increase to 20% the share of renewables in its energy mix by 2020.[10] In fact, the promotion of the renewables cause could substantially help address all three 20:20:20 targets, rather than only the last target.

Along with those targets, the EU Commission put forward in January 2014 an even more ambitious proposal for a 2030 climate and energy policy, which includes a binding GHG 'emissions reduction target of 40% [from 1990 levels] and a binding EU-level target of 27% for renewable energy' consumption by 2030.[11] However, regarding energy efficiency, the EU Commission did not provide a specific target. In February 2014, the European Parliament was even more ambitious than the EU Commission and voted (even if the vote is not legally binding) in favor of three binding targets for a 40% GHG emissions reduction, 30% share of the energy market for renewable energy, and 40% improvement

---

[7] Ibid. p. 4.

[8] That said, under the Clean Air Act and President Obama's Climate Action Plan, it is proposed to cut carbon pollution from power plants by 30% from 2005 levels by 2030. See http://www.whitehouse.gov/share/climate-action-plan

[9] For ratification history of the Kyoto Protocol, see http://unfccc.int/kyoto_protocol/status_of_ratification/items/2613.php

[10] See European Commission, Communication from the Commission, *Europe 2020: A Strategy for Smart, Sustainable, and Inclusive Growth*, Brussels 3.3.2010, COM (2010) 2020 final (at p. 11).

[11] See European Renewable Energy Council, 'Commission Against EU Leadership: Less Growth, Fewer Jobs, More Import Spending', Press Release, 22 January 2014, available at http://www.erec.org/fileadmin/erec_docs/Documents/Press_Releases/EREC_Press_Release_Commission_2030_proposal.pdf. In the words of EU Commission President Barroso, the proposal is 'both ambitious but realistic'. See Statement by President Barroso on the 2030 Energy and Climate Framework, 22 January 2014, available at http://europa.eu/rapid/press-release_SPEECH-14-50_en.htm

in energy efficiency by 2030.[12] In view of the current global situation regarding climate change mitigation, one wonders whether the EU is increasingly becoming a leader without followers.

After this introduction, Section II outlines the definition of *renewable energy sources* within the EU context. Furthermore, we present key figures relating to energy use and emissions in the EU. Section III outlines the normative setting at the levels of EU law and WTO law, and discusses how EU renewable energy policy might engage the broader normative context at play – an important part of which are the EU's obligations flowing from its membership of the WTO. Section IV analyzes current developments with implications for EU renewable energy policy, where the EU emissions trading scheme is discussed as an aspect of EU renewable energy policy. Section V concludes the chapter.

II. RENEWABLE ENERGY AND THE EU

A. Definition of Renewable Energy Sources

The term *renewable energy sources* has been legally defined within the EU context. Its content is defined in the following EU Directives:

- Directive 2001/77/EC on the Promotion of Electricity Produced from Renewable Energy Sources in the Internal Electricity Market offers the following definition: '"renewable energy sources" shall mean renewable non-fossil energy sources (wind, solar, geothermal, wave, tidal, hydropower, biomass, landfill gas, sewage treatment plant gas and biogases)';[13]
- Directive 2003/30/EC on the Promotion of the Use of Biofuels or other Renewable Fuels for Transport, while affirming the definition of renewable energy sources as it appears in Directive 2001/77/EC, further elaborates on the types of fuels encompassed by the terms 'biofuels';[14]

---

[12] European Renewable Energy Council, 'European Parliament Rejects Commission's One-legged 2030 Policy', Press Release, 5 February 2014, available at http://www.erec.org/fileadmin/erec_docs/Documents/Press_Releases/EREC_Press_Release_EP_rejects_Commission_2030_proposal.pdf; see also EurActiv, 'Parliament Back Strong EU Stance on 2030 Clean Energy Goals', 6 February 2014.

[13] OJ L 283, 27.10.2001, p. 33.

[14] OJ L 123, 17.5.2003, p. 42.

- Directive 2003/54/EC Concerning Common Rules for the Internal Market in Electricity contains the following definition: '"renewable energy sources" means renewable non-fossil energy sources (wind, solar, geothermal, wave, tidal, hydropower, biomass, landfill gas, sewage treatment plant gas and biogases)',[15] thus affirming the definition in Directive 2001; and
- Directive 2009/28/EC on the Promotion of the Use of Energy from Renewable Sources (and Amending and Subsequently Repealing Directives 2001/77/EC and 2003/30/EC) (hereinafter 'the 2009 Directive on Renewable Energy') affirms at Article 2 the definition in Directive 2003/54/EC: '"energy from renewable sources" means energy from renewable non-fossil sources, namely wind, solar, aerothermal, geothermal, hydrothermal and ocean energy, hydropower, biomass, landfill gas, sewage treatment plant gas and biogases'.[16]

The 2009 Directive on Renewable Energy repealed Directives 2001/77/EC and 2003/30/EC. Therefore, the definitions in it and in the Directive 2003/54/EC become dispositive over questions of what are deemed *renewable energy sources* within the EU context. We shall discuss the various aspects of the 2009 Directive more fully in Section III.

When we refer to *renewables* in this chapter, unless specifically stated, we refer to renewable sources of energy as juxtaposed with conventional energy sources such as hydrocarbons/fossil fuels (i.e., gasoline/petrol/oil, gas, and coal), and juxtaposed with other non-conventional sources that are, however, non-renewable – for example, nuclear power. When we refer to *renewable goods*, this is a broader concept than *renewables* and encompasses renewable tradables, including energy sources traded and technologies used in the renewable-energy generation process – for example, solar panels and their parts, and wind turbines and their parts. To avoid any confusion, the term *renewable goods* is not a legally defined term in the way that the term *renewable energy sources* is under EU law.

---

[15] OJ L 176, 15.7.2003, p. 37, Article 2§30.
[16] OJ L 140, 5.6.2009, p. 27.

B. EU Energy in Numbers

The latest figures on EU energy trends aggregated by Eurostat – that is, the EU's statistical service – relate to 2011.[17] For ease of reference, we provide tables summarizing the figures at the end of this section (Tables 8.1, 8.2, 8.3). In 2011, the energy mix relating to the EU's gross energy consumption ('Gross Inland consumption') stood at around 1,698 million tons of oil equivalent (Mtoe).[18] The Member States that consumed the most energy during 2011 were Germany (316.31 Mtoe), France (259.33 Mtoe), the UK (198.78 Mtoe), Italy (172.94 Mtoe), Spain (128.54 Mtoe), Poland (102.17 Mtoe), and the Netherlands (81.31 Mtoe).[19] Looking at how this energy was used in 2011, 33% was used for transport purposes, 26% for industrial purposes, 24.7% by households, 12.7% for services, 2.1% for agriculture, 0.1% for fishing, and 0.3% for 'other' uses.[20] Clearly, the most meaningful efforts to reduce CO_2 emissions and to maximize energy efficiency within the EU must focus on the first three fields (transport, industry, and households). The promotion of renewables in all three fields would assist the EU in meeting its environmental protection objectives, given that the use of renewables – depending on the source in question – either releases no CO_2 or releases substantially less than conventional energy sources (i.e., fossil fuels/hydrocarbons such as petroleum, oil, gasoline, natural gas, and coal).

1. Renewables

Given the purpose of this chapter, it would be useful to break down the composition of the 2011 EU energy mix figure in order to gain some insights into the EU's energy use. Renewables made up only around 10% (c. 169 Mtoe) of the 2011 gross energy consumption figure, while oil accounted for 35% (597.9 Mtoe), gas for 24% (397.6 Mtoe), 'solid fuels' – such as coal – for 17% (285.5 Mtoe), and nuclear power accounted for

---

[17] Eurostat collates annual energy data from the 28 EU Member States, Turkey, and the European Economic Area countries of Iceland and Norway. Data go as far back as 1985 for some countries, but are more generally available from 1990. As of October 2008, monthly and annual energy data collections are governed by Regulation (EC) No 1099/2008 of the European Parliament and of the Council of 22 October 2008 on Energy Statistics. See http://epp.eurostat.ec.europa.eu/portal/page/portal/energy/introduction

[18] European Commission, 'EU Energy in Figures', Statistical Pocketbook, 2013, at p. 20.

[19] Ibid. at p. 39.

[20] Ibid. at p. 72.

14% (234 Mtoe).[21] In other words, up to 76% of the EU energy consumption mix in 2011 came from conventional, highly polluting energy sources. It is worth noting that the figure relating to the share of conventional energy sources in the *global* energy mix during 2011 stood around the 81% mark.[22]

It may also be helpful, in turn, to break down the 169 Mtoe figure, that is, the figure representing the 10% share of renewables in the EU gross energy consumption figure for 2011: *biomass and renewable wastes* accounted for 114.9 Mtoe; *hydro* for 26.4 Mtoe; *wind* for 15.4 Mtoe; *geothermal* for 6.2 Mtoe; and *solar* sources accounted for 6.1 Mtoe.[23]

For context purposes, the share of renewables in *global* energy consumption during 2010 stood between 17.5% and 19.3%; the 2011 figure is likely to be close to the 16% mark, whereas the equivalent EU figure for 2011 stood at around 10%.[24] While this represents an improvement over 1995 figures (when renewables only made up 5% of the EU's energy consumption),[25] it remains substantially below the global figure. This could be worrying when considered against the backdrop of EU legislation aimed at increasing the share of renewables in the EU's energy mix up to a minimum of 20% by 2020.[26]

The 10%/169 Mtoe figure (i.e., the share of renewables in the EU's gross energy consumption for 2011) was primarily consumed by the following Member States: Germany (31.22 Mtoe), Italy (19.94 Mtoe), France (18.27), Sweden (15.75 Mtoe), Spain (14.64 Mtoe), Finland (9.07

---

21 Ibid. at pp. 20 and 40.

22 During 2011, around 81% of global energy consumption came from hydrocarbons/fossil fuels. This figure represents 10,689 Mtoe out of a total of 12,274 Mtoe. The actual breakdown is 4,059 Mtoe/c. 33% from oil, 2905.6 Mtoe/c. 24% from gas, and 2,724.3 Mtoe/c. 30% from coal. See *BP Statistical Review of World Energy*, June 2012 (at pp. 40–41), available at www.bp.com/statisticalreview

23 European Commission, 'EU Energy in Figures', Statistical Pocketbook, 2013, at p. 41.

24 Ibid. at pp. 12–13. The Pocketbook does not provide comparable world figures for 2011. International Energy Agency figures, however, suggest that during 2011 the share of renewables in global energy consumption was almost 16%, with 12.5% derived from biofuels and waste material, and 3.4% derived from what the IEA refers to as *other* sources (namely geothermal, solar, wind, and hydro). IEA, *Key World Energy Statistics*, Paris, 2013, at p. 28.

25 European Commission, 'EU Energy in Figures', Statistical Pocketbook, 2013, at p. 20.

26 European Commission Communication, *Europe 2020: A Strategy for Smart, Sustainable, and Inclusive Growth*, Brussels, 2010, (COM(2010) 2020 final), Annex I (at p. 32).

Mtoe), Austria (8.77 Mtoe), Poland (7.95 Mtoe), and the UK (7.80 Mtoe), with the remaing c. 35 Mtoe shared among the rest of the EU Member States.[27]

About half of the EU's *gross* energy consumption in 2011 was produced in the EU (namely 807.2 Mtoe out of 1,689 Mtoe),[28] with the rest having to be imported from third-party energy-exporting states. For 2011, the net energy import figure stood at 939.7 Mtoe,[29] of which only 6.7 Mtoe – that is, less than 1% – comprised renewable energy imports.[30] The highest producers within the EU for 2011 were France (135.40 Mtoe), the UK (129.16 Mtoe), Germany (124.9 Mtoe), Poland (68.87 Mtoe), the Netherlands (64.69 Mtoe), Sweden (32.17 Mtoe), and Italy (32.54 Mtoe).[31] Out of the 807.2 Mtoe of energy produced in the EU during 2011,[32] 20.1% (162.3 Mtoe) was produced from renewables.[33] The highest producers of renewable energy within the EU are: Germany (31.29 Mtoe), France (17.90 Mtoe), Italy (17.87 Mtoe), Sweden (15.75 Mtoe), and Spain (13.76 Mtoe).[34]

2. Energy mix

The energy mix compositions of EU Member States vary greatly. Those Member States whose national energy mixes contained the highest shares of renewables during 2011 were: Sweden (46.8%), Latvia (33.1%), Finland (31.8%), Austria (30.9%), Estonia (25.9%), Portugal (24.9%), Denmark (23.1%), Romania (21.4%), and Lithuania (20.3%), while the

---

[27] European Commission, 'EU Energy in Figures', Statistical Pocketbook, 2013, at p. 40.

[28] Ibid. at p. 33.

[29] These energy imports entered the following Members States: Germany (194.86 Mtoe), Italy (142.61 Mtoe), France (127.91 Mtoe), Spain (104.77 Mtoe), and the UK (72.44 Mtoe) followed, after some distance, by Poland (34.53 Mtoe). See ibid. at p. 36.

[30] The highest importers were Italy (2.07 Mtoe), the UK (1.51 Mtoe), Spain (0.87 Mtoe), Austria (0.54 Mtoe), and Poland (0.51 Mtoe). Ibid. at p. 37.

[31] European Commission, 'EU Energy in Figures', Statistical Pocketbook, 2013, at p. 33.

[32] The 807.2 Mtoe figure represents the EU-produced share of the EU's gross energy consumption for 2011.

[33] European Commission, 'EU Energy in Figures', Statistical Pocketbook, 2013 (at p. 34). Also note that 11.4 Mtoe out of the 162.3 Mtoe worth of energy produced in the EU from renewables in 2011 related to biofuels (including *bio-gasoline* and *biodiesel*). Ibid. at p. 102. NB: the source refers to 11,455 kilotons of oil equivalent (Ktoe), which amounts to 11.4 Mtoe.

[34] Ibid. at p. 34.

lowest share of renewables was in the national energy mixes of Malta (0.4%), Luxembourg (2.9%), the UK (3.8%), Belgium (4.1%), the Netherlands (4.3%), Cyprus (5.4%), Ireland (6.7%), Hungary (9.1%), the Czech Republic (9.4%), and Slovakia (9.7%).[35] The picture that these figures paint might appear counterintuitive in that it would be reasonable to assume that fully industrialized states – such as Belgium, Luxembourg, the Netherlands, and the UK – would possess the infrastructural capabilities and, most importantly, sufficient political will to take more meaningful steps to support the renewables cause.

While EU legislation aims to increase the renewables share in the EU consumption energy mix to an overall minimum of 20% by 2020, and while this obligation burdens all EU Member States, the obligation is different for each Member State. For instance, Sweden is required to increase the share of renewables in its overall *national* energy mix to a minimum of 49% by 2020, while Malta has been prescribed a punier 10%.[36] Meeting their renewables share obligations presents a considerable challenge to some EU Member States, and less of a challenge to others, given that some are closer to meeting their goals than others. For instance, the share of renewables in the national energy mix of the UK during 2011 stood at 3.8% and it ought to rise to 15% by 2020.[37] On the other hand, Estonia's share stood at 25.9% in 2011, thus fulfilling its specific obligation, namely that renewables make up at least 25% of Estonia's national energy mix.[38]

---

[35] Ibid. at p. 25. For Eurostat 2011 figures in their original form, see http://epp.eurostat.ec.europa.eu/tgm/table.do?tab=table&init=1&language=en&pcode=t2020_31&plugin=1

[36] Directive 2009/28/EC (Annex I) expressly states the national targets with regard to the specific context for each Member State. For instance, Belgium is obliged to increase the share of renewables in its energy mix (from the 2005 figure of 2.2%) to 13% by 2020, whilst Sweden is obliged to increase its share of renewables (from the 2005 figure of 39.8%) to 49% in order to achieve the overall EU figure of 20% by 2020. The highest figures are prescribed for Sweden (49%), Latvia (40%), Finland (38%), Austria (34%), Portugal (31%), and Denmark (30%), while the lowest are for Malta (10%), Luxembourg (11%), Belgium, Cyprus, Czech Republic, and Hungary (13%), and Slovakia (14%).

[37] For Eurostat 2011 figures in their original form, see http://epp.eurostat.ec.europa.eu/tgm/table.do?tab=table&init=1&language=en&pcode=t2020_31&plugin=1

[38] European Commission, 'EU Energy in Figures', Statistical Pocketbook, 2013, at p. 25.

3. Wide disparity among EU Member States in the share of renewables

The latest Eurostat figures suggest that there is also wide disparity in the share of renewables in Member States' respective energy use for *electricity generation*, *transport*, and for *heating and cooling*:

- As a point of reference, the overall EU figure for 2011 suggests that 21.7% of *electricity* generated in the EU came from renewables.[39] Those Member States which derived electricity from renewable sources the most during 2011 were: Austria (with a remarkable 66.1% share), Sweden (59.6%), Portugal (46.5%), Latvia (44.7%), Denmark (35.9%), Spain (31.5%), Romania (31.1%), Slovenia (30.8%), Finland (29.2%), Italy (23.5%), and Germany (21.3%). The Member States that derived the least electricity from renewables were: Malta (0.1%), Cyprus (3.4%), Luxembourg (4.1%), and the UK (8.7%);[40]
- During 2011, 3.8% of energy consumed in the EU's *transport* sector came from renewables.[41] At Member State level, the transport sectors of the following states relied on renewables the most: Sweden (8.8%), Austria (7.6%), Poland (6.5%), Germany (6.1%), Spain (5.9%), Latvia (4.8%), Italy (4.7%), and the Netherlands (4.6%). Those States whose transport sectors relied the least on renewables were: Denmark and Estonia (0.2%), Belgium (0.3%), Bulgaria, Slovakia, and Finland (0.4%), and France and Hungary (0.5%);[42] and
- The overall EU figure for 2011 suggests that 15.1% of energy consumed for *heating and cooling* within the EU came from renewables.[43] Again, there is disparity at the Member State level. The Member States whose heating and cooling needs were met from renewables the most during 2011 were: Sweden (64.5%), Estonia (46%), Latvia (44.7%), Finland (44.3%), Portugal (35.5%), Lithuania (33.8%), Denmark (33.6%), Austria (31.1%), Slovenia (27.3%), Romania (24.3%), and Bulgaria (23.8%). Those with the lowest share of renewables used for heating and cooling were: the

---

39 Ibid. at p. 110.
40 Ibid.
41 Ibid.
42 Ibid.
43 Ibid. at p. 109.

UK (2.2%), the Netherlands (3.3%), Belgium (4.3%), Luxembourg and Ireland (5.0%), and Malta (5.6%).[44]

4. EU's CO_2 footprint

Other relevant statistical data pertain to the EU's CO_2 footprint. The latest figures relate to 2010, during which year the EU was responsible for 12.6% of global CO_2 emissions, namely 3,941 million tons out of 31,375 million tons of global CO_2 emissions. During 2010, the highest polluting States in absolute terms were China (23.5%/7,362 million tons CO_2) and the US (17.6%/5,515 million tons CO_2).[45] While the EU is unlike China and the US in that it is not a unitary sovereign state, it has legislated to reduce its emissions by 20% in relation to its 1990 levels by 2020 and, for many – though not all – intents and purposes, the EU could be compared to other sovereign states, given that, as a bloc, it has assumed international obligations under the UNFCCC and WTO special regimes.

We list some key figures regarding EU emissions, given their relevance to the EU's environmental protection objectives and to its renewable energy efforts. Similar to how Member States are under the common obligation to increase the share of renewables in their national energy mix and to how this obligation is differentiated for each Member State, the EU's target to reduce its GHG emissions by 20% by 2020 based on 1990 levels places differentiated obligations on each Member State. For instance, while Denmark, Ireland, and Luxembourg are obligated to reduce their emissions by 20%, based on their 2005 levels of GHG emissions, by 2020, Sweden by 17% (of its 2005 levels), the Netherlands, Austria, Finland, and the United Kingdom by 16% (of their 2005 levels), and Belgium by 15% (of its 2005 levels), other Member States are permitted to increase their emission levels up to certain maxima figures, given the unequal development/industrialization levels within the EU. For example, Bulgaria and Romania are merely obliged to not exceed, by 2020, their 2005 GHG emissions levels by more than 20% and 19%, respectively.[46] In that sense, we witness a degree of equity in EU policy in that the obligation burdens fully industrialized EU Member States with a degree of proportion in relation to their emitting history and developmental needs.

---

44 Ibid.
45 Ibid. at p. 16.
46 Ibid. at p. 27.

Eurostat figures suggest that in 2010 the EU had managed to reduce its overall GHG emissions by 17% of 1990 levels.[47] In terms of how well individual Member States have fared, the figures suggest that those that have made the most headway into their GHG emissions reduction obligations under EU law have been: Estonia and Lithuania (which have reduced their GHG emissions by 60% based on their 1990 levels), Latvia (by 59%), Bulgaria (by 48%), Sweden (by 38%), the Czech Republic and Hungary (by 31%), Germany (by 27%), and the United Kingdom (by 25%).[48]

Table 8.1 EU energy figures, 2011

EU gross energy consumption	1,698 Mtoe
Renewables share in EU gross energy consumption	169 Mtoe (10%)
EU gross energy production	807.2 Mtoe
Renewables share in EU gross energy production	163.3 Mtoe (20.1 %)
EU energy imports	939.7 Mtoe
Renewables share in EU energy imports	6.7 Mtoe (<1%)

Source: Specific sources cited throughout the chapter at the initial mention of each figure.

*Table 8.2 EU renewable energy consumption in 2011**

Biomass and renewable wastes (incl. biofuels)	114.9 Mtoe (68%)
Hydropower	26.4 Mtoe (6.4%)
Wind	15.4 Mtoe (9.17%)
Geothermal	6.2 Mtoe (6.2%)
Solar	6.1 Mtoe (3.6%)

Note: * 169 Mtoe renewable energy consumed – percentages given based on this figure.

Source: Eurostat aggregates based on figures submitted by Member States. See European Commission, 'EU Energy in Figures', Statistical Pocketbook, 2013, at p. 41.

[47] Ibid. at p. 28. Note that we have arrived at the percentile values cited above – e.g., EU overall reduction of GHG emissions by 17% in 2010 – by taking the figure in the last column at p. 28, which represents the EU's overall emissions in 2010 as it relates to the absolute value in the first column at p. 28, and subtracting it by the figure in the first column at p. 28. In the case of the EU, by 2010 it has 83% of its 1990 emissions, thus a reduction by 17%.

[48] Ibid. (Regarding the method used to arrive at the percentile values, see the clarification in the previous footnote.)

Table 8.3 EU renewable energy figures at a glance

Share of renewables in:	%
Gross energy consumption in the EU	10
Electricity generation in the EU	21.7
Transport in the EU	3.8
Heating and cooling in the EU	15.1
EU renewable energy imports	<1
EU energy production	20.1

EU renewable energy figures in 2011		
Renewables share in energy consumption	Renewable energy produced in the EU	Renewable energy imports into the EU
169 Mtoe	163.3 Mtoe	6.7 Mtoe

Source: Eurostat aggregations based on figures submitted by Member States in relation to 2011. Specific sources cited throughout the present chapter.

III. PRINCIPAL ASPECTS OF THE NORMATIVE CONTEXT REGARDING EU RENEWABLE ENERGY POLICY

In this section, we aim to present the main features of the normative context applicable to EU renewable energy policy. For the purposes of this mapping exercise, we have proceeded with segregating these features along the following lines: *intra-EU* and *extra-EU*. However, this taxonomy is purely for the purposes of presenting this information, as opposed to an endorsement of the view that what are ultimately bundles of legal obligation operate in some sort of isolation from one another. On the contrary, these fuse together to become the broader normative context that comes to bear on questions that relate to EU renewable energy policy.

Furthermore, by enumerating the main features of the normative context in scope, we do not suggest that other norms under other regimes or from within the same regime, but in relation to other matters, are irrelevant to questions on EU renewable energy policy. On the contrary, the interplay of *applicable* norms seemingly flowing from different regimes and/or areas of international law operates in an accumulative and highly dynamic manner and, thus, constantly inter-regulates and inter-defines one another. Much has been written on the relationship between the various aspects of a given normative context and how they inter-relate, so we do not intend to repeat those arguments here.[49] However, for the purposes of this chapter, we hold to the conclusions of the International Law Commission's Study Group, as expressed in its 2006 report on the 'fragmentation' of international law, which urges against the artificial interpretation of norms in isolation from one another or with a strict deference towards some thematic grouping.[50]

A. The Intra-EU Aspects of the Normative Context

Several pieces of legislation deal with, or have implications for, renewable energy within the EU. EU primary legislation (namely aspects of the founding EU treaties) delineates EU competences. This has implications for EU energy policy, including EU renewable energy policy, given that it defines the matters over which the EU shares policymaking powers with EU Member States and over which it has exclusive competence.

EU competences in relation to energy fluctuate depending on the specific energy-related matters engaged. While Article 4(2)(i) TFEU refers to energy in its broad sense as a shared competence matter, there are aspects of it – for example, trade tariff policy[51] and competition rules[52] – that are squarely the preserve of the EU, to the exclusion of EU Member States. This is because these energy aspects engage the customs union and the internal market (and affect the proper functioning of both), which are matters within the EU's exclusive competence field.

Furthermore, in Section II, we referred to EU secondary legislation (namely 'Directives' adopted by the EU Parliament and the Council of the European Union, which Member States are obligated to transpose in their domestic legal orders),[53] chiefly in relation to the definition of the

---

[49] See, among others, McLachlan, C. 'The Principle of Systemic Integration and Article 31(3)(c) of the Vienna Convention' (2005) *International and Comparative Law Quarterly*, Vol. 54.

[50] ILC Report of the Study Group, *Fragmentation of International Law: Difficulties Arising from the Diversification and Expansion of International Law* (A/CN.4/L.682) (13 April 2006).

[51] Article 3.1(a) TFEU.

[52] Article 3.1(b) TFEU.

[53] http://europa.eu/legislation_summaries/institutional_affairs/decisionmaking_process/l14527_en.htm

locution *renewable energy sources*. As we shall see below, there is further EU legislation thrashing out the finer details of EU renewable energy policy.

Setting aside the environmental reasons that make the promotion of renewables pressing,[54] the reasons behind the need to mobilize state resources to promote the take-up and scale-up of renewable energy relate to the persistent lack of a competitive relationship between renewable and conventional energy sources. The reasons behind the existing market conditions are manifold and include the historic high-level subsidization of conventional energy sources, which the International Energy Agency deems to have been c. USD 544 billion during 2012 alone.[55] Against the backdrop of intensifying environmental degradation, the market 'failure' behind the fact that renewables have not sufficiently taken off has to be addressed somehow by State intervention into the market.

Intervention – as is the case within the EU and, generally, globally – often involves different policy options as means of encouraging or creating more favorable market conditions. For instance, a policy such as one that mandates the prioritization of electricity generated by renewable energy sources (renewable electricity) within the EU grid system(s) could go some way towards encouraging renewable energy production. However, alone, such a policy is unlikely to secure the viability of renewables. In that sense, some *price-supporting* policy may also be necessary. What is most common in the EU is the use of *feed-in* systems, which essentially attempt to level the playing field so that renewable electricity producers may remain in the electricity generation market.[56]

---

[54] Pachauri, R.F. & Reisinger, A. (eds) *Fourth Assessment Report of the Intergovernmental Panel on Climate Change* (Geneva: IPCC, 2007); for the synthesis report, see www.ipcc.ch/pdf/assessment-report/ar4/syr/ar4_syr.pdf. For figures on temperature increases between 1970 and 2004 to get a sense of the scale of global warming, see p. 32 of the synthesis report.

[55] For the interactive IEA database on fuel subsidies, see http://www.worldenergyoutlook.org/resources/energysubsidies/ and http://www.iea.org/subsidy/index.html

[56] In relation to feed-in systems, two options are usually encountered: the *feed-in tariff* (FIT), which guarantees a fixed price per kWh, and the *feed-in premium*, which involves a payment of an amount on top of the market price for electricity. There appears to be a shift towards the latter. See Ragwitz, M. et al., 'Recent Developments of Feed-in Systems in the EU – A Research Paper for the International Feed-In Cooperation', January 2012, available at http://www.feed-in-cooperation.org/wDefault_7/content/research/index.php. As part of their research, Ragwitz et al. have reviewed EU Member States' national renewable

However, intervening in the market and/or developing policy with trade implications in order to handle an *externality* (to the market) such as environmental degradation could give rise to concerns about market access and protectionism. In that respect, State aid has to be scrutinized to ensure that the EU project – predicated on the common market – is not being undermined. The EU has rules on these matters to ensure that policies remain compatible with the internal market. We shall list the main features of these rules below.

1. Treaty on the Functioning of the European Union: provisions on State aid

Article 107 TFEU articulates the general presumption that State aid that distorts or threatens to distort trade competition between EU Member States is, from the outset, incompatible with the internal market, and therefore prohibited. Unsurprisingly, there are exemptions to this general prohibition. These have been segregated between those that *are* compatible with the internal market and those that *may be* compatible with the internal market.

While there is no express mention of *renewable energy* or, for that matter, of *energy*, there are grounds to reasonably argue that State aid linked to environmental objectives – as is the case with renewables – may be compatible with the internal market. For instance, Article 107(3) TFEU, states that aid 'to promote the execution of an important project of common European interest or to remedy a serious disturbance in the economy of a Member State',[57] 'to facilitate the development of certain economic activities ... where such aid does not adversely affect trading conditions to an extent contrary to the common interest',[58] and any categories of aid 'as may be specified by decision of the Council on a proposal from the Commission',[59] may be compatible with the internal market. In other words, renewable energy projects that require large capital investments on the part of EU Member States could arguably be justified under the existing headings. Also, the last heading (Article 107(3)(e) TFEU) leaves the possibility open for the EU Council, acting on a recommendation by the EU Commission, to be able to approve an instance of State aid. Clearly, sufficient political will must amass for this to happen.

---

energy plans and have found FIT-related programs to be the most common (see pp. 4–5).

[57] Article 107(3)(b) TFEU.

[58] Article 107(3)(c) TFEU.

[59] Article 107(3)(e) TFEU.

2. Commission Regulation (EC) No. 800/2008 (the 'General Block Exemption Regulation')

There are dispensations in Articles 108 and 109 TFEU to enable the EU Council and the EU Commission to handle instances of State aid. Under those powers, the Council adopted Regulation No. 773/2013 of 22 July 2013[60] to enable the EU Commission to adopt 'Block Exemption' Regulations for State aid – that is to say, to allow the Commission to declare specific categories of State aid as compatible with the TFEU if they fulfill certain conditions, thus exempting them from the requirement of prior notification (under Article 108(3) TFEU) and Commission approval.[61]

The EU Commission availed itself of this dispensation and has issued Commission Regulation (EC) No. 800/2008 of August 2008 (the 'General Block Exemption Regulation' (GBER)),[62] which contains express provisions on renewables. Recital 46 of the GBER clearly states that environmental aid for investments to promote renewable energy sources should be exempt from the notification requirements regarding State aid. Further, Article 23 GBER expressly refers to 'environmental investment aid for the promotion of energy from renewable energy sources' as being compatible with the internal market, so long as it does not exceed 45% of the eligible costs,[63] though this may be up to 55% when the beneficiaries are medium-sized enterprises and up to 65% when they are small enterprises.[64] Where the investment aid benefits biofuels production, in order for the block exemptions to apply, the biofuels in question must be sustainable within the meaning of EU law, which shall be discussed further below.

3. The 2008 Guidelines on State Aid for Environmental Protection

The 2008 EU Guidelines on State Aid for Environmental Protection[65] contain a set of detailed provisions on the maxima permissible values of

---

[60] OJ L204, 31.07.2013, p. 11. Full title: Council Regulation No 733/2013 of 22 July 2013 amending Regulation (EC) No 994/98 on the application of Articles 92 and 93 of the Treaty establishing the European Community to certain categories of horizontal State aid.

[61] For background, see European Commission, 'State Aid Control', available at http://ec.europa.eu/competition/state_aid/legislation/block.html

[62] Commission Regulation (EC) No. 800/2008 of 6 August 2008 declaring certain categories of aid compatible with the common market in application of Articles 87 and 88 of the Treaty (General Block Exemption Regulation).

[63] Article 23(2) of Commission Regulation (EC) No. 800/2008.

[64] Ibid.

[65] OJ 2008/C 82/01, 1.4.2008 (text with EEA relevance).

State aid in order for it to be compatible with the internal market. There is a whole raft of grounds upon which State aid may be compatible with the internal market, including aid for: early adaptation to EU standards of environmental protection,[66] environmental studies,[67] energy saving,[68] and most importantly for the purposes of this chapter, 'renewable energy sources',[69] investment, and operating costs.[70]

In order for aid for renewable energy sources to be compatible, there is a list of provisions with criteria to be met.[71] The long and short of it is that, as a general rule, the *intensity* of investment aid – what is referred to in the 2008 Guidelines as *aid intensity* – must not exceed 60% of the eligible investment costs.[72] However, higher maxima are envisaged: namely where the beneficiary is a small enterprise, aid intensity could be up to 80%,[73] and where it is a medium-sized enterprise, it could be up to 70%.[74] Additionally, the EU Commission foresees circumstances where aid intensity could be justifiably as high as 100%;[75] however, it introduces further safeguards by requiring that the investment aid be 'granted in a genuinely competitive bidding process on the basis of clear, transparent and non discriminatory criteria ...'[76] as a safety precaution against abuse and to ensure that all market actors are able to participate.

We see in the 2008 Guidelines and in the GBER, maxima levels of State aid being set. The relationship between these two instruments is outlined in the 2008 Guidelines, which suggests that, in the final analysis, the 2008 Guidelines become dispositive over questions regarding the permissible levels of State aid, should there be any confusion or controversy.[77] Consequently, it might help to regard the 2008 Guidelines as containing the substantive rules, and, on the other hand, the GBER as containing the procedural rules on whether notification to the Commission is necessary.

66 Ibid. at 1.5.3.
67 Ibid. at 1.5.4.
68 Ibid. at 1.5.5.
69 Ibid. at 1.5.6, where the rationale of aid for renewable energy sources is outlined.
70 Ibid. at point 70, entry 21 on p. 14.
71 Ibid. at 3.1.6, §101–111.
72 Ibid. §102.
73 Ibid. §103.
74 Ibid.
75 Ibid. §104.
76 Ibid.
77 Ibid. §14.

4. Directive 2009/28/EC (the 2009 Renewable Energy Directive)

The 2009 Renewable Energy Directive[78] is the most important piece of secondary EU legislation that enshrines into legal language the EU's various renewable energy-related ambitions. It contains various provisions directed towards creating the material conditions for renewable energy to finally take off. For instance, Article 3(1) of the Directive mandates that, by 2020, at least 20% of the EU's gross energy consumption be met by renewables, and Article 3(4) mandates that, by 2020, at least 10% of each Member State's energy needs for transport be met from renewables. EU Member States are also under the obligation to draw up publishable National Renewable Energy Action Plans (NREAPs) in which they set out their national targets for the share of energy to be met from renewable sources for transport, electricity generation, and heating and cooling by 2020.[79] Furthermore, Article 16(2) provides that electricity generated from renewable energy sources should have priority in the electricity grid.[80]

Other provisions are aimed at encouraging EU Member States to collaborate with one another[81] and to collaborate with third-party States on joint projects.[82] In fact, the latter would be most helpful for the EU, given its proximity to the Middle East and North Africa (MENA) region and the potential for closer cooperation with third-party States in that region for the generation of energy from renewable sources, mainly solar.[83]

---

78 OJ L 140/16.

79 Article 4 of Directive 2009/28/EC.

80 This has not been extended to *green* gas for it to have priority in the gas pipeline system.

81 See the 'joint project' provisions under Article 7; see also Article 11 relating to 'joint support schemes' under which Member States may coordinate their renewable energy policies in a unitary manner. So far, only Sweden, along with another EEA member – Norway – has sought to do so, much to the dismay of the EU Commission. See the November 2013 Communication from the Commission, 'Delivering the Internal Electricity Market and Making the Most of Public Intervention', Brussels, 5.11.2013, C (2013) 7243 final (at p. 16).

82 See provisions under Article 9 relating to joint renewable electricity generation projects with third-party States.

83 See e.g., the estimates of the DESERTEC Foundation, a research association involving policymakers, scientists, and economists linked to the Mediterranean, which suggest that: 'Clean power from Middle Eastern and North African (MENA) deserts can provide the region with sufficient energy for urgently needed seawater desalination. In addition, desert power can supply around two-thirds of the region's rising energy demand, whilst still leaving enough

The 2009 Renewable Energy Directive is also significant for a further – more contentious – reason: its 'sustainability' criteria must be met in order for biofuels and other bioliquids to be considered when assessing whether the 2009 Directive requirements are being met.[84] For instance, in order for biofuels and other bioliquids to be considered within scope, the GHG emissions savings must currently be in the order of 35%.[85] The level of savings is to rise to 50% in 2017,[86] and, for those biofuels and bioliquids produced after 1 January 2017, to rise to 60% in 2018.[87] Also, they must not be produced from raw material obtained from land with high biodiversity value.[88]

As we shall see later, this has invoked the ire of Argentina, whose biofuels producers (along with corresponding EU biofuels producers) are set to be disadvantaged, should their products not achieve a minimum of 35% GHG emissions savings. This is because the 2009 Renewable Energy Directive makes clear that any biofuels with emissions savings below 35% cannot be taken into account for the purposes of EU targets, which instantly makes biofuel products with a lower (than 35%) emissions saving less popular. The argument, which we shall discuss below, is that this offends WTO norms, which require that *like* products be treated equally. The simplicity of a term such as 'like' is a considerably profound notion in the WTO jurisprudence. Suffice it to point out for the purposes of this section that an EU rule (namely the provisions of the 2009 Directive on the definition of *biofuel* and *bioliquid*) has not been without controversy.

Other important aspects of the 2009 Renewable Energy Directive relate to *support schemes* as a means of promoting the renewables cause at the

---

electricity for export, meeting 15 percent of European consumption. Studies by the German Aerospace Center (DLR) show that this aim is technologically and economically feasible with economic and environmental benefits for all partners'. See http://www.desertec.org/global-mission/eu-mena/

84 See Article 17 of Directive 2009/28/EC.

85 See Article 17(2). Article 19 involves a convoluted formula to be used to assess the level to which a 35% GHG emissions saving relates.

86 See Article 17(2).

87 Ibid.

88 See Article 17(3), which also defines what types of land have such value. Indicatively, this is land that has some protected status – for instance, woodlands and primary forests, areas protected by law for the purposes of protecting the natural environment, and areas where there are rare, threatened or endangered ecosystems or species.

EU and Member State level.[89] Other than offering a definition of support schemes, the 2009 Directive offers very little by way of disciplines for such schemes.[90] That said, the existing disciplines (namely those to be found in Article 107 TFEU and the 2008 Guidelines on State aid) are applicable.

5. Selected EU cases with implications for renewable energy

Electricity generated via renewable energy sources and schemes to support these have been the subject of EU judicial proceedings before the European Court of Justice (ECJ) – the predecessor to the Court of Justice of the European Union (CJEU). Below are two cases with implications for renewable energy.

5.1. Outokumpu[91] In *Outokumpu*, the ECJ had the task of examining a measure on the part of Finland justified on the basis of the need to promote renewables. In that case, renewable electricity produced domestically was effectively favored for taxation purposes over electricity produced from other means. All electricity imports were taxed at a flat rate, irrespective of energy source. Consequently, renewable electricity produced in Sweden and delivered to Finland was taxed higher than renewable electricity produced in Finland. What is more, the importer was not given the option to prove that the imports were from renewable sources. This disparity in treatment was held to be discriminatory and contrary to the purposes of the internal market.[92]

5.2. Preussen Elektra[93] In the *Preussen Elektra* case, the ECJ examined a German measure that aimed at promoting renewable electricity by requiring downstream operators to purchase a portion from renewables. Firstly, the ECJ had to consider whether the measure amounted to State aid, and found it did not, as there was neither a payment from State resources nor did the State forego any income. Secondly, the ECJ considered an aspect of the policy under scrutiny which required downstream operators to purchase this portion of renewable electricity from generators from within their area of operations. Evidently, this offended

---

89 See Article 3(3)(a), which refers to *support schemes* as one means for EU Member States to meet their 2009 Directive obligations.

90 See Article 2(k) for a definition of support schemes.

91 Case C-213/96 Outokumpu Oy [1998] ECR I-777.

92 Points 38–41 of the *Outokumpu* judgment.

93 Case C-379/98, *Preussen Elektra AG v. Scheswag AG* [2001] ECR I-2099.

the interests of renewable energy generators from other EU Member States and thus appeared to undermine the internal market. However, there were a number of considerations in *Preussen Elektra* which did not feature in the *Outokumpu* case that, in the event, led to the German measure in question not being found incompatible.[94]

Where one looks for clarity in rules, the *Preussen Elektra* case does not fully satisfy, given that there appears to be a 'grey zone' at the intersection of State aid rules and the free movement of goods (one of the fundamental 'four freedoms' upon which the EU project rests), and there also appears to have been a reluctance on the part of the ECJ to satisfactorily deal with the competition element between domestic and foreign generators of renewable electricity.[95] However, the advent of the 2008 Guidelines on State aid and the GBER have since provided more certainty for EU Member States and private actors such as downstream operators and electricity generators. Further, the specific Guidelines for environmental and energy aid (EEAG) for the period between 2014 and 2020 that the Commission intends to issue in 2014 would provide even more specific guidance to the environment–energy nexus.[96]

B. The Extra-EU Aspects of the Normative Context

For the purposes of this chapter, the most relevant agreements that relate to the broader normative context applicable appear to be the Kyoto

---

94 See points 73–81 in *Preussen Elektra*. Several considerations informed that judgment, including the fact that, since the *Outokumpu* case, the environmental protection cause had been elevated structurally by changes to the treaties (namely the Treaty of Amsterdam elevated the prominence of environmental protection, and the Treaty of Maastricht redefined the 'four freedoms' (of movement of goods, services, capital, and people) into policies rather than 'foundations') so as to be almost on a par with the fundamental four freedoms. The EU's international obligations in relation to environmental protection provided further impetus, and the liberalization of the electricity sector was at the time incomplete and efforts to promote the prioritization of renewable electricity were in their early stages. All of these are matters that could go some way towards justifying distinguishing this case.

95 See Biondi, A., Eeckhout, P. & Flynn, J. *The Law of State Aid in the European Union* (Oxford: Oxford University Press, 2004), where it is stated that: '[The case] … throws up a competition element on the internal market side even if the ECJ did not satisfactorily deal with that element' (at p. 107).

96 European Commission, 'Delivering the Internal Electricity Market and Making the Most of Public Intervention', Brussels, 2013, 7243 final (at pp. 4–5).

Protocol to the UNFCCC and the various WTO-covered agreements relating to the EU and its Member States.

1. The Kyoto Protocol and the EU

The 28 EU Member States along with the EU, in its own right, are signatory and ratifying parties to the Kyoto Protocol to the UNFCCC. The Protocol allows parties to fulfill their obligations jointly if they so wish. In 2002, the then 15 EU Member States opted to avail themselves of this dispensation when they became parties to the Protocol, and jointly committed to an overall reduction of their CO_2 emissions by 8% in relation to 1990 levels.[97] The Protocol has been incorporated in EU law by way of Decision 2002/358/EC, which approves the Kyoto Protocol and refers to the burden-sharing agreement among the EU Member States.[98]

In relation to the first commitment period under the Protocol, the EU committed to reducing its overall GHG emissions for the period between 2008 and 2012 to 92% of the 1990 level of emissions of the 15 EU Member States that in 2002 formed the European Community.[99] That is to say, to reducing emissions by 8% in relation to its 1990 levels by 2013. In relation to the second commitment period between 2013 and 2020, the EU is prepared to reduce its GHG emissions by 20% in relation to its 1990 levels.[100] What is more, as mentioned earlier, the EU is willing to pledge a 30% reduction by 2020 so long as other polluters take similarly meaningful steps towards GHG emissions abatement.[101]

---

[97] For a summary of the EU and its Kyoto Protocol commitments, see http://ec.europa.eu/clima/policies/g-gas/kyoto/index_en.htm

[98] The permissible emissions limits for EU Member States are stipulated in Commission Decision 2006/944/EC, OJ 2006 L 358/87, as well as in OJ 2006 L 367/80 as amended by Decision 2010/778/EU, OJ 2010 L 332/41.

[99] See OJ L 130/19, 15 May 2002, Table of quantified emission limitation or reduction commitments for the purpose of determining the respective emission levels allocated to the European Community and its Member States in accordance with Article 4 of the Kyoto Protocol, available at http://ec.europa.eu/clima/policies/g-gas/docs/table_emm_limitation_en.pdf

[100] This figure extends to all 28 EU Member States plus Iceland. See the *Submission by Denmark and the European Commission on behalf of the European Union and its Member States on Information on the Quantified Emission Limitation or Reduction Objectives (QELRO) for the Second Commitment Period under the Kyoto Protocol* (Copenhagen, 19 April 2012), available at http://unfccc.int/files/meetings/ad_hoc_working_groups/kp/application/pdf/awgkp_eu_19042012.pdf (at p. 6).

[101] Ibid. at p. 4.

This extra-EU instance of obligation owed by the EU to third-party States and organizations is an additional consideration in the EU's policy development, given that it is obligated to honor its international obligations. From EU practice, however, the EU exhibits a willingness to go beyond these specific commitments. For instance, the EU has unilaterally committed to reducing its GHG emission levels by 20% by 2020, which is a commitment over and above its Protocol commitments.

2. The WTO and the EU

Renewables-related complaints raised within the WTO context invariably hinge upon allegations of discrimination. The EU has been both a complainant and respondent in relation to complaints raised in the WTO.[102] The policies the EU develops along with those that its Member States develop can lead to complaints on the part of WTO peers, to which the EU and its Member States may find themselves jointly and/or severally responding. Below is a specific case regarding EU renewable energy policy vis-à-vis the extra-EU normative context.

2.1. EU and Certain Member States – Importation and Marketing of Biodiesel and Measures Supporting the Biodiesel Industry (hereinafter 'EU – Biodiesel')[103] Earlier, we alluded to the sustainability requirements for biofuels under the 2009 Renewable Energy Directive. In order for biofuels to be taken into account for the purposes of measuring the EU's performance in relation to its renewable energy targets, they must be sustainably sourced and must also achieve GHG emission savings of at least 35%.[104] Argentina – an important global biofuels producer and exporter to the EU – baulked at these provisions given that, as a consequence of the EU measures, its biofuel exports are affected as they do not achieve 35% emission savings. In addition, the issue about qualifying for the 'sustainable' classification was particularly sticky, given that Article 17 of the 2009 Directive, as discussed above, has express provisions on what types of protected and/or bio-diverse land do not qualify.

---

[102] There is also a case in the WTO regarding renewable energy, where the EU reserved its third-party rights (namely *United States – Countervailing Duty Measures on Certain Products from China*, WT/DS437). However, since the EU is neither a complainant nor a respondent in this case, it is out of this chapter's scope and therefore it will not be analyzed in this chapter.

[103] WT/DS459.

[104] Article 17(2) of Directive 2009/28/EC.

In May 2013, Argentina requested consultations with the EU and its Member States regarding the measures it felt affected the importation, marketing, and sale/demand of Argentinean biofuels in the EU. Argentina's request relates to two types of EU and Member State measures: (a) measures to promote the use of renewable energy and to introduce a mechanism to control and reduce GHG emissions; and (b) measures to establish support schemes for the biodiesel sector. Argentina considers that the measures in question are inconsistent with, amongst others: Articles I and III GATT; Articles 1, 2, 3, 5, and 6 of the SCM Agreement; Article 2 of the TRIMs Agreement; and Articles 2 and 5 of the Technical Barriers to Trade Agreement (TBT Agreement). Argentina referred to the TBT Agreement, which clearly expresses a preference for multilateralism[105] in that any technical barriers to trade – in this case, arguably, the EU's definition of '*sustainable*' – be based on international standards and not be more restrictive than necessary in addressing some legitimate objective(s) contemplated by the TBT Agreement.[106]

Argentina contests EU measures, and Member State implementation legislation pertinent to these, that define as 'sustainable' such energy sources that reduce GHG emissions by at least 35% when compared to fossil fuels. Its soya-related biofuels products reduce emissions by no more than 31%, thus not qualifying under the EU definition. Argentina further challenges an EU measure requiring that certain fossil-fuel distributors also make available *sustainable* fuel through their distribution operations, given that its biofuels would be excluded. Argentina contends that this results in treatment less favorable for its own products.

2.1.1. FACTS As the Argentinian complaint *EU – Biodiesel*[107] attests, a range of WTO rules are potentially engaged by specifications, or other measures that affect the internal sale of imports, laid down by WTO members. The two principal aspects of the Argentinian complaint are that the 'sustainability' and GHG emissions savings requirements of the provisions on *biofuels* under the 2009 Renewable Energy Directive, and in relation to Member State implementation legislation and measures, are arbitrary and unduly disadvantage Argentinian exports.[108] Argentinian biofuels exports were considered by the EU to not achieve emission

---

105 See the interplay of Articles 1.1 and 2.4 of the TBT Agreement.

106 Article 2.2 of the TBT Agreement.

107 WT/DS459.

108 See the notification of the complaint by Argentina (WT/DS459/1, at p. 3, 23 May 2013, Request for Consultations by Argentina) for the fuller account of the complaint.

savings above 31%.[109] Moreover, the options open to Argentinian exporters to prove to the EU authorities the sustainability credentials of their exports were unsatisfactory and/or burdensome.[110]

The Argentinian government, among other things, complained that the EU's 35% emission savings requirement was arbitrary, not justified scientifically, and not based on a recognized international norm or standard.[111] It also complained about EU measures (pertinent to, among other things, the 2009 Renewable Energy Directive and Directive 2009/30/EC),[112] which require petrol companies that release fuels/diesel products for consumption to also release for consumption certain amounts of *sustainable* biofuels. Argentina asserts that the measures in question discriminate against Argentinian exports, given that they do not qualify for this classification. Consequently, Argentinian exports neither qualify to be included into the compulsory scheme that burdens downstream oil companies, nor do they qualify to benefit from the import duty reduction applicable to biofuel imports considered by the EU to be *sustainable*.[113] There were further complaints in the Argentinian notification document, but they were essentially about these two matters: the 35% emission saving requirement and the use of the term *sustainable*, for which Argentinian imports do not qualify.[114]

2.1.2. LEGAL ISSUES The Argentinian government felt that the goods in question – that is, biofuels that qualify vis-à-vis its biofuel exports, which do not qualify under the EU rules – were sufficiently *alike* for the purposes of the WTO non-discrimination rules (Articles I and III GATT) for them to be afforded less favorable treatment in a manner justified under WTO rules.

The Argentinian government felt that the measures in question appeared to be technical regulations that had trade-restrictive implications for Argentinian biofuel exports. Citing Articles 2.1, 2.2, 5.1, and 5.2 of the TBT Agreement, the Argentinian government argued that the measures amounted to unnecessary obstacles to international trade, given that

---

109 Ibid.

110 Ibid. at p. 10.

111 Ibid. at p. 3.

112 Amending Directive 98/70/EC as regards the specification of petrol, diesel, and gas-oil and introducing a mechanism to monitor and reduce GHG emissions and amending Council Directive 1999/32/EC as regards the specification of fuel used by inland waterway vessels and repealing Directive 93/12/EEC.

113 WT/DS459/1, at p. 9.

114 Ibid. at p. 3.

they appeared to the Argentinian government to be more trade-restrictive than necessary to fulfill a legitimate objective. Argentina cited the TBT Agreement, which clearly expresses a preference for multilateralism, to make the point that any technical barriers to trade be based on international standards.

In relation to the requirement that petrol downstream companies make biofuels available, and to certain aspects of the tax reduction policies of the EU and its Member States, Argentina argued that, given that only EU-produced biofuels appeared to qualify for these, these measures also amounted to *prohibited*[115] and to *actionable*[116] subsidies within the meaning of the SCM Agreement.[117] Argentina also felt that another aspect of a (Polish) measure that affected the internal marketing and sale of biofuels amounted to an investment measure that violated obligations under Articles 2.1 and 2.2 of the TRIMs Agreement.[118]

2.1.3. ANALYSIS The complaint is in the consultation stages between the parties. Any discussion below is speculative and based on the brief outline of the arguments in Argentina's complaint notification[119] and in analyses of the issues by others elsewhere.

Invariably, an appraisal of these claims would depend on a determination of whether the products in question are sufficiently *like* in order to subsequently assess whether any discriminatory treatment is, in the circumstances, justified. In that sense, determinations of products as *like* do not automatically lead to the conclusion that instances of unequal treatment between *like* products are unjustified, given that the Article XX GATT general exceptions and/or other considerations – for example, under Article III:8 GATT – may also apply.

However, in this case, the products in question – namely biofuels that meet the EU sustainability and emission savings criteria, and biofuels that fail to do so – could be argued to be sufficiently *like* within the context of WTO norms. On the other hand, should the complaint come before a Panel within the context of the WTO's dispute settlement mechanism, the EU is likely to argue that the two products being compared are sufficiently distinct, given the emission savings and sustainability aspects of the biofuels that qualify. For instance, the emission saving aspects of products could set them apart and justify differential

115 Articles 3.1(b) and 3.2 of the SCM Agreement.
116 Articles 5(b) and/or 5(c) of the SCM Agreement.
117 WT/DS459/1, p. 6.
118 Ibid. at p. 11.
119 WT/DS459/1.

treatment argued on the basis of this distinction being related to the physical characteristics of the products – for example, the level of emissions released following their combustion. However, biofuels sustainably sourced and those from land outside the scope of the EU definition of *sustainable* are not any different insofar as their physical characteristics are concerned and, in such circumstances, the difference in the product to justify differential treatment is less evident.

The EU, for its part, may choose to argue that sustainable biofuels from conventional land (i.e., not under, or in need of, any natural conservation/protection regime) are sufficiently dissimilar to/unlike biofuels of uncertain or of problematic provenance. This would be a distinction of products argued in relation to differences in *process and production methods*. Arguing such grounds for differential treatment is a highly complex matter within WTO jurisprudence.

The notion of *similar* or *like* products is extremely complex and adjusts to the specific circumstances in any given dispute. In fact, there has been an *accordion* analogy to highlight the flexibility of the notion of *like*.[120] In 1970, the GATT Working Party on Border Tax Adjustments, in its report, set out the basic approach for interpreting what are *like* or *similar* products, emphasizing that there should be a case-by-case approach to allow various considerations to be taken into account – including the product's end uses in a given market, consumers' tastes and habits, and the product's properties, nature, and quality.[121]

There is much controversy as to whether differential treatment of products on the basis of process and production methods (PPMs) could be in line with WTO norms, given that PPMs do not attach to the physical characteristics of products *per se*. On the other hand, the notion of *like* is not restricted to a primary or exclusive assessment of the physical characteristics of the products in question.

Shortly after the adoption of the 2009 Renewable Energy Directive, Andrew Mitchell and Christopher Tran published a scholarly paper on the WTO consistency of the 2009 Directive.[122] Among the various issues arising at the juncture of the Directive and WTO rules, they analyzed the potential created by the 2009 Directive for there to be differential

---

[120] See the Appellate Body's comments in *Japan – Taxation on Alcoholic Beverages* (AB) (WT/DS8/AB/R), at p. 21.

[121] See Report of the GATT Working Party on Border Tax Adjustments, 20 November 1970, L/3464.

[122] Mitchell, A. & Tran, C. 'The Consistency of the EU Renewable Energy Directive with the WTO Agreements', Georgetown Business, Economics & Regulatory Law Research Paper No. 1485549, October 2009.

treatment between biofuels that satisfied the Directive criteria and biofuels that failed to do so. They felt that treating products differently on account of their emission savings could potentially be justified. However, differential treatment based on a PPM – for example, the land sustainability criterion – was most likely inconsistent with WTO rules, given that the two sets of biofuels were likely to come from two different sets of exporting countries and that there was likely, therefore, to be discrimination between WTO peers. While differential treatment may be justified under WTO rules, it should not discriminate between exporters (Article I GATT).[123]

Mitchell and Tran argue that the definition of what is 'sustainable' in the 2009 Renewable Energy Directive is a matter that engages the TBT Agreement and that, given the strong preference for international standards[124] and collaborative approaches to standards development where no international standards exist,[125] the 2009 Directive may be in breach.[126] What is more, the TBT Agreement states the necessity of a technical measure to meet an objective.[127] Therefore, Mitchell and Tran argue that the fact that the EU measure does not provide for some sort of *pro-rata* approach to the taxation of biofuel imports not fulfilling the criteria of the 2009 Directive illustrates that the measure may not be necessary when there appears to be a less trade-restrictive option (such as a *pro-rata*-based measure for those imports that do not qualify).[128]

Some commentators have taken a less nuanced approach to PPMs, finding these to be unacceptable under WTO rules,[129] while others take a

---

123 Ibid. at p. 3.

124 See Article 2.4 of the TBT Agreement, referring to international standards.

125 See Article 2.5 of the TBT Agreement, referring to the need to consult with those particularly affected, along with a duty on the part of the party taking the measure in question to account for its measure.

126 Mitchell, A. & Tran, C. 'The Consistency of the EU Renewable Energy Directive with the WTO Agreements', Georgetown Business, Economics & Regulatory Law Research Paper No. 1485549, October 2009, at p. 10.

127 Article 2.2 of the TBT Agreement.

128 Mitchell, A. & Tran, C., *supra* note 126, at p. 12.

129 See Cottier, T. et al., 'Energy in WTO Law and Policy'. Available at http://www.wto.org/english/res_e/publications_e/wtr10_forum_e/wtr10_7may10_e.pdf (at p. 20).

more nuanced approach by highlighting the various relevant developments within WTO law and practice.[130] The sounder opinion appears to be that which Potts advances in his thorough analysis of the relationship between PPMs and GATT, where he concludes:

> Our analysis of the relationship between PPM-based measures and the GATT suggests that not only is there no evidence of a legal rule against the use of such measures within the GATT, but even more, that the existence of such a rule would appear to be inconsistent with the essential logic applied in GATT jurisprudence to date … On the basis of existing GATT case law, PPM policies are fully permissible, so long as the basic non-discrimination requirements of the agreement are maintained. While such an understanding provides important inroads for the integration of sustainability interests within trade policy, it does nothing to address the systemic dis-equilibrium in the abilities of developed and developing countries to comply with specific PPM requirements.[131]

As we have stated, the *EU – Biodiesel* complaint remains the subject of consultations between the parties involved and there is no progress reported so far. However, we have presented the above to illustrate the sort of issues that the EU's environmental protection and, more specifically, its renewable energy policies have thrown up in relation to the extra-EU normative context, and also to highlight the complexity that exists at the WTO normative level.

IV. CURRENT DEVELOPMENTS WITH IMPLICATIONS FOR EU RENEWABLE ENERGY POLICY

Prioritizing the EU's competition objectives against its environmental objectives could be entirely justified where there seems to be irreconcilable tension. We have seen how EU renewable energy policy, on the one hand, is driven and conditioned by EU obligations owed by the EU to third-party States and organizations as well as by EU law, which enshrines targets (namely the 20:20:20 set of targets discussed earlier). On the other hand, EU renewable energy policy must also be consistent with the EU's other objectives, by not undermining the common market and by not exonerating instances of protectionism.

---

[130] See Potts, J. 'The Legality of PPMs under the GATT: Challenges and Opportunities for Sustainable Trade Policy', International Institute for Sustainable Development, 2008 (cf. the notes to p. 1).

[131] Ibid. at pp. 35–36.

There is opinion that supports the view that in cases of tension – particularly in the early stages of the EU emissions trading system (ETS), and before the legislative entrenchment of the renewables cause in the founding treaties (namely in Article 194 TFEU) – the EU Commission has been somewhat less zealous about enforcing competition rules. Arguably, this has been with a sense of realism and proportion on the part of the Commission in acknowledging that, where there is tension between the competition and environmental protection objectives, it might be better to suffer some instances of anti-competitive behavior in the hope that this might, on balance, advance the cause of environmental protection, more than it might harm the internal market. In fact, the Commission – in its role as 'gatekeeper' of EU competition rules and of their enforcement – becomes the mechanism that balances any conflict between EU objectives.[132]

A. Review of State Aid Rules

The EU Commission intends to review the current rules around State aid and the 2008 Guidelines. It recently issued Staff Working Documents on matters relating to renewables as part of its wider efforts to review the rules around public intervention (State aid) in this field.[133]

In a recent Communication,[134] the Commission referred to the *rationale* for this review, stating its concern that public intervention may be responsible for the relatively high price of electricity in the EU. In

[132] There has been some failure on the part of the EU Commission to enforce competition rules justified primarily in relation to the objective of getting the EU ETS off the ground. See Edward, D. 'Judging Environmental Law', in Colneric, E. et al. (eds) *Une Communauté de Droit, Festschrift für Gil Carlos Rodríguez Iglesias* (Berlin: Berliner Wissenschafts-Verlag, 2003) pp. 487–495, where Edward states that: 'Where the economic advantage of free movement of goods is the primary goal, environmental protection may justify necessary and proportionate exceptions. Where environmental protection is the primary goal, exceptions may be justified on economic grounds. In this way, programmatic statements of economic, social, or environmental objectives can become legal instruments capable of administration and enforcement' (at p. 495).

[133] See Commission Staff Working Document, 'European Commission Guidance for the Design of Renewables Support Schemes' (SWD (2013) 439 final), and Commission Staff Working Document, 'Guidance on the Use of Renewable Energy Cooperation Mechanism' (SWD (2013) 440 final).

[134] Communication from the Commission, 'Delivering the Internal Electricity Market and Making the Most of Public Intervention', Brussels, 5.11.2013, C (2013) 7243 final.

relation to that, the EU – along with its peers in the Group of 20 (G20) – is keen to encourage the phasing out of subsidies for conventional energy sources.[135] A further reason that the Commission cites behind the need to review the current rules on State aid is its belief that the policy tools to promote renewables may be outdated given that the investment environment and market conditions for renewables may have improved since the existing policy tools were initially designed.[136] As we mentioned earlier,[137] the trend is to move away from feed-in tariffs towards feed-in premium schemes, and the Commission is keen to amend rules to encourage this shift, given that it deems this to be more market-responsive.[138]

Finally, as mentioned earlier, by 2014, the Commission intends to issue new Guidelines for environmental and energy aid for the period between 2014 and 2020, and, to that end, shall, in due course, be launching a public consultation.[139] In the meantime, in the Working Documents it published, the Commission sets out in some detail its thinking on the matters in scope and certain proposals of what it would like to see adopted in future guidance.[140]

B. Extension of Environmental Impact Assessment Requirements to Conventional Energy Exploration

The EU Parliament is set to vote on extending the requirement for environmental impact assessments (EIAs) to be carried out for shale gas and other harmful conventional fuel exploration and extraction operations which were hitherto excluded from the requirement for EIAs, if they were below a certain threshold.[141] Should there be a parliamentary

---

[135] Ibid. at p. 6.

[136] Ibid. at pp. 3–4.

[137] See Ragwitz, M. et al., 'Recent Developments of Feed-in Systems in the EU – A Research Paper for the International Feed-In Cooperation', January 2012 (at p. 3).

[138] Communication from the Commission, 'Delivering the Internal Electricity Market and Making the Most of Public Intervention', Bussels, C (2013) 7243 final (at p. 15).

[139] Ibid. at pp. 4–5.

[140] See Commission Staff Working Document, 'European Commission Guidance for the Design of Renewables Support Schemes' (SWD (2013) 439 final), and Commission Staff Working Document, 'Guidance on the Use of Renewable Energy Cooperation Mechanism' (SWD (2013) 440 final).

[141] See the 11 September 2013 news item on the EU Parliament website, which states that the vote has now been postponed until a parliamentary plenary

majority and sufficient political will on the part of the Council of the European Union, this amendment would be incorporated as an Annex into the existing Directive 2011/92/EU relating to EIAs.[142] While this is not directly related to renewable energy, we cite this here – in a similar vein to the earlier discussion of the EU ETS – to make the point that other EU policies have the effect of supporting the renewables cause by introducing more, rather than less, regulation in conventional energy source exploration. As is often the case with policymaking, various policies work dynamically with one another towards a final outcome. While few policies are ever absolutely *indispensable* to a policy objective *per se*, they all – to varying degrees – contribute towards the achievement of an objective.[143]

C. The EU ETS

The EU emissions trading system ('EU ETS') – as is the case with other ETS programs across the world – seeks to internalize in the market what in economic terms is often seen as an *externality*, i.e., the damage caused by environmental degradation. It operates on the logic of 'cap and trade' according to which overall EU GHG emissions are capped and those who emit must have permits – which they may trade with one another – in order to contain EU GHG emissions.[144] In that respect, the system operates within the logic that, given the market failure to avert environmental degradation, public intervention, which places financial burdens

---

session considers this matter. European Parliament, News, 'Shale Gas: Environmental Impact Studies Vote Postponed', available at http://www.europarl.europa.eu/news/en/news-room/content/20130906IPR18833/html/Shale-gas-environmental-impact-studies-vote-postponed.

142 Directive 2011/92/EU of the European Parliament and of the Council of 13 December 2011 on the Assessment of the Effects of Certain Public and Private Projects on the Environment (OJ L 26 28.1.2012), p. 1.

143 Incidentally, this is a notion we see reflected in the WTO jurisprudence surrounding questions of how 'necessary' or 'indispensable' a trade restrictive measure might be in the greater scheme of things in order to meet a policy objective. See WTO Appellate Body Report, *Brazil –Measures Affecting Imports of Retreaded Tyres* (WT/DS332/AB/R), 3 December 2007 (at §141), where the WTO Appellate Body refers to the WTO Appellate Body Report in *Korea – Measures Affecting Imports of Fresh, Chilled and Frozen Beef* (WT/DS161/AB/R,WT/DS169/AB/R), 11 December 2000 (at §161).

144 See the official EU factsheet on the EU ETS at http://ec.europa.eu/clima/publications/docs/factsheet_ets_en.pdf in relation to the legislative history (successive Directives that relate to the EU ETS), see http://ec.europa.eu/clima/policies/ets/documentation_en.htm#Legislative_history

on emitters, becomes inevitable. The auctioning-off of emission permits – somewhat reminiscent of the indulgences issued by 16th-century Church authorities and condemned by Martin Luther, sparking the Protestant movement in Europe – is an aspect of the EU's environmental protection policy. Those who emit GHGs within EU territory are required to purchase emission credits which add to the production costs and, therefore, as the argument goes, incentivize a shift towards less polluting methods and energy sources. In reality, however, GHG emitters actually seem to be purchasing 5% of the necessary credits, given that the EU allocates up to 95% of their emission credits.

The EU ETS has been included here in the same way that other issues not directly related to the renewables cause have been included due to their implications for this issue. If effective, the EU ETS is capable of incentivizing a shift towards less polluting energy sources, which would essentially involve renewables. The not-so-good news, however, is that the protracted economic crisis that started around 2008 has meant that the consequent reduction in production has, in turn, led to a reduction of GHG emissions and, therefore, a reduction in demand for emission credits. This has led to a piling of un-auctioned/unsold emission credits and to a phenomenal drop in their price, which means – coupled by the fact that up to 95% of emitters' emission credit needs were gifted to the emitters by the EU (or, to be more precise, by the national authorities that administer the EU ETS)[145] – that the disincentive to emit GHGs has been seriously weakened.[146]

1. The EU ETS and the WTO

Given that the EU ETS is an important aspect of EU environmental protection policy and that – due to its energy market implications – the EU ETS has consequences for the cause of renewables, it is appropriate to acknowledge some complex questions relating to the interplay between

---

[145] Directive 2003/87/EC of the European Parliament and of the Council of 13 October 2003 establishing a scheme for greenhouse gas emission allowance trading within the Community and amending Council Directive 96/61/EC. See Articles 9–10.

[146] In relation to German proposals to the EU to hold back on the auctioning of additional emission credits given the current glut, see International Center for Trade and Sustainable Development, 'Merkel Signals Support for ETS "Back-loading" Proposal'(2013) *Bridges Weekly Trade News Digest*, Vol. 17, No. 35, available at http://ictsd.org/i/news/bridgesweekly/177916/. See also International Energy Agency, *Redrawing the Energy-Climate Map, World Energy Outlook Special Report*, Paris, June 2013 report (at p. 16).

the EU ETS and the multilateral trade system, and to also refer to recent developments in relation to the application of the EU ETS.

Under EU law, the offering of emission credits by national authorities to domestic emitters is not generally considered State aid when it is simply the case of implementing EU law, which allows the allocation of emission credits. That said, there is some discretion for EU Member States (the national authorities of whom allocate emission credits) to set the extent of allocations. In that sense, the EU rules on State aid may be engaged. We shall not explore this further, given that it is outside the immediate scope of this chapter; however, we have referred to it for contextual purposes. With the proposed extension of the EU ETS also to foreign operators that operate flights *with segments* within EU territory,[147] GHG emitters seek to challenge the application of the EU ETS under other rules – mainly in relation to the WTO – and this brings into focus the question of the interplay of norms that exist in separate regimes.

In terms of the interplay with WTO rules, those who object to the application of the EU ETS may argue that there is a prohibited *extraterritorial* dimension to the measure. Such a complaint could be rebutted, given that the EU intends to apply the scheme only to the portion of a flight that relates to EU territory. What is more, were the details of the policy such as to involve an extraterritorial dimension to the EU ETS, on the face of it, this would not necessarily be incompatible with WTO norms.[148]

Moreover, the accusation that the allocation of emission credits to EU operators amounts to subsidization that is incompatible with WTO rules could also be rebuttable. Within the WTO context, 'State aid' is generally

---

[147] According to the EU Commission, the EU ETS shall be extended over the EU territory segment of foreign flight operations until such time that the International Civil Aviation Organization (ICAO) adopts its planned emissions-related scheme – namely, the ICAO 'Market-Based Mechanism'. See http://ec.europa.eu/clima/policies/transport/aviation/index_en.htm

[148] Pollution and environmental degradation are phenomena that are indifferent to national borders. For instance, the health of migratory species – such as schools of tuna – is a matter for which a national government may lay down such regulations which may inadvertently have trade-restrictive effects, given that these matters may also have implications for the territory under the control of a government. See the WTO Appellate Body's comments in *United States – Import Prohibition of Certain Shrimp and Shrimp Products* (WT/DS58/AB/R), 12 October 1998 (at §168, p. 67).

examined in relation to WTO rules on subsidies.[149] However, in this case, it is important to highlight the facts of the policy: the EU intends to allocate 'free' emission credits to non-EU operators – as it does to EU operators – and require non-EU operators – again, as it does of EU operators – to purchase the remainder through the EU ETS. In that sense, non-EU operators do not appear to be either disadvantaged or treated discriminatorily when compared to EU operators, given that the policy burdens both sets of operators equally. Again, these are not matters directly related to renewable energy; however, foreseeably, any weakening of the EU ETS could potentially have negative implications for the renewables cause.

2. Towards a global carbon market?

There are difficulties when it comes to developing a single global carbon market with comprehensive coverage of economic sectors and countries. A promising intermediary step between the creation of a global carbon market with comprehensive coverage of economic sectors and countries and the current situation, therefore, could be a sectoral approach to emissions trading. Unilateral, bilateral, plurilateral, or regional arrangements could target GHG emissions reductions in specific sectors such as electricity generation, motor vehicles, aviation, shipping, cement, and aluminium, always aiming for greener or more efficient technology, as opposed to simply applying bans or restrictions. Such measures will require across-the-board cooperation.

3. Inclusion of aviation

The EU's efforts to expand its ETS to aviation could ultimately encourage exploration of greener fuel for aviation. However, thus far, the EU has faced a maelstrom of criticism for attempting to expand the ETS to aviation.[150] Regardless of the fundamental legal question at the heart of the matter, that is, whether it is 'legal or legitimate to take unilateral measures against global carbon emissions as a response to the collective

---

[149] For instance, norms existing in various agreements that may be applicable to a given nexus of WTO members, starting from the universal application agreements (the General Agreement on Tariffs and Trade, the General Agreement on Trade in Services, the SCM Agreement, and the TRIMs Agreement) and moving to those to which some – but not all – WTO members are parties, e.g., the Agreement on Government Procurement, so long as these are applicable.

[150] See Leal-Arcas, R. *Climate Change and International Trade* (Cheltenham: Edward Elgar, 2013) p. 162.

action problems that are frustrating multilateral efforts at climate mitigation',[151] the disgruntled reaction of the international community reflected the disjointed approach to climate response measures globally – an approach that will have to become more cohesive if mitigation efforts are to be realized.

The EU's current compromise means that from 1 January 2014, flights to and from countries outside the European Economic Area (EEA) will be exempt for the emissions that take place outside EEA airspace. Only the emissions from the proportion of a flight taking place within EEA airspace will be covered. This process, dubbed 'Stop the Clock', is by no means a long-term solution, given that 'aviation is the fastest growing source of greenhouse gas emissions in the transport sector and the most climate-intensive form of transport. Aviation emissions have more than doubled in the last twenty years and the sector accounts for 5% of global warming'.[152] Thus, while the attempt to include aviation in the EU ETS may not have succeeded, it did serve as a 'wake-up call' of sorts, bringing to the forefront the need for a 'principled approach', that is, a solution in which 'fundamental principles of sustainable development are observed'.[153] Possible response measures include switching to more fuel-efficient engines and aircraft designs; using 'greener' fuels; as well as more efficient use of airspace and airports.[154]

Regardless of the aviation stalemate, the EU ETS has succeeded in promoting low-carbon strategies in many major emitting industries. A growing number of countries are integrating cap-and-trade schemes into their national climate policies, such as the United States, New Zealand,

---

[151] Howse, R. in Bartels, L. 'The Inclusion of Aviation in the EU ETS', ICTSD Programme on Trade and Environment, Issue Paper No. 6 (2012), pp. 28ff. Available at http://ictsd.org/downloads/2012/05/the-inclusion-of-aviation-in-the-eu-ets-wto-law-considerations.pdf

[152] 'Grey Day for Environment as Europe Reduces its Aviation Emissions Coverage', 16 October 2013. Available at http://www.airportwatch.org.uk/?p=17951

[153] Gehring, M. & Robb, A. 'Addressing the Aviation and Climate Change Challenge', ICTSD Programme on Trade and Environment, Issue Paper No. 7 (2013).

[154] Howse, R. in Bartels, L. 'The Inclusion of Aviation in the EU ETS.' ICTSD Programme on Trade and Environment, Issue Paper No. 6 (2012), pp. 28ff. Available at http://ictsd.org/downloads/2012/05/the-inclusion-of-aviation-in-the-eu-ets-wto-law-considerations.pdf

Australia,[155] Canada and Japan. It may eventually be possible to geographically expand the EU ETS to a global level by multilateralizing current and future regional ETS in the world (e.g., in Australia,[156] Kazakhstan,[157] and Korea[158]). However, before moving forward with such schemes, one should bear in mind the potential challenges and opportunities when linking the EU ETS to other emissions trading schemes. For instance, current low carbon prices in the EU market have led to reduced investment in low-carbon technologies, and it is worth waiting to see whether the various options under consideration for reviving the market, such as reducing the number of permits traded and other longer-term structural reforms, prove successful.

In a positive step towards global cooperation on aviation emissions, the International Civil Aviation Organization (ICAO) agreed in October 2013 to develop a global market-based measure for international aviation.[159] The idea is to create a multilateral mechanism to govern GHG emissions from international aviation, to be implemented by ICAO members by 2020.[160] With the participation of ICAO's 184 Member States, perhaps the EU's vision of addressing the climate challenges posed by international aviation will actually come to fruition. In the meantime, there is much the EU can do to strengthen its position, such as supporting other countries aiming to curb aviation emissions, and working to reinstate the original terms of the EU ETS as soon as feasibly possible.[161]

4. Shipping

The attempt to expand the EU ETS to aviation also points to the logic of acknowledging another key area where exploring greener fuel seems

---

[155] Jotzo, F. & Betz, R. 'Linking the Australian Emissions Trading Scheme', Climate Strategies (2009).

[156] See similar views by the EU Commission, 'International Carbon Market', available at http://ec.europa.eu/clima/policies/ets/linking/index_en.htm

[157] Kazakhcarbon, 'The GHG Emissions Trading System', available at http://www.kzc.kz/en/legislation/ghg-emissions-trading-scheme

[158] Bloomberg New Energy Finance, 'South Korea's Emissions Trading Scheme', 10 May 2013, obtained from http://about.bnef.com/white-papers/south-koreas-emissions-trading-scheme/

[159] Available at http://www.icao.int/Newsroom/Pages/mbm-agreement-solid-global-plan-endoresements.aspx

[160] Available at http://climate-l.iisd.org/news/icao-assembly-to-develop-a-global-market-based-measure-for-international-aviation/

[161] Elsworth, R. & MacDonald, P. 'Aviation and the EU ETS – What Happened in 2012 During "Stop the Clock"?' Sandbag Climate Campaign, UK (2013), p. 8.

important: shipping. According to the International Maritime Organization (IMO), more than 90% of global trade flows engage international shipping.[162] This suggests that current levels of global trade flows and, *ex fortiori*, of global consumption would not be possible without the shipping industry, not least because of the competitive pricing of freight transport through this means. While, according to the International Chamber of Shipping, 'shipping is the least environmentally damaging form of commercial transport and, compared with land-based industry, is a comparatively minor contributor to marine pollution from human activities',[163] it remains an industry that cannot be overlooked when it comes to climate response measures: shipping causes around 3% of total CO_2 emissions.[164] So far, in relation to reducing the CO_2 emissions of the shipping industry, the IMO, and more specifically its Marine Environment Protection Committee, has put together a bundle of measures which, amongst other things, include an index system, analogous to that used to rate vehicles and electrical appliances, to classify new vessels according to their energy efficiency; a template for a Ship Energy Efficiency Management Plan for vessels, new and old alike, to monitor and improve performance in relation to CO_2 emissions; and ideas in relation to possible economic tools to encourage GHG emissions reduction.[165]

In a June 2013 proposal, the European Commission called for more robust monitoring, reporting, and verification (MRV) of GHG emissions from maritime transport, stating that introducing MRV could reduce emissions by 2%, compared to business-as-usual.[166] The draft legislation was approved by the European Parliament's industry, research and energy (ITRE) committee, despite objections that the proposed changes were too weak.[167] Still, the fact that the EU is already looking towards shipping,

---

[162] Available at http://www.imo.org/About/Pages/Default.aspx

[163] Available at http://www.ics-shipping.org/shipping-facts/environmental-performance

[164] Available at http://www.shippingandco2.org/CO2%20Flyer.pdf (last accessed 2013).

[165] Leal-Arcas, R. *Climate Change and International Trade* (Cheltenham: Edward Elgar, 2013), p. 173.

[166] See Proposal for a Regulation of the European Parliament and of the Council on the Monitoring, Reporting and Verification of Carbon Dioxide Emissions from Maritime Transport and Amending Regulation (EU) No 525/2013, Brussels, 28 June 2013. Available at http://ec.europa.eu/clima/policies/transport/shipping/docs/com_2013_480_en.pdf

[167] See http://www.euractiv.com/transport/flawed-commission-proposal-ship-news-532680

despite the backlash it received for expanding its ETS to aviation, shows a certain commitment to environmental protection. In any event, now that shipping is entering the spotlight, there is no reason why the international community should sit back and let the EU go it alone once again, only to result in the same outcry of legal objections as in the case of aviation. The importance of a global approach to including shipping in emissions trading schemes is clear, and the involvement of other UNFCCC Parties is required for a more efficient and effective response to climate change mitigation. Moreover, a pre-emptive approach, acting together, may help safeguard against measures that are too trade-restrictive.

V. CONCLUSION

As the above confirms, EU renewable energy policy is both complex and meaningful. *Complex* for it encompasses a broad set of initiatives, and *meaningful* for it goes beyond the EU's international obligations – most evident in relation to the UNFCCC and its Kyoto Protocol – and certainly much further than other global actors, such as the US, to advance the renewables cause as a means of de-carbonizing the economy and, ultimately, protecting the environment.

At the level of EU law, renewable energy policy implementation may sometimes involve tension with the EU's competition objectives. Therefore, given the centrality of the EU's competition objectives to the EU project (internal market), renewable energy policy – and, more generally, the EU's environmental objectives – can sometimes be seen to undermine the internal market.

Furthermore, detailed rules exist (2008 Guidelines on State aid for environmental protection) to guide EU Member States when they intervene in the market on the basis of advancing their, or the EU's, environmental objectives, including the EU's renewables-related objectives. What is more, at the broader normative level, EU renewable energy policy has not been without controversy. As we have seen, complaints within the context of WTO often hinge upon questions of compliance with WTO norms. The EU has found itself both in the position of complainant and respondent with regard to proceedings raised within the WTO's dispute settlement mechanism in cases involving measures linked to the renewables cause. One such case which has thrown up very interesting points of law in relation to the WTO system is the Argentinian complaint regarding the EU biodiesel classification (*EU–Biodiesel*,

WT/DS459). This case is particularly interesting as it also raises the complex issue of discriminatory treatment of goods on the basis of PPMs.

What has also emerged from this review is that the various modalities of cooperation that the 2009 Renewable Energy Directive seeks to encourage[168] – namely in relation to joint projects between EU Member States, and between EU Member States and third-party States – have been lamentably underutilized.[169] In our view, it is not a normative failure *per se*. Economics may have much to do with the reasons that joint projects have not taken off, as may also the lack of serious political will on the part of Member States' governments to incentivize these. Efforts towards harnessing, among other things, solar and wind energy from the MENA region, and from other regions surrounding the EU, would certainly enhance the EU's energy security interests and its preference for these to be met through sustainable sources such as renewable options. What is more, as the Commission acknowledges in its relevant 2011 Staff Working Documents: 'as regards the Southern Mediterranean, co-operation might additionally be motivated by the wider objective of supporting the creation of stable economic and political relations through cooperation in the field of renewable energy'.[170]

Energy cooperation with the MENA region along the lines envisaged in the 2009 Renewable Energy Directive (see for instance the Directive's provisions on the possibility of *joint projects* with third-party states) – so long as this benefits the broader communities in those States – could be a means of raising the standards of living in that region. Before the outbreak of the 2011 Arab Spring, many European states, due to their energy industry interests in the MENA region, had strategic relations with the economic and political elites in that region, which perpetuated grave human rights violations. Closer EU cooperation could potentially influence those polities in that region – which themselves are in a state of flux – to adopt more human-rights-based approaches to population governance. Joint energy projects could thus result in a win-win situation not only in relation to the North–South nexus, but also in relation to

---

[168] See Articles 7, 9 and 11 of the 2009 Directive.

[169] See Communication from the Commission, 'Delivering the Internal Electricity Market and Making the Most of Public Intervention', Brussels, 5.11.2013, C (2013) 7243 final (at p. 16).

[170] Commission Staff Working Document, 'Guidance on the Use of Renewable Energy Cooperation Mechanism' (SWD (2013) 440 final) (at p. 24).

multiple policy objectives – namely EU energy security, EU external action policy relating to human rights, and EU environmental protection policy.

PART IV

Looking forward: bridging the policy objectives of energy, trade, and environment

9. Sustainable development and mega-regionals: the TTIP and TPP

I. INTRODUCTION: USING PREFERENTIAL TRADE AGREEMENTS TO PROMOTE SUSTAINABLE DEVELOPMENT

This chapter provides an analysis from the broader perspective of sustainable development of two mega-regional trade agreements currently under negotiation: the Transatlantic Trade and Investment Partnership (TTIP) and the Trans-Pacific Partnership (TPP). It is argued that these preferential trade agreements present a more efficient vehicle through which to promote sustainable development than the multilateral trading platform. The chapter presents the future of international energy governance in the broader context of sustainability by linking multiple policy objectives: energy, trade, and environment. It further argues that the TTIP has the potential to foster sustainable development, energy efficiency, and energy security.

Trade has already proven to be a powerful tool towards achieving environmental goals. For example, the Montreal Protocol on Substances that Deplete the Ozone Layer[1] restricted Parties from trading in ozone-depleting substances with non-Parties. This served the dual purpose of encouraging wide participation (the Montreal Protocol now has 197 Parties),[2] and removing any competitive advantage that a non-Party might enjoy (that is, preventing leakage[3] to non-participating jurisdictions).[4]

1 26 ILM 1550 (1987).

2 http://ozone.unep.org/new_site/en/montreal_protocol.php

3 According to Patrick Low et al., 'carbon leakage may arise where countries implement asymmetric climate policies. When an industry in one country assumes additional costs in order to reduce greenhouse gas (GHG) emissions and those same industries in other countries incur lesser (or zero) costs, this may affect geographical patterns of investment, production and trade'. See Low, P., Marceau, G. & Renaud, J. 'The Interface Between the Trade and Climate Change Regimes: Scoping the Issues', Staff Working Paper ERSD-2011-1, available at http://www.wto.org/english/res_e/reser_e/ersd201101_e.pdf

Moreover, the success of the Montreal Protocol lies in the fact that trade was not actually restricted.[5] Climate change, however, is a far more complex issue, both connected to and giving rise to a host of other issues and areas, including greenhouse gas (GHG) emissions, clean energy technology, knowledge transfer, investment in low-carbon economies, development assistance, carbon capture and storage, and adaptation. While this makes it all the more challenging to harness trade policy towards climate change mitigation, it also presents a range of potential areas of cooperation, across different regimes and disciplines.

'Green industrial policy', as Aaron Cosbey dubs it,[6] is the crossroads for trade and climate, where we have the opportunity to purposefully shape policies in various sectors in order to promote environmental protection. According to Cosbey:

> green industrial policy … is any [such] policy that supports the development of industries that produce 'green' goods, or goods that: have better environmental performance in operation than their competitors (e.g., electric vehicles, renewable electricity-generating equipment, biofuels); directly address environmental problems (e.g. environmental remediation technologies); are produced in a way that is environmentally preferable to their competitors (e.g. organic agriculture).[7]

Thus trade, the traditional foe of environmental protection, has manifold ways by which to redeem itself. This chapter proposes several ways in which trade can promote climate change mitigation.

This chapter proposes the introduction of a regional model for promoting climate change mitigation, technology transfer and sustainable energy for all as an alternative to the present structure of the UN Framework Convention on Climate Change (UNFCCC)/Kyoto Protocol framework. Given the proliferation of preferential trade agreements (PTAs)[8] –

---

[4] Leal-Arcas, R. *Climate Change and International Trade* (Cheltenham: Edward Elgar Publishing, 2013) p. 93.

[5] Barrett, S. 'Climate Change and International Trade: Lessons on their Linkage from International Environmental Agreements', Centre for Trade and Economic Integration, The Graduate Institute, Geneva, Switzerland (2010) p. 14.

[6] See Cosbey, A. 'Green Industrial Policy and the World Trading System', ENTWINED Issue Brief 17, 2013, available at http://www.iisd.org/pdf/2013/entwined_brief_green_industrial.pdf

[7] Ibid. p. 3.

[8] Regarding the international trade terminology referring to preferential trade agreements as regional trade agreements (RTAs), it is interesting to note that Jagdish Bhagwati prefers to use the term PTA instead of RTA 'because the PTAs are not always regional in any meaningful sense. For example, the

especially in the form of bilateral treaties – in the international trading system, this section proposes creating PTAs with climate change chapters, thus embedding climate goals within bilateral/trilateral/plurilateral trade agreements. Involving major GHG emitters through PTAs and economic partnership agreements that include contingent climate mitigation efforts can be an effective avenue towards reducing GHG emissions, and could therefore move both the trade and climate agendas forward harmoniously.

Climate-related chapters could promote, among other things, trade and investment in environmental goods and services and climate-friendly products and technologies. Indeed, given how proactive developing countries are in the conclusion of PTAs, the option of climate-related PTAs would be an effective way towards a future global climate change agreement, especially since the Kyoto Protocol imposes no concrete obligation on developing countries. In this sense, climate-related PTAs can be used as a legal mechanism to further the multilateral climate change agenda, while also including major developing countries to be part of the climate change mitigation exercise. An additional option for such 'environmentally-conscious' PTAs is to include provisions related to climate change adaptation efforts. These could take the form of knowledge-transfer, capacity-building, infrastructural and agricultural support, etc. The advantage of such an approach lies not only in providing trade incentives towards GHG emissions reduction, investment in renewable energy, or other climate change mitigation goals, but also in circumventing the currently arduous multilateral trading process to utilize the ever-expanding network of PTAs around the world.

PTAs promoting climate mitigation goals can have strong benefits for economic growth in developing countries, thereby delivering both environmental and trade wins. In fact, in a 2007 speech, then WTO Director-General Pascal Lamy stated the benefits of trading with developing countries that are exporters of climate-friendly products, citing the examples of Indonesia, one of the world's top ten exporters of steam condensers; India, a top exporter of hydraulic turbines; and Malaysia, which is amongst the world's top five exporters of photovoltaic cells.[9] All these cases represent clear examples where the trade and climate agendas can work together.

US-Israel FTA is not regional'. I share his views. Bhagwati, J. *Termites in the Trading System: How Preferential Agreements Undermine Free Trade* (New York: Oxford University Press, 2008) p. xi.

[9] WTO (2007), 'Lamy: Doha could Deliver Double-win for Environment and Trade', available at http://www.wto.org/english/news_e/sppl_e/sppl83_e.htm

In apparent recognition of the potential power of PTAs to move the climate agenda forward, trade agreements are going increasingly green. This is certainly a positive step and is an affirmation that the two agendas do not have to be at loggerheads; far from it. In this respect, the US, EU, China,[10] Japan, Australia, Canada, New Zealand, South Korea, Norway, Switzerland, Costa Rica, Chinese Taipei, Hong Kong, and Singapore proposed an initiative at the World Economic Forum in Davos, Switzerland, in 2014 over lowering tariffs and other trade barriers on the USD 1.4 trillion global annual market in green goods and services.[11] The move builds 'on a 2012 commitment by the 21 countries in Apec, the Pacific Rim forum, to cut all tariffs to a maximum of 5 per cent by 2015 for 54 different classes of goods. Those range from solar panels and wind turbines to filters and other parts used in power and sewerage plants and catalytic converters for cars'.[12]

It is hoped that the proposed changes will resurrect a deal on green goods, which has thus far been at an impasse during the WTO's Doha Round of multilateral trade negotiations, which started in 2001.[13] According to the International Centre for Trade and Sustainable Development:

> these new environmental goods talks, if launched in Davos, would aim to develop a most-favoured-nation (MFN) type of pact, similar to the WTO's Information Technology Agreement. In these types of arrangements, participants take on binding commitments whose benefits are extended to the rest of the WTO membership after reaching a 'critical mass.'[14]

Given that the major GHG emitters are large economies, large PTAs such as the TTIP, the TPP, or the Regional Comprehensive Economic Partnership[15] have the potential to be extremely effective when it comes to addressing climate change mitigation. In this context, the chapter takes a closer look at two mega PTAs currently under negotiation – the TTIP and

---

[10] Donnan, S. 'China Joins Davos Drive to Cut Green Trade Barriers', *Financial Times*, 24 January 2014.

[11] See Donnan, S. 'Drive at Davos Forum to Cut Green Trade Barriers', *Financial Times*, 23 January 2014.

[12] Ibid.

[13] Ibid.

[14] See ICTSD, 'Post-Bali Trade Agenda in Focus as Davos Meetings Begin' (23rd January 2014) *Bridges Weekly Trade News Digest*, Vol. 18, No. 2. Available at http://ictsd.org/i/news/bridgesweekly/182601/

[15] On the economic role China plays in the Asia-Pacific region, see Leal-Arcas, R. 'China and the Regional Comprehensive Economic Partnership', *Journal of Global Policy and Governance*, Vol. 2, No. 2, pp. 287–304.

the TPP – and their potential for addressing climate change mitigation and sustainable development at large. Twenty-first-century trade agreements,[16] such as the TPP proclaims itself to be,[17] have an enormous potential to achieve environmental goals. Such mega trade agreements present important opportunities to include provisions that promote climate change mitigation and address other environmental challenges by, for example, reducing barriers to environmental goods and services, or by promoting green technology.[18] In today's highly interconnected world, capitalizing on trade measures to promote climate change mitigation and sustainability should not be treated as a possibility worth considering at some point down the line, but as an absolute requirement *ab initio*.

In Section I of this chapter, we propose using preferential trade agreements to promote sustainable development. In Section II we examine the TTIP in the context of sustainable development. After some introductory remarks, Section II deals with the main sustainability goals, discussing ways in which the TTIP could integrate terms ensuring protection and support of these elements. In this section, we also look specifically at the role of the TTIP in addressing issues such as raw materials, energy efficiency, and renewable energy generation. In Section III we discuss how particular provisions of the TPP's Environment Chapter have affected the parties to the TPP. The section introduces the TPP as a 21st-century trade agreement, deals with the TPP's Environment Chapter and its enforcement. The section also deals with the Articles on sustainable development of the TPP's leaked Environment

---

16 The United States Trade Representative (USTR) explains a 21st-century trade agreement as one which 'addresses new and emerging issues, incorporates new elements reflecting our values and priorities, and responds to the 21st century challenges our citizens face'. Among these challenges, a sustainable and healthy environment is a principal concern of the present century. See USTR, 'Trans-Pacific Partnership: Frequently Asked Questions', p. 1, available at http://www.ustr.gov/sites/default/files/TPPFAQ.pdf

17 On 12 November 2011 leaders of the then nine Trans-Pacific Partnership (TPP) countries announced that they had established 'a comprehensive, next-generation regional agreement that liberalizes trade and investment and addresses new and traditional trade issues and 21st-century challenges'. See http://www.ustr.gov/about-us/press-office/press-releases/2011/november/trans-pacific-partnership-leaders-statement

18 See Meltzer, J. 'The Trans-Pacific Partnership Agreement, the Environment and Climate Change', in Voon, T. (ed.) *Trade Liberalisation and International Co-operation: A Legal Analysis of the Trans-Pacific Partnership Agreement* (Cheltenham: Edward Elgar, 2014) Chapter 10.

Chapter. Section IV compares the TPP with the TTIP. The last section concludes the chapter.

II. THE TRANSATLANTIC TRADE AND INVESTMENT PARTNERSHIP

A. An Introduction

The TTIP is a proposed free trade agreement between the United States and the EU and its Member States. The United States and the EU have discussed the idea of a transatlantic free trade area for decades.[19] The TTIP is the world's largest economic relationship, accounting for nearly a third of global trade.[20] It has dominated the world economy since the beginning of the 20th century. In fact, major global economic institutions are based upon American and European values and interests. In this context, the TTIP can be a forceful engine towards addressing climate change through trade policy. Thus far, negotiations have addressed the environment and sustainable development in a more general manner. However, there does not seem to be any substantive effort towards climate change mitigation.

The TTIP was first conceived in November 2011, following a US–EU Summit and the sixth meeting of the Transatlantic Economic Council.[21] Leaders requested that the US–EU High Level Working Group on Jobs and Growth identify 'policies and measures to increase US–EU trade and investment to support mutually beneficial job creation, economic growth, and international competitiveness'.[22] The High Level Working Group

---

[19] Barker, T. & Workman, G. *The Transatlantic Trade and Investment Partnership: Ambitious but Achievable* (Atlantic Council and the Bertelsmann Foundation, 2013) [hereinafter 'Barker and Workman'], p. 1, available at www.bfna.org/sites/default/files/TTIPReport_web.pdf

[20] See http://ec.europa.eu/trade/policy/countries-and-regions/countries/united-states/

[21] 'Fact Sheet: United States to Negotiate Transatlantic Trade and Investment Partnership with the European Union' (Office of the United States Trade Representative, 13 February 2013), available at www.ustr.gov/about-us/press-office/fact-sheets/2013/february/US-EU-TTIP

[22] 'Final Report: High Level Working Group on Jobs and Growth' 1, (United States-European Union High Level Working Group on Jobs and Growth, 11 February 2013) [hereinafter 'High Level Working Group on Jobs and Growth'], p. 1 (internal citations omitted), available at www.ustr.gov/sites/default/files/02132013%20FINAL%20HLWG%20REPORT.pdf

concluded that the development of a comprehensive bilateral trade and investment agreement would provide the most benefits for the parties.[23]

1. Timeline

The time is right for the aperture of trade between these two global powerhouses. Both economies have stagnated somewhat in the wake of the global recession and the financial and the Eurozone crises.[24] Increased transatlantic exchange of investment, goods, and services would strengthen the economies, create jobs, and help to solidify the old guard as emerging markets continue to carve out increasing shares of global commerce.[25] The TTIP would be a way for both sides of the Atlantic to boost their economies without occurring additional national debt.[26]

Development of the TTIP is underway. As of March 2014, four rounds of negotiations had taken place: the first round occurred in July 2013, and the fourth round completed in March 2014. The issues and areas under consideration in the TTIP are complex and have wide-ranging implications for both parties; as expected, talks have so far progressed cautiously.

In June 2012, both sides of the Atlantic showed an interest to start negotiations for a free trade agreement (FTA) because both parties have much to gain economically if non-tariff measures are removed.[27] EU trade commissioner Karel De Gucht made a statement in June 2012 on the interim report[28] on the trans-Atlantic trade relationship in the following manner:

> The announcement of Presidents Barroso and Obama welcoming the publication of the interim report on how to deepen the transatlantic trade relationship is extremely encouraging. We are now entering the last leg of mapping out how we should tackle any eventual negotiation to boost growth and jobs through our trade partnership. I look forward to continue working with my US counterpart to complete the final stage allowing us to present both leaders with the final report as quickly as possible.[29]

---

23 Ibid.
24 Barker and Workman, p. 1.
25 Ibid.
26 Ibid.
27 Berden, K.G. et al. *Non-Tariff Measures in EU-US Trade and Investment – An Economic Analysis* (Rotterdam: Ecorys, 2009), p. xiv.
28 See http://trade.ec.europa.eu/doclib/docs/2012/june/tradoc_149557.pdf
29 See http://trade.ec.europa.eu/doclib/press/index.cfm?id=807

The official launch of the negotiations was announced by US President Barack Obama, President of the EU Commission José Manuel Barroso, President of the European Council Herman Van Rompuy, and UK Prime Minister David Cameron at the G8 Summit in June 2013. Negotiations started in July 2013. After the first round of negotiations, the EU chief negotiator said: 'The main objective has been met: we had a substantive round of talks on the full range of topics that we intend to cover in this agreement. This paves the way to for a good second round of negotiations in Brussels in October'.[30] The topics covered were market access for agricultural and industrial goods, government procurement, investment, energy and raw materials, regulatory issues, sanitary and phytosanitary measures, services, intellectual property rights, sustainable development, small- and medium-sized enterprises, dispute settlement, competition, customs/trade facilitation, and state-owned enterprises. The aim of both parties is to set the standard for the rest of the world in the development of global rules for the various issues on the negotiating table, including climate change mitigation.

The second round of TTIP negotiations concluded in November 2013, after a week of discussions. Again, De Gucht's statement included no specific mention of the TTIP's plan for addressing climate change and other environmental issues:

> We are making good and steady progress across the broad range of issues we need to tackle to make our transatlantic business environment more efficient and effective whilst preserving the protections and rights already in place for consumers. Let's keep our eye on the prize: more jobs for people in Europe, more growth for the European economy.[31]

In terms of environmental issues, the Directorate-General for Trade of the European Commission merely stated that video conferences on sustainable development were being planned for the coming weeks.[32] However, the EU has produced several initial TTIP Position Papers, one of them focusing on trade and sustainable development. The paper envisages an integrated TTIP chapter, 'specifically devoted to aspects of sustainable development of importance in a trade context – more specifically, on

---

[30] European Commission, 'EU and US Conclude First Round of TTIP Negotiations in Washington', 12 July 2013, available at http://trade.ec.europa.eu/doclib/press/index.cfm?id=941

[31] European Commission, 'EU and US Conclude Second Round of TTIP Negotiations in Brussels', 15 November 2013, available at http://trade.ec.europa.eu/doclib/press/index.cfm?id=988

[32] Ibid.

labour and the environment, including climate change aspects, as well as their inter-linkages'.[33]

A third round of week-long negotiations took place in December 2013, in which, according to the European Commission, 'negotiators made progress on the three core parts of the TTIP – market access, regulatory aspects and rules'.[34] On the environmental front, negotiations related to trade rules included discussions on access to energy and raw materials as well as environmental protection.[35] EU Chief Negotiator Ignacio Garcia Bercero stressed that talks are proceeding smoothly, saying, '… we remain on track to deliver an ambitious trade and investment deal which will boost our economies, deliver growth and, more importantly, create jobs for both Europeans and Americans at a time when they're most needed'.[36] Still, EU negotiators have expressed concerns about establishing a balance between European investment interests and upholding governments' right to regulate in the public interest, including on issues related to the environment, and have called for public consultations on the issue. In fact, a group of 14 advisors from various consumer, labor and business groups was created to help the EU Commission frame the discussions for the negotiations on such topics.[37] According to the European Commission, 'no other part of the negotiations is affected by this public consultation and the TTIP negotiations will continue as planned'.[38]

From the perspective of climate change, in addition to the typical provisions on trade, investment, government procurement and intellectual property rights – among others – inserting a chapter on climate change

---

33 See European Commission, 'EU-US Transatlantic Trade and Investment Partnership – Trade and Sustainable Development', Initial EU position paper (2013), p. 1, available at http://trade.ec.europa.eu/doclib/docs/2013/july/tradoc_151626.pdf

34 See European Commission, 'EU Chief Negotiator says EU-US Trade Deal Not About Deregulation, as Third Round of Talks End in Washington', Brussels, 20 December 2013, available at http://trade.ec.europa.eu/doclib/press/index.cfm?id=1007

35 Ibid.

36 Ibid.

37 European Commission, 'Expert Group to Advise European Commission on EU-US Trade Talks', Press Release, 27 January 2014, available at http://europa.eu/rapid/press-release_IP-14-79_en.htm

38 See European Commission, 'Commission to Consult European Public on Provisions in EU-US Trade Deal on Investment and Investor-State Dispute Settlement', Brussels, 21 January 2014, available at http://trade.ec.europa.eu/doclib/press/index.cfm?id=1015

mitigation in such an FTA would be a meaningful and effective way to reduce GHG emissions, since the US and the EU are the second and third largest emitters of GHG, respectively. Such a chapter could promote 'trade and investment in environmental goods and services and climate-friendly products and technologies'.[39] However, both the US and the EU may have differing views on the importance of climate change mitigation provisions in the FTA.

According to Sidley's International Trade Group, 'the bilateral free trade agreements with the Republic of Korea that the European Union (entry into force 1 July 2011) and the United States (entry into force 15 March 2012) concluded are likely to serve as the competing models for the initial proposed texts'.[40] When it comes to the environment, the EU–Korea FTA agreement specifically aims to promote sustainable development in Article 13.1, whereas the US–Korea FTA recognizes 'the right of each Party to establish its own levels of environmental protection and its own environmental development priorities, and to adopt or modify accordingly its environmental laws and policies', while striving for 'high levels of environmental protection'.

The TTIP presents an important opportunity to go beyond the usual platitudes and include concrete and meaningful text specifically focusing on climate change mitigation. In this regard, the EU's initial TTIP position paper on trade and sustainable development[41] is on the right track. It remains to be seen how meaningfully the final agreement deals with climate change.

2. Goals

The goal of the TTIP is to further economic growth, investment and trade between the United States and the EU. There are two main routes to achieving an expansion of trade: cutting or eliminating tariffs, and

---

[39] European Commission (2013), 'EU-US Transatlantic Trade and Investment Partnership – Trade and Sustainable Development', p. 3, Initial EU position paper, available at http://trade.ec.europa.eu/doclib/docs/2013/july/tradoc_151626.pdf

[40] See http://www.sidley.com/international-trade-transatlantic-trade-and-investment-partnership

[41] See European Commission (2013), 'EU-US Transatlantic Trade and Investment Partnership – Trade and Sustainable Development'. Initial EU position paper, available at http://trade.ec.europa.eu/doclib/docs/2013/july/tradoc_151626.pdf.

removing so-called 'behind-the-border' technical barriers to export.[42] Additionally, the TTIP aims to open markets for services, investment, and public procurement.[43] 'Behind-the-border' barriers that impede US–EU trade are mostly national regulations, standards, and approval procedures.[44] Although the two regions have similarly high-quality standards, they are not yet understood to be aligned or to be parallel; thus, national authorization and qualification of trade products can be expensive and time-consuming, hampering trade.[45] The harmonization in the TTIP of these elements would foster increased trade, and the EU has estimated that up to 80% of the benefits will come from the 'elimination of bureaucratic duplication, greater regulatory alignment, and increased access to services and procurement markets'.[46]

Primary elements in the agreement to achieve these goals include: the elimination of tariffs and other technical barriers to trade; improvement of market access for goods and services; the reduction of costs by aligning regulations and standards; the strengthening of cross-border financial investment; and the development of approaches to modern issues such as intellectual property and state-owned enterprises.[47] Ancillary aims for the promotion of transparency and cooperation will help support the strength and effectiveness of the TTIP. In addition, strong implementation, monitoring, and enforcement structures will be needed to ensure effective implementation of its policies.

3. Importance

The US–EU trade and investment relationship is already a sizeable and critical element in the global commercial scene. The total trade in goods between the two regions in 2011 was worth €455 billion.[48] The United States was the EU's third-largest supplier, selling €192 billion in goods (about 11% of total imports), and was the EU's main export market,

---

[42] 'About TTIP' (European Commission), http://ec.europa.eu/trade/policy/in-focus/ttip/about-ttip/

[43] Ibid.

[44] Ibid.

[45] Ibid.

[46] Ibid; Barker and Workman, p. 1.

[47] 'White House Fact Sheet: Transatlantic Trade and Investment Partnership (T-TIP)' (Office of the United States Trade Representative), available at www.ustr.gov/about-us/press-office/fact-sheets/2013/june/wh-ttip

[48] 'Independent Study Outlines Benefits of EU-US Trade Agreement' (European Commission), available at http://europa.eu/rapid/press-release_MEMO-13-211_en.htm

purchasing €264 billion in goods (about 17% of total exports).[49] In 2011, trade in commercial services between the two regions was worth €282.3 billion. The United States was the EU's top trade partner in this category, sending €138.4 billion (about 29% of total EU imports) and receiving €143.9 billion (about 24% of total EU exports) in commercial services.[50] Lastly, investment activity between the United States and the EU is substantial: 'In 2011, US companies invested around €150 billion in the EU and EU firms some €123 billion in the US'.[51] In the same year, the total stock of bilateral investments was around €1.3 trillion in each direction.[52]

The TTIP is estimated to have large and multifaceted benefits. The European Commission anticipates a boost to the EU economy by more than €119 billion annually, to the US economy by more than €95 billion annually, and to the rest of the world by almost €100 billion. It also may potentially create hundreds of thousands of jobs.[53]

There is great potential for the TTIP to foster sustainable development, energy efficiency, and energy security through the agreement's terms and the hopefully resultant increase in trade. However, the degree to which this potential is realized will depend largely on the quality of the environmental and energy elements and the transparency, implementation and enforcement, and monitoring provisions.

B. The TTIP and Sustainable Development

1. Central sustainability goals

In its Final Report, the High Level Working Group suggested that the United States and the EU should explore opportunities to maintain a high level of protection for the environment.[54] While developing the TTIP, both economies should keep in mind advancements made in the Sustainable Development Chapter of EU trade agreements and in the Environment Chapter of US trade agreements.[55] The United States and the EU have each set forth a number of sustainable development goals in

---

49 Ibid.
50 Ibid.
51 Ibid.
52 ibid.
53 Ibid.
54 'High Level Working Group on Jobs and Growth', p. 5.
55 Ibid.

statements regarding the TTIP and as general trade goals.[56] Additionally, as members of the World Trade Organization (WTO), the United States, the EU, and its 28 Member States, are committed to sustainable development as stated in the Preamble to the Agreement Establishing the World Trade Organization, signed in 1994.[57]

The United Nations 2005 World Summit Outcome document introduces three pillars of sustainable development: (1) environmental protection; (2) economic development; and (3) social development.[58] This definition of sustainable development provides a useful framework for analysis of the potential for the topic within the TTIP.

1.1. Environmental protection Environmental protection should be enshrined in the TTIP. Both economies have expressed a desire to include and enforce pre-existing commitments made in multilateral environmental agreements. The United States named some of these agreements in its 2014 Trade Policy Agenda and 2013 Annual Report, which cover areas including trade in endangered species, maritime and fishery issues, ozone-depleting substances, biological diversity, hazardous wastes, biosafety, and organic pollutants.[59] The EU named many of the same

---

[56] The United States mentioned sustainable development as a goal and element of its trade program in the '2014 Trade Policy Agenda and 2013 Annual Report of the President of the United States on the Trade Agreement Program'. The EU has similarly produced a 'Trade and Sustainable Development Initial EU Position Paper' for the TTIP negotiations.

[57] 'Recognizing that their relations in the field of trade and economic endeavour should be conducted … allowing for the optimal use of the world's resources in accordance with the objective of sustainable development', Agreement Establishing the World Trade Organization, 15 April 1994, www.wto.org/english/docs_e/legal_e/04-wto.pdf

[58] '2005 World Summit Outcome' (United Nations General Assembly, 25 October 2005), para 48, www.un.org/womenwatch/ods/A-RES-60-1-E.pdf

[59] 'Additional examples of MEAs [multilateral environmental agreements] where USTR [the United States Trade Representative] contributed to US policy development include the Convention on International Trade in Endangered Species of Wild Fauna and Flora, the International Convention for the Conservation of Atlantic Tunas, International Maritime Organization conventions, the Montreal Protocol on Substances that Deplete the Ozone Layer, the Basel Convention on the Control of Transboundary Movements of Hazardous Wastes and their Disposal, the Convention on Biological Diversity and the Cartagena Protocol on Biosafety, and the Stockholm Convention on Persistent Organic Pollutants', '2014 Trade Policy Agenda and 2013 Annual Report of the President of the United States on the Trade Agreement Program' (Office of the United States Trade Representative, March 2014), p. 157, available at www.ustr.gov/

international agreements as having particular importance for trade negotiations.[60]

As mentioned above, one of the most essential elements for success of the TTIP is unifying standards and regulations. Multilateral environmental agreements that have already been concluded by the United States and the EU would be a good source of developed assessments and agreed-upon standards. Their content, protections, and guidelines should be integrated into the TTIP to the degree that they are relevant.

In recent trade agreements concluded by the United States and the EU, both entities have taken a number of steps to support environmental standards and sustainable development concerns. For example, in the Environment Chapter of its Free Trade Agreement with South Korea, the United States encouraged high levels of protection for the environment and the application and enforcement of environmental laws; it outlined procedures to investigate alleged violations; it developed mechanisms and institutional arrangements to enhance environmental performance; and it created opportunities for cooperation and public participation.[61] The EU covered many of the same issues and goals in its free trade agreement with Korea, and stated that trade should promote sustainable development.[62] In an Annex, the US–Korea agreement also specifically listed multilateral environmental agreements to which both signatories were a party.[63] The integration of these agreements is useful for referencing specific environmental standards that have already been agreed upon, which would not likely be enumerated in the free trade agreement itself.

Climate change is additionally a large issue that falls under the purview of environmental protection. The EU named the UNFCCC one of the central multilateral environmental agreements that should underlie

---

sites/default/files/2014%20Trade%20Policy%20Agenda%20and%202013%20Annual%20Report.pdf

60 'EU – US Transatlantic Trade and Investment Partnership: Trade and Sustainable Development: Initial EU Position Paper' (European Commission), p. 2, available at http://trade.ec.europa.eu/doclib/docs/2013/july/tradoc_151626.pdf

61 Free Trade Agreement between the United States and the Republic of Korea [hereinafter US–Korea FTA], Chapter 20, available at www.ustr.gov/trade-agreements/free-trade-agreements/korus-fta/final-text

62 Free Trade Agreement between the European Union and its Member States, of the one part, and the Republic of Korea, of the other part [2011] OJ L127/6, Chapter 13 [hereinafter EU–Korea FTA].

63 US–Korea FTA, Annex 20-A.

the environmental protection element of the TTIP,[64] and the United States has remained involved in UNFCCC negotiations.

The TTIP should replicate the Environment Chapter and Trade and Sustainable Development Chapter of recent US and EU free trade agreements discussed above. The terms in each of these strongly promote environmental standards and the enforcement of environmental protections. Additionally, the TTIP should specifically reference standards laid out in the multilateral environmental agreements listed above and should make them enforceable by parties. The United States and the EU should consider inclusion of the UNFCCC into this group of agreements, as it would help to address the growing issue of climate change mitigation and adaptation.[65]

1.2. Economic sustainability Economic sustainability and development encompasses the idea that business, practices, and operations occur in such a way that they efficiently and responsibly use resources while avoiding the creation of environmental concerns and continuing to make a profit. One central part in creating an economically sustainable business climate in the United States and the EU is facilitating trade in sustainable and green goods, technologies, information, and services. Sustainability assurance schemes are a second tool mentioned by the EU in its Initial Policy Paper that would encourage economic sustainability.[66] Voluntary tools on the topic and fair and ethical trade initiatives could encourage these important goals while making them a desirable element in transatlantic business practices. The TTIP could have a potentially large role to play in encouraging trade in green goods and services, and could help develop and protect sustainability schemes.

In its Free Trade Agreement with South Korea, the EU specifically highlighted the economic side of sustainable development: 'The Parties shall strive to facilitate and promote trade and foreign direct investment in environmental goods and services, including environmental technologies, sustainable renewable energy, energy efficient products and services and eco-labelled goods, including through addressing related non-tariff barriers'.[67] The areas described above are of the sort that would

---

64 'EU – US Transatlantic Trade and Investment Partnership: Trade and Sustainable Development: Initial EU Position Paper', p. 2.

65 For further discussion on the link between trade and climate change, see Leal-Arcas, R. *Climate Change and International Trade* (Cheltenham: Edward Elgar, 2013).

66 Ibid. p. 3.

67 EU–Korea FTA, Article 13.6.2.

allow businesses to operate profitably and in a sustainable manner, and are central to economic sustainability. The Agreement also includes a term on sustainability structures and schemes that further economic sustainability: 'The Parties shall strive to facilitate and promote trade in goods that contribute to sustainable development, including goods that are the subject of schemes such as fair and ethical trade and those involving corporate social responsibility and accountability'.[68] The Environmental Chapters in recent US FTAs have no parallel language, although these concepts do align with stated US priorities in negotiations.

The TTIP should include an economic development term similar to the one discussed above in order to promote sustainable operations and development for businesses in both regions. Green goods, technologies, and services are essential to responsible growth and environmental protection. The term should also cover structures such as fair and ethical trade and corporate social responsibility as they encourage businesses to operate and produce goods that are in line with sustainable development goals.

1.3. Social sustainability Lastly, social sustainability is a core part of sustainable development. This pillar represents the idea that the policies, processes, and systems supporting sustainable development also improve social goals such as equality, diversity, and quality of life, etc. Although a number of areas could fall under this heading, including human rights agreements, of particular focus in discussions relating to environmental protection and sustainable development are labor standards. Both parties have named the protection of labor standards as important in trade talks, and they can be considered an important element of social sustainability.

The Trade and Sustainable Development Chapter of recent EU free trade agreements highlights the value of multilateral agreements on labor standards and the goal of increasing employment.[69] It also outlines four major principles concerning fundamental rights: (1) freedom of association and collective bargaining; (2) elimination of forced or compulsory labor; (3) abolition of child labor; and (4) elimination of discrimination.[70] All of these concepts are also tied within the agreement to the standards of the International Labor Organization (ILO).[71] Recent US free trade agreements also include a chapter on labor: recognizing the same principles of fundamental rights and the applicability of the ILO and its

---

68 Ibid.
69 Ibid, Article 13.4.
70 Ibid.
71 Ibid.

policies; encouraging enforcement of labor laws and public awareness of them; and creating institutions and mechanisms for cooperation and consultation.[72] It is clear that both parties have made labor protections an important part of free trade agreements in recent years.

The TTIP will likely include a term much like that in previous EU and US free trade agreements, recognizing the importance of labor standards and principles of fundamental rights. It should reference the ILO, of which the United States and all EU countries are members. The ILO has issued non-binding resolutions, guidelines, and codes of practice on a number of topics, as well as standards ratified by some Member States, including: the measurement of working time; safety and health in various fields of work; freedom of association; wages; working time; employment security; and child labor, etc.[73] Publications and other documents produced by the ILO could form the basis for labor standards encouraged and enforced by the TTIP if the ILO is integrated into the TTIP.

2. European Union trade policy and next generation agreements

As an international institution with agreements in its own right, it is worth examining the policies of the EU on the environment that ought to guide its TTIP negotiations. Sustainable development is an explicitly stated goal of the EU within the Treaty of Lisbon.[74] The EU has its own Sustainable Development Strategy, aiming to identify and help develop actions that allow the EU to attain its sustainable development goals through efficient resource use, realizing ecological and social innovation

---

72 US–Korea FTA, Chapter 19.

73 See 'International Labour Organization' (International Labor Organization), www.ilo.org/global/lang–en/index.htm

74 'The Union … shall work for the sustainable development of Europe based on balanced economic growth and price stability, a highly competitive social market economy, aiming at full employment and social progress, and a high level of protection and improvement of the quality of the environment', Treaty of Lisbon amending the Treaty on European Union and the Treaty establishing the European Community [2007] OJ C306/1, para 4. The EU has a similar goal for its relations with external regions: 'The Union shall define and pursue common policies and actions, and shall work for a high degree of cooperation in all fields of international relations, in order to: … help develop international measures to preserve and improve the quality of the environment and the sustainable management of global natural resources, in order to ensure sustainable development', ibid. para. 24.

potential, environmental protection and, in the end, achieving prosperity.[75] The Strategy emphasizes that global solidarity will be needed to meet the challenges of sustainable development, and that it is important for the EU to work in partnership with other nations of the world.[76] One operational objective within the Strategy is to '[i]nclude sustainable development concerns in all EU external policies … by making it an objective of multilateral and bilateral development cooperation'.[77] Thus, it is clear that the EU is internally obligated to include policies to promote sustainable development in the TTIP.

These new challenges and objectives have reformed EU trade policy. The EU Communication 'Global Europe: Competing in the World' outlines new priorities and approaches for EU trade policy that address those concerns, including access to energy resources, protection of the environment, and sustainability.[78] The EU has also stated that its practice is to include a chapter on 'Trade and Sustainable Development' in the free trade agreements that it concludes,[79] and examples of such a chapter have been discussed above. One example of such a 'next generation' FTA, which includes a chapter on 'Trade and Sustainable Development', is the one between the EU and the Republic of Korea.[80] It provides an excellent point of comparison for determining what the EU may aim to include in the TTIP with the US. The EU has also released Initial Position Papers on trade and sustainable development and on raw materials and energy within the TTIP specifically.[81] Position papers state

---

75 'Renewed Sustainable Development Strategy' (European Commission, 15/16 June 2006), available at http://register.consilium.europa.eu/doc/srv?l=EN&t=PDF&gc=true&sc=false&f=ST%2010917%202006%20INIT

76 Ibid. p 3.

77 Ibid. p. 21.

78 Commission, 'Global Europe: Competing in the World: A Contribution to the EU's Growth and Jobs Strategy', (Communication) (COM(2006) 567 final).

79 'EU – US Transatlantic Trade and Investment Partnership: Trade and Sustainable Development: Initial EU Position Paper', 2.

80 [2011] OJ L127/6. For a more in-depth analysis of the climate change provisions in the EU–Korea FTA, see Croquet, N. 'The Climate Change Norms Under the EU-Korea Free Trade Agreement: Between Soft and Hard Law', in Wouters, J., Marx, A. et al. (eds) *Ensuring Good Global Governance Through Trade: An Assessment of New EU Trade Policies and Approaches* (Cheltenham: Edward Elgar, 2015).

81 'EU – US Transatlantic Trade and Investment Partnership: Trade and Sustainable Development: Initial EU Position Paper', 2; 'EU – US Transatlantic Trade and Investment Partnership: Raw Materials and Energy: Initial EU Position Paper' (European Commission) [hereinafter, Raw Materials and Energy Position

that any such chapter in the TTIP ought to cover: trade of sustainable and climate-friendly goods, services, and technologies; sustainability assurance schemes; and corporate social responsibility standards.[82] They also state that general trade provisions, such as those on non-discrimination and the elimination of import and export duties, should apply to raw materials and energy, and any additional specific concerns related to this sector should also be developed and included in the TTIP.[83] The EU will likely offer a 'Trade and Sustainable Development' chapter that addresses these areas; alternatively, it will ensure that the same safeguards and protections are put into place in a similar term appearing in the TTIP.

C. The TTIP and Energy

1. Raw materials and natural resources

In its Final Report, the US–EU High Level Working Group on Jobs and Growth identified the raw materials and energy sector as a trade area that deserves particular attention in developing rules and modes of cooperation.[84] Energy has become a pressing issue: the increase in the world's population and the improvement of living standards have contributed to an increase in energy demand.[85] Governments are in turn thinking more strategically about energy control: how to secure a supply of raw materials and energy resources, and how to emphasize generation methods that further this goal and that protect the environment.[86]

Paper], available at http://trade.ec.europa.eu/doclib/docs/2013/july/tradoc_151624.pdf

82 'EU – US Transatlantic Trade and Investment Partnership: Trade and Sustainable Development: Initial EU Position Paper', pp. 2–3.

83 Raw Materials and Energy Position Paper, 2.

84 'High Level Working Group on Jobs and Growth', p. 6.

85 'EU – US Transatlantic Trade and Investment Partnership: Raw Materials and Energy: Initial EU Position Paper' (European Commission), p. 1. See also Leal-Arcas, R. & Filis, A. 'The Fragmented Governance of the Global Energy Economy: A Legal-Institutional Analysis' (2013) *Journal of World Energy Law and Business*, Vol. 6, Issue 4, pp. 1–58; Leal-Arcas, R. & Filis, A. 'Conceptualizing EU Energy Security through an EU Constitutional Law Perspective' (2013) *Fordham International Law Journal*, Vol. 36, No. 5, pp. 1225–1301; Leal-Arcas, R. & Filis, A. 'The Energy Community and the Energy Charter Treaty: Special Legal Regimes, their Systemic Relationship to the EU, and their Dispute Settlement Arrangements' (2014) *Oil, Gas & Energy Law Journal*, Vol. 12, Issue 2, pp. 1–42.

86 See generally Abu-Gosh, E. & Leal-Arcas, R. 'The Conservation of Exhaustible Natural Resources in the GATT and WTO: Implications for the

However, the trade of raw materials and energy has not been fully covered by the international trade and investment rules that have developed.[87] The EU has argued that the rules in the various WTO agreements do not adequately address international trade in energy and raw materials. The WTO has strong rules regarding import barriers, but weaker rules addressing export barriers, which tends to be the complicating factor in energy trading.[88] Additionally, there is no definition of 'energy services' in the General Agreement on Trade in Services, and an absence of rules governing international trade in energy goods.[89] Finally, other complications include: trade and distribution monopolies in some countries; local content requirements; and lack of transparency in licenses for exploitation or trade.[90] Thus, there is an opportunity for the TTIP to address some of these gaps and issues regarding trade between the EU and the United States, facilitating the movement of energy goods and services and potentially providing a model for energy trade liberalization by other international actors.

One of the already-anticipated benefits of the TTIP, should it successfully liberalize trade in energy and raw materials, is increased exports by the United States of liquefied natural gas (LNG) to the EU. A supply of American LNG to Europe would greatly benefit the region's energy strategy. Trade in LNG would lessen the EU's dependence on Russian gas,[91] thereby diversifying its portfolio of external raw materials sources. Currently, the US Department of Energy must approve each export of LNG abroad; however, the process is nearly automatic when the LNG is being shipped to a country with which the United States has concluded a free trade agreement.[92] This is an example of a 'behind-the-border' barrier, discussed above. Becoming a preferential partner with a free trade agreement may satisfy the EU, and no change may be needed in the US regulatory scheme to open trade. Alternatively, negotiations may encourage the United States to reduce or eliminate this permitting

---

Conservation of Oil Resources' (2013) *The Journal of World Investment and Trade* Vol. 14, No. 3, pp. 480–531.

[87] 'EU – US Transatlantic Trade and Investment Partnership: Raw Materials and Energy: Initial EU Position Paper' (European Commission), p. 1.

[88] Ibid.

[89] Ibid.

[90] Ibid.

[91] Leal-Arcas, R. 'The EU and Russia as Energy Trading Partners: Friends or Foes?' (2009) *European Foreign Affairs Review*, Vol. 14, Issue 3, pp. 337–366.

[92] Walstad, A. 'Transatlantic Trade Negotiations Reach Second Stage' (14 November 2013) 3 (221) *Natural Gas Daily* E1.

scheme or other existing tariffs or licensing programs, along with other barriers to export, so that energy products and raw materials may cross borders more freely.[93]

Market conditions may mean that the benefits in LNG trade that the EU expects may not materialize. However, since energy prices are higher in Asia, it is possible that substantial exports to the EU would only occur when Asian demand is weak.[94] Additionally, the American Henry Hub pricing system for LNG differs markedly from the current way that natural gas is priced in the EU, which is on a local market basis.[95] This may make European suppliers less interested in contracting for LNG, especially if the Henry Hub price rises above the price the European market would mandate.[96] However, it would allow European suppliers to leverage the US LNG prices in negotiations with other suppliers, and some may be willing to pay a premium for the LNG if it means a preferable security of supply.[97] The TTIP has great potential to open trade in energy and raw materials, particularly LNG, but the resulting economic benefits are not guaranteed.

The EU would like to see the inclusion of elements of the Extractive Industries Transparency Initiative (EITI) in the TTIP, arguing that it reflects the domestic legislation of the EU and the United States.[98] The EITI is an international standard of transparency for oil, gas, and mineral resources, and is developed and overseen by a coalition of actors,

---

[93] On this point, see the pertinent remarks made by Mark Kantor to the OGEMID/Transnational Dispute Management community on 26 March 2014: 'Under current US law there is blanket approval for the export of US natural gas to countries with which the US has a free trade agreement. Otherwise, … US export licenses for natural gas must be granted on a case-by-case basis. Currently, the US does not have a full-fledged free trade agreement with any EU Member State. One consequence of the TTIP … would be to eliminate the existing US requirement of case-by-case natural gas export approvals for the 28 EU Member States'. In this sense, the TTIP would be greatly beneficial for EU energy security enhancement by minimizing the EU's dependency on Russian energy.

[94] Walstad, A. 'Transatlantic Trade Negotiations Reach Second Stage' (14 November 2013) 3 (221) *Natural Gas Daily* E1.

[95] Ibid.

[96] Ibid.

[97] Ibid.

[98] 'EU – US Transatlantic Trade and Investment Partnership: Raw Materials and Energy: Initial EU Position Paper' (European Commission), p. 2.

including governments.[99] The EITI has two tiers of participation: countries that are EITI compliant and have met all the requirements of the EITI standard; and countries that are EITI candidates and are implementing EITI, but have not yet met all of its requirements.[100] The United States is an EITI candidate country, while European countries are much less active in EITI activities and only a few are showing an interest in the EITI.[101] It is possible that the EITI may be integrated into the TTIP, but with the current lack of commitment to the EITI by the parties, it may not be an easy point for negotiators to agree upon.

2. Energy efficiency and renewable energy generation

Energy efficiency and the promotion of renewable energy are central energy policy goals for both the United States and the EU. Because these technologies and product standards are closely related to the trade in green technologies, goods, and services discussed above as a form of economic sustainable development,[102] the analysis and conclusions drawn in that subsection are relevant to the goal of supporting energy efficiency and renewable energy.

One way in which the TTIP could support these goals would be to build upon the work of the Asia-Pacific Environmental Cooperation (APEC) Forum's list of environmental goods. The purpose of the List is to compile categories of products that ought to receive reduced tariffs because they are environmentally responsible.[103] One such example is renewable energy technology, such as solar panels and wind turbines; the list also includes pollution control and environmental monitoring technologies.[104] Including a term in the TTIP that specifically sets a goal to

---

[99] 'What is the EITI?' (Extractive Industries Transparency Initiative), http://eiti.org/eiti

[100] 'EITI Countries' (Extractive Industries Transparency Initiative), http://eiti.org/countries

[101] 'Other Countries' (Extractive Industries Transparency Initiative), http://eiti.org/countries/other

[102] See e.g., Leal-Arcas, R. & Filis, A. 'Certain Legal Aspects of the Multilateral Trade System and the Promotion of Renewable Energy', in Lim, C.L. and Mercurio, B. (eds) *International Economic Law after the Crisis: A Tale of Fragmented Disciplines* (Cambridge: Cambridge University Press, forthcoming).

[103] 'APEC List of Environmental Goods: Promoting Exports, Creating Jobs, and Advancing Green Growth and Sustainable Development' (Office of the United States Trade Representative), available at www.ustr.gov/about-us/press-office/fact-sheets/2012/september/apec-environmental-goods

[104] Ibid.

eliminate or reduce tariffs on behind-the-border barriers covering a particular list of renewable energy and other green technologies inspired by the APEC's list, would greatly further the goal of promoting energy efficiency and renewable energy generation.

D. Looking Forward

The parties initially set a loose goal to conclude the TTIP by the end of 2014; the current leadership of the European Commission, the Barroso Commission, is set to end in the same year, and there is a compelling reason for EU leadership to conclude a successful TTIP by that time as part of its legacy.[105] However, this goal may be unrealistic, and allowances have been made for negotiation talks to continue past that date.[106] A more likely timeline may be by the US presidential election in 2016. The results of trade talks and a signed free trade agreement may affect Barack Obama's legacy as president, thus setting one feasible deadline for US signature.

In its report 'The Transatlantic Trade and Investment Partnership: Ambitious but Achievable', the Atlantic Council and the Bertelsmann Foundation put forth three potential scenarios for the end result of TTIP negotiations.[107] The first speculated outcome is a moderate agreement that would remove a large number of barriers to trade and investment, but that would avoid resolving the most contentious issues, such as genetically modified organisms and hormone-treated agricultural products.[108] The second possible end result may be no agreement, as negotiations could stall due to a distracted focus on problematic issues, instead of upon the low-hanging fruit.[109] Lastly, with the right political momentum and mindset, the parties could reach a broad-ranging agreement that would cover most or all of the issues and policy goals.[110] The report concludes that which outcome occurs will depend largely on the dedication, focus, and interest of the governments and negotiators, their

---

105 Barker and Workman, p. 3.

106 'EU Trade Ministers Pledge T-TIP Support as Talks Enter Next Stage' (International Centre for Trade and Sustainable Development), available at http://ictsd.org/i/news/bridgesweekly/185023/

107 Barker and Workman, p. 2.

108 Ibid.

109 Ibid.

110 Ibid.

willingness to compromise, and the degree of political pressure exerted by leadership.[111]

The leading German newspaper *Die Zeit* leaked an alleged EU July 2013 draft text of the TTIP in February 2014.[112] Although the draft included sections specifically covering electronic communications and financial services, it made no mention of sustainable development, energy efficiency, or other environmental concerns.

III. THE TRANS-PACIFIC PARTNERSHIP

A. An Introduction

Following the premise that PTAs are the building blocks of multilateralism,[113] creating PTAs with sustainable growth mechanisms is a key contemporary challenge. As things stand, PTAs can either contribute or undermine sustainable development efforts. Factors such as greater negotiating power, greater regulatory cooperation and smaller numbers of parties help in regional negotiations. For example, countries that aim to include sustainable development in all their policy aspects would find greater success pursuing it through PTAs as opposed to multilaterally.[114] Furthermore, PTAs with environmental standards may help level the playing field. They can nullify competitive advantages gained from weaker environmental legislations, help environmental capacity building, and enable better understanding of environmental problems.

Arguendo, PTAs ensure greater environmental protection than multilateral environmental agreements (MEAs).[115] Concessions granted while

---

[111] Ibid. pp. 6–7.

[112] 'EU will laut Geheimdokument Sonderrechte für Konzerne', *Zeit Online*, 27 February 2014, www.zeit.de/wirtschaft/2014-02/freihandelsabkommen-eu-sonderrechte-konzerne

[113] See e.g., Leal-Arcas, R. 'Proliferation of Regional Trade Agreements: Complementing or Supplanting Multilateralism?' (2011) *Chicago Journal of International Law*, Vol. 11, No. 2, pp. 597–629.

[114] New Zealand Ministry of Foreign Affairs & Trade, 'Framework for Integrating Environment Issues into Free Trade Agreements', available at http://www.mfat.govt.nz/Trade-and-Economic-Relations/NZ-and-the-WTO/Trade-Issues/0-environment-framework.php

[115] The Organisation for Economic Co-operation and Development (OECD), 'Environment and Regional Trade Agreements' (OECD, 2007), p. 42.

negotiating a trade deal may address sustainable development concerns.[116] As a result, PTAs can effectively fulfill many objectives of MEAs. Most importantly, PTAs often contain binding dispute resolution clauses which can prove very effective in dealing with environmental disputes.

However, for developing countries, environmental commitments under PTAs may be considered akin to new barriers for exports. They also lead to regulatory fragmentation and conflicts.[117] Further, there is a fear that PTAs and sustainable development may not be compatible either because they may prejudice countries' positions in multilateral trade negotiations or because sustainable development and environmental concerns are simply not appropriately discussed in trade agreements.[118]

If indeed PTAs are to become building blocks for ensuring climate change mitigation and meet sustainable development objectives under MEAs,[119] negotiations would need to carefully balance trade, development and sustainable growth.[120] Further, the design of strategic PTAs is vital for sustainable development. This would require them to be of a relatively large size, composed of some prominent economies. The TPP fits this bill well.

1. A 21st-century agreement

The Trans-Pacific Partnership is a free trade agreement which is being currently negotiated amongst 12 Asia-Pacific nations, namely the United States, Japan, Mexico, Canada, Australia, Malaysia, Chile, Singapore, Peru, Vietnam, New Zealand and Brunei Darussalam. The parties to the treaty account for 40% of global GDP.[121] The TPP has been described as a 'comprehensive and high standard' free trade agreement which aims to

---

116 Ibid.

117 Sugiyama, T. & Sinton, J. 'Orchestra of Treaties: A Future Climate Regime Scenario with Multiple Treaties Among Like-Minded Countries' (2005) *International Environmental Agreements*, Vol. 5, Issue 1, pp. 65–88.

118 The Organisation for Economic Co-operation and Development (OECD), 'Environment and Regional Trade Agreements' (OECD, 15 June 2007), pp. 42–45.

119 Leal-Arcas, R. 'Climate Change Mitigation from the Bottom Up: Using Preferential Trade Agreements to Promote Climate Change Mitigation' (2013) *Carbon and Climate Law Rev*, Vol. 7, No. 1, pp. 34–42.

120 For proposals in this respect, see Leal-Arcas, R. 'Trade Proposals for Climate Action' (2014, forthcoming) *Trade, Law and Development*, Vol. 6, No. 1.

121 WikiLeaks, 'Secret Trans-Pacific Partnership Agreement (TPP) – Environment Consolidated Text', available at http://wikileaks.org/tpp-enviro

liberalize trade in mostly all goods and services and includes commitments beyond those established in the World Trade Organization (WTO).[122] The first formal round of TPP negotiations was held in Melbourne in March 2010 with 200 officials from Australia, the US, New Zealand, Chile, Singapore, Brunei, Peru and Vietnam.[123] Since then, several rounds of secretive negotiations have taken place, the proposed environment chapter of the TPP was leaked and there has not been much public involvement. The US entered into TPP negotiations in March 2008.[124]

The TPP is the successor of the Trans-Pacific Strategic Economic Partnership Agreement, also known as the P4 Agreement, which was being negotiated by Brunei Darussalam, Chile, New Zealand and Singapore.[125] The P4 Agreement negotiations essentially matured into the TPP to accommodate the US interest of bringing in like-minded countries. The P4 is the first multiparty PTA connecting countries in Asia, Latin America, and North America who aim to create a high standard template for an ultimate free trade agreement.[126] It also pursued total liberalization in trade in goods and services.[127] While the TPP is a separate agreement, it essentially builds upon the P4 Agreement.

The TPP is touted as providing 'a new standard of global trade and incorporating next-generation issues',[128] making it a landmark 21st-century trade agreement. To validate this, the TPP seeks to not exclude sensitive sectors such as agriculture, unlike other trade agreements, and

---

[122] Fergusson, I. et al. 'The Trans-Pacific Partnership (TPP) Negotiations and Issues for Congress', Congressional Research Service, Summary, December 2013, available at https://www.fas.org/sgp/crs/row/R42694.pdf

[123] See Organization of American States, Foreign Trade Information System, available at http://www.sice.oas.org/TPD/TPP/Negotiations/Reports/Round_I_update_e.pdf

[124] http://tppinfo.org/

[125] Hsueh, C.-H. 'A Greener Trade Agreement: Approaches to Environmental Issues in the TPP Negotiations' (2013) *Asian Journal of WTO & International Health Law & Policy*, Vol. 8. No. 2, pp. 521–542, at 522.

[126] Lewis, M.K. 'The Trans-Pacific Partnership: New Paradigm or Wolf in Sheep's Clothing?' (2011) *Boston College International & Comparative Law Review*, Vol. 34, No.27, pp. 32–34.

[127] Ibid. pp. 32–33.

[128] USTR, 'Outlines of the Trans-Pacific Partnership Agreement' (November 2011), available at http://www.ustr.gov/about-us/press-office/fact-sheets/2011/november/outlines-trans-pacific-partnership-agreement

aims for zero tariffs.[129] It also has a docketing provision to progressively include like-minded members who, however, will not take part in the negotiating process.[130] It also promotes next generation reforms in areas such as the environment and labor standards.[131]

The TPP represents an example of a mega PTA, dwarfed only by the WTO. It represents 40% of the world's Gross Domestic Product (GDP) or one third of world trade.[132] This, along with greater liberalized trade, makes it a major attraction. Robert Stumberg calls the negotiations over the TPP a roadmap towards a trading bloc other than the WTO.[133]

However, the TPP negotiations are being conducted with a level of secrecy not witnessed in any previous trade agreement.[134] No official draft of the TPP exists in the public domain, including all of its 29 other chapters (in addition to the intellectual property chapter), attracting widespread complaints. Even US Congress has been critical about the opaqueness surrounding it.[135] Concerns exist on how a '21st-century agreement' shapes up on issues such as biodiversity, environment, labor standards, and, broadly, sustainable development. Moreover, approximately only 600 'cleared advisors' representing corporations and trade

---

129 Hsueh, C.-H. 'A Greener Trade Agreement: Approaches to Environmental Issues in the TPP Negotiations' (2013) *Asian Journal of WTO & International Health Law & Policy*, Vol. 8. No. 2, pp. 521–542, at 523.

130 Nash-Hoff, M. 'The Trans-Pacific Partnership Would Destroy our National Sovereignty', Huffingtonpost Business, The Blog (3 January 2013), available at http://www.huffingtonpost.com/michele-nashhoff/the-transpacific-partners_b_2766729.html

131 See remarks by Miriam Sapiro, 'US Trade Policy: Levelling the Playing Field', Remarks at the National Association of Business Economists (25 February 2014), available at http://iipdigital.usembassy.gov/st/english/texttrans/2014/02/20140226294123.html#axzz2wrsJHNKa

132 Office of the USTR, 'Trans-Pacific Partnership Ministers Chart Path Forward on Key Issues and Confirm Next Steps on Japan's Entry', Joint Statement of TPP Ministers (30 April 2013), available at www.ustr.gov/about-us/press-office/press-releases/2013/april/joint-statement-tpp-ministers

133 See Waren, B. 'TPP Trade Negotiations in San Diego: A Dagger Through the Heart' (10 July 2012), referring to Robert Stumberg's views. Available at http://www.foe.org/news/archives/2012-07-tpp-trade-negotiations-in-san-diego-a-dagger-through

134 WikiLeaks, 'Secret Trans-Pacific Partnership Agreement (TPP) – IP Chapter' available at https://wikileaks.org/tpp/pressrelease.html

135 Public Citizen, 'Congressional Democrats Escalate Criticism of Substance, Process of Obama's First Trade Pact – the Trans-Pacific Partnership' (27 June 2012), available at http://www.citizen.org/documents/release-congressional-democrats-escalate-criticism-6-27-12.pdf

blocs are privy to the negotiating process at the expense of the general public and civil society.[136]

In this context, the whistleblower website WikiLeaks released four draft chapters of the TPP, including the Environment Chapter.

2. The need for the Trans-Pacific Partnership

The goal of the TPP negotiation process is to create a platform for economic integration across the Asia-Pacific region. The aim is to design a high-quality agreement so as to establish a foundation for economic growth for the development and creation of employment in the member countries.[137] However, the agreement has been sharply criticized by the public for various reasons, especially for lack of transparency. The leaked text of the TPP's Environment Chapter deals with what the 12 parties to the TPP propose in negotiations with regard to fisheries, biodiversity, climate change, as well as trade and investment in environmental goods and services. The United States Trade Representative's (USTR) Office of Environment and Natural Resources has stated that the US government 'is seeking a TPP environment chapter that will facilitate increased regional trade while supporting and enhancing environmental protection and conservation efforts in the Asia-Pacific region'.[138] A USTR green paper[139] on conservation and the TPP does specify the agreement's goals related to wildlife, marine fisheries and timber – however, there is no mention of climate change.

In the next section, we analyze whether the Environment Chapter of the TPP manages to introduce sustainable 21st-century environmental standards.

B. The Environment Chapter

The importance of conserving the environment for well-being on Earth has been universally recognized and various agreements have been concluded to curb environmental harm. These agreements are also

---

[136] Mauldin, W. 'U.S Says Not "Rushing" Asia-Pacific Trade Deal', *The Wall Street Journal*, 26 September 2013, available at http://online.wsj.com/news/articles/SB10001424052702303796404579099632713091994

[137] Organization of American States, Foreign Trade Information System, available at http://www.sice.oas.org/TPD/TPP/TPP_e.ASP

[138] http://www.ustr.gov/trade-topics/environment/bilateral-and-regional-trade-agreements

[139] See http://www.ustr.gov/about-us/press-office/fact-sheets/2011/ustr-green-paper-conservation-and-trans-pacific-partnership

created with a view to limit damage caused to future generations. In this context, the TPP also includes an environment chapter, which WikiLeaks released before it was finalized. Article SS.1 of the Environment Chapter reads as follows:

> Article SS.1: Definitions
>
> For purposes of this Chapter:
>
> **environmental law** means any statute or regulation of a Party, or provision thereof, including any that implement its obligations under a multilateral environmental agreement, the primary purpose of which is the protection of the environment, or the prevention of a danger to human life or health, through:
>
> (a) the prevention, abatement, or control of the release, discharge, or emission of pollutants or environmental contaminants;
> (b) the control of environmentally hazardous or toxic chemicals, substances, materials, and wastes, and the dissemination of information related thereto; or
> (c) the protection or conservation of wild flora or fauna, including endangered species, their habitat, and specially protected natural areas[140, 141]
>
> but does not include any statute or regulation, or provision thereof, directly related to worker safety or health, nor any statute or regulation, or provision thereof, the primary purpose of which is managing the subsistence or aboriginal harvesting of natural resources.[142]

The definition notably excludes sensible management of existing natural resources and aboriginal management of resources, including traditional knowledge, culture and genetic resources. Furthermore, it also excludes environmental regulations at the local body and state levels.[143]

'Environmental law' is a vast term and the above definition does not do it justice. The United Nations Environment Programme provides a brief

---

[140] 'Specially protected natural areas' – as defined by the Party in its legislation.

[141] The Parties recognize that such protection or conservation may include the protection or conservation of biological diversity.

[142] Secret Trans-Pacific Partnership Agreement, Environment Chapter Consolidated Text (November 24, 2013), available at http://wikileaks.org/tpp-enviro

[143] Kelsey, J. 'TPPA Environment Chapter & Chair's Commentary Posted by WikiLeaks: Issues for NZ' (16 January 2014), available at https://wikileaks.org/tppa-environment-chapter.html

summary of issues which could be covered under environmental law.[144] It states that it is 'a system of complex and interlocking statues, common law, treaties, conventions, regulations and policies which seek to protect the natural environment which may be affected, impacted or endangered by human activities'.[145] It also states that environmental law as a distinct system arose in the 1960s in major industrial economies and that it has been 'seen as a critical means of promoting sustainable development'.[146] Moreover, environmental policy principles such as the polluter-pays principle, the precautionary principle, and environmental justice have played a major role in environmental law reforms.

While trade is important and inevitable, it cannot come at the cost of sustainable development. Sustainable development touches upon all aspects of human well-being, including the social, economic and environmental aspects. Sustainable development has been defined in various ways; however, the landmark definition is the following, which first appeared in 1987: 'Development that meets the needs of the present without compromising the ability of the future generations to meet their own needs'.[147]

1. The need for an Environment Chapter

The leaked Environment Chapter of the TPP consists of 18 articles which deal with various issues such as multilateral environmental agreements, corporate social responsibility, mechanisms to enhance environmental performance, cooperation frameworks, trade and climate change, and trade and biodiversity *inter alia*. Various articles deal with environment, trade, and sustainable development. According to the first paragraph of Article SS.2 of the draft TPP, the objectives of the Environment Chapter are to promote mutually supportive trade and environment policies, implement a high level of environmental protection, enforce environmental laws, and enhance the capacities of the parties to address trade-related environmental issues though cooperation. The second paragraph states that cooperation among the parties to the TPP to protect the environment and manage their natural resources in a sustainable manner strengthens their environmental governance. The third paragraph

---

144 http://www.unep.org/training/programmes/Instructor%20Version/Part_2/Activities/Interest_Groups/Decision-Making/Core/Environmental_Law_Definitions_rev2.pdf

145 Ibid.

146 Ibid.

147 The World Commission on Environment and Development's report, *Our Common Future* (Oxford: Oxford University Press, 1987).

expressly mentions that it is inappropriate to use environmental legislation to restrict trade or investment between the parties to the TPP. This seems to suggest that environmental protection should not come at the cost of economic growth.

Article SS.3 refers to general commitments and emphasizes the importance of the protection of the environment in a way that supports both trade and the environment in the context of sustainable development. According to Article SS.3.4, all parties to the TPP must enforce their environmental laws in a manner so as to not affect trade or investment between the parties. On a careful reading of this paragraph, it can be seen that the drafters of the agreement have emphasized trade and investment over the environment and the effect that trade can have on the environment.

The Montreal Protocol is mentioned in Article SS.4 of the draft text. The depletion of the ozone layer has been an alarming cause of concern since the first hole in the ozone layer was found in 1985 in Antarctica.[148] This discovery startled the world and triggered the enforcement of many international treaties and national laws upholding the need for sustainable development.

2. The enforcement of the Environment Chapter

The TPP provides certain procedural measures to enforce the protection of the environment.[149] It also talks about the establishment of arbitral tribunals to decide matters of dispute that may arise.[150] Furthermore, the TPP dictates that each party shall make use or establish consultative mechanisms, such as national advisory committees, so as to regulate the proper implementation of the TTP's Environment Chapter.[151] Article SS.10 deals with the importance of cooperation so as to strike a balance between sustainable development, on the one hand, and trade and investment, on the other. Yet, this provision, though useful, does not mention the ways and means in which the balance can be struck. The agreement is also not strong enough on the enforcement mechanism. For parties to take this agreement seriously, there should be certain stringent provisions. The TPP draft text does not mention the consequences parties may suffer if they breach any article in the Environment Chapter.

---

148 Andre, C. & Velasquez, M. 'Ozone Debate: Environmentalists and Business Collide – Again', available at https://www.scu.edu/ethics/publications/iie/v3n1/ozone.html

149 Article SS.5 of the draft TPP.

150 Article SS.12.4 of the draft TPP.

151 Article SS.6 of the draft TPP.

2.1. Domestic regulations Article SS.9 of the draft TPP states various voluntary mechanisms to enhance environmental performance, which should be designed in a way that maximizes the environmental benefits of the parties and avoids unnecessary technical barriers to trade. However, terms such as 'voluntary' and 'avoidance of unnecessary barriers to trade' dilute the entire process. Firstly, 'voluntary' mechanisms would lead to a regulatory race to the bottom. The voluntary mechanisms include auditing and reporting, information sharing, and sharing expertise.[152] These mechanisms help to educate and ensure transparency and help in capacity building, essential for any new-age trade agreement. Furthermore, none of the 12 countries negotiating the agreement classifies as a least-developed country. Therefore, they would be in a position to introduce such measures over a progressive time-bound period. These mechanisms can also be helpful for potential investors. A constant fear among investors is arbitrary penalization in the garb of public policy legislation, including environmental. Audit reports from independent and reliable organizations can be a real asset for future dispute settlements.

Article SS.11 states that each party shall designate senior government representatives as a national contact point responsible for the implementation of the TPP's Environment Chapter. Article SS.12 deals with consultation and dispute resolution in case of any conflict between the parties. These obligations on the parties to formulate committees and enforce either direct or indirect laws may bring slight changes in the domestic regulation of the parties to the agreement. However, if the domestic regulations are framed in such a way so as to pursue trade and investment while keeping the environment and sustainability in mind, this particular chapter will prove to be beneficial to society as a whole, in spite of its placing a burden on the parties to introduce new domestic laws and regulations.

2.2. Corporations and sustainability Sustainability is an important consideration for corporations when dealing with trade and investment. Corporations play an important role in economic and social development. They should use natural resources with utmost care and generate less waste so as to provide for present and future generations. In the TPP's environment chapter, trade and investment have been mentioned several times, as has the notion of corporate social responsibility in Article SS.8. According to this Article, parties to the TPP should encourage enterprises operating within its territory or jurisdiction to adopt voluntarily their

[152] Article SS.9(1) of the draft TPP.

policies and principles of corporate social responsibility related to the environment, in accordance with internationally recognized standards and guidelines.[153] The wording of Article SS.8 is important to achieve sustainable development. Moreover, Articles SS.2 and SS.3 regarding the objectives and general commitments of the TPP emphasize the importance of mutually supportive trade and environment policies so as to promote sustainable development.

However, there is no mention of any particular stringent actions regarding the failure to implement these provisions. Moreover, Article SS.4, paragraphs 1 and 2 on multilateral environmental agreements emphasize the importance of the parties to the TPP showing 'mutual supportiveness between trade and environment laws and policies', whereas the third paragraph offers any TPP party whose trade or investment is affected as a result of another TPP party not being in compliance with its treaty obligations under a multilateral environmental agreement the possibility to request the establishment of a Committee to consider the matter.

C. The Trans-Pacific Partnership and Sustainable Development

1. Trade and biodiversity

While the role of conservation and sustainable use of biological diversity in achieving sustainable development is recognized,[154] the Environment Chapter is only committed to promote and encourage such sustainable use, including fair and equitable sharing of benefits without making binding commitments. A major weakness of the provision is the fact of not requiring the consent of, and including in the benefit-sharing mechanisms, local communities who are engaged in the preservation of biodiversity and genetic resources. Presently, only the Parties' consent is required.[155] This seems to be against the United Nations Declaration on Rights of Indigenous People (UNDRIP).[156] Moreover, any cooperation in the preservation of biodiversity is not absolute, but only in areas of mutual interest of the Parties.[157] This cherry picking, however, does not seem to be a sustainable model.

These provisions are weak when compared with rules in other Chapters of the TPP, including Intellectual Property, which would enable

---

153 Article SS.8 of the draft TPP.
154 Article SS.13(1) of the draft TPP.
155 Article SS.13(5) of the draft TPP.
156 Article 31 UNDRIP.
157 Article 13(7) of the draft TPP.

commercial exploitation of biodiversity.[158] Reports suggest that four countries (Malaysia, Peru, Vietnam, and Brunei) want to extend the gains from using derivatives of the genetic materials to the local communities.[159] This, however, faces opposition from the US and New Zealand.[160] Another concern is that, while parties to the TPP have the sovereign right to determine access to their genetic resources[161] and to share the gains from their utilization,[162] a US counterproposal seeks to remove these provisions.[163] Furthermore, the US proposal also attacks the rights of indigenous and local communities to maintain their traditional knowledge and practices by substituting 'commitment', as it appears in Article SS.13(3) of the draft TPP, with 'recognize the importance'.[164] However, on a positive note, the US proposal makes conservation and sustainable biological diversity use mandatory.[165]

2. Trade and climate change

Considering the presence of the US (which is the only country that has not ratified the Kyoto Protocol), it is significant that the leaked draft text recognizes climate change as a global concern and the importance of implementing commitments under the UNFCCC/Kyoto Protocol.[166]

---

[158] Kelsey, J. 'TPPA Environment Chapter & Chair's Commentary Posted by WikiLeaks: Issues for NZ' (16 January 2014), available at https://wikileaks.org/tppa-environment-chapter.html

[159] This request is consistent with Article 5 of the Nagoya Protocol.

[160] Kelsey, J. 'TPPA Environment Chapter & Chair's Commentary Posted by WikiLeaks: Issues for NZ' (16 January 2014), available at https://wikileaks.org/tppa-environment-chapter.html

[161] Article SS.13(4) of the draft TPP.

[162] Article SS.13(2) of the draft TPP.

[163] Taverner, Christine C. 'A Low Standard of Ambition at TPP Talks: Corporations Oust Environmentalists from the Negotiating Table' *Georgetown International Environmental Law Review Blog* (6 March 2014), available at http://gielr.wordpress.com/2014/03/06/a-low-standard-of-ambition-at-tpp-talks-corporations-oust-environmentalists-from-the-negotiating-table/

[164] Article SS.X(4) of the draft text of the TPP Environment Chapter of 14 February 2014, not to be confused with the 23 November 2013 Environment Chapter consolidated text of the TPP. The text of 14 February 2014 is available at http://www.redge.org.pe/sites/default/files/20140218%20biodiversity%20climate%20change%20TPP.pdf

[165] Article SS.X(2) of the draft text of the TPP Environment Chapter of 14 February 2014.

[166] On the position of the US regarding the Kyoto Protocol, see generally Leal-Arcas, R. *Climate Change and International Trade* (Cheltenham: Edward Elgar, 2013) Chapter 5.

However, the various mitigation and adaptation measures identified under Article SS.15(3) would only be in the form of 'cooperation on the complementary, trade-related, aspects of these efforts in areas of mutual interest', subject to domestic capabilities.[167] Strikingly, the locution 'areas of mutual interest' curtails cooperation significantly, and no clarification or interpretation of its ambit exists. Furthermore, while it is agreed that multiple economic and environmental policy measures exist when dealing with climate change, the draft text limits the discussion to only 'relevant and appropriate' occasions, instead of making it a continuous process.[168] Significantly, under Article SS.15(6), the Parties agree to take cooperative and capacity building measures to implement their Asia-Pacific Economic Cooperation commitments, including crucial discussions on reducing fossil fuel subsidies. It is to be noted that the US counterproposal has attempted to even forgo the term 'climate change' by substituting it with the locution 'low-emissions economy'.[169] Moreover, it has removed any reference to the UNFCCC. Furthermore, the term 'adaptation' is no longer found in the US draft, meaning that anticipation and acting upon future climate change effects would not be within the purview of the TPP, if the US draft were to be accepted.

3. Marine fisheries

Provisions in the TPP regulating fishing are littered with half-hearted measures such as the fact that parties 'shall seek' the set-up of a fishing management system[170] and affirm commitment towards preventing maritime pollution.[171] This is in spite of the recognition that parties are the major consumers, producers and traders of fisheries[172] and that overfishing is a global problem. Depletion of fishing stocks will also have an immediate impact on the economies of these countries and people's livelihoods, and therefore non-binding obligations are futile.

Furthermore, fishing subsidies are prohibited only for 'overfished'[173] stocks and vessels listed for illegal, unreported or unregulated (IUU)

---

167 Article SS.13(3) of the draft TPP.

168 Article SS.15(4) of the draft TPP.

169 See US counterproposal to the TPP Environment Chapter (14 February, 2014), available at http://www.redge.org.pe/sites/default/files/20140218%20biodiversity%20climate%20change%20TPP.pdf

170 Article SS.16(3) of the draft TPP.

171 Article SS.16(5) of the draft TPP.

172 Article SS.16(1) of the draft TPP.

173 Article SS.16(6)(a) of the draft TPP.

fishing,[174] instead of for *all* stocks, where parties shall make 'best efforts', a legally vague and unenforceable term. Such prohibition may not be effective, as most subsidies will most likely not be specifically targeted to overfished species.[175] The US has proposed that the subsidies that target the fishing of fish stocks that are overfished (Article SS.16(6)(a)) be framed in such a way that *all* overfished stocks are targeted.[176] Furthermore, subsidies are also allowed for capacity-building of non-overfished stocks. While developmental considerations influence this, a better solution would be to restrict such subsidies only to small-scale industries.[177]

It is surprising that in relation to IUU fishing, TPP parties are merely required to 'endeavor to improve cooperation'.[178] In the absence of binding dispute resolution mechanisms, no remedy exists where fish are sourced using IUU methods.

4. Trade and conservation

Article SS.17 deals with international trade in forest, wildlife, and living marine resources. The text in Article SS.17(2) says that each party to the TPP 'affirms its commitment' to ensure that international trade in flora and fauna does not harm other species by implementing its obligations under the Convention on International Trade in Endangered Species of Wild Fauna and Flora,[179] but, with the exception of the US, no other country agrees to any enforceable dispute resolution system on this issue.[180] Neither is trade done in violation of laws designed to protect flora, fauna and lumber obligatorily curtailed.[181]

---

[174] Article SS.16(6)(b) of the draft TPP.

[175] Sierra Club et al., 'Analysis of Leaked Environment Chapter Consolidated Text', 15 January 2014, p. 3, available at http://action.sierraclub.org/site/DocServer/TPP_Enviro_Analysis.pdf?docID=14842

[176] Ibid.

[177] Mulgan, A.G., 'Why Japan is Lagging on the TPP', *East Asia Forum*, 30 May 2012, available at http://www.eastasiaforum.org/2012/05/30/why-japan-is-lagging-on-the-tpp

[178] Article SS.16(14) of the draft TPP.

[179] 12 ILM 1085 (1973).

[180] Sierra Club et al., 'Analysis of Leaked Environment Chapter Consolidated Text', 15 January 2014, p. 4, available at http://action.sierraclub.org/site/DocServer/TPP_Enviro_Analysis.pdf?docID=14842

[181] Article SS.17(5) of the draft TPP.

IV. COMPARING THE TPP WITH THE TTIP ON SUSTAINABLE DEVELOPMENT

A. Scope

The TPP is fundamentally a trade agreement with a mollifying environmental chapter. Article SS.2(1) states that the objective of the Environment Chapter is to 'promote mutually supportive trade and environment policies; promote high levels of environmental protection and effective enforcement of environmental laws; and enhance the capacities of the Parties to address trade-related environmental issues …'.[182] The Chapter also recognizes the perils of encouraging trade and investments at the expense of weak environmental provisions.[183]

However, in practice this enlightenment remains merely aspirational. Article SS.2(3) proscribes using environmental legislations as a disguised restriction on trade and investment. The provision appears to be vague and broad in the absence of determining tests for 'disguised restrictions'. Further, in order to have a healthy co-existence of trade and environmental provisions, a sound enforcement mechanism is essential, which is completely absent across the Agreement. For example, under Article SS.4(3), any non-compliance by Parties who are signatories of any MEA will be scrutinized only where such non-compliance affects their trade and investments. Various other provisions of the Environment Chapter also reiterate trade promotion as the ultimate objective of the TPP, in spite of the recognition of urgent environmental challenges that the parties face.[184]

Consider this in comparison with the United States–Peru Trade Promotion Agreement (PTPA), where parties have an obligation to enforce listed MEAs[185] and ensure no violation of obligations provided under that Treaty.[186] Since there is an obligation to enforce environmental provisions, environmental rules are not considered an exception to trade rules. The TPP missed a vital opportunity in this regard. Equally, as of

---

[182] WikiLeaks, Environment Chapter of the TPP, Consolidated Text (24 November 2013), available at https://wikileaks.org/tpp2/static/pdf/tpp-treaty-environment-chapter.pdf

[183] Article SS.3(6) the draft TPP. Accordingly, no retrospective dilution of environmental laws is encouraged to strengthen trade and investments.

[184] Article SS.15.3.

[185] Article 18.2 of the United States–Peru Trade Promotion Agreement (PTPA).

[186] Articles 18.3.2 and 18.3.3 of the PTPA.

May 2014, inserting a chapter on energy trade in the TTIP was under consideration, given that energy security, in the context of sustainable development, is not an issue of just transatlantic, but global concern.

B. Enforcement

In the context of the TTIP, but also more broadly, the EU makes it clear that it 'wants its trade policy to support economic growth, social development, and environmental protection. Coherence and mutual supportiveness … are the basis for achieving sustainable development'.[187] On a close look at the Environment Chapter of the TPP, there seem to be no provisions regarding enforcement, while in the case of the TTIP, both economies have shown a clear interest in having provisions aim at the enforcement of laws and regulations in a coherent manner.

On the 26th of June 2006, the Council of the European Union launched its Renewed Sustainable Development Strategy.[188] This particular strategy puts forth the regulations with regard to sustainable development that shall govern all the EU's policies and activities. The strategy further states that the main challenge is to gradually change the 'current unsustainable consumption and production patterns and the non-integrated approach to policy-making'.[189] On a close inspection of the TPP, it can be seen that sustainable development has been given little importance in comparison, in spite of its inextricable link to the environment.

The EU report further emphasizes the reduction of environmental pollution and promotes sustainable development so as to break the link between economic growth and environmental degradation.[190] It further puts forth policy guidelines to make better laws and regulations with regard to sustainable development, including involvement of individuals and businesses in designing laws, ways to make the polluter pay, and the need to adopt the precautionary principle.[191] It also talks about the Lisbon Strategy,[192] whose aim is to make Europe 'the most competitive

---

187 European Commission, 'Sustainable Development', available at http://ec.europa.eu/trade/policy/policy-making/sustainable-development/

188 Council of the European Union, 'Review of the EU Sustainable Development Strategy', 10917/06, 26 June 2006.

189 Ibid. p. 2.

190 Ibid. p. 3.

191 Ibid. p. 6.

192 Ibid.

and dynamic knowledge-based economy in the world, capable of sustainable economic growth with more and better jobs and greater social cohesion'.[193] In contrast, the TPP has not included many provisions in its Environment Chapter, and there is scope for the Chapter's development, as its enforcement will affect the wider public.

C. Dispute Resolution

The TPP was touted as a 21st-century trade agreement. A major requirement under such an agreement is having strong enforceable environmental provisions.[194] In fact, this has been a recognized position under previous bi-party agreements between some TPP members, especially those involving the US. Resulting from a bipartisan consensus between US Congress and President G.W. Bush signed in 2007, all US trade agreements were supposed to have an enforceable environmental chapter. Therefore, the Korea–US free trade agreement (KORUS) provided for binding obligations to meet commitments under MEAs, failing which disputes would be settled through arbitration.[195]

Under the TPP, however, parties have no obligations to enforce any environmental commitments under the Environment Chapter. While the dispute resolution process is a multi-layered process,[196] including having an arbitral tribunal,[197] the arbitration report is merely recommendatory in value, as is the case in commercial arbitration.[198] In fact, parties 'shall endeavor' to agree on a 'mutually satisfactory action plan' following the report.[199] Therefore, even if a recourse is agreed to, a requesting party may have to agree on a compromise with a serious environmental violator. If indeed a 'satisfactory' solution was all that is to be gained from the dispute settlement, spending time and money over arbitration is

---

193 Lisbon European Council, Presidency Conclusions, 23 and 24 March 2000.

194 Natural Resource Defence Council, 'Green Groups: Leaked Trans-Pacific Partnership Environment Chapter Unacceptable', Press Release available at http://www.nrdc.org/media/2014/140115.asp

195 Korea–US Free Trade Agreement, Article 20.9.3(a)–(b), Article 20.9.6(a)–(c). See also Articles 21(2) and 21(4) of the PTPA.

196 Article SS.12(1) (Environment Consultations); Article SS.12(2) (Senior Representative Consultations); Article SS.12(3) (Ministerial Consultation) of the draft TPP.

197 Article SS.12(4) of the draft TPP.

198 Article SS.12(5) of the draft TPP.

199 Article SS.12(12) of the draft TPP.

utterly unnecessary. In any case, where such recourse is refused, there are no other avenues to turn to.

In the TTIP context, the EU Commission is very keen to have a strong Investor-State dispute settlement (ISDS) system, as it believes that the protection of EU investors in the US is a crucial element of the TTIP. This notion comes from the fact that, if EU investors may not have the right to appear before local US courts or local US courts cannot deal with an EU claim, then they would have no place to bring a legal action for compensation. It is in this sense that the EU Commission wishes to have an ISDS provision in the TTIP, which may have sustainable-development implications.[200] In the specific case of sustainable development, when the Parties disagree, it would be necessary to find a dispute settlement mechanism such as government consultations and impartial third-party assessments.[201]

D. Implementation

While Article SS.4(1) of the draft TPP considers the implementation of MEAs critical, it does not insist on a binding dispute resolution system for such non-compliance;[202] it merely notes that each Party 'affirms its commitment to implement' the MEAs to which it is a party.[203] Furthermore, a major challenge under the TPP is the absence of a list of MEAs to which parties affirm commitment. This is a conscious abstinence, considering the divergent interests across the board in respect of signed MEAs. For example, it is well known that the US opposes the current commitments under the Kyoto Protocol to reduce greenhouse gas emissions as they stand; the Americans are also not party to the Convention on Biological Diversity, which grants indigenous people rights over their genetic resources and biodiversity, neither have they, along with Australia, New Zealand, and Canada, signed the United Nations Declaration on the Rights of Indigenous Peoples. These positions are in tune with the political and economic compromises that such MEAs represent.

---

[200] See EU Commission: TTIP, Questions and Answers, 'Why is the EU including Investor to State Dispute Settlement in the TTIP?, available at http://ec.europa.eu/trade/policy/in-focus/ttip/questions-and-answers

[201] 'EU – US Transatlantic Trade and Investment Partnership: Trade and Sustainable Development: Initial EU Position Paper' (European Commission) 4, http://trade.ec.europa.eu/doclib/docs/2013/july/tradoc_151626.pdf

[202] Article SS.4(3), footnote 4 of the draft TPP.

[203] Article SS.4.1 of the draft TPP.

In the TTIP context, both economies are committed to the effective domestic implementation of labor and environmental standards.[204] For that to happen, the EU's view is that 'an effective mechanism should be based on transparency, regular dialogue, and close cooperation between the Parties' on any matter related to sustainable development.[205]

E. Sovereign Determination in Legislation

Another challenge of a 21st-century agreement is the leeway given to sovereign determination, while enacting environmental laws.[206] It is essential to understand that the rhetoric of developed/developing countries has not progressed. At the same time, in the absence of any such limitations in the Investment Chapter of the TPP, any environmental legislation conferring a higher standard of protection compared to existing international standards may be deemed to be too restrictive with respect to a 21st-century agreement. This may invite the attention of the dreaded investor–State dispute settlement process under the Investment Chapter. Therefore, some clarification would be required with respect to interpretation of the Environment and Investment Chapters. What is apparent is that any high level of environmental protection contemplated under Article 3(3) of the draft TPP would become redundant on current reading of the Chapter. However, unlike trade liberalization, which can be progressively realized, environmental protection and sustainable growth is already running on borrowed time.

In the context of the TTIP, the EU and the US are committed to high levels of environmental protection in order to reach 'a comprehensive and ambitious approach to trade and sustainable development issues'.[207] Moreover, in chapters on trade and sustainable development in its previous FTAs, the EU has tried to ensure that 'increased trade is mutually supporting environmental protection'.[208] As in the case of the TPP, the EU would like the TTIP to provide each Party with the 'right to regulate in order to reflect its own sustainable development priorities'.[209]

---

[204] Trade and Sustainable Development Position Paper, p. 2.

[205] Ibid. p. 4.

[206] Article SS.3(2) of the draft TPP.

[207] 'EU – US Transatlantic Trade and Investment Partnership: Trade and Sustainable Development: Initial EU Position Paper' (European Commission) 1, http://trade.ec.europa.eu/doclib/docs/2013/july/tradoc_151626.pdf

[208] Ibid. p. 2.

[209] Ibid.

In other words, recognizing each Party's right to define and regulate its own domestic levels of environmental protection as they deem necessary.[210]

V. CONCLUSION

Regarding the TTIP, one of the complaints as negotiation talks have progressed is that the process is not sufficiently transparent, and does not satisfactorily include public comment. Various elements have been built into the development of the TTIP to assuage these grievances, including: the publication of negotiating objectives prior to each round; on the US side, the creation of a Public Interest Trade Advisory Committee to provide expert input; and on the EU side, public comment periods. The TTIP, however, has the potential to become a highly successful and influential free trade agreement, with its terms possibly becoming a model structure for future trade negotiations. The United States and the EU have a great opportunity to encourage and facilitate sustainable development, green technologies, renewable energy, and an increased trade in raw materials and energy, and this chapter has discussed ways in which the TTIP can do so. It has yet to be seen whether the parties will prioritize these environmental and energy goals, whether such terms could be successful, or whether the TTIP can be successfully concluded at all.

As for the TPP, upon a close inspection of the abovementioned articles of the TPP's Environment Chapter, the emphasis seems to have been given to trade and investment above environmental considerations. To enforce laws and regulations properly, stringent laws should bind the parties to the TPP, which this agreement currently lacks.

Article SS.3, paragraphs 1, 2, and 3 deal with general commitments and have placed importance on mutually supportive trade and environmental policies as well as the protection of the environment with a view to sustainable development. Further, the Article states that the parties' domestic laws shall be for the betterment of the environment. However, upon an examination of paragraphs 4 and 6, it becomes apparent that there is a contradiction, as at first it mentions that environmental law must not be drafted in such a way as to hamper trade and investment, while paragraph 6 states the opposite.

---

210 Ibid.

The insertion of the 'Montreal Protocol' in Article SS.4.4 is important with respect to sustainability. Article SS.6 deals with setting up national advisory committees for the implementation of the environment chapter. For the set-up of the committee, certain changes have to be made in the domestic laws of respective countries. Setting up a committee also requires funds and resources, which would definitely affect developing countries, since they are economically less healthy than developed economies. Even Article SS.11 talks about establishing an 'Environment Committee' comprising senior government representatives, or their designees, of the relevant trade and environmental authorities of each party to the TPP responsible for the implementation of the chapter. This again places an additional burden on the parties.

The TPP's Environment Chapter demonstrates a lack of clarity with regard to the environment and sustainability. Even though the TPP's main purpose is trade liberalization and investment protection, there has been less focus on environment and sustainability in the chapter that was especially drafted to protect the environment.

While the TPP's Environment Chapter has touched upon crucial areas of environmental protection that can pave the way for future talks, it does not inspire. Furthermore, the TPP seems to be facing obstacles. The parties still seem indecisive on crucial matters. It therefore seems that preferential trade agreements, while conducive to greater trade liberalization, face the same concerns as multilateral trade agreements when it comes to the environment and sustainable development. It is hoped that the human race as a whole will eventually learn to move beyond short-term gains.

Index